1971

DJB C
Jan 71
(3)

S0-AIR-429

3 0301 00017961 0

This book may be kept

FOURTEEN DAYS

A fine will be charged for each day the book is kept overtime.

OC 21 70			
8-4-72 7B			
NO 9 72			
DEC 5 '72			
Due 12/14			
JUL 21 '77			
GAYLORD 142			PRINTED IN U.S.A.

Volume 2

DISADVANTAGED CHILD

HEAD START and EARLY INTERVENTION

Jerome Hellmuth, Editor

BRUNNER / MAZEL Publishers

This book is dedicated
to the memory of **Dr. Edgar A. Doll**
who devoted his life as
the constant warm friend
and defender of
the special child.

Copyright © 1968 by BRUNNER/MAZEL, Inc.
80 East 11th Street
New York, N.Y. 10003

Manufactured in the United States of America

Library of Congress Catalogue Card Number: 67-7639

SBN 87630-014-X

371.96
D611
2

Photo courtesy of the United States Department of Agriculture.

56767

CONTENTS

5

6

7

INTRODUCTION

Diversity and enthusiasm are the most striking features of contemporary pre-school education. Part of the reason for this diversity is the recent expansion of early childhood programs to include lower-class as well as middle-class children. In order to make the experience more relevant to their varied backgrounds, researchers and early childhood educators are experimenting with a wide spectrum of approaches to curriculum organization. Current programs include emphases on socialization, free play, perceptual training, language development and custodial care, as well as sundry combinations of these elements.

Project Head Start, the most massive educational intervention program to date, has both reflected and encouraged these diversities. Head Start was designed as a comprehensive, multi-dimensional program allowing for local experimentation in program emphases, while at the same time encouraging the integration of affective and cognitive oriented learning experiences. Head Start centers were required to reflect the wide range of influences which the family and social environment exert on the child's educational development, but were allowed to choose the degree of emphasis given to such components as medical care, parent participation and community involvement. Thus, the responsibilities of the pre-school program were extended to the child's intellectual, emotional, and physical development, as well as the welfare of his family and community.

This, the second volume of THE DISADVANTAGED CHILD reflects the diversities of Project Head Start and perhaps of the entire early childhood field. The volume opens with a consideration of some of the issues involved in disadvantaged status and underdevelopment in the context of the nature-nurture controversy. Later chapters discuss issues of intellectual and academic measurement, as well as problems of pediatric care and approaches to neurological and visual assessment. Chapters describing program materials give the reader a general idea of the nature of work in this area and point to specific suggestions for curriculum modification and innovation. The particular usefulness of a book such as this lies in its provocation of discussion and exploration leading to further study and improved program design.

8

There are a number of key issues dealt with in the book that require special attention: 1) the relevance of genetic and environmentalist theories for educational practice, 2) the function of assessment in education, 3) the relation of health and nutritional status to development and learning, 4) the ecology of language development and reading proficiency, and 5) the problems of evaluating massive innovations in education.

THE RELEVANCE OF GENETIC AND ENVIRONMENTALIST THEORIES FOR EDUCATIONAL PRACTICE

The collection begins with a re-examination of genetic theories related to developmental and learning problems of the disadvantaged. An eloquent plea is made for serious studies of genetic and environmentalist theories as they relate to the educational process. There can be no dispute about the need for new research, as well as thoughtful analysis of available knowledge on this subject. What remains doubtful, however, is the appropriateness of the questions presently being asked. There is enough evidence of hereditarily determined physical characteristics to at least suggest that some psychological characteristics (intelligence, temperament, response, tendencies, etc.) may be greatly influenced by genetics. But for the educator and social planner, establishing this fact is less important than determining the modifiability of these characteristics and the development of learning experiences appropriate to them. To define the developmental and learning problems of the disadvantaged as significantly genetic in origin may relieve us of some responsibility for changing the social factors sometimes thought to contribute to them, but it does not give as much of a lead as to what can or should be done to resolve these problems. Too often the retreat to a genetic theory in this area has led to defeatist attitudes.

For those of us who are concerned with developing human potential, it is the interaction between those factors contributed by heredity and those provided or **providable** *by the environment which is of crucial importance. The value assigned to a particular characteristic is in large measure determined by the circumstances under which it is called into play. The nature and variations in the genotype-environment interaction and the conditions necessary for attainment of specific goals are crucial questions to be asked in resolving the heredity-environment uncertainty.*

Since these questions have not been thoroughly investigated, we have left room for confusion and pessimism in the minds of well-meaning persons who, looking at the variety of educational improvements directed at the disadvantaged, find only modest change in pupil functioning. The fact that the interesting programs described in this book have not met with roaring success may not be a reflection of some immutable characteristic in disadvantaged children. Rather it may reflect our failure to develop programs of experience with the environment which appropriately complement the adaptive patterns of the children served. Of course we may be faced with patterns of behavioral organization that no amount or quality of experience can develop into high level academic and social functioning. If this is true, all our efforts at new approaches to education and earlier exposure will fail. But we will never know the extent to which disadvantaged children are educable until we stop blaming their heredity or their environment and move to find a better match between whatever patterns their heredity provides and the patterns available through appropriate environmental encounters. The effectiveness of a program for educating the disadvantaged should be thought of as a test of that match, and not as a reflection of limitations intrinsic to the children themselves.

THE FUNCTION OF ASSESSMENT IN EDUCATION

The task of matching learning experience input and learner characteristics should be a principal operational goal in all educational programs. Unfortunately, this concern has not been emphasized in most contemporary efforts. Instead, we have persevered in the search for "culture fair" instruments, in the attempt to establish norms for special populations, and in efforts to improve our predictions in spite of conceded weaknesses in available psychometric tests. This tradition and the trend away from it are reflected in three of the chapters of this book. It is clear that tests can be developed which tap behavioral characteristics less influenced by the culture of the individuals tested. There is evidence that certain learning environments and less culture-bound test situations reduce differences in the performance of subjects from various backgrounds. But the main thrust in educational assessment should not be the estimation of "basic intelligence." Rather the problem is to provide an understanding of the quality and style of intellectual and social functioning for use in planning educational experiences and subsequently measuring educational growth. This is not to ignore the importance of baseline scores, criterion measures or achievement predictions. However, with disadvantaged children, particularly at the preschool level, these are not the primary concerns.

The greatest contribution that assessment procedures can make is to our understanding of how these children function, under what conditions—what turns them on, what turns them off. When we turn our concern to describing intellectual function, we are beginning to speak to these issues. In order for educational assessment to be meaningful, it must deal with the processes of affective and cognitive differentiation, as these processes reflect changes in the children's relations

10

with people, ideas and things. For it is out of this dynamic qualitative analysis that designs of learning experience input more appropriate to learner characteristics can emerge.

THE RELATION OF HEALTH AND NUTRITIONAL STATUS TO DEVELOPMENT AND LEARNING

Our work has been as meagre in applying health, neurological and nutritional knowledge to learning and developmental patterns as it has been in relating educational assessment to curriculum planning. In few school or preschool settings do we find more than a superficial concern with this relationship, except perhaps as an excuse to provide a less strenuous curriculum. Where good programs exist, they are principally concerned with identifying obviously abnormal conditions and providing minimal pediatric care. Systematic attention has not yet been given to the relevance of even gross abnormalities for learning functions, despite our knowledge that impaired health or organic dysfunction influences school attendance, learning efficiency, developmental rate and personality growth. Moreover, mounting evidence supports the hypothesis that reproductive errors and developmental defects are significantly influenced by level of income.* In any large population of varied socio-economic status, the incidence of error or defect occurs along a continuum in which the frequency is greatest among those individuals for whom medical, nutritional and child care are poorest.

Despite these striking relationships, our school health services remain poor. Our nation has trailed many less wealthy countries in providing medical services for its people. The school health examination is a disgrace to the professions of medicine and education, and the development of public school medicine as a subspecialty in pediatrics is barely on the horizon. Even Project Head Start, which has made a concerted effort to provide medical services as an integral part of each center's program, has not succeeded in integrating health care and the management of learning experience. Yet it is clear that the school functioning of many of our children, and particularly those from poverty environments, could be greatly enhanced by the application of modern medicine to some of their learning problems.

Several chapters in this book deal with the health problems of Head Start children and some of the difficulties involved in providing even minimal services to them. In

*The reader should note studies by: 1) Knoblock and Pasamanick of the relationship between health status and school adjustment in low income Negro children in Baltimore, 2) Lashof of health status and services in Chicago's South Side, 3) Birch of health and learning patterns in an entire age range of school children in Aberdeen, Scotland, 4) Birch of children from indigent families in the Caribbean, 5) Porter of the health status of Head Start children sampled in Cambridge, Massachusetts

11

the brief discussion of one neurological study we get a sense of movement in a new and important direction. The concern with relating the assessment of neurological status to certain aspects of the learning process is a welcome development. In educational planning it is not so much the identification of a defect or a malfunction that is important, or even its use as an explanation for failure. The critical issue is the relevance of these defects to the design and management of learning experiences.

THE ECOLOGY OF LANGUAGE DEVELOPMENT AND LEARNING

Athough many educators continue to stress social and emotional learning as the primary focus of preschool, the compensatory education orientation of Head Start has led to greater emphasis on the development of cognitive skills. In response to the overwhelming evidence of qualitative and quantitative differences in language between disadvantaged children and their more privileged peers, a variety of programs has been designed to enrich language facility in the preschool child. Similarly, in response to parental and administrative concern with tangible evidence that Head Start improves chances for success in school, reading readiness exercises and actual reading instruction have been introduced. Both of these emphases involve more or less direct approaches to the enhancement of cognitive development and skill achievement.

The debate continues between proponents of formal language and reading programs and those who would approach readiness through socialization, confidence building, imagination and exploration. It is interesting that efforts at evaluating the impact of the direct and indirect approaches result in much the same findings. Successes and failures are found in both camps. It may be either that the emphases identified are not really different in practice, or that they are not important determinants of the outcomes measured. However, the point at issue is probably not the relative efficacy of cognitive versus affective approaches, but the ecological conditions under which cognitive and affective approaches to learning are brought into play. There is no doubt that content, form and style are important in language development; the mastery of these elements is often thought to be a cognitive task. But language facility is developed out of a social need and in a social context. Ignorance of the affective developmental tasks and conditions necessary for mastering language arts may be contributing to our confused and frequently negative results. It seems obvious that to posit academic and social development as dichotomous elements in learning is fallacious. In almost every instance they function together and are aspects of a single process. Far more important than a unilateral emphasis are concern with the manner in which each reciprocally enhances the other and the way in which ecological factors facilitate or interfere with mastery.

THE PROBLEMS OF EVALUATION MASSIVE INNOVATION IN EDUCATION

In addition to problems in measurement, evaluations of Head Start and other massive programs of educational innovation have suffered from a failure to recognize the reciprocal relationship between affective and cognitive aspects of learning. The contributors to this book join many others in calling attention to problems encountered in evaluating Head Start. They are troubled that: 1) too heavy an emphasis has been placed on demonstrating change in intelligence and achievement test scores; 2) noncognitive outcomes, i.e. changes in attitude, emotional stability, social maturity, task involvement, initiative, etc., are being ignored; 3) little attention is given to the process by which learning occurs or fails to occur; 4) change is looked for immediately following the Head Start experience, to the neglect of long-term follow-up; and 5) outcome variables studied ignore impact on the family, the school, community agencies, community morale and politico-social aspects of community life.

It is not surprising that evaluation efforts have come under heavy criticism. While the tradition of educational evaluation is long-standing, evaluations of massive programs are very new. In fact, it was not until the Coleman study of EQUALITY OF EDUCATIONAL OPPORTUNITY *that we had anything approaching a national educational assessment. One of the by-products of Head Start and other such largescale educational projects will be the development of a science and technology of program evaluation. It will of course borrow from the experimental tradition of psychology, the survey approach of sociology, the field observation and descriptive techniques of anthropology, and the enumerative and cost analysis methods of economics. What will be crucial, however, will be a greater appreciation for ecological and process analyses monitored over a long period, marked by regular assessment probes, and concerned with multiple relationships between a wide variety of input and outcome variables. The evaluation questions will not be "did it work" or "what is the impact" or even "how much gain was achieved," but rather "under what conditions does what work for whom," "what pupil characteristics require what interventions, when and how," "what relationships exist between what we do for and with children and what happens at home and in the community."*

In addition to the several theoretical issues raised THE DISADVANTAGED CHILD *includes a rich description of current program practices. The chapters concerning Head Start health care, training and follow-up present a national perspective on the problems of designing, implementing and evaluating such massive programs. These problems are further clarified by chapters describing local projects and quite specific*

13

approaches. One may even capture the enthusiasm and come to appreciate the resourcefulness that are peculiar to many of these programs. Combined with descriptive materials which appeared in Volume I of THE DISADVANTAGED CHILD *the reader should have an operational overview of Head Start and related projects of educational intervention. In this volume, a number of the more promising trends emerging from several demonstration projects are discussed. One notes the change of focus from the educator as provider of information to the process of information-sharing between the child and teacher, the child and parent, and one child and another. Of particular interest are concrete suggestions for the use of manipulative selfcorrecting toys, controlled environments, and the design of home teaching programs.*

As a number of the articles imply, Head Start may well succeed in reaching beyond the children whom it was designed to serve. It has already been suggested that the war on poverty has probably done more to provide jobs for middle-class professionals than it has done to reduce poverty for the disadvantaged. Similarly, Head Start may have a greater impact on the thinking of professional educators and policy-makers, and eventually on school programs, than it has had on the functioning of children and families burdened with poverty. The greatest impact of Head Start health services may not be seen in immediate improvements in the health of the individual children, but in a strengthening of the position that medical care is a right and not a privilege, and that the child's physical condition is an important determinant of his learning function. The increasing use of professionals may contribute to much greater variety in their use in the service professions, just at the influx of new sub-professionals may institute radical changes in our conception of the role of the teacher and other specialists. Head Start's encouragement of parent and community participation in program planning and daily classroom activities stands as an example of the movement to decrease the long-standing isolation of the public schools. As pressure from ghetto communities increases and as research makes learning needs and instructional practices more explicit, greater demands will be made on those involved in managing learning experiences. The challenge is to make education into a scientific profession, which is at the same time accountable to the communities and the pupils it is designed to serve.

Edmund W. Gordon, Ed. D,
Dept. of Educational Psychology and Guidance,
Ferkauf Graduate School, Yeshiva University, New York City;
Chairman, Research and Evaluation Council,
Project Head Start; Director,
ERIC Information Retrieval Center on the Disadvantaged

14

The following Photo Section courtesy of the Office of Economic Opportunity.

15

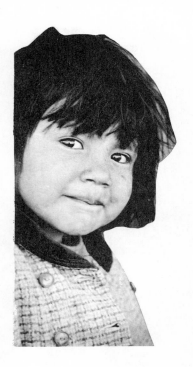

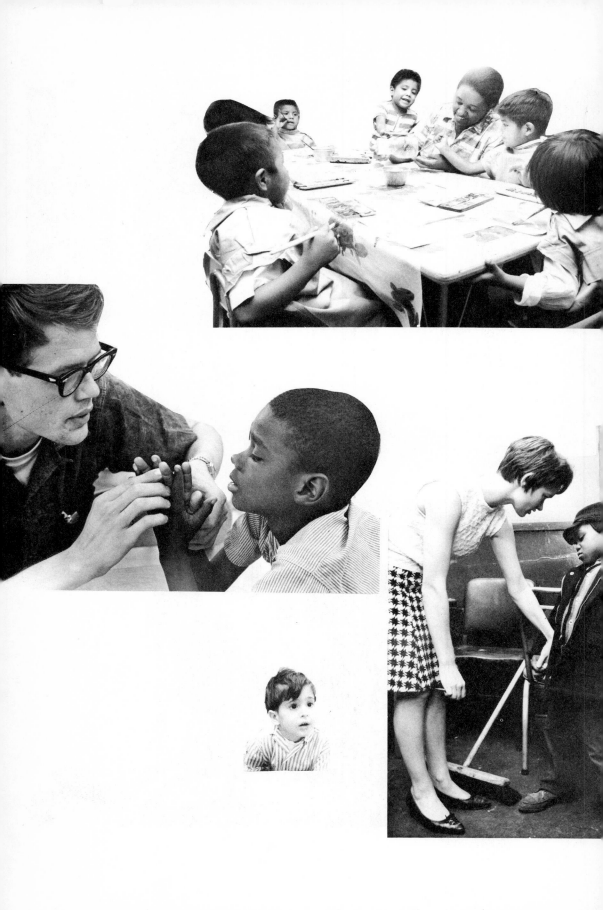

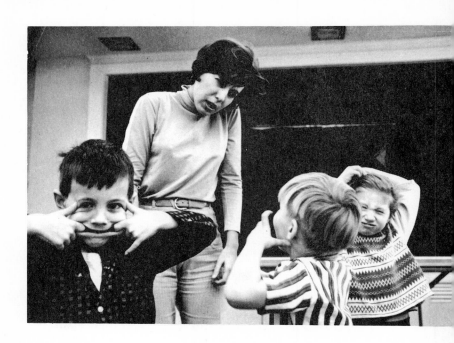

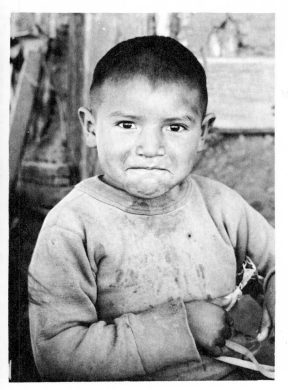

THE CULTURALLY DISADVANTAGED AND THE HEREDITY - ENVIRONMENT UNCERTAINTY

Arthur R. Jensen, Ph.D.,
Professor of Educational Psychology and Research Psychologist,
Institute of Human Learning, University of California, Berkeley,
(Written while a Fellow at the Center for Advanced Study
in the Behavioral Sciences, Stanford University)

ARTHUR R. JENSEN, Ph.D.

Is the disadvantage of the "culturally disadvantaged" only cultural? Or is it also genetic and biological? Is this the one forbidden question in the study of the "culturally disadvantaged"? Nowhere in the already vast literature that has proliferated on the topic of cultural deprivation in recent years have I found this question dealt with in a forthright, thorough and intellectually rigorous fashion. Dismissal of the heredity-environment question as unimportant or irrelevant to the problems of the "culturally disadvantaged" is quite consistent with the strong environmentalist tradition of the behavioral sciences in the United States. But in addition to this historical peculiarity in our attitudes, the heredity-environment issue also arouses fear and avoidance because of its possible implications regarding race differences in behavioral traits that are relevant to educability and other criteria of social capacity.

It is my contention that no one -- neither the culturally disadvantaged nor society in general -- will be served by shunning any body of scientific knowledge that may have some bearing on the problems now generally associated with the term "culturally disadvantaged." Ideally, the first step in attempting to solve any kind of complex problem is to achieve as thorough and accurate a description and diagnosis of the problem as possible. No physician worthy of the title would attempt to treat a patient without first diagnosing his illness; and no aspect of medical knowledge that is at all possibly relevant to the case, nor any fact of the patient's history, is categorically excluded from consideration in making a diagnosis. Behavioral scientists must approach the problems of the "culturally disadvantaged" in the same fashion. A prematurely formed theory which becomes standard doctrine or dogma can block or hinder real solutions to the problem.

It appears to me that an informal theory, at times implicit but often explicit, has grown to the status of a doctrine, if not a dogma, concerning the nature and causes of "cultural disadvantage." The doctrine is unquestioned in its basic assumption -- that the disadvantage of the "culturally disadvantaged" is entirely a result of various forms of social deprivation -- while speculation and research are concerned almost exclusively with the description and measurement of the varieties of social depriva-

29

tion, the psychological mechanisms through which deprivations produce the "culturally disadvantaged" syndrome, and the educational, social, and economic measures that might alleviate the problem. This kind of research is certainly a highly worthwhile and necessary endeavor. But as long as the focus of our collective research attention remains fixated in this one orientation which sees the whole problem as consisting only of social deprivation, to the exclusion of biological factors (genetic, prenatal, perinatal, and postnatal) that may well contribute to individual and group differences in socially relevant behavioral traits, we run the risk of severely limiting our understanding of many of the problems that have come to be categorized under the label of "cultural disadvantage". This would be unfortunate, in my view, since I take it as axiomatic that success in dealing effectively with a problem is directly related to the precision and completeness of our understanding of it. I would therefore urge that in thinking about the "culturally disadvantaged" we fully take into consideration the substantial body of research on the biological basis of individual differences. Doing this will not now answer the most important questions in the field, but without this inquiry many of the important questions are sure to remain unanswered, with consequent impairment of our capacity to discover effective courses of action.

A FAILURE OF EDUCATION

The problem of "cultural deprivation" comes to our attention most directly through certain social, economic, and educational conditions. Largely because of the rapid increase in certain kinds of demands made on the population by advancing technology, there has apparently been an increase in the proportion of the population which is unable to compete successfully in achieving the relative stability of family life, the occupational competence and advancement, or the economic self-sufficiency that the majority of persons in our society take more or less for granted as their birthrights. The bulk of this less favored segment of the population are called the "culturally disadvantaged". These persons perhaps would have been relatively less disadvantaged in the bygone days of a simple agrarian society. But the nature of modern industrial society and the kinds of educational demands that seem essential to its operations magnify the problems of those who, for whatever reason, are less favored in the competition. Furthermore, new problems are created, the worst probably being the urban ghetto, which nurtures the "culture of poverty" and produces more of the psychological disadvantage that bars so many of its inhabitants from assuming a productive role in society. Education is generally viewed as the main potential remedy. But the present crux of this solution is, of course, that the disadvantage we are trying to remedy itself seems to consist in large part of a failure of known methods of education, methods that have worked at least adequately for the majority of the population.

30

The monumental Coleman study on EQUALITY OF EDUCATIONAL OPPORTUNITY, based on over 645,000 pupils from grades 1 to 12 in 4000 of the nation's schools, has shown clearly that only a fraction (10 to 30 percent in various samples) of the variance among individuals in school achievement is attributable to differences in school facilities and other educational variables under the direct control of the school system (Coleman, 1966). The largest sources of variance in school achievement were found to be associated with family background, socioeconomic status, and race. Initial mental ability of the pupils measured during the primary grades accounts for more of the individual differences in subsequent school performance than any other single variable (Wilson, 1967). Ability measures, of course, show substantial independent correlations with social class indices and race. These studies say nothing about the overall absolute level of general scholastic performance achieved by our educational system. What they do show is that, for the most part, the large educational differences between individuals, social classes, and racial groups cannot be explained to any appreciable degree in terms of what goes on in the schools. The explanation of most of the differences must be sought in what the child brings within himself to the school. What the child brings is an amalgam of innate abilities and dispositions, acquired habits, skills, and attitudes, and a parental home with differing inclinations and capabilities for acting as a private tutorial service throughout the child's early schooling.

THE ENVIRONMENTALLY DEPRESSED

Since it would be impossible in the confines of this chapter to deal with all relevant aspects of the "culturally disadvantaged", I will deal only with those which seem most important from the standpoint of education.

Thus far I have used the term "culturally disadvantaged" only in quotation marks. The reason for the quotation marks is that I have been using the term in the poorly defined popular sense. The term, regarded by many as an outright misnomer, is so general and carries so many implicit connotations as to be practically useless for discussion of the specific problems that need to be approached through analysis and research. There would seem to be a legitimate place for the term, however, if it were clearly distinguished from more general terms such as "the poor," "the uneducated," "slum dwellers," "impoverished," "low socioeconomic status," and the like. Since "culturally disadvantaged" has come to be more or less synonymous with these other unprecise terms and carries most of their connotations, however, I will propose a new term for the purpose of clarity in the discussion that follows: the *environmentally depressed*. I will continue to use "culturally disadvantaged" (henceforth without quotes) in the popular sense to refer to those segments of the population that school authorities, welfare agencies, and Federal programs such as Head Start and the Job Corps regard as disadvantaged. There is no point in debating

31

the precise boundaries of this definition; it has none. The precise meanings I wish to give to the term *environmentally depressed* are best approached through a discussion of the distribution of measured intelligence in the population.

THREE DISTRIBUTIONS OF INTELLIGENCE

Because no one has yet discovered a true metric for the measurement of intelligence, it is not, strictly speaking, possible to prove that the distribution of intelligence in the population has any particular form, as would be possible for characteristics measured on an absolute or, at least, a true interval scale, such as height, weight, cephalic index, or income. The distribution of intelligence is assumed to be normal (Gaussian) largely because no one has thought of any good reason why it should be otherwise. Furthermore, there are good theoretical reasons, based on simple genetic models, why intelligence, if it is mainly determined by heredity, should be approximately normally distributed. The rather surprising fact of the matter is that some of the good tests of general intelligence, such as the Stanford-Binet and the Wechsler scales, yield distributions which meet more theoretical and empirical expectations than one could have reasonably predicted from the method of construction of these tests. If we make the assumption that the tests yield IQs that are on an equal-interval scale, the form of the distribution of IQs in the population makes a great deal of sense in terms of certain empirical knowledge concerning the nature of intelligence. The most striking thing about the distribution of IQs is that it is *not* a normal distribution but departs from perfect normality in certain significant and systematic ways (Burt, 1957, 1963; Wechsler, 1958, p. 106-7). Analysis of these departures from normality supports the hypothesis that the distribution is actually a composite of at least *three* relatively distinct distributions.

The observed distribution of IQs in a large and truly representative sample of the total population departs from normality mainly in three ways. First of all, the distribution is not perfectly symmetrical about the mode; it is positively skewed. That is to say, there are slightly more persons in the lower IQ range than in the higher range. Secondly, the excess in the lower half of the distribution occurs in two regions: in the very low region (below IQ 50) and in the region between about 75 and 90. Thirdly, the upper tail of the distribution (above IQ 150) has slightly greater frequencies than would occur in a perfectly normal curve, but this latter feature will be of no concern to us in the present discussion.

We can best conceive of these deviations from normality as being the result of the superimposition of two distinct distributions upon the normal distribution. The normal distribution is the main one, with a mean of 100 and a range from about 40 to 160. Individual differences in this distribution are hypothesized as being due to polygenic inheritance plus minor environmental effects amounting to not more than about 5 or 6 IQ points above or below the genetically determined IQ.

32

The simplest model of polygenic inheritance states that intelligence is genetically determined by a certain number of pairs of genes, some of which enhance intelligence while others do not. The average person would have equal numbers of enhancing and non-enhancing genes; the degree of departure from 50-50 ratio of enhancing to non-enhancing genes would determine how far above or below the mean IQ a person would stand. If the assortment of enhancing and non-enhancing genes is independent and random for each individual, the resulting values will be normally distributed. Departures from random assortment cause very little departure from normality of the distribution if the number of gene pairs allotted to each individual is fairly large. Twenty gene pairs would be quite sufficient to account for the entire range of IQs from 40 to 160; each enhancing gene would be assumed to boost the IQ by six points. The step-wise distribution would be "smoothed" by microenvironmental variations and by imperfect test reliability to yield the perfectly continuous normal curve.

The vast majority of the population is a part of this normal distribution. Though the range of IQs in this distribution goes from about 40 to 160, all the variation is caused by the same basic process, namely, polygenic inheritance. Therefore, in a biological sense none of the individuals in this distribution can be regarded as abnormal or pathological. In this respect, intelligence is analogous to height, which is inherited in a similar fashion. The short man (unless he is a dwarf or a midget) is no more abnormal than the average or the tall man. He simply inherited a different assortment of genes. But what about the abnormally short person, the dwarf and the midget? Here a different genetic mechanism comes into play, and this is true for height as well as intelligence.

This brings us to the second distribution of IQ, which is superimposed on the normal distribution. This second distribution, however, is very small, comprising only one to two percent of the population. The distribution has a mean around 35 and spreads between approximately zero and 50. (The limits are not exact.) Most individuals in this range of IQ, and virtually all of those below 40, are not part of the normal distribution of polygenically determined IQs, but are part of the abnormal distribution resulting from either severe brain damage or from what geneticists call major gene defects. These are truly pathological conditions. Certain rare, wayward genes, usually mutations, can completely override the individual's normal polygenic inheritance. Such a gene produces severe mental defect. We know that these severe grades of mental defect are not inherited in the same fashion as normal variations in intelligence but are the result of a single mutant gene. IQs below 50 occur with about equal relative frequency in all social classes, while above this level of IQ there is a substantial correlation between IQ and socioeconomic status. It is also of interest to note that children with IQs below 50 have siblings whose IQs are normally distributed around a mean of 100, while children in the IQ range from 60 to 75 have siblings who for the most part are also below average (see Gottesman, 1963, p. 276).

33

Many interesting facts such as these are explained in terms of the operation of two types of genetic process: polygenic inheritance and major genes. But we shall not be further concerned here about this abnormal range of mental defect, since it has no direct relevance to the study of the culturally disadvantaged.

The third distribution, also superimposed on the normal distribution, is composed of some unknown percentage of the population, but it is probably not more than 5 percent. This distribution is the least clearly defined; it is probably positively skewed, with a mean somewhere around IQ 85 to 90, and its range is from about 60 to 115, but the majority of cases seem to fall in the region from IQ 60 to 90. This is the group I have referred to as the environmentally depressed. It is assumed that if it were not for some environmentally caused depression of their intelligence, the individuals in this group would be distributed elsewhere at various higher points on the IQ scale. This would eliminate the slight "bulge" generally found in the 60 to 90 IQ region in the distribution of the total population. The environmentally depressed might be defined as those whose IQs are lower than their genetically determined potential by more than about 10 points. The "bulge" in the total IQ distribution created by the individuals can be eliminated by removing from the distribution those cases on whom there is independent evidence of brain damage or severe environmental handicaps in childhood (Burt, 1957, 1963). Thus it is evident that the category of environmentally depressed is not a simple one, being a mixture of biological disadvantaging effects, such as brain damage, and of disadvantaging effects due to a poor social environment. When mild degrees of brain damage or severe environmental deprivation result in lowered IQs which are nevertheless still in the above-average range, they are much less likely to be detected as forms of IQ depression. As we shall see in more detail later, there is some evidence that IQs over 100 are rarely depressed scores, but correspond closely to the child's learning ability regardless of his social class background. Many lower-class children in the IQ range from 60 to 90, however, show better learning ability than would be indicated by their IQs.

A central problem, then, is to distinguish these environmentally depressed individuals from others in the same IQ range who are part of the normal distribution, and treat them in ways that will overcome their environmental handicap as fully as possible. A second problem is to discover the precise mechanisms through which the environment causes intellectual handicaps, not only as a means to remedying the handicaps but also in order to prevent their occurrence in the first place. Too little is yet known about the differential psychology of brain damage and environmental handicaps, but it is very likely that these two classes of IQ depression have quite different implications for educational prognosis and remediation.

Non-biologic environmental depression of intelligence constitutes true environmental disadvantage. This group is handicapped educationally for essentially different reasons than the majority of individuals who are part of the normal distribution of intelligence but fall in the IQ range from 70 to 90. The large group called the culturally disadvantaged are generally treated in the literature as being the same as the group 1 have identified as environmentally depressed. If this were so, their removal from the total IQ distribution for the population would not only remove the slight "bulge" in the 60 to 90 range I have mentioned, but would leave a "dent" in the distribution in place of it. I conjecture that only some fraction of those we call culturally disadvantaged qualify for the category I have labeled "environmentally depressed." While it is possible to make a definite statement of the percentage of culturally disadvantaged children in the school population on the basis of available criteria, there are no data available at present that would permit a statement of the percentage of children who are environmentally depressed. The simple fact is that we do not know the extent to which poor environmental conditions result in depression of intelligence. The idea that the majority of culturally disadvantaged children who do poorly in school are handicapped mainly by a poor environment and poor preparation for school work is merely an assumption. It is not a demonstrated fact. At best it is a working hypothesis. The hypothesis, however, has been so generally mistaken for fact that no major attempts have been made to test its validity. If the hypothesis is wrong, many of our efforts to explain and remedy the educational problems of the culturally disadvantaged will be misguided and doomed to failure.

MISCONCEPTIONS ABOUT HEREDITY AND ENVIRONMENT

A central fact that cannot be ignored in any discussion of individual or group difference in mental ability is that the vast majority of the population are a part of the normal distribution of intelligence (as contrasted with the major gene defect and environmental depression distributions) and that the individual differences found in this normal distribution are attributable largely to hereditary factors. General acknowledgment of this fact in the literature on the culturally disadvantaged has been hindered and obscured by confusion and misconceptions concerning the heredity-environment issue. These should be cleared up before proceeding further.

The most common misunderstanding is that nothing can be said about the relative importance of heredity and environment, since it is obvious that both are absolutely essential for the existence and development of the individual. It is a mere truism that there never existed a person who did not have a biological inheritance and who did not grow up in an environment. In this sense, of course, both heredity and environment are absolutely essential, so it cannot be said that one is any more or less important than the other. But this is not the question that interests the behavioral geneticist. His question is: What proportion of the *variability (i.e.,* variance*) in a trait in the population is attributable to genetic variability and what proportion is attributable to environmental variability? The proportion of trait variance in the

*Variance (the square of the standard deviation) is a technical term with a special meaning. It is a measure of variability or dispersion among scores. Formulas for its computation can be found in any introductory textbook on statistics.

35

population attributable to genetic factors is called the *heritability* of the trait. The question, therefore, is not whether a trait is the result of heredity *or* environment, but to what extent are individual differences in the trait due to each of these factors. Quantitative genetics (also called population genetics) is the branch of genetics which deals with the methods of determining the heritability of traits (*e.g.* Falconer, 1960; Li, 1955; Fuller & Thompson, 1960, ch. 3 & 4). These methods make it possible,given certain reasonable assumptions, to obtain estimates of the proportions of trait variance (individual differences) due to heredity and environment. More refined techniques make it possible to subdivide the genetic variance into various components corresponding to known genetic processes. It is also possible to subdivide environmental variance into that associated with differences *between* families and that associated with differences *within* families (Cattell, 1960; Jensen, 967).

There are also misconceptions about the meaning of *heritablity*. The heritability of a trait is not an absolute or fixed value, like the ratio of the circumference to the diameter of a circle. A heritability estimate (called an *estimate* because it is always based on a sample from the population and is therefore subject to sampling error) is specific to the population and to the test or technique by which the trait measurements were obtained. In this respect, heritability is like any other population statistic. Thus there is no one "true" value for the heritability of a particular trait. If the environmental variability in a population decreases, the proportion of the total variability due to hereditary factors must necessarily increase, since the proportions of environmental and hereditary variance by definition add up to unity. As environmental conditions are improved for everyone in the population and true quality of opportunity increases at all levels of education as well as in the occupational and economic spheres, individual differences in ability and performance will be increasingly attributable to hereditary differences and less attributable to environmental differences. Surprising as it may seem when viewed in this light, this is the goal toward which we are actually working.

Another misconception about heritability is that it defines the limits to which variability in a given trait may be influenced by environmental factors. All that a heritability estimate tells us is the extent to which heredity and environment actually contribute to trait variability in the population on which the estimate is based. This says nothing directly about the relative importance of heredity and environment under other, different environmental conditions. When the environmental conditions differ over a considerable range in the population, however, and the heritability of a trait still is high, it is likely that only the application of very unusual environmental influences will increase the relative importance of environmental factors as a source of individual differences in the trait. There is undoubtedly some relationship between the heritability of a trait and the extent to which it can be manipulated by environmental means, but the degree of this relationship would

36

differ from one trait to another, and usually we cannot know, except through experimentation what external forces are capable of influencing a given trait. PKU (phenylketonuria) is a good example of this point. It is an inherited type of severe mental defect which can be almost completely alleviated by certain dietary restrictions shortly after birth.

This fact about PKU points up another unfortunate misconception—the idea that highly heritable traits are immutable and seal the individual's fate at the moment of conception, while acquired traits are believed to be highly malleable. Neither of these beliefs is consistenly true and the first is unduly pessimistic. Actually what a heritability estimate tells us is the principal locus of control of a given trait. For highly heritable traits the main locus of control is in the individual's internal biological mechanisms; for traits low in heritability the main sources of influence lie in the external or social environment. When we know something about the heritability of a trait, we have a better idea of where to look for means of controlling it. It would be as futile to treat PKU by means of psychotherapy as to get a person to lose a foreign accent by changing his body chemistry.

THE INHERITANCE OF MENTAL ABILITY

Studies of the inheritance of intelligence (or other traits) are based on the intercorrelations between persons having different degrees of "blood" relationship. The range of such relationships goes from identical (monozygotic) twins, whose genetic inheritance is identical, to totally unrelated persons. A typical example of such correlations is shown in Table 1, based on studies by Sir Cyril Burt, whose subjects were English children sampled more or less at random from London and its vicinity (Burt, 1955, 1958).

The correlations for physical measurements are shown for comparison with intelligence and scholastic achievement.

The correlations in Table I may also be expressed in terms of the average absolute difference between persons of differing degrees of relationship. Some of these differences are shown graphically in Fig. 1. In order to make possible direct comparisons between IQ, scholastic achievement, and height, all three measures have been converted to the same scale as Stanford-Binet IQs, with a standard deviation of 16; and since IQs and scholastic measures have somewhat lower reliability than the measurement of height, the IQ and scholastic measures have been corrected for attenuation (a statistical procedure which, in effect, removes error of measurement).

A number of important points emerge from Table 1 and Figure 1. First of all, it is clear that for intelligence and height, and to a lesser degree for scholastic achievement, the degree of correlation (Table 1) between persons decreases systematically

37

TABLE 1

Correlations for Intelligence, Scholastic Assessments, and Physical traits*

	Identical twins reared together	Identical twins reared apart	Fraternal twins reared together	Siblings reared together	Siblings reared apart	Unrelated children reared together
	N = 83	N = 30	N = 172	N = 853	N = 131	N = 287
INTELLIGENCE						
Group Test	.944	.771	.542	.515	.441	.281
Individual Test	.921	.843	.526	.491	.463	.252
Final Assessment	.925	.876	.551	.538	.517	.269
Mean	.929	.829	.539	.514	.473	.267
SCHOLASTIC						
General	.898	.681	.831	.814	.526	.535
Reading & Spelling	.944	.647	.915	.853	.490	.548
Arithmetic	.862	.723	.748	.769	.563	.476
Mean	.900	.683	.831	.811	.526	.519
PHYSICAL						
Height	.956	.942	.472	.503	.536	-.069
Weight	.929	.884	.586	.568	.427	.243
Head Length	.961	.958	.495	.481	.536	.116
Head Breadth	.977	.960	.541	.507	.472	.082
Eye Color	1.000	1.000	.516	.553	.504	.104
Mean	.965	.949	.522	.522	.495	.095

*From: Burt, C. The inheritance of mental ability. AMER. PSYCHOL., 1958, 13, 1-15.

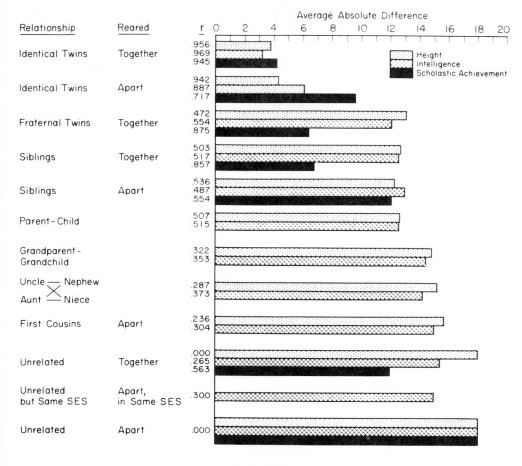

FIGURE 1

Correlations between individuals having different degrees of genetic relationship and reared together or apart. The average absolute difference between pairs of individuals is based on the same scale for height, intelligence and scholastic achievement, with a standard deviation of 16, which is the standard deviation of Stanford-Binet IQs in the normative population.

as they become more distantly related. (Conversely, the average difference between the persons becomes greater as they are more distantly related, as shown in Figure 1). Secondly, we see that height and intelligence are quite alike in this pattern as compared with scholastic achievement. Whether individuals are reared together (i.e., in the same family) or apart (i.e., in different families) has a much greater effect on scholastic achievement than on intelligence, and it has almost no effect on height. A review of all the major studies of the inheritance of intelligence and of scholastic achievement leads to the conclusion that, in general, individual differences in scholastic performance are determined less than half as much by heredity than are individual differences in intelligence (Jensen, 1967). Family environmental influ-

39

ences play a much larger role in determining school achievement than in determining measured intelligence. Note in Figure 1 that unrelated children reared together are about as much alike in school achievement as siblings reared apart.

These results from Burt's investigations based on London school children are quite typical of other studies, all of which (52 in all, as of 1963) have been reviewed by Erlenmeyer-Kimling and Jarvik (1963). They show a remarkable degree of consistency despite the fact that the studies were conducted by many different investigators having different backgrounds and contrasting views regarding the importance of heredity. They used different measures of intelligence, their data were derived from samples which were unequal in size, age, ethnic composition, socioeconomic stratification, and the data were collected in eight countries on four continents covering more than two generations of individuals. The authors concluded from this comprehensive review: "Against this pronounced heterogeneity, which should have clouded the picture, and is reflected by the wide range of correlations, a clearly definitive consistency emerges from the data. The composite data are compatible with the polygenic hypothesis which is generally favored in accounting for inherited differences in mental ability" (Erlenmeyer-Kimling and Jarvik, 1963, p. 1479).

The methods of quantitative genetics can be applied to extracting estimates of heritability (the proportion of variance attributable to heredity) from data such as the correlations in Table 1. In fact, Burt has applied what is perhaps the most elaborate and accurate of these methods to the data in Table 1 in order to obtain an overall estimate of the heritability of intelligence (Burt, 1958). The heritability (based on the individual intelligence test) is 77, which means that 77 percent of the variance in measured intelligence in London school children is attributable to heredity. The remaining 23 percent is attributable to environmental effects (16 percent) and unreliability or error or measurement (7 percent). Thus, 82 percent of the true score variance in intelligence is accounted for by hereditary factors and 18 percent by environmental factors. Burt's estimate is in close agreement with other studies. Elsewhere I have reviewed all the major studies of heritability based only on comparisons of identical and fraternal twins, the most common method for studying heritability (Jensen, 1967). The average heritability derived from these studies is 80 percent. The particular analysis that was applied to the data permits a partitioning of the environmental variance (20 percent of the total true score variance) into two components, one associated with environmental effects attributable to differences *between* families, which accounted for 12 percent of the variance, and the other attributable to environmental effects arising *within* families, which accounted for 8 percent of the variance.

In contrast, measures of scholastic achievement show a heritability (based on the average of all the major twin studies) of only 40 percent, while 54 percent of the

40

variance is attributable to environmental differences between families and only 6 percent to differences within families. This means that family influences are a powerful factor determining individual differences in scholastic performance. Children within the same family are much more alike in their school work than they are in intelligence. As shown in Figure 1, the average IQ differences between siblings reared together in their own families is about 12 points. The difference is only about half this amount for scholastic achievement.

In principle, the theoretically least ambiguous estimates of heritability are obtainable from the study of identical twins reared apart. Such sets of identical twins who have been separated early in life are difficult to find, and to date only 145 separated identical twin pairs have been reported in the literature. The three largest studies are by Newman, Freeman, and Holzinger (1937), based on 19 separated twin pairs; by Shields (1962), based on 44 pairs; and by Burt (1966) based on 53 pairs. Since each of a pair of identical twins has received exactly the same complement of genes, any difference between them must be attributable to non-genetic effects. Therefore the correlation between identical twins separated at an early age and reared apart provides a simple index of heritability. But heritability will be overestimated to the degree that there exists a positive correlation between the environments of the separated twins. The members of separated twin pairs are often placed in rather similar environmental circumstances, which would tend to produce a higher correlation between them than if they had been assigned to families in the population strictly at random. Fortunately, this objection cannot be raised to the largest of the studies of separated identical twins. Burt's 53 pairs of identical twins, separated at an early age, were reared in environments that were slightly *negatively* correlated (Burt, 1966). (The environments are classified on a six-point scale of socioeconomic stratification.) In other words, the separated twins actually grew up in somewhat more dissimilar environments than if they had been placed in differing families strictly at random. Burt's sample has the further advantage of very closely approximating the mean and standard deviation of the population in IQ and is therefore highly representative of the population distribution of intelligence. The obtained correlations between the separated twins were .77 on a group test of intelligence and .86 on an individual test (the Stanford-Binet slightly modified for suitability in the English population). The corresponding correlations for unrelated children reared together were .28 and .25. In general scholastic attainments, on the other hand, the twins were correlated only .62, as compared with a correlation of .54 for unrelated children reared together.

The largest IQ difference reported in any of the 145 separated identical twin pairs found in the literature is 24 IQ points on the Stanford-Binet (Newman, Freeman, and Holzinger, 1937). This figure should be compared with the average differences of 18 IQ points among persons in the population and 12 points between full siblings reared together in their own families. Seventeen percent of siblings reared together differ by more than 24 IQ points. The twins whose IQs differed by 24 points when they were tested as adults were reared in highly dissimilar environments in terms of their educational advantages; one left school after 8th grade while the other went on to college to become a school teacher. Also, the less advantaged twin had a record of serious illnesses in her first three years of life, while the more favored twin had always enjoyed good health. This would suggest that their IQ difference was probably due in part to non-genetic biological factors and not entirely to differences in social environment and educational opportunity. Even though there was a 24 point difference in IQ, both twins had IQs in normal range (IQs 92 and 116).

THE EFFECTS OF EXTREME ENVIRONMENTS

If heredity accounts for individual differences in intelligence to so large an extent as indicated by the evidence we have just reviewed, what are we to think of other studies which show a large boost in the IQ as a result of improvements in the environment, such as the studies of Skeels and his colleagues, which are so often optimistically cited in the literature on the culturally disadvantaged? (The upward shifts in IQ of as much as 20 to 30 points on the average that have been reported in a few studies [e.g., Skeels, 1966] are often interpreted as evidence that contradicts the inheritance of intelligence.) If environmental changes can effect a rise in IQ of 20 to 30 points, how is it possible to claim that some 80 percent of the population variance in IQ is due to heredity and only 20 percent to environment? The most common solution to this problem is to take sides on the issue and reject whichever side one wishes to believe is the contradicted evidence. Thus, by and large, writers on the subject of the culturally disadvantaged ignore the research on the inheritance of intelligence and emphasize studies which illustrate dramatic boosts in IQ as a result of improved environment. It would be interesting to compare the frequency of citation of Sir Cyril Burt's researches as compared with those of Harold Skeels in the literature dealing with the culturally disadvantaged. Both lines of evidence are important, however, and in principle it is not at all necessary to reject one in favor of the other. The two seemingly contradictory lines of evidence can be completely reconciled by hypothesizing that the environment acts as a threshold variable.

ENVIRONMENT AS A THRESHOLD VARIABLE

This hypothesis is most easily understood in terms of an analogy with the effects of the nutritional value of people's diets. A considerable proportion of the variance in adult stature will be due to non-genetic effects, namely, to differences in nutrition. But the variation in stature among persons who have grown up on a diet adequate in the required vitamins, minerals, and proteins would be determined almost entirely by their genes and hardly at all by their eating habits. No one in this category would

42

have been made appreciably taller by being given any amounts of additional vitamins and minerals. In other words, beyond a certain rather low threshold level of nutritional adequacy, further improvements in nutrition have almost no further effects on stature. Moreover, once the essential nutritional elements are maintained in the diet, individual peculiarities of tastes and eating habits are of negligible consequence as determinants of stature. Over and above the minimum daily requirement of the basic essentials, it makes little difference in a person's stature whether he habitually eats hot dogs or caviar.

A similar relationship seems to hold for the effects of environmental stimulation on the development of intelligence. All the relevant studies I have surveyed in the literature show two things: When there are large permanent boosts in IQ (i.e. greater than 10 IQ points) which are not clearly associated with changes in organic conditions, (a) the initial IQs were low (usually more than one standard deviation below the mean but rarely below 50), and (b) the child's environment prior to the boost in IQ was drastically lacking in sensory stimulation (particularly auditory) and in opportunities for interactions with other persons. When these extreme deprivations are alleviated by moving the child into a greatly enriched environment, especially by providing ample adult-child interaction, the boost in IQ takes place quite rapidly, most of it occurring in the first year after placement in a better environment (e.g., Skeels, 1966).

A well-known study by Skeels (1966) is frequently cited in the literature on the disadvantaged as an illustration of the damaging effects of early environmental deprivation and the dramtic amelioration of these effects when the children are placed in a better environment. Though the work of Skeels is interesting and important in its own right for what it may tell us about the effects of extremely early deprivation, its relevance to the understanding of the problems of the majority of children called culturally disadvantaged is highly questionable.

In brief, Skeels made follow-up comparisons of two groups of children who were reared in an orphanage from infancy. At around two years of age one group of children, called the Experimental Group (N=13), was removed from the orphanage to an institution for the mentally retarded, where they were individually "assigned" to borderline mentally retarded young women, who acted as mother surrogates. The chief occupation of each of these women was to act as a foster mother to one child. The children remained with their mother surrogates for from one to two years and then were adopted into good homes. The Contrast Group of children (N=12) remained in the nursery during the same period, and between four and five years of age they were either placed in adoptive homes or were transferred, because of low IQ or other conditions that contra-indicate placement for adoption, to an institution for the mentally retarded.

It should be noted that the Experimental Group had a mean IQ of 64 at 18 months of age, while the Contrast Group had a mean IQ of 87. After the Experimental Group had been transferred to the mother surrogate situation of 18 months (on the average), the IQs of the Experimental and Contrast groups were 91 and 62, respectively. Later testing between 6 and 7 years of age yielded average IQs of the Experimental and Contrast Groups of 96 and 66, respectively. In a follow-up of the adult status of the two groups, Skeels found that all of the Experimental group had become self-sufficient persons, quite indistinguishable from typical citizens in their communities. Their children had an average IQ of 104. But the Contrast Group did much less well: five remained inmates of institutions for the retarded and, with one exception, the others held menial, unskilled jobs. (The one exception, with an IQ of 89, was a compositor and typesetter.)

The puzzling results of this study are seldom questioned and it is seldom suggested that such a study, involving only 25 cases in all, would need to be replicated in order to inspire confidence in the generality of its findings. For example, over half (7 out of 12) of the Contrast Group who remained in the orphanage until about 5 years of age, when last tested, had IQs in the mentally retarded range (i.e., under 70). Is this a typical sample of orphanage children? Why was the Contrast Group 23 IQ points higher than the Experimental Group at 18 months of age, when both groups presumably were reared in a severely deprived environment? Five of the 12 children in the Contrast Group and 9 of the 13 in the Experimental Group showed shifts in IQ from first to last testing that are greater than the largest IQ difference ever reported between members of a pair of separated identical twins (of which 145 pairs are on record). Careful study of Skeels' monograph will raise many other questions in the reader's mind. The many peculiarities to be found in this unique set of data, based on only 25 cases, make it a dubious basis for generalizations concerning the effects of environmental deprivation.

Aside from these obvious limitations, the relevance of the study to the understanding of children commonly called culturally disadvantaged must be questioned directly. First of all, I have found no evidence that the severe early deprivation suffered by the infants in the Skeels study is at all typical of the environments of the majority of disadvantaged children. Consider Skeels' description of the orphanage environment during the first two years of the children's life: "The babies were kept in standard hospital cribs that often had protective sheeting on the sides, thus effectively limiting visual stimulation; no toys or other objects were hung in the infant's line of vision Human interactions were limited to busy nurses who, with the speed born of practice and necessity, changed diapers or bedding, bathed and medicated the infants, and fed them efficiently with propped bottles" (Skeels, 1966, p. 3) Also consider the condition of some of the children when they came to the orphanage at around one year of age, as described in the case of two baby girls who had been

44

neglected by their feebleminded mothers: "The youngsters were pitiful little creatures. They were tearful, had runny noses, and sparse, stringy, and colorless hair; they were emaciated, undersized, and lacked muscle tonus and responsiveness. Sad and inactive, the two spent their days rocking and whining. The psychological examinations showed developmental levels of 6 and 7 months, respectively, for the two girls, although they were then 13 and 16 months old chronologically" (Skeels, 1966, p. 5). This picture is quite atypical of the majority of disadvantaged children. While Skeels' Experimental Group had an average IQ of 64 at 18 months of age, culturally disadvantaged children generally perform in the normal range on infant tests of intelligence, and, if anything, tend to be slightly superior to middle-class children in perceptual-motor functions (Bayley, 1965).

It should be remembered that the stimulation afforded the Experimental Group by the mentally retarded mother surrogates was not of a peculiarly "cultural" or "middle-class" nature. It consisted largely of play and interaction with affectionate adults and other children. The mother surrogates, after all, were inmates of an institution for the retarded. Was this environment so much more stimulating and enriched for cognitive development than the homes of the majority of disadvantaged children?

It is clear that the Skeels subjects, with a mean IQ of 64 at 18 months, also were not typical of children of this IQ level; their psychological development and test performance had been decidedly depressed by severe environmental deprivations. Middleclass, home-reared children with IQs in the 60s do not show any appreciable gain in IQ over the years, and no presently known treatment boosts their IQs to a normal level. It is of great interest that despite severe early deprivation, the Skeels Experimental children later attained not only IQs in the average range, but were occupationally successful and had children of their own who were of average intelligence and did well in school. Thus, what Skeels has shown most clearly is that early environmental deprivation occurring before 2 or 3 years of age is not permanently a major handicap to mental development, provided the child at this age is brought into a normally affectionate social environment, particularly a one-to-one relationship between the child and an adult, which seems to be the single most important ingredient. In the culturally disadvantaged, on the other hand, we typically see a quite different picture: the early environment is not affectionally barren or lacking in social interactions; the child is well-developed in perceptual-motor abilities; and when moved into an enriched environment (kindergarten or first grade) at 5 or 6 years of age the child shows first a rise in verbal intelligence (probably as a result of the school's overcoming certain superficial environmental deficiencies) and then a gradual decline in IQ and scholastic performance relative to the majority of school children. This is an essentially different picture from that presented by the Skeels

45

study and others like it (many of these studies are reviewed by Hunt, 1961, pp. 19-34).

There are cases on record of even more severe and prolonged cognitive (but not affectional) deprivations than existed for many of the children in Skeels' study. The findings further suggest that the development of normal mental ability apparently is not irremediably hindered by early deficiencies in experience. A now classic case is that of Isabel, who was studied by sociologist Kingsley Davis (1947). Isabel was an illegitimate child whose "disgraced" grandparents wanted to hide her and her deaf-mute mother from the world. Isabel lived with her mother in an attic until she was discovered by the authorities at age 6½. She had lived practically all this time isolated from the rest of the family; she communicated with her mother largely through gestures. She was totally without speech and made only "strange croaking sounds." At first there was a question whether she was deaf, but her hearing was later found to be normal. Her behavior was generally strange; on the Vineland Social Maturity Scale she had a Social Age of 2 years 6 months, and on the Stanford-Binet she obtained a mental age of 1 year 7 months, putting her IQ at about 25. What is specially interesting, however, is that after some 2 to 3 years of intensive, individual, educational treatment, Isabel was behaviorally indistinguishable from the average run of her classmates of the same age; she was in the average range of IQ and scholastic achievement. She had accomplished in two years what normally would have taken six. We can never know, of course, what her level of intelligence might have been if she had grown up in an optimal environment during the six years of her life. But there remain two facts of striking importance: extreme environmental deprivation resulted, by the age of 6, in a level of development that was commensurate with the lowest level of human ability to be found in institutions for the severely defective, and, through intensive educational "therapy," it was possible to ameliorate this condition, by the age of 8 or 9, to a level of completely normal intellectual functioning.

Evidence suggests that sensory deprivation in the auditory modality, especially when it is so severe as to prevent perception of speech from an early age, is probably the most intellectually handicapping form of environmental deprivation. The acquisition and use of language is so central to intellectual functioning that children who are hindered in the acquisition of this main tool of thought by early deafness generally have IQs about 20 points below the average of their siblings (Salzberger and Jarvik, 1963). However, even the seemingly most severe forms of sensory deprivation in early life apparently do not have irreversibly damaging effects on intellectual development, as shown in the famous case of Helen Keller, who at 19 months of age suffered an acute illness which totally and permanently deprived her of both hearing and sight. From then up to age seven her deafness and blindness so retarded her mental development that she seemed scarcely human. The rest of her story is well known. When Helen Keller was seven, her remarkable tutor, Ann Sullivan, came into her life and broke through the communication barrier, so that Helen Keller was able to begin acquiring language and symbolic concepts. Despite her six years of extreme sensory and language deprivation, she progressed rapidly once she had learned to communicate. She later graduated from college with honors and became a writer of intellectual distinction.

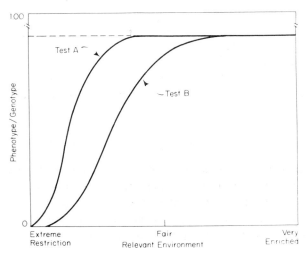

FIGURE 2

Hypothetical curves showing the relationship between the degree to which genetic potential is realized in the phenotype (performance) and the quality of the environment. Test A represents a relatively culture-free test, Test B a more culturally loaded test.

The idea that environmental stimulation has some threshold level beyond which further stimulation adds negligible increments to mental ability is illustrated in Fig. 2. The *phenotype/genotype* ratio expresses the degree to which the person's genetic intellectual potential is realized in his actual performance as measured by an IQ test. This could just as well be labeled *performance/genetic potential*. The asymptotic values of the *phenotype/genotype* ratio are assumed to be normally distributed in the population. The extent of the departure of the IQ distribution from normality due to environmental depression of the phenotype is presumably a function of the percentage of the population that falls below the threshold value on the environmental continuum. The two curves in Fig. 2 represent the functions that theoretically obtain for intelligence tests that differ in cultural loading. Test A is more "culture free" than Test B. Test A, for example, might correspond to the Digit Span subtest of the Stanford-Binet and Test B might correspond to the Vocabulary subtest. Thus, the subjects who have suffered some environmental disadvantage, we should expect to find greater discrepancies between their performances on tests of type A and type B than are found in subjects who were reared in more favorable environments.

47

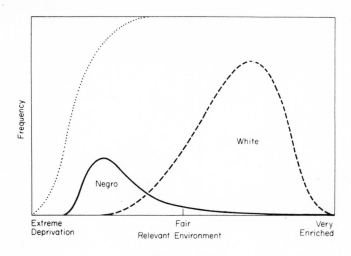

Frequency

White

Negro

Extreme
Deprivation

Fair
Relevant Environment

Very
Enriched

FIGURE 3

Hypothetical frequency distributions of Negro and white populations of the United States with respect to environmental variables relevant to intellectual development. The dotted curve represents a trace of the curve (Test A) in Figure 2, to illustrate the hypothesis that many Negroes may be reared in environmental conditions that do not permit the full development of genetic intellectual potential.

This point is illustrated hypothetically in Fig. 3, comparing the white and Negro populations, the latter having a relatively large percentage of children referred to as culturally disadvantaged. The dotted line in Fig. 3 is intended as a reminder of the curves in Fig. 2. Fig. 3 shows how the distribution of the Negro and white populations on the environmental continuum would determine their relative standing on the *phenotype/genotype* ratio. Though this picture is highly plausible, it contains many unknowns. The nature of the "relevant environment" continuum is not specifically known, and the relative standing of the Negro and white populations on this continuum is even less known. Our definition of the "environmentally depressed" refers to those individuals whose standing on the environmental continuum is such that their hypothetical *phenotype/genotype* ratio is below the asymptotic level (as shown in Fig.2).

This formulation (Fig. 3) leads to the prediction that the heritability of IQ would be lower in the culturally disadvantaged segment of the population than in the middle-class population. But no data are yet available which could test this hypothesis. It is also noteworthy that Negroes have never been included in studies of the heritability of intelligence. To the extent that the hypothesis expressed in Fig. 3 is correct, we should expect to find lower heritability estimates in random samples from the Negro population.

As pointed out previously, Fig. 2 suggests that there should be a greater difference

48

between intelligence tests having various degrees of cultural bias (Test A *vs.* Test B) for an environmentally disadvantaged group than for a more advantaged group. There is some evidence on this in the comparison of Negro and white normative data on the Stanford-Binet intelligence test, which is made up of a number of subtests that obviously differ in their degree of cultural leading. The most clear-cut difference in this respect is between Vocabulary and Digit Span. Fig. 4 shows the distribution of total Stanford-Binet IQs for Negro and white children (from Kennedy, Van de Riet, and White, 1963). (The Negro distribution is based on a random sample of 1800 elementary school children in five Southeastern States.) The overall IQ comparison is quite typical of the majority of studies of measured intelligence in Negroes and whites, which generally show some 15 to 20 points IQ difference and a smaller standard deviation (dispersion) of IQs for Negroes than for whites. But now let us compare Negro and white performance on a culturally loaded subtest (Vocabulary) and on a relatively culture-free subtest (Digit Span). The comparison is shown in Figure 5. The Negro-white difference in Vocabulary is much greater than in Digit Span. It should be noted that Digit Span is highly correlated with intelligence in the general population in which the Stanford-Binet and Wechsler

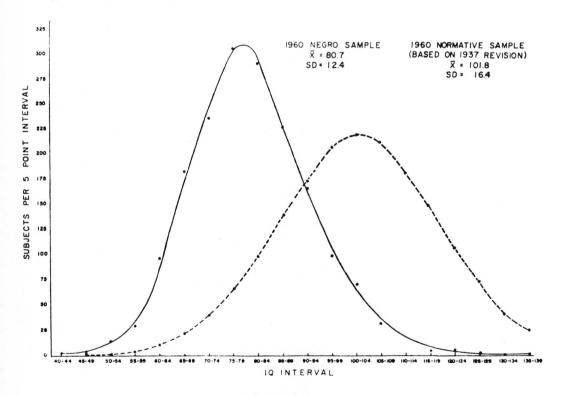

FIGURE 4

Stanford-Binet IQ distribution of Negro children in five Southeastern states (solid line) and of white children in the 1960 normative sample. (From Kennedy, Van de Riet, & White, 1963.)

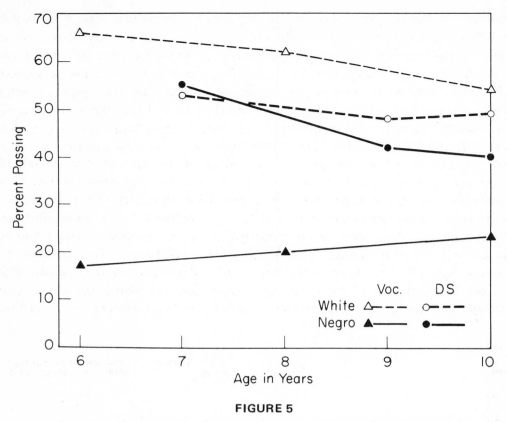

Legend (within figure):

	Voc.	DS
White	△– – –	○– – –
Negro	▲———	●———

Percent Passing / Age in Years

FIGURE 5

Percentage of Negro and white children passing the Vocabulary and Digit Span tests of the Stanford-Binet at various ages. (Data from Kennedy, Van de Riet, & White, 1963, and Terman & Merrill, 1960.)

intelligence tests were standardized, Digit Span correlates .62 with total Stanford-Binet IQ at age 2½. It correlates .75 (corrected for attenuation) with IQ on the Wechsler Adult Intelligence Scale, and it has a loading of .80 on the general factor common to all the subtests of the Wechsler (Wechsler, 1958, p. 122). Thus the results shown in Fig. 5 cannot be adequately explained merely in terms of the Vocabulary test's being a better measure of intelligence than Digit Span. The main difference between the two subtests is their "cultural" loading.

This finding, when viewed in terms of the formulation set forth in Figures 3 and 4, suggests a genetical criterion for the design of culture-free or culture-fair tests. Such tests should (a) correlate highly with standard intelligence tests when the testees are similar to those for whom the standard test meets the usual criteria of validity, and have high heritability in a group of heterogeneous socioeconomic background. These are probably the soundest criteria for determining the culture-fairness of an intelligence test. The attempt to build culture-free tests by the sole criterion of whether the test diminishes social-class differences in test performance, and doing

50

this by throwing out those items which discriminate most sharply between various socioeconomic groups, is a fallacious practice indeed. The test constructed by this criterion could not then legitimately be used to test the hypothesis that various social classes differ in intelligence; for the tests would have been so constructed as to minimize the changes of showing whatever true difference might exist between social classes. This should be as generally recognized as the principle that tests constructed so as to eliminate or equalize items that show sex differences cannot then be used to determine whether the sexes differ in intelligence.

SOCIAL CLASS DIFFERENCES IN INTELLIGENCE

We come now to the question of whether higher and lower socioeconomic groups differ on the average in innate ability. There can be no question that average differences in *measured* intelligence do exist between socioeconomic groups. Whatever dispute is engendered by the data concerns the extent to which the observed differences are determined by hereditary factors. The evidence on the whole leads to the conclusion that heredity plays a part in determining intelligence differences as a function of social class. This should not be surprising, since social class is highly related to occupation and education. The educational system and the occupational hierarchy act as an intellectual screening device, and the greater the degree of social mobility that society allows, the greater will be the tendency for innate ability to determine the individual's occupational and socioeconomic status (SES). Several different lines of evidence support this conclusion.

In the first place, the range of social class differences in IQ is about 40 points, which is about twice as much as can be reasonably accounted for in terms of all the studies we have on the heritability of intelligence. About 30 percent of the variance in school children's Stanford-Binet IQs can be accounted for by placing them into one of six socioeconomic categories according to their fathers' occupations (Terman and Merrill, 1937). Now, if 30 percent of the variance in IQ is associated with socioeconomic status, and if in essentially the same population it is found that the heritability of IQ is over 80 percent, with less than 20 percent of the total variance associated with socioeconomic status (i.e. 30 percent of the total variance) was environmentally determined; at least one-third of this variance would have to be hereditary. The point can be easily shown in the following diagram. (See page 52.)

Another line of evidence that socioeconomic differences have a hereditary component is provided by the phenomenon of "regression to the mean," which was originally discovered by Sir Francis Galton, who found that, in general, tall fathers had sons who were not quite as tall and short fathers had sons who were not quite as short. Moreover, Galton discovered a quite precise relationship between the average

51

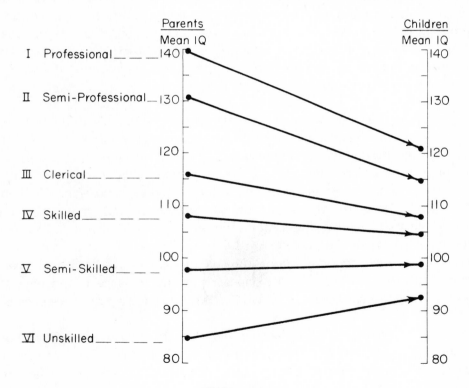

Hereditary

Environmental

Percent Variance

$0 - 10 - 20 - 30 - 40 - 50 - 60 - 70 - 80 - 90 - 100$

Within SES

Between SES

height of fathers and sons: the son's height, on the average, is just halfway between the father's height and the mean height of the population. This "Law of Filial Regression," as Galton called it, has been found to hold true not only for height but for most polygenically inherited traits. It holds true also for intelligence. This is shown in (Fig. 6. Note that for each group the children's mean IQ is almost exactly halfway between the mean of the parental group and the population mean (IQ 100). This finding could hardly be predicted precisely from any environmentalist theory of social class differences, but it is perfectly in accord with genetic expectations.

Note that the higher occupational classes, who presumably provide more beneficial

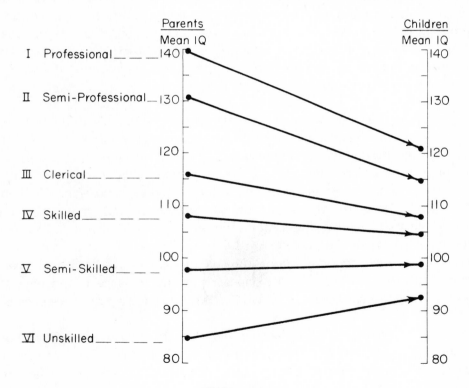

FIGURE 6

An illustration of the phenomenon of regression to the mean, originally established by Sir Francis Galton. (Data from Burt, 1961).

52

environmental influences for their children, have children whose IQs are lower than the IQS of their parents, even though many of these parents undoubtedly grew up in less favorable circumstances than they provide for their own children. The lower classes, on the other hand, have children whose IQs are higher than their parents' IQs, despite the fact that these parents generally provide meagerly for their children. It should be remembered, too, that in Figure 6 we are dealing only with group means. In reality, around each of these means there is a wide dispersion of IQs. Dull children are sometimes born to bright parents and bright children are sometimes born to dull parents.

Although the children of mentally retarded (IQ under 70) parents are often subjected to a culturally and intellectually impoverished environment, fewer than half the children of retarded parents are themselves retarded (Reed and Reed, 1965). This would be difficult to explain solely in environmental terms, although it is what we should expect from the polygenic theory of the inheritance of intelligence. In the monumental study of hereditary factors in mental retardation by Elizabeth and Sheldon Reed (1965) a number of bright (IQ 110 to 130) and definitely superior (IQ over 130) children were found in families where either one or both parents were mentally retarded (IQ below 70). Furthermore, the Reeds described the environments of most of these superior children as "extremely impoverished." Apparently, having mentally retarded parents plus extremely impoverished environment is not always sufficient to produce mental retardation or even dullness in children who are not unfavorably endowed by heredity. In fact, the majority of children from retardate unions, though for the most part reared in impoverished environments, tested in the normal IQ range of 90 to 110. (The total IQ distribution of children of retarded parents is quite skewed, however, with a preponderance of low IQs and a relative scarcity of high IQs as compared with the general population. One of the main conclusions of the Reeds' study is that some five million of the six million retardates in the United States have a retarded parent or a normal parent who has a retarded sibling.)

Finally, we can point to the interesting fact that the IQ s of orphanage children who have never known their parents are as highly correlated with their father's occupation (classified on a six point scale) as are the IQs of children who have been reared by their own parents (Lawrence, 1931). The two correlations were. 23 and .24, respectively.

RACIAL DIFFERENCES IN INTELLIGENCE

My conclusions about social class differences in intelligence cannot be safely generalized across racial groups in the United States but pertain only within racially homogeneous groups. The reason for this is that social mobility is not the same for all

53

racial groups in our society, and the individual's abilities therefore will have different chances of determining his rise or fall in the socioeconomic hierarchy depending on the extent and the nature of barriers due to racial prejudice and discrimination. In our society it should be easier to infer rather poor innate ability in native born whites who are in unskilled or menial occupations than to make the same inference in the case of Negroes or Mexican-Americans.

Although children called culturally disadvantaged are found in every racial group, attention in the United States in recent years has been focused mainly on the Negro disadvantaged, particularly those of the urban Negro ghettos. The conscience and concern of citizens in general and of educators in particular are aroused by the great discrepancy between achievements and aspirations in the Negro population. The problem is terribly complex and must be viewed on many levels: psychological, social, and economic (see Deutsch, Jensen, and Katz, 1968). It is seldom suggested that biological factors may also play a part in the relative average disadvantage of Negroes in educational and occupational attainments. Ruling out this possiblity on the basis of a social creed or by official proclamation can only restrict research and hinder our eventual understanding of the problem—and consequently diminish the changes of its solution. Given what we already know about the importance of heredity in determining individual differences in mental ability, not facing the heredity-environment uncertainty concerning racial differences in intelligence and educability as a problem for research can be justified neither scientifically nor morally. As a social policy, avoidance of the issue could be harmful to everyone in the long run, especially to future generations of Negroes, who could suffer the most from well-meaning but misguided and ineffective attempts to improve their lot in life.

So far social scientists and educators have been much too half-hearted in their attempt to determine the extent to which favorable environmental conditions can overcome the majority of Negroes' apparent intellectual disadvantage as compared with other groups. If Head Start does not produce the expected results (and so far it has not), is it because it is too little too late or is not followed up long enough and intensively enough? What has not yet been done and what is needed is an all-out effort to show what can really be done by environmental enrichment, beginning with the prenatal care of the child's mother and following through with every conceivable environmental advantage throughout infancy and all the years the child is in school.

Negro-white differences in measured intelligence have been thoroughly reviewed elsewhere (Shuey, 1966). The results of hundreds of studies are in close agreement and are most easily summarized by the statement that the average difference between the Negro and white populations is something close to one standard deviation on a

54

large variety of tests of general intelligence. (One standard deviation is 15 IQ points on most standard tests.) The meaning of this difference is that about 85 percent of Negroes fall below the average of the white population (IQ 100). Attempts to match Negro and white groups in education, socioeconomic status, and other background variables, or to statistically control for these variables, have not yet succeeded in eliminating the difference in measured intelligence. Wilson (1966), for example, used a multiple correlation to predict IQ and included race along with 10 other background variables (neighborhood, socioeconomic level, etc.) as his predictors. Race made a larger independent contribution to the prediction of IQ than any other single background variable in Wilson's analysis, which was based on a large sample of Negro and white children from the public schools in the East Bay area of Northern California.

The same generalization holds for scholastic performance as well. In the single largest comparative study we have, based on a nationwide sample of children in 4000 schools, Negroes consistently average very close to one standard deviation below whites at grade levels 1, 3, 6, 9, and 12 in tests of Verbal Ability, Reading Comprehension, and Mathematics Achievement (Coleman, et al., 1966, pp. 272-277).

Is this consistent average deficit in the Negro school population attributable entirely to social or cultural disadvantages? Some evidence in the Coleman study suggests that if the deficit is environmentally caused, the environmental factors responsible are probably not those commonly associated with economic, social, or cultural disadvantage. By far the most disadvantaged ethnic group in the United States, in terms of the usual criteria of economic and cultural disadvantage, are the American Indians. Coleman's data for the ninth grade (all regions of the U. S. combined) is perhaps most representative, since the tests are maximally reliable by this age, and the school dropout rate is not yet an appreciable biasing factor. In the ninth grade every one of the twelve social-cultural rating scales used in the Coleman study showed a lower average score for Indians than for Negroes. The ratings of the quality of the Indians' environment were, on the average, twice as far (in standard deviation units) below the Negroes' environment as the Negroes are below the average white's environment. The environmental scales were intended to assess the following: reading material in the home, items or amenities in the home, structural integrity of the home, foreign language in the home, preschool attendance, encyclopedia in the home, parents' education, time spent on homework, parents' educational aspirations for child, parents' interest in school work, child's self-concept or self-esteem, and the child's expressed interest in school and in reading. On other indices of deprivation (e.g., income, unemployment and mortality rates) Indians also are generally far more disadvantaged than Negroes.

Yet on all four of the mental tests used in the Coleman study (Non-verbal, Verbal,

55

Reading Comprehension, and Math Achievement), the mean scores for Indians significantly exceed the Negro means by about one-third of a standard deviation (Coleman et al., *Supplemental Appendix* pp. 173, 201). According to these findings the mental ability and scholastic achievement measures are not a monotomic function of cultural deprivation, at least as defined by the particular environmental indices used by Coleman et al. Yet *within* each racial group the environmental indices are positively correlated with the ability and achievement scores. Viewed altogether these results mean that some additional factor, not explicitly assessed in the Coleman study, must be hypothesized to account for the Negroes' relatively low educational achievement, which is below that of any other group identified in the study. The next step, of course, would be to conduct empirical tests of the hypothesized factors.

Patterns of Abilities

The so-called factor of *general* intelligence, which is what all kinds of test of intellectual functions have in common and causes them to be positively correlated with one another, accounts for most of the variance in standard tests of intelligence. But there are also a number of factors of more specialized abilities, and it is important to inquire as to whether various social class and racial and ethnic groups differ in these. If there are significant differences in patterns of abilities, recognition of this fact could have important educational implications. For one thing, various abilities may mature at different rates in different individuals, so that having all children learning the same thing at the same age may be far less than the optimal educational strategy. A more optimal practice might capitalize on individual and group differences rather than making them the basis for success or failure in the educational system.

An important line of research by Fifer (1965) and Lesser, Fifer, and Clark (1965) throws some light on ethnic differences in patterns of ability. The results show a remarkable consistency which make them especially interesting and worthy of further investigation. These investigators used four special abilities tests (Verbal, Numerical, Reasoning, and Spatial) to compare lower- and middle-class school children from four ethnic groups in New York City: Chinese, Jews, Negroes, and Puerto Ricans. The results are shown in Figure 7. The most interesting feature of this graph is that each ethnic group has a distinctively different "profile" of scores and, what is even more striking, this profile is the *same* in both lower and middle class. The lower class is uniformly below the middle class, but the particular pattern of abilities is peculiar to the ethnic classification. This is a provocative finding in view of the prevailing belief that social class differences are greater than ethnic difference in child rearing practices and other environmental influences which could affect the development of mental abilities. The data do not permit analysis of hereditary and environmental factors in producing these different patterns of ability, but we know

56

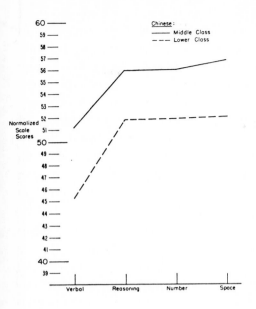

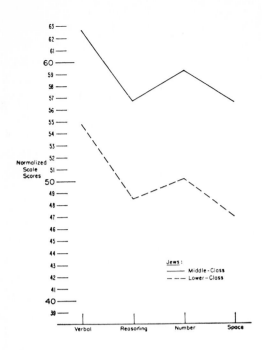

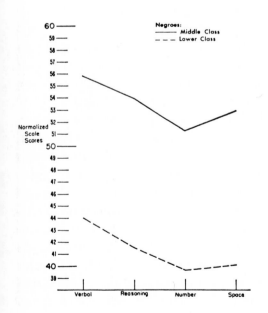

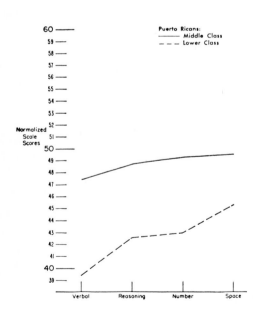

FIGURE 7

Pattern of normalized mental-ability scores for each social-class and ethnic group. (From Fifer, 1964).

57

that individual differences in these special abilities are determined almost as much by heredity as are individual differences in general ability (Nichols, 1965; Vandenberg, 1966). However, the main determinants of the ability patterns found by Lesser, Fifer, and Clark remain to be discovered. We have not yet begun to explore the possibilities of making the most of differences in ability patterns among school children, but this possibility is now distinctly feasible with the recent developments in computerized methods in instruction. It will very likely be found in the foreseeable future that a *diversity* of instructional paths will most effectively lead many children who might ordinarily not succeed in school to achieve common educational goals. The hope for improving education lies not in denying or minimizing individual or group differences but in understanding their nature to the greatest extent possible, so that they can be *used* in the design and testing of new curricula and instructional methods. We have an interesting parallel in the history of medicine. At one time physicians sought the one perfect treatment or cure-all that could be applied with equal benefit to all ailing persons regardless of the specific nature of their ills. It was an utterly vain search, and the success of modern medicine finally came about largely by improving the precision of diagnosis and discovering specific treatments for specific ailments. A similar approach seems inevitable in the future of education, as we find out more about the nature of individual differences in learning and develop the technological means of individualizing instruction.

INTELLIGENCE AND LEARNING ABILITY

Historically, the concept of Mental Age preceded that of the Intelligence Quotient or IQ. The first satisfactory intelligence tests were age scales. The idea of IQ was later invented as an index of brightness or *rate* of mental development; it expresses the ratio of Mental Age to Chronological Age: $IQ = MA/CA$. (This fraction is traditionally multiplied by 100 to remove the decimal.) If we examine the content of the usual test materials used to assess Mental Age we find that it consists mostly of specific knowledge and skills that have had to be learned. If two individuals have the same opportunities to learn the bits of knowledge or skill sampled by the test and have been exposed to these opportunities for equal amounts of time, then the amount of their knowledge can be regarded as an index of their learning rate. This is the essential logic of the IQ. The Mental Age tells us how much the child has learned, and when this is divided by the time he has spent, that is, his Chronological Age, we obtain an index of his learning rate. The construction of valid IQ tests has depended upon adequately sampling from all the learning possibilities presented by the environment. Since IQ tests were originally designed to be predictive of school performance, and since this is still their principal area of use, selection of test content has been heavily weighted with those kinds of knowledge and skills that have most in common with the types of learning expected in school. When one considers the actual content of a test like the Stanford-Binet or the Wechsler tests, it

58

seems quite amazing that these tests should work so well. And they work well indeed for the vast majority of the population. Perhaps the most convincing testimony to this fact is that such tests yield very high heritabilities, as shown previously. If the tests were not measuring some important, basically biological aspect of individuals, it would not be possible to obtain significant heritability values from the tests. The fact that the tests can predict practical criteria, such as school achievement, tells us that the tests have useful validity. But the fact that a high degree of heritability can be shown for such tests means that for the most of the population the tests get at some fundamental, biologically determined aspect of individual differences. It would seem to be most simply characterized as learning rate.

We run into difficuty, however, when we have reason to believe that there have been gross inequalities among individuals in the opportunities afforded by their environments for the acquisition of the specific content sampled by standard IQ tests. This is the familiar problem of cultural bias in tests. An intelligence test must be regarded as inappropriate for an individual to the extent that its content is sampled from a different set of environmental opportunities from those to which the individual has been exposed. And to the extent that the test is inappropriate in this sense, it fails to reflect the individual's biological potential for learning. If IQ tests fail in this way for children of low socioeconomic status in our society, we should expect that such tests would yield relatively low heritabilities in the low socioeconomic segment of the population. Furthermore, we should expect that such tests would correlate poorly with other measures of learning ability derived in situations that more or less insure equality of opportunity for learning.

Direct Learning Tests
My own research has taken off directly from this point. The basic rationale is simple: If IQ tests are essentially a measure of learning rate based on what the child has learned from his environment prior to taking the test, why not measure learning rate more directly, by giving the child something to learn in the test situation and seeing how fast he can learn it? Measures from such "direct learning tests," as we now call them, would have the advantage of insuring more nearly equal opportunity for learning and would therefore be less "culturally" biased. If such tests indeed measured the same sort of learning ability tapped by traditional IQ tests, they should correlate highly with IQ in a population for which the IQ test is culturally appropriate and in which it shows a high degree of heritability.

The first such tests I devised consisted of the recall and serial learning of a dozen common objects (Jensen, 1961). The tests were given to selected groups of Mexican-American and Anglo-American children in the fourth grade (average age of 9 years). The children were classed as Dull (IQs around 80) or Bright (IQs around 115) on the basis of standard IQ tests. The Recall Test consisted of displaying 12 common

59

objects (e.g., ball, doll, toy car, comb, drinking glass, etc.) one at a time and asking the child to name them. It did not matter what name the child used, as long as he named the object. (All the children were able to name the objects.) When all the objects were arranged on the table before the child, he was told to look them over carefully for 10 seconds so as to be able to remember them all. The objects were then returned to a large box and the child was asked to name as many as he could recall. As the child named the objects, these were removed from the box and placed again on the table. The objects that were not recalled were taken out as before and the child had to name them again. The process was repeated until the child could recall all 12 objects in one trial. His final score was the total number of unrecalled objects (simply called "errors") on all the trials up to the first perfect trial.

The Serial test followed immediately. It used the same 12 objects, but in this test each object was placed under one of 12 identical small boxes arranged in a horizontal row before the child. The child's task was to learn to anticipate which object was under each box, beginning with the left-hand end of the row. The boxes were always lifted by the examiner in the same serial order, going from left to right. The child worked at his own speed, naming the object he thought was under each box and then immediately seeing if he was right. He continued until he was able to go through the entire series without an error. His score was the number of errors made up to this point.

The results of this simple experiment are shown in Figures 8 and 9.

Both tests give essentially the same picture: the Recall and Serial Tests show a clearcut difference between Dull (low IQ) and Bright (high IQ) Anglo-American children but fail to show a significant difference between corresponding groups of Mexican-American children. Mexican-American children rated as Dull on the basis of IQ actually learned much faster than Anglo-American children of the same low IQ. It is especially interesting, however, that the Bright Mexican-American children did not show any faster learning than their Anglo-American counterparts with whom they were matched on IQ. Could it be that once the IQ is in the above average range, it reflects learning ability regardless of socioeconomic or cultural background? Several quite different experiments so far have suggested that this is the case. Culturally biased tests seem to be most unfair to children who obtain low IQs while children who obtain better than average IQs, even though they may come from rather impoverished backgrounds, do not seem to be superior to more advantaged children in the kind of learning ability tapped by our direct learning tests.

The Recall and Serial tests were given on another occasion to the same groups described above, but this time abstract objects (seven colored geometric forms) were used instead of the familiar objects. The results were essentially the same as for the

60

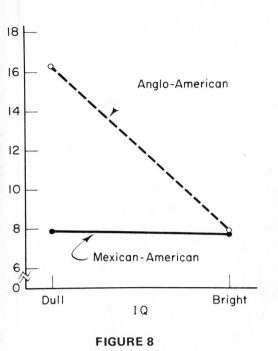

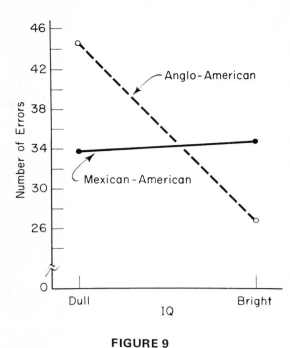

FIGURE 8

Mean error scores of Dull (IQ's 73-89) and Bright (IQ's 111-126) Mexican-American and Anglo-American fourth grade children on the Recall test for Familiar objects (Jensen, 1961).

FIGURE 9

Mean error scores of Dull and Bright Mexican-American and Anglo-American children on the Serial Learning of Familiar objects (Jensen, 1961).

familiar objects: the learning scores were correlated with IQ in the Anglo-American but not in the Mexican-American group (Jensen, 1961).

Another learning test is administered by means of the apparatus shown in Figure 10. Its technical details have been described elsewhere (Jensen, Collins, & Vreeland, 1962). It consists essentially of a screen (something like a small TV screen) on which are projected different pictures, figures, numerals, or letters. The child being tested has a panel of push-buttons, each of which corresponds to one of the pictures on the screen. The task is to discover by trial-and-error which of the pushbuttons corresponds to each of the pictures. When the child presses the correct pushbutton, he gets a "reward" (usually just the sound of a "bong"), which tells him that he made the correct response. By trying different pushbuttons every time a picture or symbol appears, he gradually learns by trial-and-error which button goes with each picture. The speed with which the child learns these connections, the number of trials he takes, and the number of errors he makes along the way to mastery all give an indication of the child's learning ability. By changing the number of stimuli (pictures) and response alternatives (pushbuttons) one can make the task as easy or as difficult as desired for a given age group or mental ability level. The task has been used with equal effectiveness on severe mental retardates and on university students.

61

FIGURE 10

The S-R apparatus for human learning as seen by the subject: the stimulus display unit (above), with reinforcement light directly under the display screen, and the response unit (below), with an array of pushbuttons. Details of the construction and operation of the apparatus are given elsewhere (Jensen, Collins, & Vreeland, 1962).

Photo courtesy of Leonard McCombe, LIFE Magazine.

62

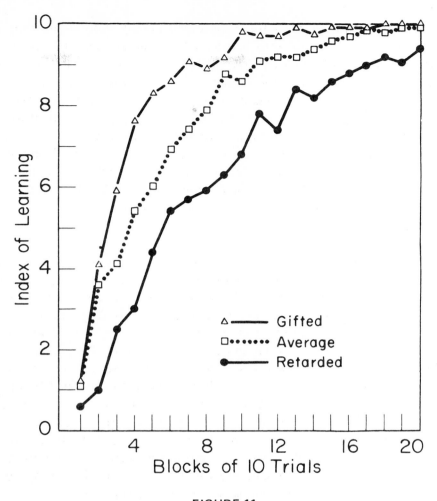

Legend:
- △ ——— Gifted
- □ ••••••• Average
- ● ——— Retarded

Axis labels: Index of Learning (y-axis), Blocks of 10 Trials (x-axis)

FIGURE 11

Learning curves of Gifted (IQ's 135+, Mean = 143), Average (IQ's 90-110, Mean = 103, and Retarded (IQ's 50 - 75, Mean = 66) junior high school students on a trial-and-error selective learning task involving six S-R connections (Jensen, 1953).

One experiment with this task involved the comparison of retarded (IQ 50-75), average (IQ 90-110) and gifted (IQ 135+) children in junior high school. The task consisted of six stimuli (colored geometric forms) and six unlabeled pushbuttons. The learning curves of the three groups are shown in Fig. 11.

Though this graph shows quite regular learning curves in the order we should expect on the basis of IQ, it conceals a highly interesting finding, *viz.*, that four of the 36 children in the retarded group had total learning scores which exceeded the mean of the gifted group. (The two fastest learners in the entire study had IQs of 147 and 65!) Yet none of the children of *average* IQ exceeded the mean of the gifted group.

63

Nor were any of the gifted below the mean of the average group in learning ability. All the low IQ children who were fast learners could be described as culturally disadvantaged. But middle-class children with low IQs are almost invariably slow learners on this task. Culturally disadvantaged children in the average range of IQ, on the other hand, do not perform significantly better on this task than middle-class children with the same IQs. It is also of interest that most of the institutionalized retardates we have tested by this means are exceedingly slow learners, even when they have had a good deal of practice on equivalent forms of the test and seem to be highly motivated. They are similarly slow in serial and paired-associate learning and are far below normal children of the same mental age (Jensen, 1965). This is what we should expect of retardation of the primary type which consists essentially of a slow learning rate.

Another set of experiments was performed by one of my students, Dr. Jacqueline Rapier (1968), who used paired-associate and serial learning tasks in which the stimuli consisted of colored pictures of familiar objects. Her subjects were upper--middle and lower-class white elementary school children. The upper-middle and lower-class children were carefully matched for IQ on both individual and group intelligence tests. A number of serial and paired-associate learning tasks were given under different conditions on a succession of days. The results were essentially the same for all tasks and conditions and can all be summarized in Fig. 12. This figure, in fact, can be said to depict the essential results of all the experiments we have conducted along these lines, so far. Correlations (not corrected for attenuation) between the learning tasks and IQ ranged from .41 to .60 in the upper-middle socioeconomic group; but in the lower-class group the correlations ranged between .01 and .22. In short, the IQ apparently reflects this type of learning ability in middle-class but not in lower-class children. None of the standard tests we have used (Stanford-Binet, Peabody Picture Vocabulary, Raven's Progressive Matrices, Hemmon-Nelson, and the California Test of Mental Maturity) seems to tap learning ability of the kind we are measuring in lower-class children, though all these tests correlate quite substantially with the learning measures among middle-class children.

A motion picture form of paired-associate learning test has been devised by Dr. William Rohwer at Berkeley. The pairs of stimuli consist of familiar objects; at times they are shown as still pictures and at other times as moving pictures, in which one of the objects in some way interacts with another, for example, a rolling ball may be shown knocking over a lighted candle. The child's task is to learn to name the second object in each pair when only the first is shown. The test consists of 24 pairs of such pictures, presented as a rate of 3 seconds per pair. Following the paired presentation only one item of each pair is presented and the child has to name the object that had been paired with it. The subject's score is the number of items recalled correctly in two trials. This brief learning task has been administered to large numbers of children in the Berkeley nursery and elementary schools. Fig. 13

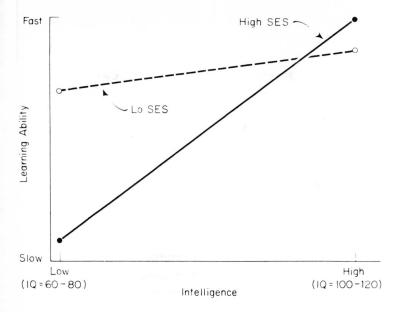

FIGURE 12

Summary graph of several studies showing the relationship between learning ability (serial and paired-associate learning) and IQ as a function of socioeconomic status.

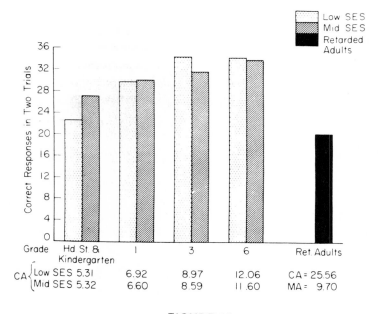

FIGURE 13

Comparisons of Low-and Middle-Socioeconomic groups at various ages with retarded adults on a paired-associate task (24 picture pairs presented two times at a rate of 3 sec. per pair.) (Permission of Dr. Wm. D. Rohwer).

65

shows comparisons of lower- and middle-class children from Head Start and kindergarten through sixth grade. The middle-class children are white; over 90 percent of the lower-class children are Negro. There is a difference of some 15 to 20 points between the groups in average IQ. As can be seen in Fig. 13, the difference between the SES groups in learning ability is negligible. To show that the test is capable of reflecting true mental subnormality, it was administered to a group of institutionalized retarded adults. As shown in Fig. 13, their performance falls below that of five-year-old children in Head Start programs, despite the fact that the Stanford-Binet mental age of the retarded adults is almost 10 years. The test scores are clearly more highly correlated with IQ (learning rate) than with mental age (amount learned).

Recently this test was given to 100 middle-class white children in private nursery schools and to 100 lower-class (mostly Negro) children of comparable age in day care centers. The groups differed 19 points in mean IQ.

In this group of very young children (3 to 5 years of age), the learning tests showed a significant difference, the mean scores of the upper and lower classes being 16 and 12, respectively. (The standard deviation is 7 in both groups.) However, the correlation between IQ (Peabody Picture Vocabulary Test) and learning scores in the middle-class group was .50 (corrected for attenuation = .67), while in the lower-class group the correlation was only .18 (corrected for attentuation = .22). The range and standard deviation of IQs and learning scores was nearly the same in both groups, so the differences in the above correlations cannot be attributed to statistical artifacts. This finding fully confirms the previous correlational findings I have reported. Thus we see that essentially the same picture emerges when we compare lower- and middle-class children (regardless of race) on direct tests of learning ability, and this picture holds across a considerable variety of procedures and subjects.

THEORETICAL INTERPRETATIONS

What theoretical interpretation can be placed on these results? For the sake of simplicity, we can reduce the alternatives to two conceptually distinct viewpoints for our interpretations. Further investigation must be directed at obtaining the information necessary for evaluating the merits of these two main hypotheses. Of course, other possible interpretations might emerge from further investigation.

The simplest hypothesis is that what we measure by means of the usual intelligence tests consists entirely of the products of learning—not just bits of information, but also attentional, perceptual, and cognitive skills, involving processes of verbal or symbolic mediation of overt behavior, and strategies for problem solving and conceptual thinking. (I have discussed these processes in detail elsewhere [Jensen,

66

1966a, b, c, d, e].) All of these "higher" processes are seen as being acquired as a result of appropriate environmental influences, and the rate and thoroughness of their acquisition, given the appropriate input, are seen as entirely a function of individual differences in the basic learning abilities. The basic learning abilities, such as those we measure in the laboratory by means of our direct learning tests, are most simply interpreted as indices of short-term memory, which is a crucial function if any sensory input is to be processed or consolidated for later recall or use in mediational processes, problem solving, and the like. The study of individual differences in these basic processes of short-term memory is a large and important subject in its own right (Jensen, 1966e, f).

The culturally disadvantaged are seen as not lacking in the basic learning abilities but only in the appropriate environmental inputs which go to make up what we call intelligence. Since it is this acquired kind of intelligence, consisting of a background of transferable knowledge and cognitive skills, that is needed in order to learn through the highly verbal and symbolic medium of the traditional classroom, culturally disadvantaged children are at an educational disadvantage even though they may be average or superior in the raw, unimplemented basic learning abilities. In the culturally disadvantaged, these abilities, as measured by our direct learning tests, correlate hardly at all with measures of acquired intelligence, such as the IQ, since the environmental input has not incuded all the necessary ingredients for the acquisition of this kind of intelligence, which correlates with ability to learn in school. Middle-class children, on the other hand, have had the necessary input, and the extent to which they have acquired intelligence from this experience is a function of their basic learning ability. Therefore, there is a high correlation between the basic learning abilities and intelligence and school performance in middle-class children. Finally, according to this view, it is the basic learning ability, rather than intelligence as such, which is controlled by hereditary factors or by environmental influences at a biological level (nutrition, disease, trauma, etc.).

The hypothesis outlined above, however, seems to run into certain difficulties. For one thing, if measured intelligence in middle-class children were as dependent on specific environmental influences as this view suggests, it would seem difficult (though not impossible) to account for the high heritability of intelligence in this population. One way of examining this matter would be to compare the heritability of basic learning ability with that of intelligence. If the hypothesis is correct, we should expect learning ability to be at least as high, if not higher, in heritability than intelligence. It would also seem hard to explain why some severely deprived children so quickly acquire average or superior intelligence once they are placed in a good environment, while other children whose environments are not so deprived, but who have good basic learning ability, still do not develop even average intelligence.

67

Another difficulty arises from the great disparity between the correlations of learning ability with IQ in lower-class and middle-class children. If the rate of acquisition of intelligence is proportional to learning ability as well as to environmental opportunities for learning, one should still expect to find a very substantial correlation between learning ability and IQ even among environmentally disadvantaged children. After all, there is considerable variance in IQ among such children. But why is so much less of this variance accounted for by individual differences in learning ability than is the case with middle-class children?

Another question is why some disadvantaged children obtain average or superior IQs. This is especially puzzling when they are not superior to many other typical disadvantaged children in basic learning ability. And their environment is often not perceptibly superior to that of the majority of lower-class children. If in order to have an IQ of, say, 120 while being reared in a poor environment required that the child have better learning ability than a child with an IQ of 120 from a good environment, why do we not find evidence of this? On the contrary, our learning tasks indicate that lower-class children with average or superior IQs are not superior in learning ability to middle-class children of the same IQ.

Finally, why do some children show a marked decrement in intelligence relative to their age group beginning at around 4 or 5 years of age, even though at this age they are usually thrust into an intellectually more stimulating environment than they have been exposed to at home? With good basic learning ability, which many of these children possess, we should expect an improvement in IQ the longer they are exposed to learning opportunities. Usually, however, the initial boost in IQ in the first months of school is lost in subsequent years, and often there is even some lowering of the IQ. It should also be noted that the IQs of adopted children are increasingly correlated with their true parents' and not their foster parents' ability level, even though the children have had no contact with their true parents. This is shown in Fig. 14. The results indicate that the specific influences of the foster parents do not override the rank order of individual differences in ability imposed by hereditary factors.

A Hierarchical Theory

Most of the difficulties mentioned above can be overcome, at least in principle, by postulating a hierarchy of mental abilities. To keep the formulation as simple as possible, while still preserving its essence, we can think in terms of two levels of mental ability, called Level I and Level II. Level I abilities involve mainly short-and long-term memory and simple associative learning. These are the functions measured by digit span and our direct learning tests of selective trial-and-error learning, recall of objects, paired-associates, and serial learning. Level II is not as easily described

68

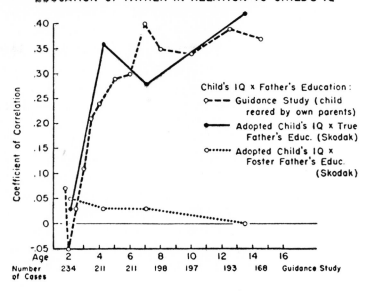

EDUCATION OF FATHER IN RELATION TO CHILD'S IQ

Child's IQ × Father's Education:
○--- Guidance Study (child reared by own parents)
● Adopted Child's IQ × True Father's Educ. (Skodak)
○⋯⋯ Adopted Child's IQ × Foster Father's Educ. (Skodak)

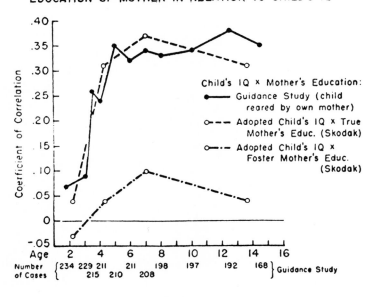

EDUCATION OF MOTHER IN RELATION TO CHILD'S IQ

Child's IQ × Mother's Education:
● Guidance Study (child reared by own mother)
○--- Adopted Child's IQ × True Mother's Educ. (Skodak)
○-·-· Adopted Child's IQ × Foster Mother's Educ. (Skodak)

FIGURE 14

Correlation between education of parents and child's IQ as a function of age. (From Honzik, 1957).

69

but presumably involves more abstract and conceptual abilities that depend upon processes such as generalization and transfer of knowledge of skills from the specific context in which they were originally acquired to similar but new situations, the combining of a number of elemental bits of knowledge or skill into more complex patterns, the use of various forms of verbal or symbolic mediation where the concrete elements of a problem need not be present for its solution, and a capacity for drawing upon appropriate memories, associations, and skills in the face of new problems to which they are relevant. These Level II functions characterize largely what Spearman meant by g, the general intelligence factor. It is mainly these functions that are tapped by traditional intelligence tests, especially those tests, like Raven's *Progressive Matrices*, which Cattell has referred to as measures of "fluid" (as contrasted with "crystalized") intelligence (Cattell, 1963). Prior to four or five years of age intelligence tests do not measure these Level II functions to an appreciable extent, as we see from the low correlation between the IQ below age four and in adolescence. Intelligence tests apparently do not begin to measure g to any great extent until after age four or five. It is after this age, too, that children's IQs begin to correlate with their true parents' intelligence, whether the children are reared by their true parents or by foster parents (Honzik, 1957).

Next, we can postulate that the genetic determinants of Level I and Level II are relatively independent and are subject to the phenomena of independent segregation and recombination of genes in the formation of the gametes (sex cells) and the zygote (fertilized egg). In brief, the biological basis of Level I and Level II processes are not genetically linked, though they may become associated through assortative mating (i.e. the tendency for "like to marry like") and geographic isolation. But while Level I processes are basic and essential to survival in almost any environment or culture we can conceive of, Level II functions may be considerably greater advantage only in more complex or technological cultures in which there is a premium on abstract and symbolic functions such as the traditional 3 R's of the elementary curriculum. The genetic basis of Level I and Level II functions would therefore be subject to different selective pressures in the environment.

But why do we find high correlations between Level I and Level II in middle-class and not in culturally disadvantaged children? The explanatory hypothesis is that Level I functions are necessary but not sufficient for the development of Level II functions. That is to say, the rate of development of Level II is causally related to individual differences in Level I, such that any deficiency in Level I, whether genetic or environmental, will result in deficiency at Level II. Individual differences in Level I, however, are not causally dependent on Level II.

Now, if we hypothesize that Level I and Level II abilities are distributed in the

70

middle-class and in the culturally disadvantaged populations as shown in Fig. 15, all of the findings I have reported can be easily "explained." This is just an hypothesis, of course, and it requires a great deal more investigation. But this hypothesis would seem so far to give a more plausible account of the various lines of evidence reviewed above than the alternative hypothesis which says that Level I abilities represent the biological basis of individual differences, while Level II abilities are entirely acquired from the environment—the Level I abilities plus environmental opportunity being the sole determinants of individual differences in Level II. The two-level model seems more convincing, especially in terms of apparent discontinuity seen in the correlations between Level I and Level II functions when we compare the correlations in lower and middle-class children.

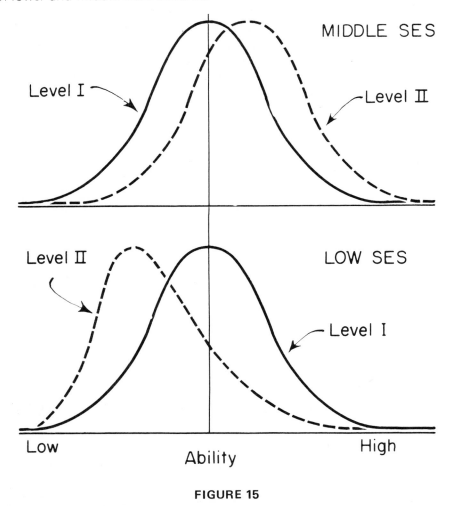

FIGURE 15

Hypothetical curves of the distributions of Level I (solid line) and Level II (dashed line) abilities in middle-class (upper curves) and culturally disadvantaged (lower curves) populations.

71

Determining the truth or falsity of these alternative hypotheses by further research is a fundamental and necessary step toward our understanding of the problems of the disadvantaged, the kind of realistic understanding we will need to achieve improvements in educational practices and policies that hopefully will make school attendance a more rewarding enterprise for this part of our population. It is quite improbable that we could ever succeed in this aim without exploring and weighing all the possible determinants of individual differences in Level I and Level II abilities: genetic, prenatal, nutritional, and social.

In future perspective, far too much is at stake to risk for long an uninformed or misinformed educational and social policy in this area of national concern. The culturally disadvantaged, and consequently the whole of society, will benefit more in the long run if behavioral scientists and educators treat these problems in the spirit of scientific inquiry rather than as a battlefield upon which one or another preordained social philosophy may seemingly triumph.

References

Burt, C. The evidence for the concept of Intelligence. BRIT.J. EDUC. PSYCHOL., 25: 158-177, 1955.

Burt, C. The distribution of intelligence. BRIT. J. PSYCHOL., 48: 161-175, 1957.

Burt, C. The inheritance of mental ability. AMER. PSYCHOL., 13: 1-15, 1958.

Burt, C. Intelligence and social mobility. BRIT. J. STAT. PSYCHOL., 14: 3-24, 1961.

Burt, C. Is Intelligence distributed normally? BRIT. J. STAT. PSYCHOL., 16, 175-190, 1963.

Burt, C. The genetic determination of differences in intelligence: A study of monozygotic twins reared together and apart. BRIT. J. PSYCHOL., 57: 137-153, 1966.

Cattell, R. B. The multiple abstract variance analysis equations and solutions: For nature-nurture research on continuous variables. PSYCHOL. Rev., 67: 353-372, 1960.

Cattell, R. B. Theory of Fluid and crystalized intelligence: A critical experiment. J. EDUC. PSYCHOL., 54: 1-22, 1963.

Davis, K. Final note on a case of extreme isolation. AMER. J. SOCIOL., 57: 432-457, 1947.

Erlenmeyer-Kimling, L., & Jarvik, L. F. Genetics and intelligence: a review. SCIENCE, 142: 1477-1479, 1963.

Falconer, D. S. AN INTRODUCTION TO QUANTITATIVE GENETICS. New York: Ronald, 1960.

Fifer, G. Social class and cultural group differences in diverse mental abilities. INVITATIONAL CONFERENCE ON TESTING PROBLEMS, Educational Testing Service, Princeton, New Jersey, 1965.

Fuller, J. L., & Thompson, W. R. BEHAVIOR GENETICS. New York: John Wiley & Sons, Inc., 1960.

Gottesman, I. Genetic aspects of intelligent behavior. In Ellis, N. R. (Ed.) HANDBOOK OF MENTAL DEFICIENCY. New York: McGraw-Hill, Pp. 253-296, 1963.

Honzik, Marjorie P. Developmental studies of parent-child resemblance in intelligence. CHILD DEVELPM., 28: 215-228, 1957.

Hunt, J. M. INTELLIGENCE AND EXPERIENCE. New York: The Ronald Press Company, 1961.

Jensen, A. R. Learning abilities in Mexican-American and Anglo-American children. CALIF. J. EDUC. RES., 12, 147-159, 1961.

Jensen, A. R. Learning abilities in retarded, average, and gifted children. MERRILL-PALMER QUART. 9: 123-140, 1963.(Reprinted in John P. DeCecco,Ed.,

73

EDUCATIONAL TECHNOLOGY: READINGS IN PROGRAMMED INSTRUC-TION. New York: Holt, Rinehart and Winston, Inc., 1964.

Jensen, A. R. Rote learning in retarded adults and normal children. AMER. J. MENT. DEFIC., 69: 828-834, 1965.

Jensen, A. R. Verbal mediation and educational potential. PSYCHOL. IN THE SCHOOLS, 3: 99-1-9, 1966. (a)

Jensen, A. R. Cumulative deficit in compensatory education. J. SCHOOL PSYCHOL., 4:37-47, 1964. (b)

Jensen, A. R. Conceptions and misconceptions about verbal mediation. In Douglas, M. P. (Ed.) Claremont Reading Conference, Thirtieth Yearbook, Claremont Graduate School, 1966. (c)

Jensen, A. R. Social class and perceptual learning. MENTAL HYGIENE, 50: 226. 239. (d) 1966

Jensen, A. R. Individual differences in conceptual learning. In H. Klausmeier & C. Harris (Eds.), ANALYSES OF CONCEPT LEARNING. New York: Academic Press, Pp. 139- 154, 1966. (e)

Jensen, A. R. Varieties of individual differences in learning. In R. M. Gagne (Ed.), LEARNING AND INDIVIDUAL DIFFERENCES. New York; Merrill, 1966. (f)

Jensen, A. R. Estimation of the limits of heritability of traits by comparison of monozygotic and dizygotic twins. PROCEEDINGS OF THE NATIONAL ACADEMY OF SCIENCES, 58: 149-157, 1967.

Jensen, A. R. Social class and verbal learning. In M. Deutsch, A. R. Jensen & I. Katz (Eds.) SOCIAL CLASS, RACE AND PSYCHOLOGICAL DEVELOPMENT. New York: Holt, Rinehart, & Winston, 1968.

Jensen, A. R., Collins, C. C. & Vreeland, R. W. A multiple S-R apparatus for human learning AMER. J. PSYCHOL., 75: 470-476, 1962.

Kennedy, W. A., Van de Riet, V., & White, J. C. A normative sample of intelligence and achievement of Negro elementary school children in the Southeastern United States. MONOGR. SOC. RES. CHILD. DEVELOPM., 28: 6, 1963.

Lawrence, E. M. An investigation into the relation between intelligence and inheritance. BRIT. J. PSYCHOL., MONOGR. SUPPLMNT., 16: 5, 1931.

Lesser, G. S., Fifer, G., & Clark, D. H. MENTAL ABILITIES OF CHILDREN FROM DIFFERENT SOCIAL-CLASS AND CULTURAL GROUPS: Monographs, Society for Research in Child Development, 30: 4, 1965.

Li, C. C. POPULATION GENETICS. Chicago: Univ. Chicago Press. 1955.

Newman, H. H., Freeman, F. N., & Holzinger, K. J. TWINS A STUDY OF HEREDITY AND ENVIRONMENT. Chicago: Univ. of Chicago Press, 1937.

Nichols, R. C. The national merit twin study. In Vandenberg, S. G. (Ed.) METHODS AND GOALS IN HUMAN BEHAVIOR GENETICS. New York: Academic Press, 1965.

Rapier, Jacqueline L. The learning abilities of normal and retarded children as a function of social class. J. EDUC. PSYCHOL., 59: 102, 1968.

Reed, Elizabeth W., & Reed, S. C. MENTAL RETARDATION: A FAMILY STUDY. Philadelphia: W. B. Saunders Co., 1965.

Salzberger, R. M., & Jarvik, L. F. In J. D. Ranier *et al.* (Eds.) FAMILY AND MENTAL HEALTH PROBLEMS IN A DEAF POPULATION. New York: State Psychiatric Institute, New York, 1963.

Shields, J. MONOZYGOTIC TWINS BROUGHT UP APART AND BROUGHT UP TOGETHER. London, Oxford Univer. Press. 1962.

Shuey, Audrey M. THE TESTING OF NEGRO INTELLIGENCE. (2nd ed.) New York: Social Science Press, 1966.

Skeels, H. M. Adult status of children with contrasting early life experiences: a follow-up study. CHILD DEVELOPM. MONOGR., 31: 3, 1966. Serial No. 105.

Terman, L. M., & Merrill, Maud A. MEASURING INTELLIGENCE. Boston: Houghton-Mifflin, 1937.

Terman, L. M., & Merrill, Maud A. STANFORD-BINET INTELLIGENCE SCALE: MANUAL FOR THE THIRD REVISION FORM L-M. Boston: Houghton-Mifflin, 1960.

Vandenberg, S. G. Contributions of twin research to psychology, PSYCHOL. BULL., 66: 327-352, 1966.

Wechsler, D. THE MEASUREMENT AND APPRAISAL OF ADULT INTELLI-GENCE. (4th ed.) Baltimore: Williams & Wilkins, 1958.

Wilson, A. B. Educational consequences of segregation in a California community. RACIAL ISOLATION IN THE PUBLIC SCHOOLS, Vol.2. Washington, D. C.: U. S. Government Printing Office, 1967.

A CULTURE - FAIR INSTRUMENT FOR INTELLECTUAL ASSESSMENT

Leon A. Rosenberg, Ph.D.,
Assistant Professor of Pediatrics and Medical Psychology
and Pediatric Psychologist, The Johns Hopkins University
School of Medicine, Baltimore, Maryland

LEON A. ROSENBERG, Ph.D.

The Johns Hopkins Perceptual Test was developed in response to a need for a brief, simple to administer, and non-verbal test of intellectual functioning for young children. The data to be presented suggests that the instrument might be relatively "culture-fair" and that the instrument might be of use with a variety of children where physical handicaps preclude the use of standard instruments. The following review will make it quite clear that we are in the midst of examining the usefulness and limitations of this test and that the instrument is still in an early stage of development.

This chapter will follow the following outline: A brief statement of our rationale for the development of a culture-fair instrument; the development of the Johns Hopkins Perceptual Test (JHPT) and our current data; a description of ongoing and future research; a statement of our expectations regarding the practical use of the *JHPT;* and a statement of the author's personal prejudice in regard to the intellectual evaluation of disadvantaged children.

The rationale we have been following for the development of culture-fair instruments involves two steps. First, does the instrument in question measure "intelligence." The usual criterion measures involve correlations with (1) school performance and (2) "established" intelligence tests. To validate a culture-fair instrument requires a restriction in the sample of subjects used. Since disadvantaged children tend to demonstrate less-than-adequate school performance and to perform poorly on current intelligence tests, correlations between a culture-fair test and these two criterion measures would be expected to be quite low due to the restriction in range of the lower socio-economic status *(SES)* subjects' scores on the criterion measures. Hence, our validity studies done with the *JHPT* involved both low and middle *SES* groups, with the correlations obtained with the more culturally advantaged group being the actual basis for statements of validity. Step two, in our methodology, moves on to the question of "culture-fairness." Our definition of "fairness" is a narrow one: a test is "culture-fair" if the obtained scores are demonstrated to be free of the influence of *SES* differences between subjects; the distributions of test scores

79

obtained from groups of subjects representing the extreme points of the *SES* continuum should be identical.

Our original objective was to produce a measure of intellectual functioning which would be of value when one was evaluating large numbers of young children. We were concerned primarily with pre-school and early school years (ages 3-6 to 7-11 constitute the maximum age range dealt with presently). The instrument had to meet several criteria:

(1) The test had to call for a simple response which would allow for the successful testing of mute, physically handicapped, or somewhat uncooperative children who might balk if asked to perform a complex act.

(2) The instrument would have to be simple to administer and score and should involve approximately 20 minutes of the child's time. The need for speed being related to our interest in producing a tool useful in large-scale testing programs but being an *individually* administered test. This approach was based on a belief that young children and low *SES* children do poorly on *group* administered tests. The instrument had to be simple to allow for non-professional technicians to successfully use it. This attribute would make the tool useful in situations where many non-psychologists would be used as testers.

(3) The items of the test should have some promise in regard to being "culturally fair."

We decided to utilize simple perceptual designs in what would basically be a discrimination task. The development of such a discrimination task poses several problems. First, how to choose the pattern or shape of the design. To reduce the effect of prior learning, these designs should be "random" and as "culture-fair" as possible. Secondly, we felt that the designs had to be ordered along a continuum of complexity by some rational means. We felt that the most promising procedure for solving these two problems was the application of information theory to shape and pattern perception presented by Attneave and Arnoult (1956). The procedures developed by these authors had two facets which were directly related to the questions raised: It allowed for the generation of perceptual patterns or shapes on a completely random basis (i.e. the experimenter had no control over what shape the figure would assume); it permitted the generation of an unlimited series of figures from the same "stimulus-domain" (i.e. the figures would be a sample of stimuli from a parent population characterized by certain determinant statistical parameters). Changing the stimulus population by known variation of one or more parameters would produce a different series of figures. The procedure for producing different stimulus populations could be seen as increasing the informational content of the individual figures.

80

Hence, different samples of figures or shapes could be ordered along a continuum of complexity if one defined complexity as the amount of information (or uncertainty) "built-in" to such a perceptual figure.

The use of information measures would also produce a second approach to the problem of defining the difficulty level of the task. The amount of information (or the degree of uncertainty) in a choice-making task is measured by the formula: $U = \log_2 k$; where U = uncertainty of information expressed in bits, and k = the number of equally probable alternatives (Garner, 1962). Hence, the difficulty level of the total task could be defined in terms of the total number of alternatives which make up the task.

Briefly, the Attneave and Arnoult process allows one to decide on the number of points or angles that a figure will have. From that point on, the exact shape that the figure will assume is beyond the experimenter's control. Square grid coordinate paper is utilized with the X and Y coordinates of each point determined by a table of random numbers. A well-defined procedure is then followed for the connecting of those points. For a better understanding of the process the reader is referred to the Attneave and Arnoult article.

The process produces a series of random designs, the shapes of which will vary greatly. It is also possible to generate a series of designs that systematically vary along a known continuum. The procedure, developed by LaBerge and Lawrence (1955), requires one to first produce a random shape by the Attneave and Arnoult method and then assign each point on the contour randomly chosen X and Y increments to its coordinates. These new coordinates are plotted and connected as a new matrix. The same increments are then added to the new coordinates and yet another figure is constructed. This process will produce a row of figures each differing from the adjacent figure by a constant amount of distortion as measured by the distance through which the points move. Any two adjacent shapes in such a row are equally spaced in terms of the total distance the points have moved.

It was decided to utilize both of these procedures to produce the needed perceptual figures. Hence, there were two types of tasks; one involving purely random figures and one using figures related to each other along a continuum of known variation.

The complexity of the task was defined in two ways: (1) The amount of information in the design itself. This was defined as the number of turns in the contour of the shape. In this case, it was the number of angles in the shape. This procedure follows the work of Attneave (1957) who demonstrated that "number of turns" was the most important variable in determining the judged complexity of random shapes. (2) The number of alternatives in the discrimination task. If the subject had

81

to choose between two figures in trying to find a match for the stimulus figure, the degree of uncertainty in that task could be expressed as one bit (or one can say that the task entails one bit of information). A task with five choices, would be a 2.3219 bit problem. The more bits of information presented to the subject, the more complex the task.

Our earliest research involved these two types of designs which were labelled as follows: Type *A* - a series of random designs; Type *B* - a series of designs varying by known increments from an original design. Types *A* and *B* designs were developed at three different information levels; designs with three points (a point being a "turn" or change in contour), four points and six points. The task for the child was to point to the design which matched the stimulus design. The youngsters were faced with either 2, 3, or 5 alternatives. Hence, the study examined the variables of number of alternatives, complexity of the designs, type *A* versus type *B*, on accuracy in a perceptual matching task.

In this first study, the subjects were 44 children who ranged in age from 3 years - 0 months to 5 years - 10 months. The occupations of their parents ranged from semi-skilled hospital employees to professional staff. The Peabody Picture Vocabulary Test *(PPVT)* was also administered to the children. The results indicated that the degree of accuracy on the perceptual task was highly correlated with both age (r = .618) and the *PPVT* raw score (.744). Partial correlation indicated that the major relationship was between the *PPVT* and perceptual accuracy.

From this data, a shorter task was chosen where a youngster would have to make a series of 30 discriminations calling for a total time expenditure of 15 minutes. The new task was administered to 22 four to five-year old youngsters enrolled in a middle-class private nursery school. The *PPVT* and Draw-A-Person *(DAP)* were also administered. The data obtained indicated a step-wise increase in difficulty level within the *JHPT,* and correlations with the *PPVT* of .566, with the Harris (1963) scoring of the *DAP* of .648, and with age of .584.

It appeared, then, that we had developed a simple, pleasant (e.g. no child at even the youngest age refused the task, although many were reluctant to do the *DAP,* and all children considered the task as "fun", "a good game", etc.), and rapid test of intellectual functioning. The uniqueness and "randomness" of the designs suggested that the task might be relatively culture-fair. The lower level of the task appeared simple enough for the very young or even the very retarded. The response required of the subject involved a very simple motor act that could be performed by physically handicapped children. The instructions might well be successfully communicated in pantomime for the testing of deaf children.

Before going on to discuss reliability and validity data, we will take a moment to describe our test procedure. Figure 1 presents a typical test situation. The child has been presented with five designs lying flat on a board. Designs which match one of the five are presented one at a time and are placed upright on the stand shown in the top center of Figure 1. As shown in the figure, the child then points to the one card in the display of five which he feels matches the upright figure. Although there are some variations, this is the basic procedure followed in the administration of the *JHPT*. Before presenting these materials to the child, we establish an appropriate "set" by utilizing plastic triangles, circles, and squares. The child is given one of each of these figures and the examiner then holds up an identical circle, square, or triangle. He asks the child to find which one of his forms matches the one held in the examiner's hand. The use of 3-dimensional forms allows the examiner to aid the child by placing the child's forms next to his own. These 3-dimensional forms are used until the examiner is certain that the child understands that a matching task is what he is dealing with. The 3-dimensional forms are then placed out of sight and formal testing begins. Each of the test items are photographs consisting of a black figure on a white background. Each photograph is mounted on heavy cardboard and is 5 inches by 7 inches in size.

FIGURE 1

The Administration of the Johns Hopkins Perceptual Test

A series of studies has been completed which answer the questions of reliability, validity, and "culture-fairness." The validity data is presented in Table 1. As expected, the correlations are lower for the "low" *SES* groups. Some additional validity data is also available. A sample of 30 institutionalized retarded children (age range of 5 to 9, mean I.Q. of 51.60, S.D. = 14.47) were administered both the *JHPT* and Stanford-Binet. The correlation between the *JHPT* raw scores and the mental ages obtained with the Stanford-Binet was .697 (there were two subjects who were not included in the study. Both could not respond to the *JHPT.* One had a Binet I.Q. of 42 and the other subject's Binet was "unscoreable"). Combining this group of 30 with 57 kindergarten and first grade students (a group attending a "slum-area" school whose Stanford-Binet I.Q. scores "piled up" in the "Borderline" and "Dull

TABLE 1

Validity Coefficients[1, 2]

(1965)		
"Middle" SES (Preschool)	r	N
JHPT x Peabody Picture Vocabulary Tests	.615**	50
x Draw-A-Person	.702**	37
x Columbia Mental Maturity Scale:	.798**	25
"Low" SES (Preschool)		
JHPT x Peabody Picture Vocabulary Test:	.449**	79
x Draw-A-Person	.356*	36
x Columbia Mental Maturity Scale:	.657**	78
(1966)		
"Middle" SES (Preschool)		
JHPT x Peabody Picture Vocabulary Test:	.756**	71
x Columbia Mental Maturity Scale:	.761**	71

$* = p \quad .05 \qquad ** = p \quad .01$

[1]All correlations are based on raw scores.

[2]The SES designations of "middle" and "low" are only rough indicators. The "middle" group were children attending private nursery schools while the "low" group were obtained from county Well-Baby clinics with many families being on welfare.

84

Normal" I.Q. ranges) we obtained an r of .572 (p < .01) between Binet M.A. and *JHPT.* Partialling-out the age variable, we obtained an r of .501 (p < .01) between Binet I.Q. and *JHPT.*

A reliability study has also been completed and has yielded data both in regard to test-retest reliability and to the degree to which one can use non-professional examiners with the *JHPT.* Two examiners were utilized. One was a 24 year-old female college graduate with no graduate level training. The second was a 15 year-old female high school student. The results are presented in Table 2 and indicate satisfactory reliability. The data suggests that more satisfactory results are obtained when the examiner is an older college level person.

TABLE 2

Test-Retest Reliability Coefficients for Three

Tests with a Time Lapse of 17 Days Between Test Sessions

Examiner	N	Test Peabody Picture Vocabulary	Columbia Mental Maturity	JHPT
15 year-old	22	.889	.894	.864
24 year-old	39	.886	.935	.933
Total	61	.888	.917	.902

Mean Test-Retest Difference in Raw Scores

Examiner	PPVT	CMMS	JHPT
15 year-old	3.81	5.55	2.71
24 year-old	1.24	7.30	- 0.36
Total	2.15	6.64	0.76

Thus far, the data appears to indicate that *JHPT* is a reasonably reliable and valid brief-test of intelligence which can be successfully administered to young children by a non-professional examiner. The validity data is limited to correlations with other tests of intelligence and no attempt has been made to predict school performance.

The assertion that the *JHPT* is a "culture-fair" instrument is based on one small

85

study. Two groups of children of different *SES* levels were compared in terms of their performance on the *JHPT,* the *PPVT,* and the *DAP.* The two groups were given the labels of "lower" and "middle" as descriptions of their social status. The labels imply difference only and do not mean that the social status of each child's family was actually determined. The "lower" group consisted of 52 pre-school children who were attending a county well-baby clinic. The clinic served an impoverished area and many of the families were receiving welfare assistance. The "middle" group consisted of 52 pre-school children attending a private nursery school which served a "middle-class" section of Baltimore City. The fact that the two groups differed in social status was quite clear, although no attempt was made to accurately determine the actual *SES* level of each group in terms of local class structure.

The two groups had equal mean ages and ranged in age from 4 to 5. Sex and race were uncontrolled with the race difference being most blatant. The "lower" group were all Negro while the "middle" group were all white. The data obtained from this hastily done and inadequately controlled study was quite promising. Figure 2 shows the distributions (ogives) of the raw scores obtained on the three tests. It is quite apparent that there was an extreme difference on the *PPVT,* less difference on the *DAP,* and much less difference on the *JHPT.* Table 3 presents the statistical tests of this data. The analysis demonstrated that the difference on the *PPVT* and the difference on the *DAP* were statistically significant while there was no significance to the obtained difference on the *JHPT.* This is the data that raised the possibility that the *JHPT* might well be a relatively culture-fair instrument.

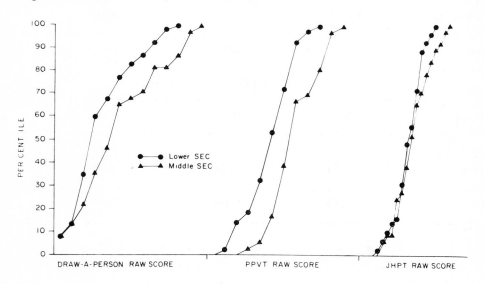

FIGURE 2

Distributions (Ogives) of raw scores obtained with three tests of intelligence administered to two different socio-economic class groups

86

TABLE 3

Tests of the Statistical Significance of the Differences in Raw Score Means Obtained on Three Tests of Intelligence Administered to Two SES Groups

Test	Size of Difference	"t"	
PPVT	9.72	4.24	$p < .0025$
DAP	3.16	2.49	$p < .025$
JHPT	.91	less than 1	

Although promising, the *JHPT* itself and the research data discussed have several limitations. Just what aspect of intellectual functioning does the test measure? Although it only requires matching of designs, the *JHPT* correlates significantly with measures involving widely different types of intellectual activity; from the concept-formation task of the Columbia Mental Maturity Scale to hearing-vocabulary in the *PPVT* to the varied skills sampled by the Stanford-Binet. We could look to the "g" factor in theories of intelligence for an answer but this question would be best resolved by a large scale factor-analytic study. At present, the exact answer to this question remains unavailable.

Is the present data sufficient to allow us to claim that the instrument is definitely "culture-fair" within the limits of our definition of that term? An analysis of the available data must lead to an answer of "no."

The study discussed above suffers from the following: (1) Age range sampled was much too limited; (2) Numbers of subjects in each group were too small; (3) The means used to establish that the two groups were different in *SES* level were too poorly defined and crudely administered leaving open the possibility that some unknown number of subjects might have been misidentified as being of "low" or "middle" *SES;* (4) The obtained data itself suggests the need for further research. The ogives of Figure 2 demonstrate not only the potential "fairness" of the *JHPT* as compared to the *DAP* and *PPVT,* but also a possible degree of difference, or "unfairness," between the two groups at the upper range of *JHPT* raw scores. At the 25th percentile, the difference between the raw scores of the two groups was .50; at the 50th percentile, it was .75; at the 75th percentile, it was 1.35; and at the 90th percentile, it was 2.50. Although no statistically significant difference was found in regard to differences between means, there is the suggestion that some *SES* influence might have affected the scores at the *upper* levels of the *JHPT.*

Hence, we can conclude that although the *JHPT* appears to be a promising tool, there is a great need for further research. Several interesting studies are in progress

87

at this time. Samples of minimally brain-damaged children are being tested with an elaborate psychological battery. The *JHPT* has been included and this data will give us excellent insights into the effect of CNS dysfunction on performance on the *JHPT.* A large number of children between the ages of 3 and 9 who suffer from various degrees of hearing impairment are being tested with both the *JHPT* and the Leiter International Performance Scale. On a smaller group of 30, we obtained an *r* of .845 between the *JHPT* and the Leiter. This larger series of subjects will enable us to determine the value of the *JHPT* in the examination of deaf children.

The *JHPT,* along with other psychological tests, is being used in research studies in other countries by several people. Data is currently being collected in Nigeria and Guatemala and plans are being made to use the instrument in Saudi Arabia. In all three studies the subjects will be pre-school age children and large group comparisons will be made. Two studies in this country are under way which will give us an opportunity to do long term follow-up in regard to achievement differences between groups scoring high and low on the *JHPT.* In both studies the *JHPT* is included in a battery of tests which will allow us to examine the relationship between the *JHPT* and these other tests. In one situation, the entire first grade of a racially-integrated poverty-area elementary school has been tested and these youngsters will be followed for some time. In the second situation, a large number of children attending a Head-Start program will be tested and followed through later school years. In regard to the question of culture-fairness, we are planning a large scale study adequately controlling for all relevant variables which should give us more definitive data in regard to this important question.

Now we come to the question of the practical use of a culture-fair instrument. Critics of this type of test-instrument quite correctly point out that the measures having the best correlation with the criterion of school success are standard, or culture-bound, tests of intelligence. This is certainly a valid statement. Both our public schools and our psychological tests are biased against impoverished people. Our social structure guarantees that large numbers of poverty-area children will be unable to succeed in school and will be unable to perform adequately on tests of their "intellectual ability." There is an additional problem, however, which these critics do not mention. In typical clinical practice, especially within school systems, individual psychometric tests are administered *not to predict school performance but to explain school failure.* Hence, the nation's school psychologists spend most of their time administering intelligence tests to children who have already done poorly in school. The finding of an I.Q. of 75, for example, is used to "explain" the child's poor school performance. Condensing the school psychologists' complicated reports to simple language results in the following typical conclusion: *the child does not do well in school because he is limited intellectually.* Some of us, however, are left with the disturbing thought that perhaps many of these youngsters fail to do well in

88

school because the school has failed to teach them. A culture-fair instrument might enable one to identify the child whose school failure is really society's failure and not his own; the lack of ability being in terms of the local Department of Education and not in terms of the child's cerebral cortex.

From this line of reasoning, I would suggest that culture-fair instruments have practical value in the following areas:

(1) Diagnosis and planning in regard to children who "fail to learn". The evaluation of intellectual potential is an important part of any diagnostic study regardless of the type of learning problem we are dealing with. Planning for such children requires one to be able to distinguish between learning difficulties due to intellectual retardation and learning difficulties due to other factors in children of normal intellectual ability. This distinction is extremely difficult to make with low-*SES* youngsters due to our present difficulties with standard tests of intelligence. A culture-fair instrument would be a valued addition to an evaluative battery in terms of just this diagnostic distinction.

(2) Pre-school enrichment programs, such as those already developed and those being developed for anti-poverty programs, require some means of identifying youngsters of different levels of intellectual potential. An educational program geared for youngsters of at least average potential might be expected to be totally ineffective, if not actually harmful, to retarded children. A culture-fair test would be of value in just such a screening procedure especially since we know that many current brief screening tools greatly exaggerate the number of retarded youngsters in the poverty population (e.g. Rosenberg and Stroud, 1966).

(3) This type of intelligence measure can also be of value in educational research projects such as attempts to compare the effectiveness of different curriculum in poverty-area elementary schools. Such studies require that one be able to control for variations in the intellectual potential of the children used in the study. A culture-fair instrument can play such a role.

The personal prejudice of the author has certainly been amply expressed in the last few paragraphs. At this point, the author's bias will be made more specific. It is my belief that the intellectual ability of the poor is distributed normally. I would expect a slight rise at the lowest end of the scale due to a greater-than-expected incidence of organically based retardation related to the greater health hazards faced by the poor than by the rest of the population. In this category would be included a higher incidence of birth injury, a higher incidence of congenital difficulties related to disease in the mother, and a higher incidence of cerebral damage in young children with such causative factors as accidental head injury, lead poisoning, etc. Subtracting out this group we are left with a large number of poverty-area people whose intellectual potential distributes normally but for whom standard tests of intelligence yield I.Q. distributions which show an extreme "pile-up" in the "Borderline" and "Dull Normal" categories. This skewness of the distribution is related to the inability of current tests of intelligence to adequately measure their ability and not to an inherited inferiority of the poor.

A similar statement can be made when the data changes from I.Q. scores to levels of academic achievement. The achievement data is greatly influenced by the academic community's failure to break through the multiple barriers of social-class difference; barriers of communication style, the lack of relevance of middle class patterns of social reinforcement, and the devastating influence of an atmosphere of apathy and despair.

Our skepticism regarding the validity of current intelligence testing results from an experience of conflict of data; too many "low I.Q." children in the lowest socio-economic status function at a level of behavioral complexity beyond that which would be normally associated with their obtained scores. In addition, I.Q. scores of deprived-area children have shown a tendency to increase significantly when those youngsters have been exposed to even mediocre educational experiences.

In support of these statements we can briefly mention data from two sources. First, Arthur Jensen's work at the University of California at Berkeley where a learning task has been developed which has been used with children of different socio-economic class levels (Jensen, Collins, and Vreeland, 1962). When the sample is restricted to middle class children, the performance on the learning task correlates quite well with the I.Q.'s obtained from standard tests of intelligence. High I.Q..middle-class children do well on the learning task while low I.Q. middle-class children do poorly. When dealing with low socioeconomic class children, on the other hand, youngsters are found who have low I.Q.'s yet who perform at a normal rate on the learning task (Jensen, 1967). Jensen's data on middle-class children indicates that learning-rate on their instrument is related to intelligence. Hence, it is quite reasonable to suspect that the poverty-area children with *low* I.Q. and *high* learning-rate are children of adequate intelligence who have been inaccurately labeled with a "low" I.Q. score. We would predict that the disadvantaged children who performed at a normal rate on Jensen's learning task would also score high on a culture-fair intelligence test.

Related to the above findings, is data from a completely different area of investigation. Eisenberg and Conners (1966) reported that a 6-week Head Start program

90

could produce statistically significant increases in I.Q. as measured by the Peabody Picture Vocabulary Test, Columbia Mental Maturity Scale, and Stanford-Binet. It might well be that what the Head Start study was dealing with were disadvantaged children with good learning capacity who scored very low on standard intelligence tests. Exposing these youngsters to the Head Start program better enabled them to demonstrate their actual level of intellectual ability. Hence, the post-testing shows significant increases. It appears that the laboratory work of Jensen and the field experience of Head Start studies complement each other quite well. Their data raises serious questions as to the true meaning of a low score on one of our standard intelligence tests received by a disadvantaged child.

Our current problem in regard to the meaning of the I.Q. with disadvantaged children might well be aided by our consideration of a statement by Binet in 1909: ". . . . . some recent philosophers appear to have given their consent to the deplorable verdict that the intelligence of the individual is a fixed quantity . . . . we must protest and act against this brutal pessimism . . . . a child's mind is like a field for which an expert farmer has advised a change in the method of cultivation, with the results that in place of desert land, we now have a harvest. It is in this particular sense, the one which is significant, that we say that the intelligence of children may be increased. One increases that which constitutes the intelligence of the school child; namely, the capacity to learn, to improve with instruction . . ."

One might equate Head Start improvement with good farming. The possible loss of the gains achieved by Head Start when these youngsters are placed in a regular school program might be equated with a situation where well nourished young plants are transplanted into very poor soil. A culture-fair instrument might well be seen as a tool which helps the farmer plan appropriately.

Part of the data discussed in this chapter has been presented in the following: (1) Rosenberg, L. A., Rosenberg, Anna M., and Stroud, M. The Johns Hopkins Perceptual Test: the development of a rapid intelligence test for the preschool child. Presented at annual meetings of Eastern Psychol. Assoc., New York, N.Y., April, 1966; (2) Rosenberg, L. A. Identifying the "gifted child" in the culturally deprived population - the need for culture-fair instruments. AMER. JOUR. ORTHOPSYCHIAT., 1967, 37, 342-343.

Supported in part by OEO contract number 510 and grants H-135 (C1) from the Children's Bureau of the Department of Health, Education, and Welfare.

References

Attneave, F. Physical determinants of the judged complexity of shapes. J. EXP. PSYCHOL., 53:221-227, 1957.

Attneave, F., and Arnoult, M.D. The quantitative study of shape and pattern perception. PSYCHOL. BULL., 53:452-471, 1956.

Binet, A. cited in Stoddard, G. D.: The I.Q.: Its ups and downs. EDUC. REC., 20:44-57, 1939; and cited in Eisenberg, L., and Conners, C. K. (1966).

Eisenberg, L., and Conners, C. K. The effect of head start on developmental processes. Presented at Joseph P. Kennedy Jr. Foundation Scientific Symposium on Mental Retardation, Boston, April, 1966.

Garner, W. R. UNCERTAINTY AND STRUCTURE AS PSYCHOLOGICAL CONCEPTS. 1962, John Wiley, Inc., New York.

Harris, D. B. CHILDREN'S DRAWINGS AS MEASURES OF INTELLECTUAL MATURITY. 1963, Harcourt, Brace and World, Inc. New York.

Jensen, A. R. Reply to inquiries concerning the article on early learning. memeo, 1967.

Jensen, A. R., Collins, C. C. and Vreeland, R. W. A multiple S-R apparatus for human learning. AMER. J. PSYCHOL., 75:470-476, 1962.

LaBerge, D. L. and Lawrence, D. H. A method of generating visual forms of graded similarity. AMER. PSYCHOLOGIST, 10:401, 1955.

Rosenberg, L. A., and Stroud, M. The limitations of brief intelligence testing with young children. PSYCHOL. REP., 19:721-722, 1966.

PEDIATRIC CARE IN PROJECT HEAD START

A. Frederick North, Jr., M.D.,
Senior Pediatrician, Project Head Start,
Office of Economic Opportunity,
Washington, D. C.

A. FREDERICK NORTH, Jr., M. D.

Ill health is one of the burdens that can keep a child from fully exploiting his environment, whether the environment be impoverished or enriched. For this reason, health must be a major consideration in any program concerned with augmenting child development. Children living in poverty have more frequent and more severe illnesses and are less likely to receive adequate health care than are more advantaged children, so health assumes an even more important role in the development of socially disadvantaged children. For these reasons, health services have been an important part of the concept of a Head Start Child Development Center.

The Head Start Health Goals

The goals of health services in Project Head Start are to ensure each child's best function by removing any existing health problems and by preventing, so far as possible, any future health problems.

The logical and practical implication of these goals define the Head Start health program. To remove health problems one must identify them—through screening tests, teachers' observations, medical and dental evaluations—and then apply a wide variety of treatments, from simple one-shot medication, to prolonged educational and rehabilitative services. To prevent future problems, one must not only provide immunizations and apply dental fluoride, one must also educate parents and children and be sure that children and their families have a source of health care for future needs. One must often change the attitudes and institutions of the community in which the children live. The elaborated goals of the Head Start health program and some of the methods suggested for achieving them are shown in Table I.

TABLE I

Health Goals of Project Head Start:

1. To improve a child's present function by:

95

A. Finding all existing health defects through:

1. Accumulating records of past health and immunization status;
2. Considering the observations of classroom teachers and other staff.
3. Performing screening tests, including tuberculin, hematocrit or hemoglobin, urinalysis, vision testing, hearing testing;
4. Interviewing the child and his parents about his current and past health and function;
5. Performing a physical examination as part of a complete health evaluation.

B. Remedying any existing defects through:

1. Applying whatever medical or dental treatments are necessary;
2. Arranging for rehabilitative services, special education, and other forms of continuing care.

II. To ensure a child's future health by:

A. Providing preventive services including:

1. Immunization against infectious diseases;
2. Fluoride treatment to prevent dental decay;
3. Health education for children and parents;
4. Introduction of the child to a physician and dentist that will be responsible for his continuing health care.

B. Improving the health of all members of the child's family through:

1. Calling attention to family health needs;
2. Introducing the family to health care services and to sources of funds for these services.

C. Improving the health of the community in which the child lives through:

1. Increasing the awareness and concern of professionals, and the general population with the health problems of poor children;
2. Stimulating and providing new resources for health care;
3. Making existing health resources more responsive to the special needs of the poor;

4. Demonstrating new skills, techniques, and patterns of care to health professionals:
5. Acquiring new knowledge through research.

Common Goals and Diverse Methods

Project Head Start is basically a system of grants to independent local community agencies to run Child Development Programs which meet certain standards. Each program, and the health component of each program, is locally initiated and is planned to meet the specific needs of its own community. While most of the goals of such a program are universally shared, there is no universally applicable method or organizational structure for reaching them. Every community has a particular group of services, facilities, funds and practices that must be pieced together to meet these goals for every Head Start child. In view of such diversity between communities, program diversity is both necessary and desirable.

Whatever methods are used, the success of the total Child Development program and the Health Services Program will depend on the quality of each of its component parts. Services must be planned and carried out by personnel who are professionally competent, aware of the community and its resources, and dedicated to bringing health care to the Head Start children. The services must be provided in an administrative, personal, and physical setting which maintains the dignity and self-esteem of each child and his parents. The program must reach out to provide services for each child, whether or not his parents show spontaneous initiative or cooperation. Services must be conceived of as part of a continuous process of health care, building on what has taken place in the past and setting the stage for better health care in the future.

PLANNING AND IMPLEMENTING
A HEALTH SERVICES PROGRAM FOR HEAD START

The task of planning a health program for a Head Start Center has many complexities. The essential elements of planning include:
1. Identifying the preventive and restorative health needs of the children involved.
2. Identifying and mobilizing services and sources of funds to meet these needs.
3. Programming services that build on past health care, and provide patterns for future health care for each child.
4. Budgeting to meet needs that are not met by existing resources.

The planning must be done not for a single child, but for a group of children with diverse needs and patterns of care. Each child must be offered not a standard set of

97

services, but an individual set of services that provides whatever he needs to insure his present and future health.

Problems in Planning

Few people in or out of the health professions have experience or skill in planning health services that will meet all of the individual health needs of a group of children, and methods for such planning have not been established or published. Problems faced by anyone planning such a program include:

1. What are the health problems to be found in a group of children?
2. What techniques will efficiently identify the children who have each type of problem?
3. What treatment or intervention techniques will be most effective in remedying the problems?
4. What financial resources and what services are available in the community which can be used to identify and treat health problems? What is their effectiveness? How can they be utilized for the benefit of the Head Start children?
5. What administrative procedures will be necessary to assure that each child gets whatever services he needs?
6. What can be done to make the future activities of the children and their families more effective in providing and maintaining good health?

Sufficient data to answer any of these questions completely does not exist. There are few program models which illustrate the successful application of what knowledge is available. Techniques for evaluating each of the problems, and for evaluating the efficacy of various programs designed to solve the problems are not well developed.

The task which at first appears simple—providing all necessary health services for a group of poor children—can be seen to be extremely complex, both in concept and execution. The following paragraphs discuss, for each of the problem areas, the knowledge that is available from Head Start experience and from other sources, and some of the implications of this knowledge for planning child health programs.

WHAT ARE THE HEALTH PROBLEMS
OF YOUNG CHILDREN LIVING IN POVERTY?

Several epidemiologic studies aimed at answering this question have provided data of only limited usefulness for program planning. Most available data are not age specific, do not consider socio-economic status, and use vague, non-specific diagnostic categories, the reliability and validity of which is highly questionable.

98

Some examples will illustrate these deficiencies. The incidence of acute medical conditions and the prevalence of chronic medical conditions, as reported in the National Health Survey, are illustrated in Tables II and III. While these data give some indication of the burden of illness to be expected in a group of young children, they have several limitations. The data were gathered in household interviews, and thus depend on parents', rather than professionals', perception of illness. The broad categories of illness which are tabulated do not allow any estimate of the severity of the conditions, or how much medical care might be required by children having these conditions.

TABLE II

REPORTED INCIDENCE
OF ACUTE MEDICAL CONDITIONS
IN CERTAIN AGE GROUPS OF CHILDREN

Incidence per 100 children

	Age 0 - 4^2	Age 3 - 6^3	Age 5 - 14^2
Infective and Parasitic Disease	72.1	71.5	50.2
Respiratory Disease	213.1	201.3	136.2
Upper Respiratory Disease		141.4	
Influenza		50.0	
Other Respiratory Disease		8.9	
Digestive Diseases	19.4	9.3	13.2
Injuries	31.3	36.7	33.7
Other Acute Diseases	37.0	35.6	22.4
Total	373.4	353.4	255.6

Source: National Health Survey

TABLE III

PREVALENCE OF CHRONIC MEDICAL CONDITIONS
AS REVEALED BY HOUSEHOLD INTERVIEWS

(Prevalence per 1,000 Children Age 0 - 16)

Infective & Parasitic Disease excluding T.B.	25
Hay Fever without Asthma	24.4

99

Asthma, with or without Hay Fever	25.7
Other Allergies	24.0
Anemia	2.9
Heart Disease	4.3
Other Circulatory Disease	4.1
Sinusitis	12.9
Bronchitis	10.1
Other Disease of Respiratory System	11.9
Hernia	5.2
Other Diseases of Digestive System	4.9
Disease of G.U. System	4.8
Skin Infective Disease	8.2
Blindness & Visual Impairment	4.1
Hearing Impairment	6.6
Speech Defects	8.8
Paralytic & Orthopedic Impairments	26.3

Source: National Health Survey

The limitations become even more apparent in Table IV, in which the prevalence of chronic disease, as revealed in the National Health Survey household interviews is compared with data from a study in North Carolina,[4] in which the prevalence and severity of chronic handicapping illness in children was judged after complete clinical assessment by a group of physicians. The household survey method yielded a prevalence of "respiratory disease" somewhat higher than the prevalence indicated by complete history and physician examination. On the other hand, the household survey yielded much lower prevalence of "vision defects" than did the clinical examination. Clearly, data from a household survey cannot accurately predict what problems will be found on clinical examinations.

In estimating the proportion of illness that was not receiving medical attention, the National Health Survey indicated that a doctor had not been consulted for a period of at least a year for 38% of the children with a chronic medical condition. In the North Carolina study, physicians examining the children judged that 42% of the children were receiving inadequate care for their handicapping condition. Neither study indicated to what extent lack of care could be found in economically deprived children of preschool age; all data were for the total group of children, age 0 - 16.

Head Start health data suffer from many of the defects of other studies, plus a few peculiar to Head Start data. Different criteria for diagnosis have been used. Records were kept with varying degrees of completeness and reliability. The likelihood of selective sampling bias, both in selection of children and in reporting of defects,

100

TABLE IV

PREVALENCE OF
CHRONIC HANDICAPPING CONDITIONS PER 1,000 CHILDREN
AS REVEALED IN TWO STUDIES

	Clinical Examination[4]		Household Survey[2]
	Total	Moderate or Severely Handicapping	
Orthopedic Conditions	60	13	26.3
Epilepsy	12	12	--
Vision Defects	123	27	4.1
Hearing Defects	49	9	6.6
Cleft Palate	3	2	--
Emotional Disturbance	106	52	--
Speech Disorder	46	12	8.8
Mental Retardation	90	77	--
Respiratory Disease	103	29	108.5
Heart Conditions	63	4	4.3
Orthodontic Problems	89	37	--
Cerebral Palsy	8	6	--
Skin Problems	77	11	8.2

makes extrapolation from Head Start incidence figures to other groups very hazardous.

Tables V, VI and VII illustrate data obtained from the Head Start health programs in the summer of 1965, 1966, and 1967, respectively. These tables show that substantial differences in prevalence figures arise when data are gathered in different ways using different diagnostic categories.

The data for 1965 were gathered from a long and detailed medical and dental questionnaire which each Head Start program was asked to complete on each child. Completeness of reporting was no better than 20% to 30%, so error due to sampling bias may be enormous.

The data for 1966 were gathered from a brief questionnaire which was completed for a sample for approximately 1% of 1966 summer Head Start children. The response rate was 77%, so little error can be attributed to sampling bias. Diagnostic categories were changed from those used in 1965. The data for 1967 were obtained

101

TABLE V

MEDICAL IMPRESSIONS, SUMMER HEAD START CHILDREN, 1965

Allergy		4.1%
Skin Diseases		2.9%
Frequent Respiratory Illness		3.8%
Tonsil-Adenoid Disease		8.7%
Anemia (Hemoglobin 10.9 gm)	(of those tested)	34.1%
Hernia		0.8%
Heart Disease		2.1%
Orthopedic Problem		2.3%
Enuresis		2.8%
Parasitic Infestation		4.2%
Convulsive Disorder		0.5%
Urinary "Infection"	(includes "abnormal" urinalysis)	2.0%
Speech Abnormality		2.3%
Hearing Impairment		1.2%
Vision Defect		7.1%
Dental Defect		44.0%

TABLE VI

DIAGNOSES IDENTIFIED IN A
1% SAMPLE OF SUMMER HEAD START CHILDREN, 1966

	Percent of children with diagnosis	Percent Newly Discovered in Head Start
Allergic Disorders	2.4%	38%
Skin Disorders	3.2%	78%
Eye & Vision Defects	4.9%	76%
Ear, Nose, Throat Disorders	8.5%	82%
Respiratory Disease	1.7%	74%
Heart Disease	3.2%	76%
Blood Disorder	1.4%	87%
Oral Problems	8.9%	82%
Gastrointestinal Disorders	1.0%	74%
Nutritional Disorders	1.9%	87%
Genitourinary Tract Disease	1.6%	76%
Orthopedic Conditions	2.2%	71%
Speech or Hearing Impairment	3.8%	78%
Convulsive Disorder	0.4%	14%

Emotional Disorder	1.0%	71%
Mental Retardation	0.6%	63%
Injuries	0.4%	32%
All Others	3.0%	84%
Positive Tuberculin Test	1.8%	of those tested
Abnormal Vision Screening Test	8.5%	
Abnormal Hearing Screening Test	5.7%	

TABLE VII

INCIDENCE OF SELECTED MEDICAL PROBLEMS 1967 SUMMER HEAD START

Anemia Noted on Examination or by Abnormal Screening Test	6.2	%
Mental Retardation or Learning Problem Requiring Specialist Evaluation	2.6	%
Skin Disease	2.4	%
Heart Murmur Requiring Specialist Evaluation	1.4	%
Bronchial Asthma	.8	%
Orthopedic Problem Requiring Treatment of Special Evaluation	.45	%
Positive Tuberculin Test	.45	%
Inguinal or Femoral Hernia	.3	%
Needed Measles Immunization	43.	%
Failed Vision Screening Test	8.	%
Dental Caries Requiring Treatment	61.	%
One or More Medical Problems Requiring Treatment or Further Evaluation	17.	%

from a sample of statistical reports submitted by approximately 80% of the summer Head Start programs. Only a few diagnostic categories were enumerated, and the diagnostic categories were more narrowly defined.

The question of whether poor children have more illness or more severe illness than do other children cannot be answered from present data. The household survey method used in the National Health Survey produces data which would indicate that poor children had a lower incidence of acute and chronic illness than did well-to-do children. This is almost certainly because middle-class parents perceive and report more illness not because the children are more ill. The best data on the relationship of social class to the incidence of illness come from several studies in Great Britain[5,6] which show that lower social class is associated with a higher incidence or prevalence of staphylococcal and streptococcal disease, tuberculosis, herpes simplex infection, gastro-intestinal infections, retarded growth, enuresis, strabismus, convulsions, speech disorders, severe lower respiratory disease,[5] mental retardation and behavior and learning disabilities.[6] Associated with the problem of describing

103

the incidence of health problems in a population is the problem of defining which conditions or findings actually constitute health problems. Several conditions mentioned in the above statistical tabulations illustrate this dilemma.

The incidence of anemia is variously reported in the statistics. Presumably, adequate studies can define the prevalence of various hemoglobin levels in the children living in any community. Unfortunately, even such studies would not indicate the importance of anemia as a health problem, since the influence of various hemoglobin levels (degrees of "anemia") on the health and performance of children are unknown. Only if anemia, as defined by a specific hemoglobin level, can be shown to have some practical consequences can it be considered as a health problem, requiring treatment or intervention.

For other health conditions, the scientific evidence is more clear, but standard practice continues to ignore the scientific evidence. For example, there is substantial evidence that umbilical hernias represent essentially no threat to health,[7] and resolve spontaneously,[8] while the surgical operation to correct this abnormality carries the real but small dangers of any surgical procedure which requires a general anesthetic. Tonsillectomy remains the most common surgical procedure performed on children,[2] despite substantial evidence that it is of no benefit in any of the conditions it purports to correct. [10]In such conditions, the "treatment" rather than the "disease" must be considered the health problem, and the extent of this problem depends on physician behavior rather than prevalence of a specific finding in a group of children.

The incidence of "mental health problems" discovered in a group of pre-school children depends almost entirely upon the orientation of the examiner. Unfortunately, no normative data are available about the behavior of poor preschool children, nor is there much data available to suggest which types of behavior in a preschool child predict behavior and learning problems in later years. Intervention or treatment techniques of proven effectiveness are also lacking. To a large extent the same considerations that apply to mental health apply to identification and treatment of minimal brain dysfunction, of speech abnormalities and of many other conditions of unquestioned importance. Should an opinion that a child is "abnormal" be considered to represent a "health problem" when "normal" is undefined and there is no evidence that what is being called "abnormal" can be modified or even that it will cause any future problem?

Even in more traditional areas of medicine, the same lack of definition of what should be considered abnormal is evident. The National Health Survey and the Head Start national data from 1965 and 1966 report "orthopedic problems" in approximately 2½% of the children examined. When the category "orthopedic

104

problem" was redefined in 1967 to include only those problems for which treatment or further evaluation seemed desirable, the prevalence in Head Start children was reported as only ½%. Clearly, a large number of conditions which are reported as "orthopedic problems" consist of minor variations such as "flat feet" a "poor posture", the practical consequences of which are unknown and which probably require no treatment or other intervention.

In summary, the problem of what health problems are to be found in a group of preschool children living in poverty cannot be answered, except by producing new data. Limitations exist in meaningful definition and categorization of health problems, and in data regarding their incidence. A group of "Best guess" estimates of the prevalence of conditions which will require special attention in program planning is given in Table VIII.

TABLE VIII

ESTIMATED PREVALENCE OF HEALTH PROBLEMS REQUIRING SPECIAL ATTENTION IN PROGRAM PLANNING

Complete Eye Evaluation Because of Failed Screening Test	10%
Eyeglasses	1%
Eye Surgery	less than 1/10%
Complete Hearing Evaluation	1-2%
Follow-up of Positive Tuberculin Test	1-4%
Iron Deficiency Anemia	10-40%
Heart Murmur Requiring Special Evaluation	1-4%
Urinary Infection	1/2%
Inguinal Hernia	1/4-1%
Skin Disease	2-5%
Asthma, Hay Fever	2-5%
Seizures	1-2%
Impaired Learning Requiring Disgnostic Evaluation	2-10%
Behavioral Abnormality Requiring Diagnostic Evaluation	2-5%
Tonsils, Circumcisions, Umbilical Hernias	0-1%

WHAT TECHNIQUES WILL BE MOST EFFICIENT IN DISCOVERING MEANINGFUL HEALTH PROBLEMS IN PRESCHOOL CHILDREN?

There are several possible ways of discovering what health problems exist in a group of young children. The most obvious is the traditional medical evaluation, or "history and physical", performed by a physician. Screening tests, performed by non—physician personnel, can discover certain health problems. Parents may

105

complete questionnaires or be interviewed by non—physician personnel to identify health problems. Teachers may identify health problems either by completing standard questionnaires or checklists or by noting and referring individual children with deviant behavior or apparent health problems.

Physicians' Examinations

The physician's examination has traditionally been considered the most certain way of identifying health problems, and it is usually the standard against which screening tests, questionnaires, or other identification techniques are judged. The physician's evaluation can be conceived of as a series of individual questionnaire and examination items, each of which is capable of discovering a certain proportion of a certain type of health problem. Which parts of the history or examination are most effective and efficient in discovering what kind of health problems in a group of preschool children is largely unstudied. Although the examination and interview are often highly ritualized, they cannot be considered to be standardized. Different examiners find different problems.[11] While a comprehensive interview, examination and evaluation by a physician appears to be the most certain way of discovering all health problems, evidence to support its reliability, or its efficiency, is largely lacking.

Screening Tests

Screening tests are procedures that can be applied to an entire group to identify that part of the group which is at high risk of having a specific health problem. Since such tests are applied to an entire population, they must be inexpensive both in material costs and in cost of professional time. They can usually be applied by non—physician personnel.

Despite long and widespread use of a number of screening tests, the precise usefulness of many of these procedures is still questionable. For example, when the Snellen Illiterate "E" Wall Chart is used to screen the visual acuity of preschool children, 8% to 10% of the children will fail to pass the screening test. However, it is not known what proportion of the children found to be "abnormal" by this screening test will actually benefit from early discovery and treatment. Nor is it clear how many children would be missed by such a test who actually might benefit from early treatment. Yet, every year millions of children are tested and are referred on the basis of this test.

Other screening tests have similar or different limitations. The screening test for anemia is limited in usefulness by a lack of knowledge of the consequences of various levels of hemoglobin as discussed above. The tuberculin test, which is both reliable and valid, produces such a low yield in some communities that its efficiency is challenged. Urinalysis produces such a high yield of abnormal tests in relationship

106

to the number of treatable medical problems finally uncovered, that many question whether it can be considered a useful screening test.[12] Screening tests for bacteriuria appear efficient and effective in discovering important urinary tract infections. However, few communities have the administrative and laboratory facilities to perform such tests efficiently.

Parent Questionnaires

Several studies have shown that questions posed to parents on a printed questionnaire, or by a non—professional interviewer, can discover a large number of children with health problems. One household survey[4] revealed that nearly 50% of children, age 0—6, were considered by their parents to have some handicapping condition. Clinical examination confirmed the presence of some abnormality in 80% of such children. While most of the conditions were mild and produced no actual functional handicap, nearly 20% of the children had a condition causing moderate or severe handicap. In addition, of the children considered normal by their parents, nearly 32% had some abnormality on examination.

Teachers' Observation

Teachers, with their prolonged chance to observe children in close proximity to other children of the same age and usually of the same social class, should be in an excellent position to identify children whose appearance or behavior deviates from that of the other children. While many have found that teachers can, indeed, identify children with a health problem, no quantitative studies are available to indicate the effectiveness and efficiency of such screening.

Based on the very limited data available, the best current procedure seems to be the utilization of all four identification techniques above. There is some evidence that each technique reveals a different group of abnormalities, although the abnormalities detected by any one technique overlap greatly with those discovered by another technique. Head Start currently recommends that teachers' observations be systematically obtained and recorded, that parents be pre-interviewed by non-physician personnel, that certain screening tests be performed, and that a physician perform a complete medical evaluation with the parent present. With the information from screening tests, parent interviews, and teachers' observations available at the time of his evaluation, the physician can probably make the most effective use of his time and talents.

WHAT TREATMENT OR INTERVENTION TECHNIQUES ARE MOST EFFECTIVE AND EFFICIENT?

Discovering health problems or defects is of only academic interest if no methods exist to treat or alleviate the conditions discovered. Of course, treatment or

107

alleviation need not imply complete cure. For example, careful explanation to a parent of the benign nature of a previously identified heart murmur does nothing for the heart murmur. But it may relieve a great deal of parental anxiety and may remove unrealistic inhibitions placed on the child's activities.

The treatment of primary tuberculosis in childhood represents a situation in which data is sufficient to make most of the necessary judgements.[13] Once a young child has been shown to have a positive tuberculin test, his chances of developing progressive pulmonary or extra-pulmonary tuberculosis, though small, are quite real and predictable. Treatment with isoniazid reduces this risk by 75% to 80%. The cost of isoniazid treatment is easily predictable, and the risks of treatment are both well known and of extremely small magnitude. In such a situation the cost and risks of treatment can be compared directly with the cost and risks of not treating, and a rational decision can be reached (in this case, almost always in favor of treatment).

In most medical conditions knowledge of the risks is not nearly so clear. Bronchial asthma is a frequent and distressing cause of disability in children. While immediate symptomatic treatment can always be justified, the justification for long term treatment is not so clear. The course of the disease when no long term treatment is applied is not accurately known or predictable, even in a statistical sense. The effectiveness of each type of treatment—hyposensitization, environmental controls, dietary restrictions, medications—is not known, nor are the risks and costs of each type of treatment or combination of treatments known. The decision for or against any type of long term treatment for bronchial asthma must be based on much weaker evidence than that which is available for such conditions as tuberculosis.

For other conditions, widely used therapeutic techniques not only have inadequate supporting data, but have a considerable amount of data showing that they are not effective. Tonsil and adenoidectomy, and umbilical hernia repair have already been mentioned. A large group of studies have tried to establish the effectiveness of psychotherapy as a technique in relieving psychiatric or behavior disorders. The majority of such studies have not shown psychotherapy to be effective.[14] Special classes for children with various educational problems have become a widespread phenomena, yet there is very little evidence that segregating children with special learning problems (or with superior learning ability) from their peers results in more learning progress than these children would have achieved without such separation. The feeling that "something must be done" is natural when one is dealing with children with problems. But the "something" should either be supported by scientific evidence or be administered in such a way that scientific evidence of its efficacy can be obtained.

The lack of scientific evidence to support many of the forms of therapy in

108

widespread use adds to the difficulties in planning a realistic and effective health program for a group of children. The fact that decisions must be made, even in the face of such factual uncertainty, lends support to two premises underlying the Head Start Health Program. One is that most decisions about which identification and treatment procedures are to be used must be made on an individual case by case basis in the community in which the problems and the resources to solve the problems are located. The other is that every health program must evaluate itself not only in terms of what it has done (inputs) but in terms of how what it has done has affected the health of the children involved (effects) and at what cost.

WHAT FINANCIAL AND SERVICE RESOURCES EXIST FOR CHILD HEALTH? HOW CAN THEY BE UTILIZED?

Every large community and most small communities contain a wide range of sources of funds and services for childrens' health care, such as those listed in Table IX.

TABLE IX

1. Private Practitioners of Medicine, Dentistry, Optometry, Psychology - individual or group.

2. Health Departments - city, county, regional and state.

3. School Health Programs.

4. Clinics - run by hospitals, medical schools or other agencies.

5. Prepaid Medical Groups.

6. Armed Forces Medical Services

7. OEO Neighborhood Health Centers.

8. Dental Service Corporations.

9. Special Voluntary Agencies and Public Agencies, such as:

    a. Catholic, Protestant, Jewish Welfare Associations.

    b. Family Service Associations

    c. Fraternal Organizations, Civic Clubs, Women's Clubs and Parent Teachers Associations.

109

d. Associations for the blind or for prevention of blindness.

   e. Associations for retarded children, cerebral palsy, crippled children and for children with special diseases.

   f. Tuberculosis Associations

   g. Mental Health Associations

10. State Crippled Childrens' Programs

11. Local and State Welfare or Public Assistance Programs.

12. Medical Assistance under Title XIX "Medicaid".

13. Insurance and Prepayment Plans.

Head Start programs are urged to utilize fully all acceptable available community resources. Such a policy serves several purposes. By conserving Head Start funds, it makes services available to a larger number of children. By introducing parents and children to resources which are a permanent part of the community, it helps ensure that the families will continue to obtain appropriate health care even after the children leave the Head Start program. By confronting existing institutions with the problems of providing comprehensive health care for poor children, it frequently makes such existing resources more responsive to the special needs of poor children and of all children in the community.

Once all resources available for child health care in a community have been identified, each one must be evaluated as to the scope and limitations of its services. The following questions must be asked in evaluating such a resource:

1. What categories of health care can be provided or funded under this program?
2. Are there special diagnostic, financial or other criteria for eligibility under this program? What are they?
3. Is this program of adequate size to meet the needs of all eligible children?
4. Is participation in this program potentially or actually restricted by complex admission, eligibility, or other administrative procedures?
5. Is the professional quality of the services offered in this program equivalent to that available in other programs in this community?
6. Is participation this program actually or potentially restricted by geographic inaccessibility of the services?

110

7. Is participation in this program actually or potentially restricted because of unpleasant surroundings, long waiting periods, or unpleasant attitudes towards the poor, the patient, or ethnic minorities?

After each potential source of funds or services has been identified and evaluated as to its applicability, a program must be devised which will utilize whatever resources are appropriate and which will fill any gaps which may be present in existing resources. The coordination of resources must be considered from the point of view of the parent and the child, not simply from the point of view of the administrator.

The final and most difficult task in evaluating local funds and services is preparing a budget that will fill the gaps in existing services. This budget must consider the cost of identifying and treating the health problems of the children involved, the cost of immunization programs and health education, the part of this cost that can be met through funding programs, the part of the services that can be provided free through existing community resources, and the cost of administering a program that will achieve these goals. Given this complex task, it is hardly surprising that many Head Start programs have found themselves under-budgeted or over-budgeted in terms of the precise health needs of the children they serve and the other resources in their community.

WHAT IS NECESSARY TO ASSURE THAT EACH CHILD GETS THE SERVICES HE NEEDS?

Attitudes

When unmet health needs are discovered in a population, the first response of professionals is usually to blame the individuals with health needs for not obtaining the necessary care. This is especially true when facilities for meeting these needs are apparently available. When children are involved, it is not easy to blame them directly for not obtaining health care, so the parents are blamed.

The general term "parent apathy" has been used to explain why a substantial portion of the population of poor children does not obtain health services, even in our well equipped large cities. Those Head Start programs which have been successful in obtaining health services for nearly 100% of the children who need them have shown that the failure to obtain treatment, attributed to "parent apathy", is actually the product of several realistic factors which can be overcome, but only by special efforts. The examining physician must explain the nature of the defect to the parent, along with the reasons for treatment and the kind of treatment needed. Someone must aid the parent in finding the needed services and provide funds for the needed services. Someone must see that the parent and child actually have transportation and that other children in the family will be cared for during the

111

visit to the physician or the clinic. Someone must carefully and repeatedly screen records to assure that recommended treatment has actually taken place. *The Program must be willing to do whatever is necessary to assure treatment and follow-up.* When these measures are taken "parent apathy" often becomes parent enthusiasm which reflects itself in better health care for the entire family. That part of the population which has been called "unreachable" is only the unreached. Their attitudes towards health care seem similar to those of people of more fortunate background.[15] Their participation in health care is low because they often have other needs of higher priority, and because the services offered to the medically indigent population in most communities are inaccessible in terms of time and distance, and often unacceptable in terms of human dignity.

It is apparent that it is not the attitudes and priorities of those who fail to obtain medical care that need to be changed, so much as the attitudes and priorities of the providers of medical care. Perhaps one of the most important benefits of massive demonstration programs, such as Project Head Start, is that they confront the providers of services with the demand to re-evaluate what they are doing. One of the results of Head Start has been to show that participation in a conscientious attempt to provide comprehensive health services for a group of poor children is a valuable educational experience for the doctors, dentists, nurses and others who provide health care. When they see parents actively and articulately concerned about the conditions in which health care is given; when they see that an aide without professional training can accomplish more in ensuring follow-up than their own stern advice to a parent; when they hear and see at first-hand that some of the children have had no previous medical or dental care; when they find that many screening tests and examinations have a much higher yield in a poverty group than in the middle-class children they may be accustomed to serving; the entire attitude of the health professional toward the need for, and possibilities for, health care for poor children is often dramatically altered. And when their attitudes are altered, the individual providers of health care are in an excellent position to alter the institutions through which their services are made available.

Administrative Methods

The administrative systems used by school health programs or well-child programs, which have been concerned primarily with screening rather than with treatment, do not adapt themselves well to a treatment oriented program such as Head Start. In addition to the plan and budget, the administration of a successful health program requires at least two types of records—individual health records and administrative records.

The individual health record serves three purposes: insuring that the individual child gets the needed corrective and preventive care, helping physicians and other health

112

workers to provide and arrange for such care, and helping the classroom teachers to mould an educational program that is especially suited to the needs of the individual child. To aid the individual child, the record must completely and concisely summarize the health findings, as determined from all sources, in a way that clearly shows which recommendations for treatment and preventive measures have been made and which have taken place. To aid in the provision of needed health care, the record must include a sufficient background of social, medical and educational information so that each health professional dealing with a child need not accumulate his own record and history. To serve the educational needs of the child, the health findings must be translated into classroom recommendations, and these must be systematically transmitted to the classroom personnel.

Administrative records are necessary to be sure that each child actually receives the medical evaluation, screening tests, follow-up and preventive measures which he requires. Such records are necessary to evaluate the effectiveness of the total health program and to aid in setting priorities for planning and budgeting follow-up care.

To aid individual programs in keeping such administrative records, a pre-packaged "Health Bookkeeping System" has been devised which will be published in the near future. Fig. 1 illustrates the basic elements of this bookkeeping system: a class roster with a novel checklist feature, and a "referral and treatment card" to be kept in a chronological tickler file. As the information from screening tests, examinations, and histories is made available, it is noted on the class list. It is marked "O.K." if the test or examination shows, or the history indicates, no need for further action. If further action is necessary, a letter "R" is entered in the appropriate space, and a referral and treatment card is filled out describing exactly what has to be done and when it is to be done. By filing the cards chronologically by date of appointment and by referring to them each week, the person responsible for health services can clearly see and plan each week's activities. As soon as all necessary action is completed, the tickler card is removed from the file and the appropriate place on the roster sheet is marked with a letter "C" indicating completion.

This simple administrative tool should help Head Start programs to assure that each child gets every service which he needs, to schedule the health program in a logical sequence, and to make periodic analysis of its progress.

FIGURE I

SUMMARY OF THE HEALTH SERVICES RECORD SYSTEM

1. The HEALTH PROGRAM CONTROL SHEET lists each child in the program. As each item of the health program is completed for each child, the control sheet is checked off in a way that shows clearly what has been done and what remains to be done.

113

HEALTH PROGRAM CONTROL SHEET

Sheet _/_ of

NAME OF HEAD START CENTER: _Community Church_   CLASS: _Miss Smith_   YEAR: _1968_

(Use the code indicated at the bottom of the page when completing these columns.)

NAME OF CHILD	TESTS					MEDICAL EVAL-UATION	DENTAL EVAL-UATION	IMMUNIZATIONS							
	TUBER-CULIN	HEMA-TOCRIT HEMO-GLOBIN	HEARING TEST	VISION TEST	URIN-ALYSIS			D. P. T.		POLIO		SMALL-POX		MEASLES	
Richard Washington	O K	R		O K	O K		O K			R		R		O K	O K
Charles Emons	O K	O K		O K										R C	
Juan Pizzaro		O K		O K				O K	J K	J K	J K	J K	O	R	O K
Elsie Jankowski	R	O K		R		R								R C	
Jack McDonald	O K	R		O K					R	C	O K	O K		O K	

The following code should be used:

	Space is to be left blank until evaluation or test is performed		R	If evaluation or test has been performed and referral for treatment is required enter an R in the first space in the column.
O K	If evaluation or test has been performed and no referral required enter O K in the spaces.		R C	When treatment has been given and no further remedial action is required enter a C opposite the R.

2. Whenever a child needs an appointment for further evaluation or for medical or dental treatment, a REFERRAL AND TREATMENT APPOINTMENT RECORD card is completed to indicate the date, time and place of the appointment, whether the appointment is kept, and whether further appointments or special services (such as transportation) are needed.

TYPE OF APPOINTMENT: _Evaluate Positive T B Test_   NAME OF CHILD (Last name, first name, middle initial): _Juan Pizzaro_

NAME OF DOCTOR (Or clinic): _George Wilson_   ADDRESS OF DOCTOR (Or clinic): _18 Center Street_

*SCHEDULE		ACTION REQUIRED FOR COMPLETING TREATMENT (Transportation, baby sitter, special services)	NOTES AND RECOMMENDATIONS
DATE	TIME		
7/20/68	2°° pm		Missed Appt.
8/1/68	3°° pm	Needs Transportation and reminder	X ray ok, INH R
10/2/68	2°° pm	" " " "	

3. The appointment record cards are filed by date, to provide a daily or weekly list of all children requiring medical or dental care.

4. At any time, a glance at the control sheet shows which children still require each type of medical or dental service. The card file shows where and when these services are scheduled.

5. A count of each column on the control sheet will provide information for periodic and final reports of what has been accomplished in the health services program.

114

HOW CAN THE FUTURE HEALTH OF CHILDREN BE PROTECTED?

Immunization with live measles vaccine is an example of almost ideal protection of future health. The administration of a single dose of measles vaccine offers more than 95% certainty that the vaccinated person will not experience measles at any time in the future.

A type of prevention nearly as successful as immunization is the addition of fluoride to water supplies and the topical application of fluoride compounds to the teeth. The addition of fluoride to the water supply reduces the incidence and severity of dental decay by 50% to 70%. Fluoride application to the teeth apparently further reduces the incidence of dental decay by 20% to 30%. The cost of these preventive measures is extremely small when compared with the costs of providing care if the preventive measures are not taken.

Unfortunately, preventive measures as direct and effective as immunization and fluoridation are not abundant. Head Start programs attempt in two other ways to protect the future health of children.

First, they attempt to change the health care patterns of the children and their families if these patterns have been unsatisfactory in the past. Children and families are introduced to physicians or clinics who are willing to provide future preventive and remedial care, and funds are located to pay for such care. There is no available measure of how successful Head Start has been in actually changing the health care patterns of the children it serves. It is not certain scientifically that patterns of health care have any substantial effect on the health of families or children. While it is true that poor families obtain less health care and have more health problems than the more well-to-do families, it is by no means certain that lack of health care causes, or even contributes to impaired health of people living in poverty. It may be that much broader social changes are necessary before the health of such people can be improved. However, choices must be made in the face of inadequate data, and the only humane and socially acceptable choice seems to be that poor people should have available to them the same system of health care as is available to the more fortunate segments of the population.

A second way of protecting a child's future health is by educating him and his parents to take whatever measures are necessary to protect future health, such as eating nutritious foods, seeking preventive medical care and early treatment for health problems, preventing accidents, personal cleanliness, tooth brushing, etc. Again, there is little evidence that health education programs do change the behavior of parents and children, nor is there much evidence that if behavior were changed,

115

the changed behavior would have any substantial impact on health. Up to the present time, it has been nearly impossible to judge the quality or the impact of health education programs in Project Head Start.

THE ADMINISTRATIVE FUNCTION

The actual transactions which change the health of a Head Start child take place between the child, the parent, and the provider of health services. The administrative function at any level is simply to make these transactions more efficient and effective and to assure that no child or family is overlooked. There are four basic administrative tools for achieving effective health services: 1) setting of mutually acceptable health goals; 2) discovering and suggesting acceptable alternative methods of achieving these goals; 3) providing advice and assistance in the implementation of these methods; 4) providing and encouraging a system of evaluation that will provide immediate and corrective feedback on the success or failure of a program or procedure.

Goal Setting

The goals described at the beginning of this paper have appeared to be non-controversial and widely acceptable. The major administrative difficulty has been in making these goals known to all participating in the Head Start programs—health professionals, school personnel, parents, and community leaders.

Methods of Implementation

For the reasons discussed in this paper, there is less consensus regarding the relative effectiveness of various methods of achieving these health goals. Administrative difficulties arise both from too rigid and too lax acceptance of suggestions. Many Head Start children did not receive measles immunization because the person responsible for their program "did not believe in" measles immunization. In view of scientific evidence in favor of measles immunization and the lack of alternative methods for preventing measles, this appears to be too lax an interpretation of the guidelines. In other instances, complete medical evaluations were repeated for children who had only recently completed them in other programs. This seemed to represent a too rigid interpretation of the suggestion that in order to discover and treat health defects, each child should have a complete medical evaluation.

Aid, Advice and Assistance

Technical aid and assistance is provided for Head Start Health programs through several channels. The booklet *Project Head Start Health Services, A Guide for Project Directors and Health Personnel* outlines the health goals of Project Head Start and provides suggestions both for administrators and for medical and dental professionals about how to achieve these goals. The application forms and instructions reinforce the goals and suggestions set forth in the Health Services Guide. Examples of successful programs and suggestions for program improvement are published in a HEAD START NEWSLETTER.

In addition to publications, certain forms and systems have been devised and made available to Head Start programs. A group of record forms for recording medical and dental care, and forms for recording teachers' health observations, have been distributed. A modification of the Denver Developmental Screening Test,[6] standardized especially for Head Start children, is available as an aid to health professionals, psychologists or teachers interested in screening for developmental progress. The "Health Bookkeeping System" described earlier in this paper, and a "Guide to Evaluation of Community Health Resource" are in preparation and should be published soon.

Probably the most important method of technical assistance is through a system of health service consultants who can meet with those planning health service for Head Start programs and deal directly with their particular problems. In the first two years of Head Start, nearly two hundred pediatricians and public health physicians made their services available to Head Start programs for both evaluation and consultation. They were able to provide technical medical advice, to help in working out administrative arrangements and in utilizing existing agencies, and to serve as advocates for the Head Start Programs and children with professional organizations, with service agencies and institutions, and with the granting agency. Unfortunately, no administrative mechanism was available to assure that each program that needed medical consultation, either to plan or to carry out its health program, actually received it, nor was it possible to assure that consultation was readily available on a continuing basis during grant preparation, planning and operation of the health programs. In October 1967, the Office of Economic Opportunity contracted with the American Academy of Pediatrics to provide health services consultation to every Head Start program in the country. Under the terms of this contract, the American Academy of Pediatrics will recruit, orient, and reimburse a group of several hundred specialists in Child Health and Development. Each of these physicians will provide consultation to a group of two to five Head Start programs in geographical proximity to his own community but not including his own community. The consultant will review the medical aspects of the Head Start application, meet with local planning committees to map out Head Start medical programs, maintain contact with program directors and medical personnel while the program is in operation, and will make a formal evaluation of the medical program.

The consultant is not expected to act for the Head Start community or direct its health activities, but rather through his professional knowledge, his knowledge of

117

health resources, and through his prestige as an expert in the field of child development, to better equip the community to act on its own.

A central role for the consultant will be to help those planning the health program, to evaluate the effectiveness of their own plans and programs, and based on this evaluation, to modify the program so that it more closely meets the needs of the Start children and their families.

A trial of this consultation system in six New England states during the summer of 1967 demonstrated that the system appeared useful and acceptable both to consultants and program directors. Such a consultation system may prove useful not only for Head Start, but for all child health programs. The developing expertise of the consultants should constitute a major resource for improving other child health services.

Evaluation and Monitoring
In order to maintain effective and efficient health services, the program must continually evaluate itself to be certain that its activities do, indeed, lead to better health and function of the Head Start children and their families.

The place of evaluation and monitoring in the system for program improvement is illustrated schematically in Figure 2.

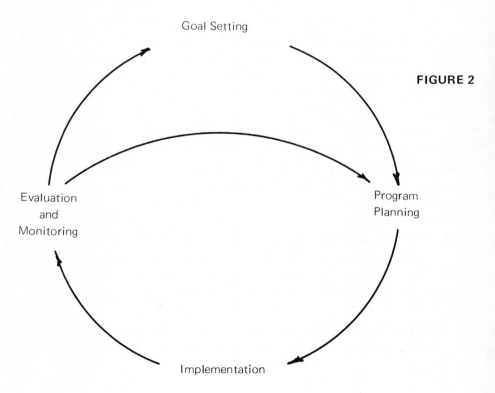

Goal Setting

FIGURE 2

Evaluation and Monitoring

Program Planning

Implementation

118

The most important part of evaluation and monitoring is objective self- evaluation by those who plan and carry out the program. These people are in a position to respond directly to feedback from the children, the parents, and other participants in the health program, and to modify the program and its techniques.

In order to evaluate whether the services offered in the program are reaching all the children in the program, certain objective statistics are necessary. The Health Bookkeeping System, previously discussed, provides not only a convenient way of assuring that each child receives the necessary services, but also a constant monitor that shows which parts of the program has been accomplished and what remains to be accomplished. The type of statistics necessary for this sort of internal evaluation is also valuable for external reporting of the accomplishments of the health services program.

Each Head Start program is asked to submit statistical reports of its activities and accomplishments. The present reporting form is illustrated in Figure 3. The questions asked force those responsible for a program to evaluate not only what has been done but what has been left undone.

FIGURE 3

Questions from Head Start Health Services Reporting Form

1. Measles Vaccine
    a) How many children received measles vaccine during the Head Start Health Program? . . . .
    b) How many did not receive measles vaccine? . . . .
       Of these, how many had been previously vaccinated? . . . .
       How many have already had measles? . . . .
       How many still need vaccination at the time of this report? . . . .
    c) How many have unknown measles immunization status? . . . .

2. Vision Screening Test
    a) How many children had a test of visual acuity (vision screening test) as part of the Head Start program? . . . .
    b) Of those tested, how many failed the vision screening test? . . . .
    c) Of those who failed the vision screening test, how many
       1) Have had no further evaluation? . . . .
       2) Have had full professional evaluation at the time of this report? . .
       3) Have been found to need eyeglasses? . . . .
       4) Have had eyeglasses prescribed and fitted and are wearing them? .
       5) Have unknown treatment status? . . . .

3. Dental Care

119

a) How many children had a dental examination as part of the Head Start Program ....
   1) How many were examined by a dentist ....
      (rather than by physician, nurse or hygienist)
b) Of those examined, how many
   Were free of dental disease ....
   Had dental caries (cavities, decay) ....
   Had other dental disease ....
   Had unknown or unrecorded findings ....
c) Of those with dental caries or other disease
   For how many was treatment recommended? ....
d) Of those with treatment recommended, how many
   1) Have completed all recommended treatment? ....
   2) Are currently receiving dental treatment? ....
   3) Have not yet received dental treatment? ....
   4) Have unknown treatment status? ....

4. a) How many children were discovered in the Head Start program to have medical problems requiring treatment or further evaluation? ....

   Of these how many, at the time of this report:

   b) Have completed all recommended evaluation and treatment? ....
      (a chronic problem, such as asthma, mental retardation, may be considered completely treated if it has been fully evaluated and is under the care of a physician or clinic that has accepted responsibility for future care).
   c) Are currently being evaluated or under treatment? ....
   d) Have had no further evaluation or treatment? ....
   e) Have unknown treatment status? ....

5. How many children had *no* medical or dental problem requiring treatment of further evaluation? ....

6. How many children had each of the following health problems:
   1. *Anemia* (either diagnosed by physician or indicated by abnormal hemoglobin or hematocrit test) ....
   2. Positive tuberculin test? ....
   3. Bronchial asthma ....
   4. Skin disease (including eczema and impetigo) ....
   5. Heart murmur requiring specialist consultation ....
   6. Mental retardation or learning problem requiring specialist evaluation ..
   7. Inguinal or femoral hernia (Do not include umbilical or ventral hernia) .
   8. Orthopedic (bone or joint) problem requiring X-rays or specialist consultation ....

120

While such an instrument measures success in getting services to children, it does not measure effectiveness in achieving better health for children except when services can be directly related to better health. A previously un-immunized child, who is now protected against measles, can be considered to have had his future health and function sufficiently modified by the immunization. The fact that a child has been examined and fitted for eye glasses does not necessarily mean improved health unless it can be shown that the eye glasses have actually improved his comfort or functional ability. As has been previously discussed, the benefits of many other services are even less certain. The statistical evaluation, therefore, usually measures not increased health of children but the effectiveness of the program in reaching all children with the services they appear to need.

Many of the goals of the health program do not lend themselves to statistical reporting. To evaluate success in meeting these goals, consultants are asked to make qualitative and subjective judgements. As is the case with program statistics, the consultants' evaluations serve two purposes. They provide immediate feedback to those planning and carrying out the program, and they provide useful information for national statistics, for changes in national guidelines, and for funding decisions. Thus, the two main evaluative tools—program reporting and consultant evaluation—each provide immediate feedback to those planning and carrying out the program and at the same time provide information that can be used to report on and to modify the program at a national level.

One element that is missing from the current evaluation system is a systematic means of recognizing what, if any, program characteristics lead to successful or unsuccessful health services programs. The consultants' reports do contain open-ended questions asking about major strengths and weaknesses of the program. From these reports we hope to compile a list of program characteristics which seem to have a critical impact on the success of the health services program. A questionnaire regarding these characteristics will then be added to the program reporting form to determine whether the impressions gathered from the consultants' reports can be statistically validated. If certain program characteristics or techniques appear uniformly useful, they can be built into future regulations or guidelines, or suggested for use in other programs.

SUMMARY AND OVER-VIEW

There is widespread consensus, though very little direct evidence, that health services can play an important role in programs directed in helping children, especially poor children, achieve their full developmental potential. Based on this consensus, and on what evidence is available, comprehensive health services for children have been incorporated as a central component of Head Start Child Development Centers.

121

The type of basic data necessary to plan a completely rational program for child health has been discussed, and the gaps in existing knowledge have been pointed out. With such gaps in basic knowledge, it is hardly surprising that there is criticism and debate about what methods will best achieve better health and function for Head Start children.

Gaps in knowledge and a lack of organizational models of proven utility cannot prevent the need for pragmatic decisions about program content and organization. However, the imperfect knowledge does dictate *first*, that diversity of program content and organization is highly desirable both in adapting to local conditions and in testing new methods; second, that each of the diverse programs must build into itself an evaluation and monitoring system that can lead both to program improvement and to more definite knowledge about the effectiveness of service techniques and organizational plans. Head Start may prove to be both an impetus and a setting for scientific investigation of many of the unsolved problems of health care for children.

CONCLUSION

Over the past two and one-half years, Head Start has brought health services to a group of young children who had been previously considered "hard to reach". While the services brought to these children can be considered to be worthwhile in themselves, perhaps the greatest health impact Project Head Start has made is not in bringing services to children, but in confronting health professionals and laymen in thousands of communities with the unmet health needs of a large group of children, and by forcing many of these people to begin to plan rational health services to meet the needs of these previously unserved children. The lessons learned from Head Start on a national scale, but more importantly on the local scale in thousands of communities, will hopefully provide impetus toward personal and institutional change that will result in better health services for all of America's children.

References

1. PROJECT HEAD START, 2: HEALTH SERVICES, A GUIDE FOR PROJECT DIRECTORS AND HEALTH PERSONNEL. Office of Economic Opportunity, Washington, D. C., 1967

2. Schiffer, C. G. and Hunt, E. P. ILLNESS AMONG CHILDREN: DATA FROM U. S. NATIONAL HEALTH SURVEY. Childrens' Bureau Publication No. 405, Dept. of Health, Education & Welfare, Washington, 1967.

3. Unpublished material from U. S. National Health Survey.

4. Richardson, W. P., Higgins, A. C., Ames, R. G. THE HANDICAPPED CHILDREN OF ALAMANCE COUNTY, NORTH CAROLINA: A MEDICAL AND SOCIOLOGICAL STUDY. Nemours Foundation, Wilmington, Delaware, 1965.

5. Miller, F. J. W., Court, S. D. M., Walton, W. S., Knox, F. G. GROWING UP IN NEWCASTLE UPON TYNE. Oxford University Press, New York, 1960

6. Drillien, C. M. THE GROWTH AND DEVELOPMENT OF THE PREMATURELY BORN INFANT. Baltimore, Williams and Wilkins, 1964.

7. Potts, W. J. THE SURGEON AND THE CHILD. W. B. Saunders, Philadelphia, 1959. p. 145.

8. Halperin, L. J. Spontaneous Healing of Umbilical Hernias. J.A.M.A. 182: 851-852, 1962.

9. Bakwin, H. The Tonsil Adenoidectomy Enigma. J. PEDIATRICS 52: 339-361, 1958.

10. McKee, W. J. E. A Controlled Study of the Effects of Tonsillectomy and Adenoidectomy in Children. BRIT. J. PREV. SOC. MED. 17: 49-69, 1963.

11. Eisner, V., Goodlet, C. B., Driver, M. B. Health of Enrolees in Neighborhood Youth Corps. PEDIATRICS 38:40-43, 1966

12. Charney, E. Current Concepts: Examination of the Preschool Child. NEW ENG. J. MED. 270:1408-1411, 1964.

13. Davis, S. D., Wedgewood, R. J. TB, PPD, and INH. PEDIATRICS 39:809-810, 1967.

123

14. Levitt, E. E. Psychotherapy with children: A Further Evaluation. BEHAV. RES. THER. 1:45-51, 1963.

15. Watts, D. D. Factors Related to the Acceptance of Modern Medicine. AM. J. PUB. HEALTH. 56:1205-1212, 1966

16. Frankenberg, W. L. and Dodd, J. B. The Denver Developmental Screening Test. J. PEDIATRICS 71:181-191, 1967.

THE NEUROLOGICAL EVALUATION OF CHILDREN IN HEAD START

Mark N. Ozer, M.D.,
Associate Neurologist,
Children's Hospital of the District of Columbia,
Washington, D. C.

MARK N. OZER, M. D.

The Head Start program was the first large scale application of remedial techniques to the problem of poor school performance in the culturally disadvantaged. The need for such a preventive program was obvious since many of these children later fail to develop adequate verbal skills and other learned behaviors in the school. This failure has been considered to be mainly a reflection of inadequate verbal training in the home and of relatively poor school programming. Another major contribution to inadequate school performance may be the variation in the central nervous system or physiological substrate available for environmental manipulation. Studies have generally described the less adequate prenatal care and increased incidence of prematurity with attendant brain dysfunction in the lower income group. (1-3) Children with learning problems have been considered as within the continuum of less severe brain dysfunction, and their difficulties are similarly related to prenatal and para-natal factors.(4)

There had been no easily administered, scorable, medical examination of brain function of children of school age. A short, scorable, standardized neurological examination is being developed for large scale use by school health physicians and pediatricians. This type of examination appeared to be particularly relevant to the evaluation of a relatively high risk group such as might be enrolled in Head Start. Such a measure would help to delineate the extent of the problem of lesser degrees of neurological dysfunction as well as to identify those individual children who would require special programming. Early evaluation in pre-school centers could thus identify the child with "neurological immaturity" prior to the "trial of school." In most instances, the child with learning difficulties is given several years of schooling as a "trial." It is only after these several years of trial and failure, often resulting in secondary emotional difficulties, that he may be referred for testing and hopefully more appropriate educational programming.

The diagnosis of neurological dysfunction has been based primarily upon the presence of motor and perceptual disabilities and certain other behavioral correlates such as excessive hyperactivity and distractibility in a group of children with learn-

127

ing difficulties.[5] The neurological examination, however, as generally administered, has been derived from that of adult clinical neurology. It is essentially concerned with the delineation of asymmetries of performance. The child, for example, with abnormalities on one side versus the other, in the lower extremities versus the upper, is identified as having neurological dysfunction. This type of neurological examination is not as useful in the delineation of developmental difficulties where asymmetries may not be found. The child with slower performance of the early motor skills and speech can be identified as significantly at risk with regard to learning difficulties at school. However, these milestones may be met within a wide range of normal. Moreover, a child may present learning problems in school without having been identified as having developmental difficulties during the first few years of life.

Many of the children with learning problems may be identified as having relatively minor motor disabilities at school entry. It is the breakdown in finer motor sequencing that may serve to separate the child with learning problems from his contemporary. Motor scales have been developed in the past, notably those of Oseretsky,[6-8] later modified by Sloan at the Lincoln School.[9] The presence of spontaneous adventitious movements has been emphasized,[10] as well as associated movements, as a measure of maturation of motor function.[11] A short, standardized, motor examination was derived which focuses on finer sequencing in a scorable fashion. Items have been selected on the basis of ease of scoring and sampling of various parameters of motor function.

Although clumsy children may be at greater risk for learning difficulties there may not be a one to one relationship between motor performance and learning school type materials. Motor performance may be considered a measure of brain function or maturation; however, there are other aspects of performance which are probably more relevant to academic learning. For example, tasks involving performance through utilization of visual and auditory or, at times, kinesthetic cues might be useful in identifying children with potential learning difficulties. Additionally such tasks could also be considered diagnostic in a more specific sense of delineating the channels by which the individual child may be most effectively taught. An example might be a task in which the child is required to follow more complex verbal instructions such as those involving discrimination of right and left and crossing the midline.[12]

In a further attempt to make the neurological examination more relevant to the identification of children with potential learning problems, the acquisition of new "sets" in the clinical setting has been included as a measure of brain function.[13] On these tasks, the operational definition of adequate brain function would be the child's ability to "catch on" to a particular task. The child is explicitly taught and

128

the number of trials required is reflected in the scoring. As an example, another task involving a measure of processing in the auditory channel is the "sound-touch" test. The child is presented with distracting sound to the ear along with touch to the hand. The rapidity with which he "tunes out" the sound over a series of trials may be considered a measure of distractibility simulating, in a clinical setting, the phenomenon described in the classroom.

The neurological examination has then been developed to probe the functions relevant to the *process* of learning in a school setting. Process is involved in at least two senses. The tasks are, whenever possible, not merely measure of present performance. An opportunity for learning is provided so that these tasks could be more specifically related to the dynamic aspects of learning. The tasks are concerned with *process* in still another sense. The types of tasks chosen were also felt to simulate in the clinical setting the behaviors required for learning in the classroom setting. The sound-touch test, for example, may be considered as simulating, in a clinical setting not only the channels of input and the learning of "sets", but also the problem of distractibility in the classroom.

This report deals with the use of an early version of such a neurological instrument in a pilot project involving a sample of Head Start children in 1965. Performance on this instrument by these Head Start children will be compared with that of other pre-school children of high socio-economic background. Longitudinal studies involving this instrument have been carried out subsequently on these Head Start children as well as others of varying socio-economic background. Studies are also pending concerning the use of such an examination on school entry to predict later school achievement.

Materials and Methods
An early version of the neurological examination described above was given to a sample of the children enrolled in Head Start in the summer of 1965. Eighty-seven children, all of whom were Negro, were examined in several urban centers. The entire population of the center was examined, selected only on the basis of age, 4½-5½ (54-65 months). Another sample of pre-school children was similarly derived from nursery schools in a suburban area of high-socio-economic background. This latter sample consisted of 117 children, all of whom were white. Both samples had approximately equal numbers of boys and girls. All children in both groups were seen by the same examiner, the author. The fifteen minute examination was performed in a room free from distraction. The child was rewarded by a piece of candy which had been in plain view during the examination. Reinforcements were offered for maintenance of behavior whenever required. Generally, the cooperation and motivation of the children was excellent.

129

The standardized format included a test for right-left discrimination as well as a series of directions involving crossing the midline. This was followed by the motor examination. The "sound-touch" test described above followed the "face-hand" test in which the child was required to identify touch on the hand as well as the face when they were simultaneously applied.[14] The scoring on this task reflected the number of cues required.[15]

The scoring on right-left discrimination involves the consistency with which the child correctly attached the labels of "right" or "left." The series of directions given is as follows:

1. Show me your left hand.
2. Show me your right leg.
3. Show me your left eye.
4. Show me your right ear.
5. Show me your left leg.
6. Show me your right hand.

The child who was consistent in identifying the side correctly or consistent in identifying it incorrectly was scored similarly for this purpose. His failure to apply the specific labels correctly was not cause for penalty. The child who was right on 3 items and wrong on 3 items was felt to be performing in a random fashion and his "consistency" score was 0.

The task involving crossing the mid-line was a series of commands, again involving body parts. The series of directions given is as follows:

1. Cross your left leg over your right knee.
2. Touch your left elbow with your right hand.
3. Touch your right ear with your left hand.
4. Touch your left foot with your right hand.
5. Touch your right knee with your left hand.

The scoring, here again, was not based on accuracy in applying the labels "right" and "left" in terms of the appropriate sides of the body; it was rather in terms of the child's following the direction involving crossing. That is, he was required to distinguish between the different labels that were applied in the context of the command; ipsilateral performance was the only behavior penalized. Failure to follow the command at all rarely appeared. No penalty was given for failure to touch the appropriate body parts. The elbows, for example, were identified by the examiner, if nec-

130

essary. The subject was also scored as correct if he touched the left leg rather than left foot when the command specifically stated "foot." It may also be noted that the first two commands perforce required "crossing over" while the remaining commands permitted an opportunity to touch the ipsilateral body part. Failure was defined by a score of 2 or below. This would indicate that the child failed to demonstrate subsequent "crossing over" even after having received the cue provided by the first two items.

The motor test consists of 20 items, each of which is usually found in the motor examination portion of the clinical neurological examination. Specific items include rapid tapping movements of feet, hopping, tandem walking as well as touching finger to nose, and rapid movements of tongue and lips. Each item is scored on a 4 point scale. The directions were amplified by demonstration by the examiner in all instances. Specific criteria have been established for scoring each of the 20 items. In general, the score *0* is given if the child does not follow the demonstrated action at all. Score *1* is given if he follows the action in part. Score *2* is given if he follows the action in large part. Score *3* is given if he follows the action completely. The total possible score is therefore 60.

The scoring on both the "face-hand" and "sound-touch" tests is based upon the number of trials required to learn the "set." Score *0* on the face-hand test indicated failure to identify touch on the hand as well as face consistently even after a series of 12 trials and with the eyes open. Failure on the "sound-touch" test was determined by the child not identifying touch on the hand when distracting sound is applied to the ear even after having been given several cues.

The data are reported in terms of 6 month intervals (54-59 and 60-65 months). Sex is disregarded for this study since each sample (Head Start and Nursery School) consisted of approximately equal numbers of each sex. On all tests, with the exception of the motor scale, statistical comparisons were made between the two groups of children (Head Start versus Nursery School) at each of the two age ranges by means of the Chi Square test for independent samples. Thus, for a particular test, comparisons were made between the two samples in terms of number of children "passing" and "failing" that test. The criteria for failure on tasks has been reported above. For the motor scale, means and standard deviations were calculated for each sample at the two age levels and test analyses were made.

Results
The following tables describe the degree of significance to be attributed to the differences between these two populations on the various sub-tests on the basis of 6 month age intervals.

131

TABLE I

Percentage with Consistency Score 0

AGE	HEAD START	NURSERY SCHOOL	x^2
55-59	37%	15%	P .05
60-65	24%	13%	Non-sig.

Table I describes the incidence of random behavior on tasks involving differentiation between "right" and "left" as distinct labels. A consistency score of 0 was found in significantly more Head Start children in the younger age group. Although the absolute incidence of failure was higher in the older Head Start children as well, it did not fulfill the criteria for significance.

TABLE II

Percentage with "Crossing" Score 2 or Less

AGE	HEAD START	NURSERY SCHOOL	x^2
55-59	54%	12%	P .001
60-65	35%	4%	P .001

Table II describes the incidence of failure to cross over even after receiving the cues provided in the first two directions. The Head Start children did significantly less well than the nursery school sample of the high socio-economic group in both age samples.

TABLE III

Motor Scale

AGE	HEAD START	NURSERY SCHOOL	"T"
54-59	N = 39	N = 60	
	X = 36.77 + 9.66	X = 35.00 + 9.49	N.S.
60-65	N = 45	N = 56	
	X = 38.87 + 8.41	X = 40.95 + 6.22	N.S.

The mean score on the motor examination was not significantly different between the two samples.

132

TABLE IV

Percentage Failing "Face-Hand" Test

AGE	HEAD START	NURSERY SCHOOL	x^2
55-59	44%	32%	N.S.
60-65	38%	32%	N.S.

The incidence of failure on the "face-hand" test was not significantly different between these two populations although the absolute incidence of failure again was higher in the Head Start population.

TABLE V

Percentage Failing "Sound-Touch" Test

AGE	HEAD START	NURSERY SCHOOL	x^2	
55-59	51%	16%	P	.001
60-65	38%	14%	P	.01

The "sound-touch" test appeared to discriminate significantly between the two populations examined across both age samples.

Discussion

The diagnosis of neurological dysfunction in the young child has been traditionally based upon the presence of motor clumsiness. Our early hypothesis that Head Start children would have a higher incidence of motor disabilities was not substantiated in this particular sample. On this traditional measure of brain maturation, there were no significant differences between this group of Head Start children and a group of children of high socio-economic status. Unfortunately, no data were available on the birth weights and possible medical complications of pregnancy in both populations. It may be stated, however, that both populations derived from an urban area relatively well served by medical facilities. There is another possible bias which may make our Head Start sample less representative of the culturally disadvantaged; the process of enrollment in Head Start in 1965 may have biased the sample by selecting the child whose parent had voluntarily sought his admission. The centers whose population was studied were also sited in areas of less severe deprivation. It is suggested that further sampling of populations without these selection biases might substantiate previous studies.

Similarly, the "face-hand" test also failed to discriminate between these two populations of disparate background in the age groups studied. As determined by these

133

two developmental measures, the so-called physiologic substrate available for learning appeared to be comparable. Nevertheless, one might expect eventual school performance in these two populations to be quite different.

Some of the other measures included in the neurological battery may help to make more explicit the behavioral deficits of the lower income pre-school child. The Head Start child did significantly less well in following directions even when they involved common labels such as "right" and "left." When determined by the "consistency" score, this difference however was significant only at a 5% level and in the younger age group studied. The deficits became much more obvious when the child was required to differentiate these labels in the context of a more complex command. When asked to cross the midline, the Head Start child could not utilize the cues provided.

This deficit in handling verbal instructions may be further delineated by the performance on the "sound-touch" test. This task requires the child to "tune out" a distracting sound in order to identify touch simultaneously applied to the hand. On this non-verbal task, the Head Start child again did significantly less well. The sound-touch test requires that the child focus on the touch and "tune out" the irrelevant background sound. Failure to attend to the figure rather than sound in such a setting may be a peculiarly sensitive measure of difficulties in auditory processing basic to the later more obvious verbal deficits of these children. Performance in the classroom as well may be peculiarly sensitive to such difficulties in handling auditory input. Attention to the instruction being provided must overcome the other distracting stimuli.

The diagnosis of neurological dysfunction, although primarily based on motor disabilities, may also be correlated with various perceptual deficits and behavior described as "distractibility" and "hyperactivity."[4] It is suggested by the present data that these phenomena may be found to a greater degree in the Head Start children than in those of high socio-economic background. Differences in performance are a function, however, of both the physiologic substrate and differences in previous training. Failure to distinguish between auditory figure and sound is perhaps reflective of the lack of clarity, order and consistency of the auditory signals in the relatively crowded, noisy environment of the Head Start child. An alternative hypothesis is that the differential in physiologic substrate is more sensitively delineated by these auditory, verbal tasks than the relatively gross motor examination. Regardless of primary origin, the apparent deficit in handling auditory input helps outline the explicit requirements of the Head Start child when contrasted to the child of high socio-economic background.

One major aim of the Head Start program is to focus more clearly on the needs of children whose eventual school performance may be expected to be quite low. Moreover, the aim is to do so at a time when remedial efforts may be most useful. The neurological examination which has been developed has been concerned with defining the problems of these children in as operational a fashion as possible. It provides a short, scorable standardized measure which is concerned with a more dynamic analysis of brain function. It may help to define the extent of the problem in various populations as well as to identify the specific child requiring special programming. It has helped perhaps to outline the special needs of the Head Start child in the pilot project here reported.

This study was supported in part by OEO Research Contract 528

References

1. Pasamanick, B. and Lilienfeld, A. Association of maternal and fetal factors with development of mental deficiency: I. Abnormalities in the prenatal and paranatal periods. J.A.M.A., 159:159-160, 1955.

2. Pasamanick, B. and Lilienfeld, A. Socio-economic status and some precursors of neuropsychiatric disorders. AMER. J. ORTHOPSYCHIAT., 26:594-601, 1956.

3. Pasamanick, B. and Knoblock, H. Brain damage and reproductive causality. AMER. J. ORTHO-PSYCHIAT., 30:298-305, 1960.

4. Kawi, A., and Pasamanick, B. Prenatal and Paranatal factors in the development of childhood reading disorders. MONGR. SOC. RES. CHILD DEVELOP., 24:2-80, 1959.

5. Minimal Brain Dysfunction in Children: Terminology and Identification NINDB MONOGRAPH 3. U. S. Dept. of Health, Education and Welfare, 1966.

6. Da Costa, M. (Translated by E. J. Fosa), The Oseretsky tests; method, value and results, (Portuguese adaptation), TRAIN. SCH. BULL., 43:1-13, 27-38, 50-58, 62-74, 1946.

7. Doll, E. A. THE OSERETSKY TESTS OF MOTOR PROFICIENCY, Minneapolis, Educational Publishers, 1946.

8. Lassner, R. Anotated bibliography on the Oseretsky tests of motor proficiency, J. CONSULT. PSYCHOL., 12:37-47, 1948.

9. Sloan, W. The Lincoln-Oseretsky tests of motor proficiency, GENETIC PSYCHOL. MONOGR., 51:183-252, 1955.

10. Prechtl, H.F.R. and Stemmer, L. J. The choreiform syndrome i. .iildren, DEVELOP. MED. CHILD NEUROL., 4:119, 1962.

11. Fog, E. and Fog M. CEREBRAL INHIBITION EXAMINED BY ASSOCIATED MOVEMENTS IN MINIMAL BRAIN DYSFUNCTION, R. MacKeith and MC.O. Bax (eds.) Little Club Clinics (National Spastic Society) 10 pp. 52-57, 1963.

12. Benton, A. L. RIGHT-LEFT DISCRIMINATION AND FINGER LOCALIZATION. Hoeber, New York, pp. 138-143, 1959.

13. Ozer, M. N. The use of operant conditioning in the evaluation of children with learning problems. CLIN. PROC. CHILD. HOSP. (Washington, D. C.), 22:235-244, 1966.

14. Fink, M. and Bender, M. B. Perception of Simultaneous tactile stimuli in normal children, NEUROLOGY, 3:27-34, 1953.

15. Ozer, M. N. The face-hand test in children: directions and scoring, CLIN. PROC. CHILD. HOSP., (Washington, D. C.), 1967 (in press).

136

EVALUATION OF PSYCHIATRIC REPORTS OF HEAD START PROGRAMS

Albert S. Hotkins, M. D.,
Chief Psychiatrist, Bureau of Child Guidance,
Board of Education, New York, New York

Leonard Hollander, M.D.,
Director of Psychiatric Services,
Jewish Child Care Association of New York,
New York, New York

Barbara Munk, M.D.,
Medical Director, East Brooklyn Mental Health Clinic, Brooklyn;
Director, Mental Health Services, Summer Program
1966 Project Head Start, New York, New York

ALBERT S. HOTKINS, M. D.   BARBARA MUNK, M. D.

LEONARD HOLLANDER, M. D.

INTRODUCTION

This paper presents highlights of material gathered from 51 child psychiatrists who participated in the mental health consultation program organized for 1966 Summer Program of Project Head Start in New York City. This mental health consultation program was in many ways so unique that the extensively gathered field-work information lends itself to discussion of paramount organizational needs, social-psychiatric issues and problems of mental health services vis-a-vis the recipients of such services.

During the Summer of 1965, some child psychiatrists participated in a program of consultation to the Head Start Operation. On last minute notice the New York Council on Child Psychiatry, then an organization of some 250 psychiatrists of Greater New York interested in Child Psychiatry, called on its members to be consultants to privately community sponsored programs of Operation Head Start. Those available were used very little but felt strongly that a more formal and organized Mental Health Service for the 3 to 6 year old pre-kindergarten children should be formulated. Hence in the Spring of 1966, a proposal for a mental health consultation program was submitted to the New York office of OEO Head Start through cooperative efforts and joint participation of the New York Council on Child Psychiatry, and the Special Assistant to the Executive Director of the Community Mental Health Board of New York City. The Office of Economic Opportunity made a special grant available to the New York Office of Head Start for this proposal for service to the privately sponsored programs for the Summer of 1966. The psychiatric services of the Bureau of Child Guidance of the Board of Education then joined in the cooperative project. This report is offered as a first experience for critical discussion and as a basis for future operative suggestions.

PURPOSES OF THE PROJECT

The consultation program was initiated based on strong conviction that the children and their families Project Head Start tries to reach are in need of active and comprehensive mental health care and that the child psychiatrist carries an important responsibility in this complex effort. Clinical findings discovered in the conventional working milieu of a child psychiatrist such as child psychiatric clinics, school and day care settings, juvenile court, mental hospitals and private practice lead to the assumption that the child population of Head Start would present similar problems which were likely to remain unidentified and unresolved, if not actively approached with preventive mental health concepts in mind. This program could be also seen as a pilot project to explore and help clarify the role of the child psychiatrist as a consultant in the educational setting and to work out methods of preventative intervention in communities which do not know how to refer themselves as contrasted to the conventional medical models.

The paucity of valid information of the behavioral elements, early child development, adaptation to group learning, family milieu and child rearing of the so called "deprived" or "underprivileged" or "ghetto" child could be expanded through field work information gathered by one of the specialists working with children, the child psychiatrist. To collect these data a guideline (Appendix No. II) for reporting observations was given to the participating child psychiatrists. The analysis of these findings is herein presented and serves as the basis for the further discussion.

METHODS

Late in June 1966, it became known that funding was approved. Three separate but parallel programs were established with funds derived from OEO. (1) The program set up by the Board of Education of New York City, through its Bureau of Early Childhood Education to serve 28,500 children. (2) 48 private community sponsored groups with individual programs to render service to some 2,700 children (3) Roman Catholic parochial schools for some 3,800 children. Due to the exigencies of administrative pressures and lack of time in setting up these programs it was not possible to include group 3 in this study.

140

ADMINISTRATION AND ALLOTMENT OF THE CHILD
PSYCHIATRIC CONSULTATION SERVICES

Board of Education Programs - The child psychiatric consultation service for the Head Start Program sponsored by the Board of Education of New York City, through its Early Childhood section, was organized by the psychiatric department of the Bureau of Child Guidance utilizing its child psychiatrists who usually worked in an educational setting, and who were available.

Two hundred and sixty-two Head Start Centers were localized in public schools of areas considered as "poverty pockets" of the city. Centers were grouped into geographic clusters of 5 or 6 schools, and each of these clusters was supervised by an educational supervisor. A center was composed of 4 classes, morning and afternoon sessions which in turn had its head teacher, teachers, teacher aides and family assistants, family workers and volunteers from the community. Fifteen children were assigned to a class determining the number of 120 children accepted in each center. The age range of the children was between 4-6 years and the ethnic composition of the classes was varied in percentage of Negro, Puerto Rican, White and Chinese children dependent on the geographic areas.

Sixteen psychiatrists participated for varying lengths of time from 4 to 8 weeks, giving from 6 to 24 hours per week in sessions of 3 hours each. Most psychiatrists spent between 4 and 5 weeks in the program giving about 5 sessions per week. The total number of 1,319 hours were spent by these psychiatrists in the 8 weeks, and each psychiatrist was assigned to 2 clusters covering a total of 1,400 children.

Privately Sponsored Programs - 48 independent organizations sponsored their private programs. These groups were composed of a variety of different community resources such as local community organizations, independent community agencies, local church groups of Baptist, Methodist, Pentecostal and Catholic denomination and some Yeshiva schools.

The settings of the programs was very diverse and sites were utilized such as churches, synagogues, settlement houses, recreational centers and public schools. These varied as widely as did the general organization of the individual (field) milieu. In some cases the location of the programs was practically on the same street as that of the public school program.

The basic structure of staff as requested by Head Start however was the same as that of Board of Education centers. A program director worked with a head teacher, teachers, teacher's aides, family assistants, family workers and volunteers.

141

Most of the centers were funded for provision of 60 children in their center, some for only 30 and a few for 120 children. The age range of the children was the same as elsewhere, between 4-6 years.

The ethnic composition of the children in most centers tended to be more homogenous depending on the particular nature of the individual sponsor. While there were many mixed groups, there were quite a few centers with only Negro, Puerto Rican, Orthodox Jewish or Chinese children. Many of the Hispanic, Jewish and Chinese children did not speak English well.

The child psychiatric consultation program for the independent sponsors was administered by the Director of Mental Health services for the Summer Program assigned to the central office of Project Head Start. In cooperation with the assigned fieldworkers of Head Start, the introduction of the psychiatric consultant into the programs was expedited.

Thirty-seven Child Psychiatrists were utilized in this area, and the individual psychiatrists were in attendance for 4 hours per week for one to two months. Twenty programs had 4 hours per week for 8 weeks; 12 had 4 hours per week for 4 weeks; 6 programs had only one 4 hour visit; 4 had no service. Six programs had their own psychiatric consultation and were not provided with resources from the pool. Two psychiatrists also worked with the Board of Education.

Projected Functional Aims of the Consultation Program were outlined as follows: Ideally the child psychiatrist should be able to provide perspectives on the problems of social psychiatry as well as plan for finding the individual child who needs consultation or referral. To achieve these aims he has to consider the specific program in terms of such problems as administration and community participation. If he can anticipate some of these problems, he must then find appropriate ways of approaching the persons with whom he has to work in order to put a preventative mental health program into action.

Variables for major consideration were the obvious diversity in all areas involved; the nature and personality of administration, sponsors, programs and communities and the specific child psychiatric consultant himself. Therefore no attempt was made to set up a preconceived model for mental health consultation; indoctrination and formulae of operation were kept at a minimum.

The consultants were all members of the New York Council on Child Psychiatry and had formal training in the speciality of child psychiatry. Their practical experience in psychiatric consultation for child care institutions and in consultation for the preschool child varied considerably. Not many consultants had been exposed to community mental health practice in under-privileged communities.

142

For the project directed by the Bureau of Child Guidance, indoctrination consisted of 2 three hour sessions; one was given by the director of Early Childhood Education to orient the psychiatrists to the realities of the program, its aims for the children and some concepts of the curriculum. The other session was a clinical orientation lecture of an expert in Early Childhood Development.

Shortage of time did not allow such formal lectures for the privately sponsored project. However, in two preliminary meetings some procedures and approaches for consultation were discussed in relation to the structure of specific private agencies and their programs.

Each consultant was advised that he enter his assigned center as a "visiting doctor" operating on his own and not in the traditional role as a member of the orthopsychiatric team.

Emphasis was given to classroom observation as the principal mode of data gathering. Rather than attempting correction of individual pathology, the focus was understanding of normal behavior and support of healthy ego components. The consultant was encouraged to use all creative approaches appropriate to the particular program to engage the community in mental health education through discussion groups with staff and community.

Finally, procedures of individual psychiatric evaluation and referral, reports and record keeping were discussed. (Appendix No. I, II and III).

The Nature of the Centers and the Introduction of the Child Psychiatric Consultation Service.
The centers under the auspices of the Board of Education were informed of psychiatric assignments by a memorandum (Appendix IV) sent to each supervisor of a cluster and their head teachers. It was outlined to them that the psychiatrist would not be used in the traditional role of the head of the clinical team, which is the usual procedure in the Bureau of Child Guidance. The cluster supervisors were advised that the function should be worked out between themselves and the psychiatrist along lines evolving from mutual experience. It was suggested that the psychiatrist spend as much time as possible observing the children, and to be utilized as a consultant rather than doing individual psychiatric examinations. However in anticipation of such requests, a brief consultation form (Appendix III) was drawn up which the psychiatrist was asked to complete, noting his findings and recommendations after an individual psychiatric evaluation.

The privately sponsored centers were notified of the assignment of a child psychiatric consultant to their program by a memorandum from the Director of Mental Health outlining utilization of the consultant in the areas mentioned above.

It was the policy of central administration that all contact with the program directors was to be effected solely through field workers who were assigned to a number of centers, in order to prevent confusion from "too many consultants". This proved to be a serious handicap since the Director of Mental Health Service, although the responsible and capable professional, was unable to clarify many questions through direct contact with the program directors. Attempt was made to meet this situation by inservice conference with the field workers to discuss the psychiatrist's visits. This conference revealed a range of attitude from full acceptance, although with misconceptions, to exteme resistance and negativism to psychiatric consultation. Similar attitudes were later noted in the visits to the centers. The pertinent memoranda were usually unnoticed in the flood of written material sent to these centers.

At the conclusion of the Summer 1966, the participating psychiatrists of both programs were asked to submit their reports along the lines of the prepared outline (Appendix II).

FINDINGS

Although these programs as outlined above were of different nature, there were similarities in findings which could be drawn from the submitted reports. These can be categorized in terms of the following: (1) Relation with the educational staff (2) Role as a physician (3) Liaison with other disciplines (4) Working with paraprofessionals and (5) Contact with parents and the community.

Relation to Education Staff - The main role that the psychiatrist played as consultant was in relationship to the teaching and administrative educational staff. In view of the limited time available for preparation of all personnel, it was to be expected that in some instances the administrators of the programs were quite surprised to see a psychiatrist appear on the scene. They were advised that the consultative function should be worked out between themselves and the psychiatrist along lines evolving from mutual experience and the specific needs of their areas. It was anticipated that in spite of specific recommendations to the contrary, the educational personnel would request that individual cases be seen. In one instance, when it became known that there would be psychiatric participation in the Head Start Program, and prior to individual assignments, request was received to examine a child to see whether or not he was retarded and should be included in the program. By and large this was the role which satisfied the educators most, namely having the psychiatrist take care of individual obstructive and difficult problem children. The initial contacts between the directors or supervisors of the programs and the psychiatrist generally had a guarded tone in an atmosphere which was usually that of vague expectation and poor definition.

144

The fact that no groundwork had been laid for the psychiatric consultant's role was partly responsible for the mixed feelings about his function. Some felt he had been sent to prepare a critique of the staff or to tell the teachers how to handle the children. Even experienced directors and staff members often felt that the psychiatrist's presence in an educational setting would provoke fear and anxiety in parents, who might feel that the psychiatrist was "looking for illness" or "labelling the child with a diagnosis". The psychologist's presence was more easily accepted as useful in assisting the education of the healthy child. This might reflect a public attitude of confusion regarding the variety of specialists in mental health work, indicating need of further clarification and education. The utilization of psychiatric talent by the Head Start staff was the product of the concept that the psychiatrist himself had of his function and the image held by the Head Start staff. His own background and the variety of circumstances under which he worked evoked various responses and helped determine his role.

The closest contacts were with the teachers since psychiatrists spent as much time as they could in the classroom, observing the children and program activities. Here the psychiatrist generally felt acutely limited since his knowledge of education methodology, and curriculum was rather sketchy. However, it was possible in most circumstances to arrive at some mutual understanding, in which the teacher gained confidence from the consultation and discussion, which clarified her understanding of the child's behavior, and any problems that the child might present. It was also quite helpful to the teacher to know that they had some support when they were faced with severe problems.

The teachers had varied backgrounds of experience. In the private Head Start Programs many were kindergarten teachers but received little supervisory help. In the Board of Education program there were many supervisors and teachers who were offered these positions and frequently were without any specific training in the pre-kindergarten areas. Some of these teachers were excellent, well trained and "intuitive"; these had little difficulty with children. Those who had the least training were quite anxious and had much more difficulty, and resented mental health "interference". They frequently felt they were the ones being observed. Most teachers who had to cope with behavior problems, poor attention span, lack of interest and disturbed object relationships had little knowledge of these problems in their prior experience. They found that it was helpful that psychiatrists could interpret to them the wide range of maturation and developmental patterns which the children presented.

Psychiatric consultants reported that initial fears were often replaced by more positive attitudes. The psychiatrist often found himself in the role of a good parent and kindly listener who was asked to confirm positions or arbitrate differences. This

145

attitude was often expressed in the sentence, "It's good to have a doctor around." Many teachers saw their aim primarily as one enhancing socialization, with educational goals of the improvement of language learning, handling of the tools of learning and "the broadening of general horizons".

Much time was spent by the psychiatrist in working with teachers who felt threatened by not being able to perform their job adequately, and who were experiencing difficulty relating to assistant teachers, fellow teachers, aides and parents present in the classroom. Marked ethnic and personal differences existed in the teachers with regard to standards for conformity, discipline and behavioral performance. Some tried to establish highly controlled situations regardless of the children's age level. Others were anxious and impatient with the children's slow progress. Some of the teachers were not able to structure the classroom activities on the pre-kindergarten level and frequently it was not possible to maintain order. This was especially true when there was a disruptive element or children of overly aggressive, anxiety and impulse ridden behavior. Most teachers were very dedicated and tried hard, were daily frustrated by the problems that beset them, included in which was the bilingual child who in many situations was hard to teach. In this regard the absence of the Spanish speaking teacher was a keenly felt deficiency.

Another area in which the psychiatrist functioned very well was in helping the teacher understand some of the group dynamics operative within the structure of the classroom. They were able to demonstrate to the teacher how many children were giving them clues of increasing anxiety. They were also able to be helped to recognize how they could utilize group procedure in order to divert some of the aggressive behavior into acceptable channels; teachers were made aware of the need to be alert to some of the stimuli from the group provoking the disruptive child. Teachers also helped to recognize that in many situations children were not able to handle the very well defined and structured material presented to them. In some instances when ordinary broken down materials with which these children were familiar was utilized, the youngsters did well.

Some of the methods used to reach the goal of dissemination of mental health principles included general teacher discussions whenever possible. In some instances when the administrator of the program was able to manage, group discussions were held with the teachers usually around one child as the focus for general discussion. At these times conferences would have content in which the principles of growth, development and maturation were emphasized, problems of symptomatic disturbances were discussed, and some attempt made to help teachers recognize their own reactions. In many situations individual conferences with the supervisor and teachers after a classroom observation were of great value. Attempt was made to discern and to help the teacher recognize some of the problems of temporary nature as well as those indicating more serious pathology. They had a tendency to overlook

146

the protean manifestations of anxiety, most notably that of separation anxiety. Signs of regressed behavior were regarded as reactions to the here and now of the classroom; the etiologic factors in the child and his family were usually not considered.

Faced with an eight week program, many psychiatrists felt that it was more important to stimulate the understanding of normal behavior than to focus on the disturbed child. They adopted the public health view of preventative measures in mental hygiene which emphasizes strengthening of adaptation by supporting healthy ego components and helping to circumvent rather than to correct individual pathology. This prophylactic orientation was reinforced by the feeling of many that the facilities for individual psychiatric consultation would never be adequate for such care. To deal with the problems in mental health and child development in terms of social and community psychiatry, directors and other staff members cooperated with the psychiatric consultant in organizing staff discussion groups. In organizing these groups at the centers, it became quite evident that there was overlapping function with the social worker and psychologist.

Some psychiatrists, by preference and circumstance, confined themselves largely to individual consultation with teachers and parents, a circumstance which emphasized their role as physician. This role was generally accepted without provoking anxiety or resistance.

Role of Psychiatrist as Clinicians and Their Observations - In many nurseries the administrative heads expressed the fact that it was "good to have a doctor around" Through medical observation, there were some cases of malnutrition, poor dentition and minor medical difficulties which were referred for proper attention, as were such questions as hearing difficulties and speech problems. There were some few cases of cerebral dysrhythmias discovered, as well as cases of possible tuberculosis. In many situations consultants who had not worked with poor children before found themselves confronted with a dilemma in which they were expected to find the stereotyped characteristics of the deprived, underprivileged or ghetto child from a poverty culture. They were however surprised to find the children generally clean, lively, healthy and alert. They were neat and well cared for on the whole, although there were some children who were very poorly dressed with multiple bruises who always appeared sleepy or appeared malnourished. These seemingly neglected children attended irregularly, and many of them dropped out of the program, but they were definitely in the minority. This gave rise to a serious question in many of the observers minds as to whether or not the program was actually reaching those children for whom the program was intended.

On the whole there were many pure psychiatric problems referred both from the

147

teachers and from the other professionals working in the program. As anticipated, a large number of individual evaluations were made, ranging from brief observation and screening to more detailed workups. A wide range of pathology was reported with a preponderance of behavior disorder, frequently considered reactive to family pathology and deprivation experiences. Anxiety reactions comprised the second most common category. Psychotic reactions came next in frequency and a similar number of organic disturbances. These were empirical proportions of the reported difficulties, and do not necessarily reflect the proportion of pathology in the children due to factors inherent in the methods of gathering the data.

Generally it was felt that about 5% of the child population was found to be disturbed enough to warrant psychiatric attention. This was more true in the psychiatrist's observation than of the teachers who were often willing to make more allowances for future growth and maturation. In most situations the psychiatrist spent a good deal of time discussing the problems of early identification of difficulties. There were many difficulties in discerning this because many speech problems were felt to be "baby talk", and were indulged by the personnel. Problems of children dressing in clothes of the opposite sex, boys participating in activities considered more applicable to girls, withdrawn behavior as well as excessive aggressive behavior were all noted, and teachers were helped to differentiate between normality and that which might lead to difficulty at a later time.

Most of the disturbed behavior was seen as clearly a result of traumatic family and environmental factors. Mental illness of one or the other parent had often resulted in the child's being shifted around among relatives and neighbors. Often other siblings had a history of emotional disturbance. The more broken the family was, the more frequently it had moved, the larger the number of siblings, the more any particular child in it was likely to be disturbed. The consultants felt that about 75% of the children functioned within normal psychic and developmental limits. Two or three in twenty showed mild symptoms of maladaptation. In most cases consultation with the teacher, case worker or parent might have prevented further difficulty and obviated later referral to a clinical facility.

As previously mentioned, there was the feeling that about one child in 20 was sufficiently disturbed as to require immediate clinical attention. Of the children in this group, half had functional disturbances rooted in a family pathology; about one quarter had signs of mental deficiency or brain damage and a further one quarter showed signs of autism or psychosis of unknown origin.

One other area which was quite gratifying to all concerned was that of intervention in a crisis which occurred while some psychiatrists were observing the class or when present at a school. In a few instances phobic situations could be relieved when the psychiatrist, applying his theoretical knowledge of children's fantasies alleviated the child's anxieties in such conditions as separation anxiety or temporary regressions due to some overwhelming situational reaction of which the personnel was aware.

It was observed that after the first 2 or 3 weeks most of the children participated very readily and smoothly. Programs varied and it was difficult to generalize, but the children were observed to be much more involved with each other when they were playing with familiar games, and playing with the unformed materials such as water, clay and paint. There were minimal relationships between children. Most of the usual and normal activity of nurseries were observed. It was interesting however that most psychiatrists observed that the communication between children and teachers was mostly on the nonverbal level with gesture and eye contact, especially when there was language difficulty. This corroborates the observations of many observers in the pre-kindergarten programs.

Both boys and girls enjoyed playing with the doll house and kitchen sets and both enjoyed dressing up in old adult clothes. They did jigsaw puzzles with zest and enjoyed finishing them. All loved jumping and dancing and the boys liked to show off their motor coordination and daring by doing climbing stunts in the playground. Finer motor coordination in the handling of tools, pencils and spoons was, so consultants thought, less developed than among more well-to-do children. Left handedness was not uncommon.

The children sought attention from the adults in the program, liked to involve themselves in games led by the adults and enjoyed the approval of the adults more than success in competition. Many of the children enjoyed close physical contact, wrestling with one another. The boys especially enjoyed clinging to or wrestling with men, if they were present.

It did seem that the children were happiest in a structured program where clues for activities were given by adults. Under these circumstances there was no overt aggressive or destructive behavior.

The children showed a high incidence of immature speech, including lisping, blurred pronunciation and often more severe speech disturbances.

Most of the programs had ample time for free play during which there was much running around and noise making. Small groups formed around toys and doll house. The boys were more attracted to cars and blocks. They often teased and wrestled one another. Leadership, when it showed itself, led to the formation of groups, rather than to fighting. Girls' play was more interpersonal and verbal than that of the boys.

149

Not a few of the three year olds seemed to be frightened and overwhelmed, both by the activities of their peers and by contact with the older groups.

The differences in children's motor and expressive behavior as well as in their object relations seemed to be related to their ethnic background. The homogeneous centers, with all Negro, Jewish or Chinese children, revealed some interesting patterns. Some groups had lived in New York for a long time, but had maintained their cultural differences, e.g. the Hassidic and Chinese children. Some differences in object relations were noted. Both Negro and Orthodox Jewish children were attention seeking and more oriented toward the supervising adult than toward their peers. However, the Negro children were more easy going and uninhibited, more clinging, more in search of physical contact. Gestures and eye contact were more important elements of communication for the Negro children and aggressive behavior seemed more culturally approved. The Negro boys enjoyed doing daring athletic feats to gain approval and were surprised at the teacher's concern and protectiveness. The Jewish children were more restricted in their physical activity and turned to adults for suggestions in play and for protection against aggressive peers.

Puerto Rican and Chinese children seemed more interested in peer relations and independent play, and were cautiously aloof to adults.

The entire Chinese group showed highly conforming behavior, long attention span and greater involvement in toys and creative materials. Chinese teachers said that education and the privilege of attending school were stressed in Chinese families, especially among recent immigrants.

Puerto Rican children were noted to be shy and fussy about accepting food.

Liaison with Other Disciplines - In general, the relationship with other discipline team members was quite varied. In many situations when other team members were available, things went smoothly and much more along usual orthopsychiatric lines. However, these disciplines had designated roles, but there was considerable overlap. The psychologist spent a good deal of time working with teachers and individual children but the social worker spent a good deal of time working with the family aides and community workers. It was only occasionally that they would present a problem for psychiatric consultation because the orientation was not the clinical but that the community had to be served.

In many situations there were many interpersonal difficulties with the numerous people that were present in the classroom. Many of the psychiatrists felt that there were entirely too many adults in these programs with the teachers, head teachers, family aides and assistant teachers involved. In view of administrative problems in the Board of Education, and the fact that there had not been adequate time for planning for social workers and psychologists, it was not possible to formulate the typical team approach. In privately sponsored centers, each center had to hire its own psychologist and social worker which they did usually on a part time basis. These disciplines were therefore mostly forced to work independently of each other and it was only in rare circumstances that a request was made for a total team approach. Problems of time made coordination between the other professionals and the psychiatrist difficult. One third of the psychiatric consultants had no contact with either of the other "team" members and had to confine their contacts mainly to director, teachers or family workers.

Few psychologists did testing, although neither director, teacher nor psychiatrist was clear as to how the test results might be used. Most psychologists did no testing, but confined themselves to program consultation, interviewing and home visiting. Social workers sometimes found themselves dealing with the child and his family problems, and gathering family information. The workers spent most of their time in offering their experience and guidance to the community personnel.

Working with Paraprofessionals - The family worker acted as a bridge between the child psychiatric consultant and the community. They were very cooperative, providing family histories on children seen for psychiatric evaluation and often proved helpful in disposition and in discussing family problems with the parents who seemed more readily accepting of their statements. Discussion groups and supportive consultation amplified this area of cooperation.

In rare cases the presence of paraprofessionals in the program (assistant teachers, family aides, teacher aides), contributed to group tensions and conflicts especially where the family worker was a leader in community affairs. In one situation, the family assistant who was an extremely verbal and militant woman, caused considerable tensions and almost destroyed the entire program because of her need to see herself as the authority and to be the person in charge of the program, controlling the teachers and dictating curriculum of which she knew very little. However, this was exceptional, and informal discussions between the psychiatric consultants and family workers proved mutually beneficial.

Contact Between Parents and the Community - On the whole there was not enough contact between the psychiatrist, the parents of the children and the community functions in which the psychiatrist potentially could have participated.

Communication with the parents was established in a number of different ways. In

151

some centers, where there was close cooperation between the director and staff psychiatrist, discussion groups on mental health and child development were set up. In the public school program this was mainly left to the psychologist and in some cases the social worker. When a child was seen for individual psychiatric evaluation, an interview with the parent was usually arranged. However, most of the contacts were through informal visits while the day's program was in progress. In the privately sponsored programs, partly due to the lack of space for individual interviews or group discussions during the day, and difficulty in organizing meetings in the evening when space would have been available these contacts were minimal. In the public school situation, where a room was set up for family visits, it was possible to "insinuate" psychiatric discussion and thinking in an unofficial manner, by joining the women in a "coffee klatch" type of discussion. This was most feasible when the psychiatrist happened to be a female. In these settings the parents did not prove suspicious or anxious about psychiatric consultation. However, in formal contacts such as groups specifically scheduled for mental health discussions, and for individual interviews, parents showed initial suspicion and anxiety about the psychiatrist's role. Once the initial anxiety was relieved, parents of all ethnic backgrounds were grateful for the opportunity to discuss the problems, especially crises of the moment. They were least interested in the *why* of behavior than how to change it in disobedient, quarrelsome and undisciplined children. Problems of speech and sleep disturbance were aired and a few inquiries were anxiously made about boys who liked to dress in girl's clothes and play with dolls. Some psychiatrists felt that once the initial anxiety was over parents often felt freer about talking to the psychiatrist than to members of the staff who had the same cultural background as themselves, since they feared criticism from their fellows. Frequently they were more interested in discussion of problems they were having with their older siblings rather than with the child who was attending the program.

The psychiatrist usually played very little role in the community planning, but was able to support some family sides and function in unusual situations. They were also quite useful in helping administrators resolve some of the interpersonal problems that existed between community people, parents, and teachers. A unique experience was that of one of the psychiatrists in the public school situation who was assigned to an area in which there was open racial strife and rioting. Fear in the school was running very high, the personnel were on guard and quite divided along racial lines. A previously harmonious situation became quite tense and upset. A parent workshop was turned into a militant political meeting when racial leaders appeared and took over. The psychiatrist felt it was her duty to see what was happening with the children and found that surprisingly they seemed to have no direct response to the community tension. However, she did observe that they were responding to the anxiety of the teachers who were equally divided and in conflict with each other. Working with the group to help the teachers recognize some of their undercurrent feelings was extremely valuable in relieving the tension in one of the schools.

152

On the whole the psychiatrist was minimally utilized in community education, community planning and was usually only the invited guest for one or two lectures as part of the general education forum which was set up by the parents. The role of community planning seems to have involved mostly the community organizers, community aides as supervised by the social worker.

Conclusions and Recommendations - The child psychiatrist attached to a prekindergarten program plays many roles. He is a consultant, teacher and clinician; he is concerned with prevention and treatment. He belongs on the one hand to a team of medical specialists in pediatrics and its sub-specialties, and on the other hand he serves on the orthopsychiatric team which includes social workers and psychologists.

Within the brief summer program of Head Start 1966, the consultants in child psychiatry concentrated on those areas where they felt they could make the greatest contribution. In an ideal situation they would be involved in all of the activities previously mentioned.

Most consultants empirically suggested that about one out of every 20 children showed behavioral and developmental disturbance requiring psychiatric and neurologic evaluation.

All the psychiatrists were quite unanimous in their praise for the program, feeling that this was and could be an invaluable adjunct to the growth and development of many children. Many expressed considerable doubt as to whether those children for whom the program was primarily designed were reached.

Since one of the important roles of the child psychiatric consultant in the Head Start Program should be to find ways of improving the child's state in school and community, he should be able to present the child's strong points and weaknesses in a form useful to the educational institution, with explicit recommendation for educational plans or specialized intervention. For the Summer Program in 1966, provision for psychiatric consultation had to be quickly improvised and procedures remained loose. Therefore, the following areas of consideration are offered for discussion and study in order to clarify the process of child psychiatric consultation and treatment implementation.

Coordination of the Mental Health Team's Activities
The need for Mental Health teamwork must be stressed again. There is need for much more cooperation between the social worker, psychologist and the psychiatrist. Further definition needs to be made of the role of each of the disciplines.

153

Follow-up and implementation of mental health recommendations are imperative if long term planning is to be done and results are to be evaluated. No single discipline can carry the burden of coordination or follow up. Procedures should be set up for providing time for regular contact to discuss planning and follow-up.

To achieve these ends, some long term, central planning and coordination should be instituted. The individual or the group charged with this would coordinate responsibilities, clarify roles and explore the possibilities for finding and training personnel; they would assist each center in obtaining appropriate Mental Health consultation, both within the program and from neighborhood facilities. In-service training for Mental Health consultation appears to be necessary for all personnel involved with the children.

Physical, Neurological, and Psychiatric efforts should be coordinated through the psychiatrist, pediatrician and nurse. Recognition of differences in approaches and open discussion of problems would help insure the close working together of those specialists for maximum help to the child.

Methods of Psychiatric Participation - Formal individual psychiatric examination was at the start a function most acceptable to the directors and head teachers. Legal obstacles such as permission for psychiatric examinations should be eliminated by obtaining this permission through inclusion in routine discussion at entry into program. This would immediately set the tone for mental health participation in the general health care of the child. After establishing himself in this way, the consultant would be able to participate more extensively in the total program, such as staff consultation, discussion groups with teachers and parents, etc. Requests for individual evaluation indicated a need for broad involvement of a consultant in Head Start in services aimed not only at the child, but at the child's family and at the community at large. Broad clinical assessment was best achieved by close consultative relationship with the teacher, observation of the children in the classroom, and understanding of the family and social forces operative in the situation. Forms of rapid and comparative evaluation of behavior need to be developed to specifically help early identification of behavioral deviation.

Diagnosis Must be Formulated in a Way Useful for the Program and Parents
Evaluating and explaining the behavior pattern of three to six year olds in a way comprehensible to educators proved a challenging and sometimes baffling task. Putting aside the problem of precise classification, the psychiatrists attempted to see and to show the relevance of patterns of behavior which require special attention.

Such patterns as withdrawal, clinging, excess crying, excess or erratic activity, bizarre or autistic behavior, depression, panic, speech and motor defects were noted.

154

Rapid changes in many of these patterns suggested that spot diagnoses required further verification to distinguish transient from persistent behavior.

Further study is needed of the meaning and usefulness of such terms as *shy, withdrawn, uncommunicative* and *slow* to more sharply define the differential approach to severe reactive behavior, maturational and developmental retardation, the brain-injured syndrome, motor and sensory defects, and autistic behavior. The high incidence of speech disturbances of various patterns and degrees of severity is a diagnostic challenge needing more explicit definition, utilizing the full clinical team approach of psychologist, child neurologist, speech specialist and child psychiatrist as vital to help clarify accurate diagnosis.

Management of Confidential Medical Records in an Education Setting

Guidelines as to the preparation and handling of clinical records should be established.

Psychiatrists did not submit written reports of their findings of individual evaluations in the private sponsored programs. In the Board of Education Program, a brief report (Appendix III) was used for individual contact. These evaluations were submitted only to clinical facilities on request, with parental consent. However, oral recommendations and comments were made to the involved staff members. Early transmission of relevant information to the public school which the child would attend could facilitate placement in remedial or special classes, help maintain those gains made during the Head Start Program and secure advancement directly into the first grade for the gifted.

Conferences and Consultations with the Educational Staff - There is a need for further study for more effective methods for explicitly formulating psychiatric impressions for such procedures and training including increased use of staff culturally consonant with the population, especially with the bilingual child.

Implementation of psychiatric recommendations should be secured by charging one individual with this responsibility.

Recruitment and Preventative Intervention - It is felt that more active participation in the recruitment of children for the program would enable psychiatrists to make early recommendations for the care of the disturbed child and help set the tone for better utilization of the Head Start Program. Some ways must be found for evaluating and then assisting isolated and deteriorated families who so far have been beyond the reach of the program. Through liaison with other clinical facilities this program could be used for the children who need this as a therapeutic milieu,

155

through sibling referral. This gives the psychiatrist the opportunity to practice preventative medicine and approach the family although the initial contact is with the young child under consideration. The psychiatrist often proved useful for "crisis consultation and intervention".

Participation in the Training of Personnel Involved in the Program - The psychiatrist was not used in any of the orientation programs for the personnel working directly with children except for one or two lectures. It is felt he could play a much more important role here.

Use of Older Siblings in the Classroom - Especially when ethnic differences were marked, the presence of adolescent girls and boys, and older siblings as classroom aides proved a very great help. These older children are a community resource whose further use should be considered and planned in detail. The adolescents enjoyed participating and functioned to bring the entire family into the Head Start Program. The additional benefit of the exposure of the extended family situation under emotionally controlled and creative supervision in the classroom again offered marked preventative features.

A great need for a male figure as an important balance in the interaction of the classrooms was also emphasized.

The programs at the various centers seemed to go best when the director was a community leader familiar with the neighborhood. His leadership requires a back-up program for lay persons, teachers, co-directors, family workers, teacher-aides, and others. For these there should be some comprehensive in-service program which would provide audio-visual materials and discussion groups.

Teacher discussion groups could clarify goals and evaluate teaching methods for the children in the program. Subjects to be discussed should include the reciprocal relationships of teacher, parent and child, as well as the mental health, learning and development of the child.

The direct contact with the school personnel and the community, the complexity of the social and psychological problems, suggested new areas for social psychiatry. Among the recommendations for further investigation were the following:

(1) Further study of the growth of learning and behavior of pre-kindergarten children, especially in the area of translating the knowledge of psychodynamic behavior of early childhood into teaching measures in the classroom.
(2) Cross-cultural studies of the child rearing patterns in the different ethnic groups and in regard to *"poverty culture"*

156

(3) Development of instruments for rapid, comparative clinical assessment and evaluation of cognitive, motor and learning development as well as patterns of emotional interaction and object relations for this age group.

The consultants felt that the role of the psychiatrist in an educational setting requires clarification at many points. How should he be used by the teacher and other lay persons? What patterns of treatment, intervention, family and crisis consultation should be set up? What should be the form of consultation with the public health physician and the pediatrician? In general, how should mental health consultation be used in the content of a Head Start Program?

The child psychiatrist who works in early childhood settings should have a background of supervised experience with nursery school children and a knowledge of the specific problems of the disadvantaged population.

The fact that 51 child psychiatrists could be marshalled in such short order for participation in this program is an indication of their great interest in the mental health of children from three to six. Some consultants' observations were directed at the value of the Head Start Program for the children and community, and at the role of the child psychiatrists in such a program.

All participants felt that Head Start is an important approach to community involvement in the fate of the child. Almost all of the children were thought to have benefited from the socialization afforded them, in spite of the short preparation time and inadequate budget.

It was strongly felt that the number of full-year Head Start Programs should be increased. More immediately, the two-month summer program should be planned to help those children who must enter school in the Fall without benefit of a pre-kindergarten program.

The experience in development of this mental health consultation program for operation Head Start was a most satisfactory one for all psychiatrists involved. All felt strongly that further implementation is essential to continue the momentum of this program which holds the promise of so many positives for the deprived child. It is preferable to approach the early childhood education program as a major opportunity to offer young children and their families the maximum in health and education through the joint efforts of concerned professionals. Our purpose in presenting these thoughts and ideas has been to help in the future planning of more comprehensive services for prevention, detection and treatment, as well as child care and education, at this critical level of development.

The views expressed herein are personal and do not reflect the official policy and endorsement of the organizations with which the authors are affiliated.

APPENDIX I

MEMORANDUM TO HEADSTART
MENTAL HEALTH CONSULTANTS   (July 1966)

The enclosed represents an outline that we hope will be useful to you in your Head Start experiences this summer. Please view this outline as a first attempt in formulating an approach to your consultation experiences. We would welcome your suggestions for its revision in order that we can develop an even more useful and comprehensive outline for the future.

This outline could not possibly cover all of the many facets of the consultation processes and clinical concerns. The attempts are to draw your attention to the following major items:

1. Program consultation, administrative processes, staffing patterns, training levels, classroom organization, feeding arrangments, recruiting processes, staff interaction.

2. Observation of children with reference to both normal and abnormal indices.

3. Operational procedures regarding diagnostic and referral services and liaison with Head Start central office staff.

4. Methods of recording your observations and your suggestions for the future improvements of the program and your participation.

The following are a few thoughts that were not directly included in the outline, but might be useful to you and to future planning.

1. How can we define more specifically the child psychiatrist's role in terms of his unique area of competence? Where does his functioning overlap with other disciplines? How does the process of consultation differ from the exercise of clinical methods?

2. Can we identify, define and emphasize the positive healthy aspects of the Head Start children (such as coping mechanisms and evidence of adequate mastery) well enough to use them as a fulcrum to promote mental health, especially where opportunities for removal of potential illness are not at hand.

3. What is mental illness in children and is it different from a psychiatric disorder? At what point can we say a child is mentally ill?

158

4. How effective has the program been in terms of recruiting "poverty children"?

5. How are we understood by the staff in the center and how well do we understand them. Are our notions about them and expectations of them real or not? Are their expectations about us accurate?

6. How susceptible are we to using labels to describe "poverty children"? How susceptible are we to rescue fantasies? How insensitive are we to the competence of those with whom we come in contact? How insensitive are we to the "stake" that others have in this program?

7. How do we react to the chaos and confusion of the Head Start organization and implementation?

It would be unrealistic to expect any of us to comprehend in so short a time the total functioning of Operation Head Start with all of its problems. It is also unrealistic of us to expect that we will perform smoothly in our new roles as consultants and to learn all there is to know about consultation very quickly. It would be unrealistic of us to assume that we had mastered all of the information about child development and psychiatric problems in young children. We must guard against a temptation to look at everything and yet see nothing or the temptation of trying to do everything and yet accomplishing little.

This program is just a beginning. The information you gather is vital for a feedback into the construction of an even better program for next year. Plans are being made now not only to collate this data, but to hold a day and a half seminar in late September where you all will have an opportunity to discuss your findings with discussion leaders who have special knowledge in the areas of our concerns. We are attempting also to involve the national Head Start office in this fall meeting so that we may compare our data with those from other parts of the country.

Barbara Munk, M.D.
Director of Mental Health Service
Project Head Start, New York City

Alan M. Levy, M.D.
Special Assistant in Child Psychiatry
New York City Community Mental Health Board

Albert Hotkins, M.D.
Chief Psychiatrist
Bureau of Child Guidance

159

Enclosure

P.S. If you have performed a formal psychiatric examination on any child and have prepared a written report of this examination with your diagnosis and recommendations, please send this report *only* to the Director of Mental Health Service, Project Head Start, New York City, 280 Broadway, New York, 6th floor. You may, however, send a copy of this report to any clinical facility to whom you have made a referral.

APPENDIX II

OUTLINE OF REPORT OF PSYCHIATRIC CONSULTATION FOR THE PROJECT HEAD START SUMMER 1966

I. **Name of Sponsor**

Location of Premises (Public School, Housing Project, Church, Synagogue, Settlement House or others).

Neighborhood of Premise (Description).

Number of participating children.

Age range, girls, boys.

Ethnic Groups (Percentage of mixed groups, predominance of one group, religious, cultural and language background, socio-economic background or others).

II. **Physical Set-up of Center (evaluation)**

How many classrooms (space.)

Equipment (kindergarten furniture, toys, dollhouse, material for creative play, art supply, puzzles, musical instruments, books or others).

Yard for outside play.

Provision for food (What kind of meals).

Rooms for conferences, recreation rooms for mothers, office space.

a) **Various Staff** - attitude, understanding and expectation of Mental Health Consultation (interested, reserved, anxious, tense, or others, understanding or confusion about role of psychiatrist and psychologist; reasonable requests; overdemanding; magical solution; frustration.)

Special attention to working relation with:

Teachers
Social worker
Psychologist (What was his role, what did he do with children)
Public Health Service (M.D., Nurse or others)

b) **How was Mental Health Consultation Utilized and Given?**

1. Form: Conferences, consultations, psychiatric examinations.
   Individual, formal, informal, casual during ongoing activities.
   Groups, formal, informal, how were they formed, who participated, how often.

2. Subjects of discussion, major questions and problems raised (describe in regard to the various staff-categories as mentioned above).
   For example, questions about:

   Program-Management
   Handling of individual children (hyperactive, crying, fighting, temper tantrums, wetting, soiling, not eating, not speaking, language barrier, unresponsive, disobedient, not separating from mother, clowning, clinging and others.)
   Mental illness and treatment (bizarre behavior, retardation seizure-disorder.)
   Procedure of psychiatric examination (S.W., Psychologist, Director, parents, record-keeping, referral.)
   Removal of a child from the program.
   Family-problems, interview with parents.
   Problems of child-rearing, mother-child interaction.
   Child-development (normal maturational levels, what to expect from this age group and others.)
   Interest in ethnic and cultural differences of behavior and expression.
   Or Other . . .
   Was Mental Health Consultation considered desirable and what approach or service was felt the most helpful?

161

III. **Staff** (Number of staff-categories, how many of each category, sufficiently staffed in each category, *evaluation* of background, training, experience, devotion, interest, working relation to others, cooperation in teamwork of working relation to others, cooperation in teamwork or authoritative attitude, all-over atmosphere of center as a unit.)

Director (Teacher, Rabbi, Clergyman, Layman or others).

Teachers (Qualification, Kindergarten teacher, P.S. teacher, female, male, age).

Assistant Teachers

Social worker

Psychologist

Family Assistant

Family Workers

Teacher Aides

Volunteers (mothers, older children or others).

Secretary

Cook and Kitchen Aide

Foreign Language Speaking Staff (Spanish, Chinese, Yiddish, Italian or others).

Provision of Public Health Service (facility)

Medical Doctor

Nurse

Dentist

First Aid

IV. **Contact with Staff-Categories**

V. **Contact with Parents or Other Laymen not Belonging to the Staff**

a) **Attitude Towards** - understanding of - expectation from - Mental Health Consultation (interested, fearful, resistant, understanding of role of psychiatrist, magical answer, angry, frustrated, sensitive, attitude in relation to ethnic, cultural, religious, socio-economic and educational background, or others.)

b) **How was Mental Health Consultation Utilized and Given?**

1. Form: Individual interview in connection with psychiatric evaluation of a child.
Individual interview for a parent, formal, informal, during ongoing activities, trips, etc.
Conferences or Workshops, casual, formally scheduled, informal.
Who participated? (ethnic groups, mothers, fathers.)
How often?

2. Subjects of discussions, major questions and problems raised

For example, about:

Child-rearing, disobedience, punishment, permissiveness, restrictions, protection, independence, expectations of conformity, responsibility, etc.
Sleeping, sleepwalking, nightmares, crying, bedwetting, thumbsucking, eating, food, clothing, Sibling-relation, fighting, play, temper tantrums, etc.
Child-development, learning.
Physical and Mental Illness (acceptance, approach, care, concern.)
Personal problems, marriage problems.
Role of father, mother, older siblings, extended families.
Feelings about Head Start program.

VI. **Program (evaluation)**

a) **Recruitment of Children**

Method (by home visits, through schools, settlement houses, church, other organizations.)
(How were mothers prepared, how was child prepared)

Acceptance for registration (age range, address or other criteria.)

163

Rejection (physical handicap, seizure-disorder, day and night enureses, soiling, gross mental retardation, emotional disturbances, no speech, not separating from mother, mother unable to bring and take child home from program, etc.)

b) **Classroom - program**

General tone and atmosphere.

Consistent curriculum during the week.

Balance between structured activity, quiet rest-time, unstructured free play and outdoor play.

Structure of group (was age and sex considered in group selection.)

Availability of sub-grouping and independent play or activity of a child.

How much wrestling, wild play, noise, destruction, and fighting was tolerated.

How much emphasis on educational goals.

How much encouragement of creativity.

Expectation of response to verbal and visual material (language).

How much stimulation of abstract thinking and perception.

How much material available and used.

Trips (preparation of children, utilization of experience, were they enriching and valuable.)

Mealtime (children sitting together; instructions about food and how to eat; were children supported and also protected from each other's rivalry and aggression during the meal.)

To what aspect of the program did the children respond best.

VII. **Educational Staff** (Observation of interaction and approach during activities, classroom, trips, etc.)

164

Teachers approach to children (personality, interested, cheerful, secure, efficient, rigid, span of patience and tolerance, overindulgent, overinvolved, imaginative, common sense, understanding of behavioral and cultural differences, handling of language barrier, disciplining, and respecting the independent attitude of child.)

Communication - verbal, non-verbal

Teachers approach to aides, assistants, and parents.

Utilization of Teacher's Aides and their relation and approach to children.

Stability of attendance of educational staff; how much turnover of staff.

Sufficient coverage at all times.

How much time passed (days, weeks) until staff was relaxed, secure in command and organized.

VIII. **Children** (Observation of behavior and interaction during various activities in the classroom, on trips, mealtime, coming and leaving.)

Physical appearance (clothing, nutrition, bruises, injuries, general impression of physical health.)

Ability to attend their needs (dressing, washing, eating, toilet.)

Relation to teacher and other adults (aloof, shy, independent, respectful, indifferent, affectionate, clinging, attention-seeking, observations in regard to behavior and cultural, ethnic background.)

Relation to peers (communication, verbal, non-verbal, conversations, group-play, games, helping each other, rivalry, teasing, provocation, fighting wrestling, destructive, comparative behavior of boys and girls, different peer-relation noticed in different ethnic groups, etc.)

Interaction of siblings, when present in the group (supportive, indifferent.)

Relation to toys (overwhelmed, just holding toys, playing constructively, sharing with others in integrated play, phantasies, verbalizations, imaginations, correct use of toys, or throwing around as weapons, persistence and occupation-time with a particular toy or play-selling.

165

Relation to creative material (painting, drawing - scribble, figures, forms - clay, paper, interest, dexterity, conception, attention span, etc.)

Preference for relation towards persons or material.

Relation to games, music, singing.

Relation to food (grabbing, anxious to protect it, taking time to eat, indifferent, rejecting, smearing, satisfied, better than at home, etc.)

Relation to discipline, structure, limit-setting, conformity, stress.

General observation of sub-grouping, leadership, independence, isolation.

How much time (days, weeks) passed until the children were seen as relaxed and accustomed to the program.

IX. **Observation of Behavior of an Individual Child Leading to Psychiatric Evaluation**

a) Speech (language barrier, immature speech-pattern, stuttering, echolalia, mutism, aphasic speech.)

b) Motor-coordination and performance (awkward, spastic, inability to complete simple puzzle, scribbling, etc.)

c) Attention span, impulse control, frustration tolerance (restlessness, hyperactivity, erratic behavior, rages, etc.)

d) Seizure-disorder, Grand-Mal, Petit-Mal.

e) Vision, hearing (misunderstanding, not following instructions.)

f) Body-movements (bizarre, stereotype, rocking, headbanging, self-destructive, biting, autoerotic.)

g) Isolated, withdrawn, autistic.

h) Moody, depressed, excessive crying, panic-reaction, freezing.

i) Aggressive, destructive, uncontrollable, etc.

166

j) Excessive clinging, helpless, anxious, frightened, separation-anxiety, fear of any change, etc., or

k) Other symptomatology.

X. **Assessment of Mental Health and Illness**

a) How many children of a class were found to function within normal limits of mental health and development.

b) How many children with mild behavioral difficulties, which needed special attention of the teacher, but could be helped by consultation with teacher about approach and handling of the child or other environmental manipulation.

c) How many children, presenting more serious behavioral difficulties and deviations, requiring special psychiatric attention.

d) How many individual psychiatric evaluations were done:

Interview with child
Interview with parent

Number of children in these Tentative Diagnostic Categories:

Behavior disorder due to family-pathology (father or mother mentally ill, alcoholism, etc.) or family sociology (neglect, broken home, violence, large sibling number.)

Behavior disorder due to Organic Brain Pathology

Maturational lag
Mental deficiency
Cerebral Palsy
Defect of Vision or Hearing
Seizure disorder
Aphasia or residual of infectious diseases
Head injuries

Behavior disorder due to severe deviation and atypical personality development

167

Autism, psychosis, severe atypical traits

Behavior disorder due to acute anxiety reaction

Acute regression

XI. **Procedure of Psychiatric Examination**

Preparation of parents (by whom?)

Receiving of permission.

Participation of Social worker and Psychologist (did Center hire them?).

Arrangement for the psychiatric interview with child.

Was parent seen individually.

Disposition Conference (with whom?).

Recommendations (who interpreted to parents?).

Record (where was information written down and kept; confidentiality!).

Referral (to which facility in the community?).

Was child accepted, how was it followed through?

XII. **Evaluation of Head Start Program - Comments and Suggestions**

Comments in regard to all above-mentioned points.

Suggestions of needs (insufficient staff-education in regard to program, parent education, mental health problems?
insufficient community work, participation, education?
insufficient facilities for referral for psychiatric care?
insufficient medical care?, etc.)

Suggestions for improvement (written material, workshops, movies for staff and community.)

Seminars for psychiatrists, research.

168

Comments about valuable points of the program.

What was the best functioning part of your center?

Barbara Munk, M.D.
Director of Mental Health Services
Project Head Start, New York City

Alan M. Levy, M.D.
Special Assistant in Child Psychiatry
New York City Community Mental
Health Board

Albert Hotkins, M.D.
Chief Psychiatrist,
Bureau of Child Guidance

APPENDIX III

HEAD START PROGRAM
Summer 1966

BUREAU OF CHILD GUIDANCE
NYC Board of Education

PSYCHIATRIC REPORT OF INDIVIDUAL CASE EVALUATION:

(To be filled out for each case you are asked to see individually. Then forward to
Office of the Chief Psychiatrist).

Referral
Date:

Name of
Child:

Add:

Date of
Birth:

Parent or
Guardian:

P.S.
& Boro.

1) **Presenting Problem:**

2) **General Clinical Findings:**
   a. Classroom Observations:

   b. Interview Observations:

3) **Diagnostic Impression:**

4) **Disposition:**

(Signature)

(please print name)

170

APPENDIX IV

BUREAU OF CHILD GUIDANCE
N. Y. C. Board of Education
80 Lafayette Street, New York 13

July 13, 1966

MEMORANDUM

From: Albert S. Hotkins, M.D.,
Chief School Psychiatrist

To: Supervisors of Operation Head Start;
Head Teachers.

Subj: FUNCTIONS OF THE PSYCHIATRIC CONSULTANT

This is the first time psychiatrists will be available in certain locations for consultation to educational personnel involved in Operation Head Start. Since this is a new undertaking, this memo is being addressed as suggestions for utilization of the psychiatrist. There will have to be a departure from the classical utilization as had been previously practiced in clinical procedures of the Bureau of Child Guidance in view of the short term nature and the special goals of this program.

Psychiatrists have been tentatively assigned to cover certain supervisors' areas. However, we would like to suggest that wherever possible a more concentrated school assignment for each psychiatrist, i.e. function in one school of an area may be of more value for everyone concerned. It is acknowledged that the psychiatrist will have to familiarize himself with the program, especially as he can assess his participation and relate to the teachers' evaluation of their own needs evolving from their experiences. We recognize that there will be particular needs in each area and as such the following broad outline is suggested.

(1) It would be advisable for the psychiatrists to spend as much time as is possible observing the children in their classroom setting in order to most effectively perform as mental health consultant, which we feel is the primary manner in which he could be utilized in this program.

Such observations can be the basis for:

a. Conferences with teachers who might have questions as to the differentiation of situational or developmental factors as opposed to that activity which represents a real pathological and

171

maladjusted behavior.

b. Suggestions to understand the individual manifestations and differences of children as related to special aspects of growth and development.

c. Suggestions in managing troublesome situations or specific questions regarding educational expectations.

d. He can serve to interpret the effects of physical processes and medical problems which the child may present either directly in a program or as elicited by the medical examination which each of these children is scheduled to have.

(2) The psychiatrist can also be used in general "in-service" conferences with teachers regarding general mental health procedures, principles of identification of that which can be considered pathology, and around any other problems in which teachers may have interest and desire some discussion.

(3) The psychiatrist can be used to confer with non-professional personnel who will be working as family aides, assistant teachers and others involved with the care of the children.

(4) The psychiatrist can be used to work with parents in groups or to help those people who are engaged in these procedures.

Lastly we would like to recognize that there will be many problems that require individual evaluation. We would like to keep this at a minimum since we would rather concentrate on a broad overall mental health consultative role. However, we do feel that there will be situations in which such evaluation will be necessary and as such we are prepared to do so. It must be kept in mind that these children if discovered to have pathology, will have to be referred to local agencies. Psychiatric participation in Operation Head Start is a distinct program away from the Bureau of Child Guidance. In view of the fact that this is a limited program, we feel that we would serve a much more important community function by participating with other disciplines in mutual sharing of ideas to the advancement of the program for these children.

Dr. Elvira Carota, School Psychiatrist, will be administratively responsible for the Psychiatric Staff. If you wish to communicate with her, she can be reached on Wednesdays (8:30 - 11:30 AM) at BE 3-7550 (BCG Hdqtrs). At other times, please call same number to reach secretary who will then contact Dr. Carota.

172

VOLUNTEERS FOR VISION

Robert A. Kraskin, O.D.,
Optometrist; Optometric Consultant to Project Head Start,
Office of Economic Opportunity, Washington, D. C.

ROBERT A. KRASKIN, O. D.

"Volunteers for Vision" was created as a result of Mrs. Lyndon B. Johnson's announcement concerning her interest and desires for Project Head Start in February, 1965. "Volunteers for Vision" is the primary contribution to Project Head Start by the Woman's Auxiliary to the American Optometric Association. Following Mrs. Johnson's report, the Auxiliary was one of the first, if not the first, volunteer organizations to offer on a national basis to do something for Project Head Start, and their volunteer effort was to be directed towards anything with which they could aid regarding vision and vision care. Mrs. Johnson's original report named specifically the predicted potential vision and eye problems expected to be encountered during the first year of Project Head Start, and it was this that prompted the initial offer on the part of the Woman's Auxiliary. Mrs. Johnson personally accepted this volunteer effort, following which her daughter, Miss Luci B. Johnson, because of her especial interest in vision and vision care, was asked to be Honorary Chairman of the Volunteers for Vision in which capacity she continues proudly today as Mrs. Patrick Nugent.

The value and purpose of Volunteers for Vision became obvious when it was realized that one of the needs of the successful Head Start programs was an adequate pre-school vision screening program that could be given by lay volunteers rather than professional vision care specialists. It was recognized that volunteer help was essential for Project Head Start. It was noted that in many areas it would be impossible to have adequate professional staffing only for the purpose of vision screening. It was also appreciated that a screening program was essentially a layman's responsibility (functioning under professional supervision and guidance) rather than professional, and the need was for vision screening rather than complete vision examination.

With the foregoing in mind, it was then realized that there was no existing accepted, organized and specifically designed pre-school age vision screening program. There were many school age and older level vision screening programs but none specifically designed for pre-school children. Thus, following their volunteering to aid the Auxiliary in any way possible, the Child Vision Care section of the Optometric Extension

175

Program was asked to develop a specific pre-school vision screening program, and this was done, and has become known as the Volunteer for Vision program.

It is significant to note that the very goal and reason for existence for the Woman's Auxiliary to the American Optometric Association has been their dedication towards "aid to the visually handicapped child", and, thus, this program provided a means to satisfy their dedication.

The Volunteers for Vision program was presented to Project Head Start specifically as the Auxiliary's contribution and was gratefully accepted, following which announcement of this program's availability was made to all Project Directors by Dr. Julius Richmond, Director of Project Head Start. The program was used in many areas and by many Head Start programs throughout the country during the initial summer program, and has continued to be utilized where requested or desired currently.* The Woman's Auxiliary has dedicated themselves nationally to this program and will continue it for Project Head Start. At the same time, the broad scope and value of such a vision screening program has been recognized, and there are now plans to expand the program. This will be covered in a later section of this discussion. It is important to note that the women doing the screening are laywomen, primarily members of their local optometric auxiliaries, however the use of this program is under professional supervision and training by optometrists specializing in children's vision care. It is also significant to note that the Volunteers for Vision encourages non-optometric laywomen to participate, and has made great use of volunteers both individuals as well as groups such as PTA, American Legion Auxiliaries, etc.

It has been estimated that over twenty percent of the one-half million children participating in Project Head Start during the first summer period were given the Volunteers for Vision screening tests. As time has gone on, with the continuation of Project Head Start both as a summer program as well as the year-round program, this percentage has grown significantly greater.

*The 1965 summer program
    Vision screening was given in 84% of the programs; another 10% had partial screening.
    V. for V. handled over 100,000 children

*The 1966 full year program
    Of a sample group, 8% were referred for additional vision care following screening as a result of being identified as problems by the screening. An additional 3.5% were already known vision or eye problems.

*The 1966 Summer program
    88% of the children received vision screeining; 10% were identified as having vision and eye problems.
    Following are samples:
    In Chicago, 16,000 children were screened, 8% referred for vision care.
    In Miami, 2000 children screened, 139 referred for vision care.

176

The Volunteers for Vision screening program continues to be the only specifically recommended vision program for Project Head Start.

Regarding the results of these tests, although official data has not been released through the Office of Economic Opportunity, it is estimated that these tests have uncovered the need for additional and more extensive investigation of visual function by professional examination of about ten percent of the total population screened. This figure correlates highly with the original estimation of need for additional vision care. It must be strongly emphasized that the Volunteers for Vision tests are not a substitute for a complete thorough professional study of visual function. They are merely vision screening tests designed to select those suspected of having visual dysfunction. Selection of those suspected as having need for vision care is not to be construed as a diagnosis. Diagnosis is dependent upon the results of the follow-up complete vision examination given by the professional specialist in vision care.

The Volunteers for Vison screening tests were specifically designed to be significantly related to the visual behavior of the child from three to six years old. These tests, from a non-clinical point of view, are simple in their design yet directed towards the investigation of an observation of basic and fundamental visual abilities. Although they are few in number, they will provide the necessary information about the child's ability in visual function that will permit adequate evaluation as to whether the child should be seen for additional and more extensive professional investigation. Needless to say, the design of the tests centered around ease of administration and simplicity in scoring. The following is a description of the tests, quoting directly from the OFFICIAL MANUAL OF INSTRUCTIONS FOR VOLUNTEERS FOR VISION.

EXTERNAL APPEARANCE of the eyes:

This consists of a careful observation of the child's eyes to determine whether there is any visible obvious sign of abnormality, disease or any condition indicating improper health or obvious faulty alignment. This is not really a test but an observation, such as any mother would make of her own child. Obvious crossed or "wall" eye posture, styes, inflammed eyes, or "runny" eyes would be cause for referral.

In the event that there is a diseased or abnormal appearance of the eyes observed, the child is immediately removed from the remainder of the screening program and a recommendation for referral for complete professional attention is forwarded to the proper local person in Project Head Start. Please bear in mind that the referrals are not made by the Volunteers for Vision. The recommendation for referral is made to Project Head Start personnel.

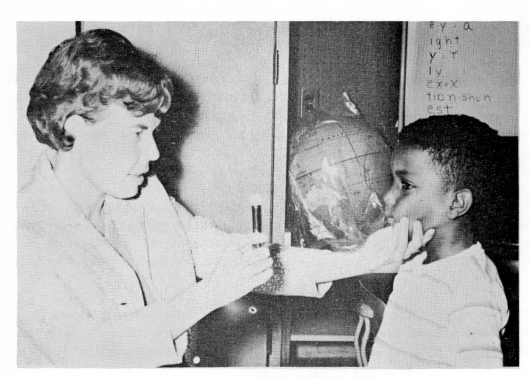

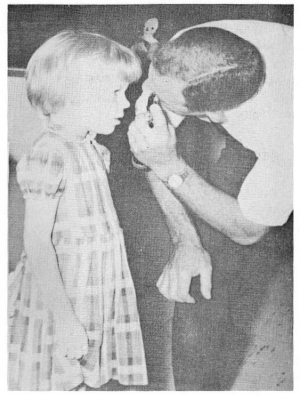

IDENTIFICATION

This test has some relation to visual acuity but also incorporates some degree of information as to how well the child can match similar visible objects. This test is taken from a battery of tests known as "Stycar." The particular part of the "Stycar" test utilized here is known as the "miniature toy test" and is well suited to the purposes of this program. Many of the children will be unable to respond to letter or tumble E charts because of the deprivation of experience in directionality.

The child is shown some toys consisting of familiar objects and is asked to name them if possible. Examples of the toys and their respective sizes are: a car (2"), and airplane (2"), doll (2"), chair (2"), knife (3½"), fork (3½"), spoon (3½"), small knife (2½"), small fork (2½"), and small spoon (2½"). There are many others that may be used as long as the 2" size and 10 foot testing distance are maintained. Two sets are necessary so that the observer, or her helper, has one set to present as test objects and the child has one set from which to choose the matching object. These objects may be obtained from most any variety or toy store. Particular attention should be paid to obtaining objects of different colors so that color matching is not a factor. For example, the two cars should be of different color.

The test is administered by displaying the card upon which the test objects are attached. The card should be of a dull gray finish and displayed at a distance of 10 feet from the child. The observer points to one of the objects and asks the child to name it, if possible. If this is not readily done, the child is asked to choose the object that matches the one being shown from the randomly displayed set in front of him. This procedure is repeated for each eye by covering one eye, then the other, with a clean card. Care must be taken to prevent touching the child's eye with the card, on hygienic basis, yet being certain only one eye can view the target.

MOTILITIES

In this test the child is being asked to demonstrate to the observer that he or she can move the eyes up and down and side to side from a central point located straight ahead of the child's eyes. In addition to these movements the child should be able to point or turn both of his eyes inward to at least 8 inches from his face.

The motility portion of the test is administered by holding a lighted penlight vertically in front of the child's eyes, some 10 to 12 inches from his face. The light should not be pointed into the child's eyes. Then the child is instructed to follow the light with his eyes. As soon as the observer is reasonably sure that the child understands the instructions, the light is moved slowly through the above mentioned directions. The observer should be alert to any lack of movement in any of these di-

179

rections, which might indicate some degree of paralysis. Also, any *gross* inability to follow the light would be suspect.

The "push-up" phase of the test is administered next by asking the child to "look at, and follow the light." Upon obtaining the child's attention, the observer moves the light toward the child's nose, all the while keeping the penlight directly in front of the child on the child's mid-line at his eye level. Both eyes should be able to follow the light inward to at least 8 inches from his eyes, preferably closer.

EYE ALIGNMENT (cover test)

Again the penlight is used as the target to be fixated by the child. The light is held 10 to 12 inches in front of the child's face at his eye level, while he is told to "look at the light." While the youngster is looking at the light with both eyes open, a cover is placed over one eye for a count of five, then removed. Observe the eye which was under cover, as the cover is removed. The observer may note one of three possibilities. First, the eyes may continue to be properly aligned; secondly, the eye that had been covered may have drifted out of line (in or out and even up or down) but quickly realigns; or, thirdly, the eye that had been covered may have drifted out of line even after the cover is removed. The behavior that is observed is noted on the examination form. This procedure is repeated covering the other eye. Next, the test is repeated following the same procedure with each eye but using a fixation target placed at 10 feet. This test incorporates observations of alignment of each eye at both near and far distances.

PERIPHERAL ORIENTATIONS (Visually Steered Controlled Movement)

This is a test that is borrowed from the series of performance tests used by Savitz, Reed and Valadian but modified in order to gain more information as to the child's ability to use visual information he obtains from his peripheral environment.

Two strips of 1 inch masking tape are placed parallel and 7 inches apart on the floor. The color of the tape should differ from the color of the floor for contrast value. The "track" should be about 8 feet long. In line with, 2 feet beyond, and 2 feet above the track, should be a toy or other attractive target to which the child's attention is directed while walking within this track. At some point 2 to 3 feet to the side of the "track" some object, such as a chair, is placed. The child is instructed to walk through the track while looking at the toy on the other end. Observe whether the child can stay within the confines of the track. If this phase is successfully accomplished, the child is asked to repeat, but this time stop when he is even with the chair. The observer should particularly note that the child watches the toy at the

180

end of the track and does not look at the chair in order to determine where to stop. The less the child turns eyes and head the better his performance on this test.

Following a review of the screening tests as described above, it is readily seen that the demands of the tests and the responsibilities of the observer are not equivalent to a complete professional investigation of and evaluation of the visual behavior of the pre-school age child. The responsibilities of the observer is not diagnostic; on the basis of the expected behavior of a child on any given test, the observer is required to make simply a judgment as to whether the behavior was as expected, and, if not, the child is referred for professional examination. In other words, it is not the responsibility of the observer doing the screening to determine whether a child has amblyopia exanopsia, myopia, faulty ocular alignment or any form of visual difficulty or visual inadequacy. Diagnosis is a professional responsibility. Idealistically, there is no question in any one's mind that the desired approach would be a complete professional investigation of every child's visual abilities, but this is impractical, and, thus, it was early determined that the most appropriate approach would be vision screening. In addition to vision screening, it has been recommended that every child be afforded the benefit of an internal eye examination with the use of ophthalmoscope to determine the health status of the internal tissue of each eye. If possible, this is to be done during the time the physical examination is given the child by the physician, or if available, an optometrist or ophthalmologist.

These vision screening tests are designed to identify the existence of a visual problem or an inadequacy or interference in visual development. Experience has demonstrated that the tests do what they were designed for. It is recognized that any impairment in visual performance may delimit the child's ability to profit from a learning situation, some impairments being more delimiting than others. It is important that those children who have inadequate ability to see clearly at either distance and/or near be given appropriate aid to do so. Certainly, it is desirable to see that those children who have existing interferences in binocular function be provided the proper professional opportunity to alleviate this interference. The existing visual problems requiring professional investigation and subsequent follow-up care are generally obvious. The less obvious are those youngsters who, as a result of their deprived environments, having had less than adequate opportunity to develop proper visual abilities, will demonstrate these inadequacies and interferences in their general behavior and performance both during the screening as well as in the classroom. It was Arnold Gesell who said, "to know a child's vision, we must know the child; and, to understand the child, we must understand the nature of his vision." These youngsters have "visual problems" in the full sense of the word but generally need supervised guidance, frequently in the classroom, rather than usual procedures such as glasses. The proper professional care in these situations may be simply in the area of professional recommendations to the classroom teacher providing suggestions for ad-

181

equate opportunities to develop appropriate visual abilities through directed experiences. The child may need guidance in using vision to "steer" his performances; he may need more specific hand-eye activities; or, he may be in need of more elaborate gross motor coordination opportunities, to name but a few of many that may be necessary to support the learning experiences that are being directed towards developing his ability to learn to learn. Great advantage may be taken of the results of these screening tests, and, the advantage that is taken of them is dependent upon the degree of coordination existing between the Head Start teachers, the screening observers, and the professional members of the community.

As a result of the experiences involved in Project Head Start that were had by Volunteers for Vision, the overall significance of such a vision screening program dedicated towards the identification of visual problems of pre-school children has been truly felt and appreciated. To expand the program so that it may function in a community over and beyond the limited group of children participating in Project Head Start, Volunteers for Vision has now been incorporated as a national community service organization. It is no longer a committee function of a local Woman's Auxiliary to an optometric society. Throughout the country, local chapters of Volunteers for Vision are being organized with the primary purpose being to do anything possible "to aid the visually handicapped child." These chapters will provide opportunities to every pre-school child for vision screening. Fundamental interests will be centered around the prevention of visual problems. In view of the fact that it is recognized that vision is the dominant process of the human being, and, further, that is via the visual process that most learning takes place, it can be well predicted that the activities of the Volunteers for Vision can be extremely significant and prove to be a most valuable community service in any and every community.

References

1. CONFERENCE PROCEEDINGS, Golden Anniversary White House Conference on Children and Youth, Washington, D. C., March 27 - April 2, 1960.

2. Skeffington, A. M. and Associates, Post Graduate Texts issued monthly by the Optometric Extension Program, Inc., Duncan, Oklahoma, 1929-1967.

3. Getman, G. N. and Associates, Post Graduate Courses issued monthly by the Optometric Extension Program, Inc., Duncan, Oklahoma, 1952-1967.

4. Getman, G. N., HOW TO DEVELOP YOUR CHILD'S INTELLIGENCE, seventh edition, Research Press, Luverne, Minnesota, 1962.

5. Gesell, A., Illg, F., Bullis, G. E., Getman, G. N., Illg, V., VISION, ITS DEVELOPMENT IN INFANT AND CHILD, Paul B. Hoeber, Inc., Harper and Brothers, 1949.

6. Bing, Lois B., and Committee on Visual Problems of Children and Youth, REPORT TO THE 1960 WHITE HOUSE CONFERENCE ON CHILDREN AND YOUTH, American Optometric Association, 7000 Chipewa Street, St. Louis, Missouri, 1960.

7. Apell, Richard, Lowry, R. W., PRE-SCHOOL VISION, American Optometric Foundation, 1959.

8. Hirsh, M. Wick, R., VISION OF CHILDREN, American Optometric Foundation, 1964.

9. Harmon, D. B., "Some Preliminary Observations on the Developmental Problems of 160,000 Elementary School Children", MEDICAL WOMAN'S JOURNAL, 1942.

10. Sheridan, M. D., MANUAL FOR THE STYCAR VISION TEST, National Foundation for Educational Research in England and Wales, 1960.

11. Savitz, R. A., Reed, R. B., Valadian, L., VISION SCREENING OF THE PRE-SCHOOL CHILD, U. S. Department of Health, Education, and Welfare, Welfare Administration, Children's Bureau, 1964.

12. Getman, G. N., TECHNIQUES AND DIAGNOSTIC CRITERIA FOR THE OPTOMETRIC CARE OF CHILDREN'S VISION, Optometric Extension Program, Inc., Duncan, Oklahoma, 1959.

13. OFFICIAL MANUAL OF INSTRUCTIONS FOR VOLUNTEERS FOR VISION, 1966 Edition, prepared by Section on Child Vision Care and Guidance, Optometric Extension Program, for the Woman's Auxiliary to the American Optometric Association.

HEAD START HEALTH:
THE BOSTON EXPERIENCE OF 1965

Paul R. Mico, M.A., M.P.H.,
President, Social Dynamics Incorporated, Boston;
Formerly Supervisor of Health Planning,
Action for Boston Community Development, Inc.,
Boston, Massachusetts

PAUL R. MICO, M. A., M. P. H.

Those who are involved in social change programs which attempt to intervene in the lives of poverty-stricken and disadvantaged peoples are continuously confronted with the glaring inadequacies of the American social-system way of life. Large numbers of people are caught up in seemingly-inescapable cycles of deprivating life situations, which foster a "survival of the fittest" climate in which Man is pitted against his Fellow-Man. The will to exist creates novel methods of coping with problems, such as "fatherless" families in cases where welfare funds would otherwise be terminated.

In general, poor people are poorly educated. They are less knowledgeable about how to things get done. They earn less money and work at less meaningful tasks. Their physical environments stifle their social growth. And they are less healthy than their more affluent counterparts.

The "target groups" which have been identified, as "handles" in the efforts to deal with the problem in its totality, give some measure of the task at hand: Fatherless and multi-problem families; disadvantaged pre-school children; school children in need of compensatory education; school drop-outs and unemployed youths; unemployed and under-employed adults; and the isolated, the addicted, and the aged.

It is perhaps the plight of disadvantaged pre-school children which strikes deepest into the social heart and conscience of America, for it is within the lives of these important people that the most significant changes can be made, if meaningful intervention can be effected. It is this aspect of our value system which has made Project Head Start the most popular program of the U. S. Office of Economic Opportunity, the Nation's anti-poverty agency; for Project Head Start is an effort to help little children who cannot help themselves.

Project Head Start, as is common knowledge by now, is a comprehensive community action program designed to intervene meaningfully in the lives of underprivileged pre-kindergarten children and their families. Its intent is to improve their educa-

187

tional, social and health potentials; enabling them to enter formal school systems less retarded than they would have been otherwise. It was started in many communities for the first time during the summer of 1965.

One of these cities was Boston. The organization responsible for it there at the time was Action for Boston Community Development, Inc. ABCD is the city's anti-poverty agency and has the broad aim of promoting social changes. It was one of the first such agencies in the country to employ a health planner so as to develop health programs for social change purposes. It was in a position, therefore, to focus as much on the health aspects of Project Head Start as on the education and social service aspects.

ABCD designed a comprehensive innovative health component for the Summer 1965 experience; and it was funded. The following is a summation of that health experience and some comments about its implications.

DESIGNING AND PLANNING

The purpose of Boston's Project Head Start health component was to provide an extensive array of diagnostic and treatment services, covering pediatric, mental health and dental health, to an expected enrollment of 1,560 children.

Attempts were made to have these health services provided through the existing resources of either the Boston School Department or the Boston City Health Department but, because of conditions existing at the time, these resources could not be utilized. Boston is rich in other health resources, however; and it was possible, therefore, to design an innovative and feasible alternative. The alternative model was to use hospitals for pediatric and dental services; to organize an ad hoc grouping of child psychiatrists and psychologists for mental health services; and to contract with the Boston School Department for nutrition services.

Coordinating Council

A Head Start Health Resources Coordinating Council was organized. Members consisted of at least one representative from each relevant health resource involved in the Head Start Project. Chairman was Robert H. Hamlin, M.D., LL.B., Professor of Public Health Practice, Harvard University School of Public Health.* This Council was responsible for establishing health policies, effecting coordination of services, for delegating the roles and functions of the various service agencies and resources taking part in Head Start, and for determining the future resolution of Head Start, health services on a permanent basis. Represented were:

*Now Vice-President for Health; Booz, Allen and Hamilton, Inc.; New York City.

188

Action for Boston Community Development
Beth Israel Hospital
Boston City Health Department
Boston City Hospital
Boston Floating Hospital
Boston School Department
Boston Tuberculosis Association
Boston University School of Graduate Dentistry
Boston University Medical Center
Children's Hospital Medical Center
Forsyth Dental Center
Harvard University School of Dental Medicine
Harvard University School of Medicine
Harvard University School of Public Health
James Jackson Putnam Children's Center
Massachusetts General Hospital
Massachusetts Society for the Prevention of Blindness
Massachusetts State Department of Mental Hygiene
Massachusetts State Department of Public Health
Tufts University School of Dental Medicine
United Community Services of Metropolitan Boston
United States Public Health Service, Region I
Visiting Nurse Association of Boston

Major Policy Decision
A major factor in the design of the Boston program was the insistence on the part of the Council representatives from the teaching hospitals that their participation in such a large service program could be justified only if the following two conditions were met:

1. A high level of quality and quantity of health services to be provided to the children.
2. A thorough evaluation of the program to be carried out. This position was accepted by the Council and planners as a matter of policy and was the single most significant determinant in the eventual design and program.

Health Services Design
To the extent that it was possible, the Coordinating Council wanted a health program that extended beyond screening and diagnosis, so as to include treatment and rehabilitation and health education. The total cost of the program was computed, on a per capita basis, to be $170.89 per child. Of this, $70.65 per child was requested and received from the Office of Economic Opportunity; and $100.24 per

189

child was contributed by the Boston health community in the form of manpower facilities and resources and medical services. Payments for services to the hospitals, mental health center, and the School Department were on a per capita basis.

The $70.65 per child allocation from O.E.O. was budgeted on the following basis:

$30.00	Pediatric Services
4.25	Public Health Nursing Services
10.00	Dental Services
6.00	Mental Health Services
5.00	Data-Processing
15.40	Nutrition Services

In addition to the per child allocation, the O.E.O. grant provided funds for a part-time medical director and a half-time health educator. One critical period in the program occurred when the budget of the initial health component was slashed drastically by O.E.O. to conform with its general guidelines allotment of $10 per child for health services. The Boston health community rallied in support of the original proposal, making its concerns known to O.E.O.; and it was eventually funded essentially as submitted.

Five hospitals agreed to participate in the program, lending the resources of their pediatric and dental departments to the task. They were: Beth Israel Hospital, Boston City Hospital, Boston Floating Hospital, Children's Hospital Medical Center, and Massachusetts General Hospital. All are major teaching institutions of great reputation. Head Start classes of fifteen children each were assigned to them on the basis of their intake capabilities and geographical location. Beth Israel was assigned 150 children; Boston City, 465; Boston Floating, 255; Children's, 405; and Massachusetts General, 270. The children attended their regular classes in the morning. Appointments for their pediatric and dental services were scheduled for the afternoon periods, with the children being escorted to the hospitals for them.

The per capita allocation of $4.25 per child was sufficient to employ five public health nurses on a full-time basis, during the period of the program. One was assigned to each of the five hospitals, to use the hospital as her basis of public health nursing services and operations.

The James Jackson Putnam Children's Center, one of Boston's finest mental health resources, accepted the organizational responsibility for the mental health services. Since there was no one Center with the resources to carry out the entire task, child psychiatrists and child psychologists from various Centers throughout the city were organized on an ad hoc basis to provide the services. They went to the classrooms during the mornings to conduct screening observations of the children.

190

Head Start administrators earlier had decided that the nutrition program should be part of the Health component. The health planners made an attempt to involve private enterprise and local service agencies in the provision of nutrition services to the children, but there were too many problems involved and not enough planning time to resolve them. A contract was then negotiated with the Boston School Department to provide a standardized mid-morning snack and bag-lunch program.

Data-Processing
The $5.00 per child allocation was sufficient to provide for data collection and tabulation services. A standardized, pre-coded health and medical record was designed. It was used by each of the hospitals. The public health nurses accepted responsibilities for seeing that proper entries were made. This record provided data regarding family and child health history, the findings of pediatric and dental examinations, and the services provided. A separate instrument for mental health data collection was designed and utilized.

Coders were recruited from among the ranks of college students and trained to transfer the data from the two separate instruments onto IBM cards. The coding was after the health program had been completed and the records collected from the various health resources. Data processing services were provided by the Boston University Computational Center.

Planning and Staff Personnel
The central staff consisted of a part-time medical director, a part-time health educator, and the five full-time public health nurses. The planning for the Health component was directed by the ABCD Supervisor of Health Planning, in cooperation with Dr. Hamlin of the Harvard School of Public Health. Dr. Hamlin was also Chairman of the ABCD Advisory Committee on Health Planning at the time.

The Project also obtained the part-time consultation services of a public-health-trained pediatrician, Dorothy Worth, M.D., who assisted in designing the medical component of the program and helping to negotiate its implementation with the various hospital pediatric departments. Also instrumental in the design of the program was Arthur Salisbury, M.D., of the Harvard University School of Public Health, and the Massachusetts Committee on Children and Youth.

Pierre Johannet, M.D., a child psychiatrist, Director of Nursery Services for the James Jackson Putnam Children's Center, was instrumental in designing the mental health component and data collection instrument, and in organizing a large group of mental health personnel to carry out this aspect of the program.

Mrs. Thomas C. Cone, a volunteer with the Children's Hospital Medical Center, de-

191

serves special recognition for her initial role in organizing volunteers for the Head Start program at that Center; and for coordinating the follow-up services of the entire project later.

The two persons most responsible for the design of the medical and dental instrument and the data processing schema were: Dr. Richard Kauff, whose services were contributed to the program on a half-time basis, courtesy of the USPHS, and the Boston City Hospital, where he was on official assignment; and Mr. Norman Goldman, Associate Director of the Boston University Computational Center, a Consultant to the Project. Dr. Kauff was later made available to serve as the part-time Medical Director of the Boston program.

Recognition is also paid to the Department of Nutrition, Harvard University School of Public Health, for the loan of Miss Sheila Cronin of its staff to help design and negotiate the nutrition service.

Innovations

This Boston approach, in general, had the following innovative facets: Five major hospitals cooperated in a common venture in Boston, for the first time; they agreed to use a standardized medical record form; pediatric staffs had their first experience with a public health nurse, and with large groups of relatively healthy children; and an insightful body of data was collected about the health status of a large number of children.

THE PROGRAM

The general objective of the Health component was to enable the children to enter kindergarten or first grade classes in the fall with a "head start" in health improvement. A review of the daily operations indicated that the program was implemented basically as planned. Classes were held in the morning, with the snacks and lunches being delivered to and consumed in the classroom. Psychiatric observers made two separate observations of the children in their class settings, using the structured observation schedules. The children visited their respective hospitals in the afternoons, accompanied by parents and volunteers, to receive their pediatric and dental services. And the Health Educator conducted health education activities with children, teachers, staff, parents, and the community.

A. REVIEW OF HEALTH SERVICES. The specific services provided to the children were as follows:

1. PEDIATRIC SERVICES

192

The general objective -- to enable her to enter kindergarten or first grade with a "head start" in health improvement.

a. Pediatric (physical) evaluation.
b. Vision testing.
c. Hearing evaluation.
d. Speech evaluation.
e. Laboratory services for anemia, tuberculosis and kidney disease.
f. Emergency follow-up diagnostic procedures.
g. Immunizations and vaccinations.
h. Drugs and corrective devices, such as glasses, hearing aids.
i. Hospitalization for conditions which cannot be deferred.
j. Emergency first aid services to head start classes.
k. Patient and parent education.

2. DENTAL HEALTH SERVICES
   a. Dental Examination.
   b. Treatment of Class IV emergencies, such as pain and infections.
   c. Topical applications of fluorides
   d. Oral prophylaxis
   e. Patient and parent education, as in techniques of toothbrushing.

3. MENTAL HEALTH SERVICES

193

a. Mental health screenings, in classroom settings.
b. Identification of those requiring more intensive diagnostic evaluation.
c. Referral and Follow-up diagnostic and treatment, on priority-need basis.
d. Consultation with teachers and staff.

4. NUTRITION
a. Mid-morning snacks: fruit juices and crackers.
b. Class "A" sack-type lunches.

B. MENTAL HEALTH. A further discussion* of the mental health services is in order, particularly in view of the findings which resulted in this area.

The possible diagnostic impressions were grouped under three major headings. Obviously in most instances only a rough or approximate impression could be derived.

1. THE SEVERELY DISTURBED. This group of children includes the children who are so severely disturbed that we would want a more intensive diagnostic work-up which would include a detailed family history as well as individual observation and possibly testing, Most of these children would probably prove very difficult if not impossible to integrate into the regular school system. Many or most of them would probably require some form of treatment and/or a special school situation. But such definite decisions would be made only after a full diagnostic work-up.

    Included under the heading are:

    a. The psychotic child (child with atypical development, infantile psychosis, autism, childhood schizophrenia). It may be advisable to recommend prompt diagnostic studies for these children, perhaps even removal from the classroom unless a special program for such a child is available.
    b. Character disturbance.
        (1) Children with severe character disturbance and severe ego defects manifested by impulsive behavior with breakdown or absence of internal controls and very low frustration tolerance. Children who exhibit marked distortions in object relations, reality testing and/or a proneness to severe regressions, without evidence of psychosis.
        (2) Children who belong to the broad category of children from

---

*Prepared by Dr. Johannet.

194

"hard core" families and reveal severe character disturbance but without impulsive behavior and hyperactivity. The disturbance may be manifested by distortions in object relations and reality testing but their behavior may show marked inhibition, restriction and anxiety.

c. Severe neurotic development. Children who show neurotic patterns in development other than the above character disturbances but to such a severe degree as to be a serious handicap to social and intellectual adaptation.

d. The possibly brain damaged child. Evidence may be on the basis of specific neurological symptoms and/or hyperactivity. It is often a very difficult diagnosis to establish even with thorough work-ups and of course we expect no more than a diagnostic impression based on certain indications.

e. Severe mental retardation without gross evidence of psychosis. These children give the impression of being so severely retarded that they could not function in regular school. Testing would eventually be required before reaching a final diagnosis.

f. Severely disturbed children possible diagnosis not definable. These children are obviously severely disturbed but the observer cannot on the basis of this present observation make a possible diagnosis. Further work-up is of course mandatory.

2. THE MILD-TO-MODERATE DISTURBANCES. These children would probably need further evaluation before a more definite impression can be arrived at. A careful evaluation of their overall adaptation to the Head Start program, evaluation of the family history, home setting, and general physical health would indicate whether a thorough psychiatric diagnostic evaluation may be necessary.

Included under this heading are:

a. Character disturbances. These represent less severe disturbances than the ones noted in group 1, categories 2a and b.

b. Neurotic development. This group includes children who show indications of neurotic patterns of symptomatology such as moderate obsessional symptoms or phobias. They may show a heightened state of anxiety or a degree of inhibition which is moderately severe. (Although immaturity is a form of neurotic development, it was felt useful to keep it in a separate category because of the implications for school adaptation.)

c. Immaturity generalized. These children show a developmental lag

195

in the several areas of motor skills, language, level of play and object relations. They usually do not show any severe symptoms or an unusually high degree of tension. They may cling to an adult or to another child. They may show some inhibitions (for example a reluctance or hesitation to try new things.) They may respond to pressure by resistance, provocative behavior, negativism or an intensification of infantile behavior.

 d. Immaturity, specified. These children show signs of immature development in one or two specific areas such as motor skills or language.

 e. Mild mental retardation. These children who appear retarded but not sufficiently so as to require special education.

 f. Moderately disturbed possible diagnosis not definable. These children appear moderately disturbed but the observer cannot on the basis of the present observation make a possible diagnosis.

3. PROBABLY MINIMALLY-DISTURBED OR NOT DISTURBED. This group would include children who appear normal or who may have some developmental disturbances not sufficiently marked to require further investigation or prevent them from making a good adjustment to a kindergarten experience.

A PROFILE OF THE HEAD START CHILDREN

A primary objective of the Project was to assure that a maximum number of children recruited be those with unmet-but-serviceable health needs. An initial effort to select children by random sampling methods, to allow for a better research design, was rejected by other Head Start staffs as being not feasible. Criteria were then established which would help assure that the children with the greatest needs would be selected.

The actual selection of the children was carried out by sponsoring agencies and there is reason to suspect that many children who should have had the benefits of Head Start health services were never reached because of the uncontrolled means by which children were selected. A brief profile of the children selected, follows:

1. Approximately 80% of the children were judged in "good or excellent" health by the examining physicians, despite what otherwise amounts to an unusually high incidence of findings.

2. Only 5% of the children had no "usual source of medical care." Sixty percent had used public clinics in the past, 25% had used private clinics.

196

3. However, 65% had had no dental experience prior to Head Start.

4. In addition, only 12, or 1%, had been known to mental health practitioners prior to Head Start.

5. Fifty-four percent had no medical insurance, about 30% did have. Thirty-one percent of the families were on ADC care.

6. The mean age of the Head Start child was 4.9 years, indicating an older group of children being selected than was attempted for recruitment. His mean weight was 40 pounds; his mean height was 42 inches; his parents were in their early 30's; and he was the third or fourth child in a family of nearly five children. The family income was earned and the income level approached the upper limits of this criterion for eligibility. The family lived in a multiple dwelling housing unit, and had 6 rooms. The Head Start child had his own bed, though he slept in a room with his brothers and sisters.

7. Fifty-three percent of the children were male; 47% female. Fifty percent were Negro; 44% white. Forty-six percent were Catholic; 39% Protestant; and 1% Jewish.

8. The family history showed evidence of Heart Disease 25%; Allergy 23%; and Diabetes 22%. Only 40% of the mothers sought prenatal care during the pregnancy period with the Head Start child, and 20% had a gestation period of 40 weeks and over. Two percent to 7% had prenatal complications, and 8% were in labor for more than 24 hours. Five percent had home deliveries.

9. Six percent of the Head Start children weighed less than five pounds at birth, 25% more than 8 pounds. There were known problems during the Infant Neonatal Course for 1% to 6% of the children, with 16% remaining at the hospital when the mother was discharged. Four percent to 8% had problems of growth and development. About half of the children had adequate immunization levels for DPT and Polio; 20% had not had a smallpox vaccination; and 65% had not had a measles vaccination.

Less than half of the children had had "childhood" infectious diseases, for the most part, with 16% having been hospitalized. Eighty percent had problems of sleep disturbance; 12%, fearful and dependent; 15% poor appetite; and 15% discipline. Nine percent had frequent falls and accidents. There were 718 hospitalizations among the group, for a mean of .44; and 847 injuries, for a mean of .45.

The systems history review showed the highest incidence problem in the following areas (selected):

Central nervous system
Speech problem, 8%

197

Neuro-musculo-skeletal (1% to 3%)
Cardio vascular (1%)
Respiratory -
    Frequent URI's, 14%
    Frequent Otitis, 10%
    Frequent Odentitis, 8%
Gastrointestinal
    Abdominal pain, 4%
Genitourinary
    Enuresis, 19%

FINDINGS AND RESULTS

Data was collected on 1,467 children or 94% of the total expected enrollment, indicating that sufficiently adequate services were provided to that number to permit the tabulation. The following reasons account for those who were lost;

1. Children were absent on the days the health services were scheduled for them and, in many cases, absent also on the days scheduled for "make up" exams.
2. Some of the 104 classes were under-enrolled, so that it is not known if the full 1,560 were actually recruited.
3. Some records were incomplete and could not be tabulated. Of the children who were examined, 1,364, or 93%, received both Pediatrics and Dental services; and 1,285, or 88%, received Mental Health services.

About 85% of those examined had been previously known to child health services or family physicians, but the ration of "previously unknown" defects found to "known" defects was nearly 3 to 1, indicating that the children were known to child health services from immunization and acute disease points of view rather than from a comprehensive pediatric services point of view. For 65% of the children, Project Head Start was a first dental experience. Only about 1% of the children had been known to mental health services previously.

Of the children examined, 77%, or 1,133, were referred for one or more conditions detected in the pediatric, dental, and mental health areas. Seven percent had findings in all three areas; 29% had findings in a single area (Pediatrics, 7%; Mental, 8%, and Dental, 26%). Of the children referred, 50% received some form of follow-up service ranging from further diagnostic tests and dental treatments to hospitalization and surgery.

Ninety-three percent of the children received pediatric examinations; 35% of those examined were referred for follow-up services; and of those referred, 32% received some form of services.

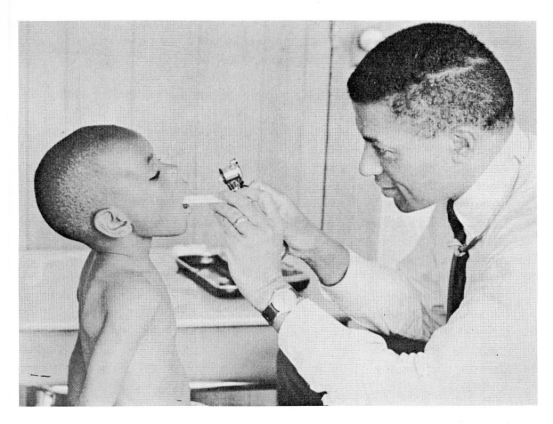

About 85% of those examined had been previously known to child health services or family physicians, but the ratio of "previously unknown" defects to "known" defects was nearly 3 to 1. Thirty-five percent of those receiving pediatric examinations were referred for follow-up services.

Ninety-three percent of the children received dental examinations. Although it was stated repeatedly that no child was found without dental disease, only 65% were referred for follow-up services. Of those 49% received some service.

Eighty-eight percent of the children were observed by the Mental Health team. Five and four tenths percent of those screened were found to be seriously disturbed and 31.4% mild-to-moderately disturbed, for a total of over 36%.

Referrals for Pediatric Diagnostic and Treatment Services
Perhaps the most startling finding of the Boston program was that of the 1,467 children examined, in all components, *1,133 children, 77%, were referred for further diagnostic and treatment services for one or more reasons.* This rate exceeded the general expectations of what would be found, prior to the Summer experience. Some insight to the nature of the problems found, based on frequency tabulations of the physical examination, follows:

199

1. *Head*--Positive findings were noted in 4% to 8% of the categories, with 3 to 4 times as many cases having been unknown previously, as known.
2. *Visual acuity*--14% positive findings, untreated.
3. *Auditor acuity*--10% positive findings, half previously unknown.
4. *Mouth, teeth, soft tissues*--40% positive findings, with only 3% having been known previously.
5. *Neck*--5% positive findings, mostly previously unknown.
6. *Chest*--Positive findings ranging from 4% to 9%, mostly unknown.
7. *Abdomen*--6% hernial findings, only 1% previously known.
8. *Genitalia*--47% uncircumcised.
9. *Musculo-Skeletal*--8% positive findings, mostly unknown.
10. *Central Nervous System*--3% findings in motor and sensory areas; 22% in emotional areas, only 1% previously known.
11. *Laboratory*--Positive findings ranging from 1% to 5%.
12. *Immunizations*--60% to 80% "no answer" indicating that data is inadequate in this area. Of those who did respond, more than half indicated inadequate immunization levels.
13. *Doctor's evaluation of child's health*--Excellent, 42%; good, 40%; fair, 12%; poor, 1%.
14. *Summary of findings*--Total findings 1,483; unusual 516; requiring referral 1,184.

Pediatric Referrals.
The 460 children, who were referred, or 35% of those examined, had a total of about 750 referrals, ranging from 1 to 7 per child, excluding dental and mental problems. That information is as follows:

	Problem	**Number of Referrals**
1.	Head	88
2.	Vision	268
3.	Hearing	154
4.	Chest	32
5.	Abdomen-hernial	30
6.	Uro-genital	13
7.	Musculo-Skeletal	20
8.	CNS - Motor Sensory	6
9.	Laboratory	41
10.	Immunization	12
11.	Tuberculosis	21
12.	Speech	42
13.	Asthma - Allergy	22

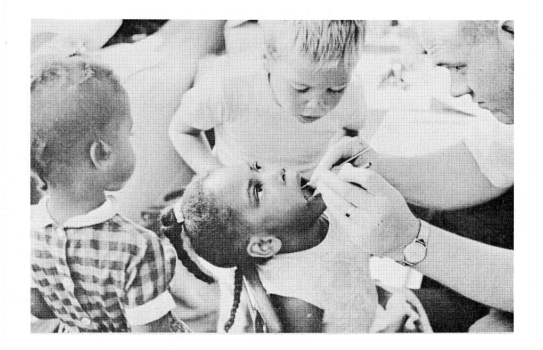

For two out of three, Head Start was the Children's first experience with a dentist. Only a few were found to be free of dental disease. Sixty-five percent, in all, were referred for follow-up services.

Dental Referrals

Dentists indicated that few children were found to be free of dental disease. Of the 1,364 individuals examined, 887, or 65%, were referred, A total of 929 referrals conditions were made, ranging from 1 to 4 per child.

As shown previously, most of the children saw a dentist for the first time as a result of Project Head Start, and most were in dire need of preventive and restorative care.

Mental Health Referrals.

One thousand two hundred eighty-five children were observed by child psychiatrists and psychologists in their classroom, with the rest having been missed as a result of being absent or because the classes could not be observed during the short summer program period.

Table 1 shows the results of the screenings. Five and four tenths percent of the children were found to be "seriously disturbed" and 31.4% "mild-to-moderately disturbed." The need for further diagnostic and evaluation services were regarded as essential.

201

TABLE 1. Summary of Mental Health Findings and Recommendations

CATEGORY	FINDINGS		RECOMMENDATIONS				
					No recommendation for diagnostic or follow-up indicated but:		
	Total Number	%	Diagnostic Evaluation Recommended	Follow-Up Evaluation	Prekindergarten Recommended	Special help in school may be necessary	Can attend regular School
Group I Considered seriously disturbed	70	5.4	70				
Group II Considered to have a mild to moderate disturbance	403	31.4	93	240	21	31	14
Group III Considered not disturbed or very mildly disturbed	812	63.2	1	4	1	3	803
TOTALS	1,285	100.0	163	244	22	34	817

" Happiness is holding hands in a running line." From a mental
health point of view, four out of five were judged ready for
kindergarten or first-grade experiences.

This particular finding differs markedly from the teachers' evaluation of their child-
at the end of the Head Start experience. Eighty percent of the children were judged
ready for kindergarten or first grade school experiences, and 20% were either regarded as not ready or with qualifications. The difference of a 39% finding on the
part of the mental health observers, and 20% on the part of the teachers, warrants
further study and research in this area.

In general, whether the high rate of morbidity referral among the Boston Head Start
children reflects an over-referral on the part of highly specialized medical technicians
or a poorer level of child health than had been anticipated, remains to be seen. In
any event, the Boston experience raises many questions which need to be pursued
by further study.

Diagnostic and Treatment Services Received
The most inadequate data in the Boston program concern the services provided to
the children who were referred. The reasons for this are as follows:

1. When the public health nurses, who were assigned to the hospital pediatric
   departments, terminated their roles at the end of the Summer Head Start Program, the primary vehicle for *follow-up of referrals* and *recording of follow-
   up services* was lost. The data reported herein includes only the services which
   had been provided to the children while the nurses were still on duty, terminated in August. The hospitals indicated subsequently that numerous appointments for follow-up services had been broken, which would have resulted in

203

services performed, had the public health nurses remained on duty. Also, hospitals continued to provide services after the nurses left to those who did keep appointments, but the data were not available for this report.

2. Referrals were made to numerous facilities, resources, and private practitioners, apart from the five examining hospitals, and no follow-up data were available from these services.

Therefore, on the basis of the data available, the following can be said. Of the 1,133 children referred for follow-up services, 566, or 50% received some form of service. Thirty-two percent of those referred for pediatric services received services; and 49% of those referred for dental services received them. Only two children received follow-up mental services. Some children received emergency services from their assigned hospitals, resulting from accidents, lacerations, and acute illnesses occurring after the examination.

Additional information volunteered by the hospitals, but not contained in the present data, reveals the following more dramatic service aspects of the Boston program:

- 3 active tuberculosis cases were discovered and were placed under treatment.
- 2 open-heart surgery operations were completed.
- 12 hernia operations were conducted.

Another significant deficiency in the Boston program concerned the lack of effective follow-up of the mental health referrals. No way was worked out for providing the psychiatric evaluations to the 67 children identified with urgent needs, because of long waiting lists and traditional time-consuming evaluative procedures. Furthermore, there was no way of preventing those emotionally immature children, who should have had the opportunity afforded by continuing Head Start or special-class experiences, from entering kindergarten or first grade. A follow-up survey conducted by the Social Service staff of Head Start indicated that 10% of the Head Start children were not in school and another 23% could not be located because of having moved from the area.

Nutrition
The mid-morning snack was modified in that juices and crackers were delivered in bulk to the classes each week, and dispensed by Head Start staff daily, rather than delivered on a daily basis by the School Department.

The lunch met the standards for good nutrition. Sack lunches were delivered daily as the basic lunch format. A survey of teachers at the end of the program indicated that many children thought the sandwiches were too dry to eat; and some foods,

204

Fried chicken, when it was served, was the favorite. The handful of children who were served hot lunches were thought to have had more satisfactory nutrition experiences than the majority who received sack lunches.

such as various lunch meats, were not liked and often not eaten. In addition, it was reported that fried chicken was served on occasion, and was universally liked by the children. From a health point of view, however, the potential food-poisoning hazard of preparing and serving fowl--in the face of lack of refrigerated storage at the Head Start classes, considering the hot summer weather which prevailed, and the several hours length of time between food preparation and food service--makes the future use of this type of food, however desirable, inadvisable under the same conditions.

One Head Start Center of five classes, a Montessori School, prepared its own lunches; and as a result, those children received daily hot lunches. Informal observations on the part of several people indicated that this was a more satisfactory experience for the children involved than the sack lunch was for the others.

Adequacies and Inadequacies of Boston Health Resources

There seems to be general agreement that the alternative of employing hospital pediatric resources to provide Head Start health services was effective and meaningful, particularly under the circumstances of time pressures which existed. Needless to say, several means of improving the feasibility and utility of such hospital resources can be made, if the use of the hospital model is to be continued. For example:

205

1. Children should be registered in summer Head Start programs much earlier in the future so that health examinations can get under way before the classes begin. This has the advantage of relieving work loads during the summer months, when many hospital and teaching staff personnel usually take vacations. It would provide more time for the examination and for better service. Someone noted that if Boston had had a significant disease outbreak during the past summer, it would have been virtually impossible to have provided the Head Start health services and meet the disease problem at the same time with the same resources.

2. Dental services were negotiated with medical people, rather than with dental personnel, and there was the feeling on the part of the dental community that the administrative decision-making resulted in the dental program getting less of the resources than had been planned in the original design. A more equitable contract would need to be negotiated for them in the future.

3. Further improvements in the staffing of the clinics need to be made, and the linkages between the hospitals and community and the schools need to be better established and strengthened.

In addition, the original resources designed for the mental health component proved to be inadequate, resulting in the mental health community having to absorb a higher cost of the actual operation than could be afforded.

The Boston program revealed, or reaffirmed, the following deficiencies in the City's community health services:

1. There is no fluoridation of public water supplies, or an alternative fluoride program, which is necessary to reduce the high, prevailing incidence of dental disease.

2. Resources for the care and treatment of dental disease are grossly inadequate for meeting the needs of the majority of the population.

3. Resources and traditional practices for providing psychiatric evaluations and treatments are grossly inadequate to meet the needs of a large population, such as Project Head Start children.

4. Comprehensive child care services for the pre-school child are relatively non-existent in Boston.

The adequacies, on the other hand, speak well for the Boston health environment:

1. Numerous excellent hospital pediatric and dental resources, which could be and were made available for the program.

2. Availability of sufficient manpower—particularly pediatricians, psychiatrists, dentists, nurses, and volunteers—to help make the program possible.

3. A high level of professional and personal interest in the Head Start children, on the part of the people who became involved in the program, as exemplified by the spirit of cooperation among the hospitals, agreement on basic standardized procedures, patient compliance with the changing Head Start policies and guidelines, and the all-out efforts to seek a change in the federal position relative to the financing of the Boston health component, which made the whole experience possible in the first place.
4. Availability of data processing resources.

Factors Which Helped or Hindered the Children From Using the Services
1. HELPED:
   Parents and aides escorted most children to the hospital and stayed with them until the services were completed. The hospital staffs were psychologically geared for this program. The children were well received and many procedures were streamlined and made more accessible to the children, as a result.

   Psychological screenings were conducted in the classroom settings.

   Parents liked the hospital approach better than the use of public clinics. The various problems they have experienced with public clinics in the past have created long-standing detrimental negative attitudes about the clinics.

2. HINDERED:
   The logistics of transporting the children from the classes to the hospitals presented numerous problems. These were increased when the modest budget item for this purpose had been eliminated by OEO and could not be restored. The volunteer and ad hoc methods employed to meet the transportation problem, varied considerably in nature and effectiveness.

   Prevailing negative perceptions and fears about doctors, dentists, shots, and hospitals were factors which had to be dealt with by staffs continually.

   Many children were absent on the days of their exams, and likewise missed the make-up clinics which were subsequently scheduled.

   Loss of the public health nurses and other staffs, at a critical point of the follow-up procedure, proved to be the most significant factor in preventing the follow-up potential from having been maximized.

Demonstrating the Role and Function of Public Health Nurses in Hospital Pediatric Departments
The hospitals exhibited great satisfactions with the nurses, with some hospitals ex-

207

pressing formal intentions to employ public health nurses on a permanent basis. The roles and functions of the nurses were described as follows:

"She will assist the pediatrician in scheduling and conducting the physical examination and administering medications and immunizations as directed. She will provide home visiting and community nursing services to those children with the greatest needs, on a priority basis, within the resources. Home visiting will be coordinated with Head Start social service home visiting services. In addition, she will visit the offices of City Health Department Nurses and Visiting Nurse Association to review their family records and avoid duplicating home visiting.

"The public health nurse will interpret her findings to the pediatric staff, and will help motivate desirable attitudes on the part of parents and children."

In practice, the nurses should have had much more help with their data collection and routine functions than was provided to them. In addition, the role and function of hospital-based public health nurses, particularly where the potential for reaching out into the homes, schools, and community exists as it does in the Head Start program, needs to be clarified and delineated to the satisfactions of the existing three public health nursing agencies: The Health Department, the School Department, and the Visiting Nurse Association.

Health-Education
The health-education potential of Project Head Start was developed to an optimal level by Health Educator. The Health Educator was employed on a half-time basis for three months, starting one week before the classes and continuing for a short period of time following the end of the program. She was responsible for arranging and carrying out health education activities with Head Start, with parent groups and volunteers, and with neighborhoods.

The Head Start program offered much opportunity for health education of parents, children, staff, volunteers, and the community--particularly in the area of maternal and child health. Parent attendance is necessary for both the child and parent for this part of the program as a health education process. Other activities were: the rest periods, the snack and lunch programs, and health and safety practices.

Initial duty consisted of planning schedules and carrying out the logistics of the medical and dental health service. In addition, the health educator presented material on community organization, neighborhood work, and health education to each of four groups of neighborhood aides, employed in the program.

208

There had been no financial appropriation for transportation in the program. The Health Educator responded by contacting the Red Cross, United Community Services, and numerous local agencies, business establishments and individual volunteers; and from these resources, the transportation needs were met.

Interdisciplinary staff meetings were held weekly. At these, the Health Educator represented the health services. All aspects of the health services, including medical and dental examinations, mental health observations, lunch program, and health education activities, were discussed at each of these. Biweekly meetings were held with the public health nurses and other health services personnel.

The Health Educator also compiled a bibliography of readily available health education resources and materials, and distributed it to nurses, social workers, coordinators, teachers, and neighborhood aides.

Recommendations
Two recommendations were suggested for supporting and strengthening the Child Health programs and services of the Boston Health Department and the Boston School Department's school health services;

1. Establish comprehensive child care service clinics in all parts of the city, to provide services to all children and young adults, under age 18, on a family basis.
2. Adding mental health services to the program of the School Department.

The strength of the health education program depended upon the effectiveness of communications. Head Start afforded many channels for health education: at conferences between parents and nurses, doctors, dentists, or others; group discussions with health personnel; classroom instructions; parent-teacher meetings; staff meetings; and home visits.

CONCLUSIONS

The Boston experience is significant in that much in-depth data were collected relative to the health status of the Head Start child. It is important to note that the children who participated were not selected from the eligible universe by a reliable sampling method. Therefore, it is not possible to generalize whether the health status of the typical Head Start child is similar to that of the typical child recruited into the Summer 1965 Boston program. It may be better, or it may be worse.

What is possible, on the other hand, is a rather insightful description of the level of health, or level of sickness, of the children who did participate. If the Boston experience has any meaning at all, then it has to be terms of delineating a public mandate

209

for improving the quality and quantity of health services available to all children everywhere. Head Start or non-Head Start.

It should be a cause for concern that large numbers of children can go throughout their preschool years and enter America's school systems without having had a thorough, comprehensive health evaluation. Although 85% of the Boston children had already been known to other child health services, the ratio of "previously unknown defects" to "known defects" found was nearly 3 to 1. The implication is that the children were known to health service previously on the basis of receiving immunizations from well-baby clinics and receiving specific treatments for specific acute illnesses. Comprehensive medical care requires thorough evaluation and follow-up.

It should be a cause of concern also that the health services of America's school systems are geared primarily for screening and preventive services only. "Screenings" will not detect many of the serious defects detected in Head Start children. Furthermore, ABCD's experience in providing health services to 16- to 22-year-old school-dropout youths strongly suggests that many of these defects go undetected throughout the aborted school experiences of the youths; and even when histories indicated that defects had been detected in school screening programs, little or no follow-up of the problems into treatment and rehabilitation resulted. The health of school-age children and youths require prevention, diagnosis, treatment, and rehabilitation; and where these are not in evidence, they should be.

And, finally, it should be a cause for concern that the health, wealth, and medical mights of America are still incapable of meeting the needs of its people. In Boston, one of the great medical centers of the world, there are simply not enough resources to meet the comprehensive health needs of Head Start children, particularly in the dental and mental health areas. What must it be like elsewhere?

Some critics of Head Start and other preschool educational programs point out that the educational advantages derived by the child who participates in them, in comparison to the nonparticipants, are rather quickly lost when both enter the formal educational system. Maybe that is so for education, but the same criticism should not and cannot be leveled against the health advantages to be derived when the proper services are provided. In this case, an ounce of Head Start is worth more than a pound of what follows.

A summarized version of this article was published in THE JOURNAL OF SCHOOL HEALTH, Vol. XXXVI, No. 6, June, 1966, pages 241-244, under the title of "A Look at the Health of Boston's Project Head Start Children."

210

References

1. American Academy of Pediatrics: 1961 Red Book: REPORT OF THE COMMITTEE ON THE CONTROL OF INFECTIOUS DISEASES. Evanston, Illinois. 1964.

2. American Public Health Association Committee on Child Health: HEALTH SUPERVISION OF YOUNG CHILDREN. Third edition. New York: 1790 Broadway.

3. Baumgartner, Leona: Medical Care of Children in Public Programs. AMERICAN JOURNAL OF PUBLIC HEALTH, 51:1491-1499, October, 1961.

4. Chaplin, Hugh and Jacobziner, Harold: A Health Program for Children in Day Care Services. PUBLIC HEALTH REPORTS, 74:567-572, July, 1959.

5. Children's Bureau: GUIDE FOR PUBLIC HEALTH NURSES WORKING WITH CHILDREN. Publication 392. U. S. Department of Health, Education and Welfare, U. S. Government Printing Office, Washington, D. C. 1961.

6. Child Welfare League of America: DAY CARE: A PREVENTIVE SERVICE. John E. Hansan, Kathryn Pemberton, Viola G. Gilfillian, Esther Eckstein. New York: 44 East 23rd Street, 10010. 1963.

7. Child Welfare League of America: DAYTIME CARE. A PARTNERSHIP OF THREE PROFESSIONS. New York. March, 1946.

8. Child Welfare League of America, Inc.: GUIDE FOR A HEALTH PROGRAM IN DAY CARE SERVICES. New York: 44 East 23rd Street. 1960.

9. Cohen, Pauline: The Impact of the Handicapped Child on the Family. SOCIAL CASEWORK, 43:137, March, 1962.

10. Cole, Minerva G. and Powell, Lawrence: Serving Handicapped Children in Group Programs. SOCIAL WORK, 9:97-104, January, 1961.

11. Delgato, G., Brumback, C. L. and Deaver, M. B.: Eating Patterns Among Migrant Families. PUBLIC HEALTH REPORTS, 76:4, April, 1961.

12. Dukelow, Donald A. and Hein, Fred V., editors. HEALTH APPRAISAL OF SCHOOL CHILDREN. A Report of the Joint Committee on Health Problems in Education of the National Education Association and the American Medical

Association. 3rd edition. American Medical Association, 535 N. Dearborn Street, Chicago, Illinois. 1961.

13. Gilbert, A. and Schloesser, P.: Health Needs of Migrant Children in a Kansas Day Care Program. PUBLIC HEALTH REPORTS, 78:(11) 989-993, 1963.

14. Gordon, John E. (ed): CONTROL OF COMMUNICABLE DISEASES IN MAN. 10th Edition. American Public Health Association, 1790 Broadway, New York. 1965.

15. Haeussermann, Elsie: DEVELOPMENTAL POTENTIAL OF PRESCHOOL CHILDREN. New York: Gruen and Stratton. 1958.

16. Harrelson, Orvis A.: Problems in Developing Health Programs for Head Start. AMERICAN JOURNAL OF PUBLIC HEALTH, 57:(7) 1187-1192, 1967.

17. Hartenstein, Hans and Richmond, Julius B.: A HEALTH PROGRAM FOR THE NURSERY SCHOOLS. Pamphlet of the National Association for the Education of Young Children, 3700 Massachusetts Avenue, N. W., Washington, D. C. 20016.

18. Hartman, Evelyn E., Wallace, Helen M. et al.: Health Problems of Infants and Preschool Children. AMERICAN JOURNAL OF PUBLIC HEALTH, 99:67-73, January, 1960.

19. Hille, Helen: FOOD FOR GROUPS OF YOUNG CHILDREN CARED FOR DURING THE DAY. U. S. Department of Health, Education and Welfare. Children's Bureau Publication 386. Washington, D. C. 20402: U. S. Government Printing Office. 1960.

20. Hornberger, Ralph C., et al.: HEALTH SUPERVISION OF YOUNG CHILDREN IN CALIFORNIA. FINDINGS OF THE 1956 CHILD HEALTH SURVEY. California State Health Department, Berkeley, California. 1961.

21. Hymes, James L., Jr.: THE CHILD UNDER SIX. Englewood Cliffs, New Jersey: Prentice-Hall. 1963.

22. Jacobziner, Harold, et al.: How Well Are Well Children? AMERICAN JOURNAL OF PUBLIC HEALTH, 53:1937-1952, December, 1963.

23. Jenkins, Gladys G.: HELPING CHILDREN REACH THEIR POTENTIAL. Chicago, Illinois: University of Chicago Press, 1954.

24. Kearsley, R., et al.: Study of Relations Between Psychologic Environment and Child Behavior. A Pediatric Procedure. AMERICAN JOURNAL OF DISEASES OF CHILDREN, 104:12-20, July, 1962.

25. Martin, E. A.: ROBERTS' NUTRITION WORK WITH CHILDREN. Chicago, Illinois: University of Chicago Press. 1954.

26. Martmer, Edgar: THE CHILD WITH A HANDICAP. Springfield, Illinois: Charles C. Thomas. 1959.

27. Maryland State Department of Public Welfare and the Governor's Commission to Study Day Care Services for Children: DAY CARE FOR CHILDREN. . . A PREVENTIVE SERVICE. Proceedings of Maryland's First State-wide Conference on Day Care Services for Children. 301 West Preston Street, Baltimore, Maryland 21210. October 1963.

28. May, Charles D. (ed): MEDICAL RESPONSIBILITIES FOR THE DISPLACED CHILD. Report of the Forty-third Ross Conference on Pediatric Research. Ross Laboratories, Columbus, Ohio. 1963.

29. Morris, Nomi, Peters, Ann DeHuff and Chipman, Sidney S.: Children in Day Care: A Health-Focused Look at Current Practices in a Community. AMERICAN JOURNAL OF PUBLIC HEALTH, 54:44-52, January, 1964.

30. Murphy, Lois B.: Effects of Child Rearing Patterns on Mental Health. CHILDREN, 3:213-218, November-December, 1956.

31. N.A.E.Y.C.: SOME WAYS OF DISTINGUISHING A GOOD SCHOOL OR CENTER FOR YOUNG CHILDREN. Washington, D. C. 20016; National Association for the Education of Young Children. 3700 Massachusetts Avenue, N. W.

32. N.E.A. and A.M.A.: HEALTH APPRAISAL OF SCHOOL CHILDREN, 3rd Edition. A report of the Joint Committee on Health Problems in Education of the National Education Association and the American Medical Association, 1961.

33. New York City Health Department: GUIDE FOR THE HEALTH PROGRAM IN THE DAY CARE AGENCY FOR YOUNG CHILDREN. 3rd Edition. 100 Worth Street, New York. 1956.

34. Office of Economic Opportunity: GUIDE SERIES FOR PROJECT HEAD

213

START, 2, MEDICAL. Washington, D. C. 1965.

35. O.S.D.H.: SUGGESTED PLAY MATERIALS FOR CHILD'S GOOD GROWTH AND DEVELOPMENT. Oklahoma City, Oklahoma: Oklahoma State Department of Health. Dorothy D. Driver, Compiler.

36. Richmond, Julius B. and Caldwell, Bettye M.: PEDIATRIC ASPECTS OF DAY CARE. Paper presented at the 1964 Annual Meeting of the American Public Health Association. New York.

37. Schiffer, Clara G. and Hunt, Eleanor P.: ILLNESS AMONG CHILDREN. Children's Bureau Publication 405. U. S. Department of Health, Education and Welfare. Washington, D. C.: U. S. Government Printing Office. 1963.

38. Siegel, Earl and Bryson, Sylvia A.: A Redefinition of the Role of the Public Health Nurse in Child Health Supervision. AMERICAN JOURNAL OF PUBLIC HEALTH, 1015-1024, July, 1963.

39. Siegel, Earl: Health and Day Care for Children of Migrant Workers. PUBLIC HEALTH REPORTS, 79:(10) 847-852, October, 1964.

40. Spock, Benjamin and Lerrigo, Marion: CARING FOR YOUR DISABLED CHILD. New York: Macmillan. 1964.

41. Spock, Benjamin and Lowenberg, Miriam: FEEDING YOUR BABY AND CHILD. Pocket Books. 1956.

42. Stuart, Harold C. and Prugh, Dane G., editors. THE HEALTHY CHILD--HIS PHYSICAL, PSYCHOLOGICAL AND SOCIAL DEVELOPMENT. Cambridge, Mass.: Harvard University Press. 1964.

43. Tuuri, A. L., Johnston, H. L. and Harting, D.: Adapting Immunization Programs to Special Groups. PUBLIC HEALTH REPORTS, 72:4, April, 1957.

44. U. S. Department of Health, Education and Welfare, Welfare Administration, Children's Bureau. CHILDREN IN DAY CARE, WITH FOCUS ON HEALTH. Washington, D. C.: Government Printing Office. 1967.

45. U. S. Department of Health, Education, and Welfare: Children's Bureau. CHILDREN IN MIGRANT FAMILIES. A REPORT TO THE COMMITTEE ON APPROPRIATIONS OF THE UNITED STATES SENATE. Washington, D. C. 20402: U. S. Government Printing Office. 1961.

214

46. U. S. Department of Health, Education and Welfare: Children's Bureau Publication No. 427. HEALTH OF CHILDREN OF SCHOOL AGE. Washington, D. C. 20402: Government Printing Office. 1964.

47. U. S. Department of Health, Education and Welfare: Children's Bureau Publication No. 30, YOUR CHILD FROM ONE TO SIX. Washington, D. C. 20402: U. S. Government Printing Office. 1962.

48. U. S. Department of Health, Education and Welfare: Children's Bureau Publication No. 324. YOUR CHILD FROM SIX TO TWELVE. Washington, D. C. 20402: U. S. Government Printing Office.

49. Wallace, Helen M.: HEALTH SERVICES FOR MOTHERS AND CHILDREN. Philadelphia, Pennsylvania: Saunders. 1964.

50. Welfare Planning Council, Los Angeles Region: STANDARDS FOR HEALTH SUPERVISION OF PRESCHOOL CHILDREN IN DAY CARE FACILITIES. Prepared by Technical Advisory Subcommittee, Day Care Committee. Los Angeles, California: 731 South Hope Street, February, 1965.

51. Wilson, Eva D., Fisher, Katherine H. and Fuqua, Mary E.: PRINCIPLES OF NUTRITION. (Revised Edition). John Wiley. New York. 1965.

52. World Health Organization: Technical Report Series No. 256. THE CARE OF WELL CHILDREN IN DAY CARE CENTERS AND INSTITUTIONS. Report of a Joint U.N. W.H.O. Expert Committee. Geneva, Switzerland, 1963.

SUBCULTURAL DIFFERENCES IN CHILD LANGUAGE: AN INTER–DISCIPLINARY REVIEW

Courtney B. Cazden, Ed.D.,
Graduate School of Education,
Harvard University,
Cambridge, Massachusetts

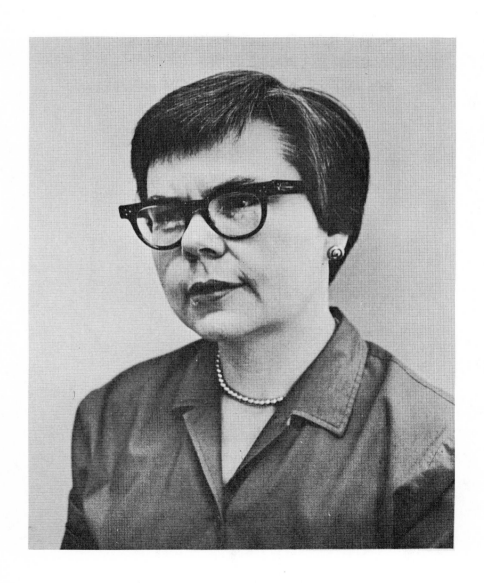

COURTNEY B. CAZDEN, Ed.D.

The argument over whether children from Harlem or Appalachia should be called "culturally different" or "culturally deprived" is more than an empty terminological dispute. It reflects a basic and important question: Is the concept of cultural relativity valid in this subcultural context or not? More specifically, in what ways is the language used by children in various subcultural groups simply different, and to what extent can the language of any group be considered deficient by some criteria? It is the purpose of this paper to explore a large body of literature bearing on the basic question.

Necessarily, this review of the literature will be an inter-disciplinary one. Linguists describe the nonstandard dialects of English in formal ways. Developmental psychologists find variations in the rate of language acquisition by children that correlate with variations in status characteristics, e.g., of social class or ethnic background. Anthropologists and sociologists suggest that not only language, but speech, is structured. Under the heading of ethnography of communication or socio-linguistics, they examine the inter-individual functions that language serves in subcultural settings. Lastly, experimental psychologists studying the intra-individual, or mediational, role of verbal behavior are becoming interested in the individual and group difference among their subjects.

I will discuss these four strands of research in turn, not trying to list all the studies and their findings but concentrating instead on an analysis of significant issues. However, even though some of this work has been stimulated by pressing educational problems, the educational issues would require such a lengthy discussion in themselves that they must be considered as falling outside of the scope of the present paper.

NONSTANDARD VERSUS STANDARD ENGLISH

Dr. Martin Luther King, speaking in Selma, Alabama, just before the civil-rights march to the state capital, said:

219

*Those of us who are Negroes don't have much. We have known the long night of poverty. Because of the system, we don't have much education and many of us don't know how to make our nouns and our verbs agree. But thank God we have our bodies, our feet and our souls (***New York Times** , March 22, 1965, P. 1).*

As will be seen, Dr. King's example is pertinent in a discussion of standard and non-standard English.

Standard English has been defined as "the particular type of English which is used in the conduct of the important affairs of our people. It is also the type of English used by the socially acceptable of most of our communities and, insofar as that is true, it has become a social or class dialect in the United States" (Fries, 1940, p. 13). Nonstandard English, by contrast, refers to dialects which deviate from the standard in pronunciation, vocabulary, or grammar. Social or class dialects are thus usually grouped into three main types: Standard English, common or popular English, and vulgar or illiterate English. However, the methods of distinguishing or describing the latter two types also vary in themselves.

Methods of Describing Nonstandard English

The differences between nonstandard dialects and Standard English have been described in three principal ways: in terms of frequency of errors, of contrastive analysis, or of transformational grammar. The oldest method, now discarded, is simply to count "errors" or deviations from Standard English and express the sum as a percentage of total use of a particular part of speech (e.g., pronouns), or as a percentage of total words used. Three studies of child language (Templin, 1957; D. R. Thomas, 1962; Loban, 1963) provide information on such deviations. All three find that verb usage is the most frequent source of errors: specifically, violation of subject-verb agreement; deviant use of the verb *to be,* "especially for Negro subjects whose parents have migrated from the rural South" (Loban, 1963, p. 52); use of present for past tense; and use of *got* for *have.* * Other frequent errors are wrong forms of the pronoun, double negatives, and the use of *ain't.*

A second method is to describe nonstandard forms of English in terms of a contrastive analysis, a technique adapted from research on foreign language teaching. This defines the points of maximum interference between the phonology, morphology or

*This last instance deals primarily, of course, with *got* used as a transitive verb in a present-tense construction for *have* in the sense of "to possess, own, hold," etc., not with *got* as a past participle used with some form of *have* as an auxiliary verb. The writer recognizes that any discussion of *got*-versus-*have* is soon diverted into historic arguments on English usage, divergent British- and American-English practices, literary precedents running from Shakespeare to Shaw, and so on and so on—all of which are beyond the scope of this review. Moreover, it is my impression that the use of *got* is increasing among speakers of Standard English; built into the definition of Standard English is the concept of the changing norm.

220

syntax of the speaker's native language and the "target language" which he is trying to learn. Thus a contrastive analysis would pinpoint, for example, the problems of learning English for a native speaker of Hindi. The same technique could be applied to the teaching of Standard English to speakers of nonstandard dialects.

However, this method entails making a separate analysis for each nonstandard dialect—regional, foreign-language background, or social class. Work is now in progress for Negro and Puerto Rican speech in New York City (Labov, 1965); for Negro and white middle- and lower-class speech in Chicago (Davis and McDavid, 1964; Pederson, 1964); for the speech of Negro students at Tougaloo College, in Mississippi (Beryl Bailey)*; and for the speech of school children in Washington, D. C. (Center for Applied Linguistics, 1965). These are particularly promising studies of language behavior and the psychological and sociological factors related to it. The Center for Applied Linguistics is also stimulating as well as coordinating activities in this field.

The third method uses the approach of "transformational grammar." Very briefly, each dialect is described in terms of the rules underlying it (descriptive, not prescriptive rules), and the rules for different dialects are then compared. A readable exposition of the basic theory is set forth by O. C. Thomas (1965). Rosenbaum (1964, p. 30) comments that the transformational approach "permits a precise and insightful characterization of the relatedness between grammatical systems" and notes some of the ways in which it seems to hold promise for dialect study. To date, the only example of this approach is Klima's (1964) analysis of the use of interrogative and personal pronouns in four "styles"—elegant or literary English, two intermediate styles, and vulgar English as found in the novels of Nelson Algren.

Nonstandard English as Deficient
There are both social and psychological criteria by which nonstandard speech might be considered deficient. The evidence on social grounds is the more conclusive. There is little question that speaking a nonstandard dialect is a social liability, creating a barrier to the speaker's acceptance in the dominant culture. As Jespersen ([1946], 1964, pp. 70-71) has observed:

> *[It is to the advantage of the children to speak Standard English] not only materially, because they can more easily obtain postions in society which now—whether one approves it or not in the abstract—are given by preference to people whose speech is free of dialect, but also because they thus escape being looked down on on account of their speech, and are therefore saved from many unpleasant humiliations. Apart from all this, merely by reason of their speaking they have a better chance of coming in contact with others and getting a fuller exchange of ideas.*

*Personal communication from Beryl Bailey, 1964.

221

Putnam and O'Hern (1955) provide recent evidence that features of nonstandard speech are indeed perceived and negatively evaluated by Standard speakers. Just which features elicit the most unfavorable reactions from teachers, employers, etc., is one of the points under study in several of the contrastive analyses referred to earlier.

Whether nonstandard English is, in addition, a cognitive liability to the speaker is much harder to determine. First, Standard English might be a more powerful means of communication. But all other things, such as vocabulary, being equal there is no evidence that this is so. "It is generally the very small points that are fixed upon as objectionable, often insignificant things that hardly affect the value of the language as a means of communication" (Jespersen [1946], 1964, p. 56n.).

Second, the child who speaks a nonstandard dialect may have difficulty understanding his teacher and his schoolbooks. The evidence on this point is unclear. Cherry (1964) reports a pioneer attempt to use the Cloze technique "to evaluate the extent to which information is successfully communicated from teachers to pupils of various social backgrounds and the degree of effective communication among children from different social backgrounds" (p. 23). Words were deleted according to a predetermined sequence from samples of teacher and peer-group speech, and the child's comprehension was measured by his ability to replace the exact word or suggest a substitute that made semantic or grammatical sense. Despite methodological problems in oral presentation of the speech samples and in the reliability of the scores, there were three major results: (1) social-class differences in understanding teacher speech were more apparent among fifth-graders than first-graders, but this effect was not maintained when intelligence was controlled statistically; (2) there were no social-class differences among fifth-graders in comprehending lower-class peer speech, but middle-class children were significantly superior to lower-class children in comprehending middle-class peer speech, and this effect was maintained even when intelligence was controlled; (3) Negro-white differences in these receptive language skills were virtually absent. In interpreting these results, we should note that while lower-class fifth-graders had more trouble understanding middle-class peer speech, the decreased comprehension across social-class lines was not reciprocal. The middle-class children understood lower-class peer speech as well as did the lower-class children. This finding suggests that dialect differences are confounded with other linguistic variables, such as vocabulary load and utterance complexity.

Here is a key problem. It is hard to determine whether nonstandard dialects are, "other things being equal," just as good a means of communication as Standard English. For such "other things" as the total repertoire of words and grammatical patterns are, in fact, rarely equal. Fries (1940, p. 287f.) reached the following conclusion:

222

Over and over again....it appeared that the differences between the language of the educated and that of those with little education did not lie primarily in the fact that the former used one set of forms and the latter an entirely different set. In fact, in most cases, the actual deviation of the language of the uneducated from Standard English grammar seemed much less than is usually assumed....The most striking difference between the language of the two groups lay in the fact that Vulgar English seems essentially poverty stricken. It uses less of the resources of the language, and a few forms are used very frequently.

Fries's language samples were taken from the correspondence of American citizens with agencies of the federal government, and it could be argued that the writers of Vulgar English were particularly impoverished in meeting the demands of that task. However, Loban obtained comparable results from an analysis of oral language of children in an informal interview. Thus it seems unlikely that the relative position of high and low social-class groups on a richness-impoverishment dimension can be explained wholly in terms of each given situation.

Loban (1963) used a two-level analytical scheme developed for his research. In the first level, utterances were classified into one of nine structural patterns—e.g., subject-verb-object *(George eats onions),* or subject-linking verb-predicate nominative *(Onions are roots).* In the second level, the component parts of these nine patterns were examined. From a comparison of the speech of a high group and a low group, selected on the basis of language ability but contrasting on socio-economic status as well, Loban (1963, p. 46) concludes:

*All these subjects...use the relatively few structural patterns of the English language. Thus structural pattern reveals less remarkable differences than does dexterity of substitution **within** the patterns. The important differences show up in the substitution of word groups for single words, in the choice and arrangement of movable syntactic elements, in the variety of nominals, and in strategies with prediction.*

In other words, there is evidence that not only do nonstandard dialects use different rules once a particular construction has been selected (the so-called "errors") but, more importantly, people speaking these dialects tend to use fewer of the optional constructions in their native language and to fill all the slots in their constructions from a smaller set of words.

Sometimes a single utterance can be categorized in several ways. Take the case of verb usage and, specifically, this example heard from a five-year-old in a day-care center: *My Mommy help me.* It can be considered as containing an error at the morphological level of linguistic structure in the failure to observe subject-verb agreement in the third person singular. Such errors are common in nonstandard dialects, as has been seen above. But the same utterance can be considered evidence of impoverishment, in failing to encode a particular meaning in a unique way by taking advantage of the rich possibilities afforded by English verb auxiliaries. The weakness of *My Mommy help me* as a communication lies in the use of an unmodified lexical verb instead of one of many alternatives, such as *My Mommy did help me* or *My Mommy would have helped me.* (However, see Stewart, 1965, for evidence that nonstandard dialects make different, not simply fewer distinctions.) Further, since the use of unmodified lexical verbs like *help* precedes developmentally the emergence of more complex constructions, the same utterance can be considered an example of retardation. I will suggest later that such ambiguity in interpretation poses a serious problem in the attempts to establish dialect-free scales of language development.

The question of whether nonstandard dialects are deficient or just different is sometimes glossed over by the statement "you can say anything in any language." It may be true that any language has the resources available, in words and grammatical constructions, to encode any meaning in some way (although Hymes, 1961, offers an opposing view). What is meant by such "resources" is the contents of a complete dictionary. In this sense English is as good as, but not better than, French or Russian. However, when we shift from the difference between English and French to that between the speech of a middle-class child and a lower-class child, we aren't looking at the total of what is available in language as a set of symbols but only at what is actually used by certain individuals at the moment of framing and utterance. This is one distinction between language and speech, and it's a sign of confusion between the two to inject the idea that "one language is as good as another" into the controversy over the verbal inadequacies of children in some subcultural groups. In general, then, it is probably true, to quote Loban (1963, p. 85), "Subjects who are rated as most proficient in language are also those who manifest the most sensitivity to the conventions of language. The subject who, despite unconventional usage, exhibits verbal linguistic skill is the exception." But while a correlation between deviation from Standard English and impoverishment exists, it can't be explained on any intrinsic grounds. The causes must therefore lie in historical and sociological factors—such as isolation, discrimination, or distance from foreign-language background—and the degree of correlation will therefore vary from one subcultural group to another.

STAGES ON A DEVELOPMENTAL CONTINUUM

The findings of those studies of language development that make subcultural com-

224

parisons have become rather widely known. Therefore, I will devote less space here to a summary of that work than to two related topics: an outline of the mediators by which such gross environmental variables as social class may affect language development, and an exploration of the problems which dialectal differences pose for the establishment of developmental scales.

Studies of Language Development

In addition to the work of Templin (1957), D. R. Thomas (1962), and Loban (1963) already touched on, the studies by Irwin (1948a, 1948b) and Lesser, Fifer, and Clark (1965) should be mentioned. Research by various members of the Institute for Developmental Studies (e.g., Deutsch, 1963; John, 1963; Keller, 1963; Cherry, 1965; Deutsch and B. Brown, 1964; John and Goldstein, 1964) is cited elsewhere in this review. Except for the work by Lesser, et al., these studies divide their subjects by social class only. They deal with three aspects of language development: phonology, vocabulary, and sentence structure (today more often termed grammar). The findings can be quickly summarized. On all the measures, in all the studies, children of upper socio-economic status, however defined, are more advanced than those of lower socio-economic status. Nevertheless, some points merit additional comment.

Phonology. Irwin's (1948a, 1948b) work is striking in that it pinpoints the early age at which environmental differences impinge on phonological development. Comparing the number of sound types and tokens produced by infants from birth to 30 months, he found that the infants from higher-status families had significantly higher scores for the last year of the period than did those from lower-status families. In other words, the developmental curves separated at 18 months of age.

Vocabulary. The study by Lesser, et al. (1965) is included here because language development was measured with a vocabulary test, but the import of this research extends beyond that to intellectual development as a whole. The purpose was to examine the pattern of four mental abilities (verbal, reasoning, numerical, and space) among first-grade children in New York City from middle and lower social-class groups and four ethnic backgrounds—Chinese, Jewish, Negro, and Puerto Rican. Care was taken in preparing the test materials and in obtaining examiners from the child's own subcultural group to insure that "observed differences . . . reside in the respondents and not in the test materials themselves" (p. 13). Verbal ability was measured by a 60-item vocabulary test, one-half pictures and one-half words, administered in the child's native language, or English, or a combination of both.

Probably the most important finding is that ethnic background and social class have different effects. Ethnic background affects the pattern of mental abilities, while social-class status affects the level of scores across the mental-ability scales. Specifi-

225

cally, on *verbal ability* Jewish children ranked first (being significantly better than all other ethnic groups), Negroes second and Chinese third (both being significantly better than the Puerto Ricans), and Puerto Ricans fourth, On *space,* by contrast, the rank order was Chinese, Jewish, Puerto Rican, and Negro children. But in all four ethnic groups, on all scales and subtests, the middle-class children were significantly superior to the lower-class children. As Lesser and his co-workers (1965, p. 83) observe:

> *Apparently, different mediators are associated with social-class and ethnic-group conditions....The importance of the mediators associated with ethnicity is to provide differential impacts upon the development of mental abilities, while the importance of mediators associated with social class is to provide pervasive (and not differential) effects upon the various mental abilities. This conclusion allows selection among several explanations offered to interpret cultural influences upon intellect activity.*

The same investigators also found that social-class position has more effect on mental abilities for the Negro children than for other groups, and that on each mental-ability test the scores of the middle-class children from the four ethnic groups resemble each other more than do the scores of the lower-class children. All the findings are discussed in the light of previous studies. For instance, the superior verbal ability of the Jewish children appears in many other studies. On the other hand, the verbal inferiority of the Puerto Rican children has been contradicted by other evidence (e.g., see Anastasi and de Jesus, 1953). Lesser, et al. discount the possible effects of bilingualism.

Although measures of vocabulary consistently yield social-class differences in the scores, significant questions relevant to the difference-deficiency issue remain unanswered. Tyler says that "lower-class children use a great many words, and a number of them use these words with a high degree of precision; but facility with words commonly used by the lower classes is not correlated with success in school" (Eells, Davis, Havighurst, Herrick, and Tyler, 1951, p. 40). Does Tyler mean that children from different status groups know and use different words? If so, how can this be reconciled with Templin's (1957) results on the Seashore-Eckerson Test in which the sampling of words from an unabridged dictionary results in a bias in the direction of common, easier words (Lorge and Chall, 1963)? Or how can it be reconciled with the results obtained by Lesser, et al. on the tests described above? Or does Tyler mean that lower-class children use "slang" from a different "dictionary"? How does this relate to Nida's (1958, p. 283) suggestion that "subcultures have proportionate-

226

ly more extensive vocabularies in the area of their distinctiveness"? Can one speak of the vocabulary of an idiolect or a dialect as structured? Is Tyler implying that, even for vocabularies similar in size, children from different groups may know fewer words in common than children from the same group? Conceivably, quantitative measures may conceal wide variation in overlap.

It has also been remarked that the language of the lower-class child is rich in something called "expressiveness." Cohn (1959, p. 439) speaks of "the great power of lower-class language to express emotions, a power ordinarily exploited with a clear conscience only by novelists." Is this just a romantic view in which the cliches of one subculture are perceived as creative expression by the listener from a different culture? Or does it mean that lower-class children use a small vocabulary in varied and novel ways, compensating by inventive encoding for what they lack in availability of single words? Or does it refer not to language as a code but to what it is used to say?

Sentence Structure. The most common measure of development in sentence structure, or grammar, is mean length of response (MLR), usually in words although it should be in morphemes. The validity of such a global and summary kind of measure rests on the widespread finding that it increases with age, and on more recent discoveries by Brown and Fraser (1964) and Bellugi (in press) of a close correspondence between mean length and the emergence of specific grammatical features in the speech of children under 4 years of age. We should not assume, however, that the correlation between length and complexity remains high at older ages. An average can include very short and very long. Thus, even if the MLR for two status groups were similar, the lower-status children might be speaking either in short sentences or connecting simple strings of words with "and" while the upper-status children utilize more complex syntactical patterns.

In a frequency distribution of the written sentences from Standard English and Vulgar English samples, Fries (1952, pp. 291-292) found that even though average lengths were similar, 23.46 and 23.16 respectively, the mode (most frequent length) in Standard English was 21 words, while Vulgar English had a mode of only 11 words but included more very long sentences. The same phenomenon can explain Templin's (1953, p. 79) finding in her study of children 3-8 years old, that while the MLR is the same or higher for upper-status children at all ages, the standard deviation of length-of-response scores is the same or higher for lower-status children above the age of 4 years.

Mediating Variables

In measuring aspects of the environment which correlate with the growth of intelligence and academic achievement, Wolf (1964) and Dave (1963) distinguish between

227

status and *process* variables. Examples of status variables are the income of the family and educational level of the parents; examples of process variables are the nature of intellectual aspirations for the child and the academic guidance provide in the home. In short, the contrast is between what parents are and what they do. In a sample of all the fifth-grade children in a Midwestern community, Wolf obtained a multiple correlation of +.76 between the process variables and intelligence; Dave obtained a multiple correlation of +.80 between the process variables and achievement. These contrast with usual correlations of +.40 to +.50 between intelligence of achievement and usual measures of socio-economic status. (See Bloom, 1964, pp. 24 and 79, for summaries of these two studies.)

In this sense, the widespread finding of a significant positive correlation between social class (a cluster of status characteristics) and the rate of language development begs the important question of what mediating process variables may be operating. I have therefore adapted the categories used by Gray and Klaus (1964) and will outline the features of the environment that may be critical under three headings: context, or the non-verbal setting in which the language occurs; stimulation; and responses to the child's speech. Some of these may have a "differential" impact on language development, while others may have a more "pervasive" impact on cognitive development in general (Lesser, et al., 1965). Unfortunately, we are not yet able to separate these two sets of variables.

Context. Five features of the non-verbal context may be important: the affective quality, whether the child talks to adults or other children, how varied the contexts are, the prevailing signal-to-noise ratio, and conversation versus television. These will be discussed in order.

AFFECTIVE QUALITY—There is widespread emphasis on the key role in language development of the mother-child relationship. It is difficult to test the specific influence of that relationship, however, because warm feeling and lots of talk tend to occur together. This confounding is present when home care is contrasted with institutional care (e.g., Provence and Lipton, 1962). It is also present when the home environments of high and low scores on reading readiness tests are compared (Milner, 1951).

ADULTS VERSUS CHILDREN—Children talk with adults and other children, and the relative amounts of such talk vary greatly among subcultural groups. Which has the greater influence on language development is still an unresolved question. On one side of the issue are those linguists who argue that children speak more like their peers than like their parents. This is the view of Jespersen (1922) and Hockett (1950). And more recently, Stewart (1964, p. 14n.) has observed:

228

It is easy to find cases involving second- or third-generation Washington [D.C.] Negro families in which the parents are speakers of a quite standard variety of English, but where the children's speech is much closer to that of the newer immigrants [from the South] .... This phenomenon, incidentally, seems to support the theory that children learn more language behavior from members of their own peer group than from their parents, and suggests that educator concern over the quality of "language in the home" may be misplaced.

On the other side are those psychologists who offer convincing evidence that the speech of children without siblings, who presumably have more opportunity for conversation with parents, is generally superior. Examples can be found in the studies of Koch (1954), Nisbet (1961), and most recently in Vera John's finding[4] of a birth-order effect on language development within a sample of lower-class Negro children.

No doubt, studies of conversation among children could help resolve this issue, but such studies are rare. One example is Smith's (1935) analysis of the mean length of utterance of 220 children, from 18 to 70 months in age, in two situations—at play with other children and at home with adults. The children used longer sentences in conversation with adults, probably because they answered fewer questions, gave fewer imperatives, and generally engaged in more connected discourse with less active play and fewer interruptions.

Only a possible direction for resolution of these seemingly conflicting claims can be suggested. Extrapolating far beyond the present evidence, and using a computer analogy, I wonder if the opportunity to talk with adults may largely determine the complexity of the "programs" for constructing and understanding utterances which a child can handle, while conversation with peers has more effect on specific details of those "programs" such as features of phonology and morphology.

CONTEXTUAL VARIETY—A child's language develops within contexts of greater or less variety. Deutsch and Brown (1964) suggest that variety in family activities increases verbal interaction. Ausubel (1964) writes of the desirability of a wide range of objects which can serve as referents for speech. John and Goldstein (1964) report that a group of lower-class Negro four-year-olds had trouble on the Peabody Picture Vocabulary Test with such action words as *digging* and *tying.* They suggest that a word like *digging* differs from one like *Coca Cola* in the stability of the word-referent relationship: "Gerunds such as *tying* were failed, not because the children were deficient in experience with the referent, but rather because they had difficulty in fitting the label to the varying forms of action observed and experienced" (p. 269).

*Personal communication from Vera P. John, 1965.

229

They argue that the process of generalization and discrimination involved in learning the meanings of more abstract words does not come about simply through "receptive exposure" to many examples but through "active participation with a more verbally mature individual (p. 273). The benefits of variety in non-verbal experience may depend on the availability of help in encoding that experience in words.

Varied surroundings can stimulate and reinforce different functions of language. Bernstein (1962a, p. 32) contrasts "restricted" and "elaborated" codes, and asserts that working-class speech is characterized by a restricted code which "is played out against a background of communal, self-consciously held interests which remove the need to verbalize subjective intent and make it explicit." It may be that during the period of language learning those children who are confronted with a narrow range of close personal contacts learn only the economical mode of communication that suffices within that small circle. A related hypothesis is suggested in Frake's (1961) study of folk taxonomies: ". . . the greater the number of distinct social contexts in which information about a particular phenomenon [e.g., skin disease] must be communicated, the greater the number of different levels of contrast into which that phenomenon is categorized" (p. 121).

SIGNAL-TO-NOISE RATIO—Deutsch (1963) discusses the relevance to language learning of the overall signal-to-noise ratio prevailing in the daily environment. One characteristic of slum living which may contribute to language retardation is the high noise level, not only in the literal sense of noise but in the minimum of non-instructional conversation directed toward the child. This situation is ideal for inducing habitual inattention. The child may learn to "tune out" both meaningless noise and the occasional meaningful stimuli, with the result of an absolute decrease in effective stimulation.

CONVERSATION VERSUS TELEVISION—Lastly, what about television? Children from lower-status groups watch as much TV as high-status groups, if not more (Keller, 1963; Wortis, et al., 1963). Why isn't this extra language stimulation more beneficial? Is the critical difference passive listening to a monologue versus active participation in a dialogue? If so, then what of the supposed benefit of listening to stories? Is attention to language reduced when it is embedded in the context of constantly changing visual stimuli. There is evidence that TV has some positive effect on vocabulary (Schramm, Lyle, and Parker, 1961), but research is needed on what children attend to while watching TV and how they process the language heard in this context.

Stimulation. Language stimulation can vary both in quality and in quantity. The quality of the stimulus in turn can vary along lines of conformity to Standard English, variety, and sequence.

230

CONFORMITY TO STANDARD ENGLISH—Ervin (1964, p. 163) states: "Children's grammar converges on the norm for the community in which they live." If that norm is not Standard English some of the effects may resemble retarded speech, as we have seen, and may be unfortunate from other standpoints. But when we study the rate of language development as such, a child's progress should be judged in terms of his approach toward the norm for his particular language community. Whether the nature of that norm can itself affect development is an open empirical question.

In the studies cited earlier, Wolf (1964) and Dave (1963) found that a rating of opportunities provided in the home for enlarging vocabulary and using a variety of sentence patterns correlated highly with both intelligence and achievement, while a judgment by the interviewer of the quality of language usage of the mother did not. Dave (1963, p. 114) was thus led to observe, "This may imply that the quality of language usage of the parents, and the extent of verbal interaction among family members, are quite independent characteristics."

LINGUISTIC VARIETY—Variety in the non-verbal setting in which language occurs has already been discussed; here we are dealing with the variety in the words and grammatical patterns which the child hears. Razran (1961, p. 126) reports a Soviet experiment on the role of both kinds of variety in the development of lexical meanings. A group of nine children, 19 months old, were given 20 simultaneous exposures to a book and a sentence about a book. Three children received a single book and a single sentence; three received a single book and 20 different sentences; and three received 20 different books and a single sentence. Learning, as measured by the child's ability to select a book from a group of objects, was greatest for the varied language group, next best for the varied referent group, and practically nonexistent for the first group.

Another approach uses the "type-token" ratio. Briefly, the number of tokens—e.g., the total number of instances of plural nouns that a child hears—is an indication of the sheer quantity of language stimulation. The number of types—e.g., the number of different nouns which the child hears pluralized—is a measure of variety. Miller and Ervin (1964) have asked whether greater variety, as measured by the type-token ratio, plays a role in the development of grammatical meanings, specifically in the child's developing use of the plural inflection. Starting from non-contrast (e.g., using *boy* for both singular and plural), the child occasionally uses contrasted forms, then correctly contrasts all familiar words, and finally generalizes to irregular nouns *(foots)* and, in an experimental situation, to nonsense words *(biks)*. Contrast with familiar forms always precedes generalization to nonsense forms, but the time lapse between the two stages varies. Miller and Ervin (1964, p. 33) therefore point out, "We do not know whether it is the variety of types or the frequency of tokens show-

231

ing contrast which is crucial in determining the length of time before generalization occurs." The question at issue is whether increased variety, often termed "richness", adds anything to increased quantity along. It is at least a hypothesis to be explored that variety does aid the child, in and of itself; and, conversely, that language that is impoverished is harder to learn, not easier.

Three arguments can be suggested for this hypothesis. First, if as Cofer has commented, "learning of inflectional and syntactical skills is akin to concept formation" (Cofer and Musgrave, 1963, p. 198), then variation in irrelevant features (e.g., particular count nouns) may aid learning of the concept of inflectional marking of plurality. Second, increased variety of language stimulation may enhance attentional processes in the child (Fiske and Maddi, 1961). Third and purely theoretical, if the process of first language acquisition is akin to scientific theory construction in which hypotheses are tested against available data, as the transformational grammarians argue, then a meager set of data could be a hindrance. Fodor (MS) makes this argument explicit:

> *If parents do simplify the syntax of their speech when they address children they may make it* **harder** *for the child to learn the correct syntactic analysis of his language. Rules that hold for selected sets of simple sentences may have to be abandoned in the light of examples of sentences of more complicated types.*

In contrast to variety are well-learned routines. These may include sentences such as *I don't know;* they may also include bits of nursery rhymes and songs and, perhaps most important of all, phrases from books read to the child many times. It has been a long time since Carroll (1939, p. 222) suggested, "An interesting investigation could be set upon the hypothesis that learning of rote material is an important factor in speech development." That investigation still remains to be done.

SEQUENCE—In analyzing the detrimental effects of the slum environment, Deutsch (1963, p. 168) suggests that "in addition to the restriction in variety . . . it might be postulated that the segments made available to these children tend to have poorer and less systematic ordering of stimulation sequences, and would thereby be less useful to the growth and motivation of cognitive potential." Variety can be described in absolute terms, e.g., by the type-token ratio, but sequence cannot. For while an optimal sequence may incorporate some absolute dimension of complexity, there remains as a relative component the "match" between the stimuli the child encounters in his environment and the cognitive structures which determines his readiness to respond to them (Hunt, 1961).

This match can be improved in two ways. The adult might provide a rich and varied

232

supply of stimuli and let the child find what he needs. This was the principle involved in the self-selection feeding practices of some years ago; it is also the principle recommended by the Montessori method (Hunt, 1964). Applied to language development, this principle would predict that if a child has the chance to hear a sufficiently varied and large sample of well-formed sentences, he will take from it what he needs for the acquisition of his own language system. Alternatively, the adult might preselect certain stimuli for the child. Such preselection could be either purposeful or fortuitous. For first language learning it would have to be fortuitous, since no one knows enough about what the child is doing to plan his curriculum.

QUANTITY—Finally, the language stimulation available to a child can and does vary in quantity. It seems intuitively obvious that differences in quantity should affect language development, although frequency of exposure may matter only up to some threshold, beyond which no additional benefits may accrue. But severe problems face any attempt to separate the effects of frequency of stimulation from the effects of responses to the child's speech.

Response to the Child's Speech. It is still an open question whether some category of response, such as reinforcement or feedback, is necessary or at least very helpful to language development, or whether rich stimulation or exposure is sufficient. For the most part, the theoretical controversy is carried on between experimental psychologists who attempt to substantiate their theories of human learning by fitting them to the child's strikingly successful acquisition of language (e.g., Staats and Staats, 1963), and linguists and their cognitive psychology associates who derive implications for the process of acquisition from the transformational model of language structure (e.g., Fodor, MS.; Lenneberg, 1964; Katz, in press; McNeill, in press). A review of the arguments is outside the scope of this paper. I will only suggest one way in which reinforcement may apply, then review several empirical studies.

Whether reinforcement applies to any of the actual content of the language learning process—to any aspect of phonology, vocabulary, or grammar—it may apply to the child's interest in, valuing of, and motivation toward language. It may affect his attentiveness, regardless of what is happening while he is attending. It seems to me that some global effect such as this, ill-defined as it is, is necessary to explain the role of the Jewish tradition in consistently producing an impact in the direction of superiority in verbal development. (*See* Lee, 1960, for a description of this subculture.) At the opposite extreme is the isolated and hopeless situation of many mothers on Aid to Dependent Children, where "the reduction of absolute power undercuts the motivation for protracted verbal exploration of action possibilities" (Strodtbeck, 1965, p. 108).

233

Studies of infant vocal behavior have been widely cited in support of reinforcement theories of language learning. Detailed comparisons have been made of caretaking activities of parents in homes and of adults in institutions (Rheingold, 1960, 1961; Provence and Lipton, 1962). There is notably more talking to the infants at home—five to nine times as much, according to Rheingold's time-sampling data. There is likewise more vocalizing by the infants themselves. Experimental studies with infants—such as those of Rheingold, Gewirtz, and Ross (1959) and Weissberg's (1963) carefully controlled follow-up study—offer convincing evidence that reinforcement rather than stimulation is operating. But it is questionable whether any results should be generalized across the discontinuity which separates pre-linguistic babbling from true verbal behavior.

Irwin's (1960) experimental study with slightly older children has been widely cited in support of the value of added stimulation. He induced working-class mothers to read to their children for 20 minutes a day from the time the children were 12 months until they were 30 months old. The result was a significant increase in production of speech sounds, both in tokens and in types. Irwin interpreted this result as a response to the systematic increase in the "speech sound stimulation" (1960, p. 189). While reading could indeed have provided an increased quantity of stimulation alone, it is possible and even likely that in the course of reading the mothers also responded to the vocalizations of the child which the reading may have prompted. Moreover, we do not know how this induced attention to the behavior of her child may have affected the mother's response to him during all the non-reading parts of the day. Once a child has started to speak, it is not feasible to withhold response even for experimental purposes. Consequently, the effects of exposing a child to language and of responding to his language become confounded.

It is commonly assumed (e.g., Ausubel, 1964; Bloom, Davis, and Hess, 1965) that where language has developed well something termed "corrective feedback" has been in ample supply. For this to exist, the child must make errors and the adults must recognize those errors. Parents to seem to correct errors in naming, e.g., of *cat* for *dog,* and feedback may be very important for the learning of vocabulary. But errors of a non-referential nature seem to be largely ignored.

Miller and Ervin (1964, p. 26) give this summary of errors in the speech of two-year-old and three-year-old children:

> *Most of the mistakes or deviations from the model can be classified as omissions (***I'll turn water off*** for ***I'll turn the water off***), overgeneralization of morphophonemic combinations (***foots** for **feet,** a owl *for* **an owl, breaked** *for* **broke***), the incorrect use of a function word with a subclass of a lexical class (using* **a** *with mass nouns and*

234

*proper nouns), or doubly marked forms (adding the possessive suffix to possessive pronoun, **mine's**).*

While no frequency counts are yet available, it is safe to say that except for the category of omissions the proportion of errors in the young child's speech is remarkably small. Furthermore, it is my impression that adults without special training do not "hear" such errors even when they are made. Persons trained to be attentive often cannot catch them except under special conditions, such as repeating tape recordings at half-speed. Ordinarily, we hear what we expect to hear—normal English speech. Not surprisingly, R. Brown and his colleagues (conference discussion in Cofer and Musgrave, 1963, p. 203) found "little correction of children's speech by their parents." Furthermore, there is no evidence that the non-verbal responses of adults match in any way the degree of the child's approximation to the adult model.

Sentences containing errors of omission are one exception to the generalization that errors of a non-referential nature are largely ignored. Such sentences constitute the typical "telegraphic speech" of the young child (Brown and Bellugi, 1964; Brown and Fraser, 1964), and a gradual filling in of the omitted morphemes is the most prominent change characterizing the child's acquisition of grammar. From transcriptions of the speech of two children with their respective graduate student parents, Brown and his colleagues discovered that to the child's telegraphic utterance, e.g., *Mommy lunch,* the parent often responds with the nearest complete sentence appropriate to the particular situation, e.g., *Mommy is having her lunch.* To the content words of nouns, verbs or adjectives in the child's speech, the parent adds mainly the functors: auxiliaries, prepositions, articles, pronouns, and inflections.

Expansions seem to constitute perfect examples of feedback. In fact, they constitute the one category of adult responses where the nature of the assistance to the child can be specified. Again, to quote Brown and Bellugi (1964, p. 143):

> *By adding something to the words the child has just produced one confirms his response insofar as it is appropriate. In addition, one takes him somewhat beyond that response but not greatly beyond it. One encodes additional meanings at a moment when he is most likely to be attending to the cues that can teach that meaning.*

In discussing the optimal sequencing of stimuli, I suggested that if it does occur in the language learning process it must occur fortuitously. Expansions, by their very nature, provide such sequencing. No one has suggested that parents expand with any conscious tutorial intention. It seems simply to be one spontaneous way of keeping the conversation with a young child going.

Discovery of the category of expansions made possible a new attempt to separate the effects of exposure and contingent response. At first it seemed this might be possible even in natural observations, and that it would therefore be informative to compare the emergence in the child of grammatical construction heard in the adult's non-expanding speech with those appearing in the adult's expansion of the child's telegraphic utterances. Brown* found that for his two subjects the order of emergence of some 40 different grammatical constructions can be well predicted (rank order correlation near .80) by the frequency with which the same constructions are used by the mothers. But the constructions more often used in the parents' non-expanding speech were also the ones more often expanded. The confounding of the two variables was still present.

Part of the present writer's own research (Cazden, 1965) was an experiment designed to separate adult expansions from adult modeling of well-formed sentences. The subjects were 12 Negro children, 28-38 months old, attending an urban day-care center. One group (expansion) received 40 minutes a day of intensive and deliberate expansions; another group (modeling) received 30 minutes a day of exposure to an equal number of well-formed sentences which deliberately were not expansions. One of two tutors, trained for the research, talked with each child in these two groups in an individual play session every school day for three months. A third group (control) received no special treatment. Six measures of language development were used, one being a structured sentence imitation test. The other five were measures of spontaneous speech—mean length of utterance, complexity measures of noun and verb phrases, percentage of copulas supplied, and percentage of sentences which included both subject and predicate.

Contrary to predictions, the children who received the non-expanding language stimulation gained the most. One possible explanation is that as the concentration of expansions goes up, in this case far above that occurring in natural conversation, the richness of the verbal stimulation goes down. By definition, expansions are contingent on the child's speech, in content as well as in timing. To the extent that they are pure expansions, just filling in the child's telegraphic utterance to make it a complete one, they will have less variety of vocabulary and grammatical patterns than the adult's non-expanding speech normally contains.

In summary, a tentative resolution of the stimulation-reinforcement controversy can be suggested. Reinforcement, in the classical sense, probably operates to increase vocalizations at the babbling stage of infancy. But once true language begins to develop there is no clear evidence that any specific kind of adult response, verbal or nonverbal, aids the child's progress. Natural observations and the few existing manipula-

*R. Brown, unpublished memorandum, 1964.

236

tive studies are consistent with the hypothesis that is is the amount and richness of language stimulation available in the context of face-to-face interaction which is most important. Differential access to such stimulation by children from different subcultural groups can be explained by differences in the conditions of their lives, as outlined above under "Context."

Developmental Scales

There is general hope that current research on the acquisition of language [*] will eventually make possible developmental scales which will be more valid measures than mean sentence length (Carroll, 1961). Little consideration has thus far been given to problems which dialect differences pose in establishing such scales. Ervin and Miller (1963, p. 126) recognize the problem: "Adult usage differs in the various subcultures of any community. A good developmental measure for general use should include only those features common to all adult speech in the presence of children." The author faced this problem in the research reported above (Cazden, 1965). I needed to measure the grammatical development of working-class Negro children, but had to devise scales from data on the language of two children from graduate-student families. Because that experience suggests that the problems posed by dialect differences will not be easily solved, it will be recounted in some detail.

The grammatical structure of child speech can be scaled along at least three dimensions—developmental sequence, structural complexity, and conformity to Standard English, Complexity undoubtedly influences the sequence of emergence but is not in any one-to-one correspondence with it.

Two examples may clarify this point. Brown and Bellugi (1964) have studied the development of the noun phrase. They found that in the first stage any modifier was used with any noun. When the differentiation process began, articles were separated out of the class of modifiers. The children said *A blue flower* but not *Blue a flower.* Only later did they use two modifiers other than articles before a noun (*My blue flower).* Therefore, on a weighted index, *Flower, Nice flower, A blue flower,* and *My blue flower* may be scored from 1 to 4, respectively. There is no objective difference in complexity which dictates this separation of articles from other modifiers. *A blue flower* and *My blue flower* each contain three units in a common pattern. Yet the developmental sequence is clear.

Verb forms present a contrasting case. The sequence of *I drop, I dropping,* and *I'm dropping* represents both increasing complexity and sequence of emergence, and the forms may be accordingly scored 1, 2 and 3, respectively. But what of the past tense *dropped?* On the basis of complexity it should be grouped with *dropping,* as a verb

[*]See Bellugi and Brown (1964) for a report on current research in this area.

237

plus one additional element, but its period of emergence is definitely later. If we knew exactly when it appeared in relation to other forms, it could be scored accordingly. Since we don't know, the decision has to be made on grounds of complexity: *dropped* thus receives 2 points.

Conformity to Standard English is another possible criterion—one I deliberately did not apply. Thus *a trees* and *a coffee* were each given full credit on the noun-phrase index. But conformity did intrude. Sometimes deviations from Standard English left the meaning ambiguous. If the child said *Her go upstairs,* clearly *her* was being used in the subject position. But if the child said *He wet him bed,* it was not equally clear whether *him* was being used as a possessive pronoun. Sometimes non-standard forms raised problems in scoring even when the meaning was clear. The children in my sample often used an auxiliary with an unmodified verb, such as *He's go* or *I'm put.* These patterns hadn't been anticipated, since they had not appeared in Brown and Bellugi's data. Strictly on a criterion of complexity, *I'm put* would be counted as two verb elements, along with the more familiar *He going* or *I putting.* Dialect differences also made it impossible to measure the use of negation. Basis for such an analysis had been provided by Bellugi's (in press) study of the sequence of emergence of particular negative forms, but many of the utterances of the subjects in my study could not be placed on Bellugi's scale. First, the frequent use of *got* and *ain't got* produced a construction where the negation appeared after the verb, as in *I got no crayons.* Second, multiple negatives (*I not kiss no people*) were more frequent and seemed to appear at earlier stages than in Bellugi's data. In the end, I gave up the attempt to do this analysis.

I have already suggested that, ideally, a child's language development should be evaluated in terms of his progress toward the norms for his particular speech community. My reliance on complexity more than on developmental sequence as a criterion for evaluation helped make possible the transfer from one dialect to another. A scale which accepts alternate forms of the complexity on which it is based can be applied cross-culturally more appropriately than one based on sequence of emergence. Though the latter is otherwise the superior criterion, it is more likely to penalize departures from a preconceived norm. This issue of "dialect-fair" scales of language development may become as significant in the future as that of "culture-fair" tests of intelligence has been in the past.

DIFFERENT MODES OF COMMUNICATION

To view the language of subcultural groups as different modes of communication, it is necessary to go beyond the structured system of symbols and the rate at which parts of that system are learned to the functions the language serves in actual verbal behavior. This requirement is one version of the contrast between language and

238

speech, which is at once so important and subject to many interpretations.

The two main categories of language functions are, as Carroll (1964, p. 4) has stated them, "(1) as a system of responses by which individuals communicate with each other inter-individual communication); and (2) as a system of responses that facilitates thinking and action for the individual (intra-individual communication)." In this paper I use the term "mode of communication" to refer to both subsystems of language functioning, which are somehow intimately related. I say "somehow related" because we do not know how overt speech becomes internalized into covert thought, particularly in the case of the growing child (John, 1964). Of great importance for the study of subcultural differences in child language, we don't know how variation in the use of language for inter-individual communication affects its use as an intra-individual cognitive tool. For reasons that have to do with the intellectual history of the behavioral sciences, the two functions of language have been studied in separation. One reason for subsuming my discussion under one term, "different modes of communication," is to emphasize the importance of their relationship.

Inter-individual Communication
A statement by Hymes (1961, p. 57) is immediately pertinent here:

> *In a society, speech as an activity is not a simple function of the structure and meanings of the language or language involved. Nor is speech activity random. Like the languages, it is patterned, governed by rules; and this patterning also must be learned by linguistically normal participants in the society. Moreover, the patterning of speech activity is not the same from society to society, or from group to group within societies such as our own.*

How speech activity is patterned is the focus of a new inter-disciplinary study, the ethnography of communication. More recent publications by Hymes offer both an overview of the field (Hymes, 1964b) and a provocative discussion of the inadequacies of the description given by the transformational linguists of the capabilities of language users (Hymes, 1964a). Overlapping with an ethnography of communication, but not confined to naturalistic observations, is another inter-disciplinary field, socio-linguistics (see Ervin-Tripp, 1964). Both deal with the questions of who says what to whom, how, and in what situations.

Studies of subcultural differences in inter-individual communication have been carried out by Bossard (1954), Schatzman and Strauss (1955), Bernstein (1959, 1960,

---

*In this regard, see Hymes (1963) for the viewpoint of those in the field of linguistics, and Cronbach (1957) for those in psychology.

239

1961, 1962a, 1962b), Loban (1963), and Lawton (1964). (The work of Hess and his colleagues will be considered in the next section.) These studies are quite different, and the story of their work will not be a connected one. But each raises interesting issues for further exploration.

Bossard (1954) was a pioneer in what used to be called "the sociology of language." He analyzed the mealtime conversations of 35 families and found differences in amount of talk per unit of time, in range of vocabulary, in the use of imagery, in the extent to which children were interrupted, and in whether the talk was child- or adult-centered—with social class "the most important line of cleavage in our language records" (pp. 190-191). Studies by Milner (1951) and Keller (1963), previously cited, found that lower-class children are more apt to eat alone or with siblings, and less apt to eat with adults, than middle-class children. What Bossard's work indicates is that children not only participate in different speech situations, but that even where the situation is a common one, family mealtime conversations, the patterns of speech activity vary along social-class lines.

The study by Schatzman and Strauss (1955) is included here even though the subjects were adults, because it raised important questions about inter-group versus intra-group communication. Twenty subjects, 10 upper-status and 10 lower-status individuals selected from the extremes of income and education, were interviewed in a small Arkansas town after a tornado. The authors summarize the difference in the resulting narratives of members of the two groups:

> *The difference is a considerable disparity in (a) the number and kinds of perspectives utilized in communication; (b) the ability to take the listener's role; (c) the handling of classification; and (d) the framework and stylistic devices which order and implement the communication (p. 329).*

In analyzing these differences, Schatzman and Strauss express two different ideas. On the one hand, they say that the upper-status subject is better able to make his meaning explicit because he has been more often in situations where this is necessary, whereas the lower-status subject is accustomed to talking about his experiences only with people with whom he shares a great deal of previous experience and symbolism. By this view, the experience of the upper-status speaker has taught him how to encode more information. Yet, on the other hand, the authors also seem to assert that the important variable is not how much information the speaker has encoded, but the extent to which communication of it from speaker to listener may be impeded by "differential rules for the ordering of speech and thought" (p. 329). These rules, describing the structure of speech, are independent of those describing the structure of language, referred to earlier in the discussion of dialects. Subcultural dif-

240

ferences in both kinds of rules may bave been tapped in Cherry's (1965) study of communication in the classroom.

Bernstein's work in Great Britain is cited in virtually every discussion of the influence of subcultural differences—in this case, social class—on language and cognition. It is cited, but rarely is it subjected to the analysis it deserves. He set out "to find a way of analyzing some of the interrelationships between social structure, language use, and subsequent behavior" (Bernstein, 1962a, p. 31). He postulated the existence of two codes, restricted and elaborated. These are defined in terms "of the probability of predicting which structural elements will be selected for the organization of meaning"—highly predictable in the first case, much less so in the second. Further, the first is considered to facilitate "verbal elaboration of intent," the second to limit "verbal explication of intent" (Bernstein, 1962b, p. 233).

So far, he has reported one experiment testing three hypotheses related to these codes: that they can be distinguished, that their use is associated with social class, and that their use is independent of measured intelligence. For a non-linguistic measure of the verbal planning functions associated with speech, he drew on Goldman-Eisler's (1958) research on the nature of hesitation phenomena. Goldman-Eisler differentiates between two kinds of gaps in the continuity of speech-production: breathing, related to the motor dimension; and hesitations or pauses, related to the symbolic dimension. Measuring the frequency and duration of pauses, she found that they anticipated a sudden increase in information as measured by transitional probabilities:

> *Fluent speech was shown to consist of habitual combinations of words such as were shared by the language community and such as had become more or less automatic. Where a sequence ceased to be a matter of common conditioning or learning, where a speaker's choice was highly individual and unexpected, on the other hand, speech was hesitant (1958, p. 67).*

Using Goldman—Eisler's procedures, Bernstein analyzed the verbal behavior of a group of 16-year-old boys. From 61 lower-status messenger boys and 45 (British) "public school" boys he selected five subgroups of 4 or 5 boys each, arranged so that their speech patterns could be compared while holding social class or verbal and non-verbal intelligence constant. An unstructured discussion of capital punishment was held with each subgroup, with only one special provision: "It was thought the working-class group would find the test situation threatening and that this would interfere with the speech and consequently all working-class groups had two practice sessions (one a week) before the test discussion" (1962a, p. 37). Analysis of the recorded group discussions confirmed all three of his hypotheses in regard to the "codes."

241

Bernstein (1962b) acknowledges the limitations of a small sample and a discussion topic which may not have had the same significance for the two social-class groups. But he has not raised the question of the possible effect of the two practice sessions on the fluency of the working-class speech. Fluency, as measured by the hesitation phenomena, was taken as the operational definition of predictability, and that in turn was the defining attribute of the restricted code. Any influence of the practice sessions would have been in the direction of greater fluency. But sound research procedures requires that bias, if unavoidable, should work against one's hypothesis, not for it. The experiment has since been replicated by Lawton (1964)—but the analysis of the hesitation phenomena is not yet available and he does not indicate whether he repeated the practice sessions for the working-class group.

Of greater importance is that Bernstein's theory reaches beyond verbal behavior to cognitive functioning in general. He believes that differences in the habitual modes of speech arise out of "a different way of organizing and responding to experience" (1959, p. 312), and that they accordingly "create and reinforce in the user different dimensions of significance" (1960, p. 276). In other words, speech is seen as both effect and cause: "In some way the form of the social relationship acts selectively on the speech possibilities of the individual, and again in some way these possibilities constrain behavior" (1962a, p. 31). Further, be believes that the nature of the restricted code has far-reaching implications for the behavior of its speakers: a low level of conceptualization, a disinterest in process, a preference for inclusive social relationships and group solidarity, and socially induced conservatism and acceptance of authority (1961, pp. 300-303).

With these last assertions we are right in the middle of the well-argued controversy over the Whorf hypothesis that language conditions our perceptions of and responses to the environment. Bernstein's version of that hypothesis may be a particularly interesting one. Whorf was interested in the influence of the structure of language, whereas Bernstein is interested in the influence of the structure of speech activity. Hymes (1964b, p. 20) suggests that the latter is the more fundamental question: "What chance the language has to make an impress upon individuals and behavior will depend upon the degree and pattern of its admission into communicative events." But Bernstein's formulation is a hypothesis, nonetheless.

It is not possible to review here the arguments for and against the strong ("language determines") and the weak ("language predisposes") versions of the Whorf hypothesis. It is sufficient to report the widespread agreement that evidence of differences in language, no matter how extreme, cannot be used both to suggest and to prove differences in feeling, thought, or other non-verbal behavior. The claimed effects of language or speech differences on ways of perceiving or responding must be demonstrated and not merely assumed, and their proof must involve independent measures

242

of linguistic and non-linguistic behavior (Carroll, 1958). Since all of Bernstein's data deal with speech, there is so far no supporting evidence for the broader implications of the differences he reports.

Bernstein is dealing with a topic of great interest today, and he has engaged in theory construction in a field where theory is sorely needed. The danger is that those reading the widespread references to his work may take his assertions as proven fact, rather than as hypotheses to be tested. The result could be a stereotype of working-class children and adults as unfortunate as the now-discredited stereotype of limited genetic potential. Schorr (1964, p. 911) retells a poignant admission by sociologists that, "according to all that they knew of it, the [civil rights] sit-in movement should never have happened." At least sociologists were in no position to make their erroneous prediction come true. But educators are among the readers of the frequent references to Bernstein's work, and through them the danger of a self-fulfilling prophecy is a real one.

One other point merits examination before leaving Bernstein's work. Earlier, I mentioned that he found a social-class difference in the use of what he calls "egocentric" and "sociocentric" sequences. The former refers to the sequence *I think,* which is more used by middle-class speakers. The latter refers to terminal sequences such as *isn't it, you know, ain't it, wouldn't he*—"sympathy circularity sequences" (1962b, p. 223)—used more by lower-class speakers. Bernstein considers both egocentric and sociocentric sequences to be ways of dealing with uncertainty, with quite different results. For example, he has stated (1962b, p. 237):

> *Inasmuch as the S.C. [Sociocentric] sequences...invite implicit affirmation of the previous sequence, then they tend to close communication in a particular area rather than to facilitate its development and elaboration...The "I think" sequence, on the other hand, allows the listener far more degrees of freedom and may be regarded as an invitation...to develop the communication on his own terms.*

His interpretation of the function of these two modes of communication contrasts with one of Loban's findings. Loban (1963, pp. 53-54) has reported:

> *Those subjects who proved to have the greatest power over language by every measure that could be applied...were* **the subjects who most frequently used language to express tentativeness.**...*These most capable speakers often use such expressions as the following:*
>
> *It might be a gopher, but I'm not sure.*

243

That, I think, is in Africa.
I'm not exactly sure where that is.

The child with less power over language appears to be less flexible in his thinking, is not often capable of seeing more than one alternative, and apparently summons up all his linguistic resources merely to make a flat dogmatic statement.

Remembering that his high language group was also higher in socio-economic status, we see that Loban, in a study of elementary school children in California, and Bernstein, in a study of adolescents in England, both found that higher-status subjects say *I think* more than lower-status subjects do. What is striking is the ease with which two interpretations are placed on the common finding. Bernstein contrasts *I think* with *ain't it,* and finds an egocentric-sociocentric contrast. Loban groups *I think* with *I'm not exactly sure* as examples of cognitive flexibility.

Intra-individual Communication
The use of language as a cognitive tool for intra-individual communication places its own demands on some special set of inner resources. Jensen (in press) sees it as depending on the existence within the individual of a hierarchical verbal network "which environmental stimuli, both verbal and non-verbal, enter [into] and ramify. . . . A great deal of what we think of as intelligence, or as verbal ability, or learning ability, can be thought of in terms of the extensiveness and complexity of this verbal network and of the strength of the interconnections between its elements." There are at least two variables here: the number of elements and the quality (which could be further subdivided at least into complexity and strength) of their connections. In discussing measures of vocabulary, I reported studies which found subcultural differences in the repertoire of words or grammatical patterns available or used. A repertoire can be defined by a list and is synonymous with the number of elements in the network. But network has a second attribute which repertoire does not—the structure or relations of its parts. We know little about subcultural differences in the use of this verbal network in purely mediational, covert ways, because few experimental psychologists have been interested in individual differences, much less group differences, among their subjects.

The work of Jensen (1963a, 1963b, in press) indicates important directions for such research. He reports an experiment (Jensen, 1963a) in which gifted, average, and retarded junior high school students, predominantly middle-class, were presented with a multiple stimulus-response problem. On the first presentation of 200 trials, only students in the gifted and average groups gave evidence of learning. Students in the retarded group were given additional trials on subsequent days until their performance also rose above the chance level of correct response. Each day a new procedure

244

was used: first verbal reinforcement by the experimenter, then stimulus naming by subject prior to responding, stimulus naming while learning, and last, enforced delay of response following reinforcement. All three groups were then tested on a similar but harder task. Here the groups still differed significantly, but the retarded group showed marked improvement. An unusual feature of the data was that the retarded group, while as homogeneous in I.Q. as the other two groups, was far more heterogeneous in learning ability. The Mexican-American children, who constituted one-third of the retarded group, were significantly lower than the rest of that group on the first test but then improved markedly.

In discussing these results, Jensen (1963a, p. 138) suggests:

> *The normal and fast learners in the retarded group are not really retarded in a primary sense, but are children who, at some crucial period in their development, have failed to learn the kinds of behavior which are necessary as a basis for school learning....The habit of making verbal responses, either overtly or covertly, to events in the environment seems to be one of the major ingredients of the kind of intelligence that shows itself in school achievement and on performance tests. Without this habit, even a child with a perfectly normal nervous system in terms of fundamental learning ability will appear to be retarded, and indeed is retarded so long as he does not use verbal mediators in learning. Some of the fastest learners among our retarded group, for example, were those who showed no appreciable learning until they were required to make verbal responses to the stimuli.*

Jensen (1963b) also reports an experiment by Jacqueline Rapier in which Mexican-American children who were taught verbal mediating links spontaneously used them to form new associations. He suggests that comparisons of the amount of gain in learning ability from such instruction can be used to separate retardation due to neurological causes from retardation due to a verbally impoverished environment. In addition, he gives (Jensen, in press) extensive proposals for further research.

We do, however, know something about group differences in characteristics of the verbal network. Three studies are available on subcultural differences in word-association responses. In one dating back almost half a century, Mitchell, Rosanoff, and Rosanoff (1919) found that Negro children, ages 4-15, from New York City were less apt to give a common specific reaction (e.g., *chair* to the stimulus *table*) than white children of the same age, and correspondingly more apt to give idiosyncratic reactions. Since commonality of response increases with age, the authors concluded

245

that the Negro children were developmentally immature. The other two studies, both current, deal with another trend in word-association responses. This developmental trend, related to increasing commonality, is the shift from syntagmatic responses (*deep . . . hole*) to paradigmatic responses (*deep . . . shallow*). In an all-Negro sample of first- and fifth-grade children, John (1963) found significant social-class differences only in the first-grade latency scores. Entwisle (1966) also found very slight social-class differences between high-status urban Maryland elementary school children, matched for I.Q., but some retardation for rural Maryland children at the lower I.Q. levels, and further retardation in an Amish group. Recent evidence thus shows that status differences are less dramatic for word-association measures than for other measures of verbal ability, and that those differences decrease, rather than increase, with age. The tendency to give common and paradigmatic responses reaches an asymptote during the age range being studied, and the initially retarded children do catch up.

Vocabulary tests indicate whether certain items are part of a person's verbal network and thereby provide estimates of its total size. They can, if the definitions are scaled, provide additional information on network structure. Carson and Rabin (1960) matched three groups of fourth- to sixth-graders—Northern White, Northern Negro, and Southern Negro (recent in-migrants)—on the Full Range Picture Vocabulary Test. They then administered the same test as a word vocabulary test and grouped the definition into six levels. For example, the six levels for *wagon* could be: (1) a *vehicle*—categorization; (2) *a cart*—synonym; (3) *a wooden thing with four wheels*—essential description; (4) *you ride in it out West*—essential function; (5) *it bumps into people*—vague description or function; and (6) complete error. Even though the groups were matched when the task required only finding a picture to match a word, the Northern White children gave significantly more definitions from levels 1-3 and the Southern Negro children least.

Spain (1962) analyzed definitions given by "deprived" and "non-deprived" elementary school children in central Tennessee. Ten stimulus words were carefully selected to insure that both the word and its superordinate (e.g., *bread* and *food*) were of high frequency and familiar to local first-graders. Definitions were categorized as generic (superordinate), descriptive, and functional, He found that functional definitions remained the predominant response for the deprived children at all age levels; descriptive definitions increased with age at a rate similar for both groups; and that generic definitions increased most sharply for the non-deprived, while the deprived group showed a 4-year lag in this mode of response by the end of elementary scnool.

The use of language in relation to cognition can also be tapped by categorizing tasks. In general, status differences on such measures increase with age (e.g., see John,

246

1962). But here the line between studies of language and studies of concept formation disappears, and the limitations of this paper preclude a proper review of such research.

Nevertheless, mention must be made of the large-scale project of Hess and his associates at the University of Chicago, reports of which are now beginning to appear in the published literature (Hess and Shipman, 1965a, 1965b). This is a particularly important study because it relates intra-individual and inter-individual modes of communication. It has been planned as a test of the Bernstein hypothesis of a relation between the child's cognitive development and the mother's verbal ability, maternal teaching style, and characteristic mode of family control. In all, 160 Negro mothers from four socio-economic levels were interviewed, tested, and brought to the university for a structured session of mother-child interaction. Each mother was taught three tasks—two sorting tasks and the use of an Etch-a-Sketch board—and then asked to teach those tasks to her four-year-old child. Her maternal teaching style was monitored and analyzed. The children were subsequently tested by being asked to sort new material and give a verbal explanation. (See Bing, 1963, for similar use of an experimental teaching situation to study mother-child interaction.)

Preliminary results indicate that, while there were no social-class differences in affective elements of the interaction or in persistence of the mothers or in cooperation of the children, on at least some of the performance measures social-class differences were in the direction expected. Hess and Shipman (1965a, p. 192) have reported:

> *Children from middle-class homes ranked above children from the lower socio-economic levels in performance on these sorting tasks, particularly in offering verbal explanations as to the basis of sorting. These differences clearly paralleled the relative abilities and teaching skills of the mothers from the different groups.*

Additional information on a subset of this sample is available in Stodolsky's (1965) doctoral research. One year after the original data had been collected, she administered the Peabody Picture Vocabulary Test and Kohlberg's Concept Sorting Test to 56 of the original 160 children from three of the four socio-economic groups. The children's scores were then correlated with a selected set of maternal variables from the previous year to find the best predictors. She found that there were significant social-class differences in the vocabulary scores of the children, and that a set of maternal variables predicted those scores with a multiple correlation of .68. The best single pair of maternal variables, in this respect, proved to be the mother's score on the vocabulary part of the W.A.I.S. and one of the indices of teaching style. The latter was the "discrimination index" that measures the extent to which the mother isolates task-specific qualities of the environment. While scores on the W.A.I.S. dif-

247

ferentiated among the mothers on social-class lines, scores on the discrimination index did not. In other words, there is an interaction between characteristics that are class-linked and those that are not.

The entire Hess project is planned to continue until the children have completed four grades of school, with further data being collected on both the mothers and children. Hopefully, analysis of all the data will proceed beyond a test of the Bernstein hypothesis to provide a differentiated picture of how the maternal variables interact in affecting the verbal and cognitive behaviors of the child.

SUMMING UP

In conclusion, the relative space devoted to the three main divisions of this paper is a rough guide to the extent of our present knowledge. We know little about dialect differences as yet; but we should learn much, about urban Negro speech in particular, from the contrastive studies in progress. Relatively, we know the most about language development. Here the evidence of retardation among lower-class children is extensive, and future work will probably concentrate on more precise analysis of the process variables that mediate this relationship. We know very little about differences in language function. Basic research is needed in this area on ways of categorizing the functions that language serves in natural speech communities, and on ways of analyzing the mediational use of language as well.

At the present time, we cannot completely resolve the difference-deficiency issue on which this review has focused. Children who are socially disadvantaged on such objective criteria as income and educational level of their parents do tend to be deficient on many measures of verbal skills. But the concept of subcultural relativity is nevertheless relevant. We must be sure that developmental scales of language development do not distort our assessment of children who speak a nonstandard dialect. We must be equally sure that studies of language function do not simply reflect the predilection of the investigators. In short, subcultural relativity provides an essential perspective for objective analysis and for any program of planned change. Unfortunately, when pressure for change is great, the danger exists that such perspective may be discarded just when we need it most.

An earlier version of this review was submitted as a special qualifying paper to the Harvard Graduate School of Education. The author is grateful to Professors Robert Anderson, Roger Brown, and Robert Dreeben for helpful comments and criticism. This revision was supported by Contract OE5-10-239 of the U. S. Office of Education with the Center for Research and Development on Educational Differences, Harvard University.

Reprinted from MERRILL-PALMER QUARTERLY OF BEHAVIOR AND DEVELOPMENT Volume 12, No. 3, 1966. Copyright 1966 by Merrill-Palmer Institute.

References

Anastasi, Anne & De Jesus, Cruz. Language development and non verbal I.Q. of Puerto Rican children in New York City. J. ABNORM. SOC. PSYCHOL., 48:357-366, 1953.

Ausubel, D. P. How reversible are the cognitive and motivational effects of cultural deprivation? Implications for teaching the culturally deprived child. URBAN EDUC., 1:16-38, 1964.

Bellugi, Ursula. A transformational analysis of the development of negation. In T. Bever & W. Weksel (Eds.), PSYCHOLINGUISTIC STUDIES: EXPERIMENTAL INVESTIGATIONS OF SYNTAX. New York: Holt, Rinehart & Winston, in press.

Bellugi, Ursula & Brown, R. (Eds.) The acquisition of language. MONOGR. SOC. RES. CHILD DEVELPM., 29:No. 1 (Serial No. 92), 1964.

Bernstein, B. A public language: some sociological implications of a linguistic form. BRIT. J. SOCIOL., 10:311-326, 1959.

Bernstein, B. Language and social class. BRIT. J. SOCIOL., 11:271-276, 1960.

Bernstein, B. Social class and linguistic development: a theory of social learning. In A. H. Halsey, Jean Floud & C. A. Anderson (Eds.), EDUCATION, ECONOMY AND SOCIETY. Glencoe, Ill.: Free Press, Pp. 288-314, 1961.

Bernstein, B. Linguistic codes, hesitation phenomena and intelligence. LANG. & SPEECH, 5:31-46, 1962. (a)

Bernstein, B. Social class, linguistic codes and grammatical elements. LANG. & SPEECH, 5:221-240, 1962. (b)

Bing, Elizabeth. Effect of child-rearing practices on the development of differential cognitive abilities. CHILD DEVELPM., 34:631-648, 1963.

Bloom, B. S. STABILITY AND CHANGE IN HUMAN CHARACTERISTICS. New York: John Wiley, 1964.

Bloom, B. S., Davis, A., & Hess, R. COMPENSATORY EDUCATION FOR CULTURAL DEPRIVATION. New York: Holt, Rinehart & Winston, 1965.

Bossard, J. H. S. THE SOCIOLOGY OF CHILD DEVELOPMENT. (2nd ed.) New York: Harpers, 1954.

Brown, R. & Bellugi, Ursula. Three processes in the child's acquisition of syntax. HARVARD EDUC. REV., 34:133-151, 1964.

Brown, R. & Fraser, C. The acquisition of syntax. In Ursula Bellugi & R. Brown (Eds.), The acquisition of language. MONOGR. SOC. RES. CHILD DEVELPM., 29, No. 1 (Serial No. 92):43-79, 1964.

Carroll, J. B. Determining and numerating adjectives in children's speech. CHILD DEVELPM., 10:215-229, 1939.

Carroll, J. B. Some psychological effects of language structure. In P. Jock & J. Zubin (Eds.), PSYCHOPATHOLOGY OF COMMUNICATION. New York: Ginn & Stratton, Pp. 28-36, 1958.

Carroll, J. B. Language development in children. In S. Saporta (Ed.), PSYCHOLIN-GUISTICS: A BOOK OF READINGS. New York: Holt, Rinehart & Winston, Pp. 331-345, 1961.

Carroll, J. B. LANGUAGE AND THOUGHT. Englewood Cliffs, N. J.: Prentice-Hall, 1964.

Carson, A. S. & Rabin, A. I. Verbal comprehension and communication in Negro and white children. J. EDUC. PSYCHOL., 51:47-51, 1960.

Cazden, Courtney B. Environmental assistance to the child's acquisition of grammar. Unpublished doctoral dissertation, Harvard Univer., 1965.

Center for Applied Linguistics. URBAN LANGUAGE STUDY: DISTRICT OF COLUMBIA PROPOSAL. Washington, D. C.: Author, 1965.

Cherry, Estelle. Children's comprehension of teacher and peer speech. CHILD DEVELPM., 36:467-480, 1965.

Cofer, C. N. & Musgrave, Barbara (Eds.) VERBAL BEHAVIOR AND LEARNING. New York: McGraw-Hill, 1963.

Cohn, W. On the language of lower-class children. SCHOOL REV., 67:435-440, 1959.

Cronbach, L. J. The two disciplines of scientific psychology. AMER. PSYCHOLO-GIST, 12:671-684, 1957.

Dave, R. H. The identification and measurement of environmental process variables

250

that are related to educational achievement. Unpublished doctoral dissertation, Univer. of Chicago, 1963.

Davis, A. L. & McDavid, R. I., Jr. A description of the Chicago speech survey: communication barriers to the culturally deprived. Ithaca, N. Y.: Cornell Univer., PROJECT LITERACY REPORTS, 2:23-25, 1964.

Deutsch, M. The disadvantaged child and the learning process. In A. H. Passow (Ed.), EDUCATION IN DEPRESSED AREAS. New York: Teachers College, Columbia Univer., Pp. 163-179, 1963.

Deutsch, M. & Brown, B. Social influences in Negro-white intelligence differences. J. SOC. ISSUES, 20:24-35, 1964.

Eells, K., Davis, A., Havighurst, R. J., Herrick, V. E., & Tyler, R. W. INTELLIGENCE AND CULTURAL DIFFERENCES. Chicago: Univer. Chicago Press, 1951.

Entwisle, Doris R. Developmental socio-linguistics: a comparative study in four subcultural settings. SOCIOMETRY, 29:67-84, 1966.

Ervin, Susan M. Imitation and structural change in children's language. In E. Lenneberg (Ed.), NEW DIRECTIONS IN THE STUDY OF LANGUAGE. Cambridge: M.I.T. Press, Pp. 163-189, 1964.

Ervin-Tripp, Susan M. An analysis of the interaction of language, topic and listener. In J. J. Gumperz & D. Hymes (Eds.), The ethnography of communication. AMER. ANTHROP., 66, No. 6, Part 2:86-102, 1964.

Ervin, Susan M. & Miller, W. R. Language development. In H. W. Stevenson (Ed.), Child psychology. YEARB. NAT. SOC. STUD. EDUC., 62, Part I:108-143, 1963.

Fiske, D. W. & Maddi, S. R. FUNCTIONS OF VARIED EXPERIENCE. Homewood, Ill.: Dorsey Press, 1961.

Fodor, J. A. How to learn to talk: some simple ways. Unpublished MS., undated.

Frake, C. O. The diagnosis of disease among the Subanun of Mindanao, AMER. ANTHROP., 53:113-132, 1961. Reprinted in D. Hymes (Ed.), LANGUAGE IN CULTURE AND SOCIETY. New York: Harper & Row, Pp. 193-211, 1964.

Fries, C. C. AMERICAN ENGLISH GRAMMAR. New York: Appleton-Century, 1940.

Fries, C. C. THE STRUCTURE OF ENGLISH. New York: Harcourt, Brace, 1952.

Goldman-Eisler, Frieda. Speech analysis and mental processes. LANG. & SPEECH, 1:59-75, 1958.

Gray, Susan W. & Klaus, R. A. An experimental preschool program for culturally deprived children. Paper read at Amer. Ass. Advancement Sci., Montreal, December, 1964.

Hess, R. D. & Shipman, Virginia. Early blocks to children's learning. CHILDREN, 12:189-194, 1965. (a)

Hess, R. D. & Shipman, Virginia. Early experience and socialization of cognitive modes in children. CHILD DEVELPM., 36:869-886, 1965. (b)

Hockett, C. F. Age-grading and linguistic continuity. LANGUAGE, 26:449-457, 1950.

Hunt, J. McV. INTELLIGENCE AND EXPERIENCE. New York: Ronald Press, 1961.

Hunt, J. McV. The psychological basis for using pre-school enrichment as an antidote for cultural deprivation. MERRILL-PALMER QUART., 10:209-248, 1964.

Hymes, D. Functions of speech: an evolutionary approach. In F. C. Gruber (Ed.), ANTHROPOLOGY AND EDUCATION. Philadelphia: Univer. Pennsylvania Press, Pp. 55-83, 1961.

Hymes, D. Notes toward a history of linguistic anthropology. ANTHROP. LINGUISTICS, 5:59-103, 1963.

Hymes, D. Directions in (ethno-) linguistic theory. In A. K. Romney & R. G. D'Andrade (Eds.), Transcultural studies in cognition. AMER. ANTHROP., 66, No. 3, part 2:6-56, 1964. (a)!

Hymes, D. Introduction: toward ethnographies of communication. In J. J. Gumperz & D. Hymes (Eds.), The ethnography of communication. AMER. ANTHROP., 66, No. 6, part 2:1-34, 1964. (b)

Irwin, O. C. Infant speech: the effect of family occupational status and of age on use of sound types. J. SPEECH HEARING DISORDERS, 13:224-226, 1948. (a)

Irwin, O. C. Infant speech: the effect of family occupational status and of age on

252

sound frequency. J. SPEECH HEARING DISORDERS, 13:320-323, 1948. (b)

Irwin, O. C. Infant speech: the effect of systematic reading of stories. J. SPEECH HEARING RES., 3:187-190, 1960.

Jensen, A. R. Learning ability in retarded, average, and gifted children. MERRILL-PALMER QUART., 9:123-140, 1963. (a)

Jensen, A. R. Learning in the preschool years. J. NURSERY EDUC., 18:133-139, 1963. (b)

Jensen, A. R. Social class and verbal learning. In M. Deutsch, A. R. Jensen, & T. F. Pettigrew (Eds.), SOCIAL CLASS, RACE AND PSYCHOLOGICAL DEVELOPMENT. New York: Holt, Rinehart & Winston, in press.

Jespersen, O. LANGUAGE: ITS NATURE, DEVELOPMENT AND ORIGIN. London: George Allen & Unwin, 1922.

Jespersen, O. MANKIND, NATION AND INDIVIDUAL FROM A LINGUISTIC POINT OF VIEW. (Originally published, 1946) Bloomington: Indiana Univer. Press, 1964.

John, Vera P. The intellectual development of slum children. AMER. J. ORTHO-PSYCHIAT., 33:813-822, 1963.

John, Vera P. Position paper on pre-school programs. Unpublished manuscript prepared for Commissioner Keppel. Yeshiva Univer., 1964.

John, Vera P. & Goldstein, L. S. The social context of language acquisition. MERRILL-PALMER QUART., 10:265-275, 1964.

Katz, J. THE PHILOSOPHY OF LANGUAGE. New York: Harper & Row, in press.

Keller, Suzanne. The social word of the urban slum child: some early findings. AMER. J. ORTHOPSYCHIAT., 33:823-831, 1963.

Klima, E. S. Relatedness between grammatical systems. LANGUAGE, 40:1-20, 1964.

Koch, Helen. The relation of "primary mental abilities" in five- and six-year-olds to sex of child and characteristics of his siblings. CHILD DEVELPM., 25:209-223, 1954.

Labov, W. Stages in the acquisition of Standard English. In R. W. Shuy (Ed.), SOCIAL DIALECTS AND LANGUAGE LEARNING. Champaign, Ill.: National Council of Teachers of English, Pp. 77-103, 1965.

Lawton, D. Social class language differences in group discussions. LANG. & SPEECH, 7:183-204, 1964.

Lee, Dorothy. Developing the drive to learn and the questioning mind. In A. Frazier (Ed.), FREEING CAPACITY TO LEARN. Washington, D.C.: Association for Supervision and Curriculum Development, Pp. 10-21, 1960.

Lenneberg, E. H. The capacity for language acquisition. In J. A. Fodor & J. J. Katz (Eds.), THE STRUCTURE OF LANGUAGE: READINGS IN THE PHILOSOPHY OF LANGUAGE. Englewood Cliffs, N.J.: Prentice-Hall, Pp. 579-603, 1964.

Lesser, G. S., Fifer, G., & Clark, D. H. Mental abilities of children in different social and cultural groups. MONOGR. SOC. RES. CHILD DEVELPM., 30, No. 4 (Serial No. 102), 1965.

Loban, W. D. THE LANGUAGE OF ELEMENTARY SCHOOL CHILDREN. Champaign, Ill.: National Council of Teachers of English, 1963.

Lorge, I. & Chall, Jeanne. Estimating the size of vocabularies of children and adults: an analysis of methodological issues. J. EXP. EDUC., 32:147-157, 1963.

McNeill, D. Developmental psycholinguistics. In G. Lindzey (Ed.), HANDBOOK OF SOCIAL PSYCHOLOGY. (2nd ed.) Reading, Mass.: Addison-Wesley, in press.

Miller, W. & Ervin, Susan. The development of grammar in child language. In Ursula Bellugi & R. Brown (Eds.), The acquisition of language. MONOGR. SOC. RES. CHILD DEVELPM., 29, No. 1 (Serial No. 92):9-34, 1964.

Milner, Esther. A study of the relationship between reading readiness in grade one school children and patterns of parent-child interaction. CHILD DEVELPM., 22: 95-112, 1951.

Mitchell, I., Rosanoff, Isabel R., & Rosanoff, A. J. A study of association in Negro children. PSYCHOL. REV., 26:354-359, 1919.

Nida, E. A. Analysis of meaning and dictionary making. INTERNAT. J. AMER. LINGUISTICS, 24:279-292, 1958.

254

Nisbet, J. Family environment and intelligence. In A. H. Halsey, Jean Floud, & C. A. Anderson (Eds.), EDUCATION, ECONOMY AND SOCIETY. Glencoe, Ill.: Free Press, Pp. 273-287, 1961.

Pederson, L. A. Non-standard Negro speech in Chicago. In W. A. Stewart (Ed.), NON-STANDARD SPEECH AND THE TEACHING OF ENGLISH. Washington, D. C.: Center for Applied Linguistics, Pp. 16-23, 1964.

Provence, Sally & Lipton, Rose C. INFANTS IN INSTITUTIONS. New York: Internat. Univer. Press, 1962.

Putnam, G. N. & O'Hern, Edna M. The status significance of an isolated urban dialect. Language dissertation No. 53, LANGUAGE, 31, No. 4, Whole part 2, 1955.

Razran, G. The observable unconscious and the inferable conscious in current Soviet psychophysiology: interceptive conditioning, semantic conditioning, and the orienting reflex. PSYCHOL. REV., 68:81-147, 1961.

Rheingold, Harriet L. The measurement of maternal care. CHILD DEVELPM., 31: 565-575, 1960.

Rheingold, Harriet L. The effect of environmental stimulation upon social and exploratory behavior in the human infant. In B. M. Foss (Ed.), DETERMINANTS OF INFANT BEHAVIOR. London: Methuen, Pp. 143-170, 1961.

Rheingold, Harriet L., Gewirtz, J. L., & Ross, Helen W. Social conditioning of vocalizations in the infant. J. COMP. PHYSIOL. PSYCHOL., 52:68-73, 1959.

Rosenbaum, P. S. Prerequisites for linguistic studies on the effects of dialect differences on learning to read. Ithaca, N. Y.: Cornell Univer., PROJECT LITERACY REPORTS, No. 2:26-30, 1964.

Schatzman, L. & Strauss, A. Social class and modes of communication. AMER. J. SOCIOL., 60:329-338, 1955.

Schorr, A. L. The nonculture of poverty. AMER. J. ORTHOPSYCHIAT., 34:907-912, 1964.

Schramm, W., Lyle, J., & Parker, E. B. TELEVISION IN THE LIVES OF OUR CHILDREN. Stanford, Calif.: Stanford Univer. Press, 1961.

Smith, Madora E. A study of some factors influencing the development of the sentence in preschool children. J. GENET. PSYCHOL., 46:182-212, 1935.

255

Spain, C. J. Definition of familiar nouns by culturally deprived and non-deprived children of varying ages. Unpublished doctoral dissertation, George Peabody College for Teachers, 1962.

Staats, A. W. & Staats, Carolyn, K. COMPLEX HUMAN BEHAVIOR. New York: Holt, Rinehart & Winston, 1964.

Stewart, W. A. Foreign language teaching methods in quasi-foreign language situations. In W. A. Stewart (Ed.), NON-STANDARD SPEECH AND THE TEACHING OF ENGLISH. Washington, D. C.: Center for Applied Linguistics, Pp. 1-15, 1964.

Stewart, W. A. Urban Negro speech: socio-linguistic factors affecting English teaching. In R. W. Shuy (Ed.), SOCIAL DIALECTS AND LANGUAGE LEARNING. Champaign, Ill.: National Council of Teachers of English, Pp. 10-18, 1965.

Stodolsky, Susan. Maternal behavior and language and concept formation in Negro pre-school children: an inquiry into process. Unpublished doctoral dissertation, Univer. of Chicago, 1965.

Strodtbeck, F. L. The hidden curriculum in the middle-class home. In J. D. Krumboltz (Ed.), LEARNING AND THE EDUCATIONAL PROCESS. Chicago: Rand McNally, Pp. 91-112, 1965.

Templin, Mildred C. CERTAIN LANGUAGE SKILLS IN CHILDREN: THEIR DEVELOPMENT AND INTERRELATIONSHIPS. Minneapolis: Univer. Minnesota Press, 1957.

Thomas, D. R. Oral language, sentence structure, and vocabulary of kindergarten children living in low socio-economic urban areas. Unpublished docotral dissertation, Wayne State Univer., 1962.

Thomas, O. C. TRANSFORMATIONAL GRAMMAR AND THE TEACHER OF ENGLISH. New York: Holt, Rinehart & Winston, 1965.

Weissberg, P. Social and non-social conditioning of infant vocalizations. CHILD DEVELPM., 34:377-388, 1963.

Wolf, R. M. The identification and measurement of environmental process variables related to intelligence. Unpublished doctoral dissertation, Univer. of Chicago, 1964.

Wortis, H., Bardach, J. L., Cutler, R., Rue, R. & Freedman, A. Child-rearing practices in a low socio-economic group. PEDIATRICS, 32:298-307, 1963.

256

ANALYSIS OF STORY RETELLING AS A MEASURE OF THE EFFECTS OF ETHNIC CONTENT IN STORIES

Vera P. John, Ph.D.,
Associate Professor,
Dept. of Educational Psychology and Guidance,
Ferkauf Graduate School of Education,
Yeshiva University, New York, New York

Tomi D. Berney,
Ferkauf Graduate School of Education,
Yeshiva University, New York, New York

VERA P. JOHN, Ph.D.

The fostering of language skills is given serious attention in all our compensatory programs for disadvantaged children.

Although the literature on language acquisition in young children is extensive, most of the old, and many of the more recent studies, are dominated by what might be called "a single work" approach. The measuring of children's language skills by means of vocabulary tests is one example of this tradition. Related to the lack of attention given in past research to sequential speech as a measured response, is a similar flaw in the choice of stimuli used to *elicit* speech on the part of young children.

It was the purpose of this investigation to examine the psychological impact of stories and story books upon pre-school children drawn from a variety of ethnic backgrounds by means of standardized retelling of the stories. The selection of a research problem of this type was motivated by theoretical as well as practical considerations.

Traditionally, a series of unrelated stimulus words, pictures, or objects are used in measuring children's verbal skills.(7, 10) Both the input and the output produced by these methods may be unrepresentative of the process of verbal communication and language learning. Young children listen to, and acquire language, when exposed to the flow of speech of those around them. One of the ways in which their language, and imagination, is stimulated is by being told tales, or being read to. It seemed that a meaningful way of gathering representative samples of children's sequential speech might be through a standardized 'story retelling' technique. Such a technique (to be described in detail below) is suitable for minority, non-English speaking, or bilingual children; as well as for children raised in urban middle-class environments. The examination of the transformations that the stories undergo when retold by children, it was projected, might reveal the patterns of variations for the children with varying degrees of experience with language.

259

Much of the current emphasis upon language enrichment in pre-school and compensatory programs is based upon the findings, summarized by Cazden as follows: "on all the language measures, in all the studies, the upper socio-economic status children, however defined, are more advanced than the lower socio-economic status children. However, in some studies, certain non-verbal measures fail to reveal social class differences." (1) There has been considerable evidence, though perhaps overstated in the quoted summarization, that low-income children are deficient in verbal skills. However, most of the studies are based upon English-speaking Negro and white children, residing in urban centers. There has been limited information to date concerning the language skills of other minority, low-income children in the USA.

One of the broad objectives of this study was as follows: to discover whether the standardized story retelling technique could be used to gain language samples from young low-income children drawn from a variety of *ethnic* and *language* backgrounds; rural, as well as urban. By discovering whether this method was applicable to gathering sequential samples from children raised under such widely varying circumstances, we hoped to perfect a tool optimally suited for *monitoring* changes in language skills as a function of educational intervention.

Most of the crucial problems related to language enrichment in pre-school classrooms are a source of debate. Psychologists and linguists have reached no consensus on a workable plan of intervention, thus, the classroom educator often has to experiment on his own. One of his concerns relates to the use of books as a medium of directed growth. There is a recurrent controversy which relates to the types of books and stories of greatest intrinsic interest to children raised in poverty: Do children respond with greater attentiveness, accuracy of detail, and general pleasure, to stories with heroes representing their own ethnic groups, as contrasted with animal stories, or heroes drawn from the mainstream of American life?

In this investigation, we attempted to answer a number of questions. We approached these questions in a number of ways.

First, this study was aimed at discovering patterns of language performance, as measured by the story-retelling technique among five groups of preschool children: Negro, Puerto Rican, Mexican-American, Sioux Indian, and Navajo. In view of the wide scope of the current preschool programs, it seemed imperative to gather as much data concerning young children enrolled in these programs as was compatible with the major goals of this study, and feasible within the time limitations of this investigation. A particular stress was placed upon the gathering of background information concerning American Indian children because of the paucity of extant information.

260

Second, the impact of storybooks of differing ethnic content was examined in a controlled manner. The question whether children retell with more accuracy a story set in a familiar context in contrast with an unfamiliar setting was explored.

Third, the use of books in Head Start programs, representing widely divergent ethnic communities, were examined. Careful observations were made concerning the effectiveness of different types of books with children drawn from rural and urban, Negro and Indian, Mexican and Puerto Rican communities.

DESIGN OF THE STUDY

Description of the Centers
The children serving as subjects in this project attended Head Start preschool centers in New York, California, South Dakota and Arizona-New Mexico. A total of twelve centers were represented. Head Start center locations were chosen in order to include areas with high concentrations of selected ethnic groups.

New York
Four New York Head Start Centers were used during the summer of 1965. These were located on the upper West Side of Manhattan (Bloomingdale Project), P.S. 90 (Harlem), Haryou Center (Harlem), and P.S. 15 (Lower East Side).

Enrolled in each class on either full or half session were from 10 to 25 children. There were one or two teachers, one or two aides, and in some classes, volunteers and/or parents.

The two Harlem centers were similar as to ethnic composition (Negro) and the socio-economic status of the students ("lower class"). The "Bloomingdale" center, while ethnically similar to P.S. 90 and Haryou, was socio-economically higher ("upper-lower class"). P.S. 15, the center on the lower East Side, was composed mainly of bilingual Puerto Rican children, many of whose parents were unemployed and receiving welfare payments, making this a center of mostly "lower-lower class" children.

California
Two Head Start Centers were selected in California during the summer of 1965.

The Indio Head Start Center was composed mainly of Mexican-American lower class children, most of whom were English-speaking. In Sausalito, the children were Negro, and covered a wide range of social classes, extending from "lower-low" to "middle class".

261

South Dakota (Sioux Indian)

Rapid City and La Plant were two South Dakota Centers with heavy enrollment of the Sioux Indian children. During the summer of 1965, the Rapid City Center included some Mexican, Negro and white children, as well as urban Sioux children; the La Plant center was composed solely of rural Sioux Indian children on the Cheyenne River Reservation. All the South Dakota children were fluent in English. In Rapid City, the classes of 14-18 were held on half-session. There was generally one teacher and two volunteers per class. The average socio-economic status of the children was "lower-class". In La Plant, 14 children attended the pre-kindergarten class which was held on half-session. There was one teacher, a paid aide, and two volunteers in the class. This group had the lowest average socio-economic status level of all our groups; most of the parents were unemployed.

Arizona - New Mexico - Navajo

In the Arizona-New Mexico centers, all of which were part of the Navajo Indian Reservation, the children represented had the greatest population variations within the Indian samples. These centers were located at the towns of Shiprock and Chinle; and the rural villages of Greasewood and Many Farms.

In Shiprock, New Mexico, the primary language of many of the children was Navajo. There were two male teachers, neither of whom were bilingual. The five female aides, however, were fluent in the Navajo language and also spoke some English. Shiprock was one of the larger reservation communities, with a population of 5,000, many of whom could neither speak nor read English.

34 children were enrolled in the Chinle Head Start programs. There was one teacher, three paid aides and a volunteer. The class was divided into two groups, one English-speaking and one Navajo-speaking. Chinle itself is a community of 500 inhabitants, the majority of whom do not speak English. Many of the people have either a very low income, or are unemployed, the result being that a large percentage of the population are recipients of welfare payments. The majority of children enrolled in the pre-school live within one mile from the center. These are generally the children who will attend school regularly and take full advantage of opportunities offered them. Their parents are over the poverty line in income. Those living in secluded areas are not able to attend school or other community functions, due to poor road conditions.

The Greasewood community has a population of 1,000, many of whom are employees of the Federal Schools in the area. Those living in the immediate area of Greasewood speak English, although many are bilingual. Individuals living outside the area speak mainly Navajo. There were over 64 children enrolled, divided into two groups of those who live in the community and speak English, and those who

262

ride the bus to school and speak Navajo. There are two teachers, one of whom speaks Navajo, and six aides.

Many Farms, Arizona, was the smallest Navajo community used in this study. It has a population of 500, the majority of whom speak Navajo and are of very low socio-economic status. Many of the parents whose 30 children were enrolled in Head Start were employed by the Federal Government, and consequently spoke English and were of a higher social class than others in the community. The pre-school class, supervised by a teacher and aides, was largely split into those children whose only language was Navajo, and those whose only language was English.

SUBJECTS

Ethnic group membership
The subjects in this study were members of one of five ethnic groups: There were 46 Negro children enrolled in New York and Sausalito, California preschools, 22 Puerto Rican subjects in New York, 10 Mexican-American children in California, 16 Sioux and 48 Navajo children; for a total of 142 subjects, including 72 boys and 70 girls.

Language
Many of the subjects were bilingual or did not speak English. One-third were administered standard tests and the experimental task in languages other than English (Spanish and Navajo). The children were encouraged to choose the language in which they felt most competent.

Age
The children in this study ranged in age from 3.5 to 6.5 years. No child with previous pre-school experience was included. The majority of children were five years old at the time of testing, and were divided into four age groups: under 4 years 7 months; 4 years 7 months to 5 years 2 months; 5 years 2 months to 5 years 9 months; and over 5 years 9 months.

SES
The socio-economic status of each child was determined by using a modified form of the socio-economic status scale developed at the Institute for Developmental Studies, New York University, utilizing the Empey Scale of occupational prestige. The large majority of study children were drawn from low income non-white families, thus the traditional designations of low, middle and upper class or of SES I, II, and III were too inclusive for this group of subjects. Therefore, while class determination was based upon occupation and education of the main support of the family, group I signifies only those children whose families received the bulk of their income from public assistance, the head of the family usually being unemployed.

263

Group 2 includes those children whose parents had not completed any high school, who were laborers, unskilled or semi-skilled workers, job trainees or domestic servants, but were not receiving public assistance. Group 3 includes those subjects whose parents had at least some high school education or better, were employed as skilled laborers or low level white collar workers. Group 4 included those children whose parents had completed some college and were employed as highly skilled technical workers, high level white collar workers, or held professional jobs. There were 34 subjects in group I ("lower-lower class"), 80 in group II ("lower class"), 21 in group III ("upper-lower class"), and 7 in group IV ("middle class").

Birth Order

Although we had originally planned to collect data as to the birth order of each subject, we found that this information was lacking on over 12% of our subjects. Of the remaining group, the distribution was one-third first borns, and two-thirds latter borns.

TABLE I

Demographic Characteristics of Study Subjects

A. Ethnic Membership

    46 Negro (New York and California)
    22 Puerto Rican (New York)
    10 Mexican (California)
    16 Sioux (South Dakota)
    48 Navajo (Arizona-New Mexico)

B. Language

    96 English
    46 Non-English
    17 Spanish
    29 Navajo

C. Age

    5 under 4 years, 7 months
    39 4 years, 7 months to 5 years, 2 months
    58 5 years, 2 months to 5 years 9 months
    40 over 5 years, 9 months

D. Sex

264

72 Male
70 Female

E. Socio-economic-status

34 SES I
80 SES II
21 SES III
7 SES IV

F. Birth Order

33 First born
    (9 Only-children)
91 Latter born
18 Insufficient information

Librarians

College students were trained as "librarians", and each was assigned to one center, or in the case of the Navajo reservation, to a group of centers. They were responsible for administering Head Start tests, noting reactions of the children to various books, recording information that pertained to the classroom reading, and conducting interviews with parents and teachers. Librarians of the same ethnic background as the children were chosen where possible. It was also necessary that the librarians working with Puerto Rican, Mexican or Navajo children be fluent in Spanish or Navajo as well as in English.

During the first few weeks of the program the librarians got to know the children, read them stories, and gradually oriented them to the story-retelling routine. During this period the librarians also assembled a complete file on each child participating in the study. The study children consisted of the entire enrollment of the class to which the librarian was assigned. A special kit of books was selected and given to each librarian, who collected information concerning the children's reactions to the books, and recorded them on a standard form.

During the second half of the summer program, the librarians worked with each of the children individually. All of the children were first read CURIOUS GEORGE, by H. A. Rey, and told to retell it. Then half of the children were selected at random and were read ONE OF THESE DAYS (a book specially commissioned for this study) set in their own ethnic background.(9)

265

EXPERIMENTAL PROCEDURES

The Story Retelling Technique

This technique is the central feature of this study. It is a task which was designed in the context of an earlier study by the author, but it is still in its developmental phase.(5) The purpose of administering the story retelling task to children is to obtain a representative sample of sequential language. The analyses to be performed with such data are of wide diversity. Among these are formal, linguistic analyses as well as content and stylistic treatments. The task can be most broadly compared to attempts assessing *cognitive* style in children.

Techniques similar to the experimental task in this study have been used in the past. Clinicians have looked at story-completion, and story telling as projective material. Their methods of analysis reflect this orientation. Currently, techniques are being developed to assess concept attainment via the retelling of short stories.

The choice of stories as stimulus materials are not accidental. Children respond to a sequential input differently from their responses to single word or phrase stimuli. Though level of verbal performance is measured by many tasks requiring but pointing or short responses, these approaches have serious shortcomings. It was our purpose to discover how a child selects from, and organized, the continuous flow of stimuli--a process which is truly representative of his everyday verbal environment. It is with this complex process in mind that the Story-Retelling Technique was developed. It was hypothesized in this study that systematic variation in response will occur when children were read a single story set in two different ethnic contexts. With this in mind, two versions of the same story were constructed which differed only in ethnic context as represented by the illustrations. The illustrations were selected to depict, as faithfully as possible, two rather different environments. The Negro version of the story was set in a crowded city slum; the American Indian version endeavored to depict life on an Indian reservation.

The procedure for the story retelling was as follows: First the librarians read to the children individually while the children looked at the corresponding pictures. After the reading was finished, the subjects were given the pictures without the text, and asked to retell the story by means of the pictures. Each picture was shown separately, and in its proper sequence. The whole session was taped in the language of the child's choice.

The detailed analysis of the re-told stories was carried out only with the experimental story, thus, children were assessed on a performance with which they had some familiarity; this was evident in that the majority of children took less than eight minutes to retell the story to them.

266

The speech samples obtained under these conditions excelled the quality and quantity of speech productions of the same children in their classrooms. From this it would appear that the method of story retelling is a flexible approach to gathering linguistic samples from young, bilingual, economically disadvantaged children.

Peabody Picture Vocabulary Test
To obtain intercorrelations between the experimental task and standard measures of language competence, we chose the PPVT for inclusion in the test battery.

Behavioral Analysis
Though the major focus of this study has related to the gathering of language samples, it seemed reasonable to include some other measures of the subjects' behavior as well. The choice of the OPERATION HEAD START BEHAVIOR INVENTORY was one of convenience. The Inventory was completed for each child by his teacher.

It was possible to compare some of the findings of this study, (as related to the correlation of social-emotional characteristics to verbal performance) with that of R. Hess as reported in "Techniques of Assessing Cognitive and Social Abilities of Children and Parents in Project Head Start."(4)

Parent Interview
In this study, it was not possible to carry out intensive parent interviews. Consequently, we designed a very simple and short questionnaire, the purpose of which was to gather information concerning socialization patterns among low-income families. Of particular interest to us has been the question: what is the social network in which young low-income children are raised? Previous information pointed to the importance of siblings and cousins as nearly exclusive playmates of children raised in a ghetto housing project.(8)

The 14-item scale ranged over following topics: a. Parent's perception of Head Start experience (including what their children may have told them about it.) b. child's social relationships within the family, c. parent's perceptions of child's verbal skills, and d. "what kinds of things does your child do that pleases you most?"

'Book kit'
Each librarian was provided with a standard kit of ten carefully chosen books; including:

THE CAT IN THE HAT, Dr. Seuss
CURIOUS GEORGE, H. A. Rey

267

CURIOUS GEORGE GETS A JOB, H. A. Rey
GILBERTO AND THE WIND, Marie Hall Ets
HAPPY BIRTHDAY TO YOU, Dr. Seuss
THE LION AND THE RAT, Brian Wildsmith
MAY I BRING A FRIEND, Beatrice Schenk de Regniers
SHAPES, Miriam Schlein
SNAIL WHERE ARE YOU?, Tomi Ungerer
WHISTLE FOR WILLY, Ezra Keats

The kit was chosen so as to include three different types of books: 1) Books of ethnic identification, such as WHISTLE FOR WILLIE, and GILBERTO AND THE WIND, 2) Non-verbal books, such as SNAIL WHERE ARE YOU? and SHAPES, and 3) Classic children's books such as CURIOUS GEORGE, Dr. Seuss' books, THE LION AND THE RAT, and MAY I BRING A FRIEND?

DATA ANALYSIS

Story Retelling Task

The following background characteristics were complete enough to be used in the quantitative analyses: ethnic membership of the child, his age and sex, his preferred language in the testing situation, and his socio-economic status.

In this and previous studies by the author, the emphasis has been to look at retold stories as patterned verbal output. The patterning is thought of as twofold: linguistic and cognitive. Children transform the input story into their own phrases (reflecting their level of syntactical and vocabulary development). In addition, they selectively recall features of the original story, a process of cognitive import.

Verbal skills are often equated with verbosity. Frequently, low-income children have been described as wordless, shy, non-verbal, withdrawn. In this study, fewer than ten out of the 142 children could be characterized in this manner. Our most interesting finding was that the vast majority of the low-income children tested, performed their verbal task in an active and participating manner.

Good participation on the part of these subjects may be due to two factors: the type of task administered (story-based), and the relationships between testers and children. The children were familiar with the librarians by the time they were taped. Ease in a testing situation is of particular importance to young Indian children, who tend to shy away from competitive situations.

Originally, we intended to analyze the obtained material *linguistically,* and for

268

'cognitive style'. However, the incredible variability of the obtained stories (retold in three languages, ranging from 10 phrases to 80 phrases) made such a task too formidable for a one-year study. Detailed linguistic analyses are projected for the future.

Instead, four types of analyses have been carried out:

Output
First, the protocols were analyzed for output measures. The basic unit for all analyses is the phrase. In most instances this consisted of subject and predicate constructions. Since it was difficult to apply a formal phrase analysis to these protocols, the empirical criteria of pauses, minimal phrase units of meaning, and occasionally, stress contours, were used for specifying phrase units.

Two measures were developed for counting the number of phrases produced by the children which were based on the story. (a) Stimulus-derived (SD) phrases, which reflect information present in both **pictures** and **test** of the story, and (b) Story-relevant-inferred (SRI) phrases which reflect information which could have been gained by the child only through the text, i.e. including only those story features which are not pictorially represented.*

In the senior author's previous study of story retelling (5). the subjects were 1st grade Negro children ranging in socio-economic status from low-to-middle class. No significant relationships were found in that study between socio-economic status, sex and verbal output. Similarly, in a study by Deutsch, et al (2) output did not correlate with socio-economic status. In this investigation, age, sex, and socio-economic status failed to show significant variations with verbal output. The differences in output were striking, however, when children of differing ethnic backgrounds were compared. The Indian children, both Sioux and Navajo retold the story with significantly fewer phrases than the Mexican, Negro and Puerto Rican children. These differences were greatest when Negro and Navajo children were compared, (the former producing twice as many phrases, on the average.) See Table II for quantitative analyses.

The length of time used for retelling was another measure. Linear time measurements, in absolute terms, parallel those of the total verbal output; Negro and Mexican children took longer to complete this task than the children in the other three groups.

Correlational analyses were carried out for all measures and all classificatory variables. Of interest here are the correlations of ethnic group membership and language, with verbal output.

*These distinctions were developed in cooperation with Mrs. Jane Ingling, and Miss Vivian Horner.

TABLE II

Number of Phrases as a Function of Ethnic Group and Social Class Membership

ANOVA

Source	df	mss	F
A (Ethnic)	4	1207.674	8.727 (.001)
B (SES)	3	317.736	2.296
AXB	12	158.017	1.142
Within	122	138.386	

Test of Mean Differences

Treatments		Navajo	Sioux	Puerto Rican	Mexican	Negro
	Means	15.17	17.50	26.13	30.20	31.31
Navajo	15.17		2.33	10.96*	15.03**	16.14**
Sioux	17.50			8.63	12.70**	13.81**
Puerto Rican	26.13				4.07	5.18
Mexican	30.20					1.11
Negro	31.31					

* .05

** .01

Total   M = 23.45

SD = 14.027

Ethnic group membership and number of phrases

Negro:	+.3893	(N-46)
Puerto Rican:	+.0831	(N-22)
Mexican:	+.1331	(N-10)
Sioux:	-.1503	(N-16)
Navajo:	-.4202	(N-48)

The additional calculations which were related to verbal output consisted of the effects of the language used by the child, and story version upon total number of phrases. Both English and Spanish speaking children retold longer stories than the Navajo speaking children. Of interest is the way in which many of the Puerto Rican children relied upon both languages (English and Spanish) while retelling the story. For example, to picture 9, one of the little girls gave the following response: "The boy, the boy? the boy sleep with the baby, and this the baby. The baby sleeps. Luna."

270

Contrary to the original predictions, the ethnic context of the story did not effect verbal output or length of time of retelling to any significant extent. Negro and Puerto Rican children tended to produce slightly longer stories when retelling the Negro (city) version of the story, while Mexican children were more verbose in retelling the Indian version.

Accuracy of Retelling

This notion implies that the retold stories can be measured for the degree to which they replicate the stimulus story. In this study, the stories produced by the children were greatly abbreviated, and substantially modified.

The percentage of the original story retold by the children (not verbatim, of course) ranged from 2% to 34% of the text, using the combined SD and SRI phrases as an index. However, when the comparison was made between the two versions of the story, the results with the Negro sample were as follows:

SD (Negro version) 8.09	SRI (Negro version) 7.363
SD (Indian version) 7.66	SRI (Indian version) 7.333

(These means are based upon N's of 22 and 24 respectively.)

The only group of children who were differentially affected by the two versions of the story, as measured by the accuracy index, were the Mexican children. They produced twice as many stimulus-derived items when presented with the Indian version of the story than when tested with the Negro version. Unfortunately, this group was so small (N of 10) that it is impossible to generalize from this result.

The assumption was made that SD phrases reflect a largely perceptual orientation to the task of retelling, and that SRI items measure cognitive skill, and are indicative of a more complex internal process. In view of such an assumption, it was interesting to find significant social-class and birth-order differences in a previous study of 60 children drawn from three SES groups.(5) These young Negro first graders differed significantly in the amount of SRI phrases they produced when analyzed for SES differences. At the same time, no differences were found in the total number of phrases in the retelling of CURIOUS GEORGE, the story used for this previous investigation.

Although in the present study we were interested in the correlation between SES and accuracy measures, because of the narrow range of SES, we did not expect highly significant results. However, it was interesting that a positive correlation coefficient, based upon an N of 142 is +.1635. None of the other measures of retelling performance correlated with SES.

271

An analysis of a socio-economically *matched* sample of New York and California Negro subjects produced significantly larger SD and SRI phrase counts for the California group. We interpreted these differences by assuming that subtle features of the environment, not reflected in a gross measure of SES status, were at work. These could be many: the children's freedom to roam, the safety of a rural environment without the usual remoteness and isolation, the absence of harsh winters, and perhaps, the absence of the deep frustrations most poignantly experienced by the residents of a sprawling, congested urban ghetto.

TABLE III

**Output Comparisons between Matched
Groups of California and New York Negroes
(N = 9 pairs)**

	California	New York	Mean Difference	Mean Number of Phrases p
Total phrases	52.7	22.4	30.3	.005
SD	11.0	6.3	4.7	005
SRI	9.7	4.3	5.4	.01

Though the comparisons between the two groups of Negro children are based only upon a few children (N = 18), the magnitude of the obtained differences, as shown in the above table, are impressive. It is possible that on standardized tests of verbal skills and intelligence, a similar gap in achievement would not be demonstrated. The California children had an active, exuberant approach which might be an attitudinal as well as a cognitive determinant of their rich performance on this task. A comprehensive study, far beyond the confines of this investigation would yield the needed answers to the questions raised in this study concerning variations due to "ethnographic" factors.

Cognitive Style

The following ratio measure emerged as useful in determining cognitive style in retelling: action versus descriptive phrases. The experimental story is replete with action. The majority of the children reflect this story characteristic in their retellings; on the average, the ratio of action/descriptive phrases was two to one. However, the children who were least able to deal with this task, whose stories qualitatively appeared weakest, deviated from this ratio, in favor of more descriptive than action phrases. Often they just labeled the person, sometimes they described the objects in a particular picture, as for example in this protocol:

272

A.D. (Navajo)

1. Medicine

2. Horse

3. House

4. Girls

5. I don't know. I don't know. (Pause) A boy . . .this is corn.

6. Medicine.

7. He comes down and then he goes up again (pause) medicine.

8. "faster, faster" he said . . . so his hair is blowing.

9. The baby went to sleep . . . so. . . the boy went back.

10. Straw doll (pause) a man . . . a lady.

In this story, the child responded with descriptive phrases to seven pictures out of ten. This tendency was different from the overall trend, in which children, on the average, gave twice as many *action* as *descriptive* phrases. (Mean number of action phrases for 142 subjects: 8.493, and mean number of descriptive phrases: 4.725.)

The Effects of Story Version
There were no significant differences in verbal output for the two versions of the story. But when the distribution of *descriptive* phrases was assessed, the analysis of variance calculations pointed to the interaction of ethnic membership with story version. (See Table IV) Surprisingly, the Puerto Rican and Navajo children retold the Negro version of ONE OF THESE DAYS with more descriptive phrases than when they (the other, randomly selected half of the subjects) were presented with the Indian version. And the Mexican children retold the Indian version with a greater number of descriptive phrases. The narrative of the Navajo children, retelling the Negro version, was replete with descriptive *labeling,* (e.g. man and boy). This was particularly true of those subjects whose story was replete with two or three times the average number of descriptive phrases. These children failed to retell action sequences, and consequently, their stories appeared somewhat lifeless, and lacked continuity.

273

TABLE IV

Number of Descriptive Phrases as a Function of Ethnic Group Membership and Story Version

ANOVA

Source	df	mss	F
A (Ethnic)	3	18.465	1.154
B (Story)	1	32.185	2.012
AxB	3	64.855	4.054 (.01)
Within	118	15.996	

Test of mean differences

Treatments		M-N	PR-I	Nav-I	Neg-I	Neg-N	M-I	Nav-N	P-N
	Means	2.75	3.46	3.96	4.58	4.77	5.50	5.76	9.22
Mex. x Neg.	2.75	----	0.71	1.21	1.83	2.02	2.75	3.01	6.47*
P.R. x Ind.	3.46		----	0.50	1.12	1.31	2.04	2.30	5.76*
Nav. x Ind.	3.96			----	0.62	0.81	1.54	1.80	5.26*

** = .01
 * = .05

Ethnic Membership and Cognitive Style

The traditional image of the quiet, contemplative Navajo child emerges when his retold story is compared with that of the urban Negro child. Navajo children include half as many action phrases in their retold stories as the Negro children. However, a similar ratio difference exists in the total verbal output of these two groups; the average length of the Negro child's retold story is twice as long as that of the Navajo child.

It is interesting to compare some of the other groups in this study as well. The total verbal output of Puerto Rican children is not significantly different from their Negro neighbors. But in their productions of action phrases the two groups differed sharply. As shown by Table V Negro children included many more such phrases when retelling ONE OF THESE DAYS than did the Puerto Rican children.

274

TABLE V

Number of Action Phrases as a
Function of Ethnic Group and
Social Class Membership

ANOVA

Source	df	mss	F
A (Ethnic)	4	117.971	4.725 (.001)
B (SES)	3	7.105	.284
AxB	12	7.643	.306
Within	122	27.967	.306

Test of mean differences

Treatments		Navajo	Puerto Rican	Sioux	Mexican	Negro
	Means	**5.48**	**6.59**	**9.12**	**11.00**	**11.78**
Navajo	5.48	----	1.11	3.64	5.52**	6.30**
Puerto Rican	6.59		----	2.53	4.41**	5.19**
Sioux	9.12			----	1.88	2.66
Mexican	11.00				----	0.78
Negro	11.78					----

* .05
** .01

Perhaps more surprising than the above trends, are the differences in action orientation found between two groups of Indian children, as shown below in Table VI. While Sioux and Navajo children differed little in length of their stories, the former produced more action phrases/total number of phrases than any of the other groups of children represented in this study. ine Sioux stories were short but replete with action.

None of the Sioux children fall in the low action-high descriptive category, while more than 25% of the Navajo children retold their stories in this manner. For long, there has been a tendency to generalize about Indians, to view them as a single group. But cultural traditions, and the varying impact of their natural environments, have contributed to wide differences among American Indian groups. The Sioux have been known as outstanding warriors (the best light cavalry of the Americas), a

275

TABLE VI

**Action/Descriptive Ratios of
Sioux and Navajo Children**

	Sioux	Navajo	Both
2A/D	10	19	29
A/D	6	16	22
A/2D	0	13	13
	16	48	64

chi-square = 6.5 (p .05)

history they still cherish. The Navajo, on the other hand, are people who value harmony and beauty. Although it seems far-fetched, it is possible that the types of differences in story retelling observed among these two groups of children are reflections of *culturally patterned* differences.

One of the first questions asked, was: do the children comment about the child-hero of ONE OF THESE DAYS, do they identify him as Negro or Indian?

Half of the Sioux children spoke of James as "that Indian boy" or "that Indian", while none of the Navajo children mentioned the Indianness of the hero, when presented with that version. This is a curious difference; it may relate to the fact that Sioux children are raised in, or close to, mixed communities, while Navajo children, on the whole, live in all-Indian communities.

The ethnic identity of the hero was mentioned more often by the children when they were presented with the Indian as contrasted with the Negro version.

While the Navajo children did not comment upon the Indianness of James, they responded differentially to the illustrations. When presented with the Indian version, children labeled objects of cultural significance to them. For instance, they mentioned the *corn doll, medicine bag* (the object used as a bag to correspond to the piggy bank in the Negro version). Perhaps the most interesting illustration of this trend was a 'case of mistaken identity'. The first illustration of this story depicts the father and the son, talking. The father points upward toward the moon. Some of the Navajo children referred to this picture by saying "corn pollen". The gesture reminded them of the Navajo religious ceremony in which corn pollen is sprinkled.

The children, when retelling ONE OF THESE DAYS varied enormously in their exclusions and inclusions of story elements. The majority of the children did refer to

276

the baby sister or doll in the story, as well as to the pony. No other object or feature appeared with the same regularity. The Navajo and Sioux children commented about the moon more often than did the city children, who, on the other hand, referred to the piggy bank or money frequently.

A striking feature of some stories, absent from the original text, were details reflecting a preoccupation with violence. Some of these statements were as follows: "and he killed the doll with laughing"; or, "he('s) punishing him". Meaning, we think, that the father is punishing the boy. In another story, these phrases appeared: "He walked up on the moon. He going to try to kill him. And he see this up here. He ain't going to hold that no more. He gonna try and kill him, then."

These unexpected details of fear and violence were only present in the retold stories of city children, though experience with a violent reality was not absent in the lives of some of the Indian children.

Interrelationship of Task Measures
The continuing assessment of a new technique, such as the Story-Retelling task, implies a continuing examination of the newly elaborated measures. In this section, some of these assessments will be presented.

In this study, two types of phrases were differentiated, inferential and descriptive. This dichotomy is represented by the SRI (story-relevant inferred) and SD (Stimulus derived) items. If, indeed, SRI phrases correspond to a complex process, then it is likely that they will be preceded by long pauses. In contrast, the relatively, simpler descriptive phrases will not be preceded by long, but by short pauses.* In other words, time as measured by the duration of pauses was used as an indicator of an internal process of complexity, a procedure akin to that used by Frieda Goldman-Eisler (3), and by Harry Levin (6).

It was found that SRI (inferential) phrases were preceded by a greater number of long than short pauses, while SD phrases were *not* preceded by a significantly greater number of long pauses. These findings are not as clearcut as the prediction would imply. The data is presented in Table VII; this analysis is based upon the protocols of the New York Negro children. (We endeavored to choose a single, relatively homogeneous group for these calculations.) The relationship between pause length and sentence type was examined additionally by means of correlations. These findings are also included in Table VII.

It is difficult to determine whether these findings are effected by confounding

---

* Pauses were grouped according to duration; short pauses where those of two seconds and less, long pauses lasted more than two seconds.

variables. For instance, each time a child is presented with a new picture he takes longer than two seconds to produce his first phrase, regardless of the type of phrase he is emitting. In addition, inferential phrases, as presently scored in this task, are uneven as to complexity. The retelling of dialogue, or melodious phrases such as "high-low", "high-low", (referring to the way in which James' brothers snore) are all scored as SRI. They are added to the more difficult sequencing phrases. In future research, an attempt will be made to 'purify' this measure, and replicate some of these analyses.

TABLE VII

Pause Length and Phrase Type Analyses

Contingency Analysis

| | Mean Number of Phrases | | (N = 37) | |
	Preceded by Long Pause	Preceded by Short Pause	Mean Difference	p
SRI	4.54	1.94	+2.59	.01
SD	4.08	3.00	+1.08	NS

Correlational Analysis (N = 114)

	Long Pauses	Short Pauses
SRI	.5239	.3485
SD	.3713	.2986

The measure of stimulus-inferred phrases requires further refinement; the SRI score did not emerge as discriminating as in previous studies of Story-Retelling. However, in this study, SRI was the only task-derived measure to correlate significantly with socio-economic status, and with scores on the Peabody Picture vocabulary test. It does seem likely that an improved SRI measure will be of use as a predictor score for verbal learning in the classroom. This is one of the hypotheses being explored in a current study.

Reliability Calculations

The question, how reliable is the story retelling task, is an obvious one, although it is a hard question to answer. Reliability calculations are traditionally based upon tests which have an equal number of items, and therefore appropriate for split-half

278

reliability calculations. This method is not applicable to a technique in which the very length of the response is a variable which reflects performance skills. An assessment of reliability by means of parallel forms presents different problems. However, in this initial stage of our work with the story-retelling task, correlational analyses of the performance of children based on two books (CURIOUS GEORGE and ONE OF THESE DAYS) is used as a preliminary indicator of test reliability. It was our feeling that, in a broad sense, the two sets of retold stories are *two samples of retelling behavior*, and consequently, a correlational analysis of the obtained scores is of relevance to test reliability. The data is shown in Table VIII.

TABLE VIII

**Correlations of Story-Retelling Measures of
Forty Subjects* Based on
Two Retold Stories by Each Subject**

Measure	Correlation coefficient (Pearson r)
Number of phrases	.577 (significant at .005)
Action phrases	.434 (significant at .01)
Descriptive phrases	.570 (significant at .005)
Stimulus derived	.484 (significant at .005)
Stimulus inferred	.722 (significant at .005)

*Except action and descriptive phrases, where N is 31.

The Navajo children's retold stories were both in Navajo and in English; the scoring and correlational analyses were based upon a translation of the Navajo tapes into English by the librarian. This fact might have had some bearing upon the obtained correlation coefficients, particularly as effecting the action phrases, because the translation of Navajo verb phrases into English was particularly difficult.

In addition, correlations were obtained for inter-rater reliability, and, as shown in Table IX, were quite high.

In sum, the correlational analyses presented in this section (though they are fragmentary) lend support to our working hypothesis: namely, that the Story-Retelling Technique is a measure which can be used to compare *groups* of children, drawn from varied backgrounds, for differences in performance on a sequential language task.

279

TABLE IX

Inter-rater Reliabilities of
Story-Retelling Measures
(2 judges)

	r
Number of Phrases	.98
Action Phrases	.86
Descriptive Phrases	.99
Stimulus-Derived	.86
Story-Relevant Inferred	.99

Behavioral Rating Scale

The teachers of children enrolled in Child Development Programs were asked to fill out a Behavioral Rating Scale. Eighty-nine of the subjects in this study (representing the Navajo, Negro and Puerto Rican groups) were thus rated. It is difficult to compare across ethnic lines with this instrument, because the teachers making these ratings did not, in most instances, have cross-ethnic experiences. Thus, a more meaningful way to analyze these ratings is to see how scores on the Behavioral Rating Scale correlate with measures obtained on the experimental tasks.

The experimental measures chosen for correlational analyses between behavioral ratings and verbal performance were as follows: accuracy measures (SD and SRI), stylistic measures (action and descriptive) and scores on the Peabody Picture Vocabulary Test. (Only 36 children had both PPVT scores and ratings on the Behavioral Rating Scale.)

A number of significant relationships were obtained in the correlations of language and behavioral measures. Both accuracy measures (SD and SRI) were found to be related to teachers' ratings. Those children who included a large number of stimulus derived phrases in their retellings tended to be rated as high in achievement motivation. Children who were rated low on timidity and aggression excelled others in their story-relevant inferred scores. Of particular significance is the correlation obtained between verbal-social participation and the SRI score. In addition, the correlations reveal a positive relationship between action phrases with achievement motivation and verbal-social participation. A negative correlation exists between timidity in behavior and the depiction of action in the retold stories.

Though only a small number of children had both vocabulary test scores and behavioral ratings, the finding of a positive relationship between independence and the PPVT is statistically significant. The data appear in Table X.

280

The evaluation of these findings is enhanced by the consistency between our results and those obtained by Hess and associates in their Chicago Head Start study. (4) The measures of cognitive performance used in their study were as follows: Stanford Binet, Pre-School Inventory, National Percentile Rank Achievement Test (number and number readiness). These tests measure a broader range of cognitive skills than the measures used in this study. Nevertheless, the findings are similar; aggression and timidity were shown to relate negatively to cognitive performance in both studies, while Verbal-Social Participation, Achievement, and Independence are positively related to cognitive performance, again a finding which is the same in both studies.

The relationship between measures of language-cognitive performance (SRI) and verbal-social participation appear promising, a fact which supports our contention that this technique might be used as a predictor for classroom verbal learning.

TABLE X

Correlations of Behavioral Inventory Ratings and Experimental Measures

Behavioral characteristic	Experimental measure	r	p
High Aggression	Low SRI	(-.191)	.05 (N=89)
High Verbal Participation	High Action	(.208)	.05
High Verbal Participation	High SRI	(.254)	.025
High Timidity	Low SRI	(-.246)	.025
High Timidity	Low Action	(-.320)	.005
High Independence	High PPVT	(.417)	.01 (N=36)
High Achievement Motivation-High SD		(-.211)	.05
High Achievement Motivation-High Action		(-.352)	.005

Parental Interviews

Forty-two parents out of a possible 50 have been interviewed on the Navajo reservation. The responses reflected an emphasis upon a close family life, a value deeply held by the majority of Navajo people.

An interesting picture emerged, when parents were asked what about their pre-school child pleased them. Six major characteristics were noted. Over half of the

281

respondents ascribed a quality of helpfulness to their children. The second-most popular characteristic dealt with interest in learning in school (meaning pre-school, or course). Eight of the mothers mentioned the acquisition by their children of educational skills, four mothers listed good sibling relationships, and four praised their children for desirable personality characteristics. Analyzing these response patterns according to the socio-economic status of the parents, it was found that those parents listing educational skills and personality values were of a slightly higher socio-economic status than those who stressed helpfulness and obedience.

Below, we have included the entire answer to the question, "What kinds of things does your child do that please you most?". because we felt it expressed well the feelings of many parents toward Head Start. The child involved is a five-year-old Navajo boy.

> "The thing that pleases me most is that before he actually started school, my child can write his name, he can count, he does a little multiplication, and he knows his A, B, C's. He has also realized that there are other children in the world besides his family, and I think he has learned to get along with them. With this background, I believe he is ready to start in the regular school program.

> "None of my other children have had this type of training before and it was kind of hard for them. I would take them to school the first day of school and they would always follow me home, because they don't understand that they will come home at the end of the day. E. has learned early and I know I won't have any trouble with him. The only thing he is afraid of, as he always says, 'My school at the chapter house is really easy, but the big school will be hard.' "

Assessment of Books Used in Head Start Centers
Analysis of 'kit' books

The most popular books were WHISTLE FOR WILLIE, CURIOUS GEORGE, and GILBERTO AND THE WIND. These were closely followed by CURIOUS GEORGE GETS A JOB, and THE LION AND THE RAT. Least enjoyed by the children were MAY I BRING A FRIEND? and HAPPY BIRTHDAY TO YOU.

Verbal stimulation scores were assigned. Those books producing the largest amount of verbal response were: CURIOUS GEORGE, GILBERTO AND THE WIND, THE LION AND THE RAT, and WHISTLE FOR WILLIE. The books producing the least amount were HAPPY BIRTHDAY TO YOU and SNAIL WHERE ARE YOU? In

282

addition, books were ranked according to their usefulness in a learning situation. CURIOUS GEORGE, GILBERTO AND THE WIND, THE LION AND THE RAT and SHAPES were the highest ranking books on this measure.

Thus, two books (CURIOUS GEORGE, GILBERTO AND THE WIND) received high scores on all three measures, and two books (WHISTLE FOR WILLIE and THE LION AND THE RAT) received a high score on two. Four books (SNAIL, WHERE ARE YOU?, HAPPY BIRTHDAY TO YOU, MAY I BRING A FRIEND?, THE CAT IN THE HAT) received low scores on all three measures.

Individual Analyses
Twelve books were analyzed for individual children in the Sioux Reservation Head Start Centers. The CURIOUS GEORGE books, ANDY AND THE RUNAWAY HORSE, WHISTLE FOR WILLIE, and THE THREE LITTLE PIGS were the best received of the books.

Discussion and Conclusions
The question, *'What is the impact of ethnic content in story books?'* has been a much debated inquiry. Educators who are specialists in Early Childhood questioned whether the preoccupation of poverty workers with realistic stories in naturalistic settings was justified. In this study, two somewhat contradictory findings are of relevance to this debate.

We found that WHISTLE FOR WILLIE, a 'new look' story book with a small Negro boy and his dog as the heroes, was the most favored of the kit books. The appeal of this book was twofold; the familiarity of the events and setting seemed effective; in addition, the children of all ethnic groups enjoyed 'whistling.' CURIOUS GEORGE, the tale of the mischievous monkey, was a close second among the books evaluated in this study. This book is a classic among children's books; the realistic world of the young minority child is not reflected, directly, in its plot. It is possible, that the recent and insistent emphasis placed upon the *shared* ethnicity of reader and story figures might be overestimated, although there were indications, in this study, that children pay attention to, and often welcome, a story about a child like themselves. (The frequency with which the Sioux Indian children commented upon the Indianness of James, the hero of ONE OF THESE DAYS, is of interest in this regard.)

It would seem then, that the inclusion of 'ethnic' books in a pre-school library is a necessary and useful component of a program aimed at non-white children.

But, contrary to the original predictions, Negro children, in this study, did not retell more accurately, or more abundantly ONE OF THESE DAYS when presented in the

283

urban, Negro setting. There were no quantitative differences in the retold stories as a function of story version. This lack of a differential response was interpreted in the following way: In the context of an enriched program in which 'ethnic' books were made available to the children, the singular repetition of a book, with a Negro family as its focus, has no special effect.

Among the Navajo children, who had no access to printed storybooks with Indian children in them, and whose experience with books of any kind was limited, the impact of the two versions of ONE OF THESE DAYS was more complex. When confronted with the Negro version, many of these children gave a series of labels, or short descriptive phrases. They did not include dialogue, or retell the action sequences of the story. It was as if they had difficulty entering into, or identifying with the story, its people, when it was set in the Negro context.

In summary, it appears that the ethnic context of a story is a subtle variable; its impact depends upon a variety of factors. Among these may be the relative scarcity or abundance of books representative of the child's own environment. Another factor is the insularity of an ethnic group--the frequency with which children interact with members of other ethnic groups.

Story-Retelling Technique
The consistent and intriguing findings in this study relate to features other than the ethnic content of books. Variations in retold stories as a function of ethnic membership and language spoken yielded interesting results.

In this investigation, much progress has been made in the adaptation of the Story-Retelling Technique to varied field conditions, to speakers of diverse languages, and in the quantification of the stories themselves.

Two major applications of this technique are envisaged by the authors. The first of these is the expanded use of this task for *comparative,* cross-cultural research; the second is the *monitoring* of language growth in young children, by repeated retelling of stories. Many of the traditional techniques of language assessment have been found limiting by contemporary workers in the field of language research. Measures of vocabulary (productive or receptive) give but a narrow picture of the ways in which children use language. Lacking a common verbal input, projective tasks, such as the Thematic Apperception Test, present difficulties in intra-personal or group comparisons. The currently popular imitation tasks assume a high degree of cooperation on the part of young children in the testing situation, but these tasks lack in intrinsic interest. Recognizing these limitations, it seemed useful to attempt to refine a technique which is applicable to the assessment of language skills of children of diverse backgrounds.

284

The following features of verbal behavior have been assessed with this technique:

Output Variables
The verbosity of children can be misjudged by teachers, as well as by psychologists. Many young, bilingual children, or children who are speakers of low-status dialects, tend to withdraw from speaking when in front of other children, or when confronted by strangers. But, language samples can be gathered from such children by training teachers, or 'librarians' to administer a task, such as Story-Retelling, to the child in an individual session, in his own language. If the testing situation is standardized, measures of the child's rate and volume of language, derived from his retold story, can be compared with the performance of other children.

How important is verbal output as an indicator of verbal competence? To date, the results are contradictory. In the case of the toddler, sheer volume is an indicator of verbal growth. But in the case of preschool, and grade school children, low, non-significant correlations have been found between verbal output and verbal meaning measures, or output and intelligence. The susceptibility of verbal output to the *social conditions* in which language is elicited might contribute to the indefinitiveness of our current knowledge. The measurement of verbal output is one of the trickiest tasks confronting the psycholinguist.

Measures of Accuracy of Story-Retelling
The recall of text-based phrases, without a pictorial cue to aid the child in this recall, assumes that the child is engaged in active and careful listening. It is possible that the SRI index can be used as a predictor of children's *verbal learning* rate in the classroom. The usefulness of this measure as a predictor is currently being tested.

Stylistic Measures
The retelling of action sequences in ONE OF THESE DAYS, as contrasted with stories replete with descriptions, or labels, differentiated sharply among children drawn from different ethnic groups. This index also reflected differences in story version. Negro and Mexican children produced more active stories than the Puerto Rican, Navajo and Sioux children. However, when action phrases were looked at as a percentage of the total number of phrases produced, the Sioux Indian children emerged in a different light. Theirs were short but action-packed tales.

This penchant for the retelling of what is happening seems to be an indicator of cultural differences. In examining what is a good or balanced story, an action/description index was developed, and proved to be a good indicator of subjectively perceived differences in the quality of the retold stories.

285

Additional Remarks

In this study, only a limited start was made toward the assessment of books used in pre-school centers. Nevertheless, it appears that it is possible to collect information concerning children's book preferences, and that a cohesive picture of preference does emerge from such observations. It seems that this crucial area for language development and reading-readiness skills needs additional, extensive exploration among low-income children.

In this study, a novel approach to the gathering of data was developed for children drawn from diverse backgrounds. We utilized young college students of the same ethnic background as the children (Navajo, Mexican - American, etc.).

The contribution of these people has been very successful: first, they were a much-needed bridge between the children's own community and the school. Secondly, they helped the children move in cognitive functioning from informal tasks to more formal learning.

While flexible and effective with the children, they also became sophisticated in methods of data gathering. We are aware that the type of language samples which these people obtained could not have been gotten in any one-shot assessment technique.

The wealth of language and information on intellectual strengths of children of diverse backgrounds has led us to conclude that widely-held myths of the ineducability and intellectual inferiority of low-income children is open to serious challenge. Such myths can only be based on certain types of superficial assessment.

Our success with a novel technique of language elicitation strengthens our contention that in designing educational programs for low-income children, great care should be taken to develop adequate techniques for both instruction in, and assessment of, language skills.

(Based upon final report of Office of Economic Opportunity Research Project No. 577)

286

References

1. Cazden, Courtney. Subcultural Differences in Child Language: an Inter-Disciplinary Review, MERRILL-PALMER QUARTERLY. 12 (3):191, July 1966.

2. Deutsch, M., Maliver, A., Brown, B. and Cherry, E. COMMUNICATION OF INFORMATION IN THE ELEMENTARY SCHOOL CLASSROOM. Cooperative Research Project No. 908. April 1964.

3. Goldman-Eisler, F. Hesitation and Information in Speech, INFORMATION THEORY, 4th London Symposium. Butterworth, London, Pp. 162-174. 1961.

4. Hess, Robert D. Techniques of Assessing Cognitive and Social Abilities of Children and Parents in Project Head Start, Final Report on Research Contract OEO-519, Univ. of Chicago, 1966.

5. John, V. and Horner, V. The analysis of story-retelling as a measure of language proficiency. Paper presented at the Annual Meeting of The American Psychological Association, September, 1965.

6. Levin, H. and Silverman, I. Hesitation Phenomena in Children's Speech. March 1963. Mimeographed Report.

7. McCarthy, Dorothy. Language Development in Children. In: MANUAL OF CHILD PSYCHOLOGY. L. Carmichael, editor. New York: John Wiley and Sons, Inc., 1946; 1954; (1946, pp. 476-581; 1954, pp. 492-630.)

8. Millon, Clara and John, Vera. Unpublished summary of parent interviews conducted in Rochester, New York, Spring of 1961, and Fall of 1965.

9. Pomerantz, Charlotte. THE MOON PONY, New York: Young Scott Books, 1967. (An abbreviated, pre-publication version of this book was used in the study.)

10. Templin, Mildred C. CERTAIN LANGUAGE SKILLS IN CHILDREN. Minneapolis: University of Minneasota Press, 1957.

HEAD START AND FIRST GRADE READING

Wallace Ramsey, Ph.D.,
Professor, School of Education,
University of Missouri, St. Louis, Missouri

WALLACE RAMSEY, Ph.D.

Deprivation in infancy and early childhood is thought to have a debilitating effect on later school success, particularly in learning to read. It is reasoned that children who do not have the experiences usually obtained during the pre-school years have insufficient background for reading. The lack of practice in hearing and using the typical language patterns of Standard English handicaps a child in learning to read those same patterns, language specialists believe.

Head Start programs are usually designed to compensate for the lack of experience and the barrenness of language practice found in deprived children. Teachers in such programs take children on field trips, read stories to them, show films, and utilize other audiovisual aids in an attempt to expand their breadth of knowledge and experience. Along with this activity there is much oral language interplay between teachers and pupils, and between one pupil and others. Children are *encouraged* to talk to the teacher so they will gain increased familiarity with the language in a very functional way.

There is little disagreement on whether or not Head Start programs have the potential to effect such changes in a majority of children attending them. Whether they actually *do* is less certain--the problem simply hasn't been researched very thoroughly. Those who have observed very many Head Start children feel confident that such changes occur. Whether the effect on *later* reading achievement is marked is even less certain. Recent reports in educational literature suggest that reading achievement is not favorably affected unless the first grade reading program is designed to capitalize on the effects of Head Start[7]. The study reported in this paper sheds additional light on the problem.

In Scott County, Kentucky, in September, 1965, 152 first graders who had attended Head Start the previous summer were intermixed with 192 non Head Start children in fifteen classrooms. The children labeled the "Head Start Group" in this report had experienced an eight-week program in classes of fifteen pupils taught by certified first-and second-grade teachers. The teachers had attended the University of

291

Kentucky for one week of training to qualify them as teachers in the Head Start program.

During the eight weeks of Head Start the children were involved in an experience-oriented program, one designed to increase their knowledge of their surrounding world. Teachers utilized various types of real and vicarious experiences to bolster the children's supply of information and language facility. In an informal atmosphere emphasis was given to increasing children's stock of ideas and their verbal fluency.

In the fall following Head Start the children entered the first grades in the five consolidated schools in two systems. Assignment to classrooms was random with regard to Head Start and non Head Start attendance. Their first grade teachers had graduated from four year accredited programs of teacher education. Each had minimal training in the teaching of reading--the one course required for certification.

The approach taken to reading instruction can best be described as formal and traditional, with basal materials being used in classes utilizing in-class grouping to care for individual differences.

Classrooms were supplied with basal reading textbooks by the State Department of Education, the usual practice in Kentucky. Charts, supplementary readers, and supplementary phonics materials (used in twelve classrooms) were purchased from P.T.A. funds or from local school funds. Small collections of appropriate trade books were used by the children in each room. The yearly per-pupil cost of education was under $400 in the two districts.

Three classrooms enrolling eighty-two children used GINN BASIC READERS (which provided for an early emphasis on learning to read whole words followed by an analytic approach to phonics) and attended school in half-day sessions until approximately December first. The remaining classrooms used PHONETIC KEYS TO READING, which provided for early emphasis on phonics. The latter group attended school a full day from the beginning of the year.

Gathering Research Data
Early in the school year permission was obtained from school officials to study the situation and gather data to determine the effects of Head Start on reading achievement. In such studies (involving comparisons of group performance) the Hawthorne Effect often influences results. In order to reduce the chances of this happening, the researchers decided to use results of the tests *usually given* by the schools (the Metropolitan Reading Readiness Test and the Stanford Achievement Tests) and to give only one extra test--the California Test of Mental Maturity. It was given to all first graders early in December. Data from cumulative records were used in determining

292

the socio-economic status of the children. Information concerning the children was gathered with little fanfare and all publicity concerning the study was avoided. Since all of the first grade teachers were teaching both Head Start and non Head Start children, the teacher variable was held constant.

Differences Between the Groups
The data were analyzed to determine the similarities between the two groups. They were found to contain similar ratios of boys to girls (49%-51% in Head Start versus 48%-52% not in Head Start.) The Head Start group contained a significantly higher proportion of Negroes (30% as compared with 3½% in the non Head Start group.) The following table shows the differences in the occupational status of parents.

*Occupational Status of Parents

Occupational Level	Head Start	Non Head Start
Unskilled	37.5%	25.5%
Skilled	47.9%	43.2%
Professional	14.6%	31.3%

*Occupations were categorized by use of the "Socio-Economic Scale of Occupations" devised by A. M. Edwards.

The figures reveal that the Head Start group clustered toward the unskilled end of the distribution. The differences between the two groups in occupation of parents was significant at the .01 level.

The Metropolitan Reading Test scores of the non Head Start group averaged slightly higher than those of the Head Start group but the difference was only marginally significant at the .15 level. Of some significance is the fact that over sixty percent of both groups ranked below the fiftieth percentile in readiness. Both groups had a median in the third decile.

In mental age the non Head Start group had a mean four months higher than the other group--a difference significant at the .02 level. In each group a large proportion of the children had mental ages below 6.6 years--the minimum mental age at which a child is likely to learn to read with ease (56% in Head Start as compared with 47% in the non Head Start group.)

A comparison of mental age scores and those from the readiness tests gives rise to interesting speculation. The mental-ages-in-months pattern is an almost normal curve but the pattern made by the readiness scores is almost random--with peak popula-

293

tion in the lowest decile. This suggests to the writer that the reading readiness test measured the results of pre-school experiences that were more formal than those experienced by the children in this study.

Comparisons were made of other important variables for which information was available. These included chronological age, state of the family (broken or intact), number of children in the family, sibling rank of the child, and presence of health limitations. There were no significant differences between the two groups in any of these variables.

Comparison of Achievement Gains
At the end of the year a high proportion of both groups (over sixty per cent) scored below the expected grade level but there was no significant difference in the mean reading levels of the two groups. A higher proportion of the Head Start group scored very low (35.5% scored below 1.5 grade level; 22% of the non Head Start group scored that low.)

To determine which of the measured variables made a significant difference in the reading achievement of the two groups, they were statistically equated for each of several variables and achievement levels were compared.

The Head Start Negro mean in reading was a month higher than the non Head Start Negro mean but the difference was not found to be significant. In the socio-economic levels for whom Head Start is designed, the two groups exhibited no significant difference in average achievement. The same was found to be true when the groups were equated for readiness scores.

The groups were equated for mental age and achievement was compared. In the 71-80 months mental age range the non Head Start group had a higher mean reading score--significant at the .06 level. An examination of the results revealed that in this study the child of 6.6 years of mental age was helped by Head Start but not enough to bring him up to his non Head Start counterpart in reading achievement at the end of first grade. However, the brighter Head Start child achieved as well as the brighter non Head Start child.

Summary and Implications of the Study
A similar number of Head Start and non Head Start children were intermixed in first grade classrooms using a typical basal reader-in-class grouping reading program. The two groups differed in several ways. The Head Start group came from lower socio-economic levels and contained a higher proportion of Negroes than did the non Head Start group. The former group measured less ready to read and had a lower mental age than the latter.

294

Despite the differences noted above, in a straight, unequated comparison of the reading scores of the two groups there was no significant difference in reading achievement at the end of the year. This indicates that the Head Start program attained some measure of success in accomplishing one of its important goals: preparing children for better academic learning. Even though several factors reduced the chances for success of the Head Start group, their average level of achievement was up to that of the more favorably disposed non Head Start group.

A further examination of the test results is sobering: the Head Start group had a higher proportion of poor readers--those scoring below 1.4 grade level at the end of the year than did the non Head Start group. It appeared that a hard core of potentially poor readers was helped very little by the Head Start program.

This writer feels that the factors which influence the usual academic retardation of disadvantaged children are too numerous and too complicated to be offset by a Head Start program of eight weeks duration. A kindergarten program lasting a full year and being of a compensatory nature and quality would have better met the readiness needs of the children involved in this study--as well as those of most children for whom Head Start is intended.

A FURTHER LOOK

Most Head Start programs are clearly experience oriented and are designed to enrich the lives of disadvantaged children. Providing programs full of new experiences helps disadvantaged children to begin school more nearly ready to read. It is questionable however, if the traditional basal reader oriented reading program most effectively capitalizes on the effects of Head Start.

The needs of experience-starved and language under-developed six-year-olds are not met by basal reader stories in typical first grade materials. This is true whether such children are from Appalachia or the inner city. (Teachers in the inner city do have the advantage of being able to utilize basal readers more nearly suited to their groups, such as the BANK STREET READERS or the DETROIT READERS. Teachers from Appalachia do not have such suitable material available for their groups.) The basal approach can be particularly sterile and unproductive when taught by teachers who have been using it a number of years.

The language experience approach (described by Allen and Lee,[1]) would allow children and teachers to create their own stories, using experiences and language patterns that are typical of the children involved. The research of Stauffer[5] Vilscek and others[6] in Delaware and Pittsburgh in using the language experience approach with disadvantaged children is evidence supporting this contention.

295

Any reading program, and particularly one involving disadvantaged children, is greatly influenced by the level of competence of the teachers involved. A systematic program of skill development can be provided by a teacher of limited imagination and skill--when she follows a basal reader guidebook. Many first grade teachers do not possess the level of knowledge, degree of creativity, or the amount of self confidence needed to work out a skills program to fit language experience stories and the needs of individual children. Until ways can be found to help teachers acquire these traits, or schools to find teachers with such traits, Head Start can not be followed up in the manner so greatly needed.

Another problem arises from the fact that disadvantaged children come from environments in which they have had very little undivided attention from an adult. They need teachers who can find time to listen to them and provide language models and feedback that will help them to achieve greater maturity in language. Adult stimulation is needed to encourage them to engage in the kind of language activity that leads to higher level of linguistic development. This means, obviously, that a way must be found to reduce the pupil loads of first grade teachers of Head Start children--or they must be provided with well trained aides who can properly fulfill the role of "listener" to the children.

In St. Louis schools the "Rooms of Twenty" have been so signally successful in improving the language skills of disadvantaged Negro children that the school system is rapidly increasing the number of rooms of this type[2]. The rest of the nation should profit from the success of the innovation. It provides evidence that reducing the pupil load can result in some rather spectacular results.

About one-third of the children in the study described in this paper were Negro. The average reading achievement of the Negro Head Starters was below that of the White Head Start children, but not seriously so. This was probably due to factors not revealed by the study. Several teachers of Title I E.S.E.A. remedial reading programs have reported to the writer the very real differences in phonology and syntax between the speech of Negro and White children cause difficulties for them in teaching reading. That such differences exist has been substantiated by Labov[3] and Shearer[4]. Labov reports a study he did in Harlem. Shearer reports nation-wide studies done by Dr. Charles Hurst Jr. of Howard University. Both men have documented the differences in phonology and syntax.

In any area in which large numbers of Negro children are enrolled, a study of their specific speech habits needs to be made and the results used to alter the basic patterns of teaching *all* phases of language to them. Negro speech has been described as a "colorful, inventive, mellifluous dialect" and a "language system that has its own

296

consistent rules."[4] When teachers downgrade it and insist that it must be completely replaced by Standard English they are compounding their problems.

The writer is not in sympathy with programs of reading instruction used in some urban school systems enrolling large numbers of Negroes--programs which take a pure phonics approach to reading and attempt to re-make the phonology of Negro children in the process. Such programs may satisfy the desire of school administrators for a more "academic" or "basic" curriculum--but they fail to appreciably affect either the speaking habits or reading ability of the children involved. They represent the kind of insisted-upon conformity to White standards (regarded as innately "superior" by the majority) and repudiation of Negro standards that tends to aggravate race relations and inflame extremists.

A solution to the problems of teaching Negro children to read will be nearer when we admit that the Negro child is now being forced to use beginning reading materials written in an unknown language, Standard English--a language that is, in several respects, a *foreign* language to him. His task in learning to read is doubled--he must learn to *read* a foreign language at the same time he is learning to speak it, a practice not condoned by linguists.

This writer proposes the use of an approach that may seem drastic to many purists. Early reading material for Negro children (or any disadvantaged dialect group) should be written in their dialect--with its phonological and syntactical deviations from Standard English represented in graphic form. By doing this the child who says "I be heah by fo' o'clock" or who tells where John is by saying, "He home now" can be helped to read earlier and with satisfaction.

The Negro child's inability to speak Standard English need not retard his reading development. He can be taught to read his non-standard dialect now while he is being taught to *speak* Standard English (probably as a "second language" taught by oral-aural methods by teachers working in a language laboratory situation.) Once he has learned to speak Standard English (a necessary tool for survival in a nation in which the dialect is the *lingua franca*) the child can be taught to read it. The use of a synthetic alphabet, such as I.T.A. or Unifon, might facilitate the whole process and prove to be advisable.

SUMMARY

A Head Start type program holds a lot of promise for the future. However, experimentation with various patterns of organization, and with different types and lengths of programs, in needed. The writer feels that a program of one or two full years in duration is likely to be necessary to achieve the desired results.

297

Of very great importance is the approach taken in teaching reading to the "graduates" of Head Start. It should be one that naturally supplements and follows up what is *begun* in Head Start. The usual basal program doesn't do this; a language experience approach is more likely to do it, especially if the material is written in the children's own dialect. Much more research will help educators to refine their techniques so that Head Start can be helped to achieve its full promise.

References

1. Allen, Roach V. and Dorris May Lee. LEARNING TO READ THROUGH EXPERIENCE. New York: Appleton-Century-Crofts, 1963.

2. Kottmeyer, William. "Hard Times and Great Expectations, An Account to the Community of the Condition of the St. Louis Public Schools." St. Louis, Missouri: The Board of Education, September, 1967.

3. Labov, William. "Linguistic Research on Non-Standard English of Negro Children" in Anita Dorr (Editor) PROBLEMS AND PRACTICES IN NEW YORK CITY SCHOOLS. New York: New York Society for the Experimental Study of Education, 1965.

4. Shearer, Lloyd. "Americans Who Can't Speak Their Own Language." PARADE, THE ST. LOUIS POST DISPATCH, June 11, 1967, pages 6-7.

5. Stauffer, Russell G. "The Effectiveness of Language Arts and Basic Reader Approaches to First Grade Reading Instruction," THE READING TEACHER, 20, No. 1 (October, 1966) pp. 18-24.

6. Vilscek, Elaine, et.al. "Coordinating and Integrating Language Arts Instruction in First Grade," THE READING TEACHER, 20, No. 1 (October, 1966) pp. 31-37.

7. Paul Woodring (Ed) "Schools Make News," SATURDAY REVIEW, September 16, 1967, p. 91.

298

AN AUTOTELIC RESPONSIVE ENVIRONMENT NURSERY SCHOOL FOR DEPRIVED CHILDREN

John H. Meier, Ph.D.,
Associate Director, The New Nursery School Research Project,
Colorado State College, Greeley, Colorado

Glen Nimnicht, Ed.D.,
Associate Director, The New Nursery School Research Project,
Colorado State College, Greeley, Colorado;
Program Director, Far West Laboratory
for Educational Research and Development

Oralie McAfee, M.A.,
Head Teacher, The New Nursery School,
Colorado State College, Greeley, Colorado

JOHN H. MEIER, Ph.D.

GLEN NIMNICHT, Ed.D.

ORALIE McAFEE, M. A.

Part I

RESEARCH RATIONALE SUPPORTING EARLY INTERVENTION

A conservative estimate (Ferman, Kornbluh, and Haber, 1965, p. 84) states that eleven million children in the United States are environmentally deprived. That is, their environment has not only failed to prepare them to meet the expectations of their school and society, but it defeats them before they start and probably prevents them from realizing much of their intellectual potential.

In the main these children come from impoverished, low-class homes. Their cultural and social background has not prepared them for school and the demands that will be made upon them in school, but they do have a cultural and social system. To say they are economically deprived does not say half enough because the problem is not just one of poverty.

> To all too many people, poverty means merely the absence of money. This is a definition influenced, perhaps, by the belief in American society that if money is lacking, work and determination will provide it, and that in our affluent society no one need starve. Admittedly, nobody starves today and apples will probably never again be sold on the street corners. But it must also be remembered that poverty is not merely a question of food, or of money, or of determination. For poverty deprives the individual not only of material comfort but also of human dignity and fulfillment. Its causes are much more complex, and its cure requires more than merely a relief check or the creation of one or two programs of training and retraining. It must be realized that, because of the growing complexity of modern society, the disadvantaged, in particular, more and more lose the very ability to make choices, to be responsible, to know what must be done, and to take action. In short, poverty has today become a complex interlocking set of circumstances caused by and in turn reinforcing each other, that

301

combine to keep the individual without money, without help, without work. It can truly be said that today those people are poor who can least afford it.

—From Hearings before the Select Committee on Poverty of the Committee on Labor and Public Welfare, United States Senate, 88th Congress, Second Session on S.1642.

Whether these children are white (or Anglo), Negro, Indian, Spanish-American or Puerto Rican, their whole environment impinges upon them and makes it almost impossible for them or their children ever to leave their urban or rural slum except to migrate to another slum. They are caught in a cycle of poverty.

The cycle of poverty means this: The environmentally deprived child enters school, fails because of his background, and drops out of school as soon as possible. He returns to his slum with its emotional frustrations, crime, mental turmoil, and unemployment only to raise the next generation to repeat the same cycle. This was not always the case; many immigrants, both from foreign countries and around rural areas, passed through the slums of our great cities on their way to a better life. Now at least a fifth of our population currently lives in poverty (defined as an annual income of less than three thousand dollars) with little prospect of anything better. For one reason or another (especially old age, the absence of a man in the household, lack of education, racial discrimination or a combination of these) the impoverished cannot contribute to production, so they are not given the means to consume. Of the 32,000,000 people in Lampman's impoverished population, 8,000,000 were sixty-five years or older; 6,400,000 were non-white; 8,000,000 were in households headed by women; 21,000,000 were in units headed by a person with an eighth-grade education or less (Lampman, 1965, p. 181).

What Does it Mean to be Caught in this Cycle?
The first effect is less chance to survive birth and infancy. For example, the infant deaths are 300% lower in the Queens borough in New York City of upper-lower class and lower-middle class residential area than in Negro Harlem (Tunley, 1966, p. 42). In 1964, for the nation as a whole, the infant mortality rate during the first 28 days of life was 64% higher for non-white (including Spanish-surnamed) children than for white children. From one month to a year the rate of non-white deaths (14.6 per 1,000 live births) was nearly triple that of white infant deaths (5.4) according to a recent report by Hunt and Huyck (1966).

If the non-white survives birth and infancy, he still has a lower life expectancy than his white counterpart. If he is non-white, his life expectancy is seven or eight years lower than that of a white person. Even this statistic is misleading. It is not the skin

302

color that makes the difference; if the statistics showed life expectancy according to social class, the differences between upper and lower class would be greater than the difference between white and non-white. In effect, we are talking about the culture of deprivation about which Harrington has already written so poignantly (1962).

Of course, part of this reduction in life expectancy is due to the poor health that is more common among the deprived. Figures from a survey by the Children's Bureau of Health Education and Welfare, if taken at face value, might suggest that physical disorders are less frequent among the poor (Coll, 1966, p. 3). Based upon household interviews to determine chronic illnesses among children under 17, the following breakdown is obtained:

Family Annual Income	Chronic Illnesses in Children Under 17
4,000 or less	207.2*
4,000 - 6,999	222.6
7,000 or above	261.4

*The rates are per thousand

A closer examination of the chronic conditions presents a different picture. Hay fever, asthma, and other allergies account for 20.0% of the reported chronic conditions in families with incomes of 4,000 or less in contrast to 40.1% in the 7,000 and over group. Easily recognized and serious illnesses such as paralysis and orthopedic impairments account for 13.8% of the illness among the poor and 9.7% of the illness in the top income group.

As Harrington (1962) points out, the notion that mental illness is a disease of the affluent is false. The disadvantaged are more likely to be mentally ill than the middle and upper-class. Hollingshead and Redlich (1960) tabulated some revealing relationships between mental illness and social classes in their study of New Haven, Connecticut. The social class breakdown goes from the upper class (I) to the lower class (V). The rates are per 100,000 by class. In the first column the rates are for patients who entered treatment for the first time between June 1, 1950 and December 1, 1950. The second column shows re-entry of former patients from treatment during the same period. Column three shows the number of patients who were in treatment before June 1, and remained in treatment throughout the period under study.

In other words, the percentage of people from the lower class who were under treatment was four times as great as the percentage of the people in upper classes I and II, and more than two and one-half times as great as lower-middle class IV. The

303

Class	Rate Column I	Rate Column II	Rate Column III
I-II	97	88	368
III	114	68	346
IV	89	59	516
V	139	123	1406
Total	104	76	638

percentage entering treatment was approximately 50% higher in the lower class V than in classes I, II, and IV and the percentage returning for additional treatment shows approximately the same differences. The conclusion one must reach is that a higher percentage from Class V enter treatment in the first place, more return for additional treatment, and more remain longer under treatment.

Not only are the poor more susceptible to illness, they are more likely to be mentally handicapped. Tunley writes, "Indeed most authorities agree that retardation could be cut in half if we applied what we already know about such familiar hazards as faulty metabolism and German measles" (1966, p. 43). Unfortunately, this knowledge is not applied within the very group which cannot afford to buy pre-natal care of pregnant women. This accounts for much of the diagnosable mental retardation. A deprived environment probably accounts for most of the mental retardation that cannot be explained by some diagnosable organic cause. The evidence is accumulating daily to demonstrate the close relationship between the environment and mental development. It comes from animal studies, experimental research studies involving humans, and sociological case studies. Since the review some ten years ago by Kirk and Kolstoe (1953, pp. 400-416), as well as its precedent by Hunt and Cofer (pp. 971-1032 in Hunt, Ed., 1944) approximately twenty years ago, there has been a considerable increase in psychological and educational research concerning persons who are mentally handicapped.

In the past, the so-called educable mentally handicapped child was commonly handled in numerous special ways. Since the turn of the century, practices have ranged from special public school classes to absolute exclusion and isolation or first grade for an additional year's maturation; in others he has to be failed one or more times in the regular program before being considered for placement in a special class.

> *Keeping the child at home until he has matured sufficiently to attend the regular grades is based on the assumption that maturation is the only factor to be considered. If, however, a lack*

304

of training in the home has retarded the child's development, keeping him at home only accentuates the effects of such factors....Allowing the child to fail in school for the first two or three years is likewise considered unsatisfactory. Such an experience for children during their formative years may produce inhibitions and poor attitudes toward learning when they do become ready for instruction; it may produce a distaste for school in general. School failure at this age level is considered a deterrent to good personality development (Kirk, 1958, pp. 1-2).

The preceding quotation questions several of the traditional practices employed in the area of mentally handicapped children. Very little positive consideration in terms of special school programs has been given to the child whose problems are essentially cultural in etiology (cf. Martin, Meier, Reed, and Welsch, Eds., 1963 and Nimnicht and Meier, 1966).

Adding turbulence to already cloudy waters were psychodiagnostic discrepancies and even anachronism, as the following citation purported:

Because of the continuing tendency of many special educators and researchers to base decisions and actions on unwarranted assumptions, and considering the diligent research of those who have provided a few answers during the past years, it is desirable to re-examine some of Goldstein's facts, determine their right to this label, and offer other possibilities for consideration. Unfortunately, much of Goldstein's position of ten years ago is, today, accorded almost universally unqualified acceptance by teachers, authors, other professionals and institutions of higher learning. Therefore, the purposes of this paper seem clear; to provoke the creative to seek answers; and to instill a healthy unrest in all who work with mentally subnormal (Blatt, 1960, p.49).

Historically, only a few experimentally minded individuals demonstrated an interest in mentally handicapped people. The attitude long prevailed that only institutionalization, special education, or training was needed on the basis of what later proved to be an inaccurate diagnosis (Cutts, 1957, and Garfield and Affleck, 1960). However, when the federal government, especially encouraged by the personal interest and support of Presidents Eisenhower, Kennedy, and Johnson, appropriated substantial sums of money to support research into the causes and prevention of mental retardation, public as well as professional activity in this area increased in direct proportion.

As part of a cross-cultural approach, Dennis (1960) presented data concerning the behavioral development among 174 children, aged one year to four years, in three Iranian institutions. A significantly greater retardation was evident in children living in two of the institutions compared to the near-normal development of those living in the third one. This was attributed solely to the lack of handling, including placing in a sitting and prone position, at the former two institutions. It was concluded that restriction of specific kinds of learning opportunities severely affected behavioral and motor development.

There had been considerable controversy regarding the inheritance of mental retardation versus the effects of environmental deprivation. It was considered meaningless to discuss this problem as stated because it was illegitimate to classify all cases of mental deficiency (i.e., heredity, brain injury, cultural deprivation, etc.) into one category. It appeared that the lower grades of mental retardation occurred in all classes of society. These cases were usually organic in etiology, some being specifically identified as arising from rare recessive genes, which was discussed in a later section of this review. The majority of the higher grade or borderline groups appeared to come from parents of lower socioeconomic status and were thought to be the results of cultural deprivation or disadvantage. Since the diagnostic category of mental handicap included both mild and severe retardation, much confusion about the above etiological considerations was to be found in the literature (Rothstein, 1961).

Some of the effects of environmental enrichment on changes in measured intelligence have been investigated. Alper and Horne (1959) conducted a twenty-year longitudinal study of institutionalized mental defectives and found very few extreme shifts in intelligence quotients. Pinneau (1961) reported many similar studies in his quite thorough treatment of some of the statistical reasons for changing intelligence quotients with especial reference to the 1960 revision of the STANFORD-BINET INTELLIGENCE SCALE.

On the other side of the coin, Garfield, Wilcott and Milgram (1961) reported a study of individuals who were institutionalized for mental handicaps and later released as not mentally defective. The implications of such misdiagnoses were considered to be formidable and gave great incentive for studies such as the present one.

A rather strong statement in favor of environmental influence was contributed by Knobloch and Pasamanick (1956):

> *Even though there are lacunae in the evidence, the patterning of almost all of the recent studies, ours as well as others, points the total picture overwhelmingly in one direction. The geneticists will*

306

need to give more than **post hoc** *data, and will require experimental or better controlled epidemiological studies than have previously been offered to support their views. Otherwise, scientific parsimony seems to lead one to the conclusion that at the present time the most useful theory is that while man's fundamental structure and consequently his basic functioning is genetically determined, it is his sociocultural milieu affecting biological and psychological variables which modifies his behavior, and, in the absence of organic brain damage, makes one individual different from the next (p. 16).*

Stein and Susser (1963) found in a study of 50 adults, classified in school as educationally subnormal and recommended for special schooling, that in 20 cases there was evidence of brain damage or other serious handicaps to learning. In the remaining 30 cases there was no such evidence. When the families were divided into lower-social class and others, Stein and Susser found that the twenty with brain damage or other serious defects came from all social classes but all 30 of the others (clinically normal) came from the lower class.

Rosenzweig (1966) reports on a study with rats. When the animals were about twenty-five days old they were assigned to an enriched environment. The animals were housed in groups of 10 to 12 in a large cage with toys such as ladders, wheels, boxes and platforms. The animals were given a daily half-hour exploratory session in a pattern of barriers. At about 30 days some formal training was given in a series of mazes. In the impoverished condition the animals were housed in individual cages with solid side walls and were kept in a separate, quiet, dimly-lighted room. At the end of the 80 days, the brains were removed and dissected. Rosenzweig reports:

The results demonstrate that the ECT (enriched environment) rats consistently develop greater weight of cerebral cortex than do their impoverished littermates. Overall, the cortex of the enriched rats weighs 4% more than that of the restricted rats (p. 001), and four-fifths of the pairs show a difference in this direction. Further experiments that we have done indicate that it is possible to modify selectively one or another region of the cortex, depending upon the particular program of enrichment used. For example, raising rats in the dark results in measurable shrinkage of the visual cortex. If the environment is complex, the dark raised rats develop heavier somesthetic areas than light raised littermates (pp. 323, 324). The experimenters also found chemical changes in the brains of the rats which favored the enriched group and they have some evidence to indicate that the brain changes run parallel with changes in problem-solving ability. Bloom (1964) and Hunt (1964)

307

make strong cases for the importance of early enriched environments to best develop human problem-solving abilities; the first five years seem to be exceedingly crucial in this regard.

Studies with children have demonstrated that the first born is more likely to be gifted or eminent than are his siblings (Jones, 1954). Twins on the average have IQ's several points lower than singletons; pairs of siblings spaced further apart in age do better on intelligence tests than those born closer together (Hunt, 1964, p. 341); the older or only child is more successful in first grade than younger siblings (Churchill, 1960). Hunt's hypothesis is that siblings born close together do not get all the adult attention and stimulation they need for full development. The relatively larger family size and younger family head of the poverty group does not augur well for each child's optimum development in view of this hypothesis (Ferman, Kornbluh and Haber, 1965, p. 34 and Mittlebach and Marshall, 1966, p. 41).

Another kind of evidence that illustrates the effects of environmental deprivation on young children comes from case studies similar to that reported on Anna, an illegitimate child, who was kept in an attic-like room with little care or attention for the first six years of her life. At the time she was discovered and removed from her mother's home she could not speak, or walk, or gesture or feed herself. She was so apathetic that is was hard to tell whether or not she could hear. Two years later Anna had progressed to the point where she could walk, understand simple commands, feed herself, achieve some neatness, understand people, etc. But she still did not speak. Her hearing and vision were normal. At age ten she had started to learn to speak. In the school for retarded children she could call attendants by name and she had a few complete sentences to express her wants (Davis, 1949, p. 40). Davis, who wrote the case study of Anna, writes that there is a possibility that Anna may have been congenitally deficient, but he thinks that it is likely that Anna might have had a normal or near-normal mental capacity if she had not been isolated for six years.

Davis reports on a very similar case. Isabelle was discovered after spending most of her first six years in a dark room with her mother, a deaf mute. Isabelle had no speech; she made only a strange croaking sound. "The general impression was that she was wholly uneducable" (Skeels, 1965, p. 33). Under a special program of training she covered six years of learning in two years and according to Davis, her I.Q. test score tripled in a year and a half. (This statement was based on the fact that at six and a half her score on a Stanford Binet was 19 months.) At 14 Isabelle was in the sixth grade (still two years behind in school) and the teacher said that she participated in all school activities as normally as other children.

Other studies point in the same direction. Skeels (1965) reports on 13 infants who were moved from the unstimulating environment of an orphanage to a residential

308

center where they received considerable attention and affection. Twelve similar children remained in the orphanage. The children who received the attention showed an average gain of 27.5 I.Q. points in 19 months while the other group had an average loss of 27.2 I.Q. points in 21 months. All of the 13 children who were removed from the orphanage were placed with families and now are young adults. All are self-supporting, eleven are married. Their average attainment in school is the 12th grade. Their occupations range from domestic workers to professionals. In contrast, of the 12 who remained in the orphanage one died in adolescence after living in an institution for the mentally retarded, four are still wards of institutions, one is married and one is divorced. Their average attainment in school was the third grade, half of them are unemployed, and except for one person, the balance are unskilled laborers.

These studies report extreme cases, but the evidence is growing that the same kind of effect, to a lesser degree, can be observed in environmentally deprived children whether they come from the slums of city or from the rural countryside. In other words, a loss of intellectual ability seems to be a by-product of the culture of poverty.

Poverty for a Fifth of our Population is not a Necessary Condition.
The irony is that this poverty exists and persists in the most affluent society in the history of the world at a time when that society has the means to offer its citizens education from early childhood to old age, to provide ample health and medical care for its citizens, and to help the entire world achieve the same ends. Why? Why hasn't our society broken the cycle wherein poverty and deprivation begets poverty and deprivation? Because the vast majority of Americans assume that this is the way it has to be because we live in a world of scarcity and people can consume only according to the contribution they make. The truth is that our society in the United States is not one of scarcity but one of plenty in which no one has to live in poverty. The problem is how can we help one-fifth of the people in the country participate in our affluence without destroying their self-respect. Galbraith in his book THE AFFLUENT SOCIETY (1958) traces the development of the central tradition in economics since the time of Adam Smith (1723-1790), David Ricardo (1772-1823), and Thomas Robert Malthus (1776-1834). That tradition has been to conceive of the world as a place of scarcity of goods where the lot of the masses was to live at a subsistence level. With the exception of the elite in society, man participates in the consumption of goods to the extent of his contribution to their production. The industrial revolution has slowly improved the living conditions of the masses, and specializations and skills have enabled some more to consume. But the theory has remained the same, and the reasoning behind this theory is that an expanding economy will provide full employment. Increased production increases the number of jobs and hence, income, which in turn increases the ability of the workers to consume more goods.

When this theory is applied to our present situation in the United States the theory is no longer valid because the application of cybernation, which is the use of automation and computers to perform a great variety of tasks, makes it possible to expand production without a corresponding expansion in the work force. Cybernation has the potential to change our world from a world of scarcity to a world of abundance. The problem is no longer how to increase production but how to increase consumption. Buckingham (1962) estimates that each computer that is placed in operation replaces thirty-five people and changes the jobs of an additional 105 people. Ten thousand computers are now produced in the United States each year and the rate will increase. From one point of view, 350,000 individuals are freed from uninteresting routine labor and 1,050,000 more have more interesting or at least different jobs each year. It also means that 350,000 individuals are unemployed and, therefore, do not have the ability to consume the goods and services of others. This in turn reduces the demand for these goods and services and the labor that produces them, which reverses the aforementioned traditional economics.

Confronted with cybernation, the conventional solution to the problems of unemployment or underemployment breaks down because increased production does not mean increased employment. The official rate of unemployment has remained at above 5.5% during the sixties. (The Vietnam war has temporarily modified these figures.) The unemployment rate for teenagers has been rising steadily and in 1964 was about 15%. Cybernation does not exclusively replace workers who are on the job—it is increasingly replacing the worker who will never get the job. The unemployment rate for Negro teenagers was about 30% in 1964, and at the same time unemployment rate for teenagers in some minority ghettos exceeded 50%.Unemployment rates for other minorities is similarly unfavorable. In Denver, Colorado, in 1960, 8.7% of the population had Spanish surnames, but 30.2% of the individuals receiving welfare had Spanish surnames; this represented 20% of the Spanish surnamed population in the city.

Besides the 5.5% of the labor force who are officially designated as unemployed, nearly 4% of the labor force sought full-time work in 1962 but could find only part-time jobs. The official unemployment rates count only those individuals who sought a job recently. There are many individuals who would like to find jobs but have not looked because they believe, and often realistically, that there are no employment opportunities for them. This phenomenon applies particularly to the young, the old, and the minority groups.

The number of people who have voluntarily removed themselves from the labor force is not constant but rather continues to increase. This decision is a difficult one to revoke either economically, socially, or psychologically. The older worker calls himself "retired"; he cannot accept work without affecting his social security status. The worker in his prime years is forced to go on relief, and in most states becoming a relief recipient brings about such fundamental alterations in an individual's situation that a reversal of the process is always difficult and often not feasible. The teenagers realize that there are no jobs for them nor is there a dignified alternative. These people and their dependents make up a large part of the hard core of poverty in this country. Increased production and a rising standard of living for the rest of the population does not change the situation of the impoverished segment of the population. It only increases the frustration because the differences between it and the rest of the population become even greater. There is no reasonable likelihood of the trend's reversing itself. The poorest 20% of the population received 4.1% of the income in 1944 and 4.9% in 1963.

The federal government is currently taking some short-range steps to improve the situation. The Job Corps is one example--it will take some teenagers off of the street, give them temporary employment and additional training and education, but it will not solve the problem of providing permanent employment for unskilled teenagers. Adult retraining programs have varied widely in their effectiveness. The most effective have been those that retrained workers who are not in the group we are talking about; the least effective have been for the group with which we are dealing. There are two principal reasons for their failure--one, these people do not have functional literacy (cannot read and write at the fifth grade level) so they are not considered retrainable; two, these people have already given up and do not seek new opportunities because they know (whether in reality they are right or wrong) that it will not make any difference.

What can we expect in the future? In all probability, the entrance of youth into the labor market will be delayed, workers will be retired earlier, and the work week will be shortened to enable more people to participate in the work that is available. There will be acute shortages of professional and managerial people. Many socially useful services will be expanded. For example, we'll probably have twice as many people working in education twenty-five years from now as we have today.

Education alone will not solve the problems of poverty, but any long-range solution to the problem must involve educating the environmentally deprived children so that they can earn their share in our affluent society, and this brings us back to our major thesis: *Education must begin before the child enters the first grade!* The failure begins in the first grade and increases year by year. For example, Churchill found that in Fort Morgan, Colorado, in 1960, only 7% of the first grade children from lower socio-economic homes were doing above average work in school whereas 54% were doing below average work. By the time these children reach the fifth grade they will be doing comparatively less well in school. Deutsch (1964) and his associates have called this the cumulative deficit phenomenon--the longer these

311

children remain in school, the greater becomes the difference in academic achievement between them and middle class children. Deutsch reports significant decreases in I.Q. test scores for Negro and white children from lower social class status from the first to the fith grade. In general, by the time these children reach fifth grade, they are two to three years behind in reading ability. Under normal school conditions, the child is already an educational drop out. The question that remains is will the school be able to keep the child in school until he reaches the legal age to drop out, or can the child find a way out sooner? There is strong reason to believe that the child often wins. For example, in 1960 in Colorado, 24% of the Spanish-surnamed people over twenty-five had completed four or fewer years of school and only 18.3% had completed high school. Of course, this includes some immigration from Mexico and many older people with low levels of educational achievement. The figures tend to understate the case, however, because not all Spanish-surnamed people in Colorado are economically deprived. At the same time, only 3.2% of the Anglos and 8.3% of the non-white population had less than four years of school. Out of 154 Spanish-surnamed children who started school in 1952 and 1953 in Greeley, Colorado, 43 (29%) graduated, one died, 48 (30%) are known drop-outs, 40 (20%) moved and what happened to 23 (15%) is unknown. Probably at least 50% of these last two groups are really drop-outs who reported they were moving and either never moved or never returned to school in the new community. Although much of the data cited here is specific to our target population and is drawn from local sources, it is generally consistent with more global reports based on national figures. Hence, we believe that whatever intervention techniques prove efficacious with our experimental sample population will have good chance of success with similar groups elsewhere.

Many children from deprived environments will be classified as mentally retarded children by the time they reach the third grade. According to the I.Q. test scores on the Stanford-Binet and Peabody Picture Vocabulary Tests, at least six (20%) of the thirty children who attended the New Nursery School (Nimnicht and Meier, 1966) the first year could have been legally classified as educable mentally handicapped children. If Deutsch's cumulative deficit phenomenon is correct, at least another three or four would probably have tested that way by the time they entered the third grade. Incidentally, much screening of children for educable mentally handicapped children begins in earnest near the end of second grade, when reading ability or disability makes the differentiation more pronounced. It is very doubtful that any of these children are mentally retarded in any but a functional sense of the term and yet the irony is that they will be placed in special education programs which typically offer prophecy fulfilling academically diluted programs. Meier (1965) noted the disproportionate number (more than 50%) of Spanish-surnamed children in special education classes for the mentally handicapped in Weld County, Colorado, which has only 12.2% Spanish-surnamed inhabitants (Boucher, 1964).

312

Much of the problem is one of the accurate evaluation and prediction of the environmentally deprived child's potential (Meier, 1967). With the recent mushrooming of educational programs for such children, charges of discrimination have been leveled at the standard tests on the basis that they are culturally biased. Goodlad (1966) in discussing the stability of the I.Q. score, made the interesting observation that this was due largely to the persistence of the environment. Wechsler (1966) elaborated on this notion as follows:

> *The I.Q. has had a long life and will probably withstand the latest assaults on it. The most discouraging thing avout them is not that they are without merit, but that they are directed against the wrong target. It is true that the results of intelligence tests, and of others, too, are unfair to the disadvantaged, deprived and various minority groups but it is not the I.Q. that has made them so. The culprits are poor housing, broken homes, a lack of basic opportunities, etc., etc. If the various pressure groups succeed in eliminating these problems, the I.Q.'s of the disadvantaged will take care of themselves.*

More specifically, Ausubel (1963) makes the following observations regarding the process of cognitive development.

> *It is reasonable that whatever the individual's genic potentialities are, cognitive development occurs largely in response to a variable range of stimulation....Characteristic of the culturally deprived environment, however, is a restricted range and a less adequate and systematic ordering of stimulation sequences. The effect of this restricted environment includes poor perceptual discrimination skills; inability to use adults as sources of information, correction and reality testing, and as instruments of satisfying curiosity; an impoverished language system and a paucity of information concepts and relational propositions. His abstract vocabulary is deficient and his language related knowledge, such as number concepts, self-identity information, and understanding of the physical and geometric and geographical environment is extremely limited (pp. 2-3).*

In a study of drop-outs in Fort Morgan, Colorado, Stevens (1964) found that among high school graduates, 2% had repeated a grade two times, 6% had repeated one year and 92% were at grade level or above. Among the drop-outs, on the other hand, 14% had repeated a grade two times, 29% had repeated one year and 57% were at grade level. The drop-outs had lower grades and lower test scores on achievement and mental ability tests; however, 20% ranked at or above the 65th percentile on tests of

313

mental ability. On reading ability, half of the drop-outs fell below the 20th percentile, one-fourth fell between the 20th and 50th percentiles, and one-fourth fell above the 60th percentile. The drop-out typically does not participate in extra-curricular activities and is absent from school more than most other students. Stevens used Warner's classification of occupations in which Level I contains the highest or most desirable occupations and Level VII is the least desirable category of occupations. No drop-outs came from Level I and II, 2% came from Level III, 10% came from Level IV, 36% from Level V, 29% from Level VI and 24% from Level VII were drop-outs, 30% in Level VI were drop-outs, 16% in Level V. Fifty percent of the drop-outs came from homes where the father had less than eight years of schooling. Drop-outs tend to associate with other drop-outs. Forty-eight percent of them come from families with six or more children and only 19% come from families with one or two children. None of these findings are particularly startling or unexpected--most research on the subject has found the same relationships, but when Stevens developed his model to identify potential drop-outs the description of the environmentally deprived child started to emerge. Stevens hypothesized that the critical number of drop-out characteristics that are associated with a drop-out is four and 82% of the drop-outs in his study had five or more drop-out characteristics. In other words, a drop-out can be described as follows: He is retarded one or more years in school and does not participate in extra-curricular activities. The principal wage earner's occupation is in the lower two levels, the father has less than eight years of school and older brothers and sisters have dropped out of school. He can also be described as being below the 49th percentile in mental ability, low in reading ability, absent more than ten percent of the time, his father has less than eight years of school and he associates with other potential drop-outs (Stevens, 1964).

At the time this individual drops out of school, he has already experienced several years of failure. The school has not helped to overcome the initial handicap he starts with but rather, has exaggerated it. Studies such as EQUALITY OF EDUCATIONAL OPPORTUNITY by the U. S. Office of Education documents this point on a national scale*. The report is broken down by race but the results reflect the differences in environment, not racial differences among which the Negroes traditionally represent the environmentally deprived.

> "With some exceptions--notably Oriental Americans--the average minority pupil scores distinctly lower on these tests at every level than the average white pupil. The minority pupils' scores are as much as one standard deviation below the majority pupils' scores in the first grade. At the 12th grade, results of tests in the same verbal and non-verbal skills show that, in every case, the minority

---

* It is interesting and surprising to read that the Spanish-surnamed person is even worse off than the Negro in Colorado (Mittlebach and Marshall, 1966, pp. 37-46).

314

scores are farther below the majority than are the 1st graders. For some groups, the relative decline is negligible; for others, it is large.

Furthermore, a constant difference in standard deviations over the various grades represents an increasing difference in grade level gap. For example, Negroes in the metropolitan Northeast are about 1.1 standard deviations below whites in the same region at grades 6, 9, and 12. But at grade 6 this represents 1.6 years behind, at grade 9, 2.4 years, and at grade 12, 3.3 years. Thus, by this measure, the deficiency in achievement is progressively greater for the minority pupils at progressively higher grade levels.

For most minority groups, then, and most particularly the Negro, schools provide no opportunity at all for them to overcome this initial deficiency; in fact, they fall farther behind the white majority in the development of several skills which are critical to making a living and participating fully in modern society. Whatever may be the combination of nonschool factors--poverty, community attitudes, low educational level of parents--which put minority children at a disadvantage in verbal and nonverbal skills when they enter the first grade, the fact is the schools have not overcome it (p. 20).

The fact that the drop-out is more likely to be a juvenile delinquent or unemployed as an adult has been well documented elsewhere. For example, Otis (1963), reporting for the President's Committee on Juvenile Delinquency and Youth Crime and Its Implications for Education, estimates that 95% of the 17 year old juvenile delinquents are school drop-outs, 85% of the 16 year old delinquents, and 50% of the 15 year old criminals are school drop-outs (1963, p. 3). In 1962, the direct cost of juvenile delinquency was estimated at 200 million dollars and the loss of property was 115 million. And, of course, following the same pattern, the most likely person to be unemployed is the school drop-out. So we have the complete cycle, early failure in school leads to dropping out of school to juvenile delinquency and adult unemployment. The evidence seems to be clear--early childhood education is a necessary intervening antecedent if the environmentally deprived child is to be given a chance to obtain the education he needs to break out of the cycle.

We are not offering nursery school education as a panacea to solve all the problems of poverty, discrimination, prejudice, unemployment and juvenile delinquency, but it is a necessary antecedent. Unless these children can enter school with a reasonable chance for success, they will not benefit from the school program, even programs allegedly tailored for them. For example vocational education can't be effective

315

unless children remain in school long enough to become eligible. Most adult retraining programs depend upon functional literacy (the ability to read at the fifth grade level), and all of them depend upon motivation for self-improvement.

Part II

THE NEW NURSERY SCHOOL*

The particular concern at the New Nursery School is for 45, three- and four-year-old environmentally deprived Spanish-surnamed children.** In addition to environmental deprivation, these children have a different culture and language. We believe that if we can demonstrate the effectiveness of a carefully designed nursery school program with these children, a similar program will benefit other environmentally deprived children.

The Facilities

The New Nursery School is located in a house near neighborhoods where most of the children live (see Figure 1). We chose the house because we wanted a noninstitutional setting within walking distance of as many of the children as possible. The house is near a public school so many of the children come and go with older brothers and sisters. The house is adequate for our needs and we apparently have been accepted by the parents. Even though the school is unoccupied from 4:30 p.m. to 8:30 a.m., we have not suffered from any serious acts of vandalism nor has any equipment been taken from the yard.

*The school is called the New Nursery School because the approach is different from that of most nursery schools presently being operated in this country, but the basic approach can be traced back to similar schools founded by Maria Montessori, over fifty years ago in Italy. We are particularly indebted to Martin Deutsch of New York University and Omar K. Moore of the University of Pittsburgh, both of whom are currently conducting studies on early childhood education. We have incorporated many of Deutsch's and Moore's ideas in our school. The school is located in Greeley, Colorado and operated under the auspices of Colorado State College.

**In the main, these children are Spanish and Indian. The designation Spanish-American or Mexican-American is used interchangeably by the general population, but the individuals involved make distinctions according to their family's origin. Some families came from Spain, settled in the Southwest when it was still under Mexican rule, and intermarried with the Indians; others settled first in Mexico, and then moved to the United States. Regardless of origin, some individuals prefer to be called "Spanish-American" because of the derogatory way in which "Mexican" or "Mexican-American" has been used in the past. To simplify writing, we will refer to the group as Spanish-surnamed.

317

FIGURE 1

The New Nursery School as seen across part of the play yard in back.

The instructional space in the school consists of an "L" shaped room and two responsive environment booths that are approximately seven feet by seven feet. The "L" shaped room contains an art area, a dress-up area, a block corner, a reading corner, a listening corner, a manipulative toy area and a concept formation area. The reading, listening and manipulative toy areas are clustered in the smallest part of the "L", the noisier activities are in the other part of the room. Cubicles for each child's coat and boots are located on an enclosed porch adjacent to the main room. In addition to the instructional space, the New Nursery School has a bathroom, and office, conference rooms (in the basement) and observation areas (equipped with one-way windows) looking in on the main classroom and each responsive environment booth. The observation areas allow us to inconspicuously record and film or videotape anything that takes place in the learning areas and make the school a demonstration and behavioral science research center as well as a unique learning environment (see Figure 2).

The Objectives of the Program:

1. To develop a positive self-image;
2. To increase sensory perceptual acuity;

318

FIGURE 2

Floor plan of the combination school and behavioral sciences laboratory.

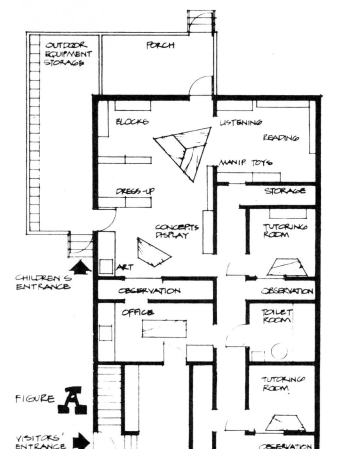

3. To improve language skills;
4. To improve problem-solving and concept formation abilities.

These four objectives closely parallel Deutsch's objectives at the Institute of Developmental Studies at New York University. We chose these four objectives because the studies and research indicated that environmentally deprived children had not developed in these areas to the extent that one would expect from observation of other normally privileged children. This lack of development logically seems to be related to their environment.

The Approach

The entire school program is organized as an *autotelic responsive environment* as Moore has defined it. The reader who is familiar with nursery school education will note that many outstanding nursery school programs in the United States have been operated more or less as responsive environments without saying so, but we believe it is essential to state these principles explicitly because of their importance in

319

formulating curricula and procedures and in evaluating the results. Moore and his colleague, Anderson, have defined an activity as autotelic if the activity is done for its own sake rather than for obtaining rewards or avoiding punishments that have no inherent connection with the activity itself.

Moore has defined a responsive environment as one which satisfies the following conditions:

1. It permits the learner to explore freely;
2. It informs the learner immediately about the consequences of his actions;
3. It is self-pacing, i.e., events happen within the environment at a rate determined by the learner;
4. It permits the learner to make full use of his capacity for discovering relations of various kinds;
5. Its structure is such that the learner is likely to make a series of interconnected discoveries about the physical, cultural or social world (Moore, 1963, p. 2).

The definition of a responsive environment points out important differences between our approach and a Skinnerian (neobehavioristic) approach. Notice the emphasis on "free exploration" and "discovering relationships". In a responsive environment, the child is not shaped to perform a given task. The objective is not to teach the child something step by step but to place him in a situation where he can make his own discoveries. In our judgement, this aspect of the responsive environment is more important in the long run than the fact that a child may learn to read and write. This is, of course, speculative at this time and we have no longitudinal evidence to support or refute our contention.

By insisting that all activities are autotelic and avoiding unrelated rewards or punishments we create a situation where we know the child is doing something because he wants to and not because an adult is applying pressure to have the child accomplish some task that the adult has decided the child is ready to do. This means that in observing the child's behavior in the classroom, we can assume we are seeing the child make choices and carry out certain activities that are not pressed upon him by an adult. Thus, we can study curriculum development and the relationship between maturation (including high and low probability behaviors) and learning without fear of pushing the child beyond his capacity or developmental level.

The notion of a responsive environment is equally important. We control what the child will do by the choices we make about what to include in or exclude from the classroom. Once the child enters the room he is free to explore. He can spend as much time on any activity as he likes; no one will ask him to stop one activity to

320

begin another. This has some interesting consequences. For example, the concept of attention span must be modified. These children do have a short attention span if they are required to do what the adult wants them to do when the adult wants them to do it. But, when the children are allowed to choose their own activities, this no longer holds. Many children have been read to for an hour and a half. One child painted 25 pictures without stopping. Another spent the whole three hours, except for time out for refreshments, playing a game which required him to recognize and match pictures. Some children will spend over half of their time, particularly at the beginning of the year, playing with the blocks. As the year progresses, their activities become varied and they spend more time in the reading corner, the listening corner or the manipulative toy area. We have group activities such as singing and story telling, but no child is required to take part. At the beginning of the year several (five or six out of fifteen) will choose not to come to the group, but day by day they scoot closer until they have joined the group. After that, it is a rare occasion when a child chooses not to participate.

The notion that the environment informs the learner immediately about the consequences of his actions determines the kind of equipment that is used, the way it is used, and the behavior of the teacher and her assistants. The learner is informed either by the self-correcting toys, machines, other children, or the teacher. Most of the manipulative toys are self-correcting. The nesting and stacking toys go together or stack in only one way; the puzzles are the same. Concentric circles, squares, or rectangles must fit inside each other to complete the pattern, and so forth. The Language Master is an example of a machine that tells the child about the consequences of his actions. The Language Master records and plays back sound recordings on two channels on magnetic tape located across the bottom of cards that vary in size from 8½" by 11" to 3" by 6". One can write or draw on the card so that a child sees and hears something at the same time. The child can operate the machine without assistance, and he is free to play with it. For example, on a single color card we put a spot of red paint or paper, write the word *red*, and record, "This color is red".

The application of the concept of an autotelic responsive environment concept to the organization and methods of teaching in a nursery school classroom has many worthwhile effects. The child is free to spend as much time playing with the colors as he wants or if he wants to know the name of a specific color he can go and find out--the machine will give him the necessary feedback. We have also installed a modified juke box for a simple random access information retrieval system by which children can have books read to them, songs sung to them or receive other auditory input.

The teacher and her assistants are another source for the child to use in finding out

321

the consequences of his acts. The important thing for the teacher and assistants to remember is that they are a part of a responsive environment and respond to the child as he spontaneously encounters and manipulates his surroundings--*they do not teach, they assist children's learning.* This statement will become evident as we elaborate upon the specific approaches we use to obtain the objectives of the school. In general we:

1. Discourage adult initiated conversation but encourage child initiated conversation
2. Never ask a child if he wants to be read to but always read to him when he asks to be read to
3. Avoid asking a child to give up one activity to do something else
4. Never insist that all children come to a group activity

Most of a child's three hours in school is spent in self-directed activities such as painting, working puzzles, looking at books, dressing up, building with blocks, and a host of other activities. About fifteen minutes a day are devoted to group activities such as singing, listening to a story, or participating in planned lessons. If a visitor were to walk into the school as the children are arriving in the morning, he could expect to see one or two children go immediately to paint or play with clay, three or four children settle down in the block corner, two or three children head for the listening corner to listen to a record that they select on the remote controlled juke box or to play with the Language Master, three or four children select a manipulative toy, the alphabet board, or a wood insert puzzle to play with, one child asks to be read to and one or two children ask to go type. At mid-morning several of the children will still be at the same activities. Others, perhaps five or six, will be gathered around the teacher playing a game with colors or simple concepts, some child will be joining the group while others are going to another activity, when the children have lost interest the teacher will introduce a new game or go to another game. Late in the morning or afternoon the visitor will find most of the children outside, one or two might still be in the room with a teaching assistant, and one might be in the typing booth.

Once each school day a booth assistant asks a child if he would like to play with the typewriter. If he says "yes", the assistant takes him to one of two booths equipped with an electric typewriter. The child is allowed to play with the typewriter for as long as twenty minutes. The child begins in the booth by simply playing with the typewriter. The assistant answers his questions and names the symbols he strikes, such as, "x", "a", "y", "comma", "space", and "return". The child will move from this first phase to finding and striking a letter that is shown to him. The child will move on to typing words and eventually to dictating stories to the booth assistant who transcribes the stories. Finally, he will transcribe his own stories.

322

Moore has had extremely good success in enabling three- and four-year-old children to read using such procedures; but, like Moore, we are not so concerned about the children's learning to read at an early age as with the mental process involved in discovering such relationships as the association of sounds with symbols and the discovery of the rules for a new game as we move from one phase to another. Obviously, if the child can see a form such as *A* on a piece of paper, find the same form on the keyboard of a typewriter and hear a booth assistant say "A", we are accomplishing one of our prime objectives, that of helping the child to perceive different forms and discriminate among sounds.

RATIONALE FOR OBJECTIVES AND SOME STRATEGIES FOR MEETING THEM

Developing a Positive Self Image

We know from research (Goodman, 1964 and Deutsch, 1964) and from our own observations that children at the ages of three and four are beginning to develop a sense of self awareness, frequently called a self-concept, and an awareness of ethnic and race differences. The way a person views himself is the way he will behave. If he sees himself as successful, good looking, and popular with his peers, he will behave in one way; if he sees himself as a failure, unattractive, and rejected by his peers and society, he will behave in a different way. Children with adequate intellectual ability, who nevertheless perceive themselves as poor students, often will not do well in school. The Negro who knows that in our society it is desirable to be white but sees that he is black tries to straighten his hair and bleach his skin.

The development of a self-image begins with the interaction between a mother and her baby. The family continues to shape the self-image by the way the child is reared--what he is told to do or not to do, the rewards and punishments he receives, the amount of attention he obtains. As the child comes in contact with the neighborhood and community, his self-concept is further shaped by his peer group and by powerful figures like the storekeepers, policemen, and teachers. Each provides him with clues about how people think about him and his kind.

We assume that the children we are dealing with have an inferior image of themselves and their ability to cope with the everyday problems of existence in a hostile society. The families are larger than most, living on the borderline between integration and disintegration as a family unit. They are headed by defeated and often mentally ill adults; if the father is in the family, his position is insecure; he cannot guarantee support for his wife or food for his children; the mother is often more likely to obtain employment than the father, which takes her out of the home with no one to replace her and no labor-saving devices to help when she comes home. The defeat and illness of the adults is passed on to the children. A tired,

323

worried mother has little time and energy to give to a child, regardless of how much she might love him. Each child compounds her problems and, as mentioned in greater detail in Chapter I, the child misses the attention the mother should provide for his optimum development and soon he learns the fact that his existence only creates problems. The seven year old Gabriel, a Puerto Rican boy who lived in San Juan and New York City certainly knew that he is unwanted.

> *"I think my mama' doesn't love me. When children are left alone all the time, it means their mama' do not love them. Isn't that right?...."Felicita (his mother) was going to take Angelito and me to our papa' and leave us with him because he stopped sending money to buy us clothes and shoes. Someone told him something bad about Felicita and the money stopped coming. Felicita went to court so they would make Angel take us but he didn't want us either" (Lewis, 1966, pp. 55-56).*

The child escapes from the home to the streets and neighborhood which reinforce the self-concept the family has helped him to develop. If he is brown or black or his name is Hernandez, the child learns that he is not the same as "whites" or "Anglos." He not only is unwanted and a problem at home, but he has the wrong color of skin and the wrong name. To live in an integrated neighborhood instead of a segregated one only helps him learn this sooner.

The self-concept that emerges is the antithesis of a positive self-image. The individual tries to cope with a nearly overwhelming environment in which he finds himself. In fact the environment encourages the development of a sense of powerlessness over decisions that affect him. He feels that these decisions are made by others and are beyond his control. This not only has the effect of alienating the child from the social power structure (Seeman, 1959) but the concomitant sense of frustration engenders hostility and aggression toward external authority figures and institutions.

One behavioral problem which frequently implies emotional maladjustment in the minds of school personnel is aggressiveness. Eron, *et al* (1958), carried on an elaborate study of aggressive behavior. The research plan was to study the complete third-grade population in Columbia County, which included approximately 1,000 pupils per year, over a three-year period, and to hold interviews with their parents. A report gave results for some sixty families, in which there was found to be: (1) no relation between aggression at home and aggression at school, (2) a consistent relation between intensity of punishment by father and aggression in the children, and (3) an inverse relation between aggression and socioeconomic status. On the latter point, the authors made some very relevant observations. They reported, for example, less aggressive children in the old Yankee families than among more recent

324

immigrants, which difference probably involved a socioeconomic factor as mentioned earlier. The report also stated that social participation by the parents was inversely related to their children's aggression, as was the social mobility aspiration of the mother for her children.

These findings were corroborated by Bandura and Walters (1963), who demonstrated the importance of social learning or imitation in the formation of an aggressive personality. Thus, one's cultural heritage was seen to be directly related to the school's acceptance of his behavior, which was in turn evidently related to acceptance and achievement in the academic world. Those who were making a poor school adjustment, insofar as stereotyped middle-class criteria were concerned, were being penalized for what was sociologically speaking quite an appropriate adjustment to their own cultural group (cf. Bendix and Lipset, 1957: Eisenberg, 1958: Freedman and Hollingshead, 1957; Frumkin, 1955; Hollingshead and Redlich, 1958; and Leacock, 1957). Thus, the child's basic drive for academic competence (White, 1959) is frustrated in the traditional school setting by the ironic side effects of his parents' typical failure to achieve upward mobility within and consequent overt and subtle manifestations of aggression toward the system. Studies in levels of aspiration support this notion in that repeatedly disappointed people tend to set either unrealistically high or ridiculously low goals for themselves; when these individuals are parents and identificands or models, their children learn to set goals similarly. The self-fulfilling prophecy of a negligible chance of worldly success that a child develops in imitation of parental attitudes adversely affects his self-concept and consequent performance wherever he is.

The first requirement in a school for environmentally deprived children, therefore, must be to help the child develop a positive self-image and the younger the child is when this begins, the better (see Figure 3). The entire environment of the New Nursery School has been organized to foster a positive self-concept.

The school is staffed with Anglos, Spanish-American, and Negro teachers and assistants. This is intentional and the placement of Anglos first is also significant. The *presence* of Anglo adults who accept the child, who help him, who talk, read, and play with him--who communicate through work and actions that the child is important, *helps* to offset the negative effects of the rest of the Anglo community.

The responsive environment contributes to the development of a positive self-concept. The child is free to explore and use anything within his sight or reach. Since the environment is self-pacing and non-competitive, he is not compared unfavorably with someone who can speak better or build better. Instead, he is free to do those things he can do and to do them as long as he likes. Some people express the concern that this is an unreal situation and therefore may be harmful. The world

325

FIGURE 3

Many occasions are proved for children to express their self-concepts (upper) or to dramatize their feelings about themselves and others, and sometimes review themselves as they were recorded on videotape (lower).

326

in reality, especially starting in school, is competitive, comparisons are made, and some individuals do advance more rapidly than others. In preparation for such a situation, these critics reason, the individual must develop a realistic self-concept; otherwise, he has no way to establish realistic levels of aspiration and the concomitant ego-protecting psychological mechanisms that go with a realistic level of aspiration. In other words, if the individual aspires to the unattainable, he must adopt some sort of defense mechanism to cope with his failure and this results in poor mental health. This reasoning may be sound but it is our contention that the environmentally deprived child's world offers an over-abundance of opportunity for him to discover that the world is competitive. What he needs most is to experience some measure of initial success.

In a responsive environment, the child is placed in a situation where he can make discoveries about his physical and social world. This also means that real opportunities exist to praise the child and his accomplishments when he makes those discoveries. This sounds as though it is inconsistent with the concept of autotelic activities because praise for an activity is certainly extrinsic to the activity. The crucial point is that participation in the activity is not dependent upon external rewards or punishments but is done because it is intrinsically interesting. For example, in truly amateur sports, the participant does not (or should not) play because of the rewards or punishments but because he likes the game; competence, however, does receive praise. This point may seem to be a fine one, but we believe it is important in developing and establishing activities which are autotelic and do not *depend* upon extrinsic motivation. This does not remove the possibility of some positive reinforcement for competent performance.

The general rules concerning adult-child relationships are designed to aid in developing a positive self-image. The reason we insist that the adults do not initiate conversations with children but allow the child to initiate the conversations is that too often adult-initiated conversations are demeaning or threatening. The adult conversation that starts off with "My name is Glen. What's yours?" is usually demeaning. It continues with "What are you playing?" "Are you having fun?" etc. Whereas the child will start with "My daddy is going to Arizona," or "I saw a policeman yesterday," or "I saw that on television," or "We got pig." The child usually starts with a statement, not a question, and it is the basis for a real exchange rather than the I-question-you-answer approach of adults. The simplest question asked by an adult, such as "What is your name?", can be threatening because it requires a response. "Hello" is better, just as "Good morning" is better than "How are you today?"

Allowing the child to initiate the conversation also has the effect of saying to the child "what you have to say is important--you're important!"; therefore, we try

327

never to by-pass a child-initiated conversation but to encourage them whenever possible. For example, we serve milk to five or six children at a time rather than to all fifteen at once. With five or six children and one adult at a table, conversation among all of the children and the adult is possible, but with fifteen children only a few can participate.

Another general rule is that the assistants and teacher use the child's name when speaking to him and write the child's full name on all pieces of art work. We also play many games with the children to help them learn their names. The teacher or an assistant takes the Language Master and some blank cards into the large group room. When a child shows some interest the adult will say, "Juanita, let's write your name on this card," and then the adult records, "This card belongs to Juanita." The child can then run the card through the machine and hear, "This card belongs to Juanita": and can record her own name on the card. Initially the child can only record "Juanita," but with some practice he can record the complete sentence. After five or six children have gathered around and have their names printed on cards, we play another game. The teacher holds up a card and says, "The person whose name is on this card can play it." Of course, there are mistakes - Michael will pick Michelle's card - but in a few tries most children will recognize their own names and we get this kind of reaction from the children, "That's you saying my name," or "That's me saying my name." This also increases auditory discrimination and expressive language skills about which we'll speak in greater detail later.

We borrowed another specific technique to build a positive self-image from the Institute of Developmental Studies in New York City by simply having a cubicle or "cubbie" for each child where he keeps his coat, overshoes and art work. In each cubicle we place the child's picture so he might think, "That's me," "my place" and "my picture."

Developing the Senses and Perceptions
Developing the senses and perceptions is usually considered a natural part of a child's development. He learns at his mother's knee to listen for certain sounds and relate them to objects. He learns that certain colors have been named red, brown, or green. He will make simple mistakes like calling something that is colored green, red, because he thought the object was called red; but someone is there to say, "No, that is not red, but this is; so is your sweater." He touches, wonders, and asks, "What's this?" He listens to someone reading a book about trains, hears a train, then someone saying, "Listen, that is a train."

The degree to which he develops his senses and perceptions depends to some extent upon how good the senses are; obviously a blind person cannot see colors, but it also

328

depends upon how rich the environment is and how much assistance he receives. In the study Dennis made (reported earlier) the missing elements in the child's environment in the orphanage were the things and people to help develop his senses. Obviously the senses are the tools of the mind, and its function is as restricted as the senses that serve it. A case study like Helen Keller's does not contradict this statement, but reinforces it. Her development was dependent upon the teacher's ability to reach Miss Keller through the sense of touch.

Even when a child has a rich environment and assistance from adults he probably does not achieve anything approaching optimum development of the senses and perceptions. Kipling's KIM is a classic example from literature of how, with special training, an individual can see and perceive far more than the average individual would see. Of course the artist, the architect, and the musician are far more sensitive to color and design or music than most people in the general population. We have learned that with some help three and four year old children are very sensitive to differences in colors and shades of color. For example, after the child has had some practice, the teacher can point to one shade of blue out of a group of four paint samples, and the child can go elsewhere and return with a paint sample that has the same shade of blue. As another example, a group of New Nursery School children were finding objects in the room that were the same color as their clothing. Benny tried several shades of blue against a new pair of blue jeans; dissatisfied with any of them, he tried something black, but that didn't work either. He finally gave up.

When the environment is not rich in materials for the development of the senses and perceptions and in some instances actually works against their development, and when the necessary interaction with adults is minimal or non-existent, we can predict that the development of the senses will be retarded. This is probably true for most deprived children. A deprived child's surroundings are often drab. The unpainted exterior of his house blends with the dirt yard. His mother's concern is not that the table setting should be color-coordinated and the food provide a contrast pleasing to the eye. Her concern is that there is food on the table. The perceptual materials available are not interpreted as fully as in the middle-class home, where the child hears language that enables him to label colors, discriminate between colors, and learn the terms that are commonly used to compare colors, such as the following:

"Today you can wear your pink skirt and pink stockings."
"Oh Greg, look at your socks! One is gray and one is black.
 Go find a pair that match."
"Those two shades of green just don't go together."

We refer to pegs and pegboards, color cones, nesting cups, depth cylinders,

329

Cuisenaire rods, puzzles, alphabet boards, and other like items as "manipulative toys."

This means equipment specifically designed to help the child discover, through play, certain concepts about the physical world. As he puts together, takes apart, stacks, matches, nests, groups, and rearranges, he not only observes, but actually participates in the physical manipulation of these materials.

The importance of this physical manipulation can hardly be over-emphasized. Montessori observed that "among the various forms of sense memory that of the muscular sense is the most precocious...The association of the muscular-tactile sense with that of vision aids in the development of the perception of forms and fixes these perceptions in the child's memory" (Montessori, 1912, p. 198-199).

Modern curriculum materials recognize the muscular-tactile sense as an aid to learning. The American Association for the Advancement of Science Publication, Science - - A Process Approach, (Book II, 1964, p. 7) has this suggestion for recognizing and using geometric shapes. "Have the children run fingers around the rims or edges of things. In this way, they will become much more familiar with the shapes they are studying."

As stated earlier, recent research has focused upon the importance of sensory impressions to the senses, all the senses, in the development of cognitive abilities. These studies have particular relevance for those concerned with the education of the disadvantaged child, as they emphasize the importance of the selection and use of equipment the child can look at, feel, listen to, and move around.

Consider for a moment the contrast between the middle class home and lower class home. In the middle class home, the child is surrounded by "things." His parents provide him with the latest educational toys; when interest in those lags, he pulls the books from the shelves and builds with them, then goes to the kitchen in search of cans to stack, pots and pans to fit lids on and nest.

The lower class home is lacking in many of these things. The Christmas toy is likely to be ill-chosen and soon broken. Often the home is equipped with the minimum essentials for living. The household equipment that children have traditionally regarded as their best toys is either lacking or in such short supply that there is none for play. Furthermore, the potential stimuli that are present are often cluttered, or disorderly.

The school should compensate for these lacks by providing a situation where maximum learning can take place. For example, the two-year-old middle class child

330

fitting rings on a color cone doesn't need verbal help from his mother at that time. He is surrounded by words and experiences of "largest," "smallest," "this comes next," and as he grows he will sort these experiences and come up with workable concepts. The casual observer who observes this process by which most children grow and learn in such a "natural" way may be inclined to believe that it happens as a result of development or maturation alone. Even among teachers and researchers there has been a tendency to stress the importance of development and maturation and overlook the differences in environment. A four-year-old without the richness and variety of experiences the middle class child has, without a vocabulary to think about them or talk about them, is in a different situation. He needs a period of time to work (play) with suitable manipulative toys, with verbal interaction with the teacher and other children to provide symbols (words) for what he is doing or has done. *THE EXPERIENCE ALONE IS NOT ENOUGH.*

In other words, simply placing the three, four, or five-year-old child in the enriched environment (in this case, manipulative toys) will not, by itself, make up for what he didn't have at one, one-and-a-half, or two years of age. The timing is wrong, and the supporting elements (speech, encouragement) are missing.

Working with manipulative equipment is a sensory-motor experience which is important in itself, and also essential to the development of other skills, such as the symbolic operations necessary in arithmetic and reading. John Holt, in a chapter called "Real Learning" (1964) gives vivid observations of fifth and sixth grade children working with Cuisenaire rods who "saw," for the first time, what they had been trying to do with symbols.

Emphasis on the cruciality of verbal interaction does not imply that the teacher subjects the child to a barrage of words. It is the appropriate word at the appropriate time that will make the difference. (For a more complete discussion of this, see the section on language development.)

The following pages contain some suggestions for using manipulative toys in a nursery school for disadvantaged children. All these toys are readily available and sources are given on the equipment list. Many of them are self-correcting, which makes them even more valuable for the child, for he can proceed at his own pace and in his own way. As rapidly as possible we will replace all toys that are not self-correcting with others that are.

The suggestions given below run, in general, from simpler to more complex in each section. However, this "sequencing" does not mean that a child has to progress this way or that a teacher should hesitate to introduce a "harder" game if she thinks a child is ready for it. We don't know enough about the way children think and learn to say that one thing must follow another in their learning.

331

Decide in advance what the various toys will be called and make sure all aides and volunteers in a particular classroom use the same terminology. Sometimes the decision is arbitrary, for there are no right names for many of the toys. But, be consistent. The stacking parts of a color cone can be called "rings," "disks," or "circles," but it is very confusing to the child to have them called all three. Let that kind of flexibility come after he is sure of one label.

Make the terminology as exact as possible. If the child has to learn a label, and most of them do, he should learn an exact one. Using the color cone as an example again, the stacking parts could be called "stackers," but so could nesting cups, blocks, gears, parquetry blocks or many other toys. They could be called "doughnuts," but they are not soft, nor can you eat them. An observation "like a doughnut" is to be encouraged and the teacher echoes, "Yes, the ring has the same shape as a doughnut," but not labeling the rings (disks, circles) "doughnuts."

When introducing the following games start with an interested child or two and let others take turns or join in as they see fit. Above all, keep these enrichment games casual and fun.

NESTING CUPS

I. Nesting Cups - round or hexagonal (see Figure 4)

    A. Play can be stimulated by presenting manipulative equipment in different ways. The nesting cups can be spread out in a row, either upside down or right side up; they can be grouped according to color.

    B. The nesting cups can be used to build towers. The easiest way to introduce this is to have one built, then the children can try to duplicate it. After they can build with the largest cup as the base, let them try building with the smallest cup as the base. Give only verbal help such as, "Look at the cups that are left, and pick out the largest (or larger as the case may be) one to try next."

    C. After the tower is built, the teacher can help the child count the number of cups in it, pointing to each cup as she and the child count.

    D. Size comparisons can also be made - - "Which tower is the tallest (or taller)?" "Which tower is the shortest (or shorter)?" A few cups can be removed from one or more of the towers, so that the comparative heights are different and a comparison can be made again. "Now which tower is the tallest?" (See concept development.)

332

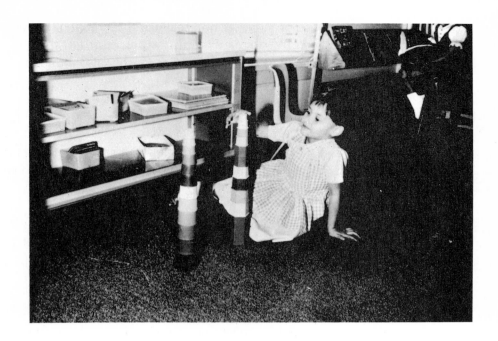

FIGURE 4

A child matches a model tower made of Nesting Cups.

II. Stacking Rings or Disks

A. The color cones can be presented with the largest ring either on the top or the bottom. The rings may also be spread on a shelf, or both sets combined and grouped according to size. The commercial sets that are available are multi-colored. This equipment would be better if it were all one color. If the rings or disks are wood a non-toxic paint can be used to make each set a uniform color. The reason for using a uniform color is that the stacking rings are primarily to develop perception of size - not color. The colors add an unnecessary variable and some children learn that the red ring goes on the green ring instead of looking for the next smaller ring.

B. The terms of relative size to be used are "smallest, smaller, largest, larger." When a child is working to get the rings on so that they are graduated from largest to smallest, or the reverse, do not suggest that the colors indicate the proper order. In other words, don't say, "Try the green ring next." Say, "Look at all the rings you have left and pick out the largest (or smallest if the child is working from smallest to largest ring) to try next."

333

C. Although the color cone is not really self-correcting, children can be shown that when the rings are not in the proper order, there is a "bump," when they feel the cone. The children can also build a ring tower without a center.

III. Barrels

A. The barrels, if nested, are self-correcting and really need no instruction. To build a tower with the barrels, see the suggestion concerning the nesting cups. The barrels will stack in any order, however.

B. A listening game can be played by letting the children put various small toys and objects in the barrels, then having other children or the teacher guess what is inside "just by listening" as the barrel is shaken.

IV. Peg Boards

A. When the pegs for peg boards are presented with colors mixed, teachers can make suggestions such as the following:

1. "Put all the red pegs in first."
2. "Take out all the blue pegs and put yellow pegs in their place."
3. "Take out all the green pegs."

When pegs are presented sorted according to color, let a child choose the color, or colors, he wants to play with. As designs appear, teachers can comment. "You've made every other row blue."

After shapes have been discussed, the children can use rubber bands to make various shapes on the pegboards.

V. Puzzles - When we speak of puzzles we are referring to a good quality wood inlay puzzle such as Sifo Puzzles.

A. A puzzle's primary purpose is to focus the child's attention on different shapes and forms as he attempts to work the puzzle.

Avoid direct questioning of the child about the names of the objects pictured in the puzzle. If he knows, there is no point in a question. If he doesn't know, he may feel threatened. This caution does not imply that a teacher should never ask a question. It does mean that the teacher

334

should not sit down and ask, "What is this?" "What is this?" "What is this?" as she points to each puzzle piece in turn. In answering the child's questions use sentences. "That is a picture of an ear of corn." "That vegetable is a tomato."

Puzzles can also be used in verbal development and concept formation, as the teacher cannot assume that the children have labels or concepts for the objects pictured in the puzzle. In fact, the teacher of deprived children can assume that the children do *not* know what the objects are.

Accurate labels and concepts can be provided in a variety of ways. Conversation, real objects, field trips, replicas, books, records, and pictures are all appropriate.

For example, the teacher can help the child by saying, "You are working the puzzle with the three little pigs on it. Remember when we listened to the record about the three little pigs?"

To help the child relate the pictures in the puzzle to real objects and the symbolic representations of the same thing, the teacher should be alert to the possibilities of correlating related resources. Gingerbread men eaten at snack time can serve to introduce (and give both label and meaning) a new gingerbread man puzzle. A picture of a gingerbread man could be pasted in the room and brought to the table. Following snack time a record of The Gingerbread Man, with the accompanying book could be played. Another day the children and teacher can tell the story using flannel board figures.

Real fruit should be related to the puzzle with pictures of fruit.

B. The child should work the puzzle he selects without interference from the teacher. The ability to see the spatial relationships involved must be developed *by the child;* he does this by working the puzzle. The goal is not that the puzzle be completed; the goal is that the child perceive the various shapes and forms and their relationship to the whole.

    If a child attempts a puzzle he cannot complete, let him leave it. The teacher or another child can work it.

C. After the child has mastered the beginner inlay puzzle, he can attempt to work the puzzles blindfolded.

335

D. Children who are adept at working puzzles can find challenge in working a puzzle without the board which contains the pieces and give the outline to the puzzle. Some even enjoy fitting the pieces together paint side down as well as paint side up.

E. The teacher can play the game "Which Piece is Missing," by having the child or teacher close his eyes while another person removes a piece from a puzzle. The child then opens his eyes and identifies the piece which is missing. Some children simply point, in which case the teacher supplies the sentence for them. Do not press the child.

F. "Which one doesn't belong in this group?" can be played with beginner puzzles (see problem solving).

Start with beginner inlay puzzles (coordination board, fruits, vegetables, animals) where the outline of the piece remains clear after the piece is removed. Advance to removing two or more of these pieces from the puzzle at a time. This is slightly harder, and also requires a longer sentence, "The pear and the apple are missing."

Other puzzles can also be used for this game after the children have grasped the idea. Be sure the piece removed is recognizable, such as the wheel of the locomotive, baby bear's head, or as one child said, "him pants," meaning baby bear's pants.

VI. Geometric Shapes (see Figure 5) - The puzzles with geometric shapes, (called coordination boards) have two circles, two squares, two rectangles and two triangles arranged in parallel rows. Each geometric shape is painted a different color which is the same as the color on the board that surrounds that piece. For example, one triangle is painted blue and the other one is painted gray.

At the beginning of the year the child just plays with the puzzle. As the children become more familiar with the shapes, the teacher can have the child close his eyes, then put one of the puzzle pieces in his hand and let him try to name the shape just by touch. Show the child how to run his fingers around the perimeter of the shape, both the shape that is removable and the shape that is left on the board. Start with the shapes that have obvious distinctions, such as the circle and the triangle, then advance to the square and rectangle. After the children have become familiar with the puzzle, the teacher can show them how to turn the pieces painted side down, interchange the colors, then guess the color of a specified shape. The procedure is as follows:

336

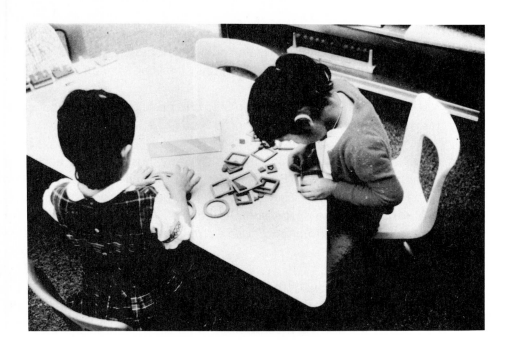

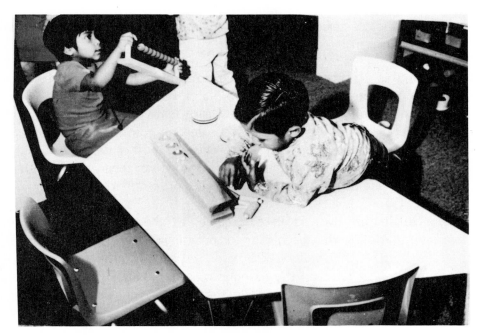

FIGURE 5

Children need many opportunities to learn about geometric shapes. Concrete experiences educate the kinesthetic modality about shapes which will later become abstract forms.

337

1. The teacher or child should turn the pieces painted side down, and interchange all of the pieces that are the same shape. (Interchanging only part of the pieces implies a certain sophistication of strategy on the part of the child, and usually comes only late in the year, if at all.)

2. The teacher or child then points to one piece and asks, "What color is this triangle (circle, square, rectangle)?"

3. The other player guesses the color. Any answer from a child is acceptable, "Blue" or "Is Blue," or simply pointing to the background color he wants to select. The teacher should use a sentence which gives both the name of the shape and the color. "That circle is yellow," or "That circle is colored yellow." Use a similar sentence to echo a child's word or phrase.

4. The teacher or child then turns the piece paint side up, and the players decide if the answer was correct. If the teacher is guessing, she can ask, "Am I right?" If the child says, "No," perhaps he can tell her "What color is it?"

5. The piece selected should be turned paint side up. Continue with other pieces of the puzzle.

A game of this type has many learning possibilities. In addition to learning color and geometric shape recognition and names, the children learn to proceed in a logical fashion. That is, they learn that you cannot guess the color until the pieces are paint side down and someone points to a piece, that you have to turn the piece paint side up to check the other person's guess. First this step, then the next, then the next. This does not mean to imply that the child cannot make up his own game with other procedures.

Problem solving is involved in this game, as the children devise various strategies for fooling the teacher or for deciding which color to guess. Since the circles can be only yellow or brown, the squares orange or purple, the rectangles green or red, and the triangles blue or gray, and these colors show clearly in the background of the puzzle, the child who guesses wildly either has not seen this connection or is mislabeling the colors.

The child who knows the circles must be either brown or yellow has greatly increased his chance of successfully solving the problem. The child who goes a step further and *knows,* if he sees the brown circle paint side up, that the other circle must be yellow, is using his problem solving abilities with complete success.

338

Interchanging only part of pieces should be done by the teacher only after a child has caught on to the idea that usually the yellow circle is in the brown background and the brown circle in the yellow background. This change in strategy makes the game more difficult.

AUDITORY DISCRIMINATION

The following activities are listed under developing the senses and perception, but like many other activities under this major objective they are closely associated with language development and problem solving. The need for developing auditory discriminations is elaborated upon in the next section on language development.

I. Listening and Identification with Aural Cues Only

   A. An assisting teacher should go out of sight of the children, but close enough to be heard. She should make familiar noises which the children are to identify. The teacher can try to elicit from the children the action verb, (*"sweeping* the floor") but should accept others. The teacher can tell the children, *"Say* what Miss Gray is doing." Suggested activities are as follows: Crumpling paper, turning pages of a book, whistling, cutting paper, singing, humming, bouncing a ball, sweeping the floor, stomping feet, snapping fingers, clapping hands, hammering, and playing musical instruments with which the children are familiar. Each classroom would have its own familiar noises which should be used.

   This activity is good for diagnostic purposes. Frequently children can imitate what the teacher is doing, but they cannot say it. This is the signal for the teacher to develop appropriate activities for language development. For example, our children could hum in imitation of the hidden teacher, but they had no word to describe what they were doing.

   During music period for the next several weeks, the children and the teacher hummed a great deal, talked about humming, how humming was done, and how it was different from singing. LISTEN TO MY SEASHELL, combines well with this activity.

   B. The teacher can drop, on a table or the floor, small objects with which the children are familiar. The children should "Listen to the sound the peg (or whatever it is) makes." After this has been done, the same procedure can be repeated out of sight of the children to see if they can identify the object by the sound it makes when it drops. Be sure to have some things that make almost no sound, such as a soft hat, or a scarf.

339

C. Montessori sound cylinders, small cans or boxes, or plastic containers can be used for this discrimination. The material consists of several containers, which can be paired according to the sound they make when they are shaken.

The Montessori materials are wood cylinders, with red tops on half of the cylinders, blue tops on the other half. The child is to shake a cylinder, then find another one with a top of the other color, that has the *same sound* as the cylinder he has.

A teacher who is making this material should not introduce the element of color, as it adds an extraneous factor. Neither should there be any other clues, such as numerals or letters on the containers, for the child quickly notes the numerals and pairs according to them, rather than according to sound.

Put the same quantity of the same material in each of two containers and tape or fasten securely. Suggested materials are salt, rice, beans, a penny, small nails, and so forth. Experiment to see what materials, in the containers you have, give sounds that can be paired. It is not necessary or desirable that the child be able to guess what is making the sound.

Instruction to the child should be, "Find another box (jar, can) that makes the *same sound* as the one you have."

II. Listening and Identification with Recorded Aural Cues.

Identifiable sounds can be recorded on the "instructor" portion of a Language Master card. Some care will need to be taken to make sure the sounds are identifiable. Suggested sounds are as follows: Telephone ringing, water being turned on and running, whistling, a door slamming, and typing. No picture is placed on the card. (It is wise to lightly write the identification of the sound on the back of the card for the benefit of assisting teachers.) The child simply listens to the card in the Language-Master and tries to identify the sound. If he wants to, he can record the identification on the "student" track.

The teacher's ability to handle incorrectly identified sounds is important. It is better simply to give verbal praise when the child is correct and ignore when he is incorrect. Then opportunities should be made to see, hear, and identify these sounds as they are being made. When the child goes back to the machine he will have an opportunity to correct his own mistakes.

340

Later, pictures illustrating the sounds that are recorded can be placed on the table. As the child identifies the sound, he can select the picture of the thing that makes the sound.

II.   The teacher (or a recording) can imitate sounds that different animals make, and the children can identify them.

IV.   Records and books which emphasize different sounds and the identification of them are good to use. "The Noisy Books," by Margaret Wise Brown, are an example of this kind of record. Records which give an aural signal to "turn the page" force the children to listen closely so they can stay in the right place.

COLOR LOTTO

Although it is certainly not essential that the child have interpretive language to discriminate between colors, he does need to have a certain amount of language as a tool to make his perceptions functional. Maria Montessori said, "However desirable it may be to furnish a sense education as a basis for intellectual ideas, it is nevertheless advisable at the same time to associate the language with these perceptions" (Montessori, 1964, p. 177).

The teacher must be aware of the importance, in talking about color, of being specific and unambiguous. As stated earlier (see Language Guides for Teachers of Young Children), children who do not know the color names may easily become confused and actually learn the wrong things if the teacher says, "This is yellow" or "Point to the red." Give the child enough information by naming the substance that has the attribute color, as well as naming the color. Say, "This crayon is yellow," "Point to the red block," "The color of her dress is blue," or "He has a blue shirt." Hearing the color names used with many different objects will enable the child to isolate the attribute "color" and begin to form concepts of what it is people mean when they say "blue," "orange," or "color."

Obviously the equipment, games, and procedures described on the following pages are not restricted to developing the senses and perceptions, but this is the major focus.

The Color Lotto Game

The equipment for this game must be made, as it is unavailable commercially. Cardboard or construction paper could be used, but we recommend sturdier material, such as felt or painted Masonite.

The following supplies are needed:

341

1. Four pieces of Masonite, each nine inches square.
2. Plastic tape (such as Scotch "Mystic" tape) or glue.
3. Nine pieces of colored felt, large enough to cut nine, three inch squares. Start with red, yellow, blue, green, white, black, orange, brown, and purple. As the children progress, finer discriminations can be presented on a different set, such as dark blue and light blue, dark green and light green, red and pink.

Tape (or glue) the different colored squares of felt to the Masonite. Arrange the colors in a different way on each board, so the children do not memorize the order in which the colors appear.

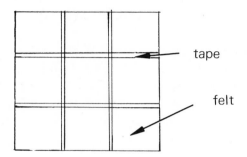

For initial presentation of this material, put boxes with a square of each color felt in each box, on a table. Let the children play with the material as they wish for a few days to become thoroughly familiar with it.

Introduction of games proceeds as follows:

Collect all the smaller squares and group them according to color. Hold up a square of each color in turn and say, "Find a square on your board which is the same color as this square." If the child does not point to the corresponding color square, but says, "I have one," say "Show me where it is." When he points correctly, give him one of the squares to put on the corresponding color on his board.

After all the squares are distributed, a reverse process can be used to remove the colored squares. The teacher has a square of each color felt. She holds them up one at a time and says, "Take off (or remove) a square that is the same color as this one."

As the children remove the pieces of felt, they can help the teacher group the pieces according to color, so they are ready for the next game.

The next step is to use the name of the color as well as the visual clue. Hold up a

342

colored piece of felt and say, "Find a square on your board which is red, the same color as this square."

Say, "Show me where it is." (After the child points automatically, this step can be omitted.) Then say, "Tell me *what color* it is." If the child cannot, supply the sentence, "That color is red," and give him the colored square.

The felt pieces can be removed using the same procedures. "Take off a square which is red, the same color as this square." . . ."Tell me what color the square was."

In the next level of this game, aural clues only are used. The teacher does not hold up a colored piece of felt, but only says, "Find a square on your board which is red." . . . . . "Show me where it is." . . . . . "Tell me what color it is.

Again, the felt pieces can be removed from the board using the same procedures.

As children become familiar with the way the game is played, they can take turns being the "teacher." However, care should be taken that the other children do not become bored by a child who does not proceed properly and with enough speed.

COLORS AND PROBLEM SOLVING

Using the Language Master with Colors
The following learning episode is designed to accomplish three things: (1) to help the child learn the names of the colors (develop the senses); (2) to help the child learn to arrive at correct answers by eliminating wrong responses (cognitive development) and (3) to determine how many of the colors the child can identify (evaluation).

Before starting with the children prepare the eight language master cards by either painting a different color on each card (black, white, red, orange, yellow, brown, green, and purple) or, instead of the paint, paste colored construction paper on the cards. Print the name of the color on the card and record on the instructor's channel, "The color on this card is red."

The language master should be set up in an area where the child can be isolated from the rest of the children.

Go into the classroom with the color cards in your hand. The first time ask a child you know if he would like to play a "new game with colors," and take him to the booth. The child can introduce the next child to the new game with colors. After each child has had the first experience simply show the child the colored cards and ask if he wants to play with them in the booth.

343

In the booth, hold up one card and ask, "What color is this?" Pause about three seconds. If the child does not respond, assume that he does not know the name for the color and record that on a form like the one on the next page. In any event after three seconds say, "Let's find out," and show the child how to run the card through the machine. Repeat the process with all the cards but after the first time, let the child run the card through the machine. Pantomime or demonstrate how the card goes through the machine rather than telling the child. If he puts the card through backwards or upside-down, no harm has been done; he receives no response so he knows something is wrong. Simply turn the card the correct way, demonstrate how to place it in the machine and let him try again. After you have gone through the cards once or twice, show him how he can record the name of the color. You will have to operate the record lever and run the card through the machine. The first time recorded, so say, "I'll say the color first and then you say it." If you say the color just as you start the card through the machine, the child's response will be recorded. Later the child can record the complete sentence.

Allow the child to play with the colors as long as he likes. When he knows three colors so well he never makes a mistake, hold up those three cards plus one with an unknown color. Say to the child, "Point to the green (the unknown) color." When he points to a card, do not say yes or no, but say "Find out." Let him run the card through the machine. If he pointed to the wrong card, have him find the right one by running the cards through the machine.

Note the difference in approach at this point and when the child first enters the booth. Each time the child plays with the colors, the first procedure is to test his ability to *say* the names of the colors and the results should be recorded. At this point, however, our concern is with developing problem solving ability and we are using the colors to accomplish this end. Therefore, we do not want to confuse the child's ability to say "yellow" and his ability to determine that red or green or blue is not yellow. So we ask the child to point to yellow. As you repeat the process with different cards, observe to see if the child is learning to eliminate wrong responses. To test the learning to identify different colors that have taken place, combine two or more of the colors that were not know when you started and ask him to point to one of the unknown colors.

Remember, the child is free to say no when you ask him if he wants to play; don't ask him again that day. If he asks to go later, take him. The child can leave the booth anytime he wants to; don't try to detain him. If he leaves he cannot come back that day.

THE ALPHABET BOARD

The alphabet board is an inexpensive magnetic chalkboard to which can be taped

344

FIGURE 6

After the child is able to match the blocks to their silhouettes on the shelves (upper) he learns to match letters to their silhouettes on the magnetic base (lower).

345

any one of a series of four paper overlays (see Figure 6). Approximately half the upper-case letters in the alphabet are silhouetted on the first overlay. At the New Nursery School we are currently using A, B, C, D, E, H, K, M, R, S, T, U, and W. The major consideration that influenced our choice was to avoid such combinations as C and G; D, O, and Q; U and V; W, X, and Y, letters that have similar shapes. The second overlay contains all the upper-case letters in the alphabet; the third overlay displays one-half the lower-case letters and the fourth displays all of the lower-case letters. Other overlays presenting grouping of letters similar in form can be used to keep the game challenging. For example, O, C, G, Q, could used, or M, N, W. The letters that are silhouetted on the overlays are the same size and shape as plastic letters that have a magnet in them, so the purpose of the game is for the child to match forms by placing "A" over "A", "C" over "C", etc.

To a great extent the game is self-correcting--the child becomes aware of his mistakes as he plays. But he is likely to make mistakes like placing the X over the Y and the Y over the X even though he knows that something is wrong. In this event, the teacher simply removes these two letters and says, "Try again."

The child probably will not recognize the letters as such and discoveries like "That (pointing to the M) is in my name," will come some time later.

We do not say that the shapes are letters in the alphabet nor try to identify them in any way. The purpose of this learning episode is to develop the child's senses and perceptions be matching various shapes. The obvious advantage is that the alphabet becomes important when the child learns to read.

The introduction of the alphabet board should follow the usual pattern. The teacher or an assistant locates the board in some convenient place and waits until a child shows interest. If no one seems to be interested, the teacher can stimulate interest by matching some of the letters. When a child does become interested, the teacher should show him what to do. After the first child has started, probably a number of children will gather and want to play. The teacher can keep order by pointing out who will have the next turn. In a situation such as this, we do interrupt a child's activity by letting some other child have a turn when the first child has finished matching the letters once or twice. After this initial introduction, however, a child should be allowed to match the letters as long as he likes. As the first overlay becomes too easy, it should be replaced or a second board with another overlay added so the child can play at the level of difficulty he chooses.

The teacher or assistant should observe the kinds of mistakes each child makes and the length of time it takes to correct those mistakes.

346

LANGUAGE DEVELOPMENT

Obviously the development of language in young children is crucial if they are going to be able to communicate effectively, but of equal importance is the internal use of language in the thought process. A language is required to go from things - oranges, apples, peaches, potatoes, carrots, peas - to categories such as fruits, vegetables, or food (see Figure 7). Over, under, and between are relational concepts that can only be thought of in some language. So, before we can become concerned about concept formation - and problem solving, we must first be concerned about developing verbal and listening skills in a language.

As Alfred North Whitehead pointed out, learning to speak and understand a language is the most difficult learning task we ever face. It comes before the educator can simplify learning by breaking it down into areas such as reading and arithmetic then proceeding from the simple to the complex. Because language develops in the pre-school years we act as though it occurs almost by osmosis.

FIGURE 7

The above category of fruit showing many specific kinds is a display in the concept formation area. Displays are changed weekly helping children to develop language concepts by abstraction.

347

However, careful observation shows that even under the best of circumstances, acquiring a language is a long tedious process of trial-and-error. We can eliminate some of the trial-and-error and speed up the process by applying knowledge derived from a careful analysis of what is involved in learning a language. This is precisely what we need to do in working with environmentally deprived children.

Again we need to be careful about generalizations. Because a child is Spanish-American, Negro, or comes from an impoverished home it does not necessarily follow that he has not developed an adequate language or verbal and listening skills. But the conditions we mentioned earlier go together to produce environmental deprivation and do adversely affect optimal language development.

The fact that a child comes from a crowded home increases the chance that (1) he receives less adult attention, (2) he hears more adult to adult conversation that is difficult to understand, and (3) there is more noise. The first assumption means that he is not listened to, praised, and corrected as much as a child from an uncrowded home. The next two assumptions mean that he does not have an opportunity to sort out words (labels) and attach them to the correct object or activity and that he tends to tune out the noise and meaningless conversation - he stops listening.

The fact that the child comes from an impoverished home increases the chance that the environment is less verbal than in most middle-class homes, the language used is more action oriented, and the child probably spends more time passively listening to and looking at TV than most children. The assumption that the home is less verbal and more action oriented means that the child learns to understand in short sentences or phrases - "Come here." "Shut up!" "Let's eat." "Go to bed." - with meaning often conveyed by voice quality, gestures, words used with action, and the force with which something is said. What is lost is the ability to understand longer and more complex sentences with the explicitness that characterizes middle-class language.

The assumption is often made that the children at least have television and that this is beneficial to language development. This is a very questionable assumption. The child generally has access to television and uses it, but all experiences via television are vicarious and it is largely a passive activity. What the child needs is an opportunity to hear *and* be heard. Our problem in teaching verbal and listening skills is not that the children speak Spanish instead of English (in reality some speak only English, others only Spanish, but most speak a corrupted form of both). Our problem is that the children have developed a functional language for use outside of school, but have not developed a functional language - either Spanish or English - that will enable them either to understand what is being said in a typical school room or to develop the language they need as a conceptual tool.

348

If we operate on the assumption that the children have not developed a functional school language, we can start with the question of how to help them learn such language. We do not know exactly how children learn language, but we do know exactly how to aid them in the process and eliminate some trial-and-error in the process.

We can start with a few general propositions and then become more specific. PROPOSITION 1: *The more opportunities the child has to be listened to with the appropriate help the more likely he is to develop verbal skills.* We have said that the child is developing language that is appropriate for his use in his home environment so for several reasons we do not want to create the impression that his native domestic language is wrong. As we mentioned earlier, a major objective of the program is to develop a positive self-image. One does not aid that objective by constantly correcting the child's speech. Also, there is always some risk of creating psychological distance between the child and his family which is undesirable in itself and would be educationally unsound. If the child corrects adults and older siblings, they are likely to become resentful and as a consequence oppose the school. This opposition probably will not be an overt and conscious act or statement against the school, but an unconscious resentment which nevertheless tends to force the child back into the "correct" use of the language. "Don't be a show off. Don't be uppity with me. Don't tell your Dad what to say." In this situation, even when it is a subtle form of adolescent rebellion, the school will probably lose, so the task is to develop a second language - the language of the school - regardless of what the first language might be.

It follows, then, that the teacher never corrects the child's language. The teacher either says, "This is what we say in school," or echoes the statement using the correct school form and construction. As a general rule the teacher should never initiate a conversation, but wait until the child initiates the conversation. This refers back to developing a positive self-image as well as to giving the child every opportunity to speak and be listened to.

PROPOSITION 2: *The clearer the reference points are in developing verbal skills the more likely the child is to make the correct association, and to learn something correctly the first time eliminating the problem of unlearning-relearning.* The implications of this proposition are clear and it is easy to apply once we become aware of its importance. Adjectives should *not* be used as nouns. If you say, "Hand me the red," instead of, "Hand me the red paper or paint," the child may not be sure of the name for paper and think that it is *red*. A good example is the child who said, "Teacher, I want more yellow," and when the teacher handed him the yellow paint he said, "No, that yellow," and pointed to the blue paint. The same notion applies in using a noun instead of a pronoun, i.e., the paper is red, the cloth is velvety, the wood is smooth, instead of this is smooth, this is velvety, etc.

349

To make certain the reference point is initially clear, the language should be related to real objects or actions instead of to pictures or illustrations. If you want to teach the concepts of "on," "under," "between," etc., start with something like a ball. "The ball is *on* the table," "The ball is *under* the table," "The ball is *between* the books." Illustrate each statement by placing the ball in the correct position. After many experiences with the real object, pictures can be used.

Environmentally deprived children appear to learn nouns easier than verbs so when the teacher is helping a child to learn verbs, the teacher should be certain that the child already knows the nouns. A good way to teach verbs in a specific way and to eliminate ambiguity is by telling a child what he is doing on the playground. "Juanita walks on the board," or "Jessie jumps down," "Mary rides a play horse," and finally, "Juanita is walking on the board. Juanita has walked on the board."

The teacher should also avoid ambiguous expressions such as big and little, when she means short and tall or short*est* and long*est* or small*est* and larg*est*

PROPOSITION 3: *The child needs specific assistance in learning how to listen.* This means presenting sounds in clear, unambiguous ways and training children to listen for specific sounds such as their names in a song or the bark of a dog.

THE RESPONSIVE ENVIRONMENT BOOTHS

The learning that takes place in the responsive environment booths is related to all four of our major objectives, but the development of language skills and problem solving are the major purposes served by the booths. We also use them as testing booths, as places to test new procedures before introducing the procedure into the general classroom, and as a place to experiment with new equipment such as the Language Master. Nevertheless, their major purpose is to provide a nonautomated responsive environment using electric typewriters, Riteline copy holders, tape recorders, Language Masters and chalkboards. Not all of the booths are equipped with all of this equipment, but it is available. The basic equipment is each booth is a typewriter, copy holder, and chalkboard. As we have pointed out in Chapter I, the entire school is organized as a responsive environment, but the booths are a purer application of the concept within a limited and controlled environment.

The child moves through four phases in the responsive environment booths: (1) free exploration (2) search and match (3) word construction (4) reading and writing. The instruction we give the booth assistants details these four phases. The following is quoted from our guide for booth assistants:[*]

[*] In developing this guide we have drawn heavily upon the work of Omar K. Moore as it is reported by him in Autotelic Responsive Environments and Exceptional Children (1963), and in personal conversations with Moore and Anne Shrader.

350

Tutoring booths are a responsive environment because:

(1) They permit the learner to explore freely.
(2) They inform the learner immediately about the consequences of his actions;
(3) They are self-pacing, i.e., events happen within the environment at a rate determined by the learner;
(4) They permit the learner to make full use of his capacity for discovering relations of various kinds, and;
(5) The structure is such that the learner is likely to make a series of interconnected discoveries about the physical, cultural or social world. (Moore, 1963, p2).

The booths are also designed for autotelic activities; that is, activities that are done for their own sake rather than for obtaining rewards or avoiding punishments that have no inherent connection with the activity itself.

Rules for the child in coming to the typing booth are:

(1) Say to the child, "Now it is *your* turn to play with the typewriter."
(2) He need not come to the booth if he refuses.
(3) He can leave when ever he wishes.
(4) He must leave when his time is up (20 minutes maximum stay).
(5) He need not explain his coming or going.
(6) He goes to the booth to which he is assigned for the day.
(7) If he says he wants to leave, or starts to leave, he may come back again the next day, but not the same day.

Rules for the booth assistants are:

(1) A child is asked only once a day to come to the booth; if, after refusing, the child later asks to come, he is allowed to do so;
(2) He is never asked to come to the booth if he is obviously involved in another activity.
(3) The booth assistant is a part of the responsive environment and only responds to the child, that is, he answers questions, announces letters as the child strikes them, etc. The assistant should be friendly and responsive, but does not direct nor teach the child. The child is allowed to discover and learn for himself.
(4) The *only* punishment used in the booth is to say, "I'm sorry, your time is up;" at which time the child is taken back to the main room.

Prior to entering the booth, the child's fingernails are painted with tempera colors. There is a match between the nail colors and the colored typewriter keys so that the

351

child may match, if he so desires, his fingers with the corresponding colors on the keys. If the child asks why his fingernails are being painted, he is told, "It's part of the game." The match between nail colors and key colors is not pointed out to the child, nor is the matching enforced. Some children discover the match and continue using the touch system throughout the year, others do not.

The activities in the booth move through four phases.

Phase I: Free Exploration

The first time you take a beginning child into the booth, select a child who has already been in the booth and ask that child to show the beginner the booth and the game. Let them explore freely then return to the room. On the day following this first experience the booth assistant invites, ("It's your turn to play with the typewriter now,") the child to come into the booth. Avoid asking the child when he is obviously involved in some other interesting activity.

As the child strikes the letters and symbols, the assistant names them. If the child hits more than one key at a time, turn the typewriter off, free the jammed keys and turn the machine on. If the child again hits several keys at once, the same procedure is followed, but the typewriter is turned off as soon as the child starts to strike more than one key at a time. It is left off until the child starts to punch one key at a time. Repeat this process until the child discovers for himself why the typewriter doesn't work when he strikes more than one key at a time. If key jamming becomes a persistent and dangerous (to the typewriter) behavior, he is told, "Use just one finger at a time." These words are spoken in completely friendly and nonpunitive tone of voice and the statement repeated no more than twice in a single session.

The first time the carriage reaches the right hand margin, the child probably will not know how to return the carriage. After allowing some time for the child to explore, press the return key and say, "See what happens when I press this?" After this first demonstration, the typewriter is turned off when the carriage reaches the end until the child presses the return key.

As far as the child is concerned, he is not learning the names of the letters, numbers, and punctuation marks. He is learning to associate abstract symbols and sounds. He will probably react to "A", "X", "5", and "question mark," in the same way and learn the name "question mark" as easily as "A" or "B". If a child demonstrates knowledge of letters or numbers, this is noteworthy and should be included in the report.

The child will indicate in one way or another when it is time to move to the next

352

phase. Some children will name the letter or number before the booth assistant does. Others will start to lose interest and the time they spend in the booth will decrease.

When a child loses interest, he quickly turns to something else. Some begin talking to the booth assistant about topics which may range from Batman to daddy's being in jail. One little girl created a make believe world playing house - the booth assistant being mommy. If a child initiates conversation in the booth, you should respond. We want to encourage child initiated conversation where ever it occurs, but be alert to the fact that this may be an indication that the child is losing interest in the activities.

Phase II: Search and Match

Step 1.

To introduce a child to phase two display the magnetic chalkboard with the overlay of the chart showing the typewriter keyboard. Lock the typewriter in upper case; seat the child at the typewriter; select one of the upper case plastic letters; and, as you say the name of the letter, place the letter on the magnetic chalkboard over the colored circle that corresponds to the color and placement of the letter on the typewriter. Do not tell the child that he is beginning a new phase or playing a new game. Let him discover this for himself. If he asks what the chart is, say it's part of a new game; if he points to the letter, name the letter; but let him discover what the new game is and what the rules are. Of course, the game is for him to find the letter on the keyboard that is the same as the one on the chart and strike it; when he does, the typewriter works. Be patient at this point; your inclination probably will be to help the child solve this problem, but don't.

The child may try many things to make the typewriter work: Some children begin an extended exploration of the typewriter, looking under it, behind, around, and inside it. Others seem to think like some housewives and believe they can make the typewriter work by banging it. Still other children behave like college freshmen, striking keys at random apparently hoping to find the right answer by chance, but some children will systematically touch every key until the typewriter works. A few study the keyboard not touching anything until they see the correct letter and then with apparent elation strike that key. These few have obviously discovered the rules to the game and the others will if you let them. So far all of the children who have reached this phase have made this discovery without aid from the booth assistant. If you are in doubt about a child's ability to make this discovery, ask the senior booth assistant to observe before you decide to prompt the child. What you can do is to continue to repeat the name of the letter or symbols at about five second intervals. If the child is not looking at the typewriter or the chart, point to the letter as you

353

say it to focus his attention on the letter. After the child has found the first letter place another one on the chart and repeat the process. As the number of symbols increases it may become difficult for the child to keep the letter he is searching for in mind. In that event remove from the chart the letters the child has already found.

Some children will want to place the letter on the chart. Let them; if the letter is misplaced locate it where it belongs without comment. Be certain at the end of the session to record the symbols the child found and those he had difficulty locating. The next day the booth assistant should start with one or two familiar letters so the child can easily recall the rules of the game, then present new symbols. When the child can match all the letters and symbols or begins to lose interest in the game, it is time to move on to the next part of phase II. During this phase a child may regress to a simpler game by indicating he wants to play the other game. When this happens, be certain to remove the magnetic board so that it is clear that you are now playing the first game (free exploration). So long as a piece of equipment remains displayed you are to play the game with that equipment. If the child is to understand the rules you must be consistent.

Phase II.

Step 2

To begin this step have the Riteline displayed with a roll of upper case letters ready for use. When you and the child are seated, display the first symbol or letter and allow the child to search and match. Again let him discover the rules to the new game. Name and display one letter at a time until you have completed the roll. Be certain to record the last letter the child finds so that the booth assistant will know where to begin the next day. Probably most children will want to play with the Riteline and push the lever to make the next letter "come up." To prevent a child from changing the display before he finds the letter, hold your thumb under the bar of the Riteline, but after the child has typed the letter let him change the letters if he wants to do so. If the child is having trouble finding a letter you may want to let him go on to another one; in that event change the letter yourself. One rule of this game is that the child can push the bar to change the display if and only if he finds the letter or symbol that is displayed.

After the child has been through the roll with upper case letters once or twice, change to the roll that displays the arrow to the left of the upper case letters. The child should recognize this as the same symbol that is on the upper case lock key. The child should strike the upper case lock key before he strikes the letter. There are only five of these letters. You will notice that the next series of five displays has the

354

arrow plus two upper case letters. This series is to help the child discover the left to right sequence and it is leading up to the next stop of searching and matching for upper and lower case letters.

During step two, the child should spend about one day out of five, or longer if he likes, playing games at the chalkboard. The first game is based upon the Alphabet cards. The booth assistant should write the letters on the chalkboard as they appear on the cards with four upper case letters spaced across the top of the board and the same letter in lower case along the bottom of the board, but in a different order. On the first set of fourteen cards, three of the four letters have similar shapes for the upper and lower case. The child can easily make the connection between "R", and "r", by eliminating the wrong answers. This has three important consequences: 1. The child is learning the different forms of the same letter; 2. he is allowed to discover them for himself, but is aided in making the right choice; and 3. he is learning to arrive at the right answers by eliminating the wrong answers.

After you have written the letters on the board, give the child the chalk and ask him to draw a line from upper case "C" to "c"; (if necessary, illustrate what you want him to do) from upper case "V" to lower case "v"; from upper case "W" to lower case "w"; and from upper case "R" to lower case "r". After the first one or two times, the child will know the rules of the game, and you should not talk him through the next group of letters.

Observe carefully the sequence the child follows in drawing his lines. Does he link the letters that are similar in upper case and lower case before he links the one with dissimilar forms? What combination of letters causes difficulty? If at first the child does not make the connection between the letters on the board and the letters on the typewriter, watch carefully for some indication that he has made this connection. Using the first set of cards, you will not know when the child can recognize the upper and lower cases of the same letter, because he can arrive at the correct answer by eliminating the wrong ones. Go through all the cards in Set I once or twice, and then switch to the card in Set II. These seven cards have two letters with similar upper and lower case forms and two letters with dissimilar upper and lower case forms. Care has been taken, however, that the forms of the letters are not similar to each other; there are no combinations of d's and b's, or p's and q's, for example. If the child has difficulty, go back to the first set. After the child can make the correct associations on the second set of cards, use Set III which has three letters to test the child's ability to associate upper and lower case letters.

Phase II

Step 3 (See Figure 8 on next page.)

355

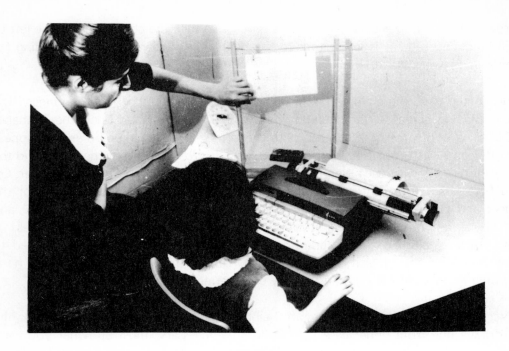

FIGURE 8

A child has reached Phase II Step 3 and is now learning how to recognize the lower case forms of the upper case alphabet she has mastered.

For this step the Riteline should be displayed with the roll that shows the arrow for upper case, a letter, the arrow for lower case and the same letter in lower case (A a). The child should strike the symbols in sequence and type Aa. You should say, "upper case A, lower case a." Follow the same basic procedure as outlined in step two of phase two. Remember the child can go back to any other game, but keep the rules clear by changing equipment.

Phase III Word Construction

During this phase there are two major activities - learning words and writing on the chalkboard.

Start this phase by asking a child, "Would you like to type a word?" There are three possible responses. "Yes" or "What is a word?" are the most probable, but it is possible a child will say no. If a child does say no, return to Phase II, but ask again the next day. If the child says yes, ask, "What word do you want to type?" Print the word on a Language-Master card, and then record the work on the card. Be certain that you make the letters the same way they appear on the typewriter. If the word is a proper noun, the first letter should be upper case. After you have written the

356

word, allow the child to type it. Expect some mistakes such as spacing between the letters or no space after the word. You should continue to turn the typewriter off if a child starts to make a mistake. For example, if he forgets to shift from upper case to lower case or forgets to space between words, turn the typewriter off and say, "Lower case c" or "Space," as the case may be. Spell the word as the child types it, and say "space" after the last letter. Continue to allow the child to select new words, write the child's name on a card, place it on top of the cards with his words, and tell him, "These are your words, and we will keep them for you."

Remember these words are the child's.[*] Allow him to type any word he chooses regardless of how difficult it may seem to you. If the child cannot think of a word he would like to type, encourage him to talk to you about anything of interest to him; after some conversation, return to the original question. You may suggest words, but they should come from his conversation or from something he has said in the room (ask the teacher) or something you have observed that he is interested in. Each child will choose different words that are strong, meaningful words for him. If the words are important to the child, he will remember them and can tell you what they say the next day. In some instances a child will not think of words he wants to type, or he will become bored after typing two or three words. In both cases the child may name anything that comes to his mind. For instance, one child started with "Volks", "Rambler", "Dr. Nimnicht", then, looking around, chose "door" and "window". The next day he remembered the first three, but had forgotten door and window. In such a circumstance, say, "Those are not good words for you," and throw these cards away unless the child asks to keep them.

Each day when the child comes into the booth *allow* him to type his "old" words, and add one or two new ones. If he does not want to type all of the words he has previously learned, go through the cards and have him identify the words; or let him run them through the Language-Master.

About one day out of five should be spent at the chalkboard showing the child how to print some of the words he has learned.

If the child does not know what a word is, use his name and "typewriter" as examples. Then ask if he can think of a word. A few examples should be all that is needed for the child to understand what you mean by "a word."

During this phase, at least part of the time, have all of the equipment displayed so the child can choose his activity, and you can move freely from one to another.

---

[*] Sylvia Ashten Warner's book TEACHER (1963) is a good reference that will give you added insights at this point.

357

Phase IV: Writing a Story

Phase IV should begin when the child starts to lose interest in typing new words or when he has a list of fifteen or twenty words. At that point ask the child if he would like to tell a story using his words. The story may only be one or two sentences; but if it is a story to the child, *it's a story.* As the child tells you the story, record it, write it down, and then type it for the child. Be sure to make a carbon copy for the file - the child gets a copy of his story. In some instances a child might ask to type his own story - fine! Help him by dictating the story as he types it, spelling the words that he does not know. In the event the child does not ask to type his own story, after the child has told you two or three stories that you have typed, ask him if he would like to type his own story and follow the procedure mentioned above.

Phase V: Reading and Writing

After a child has a list of fifteen or twenty words he recognizes and has written a few stories, he is ready to read. Ask him to choose a book that he likes and bring it to the booth with him. Print the first few sentences of the book on paper, but expose only one line at a time on the Riteline, and have the child type it. Read each word as it is typed and each sentence after it is complete. After the first session type the story out in advance. The child's paper should be saved from day to day so he can see the whole story. After finishing the book, help the child read the book and then his typed copy.

From this point on, the child may choose his own activity in the responsive environment booth. He may type his own words, write and transcribe a story, write on the chalkboard, read a story, or read and type a story.

DEVELOPING CONCEPT FORMATION AND PROBLEM SOLVING ABILITIES

We pointed out in Chapter I the growing evidence that early deprivation prevents optimum intellectual development, but many individuals in the field of early childhood education resist the idea of any experiences provided specifically for developing the cognitive abilities of young children. One reason for the resistance is the notion that early training is wasted effort--the children have not reached the level of maturation when they are ready for such learning. Another notion is that efforts to teach cognitive activities to young children are inherently harmful.Both of these notions need to be examined.

The notion that early training is of little or no value is supported by a number of studies that were made in the 1920's and 1930's. One of the best known is a study by Josephine Hilgard.* Since the study is a good example of the learning versus

*J. GENETIC PSY., 41: 36256, 1932.

358

maturation studies, and has had an important influence on the thinking of many important educators and psychologists, we are presenting a summary. The study was first reported in the Journal of Genetic Psychology in 1932 and Arthur Coladarci of Stanford University reprinted it in his book of reading in educational psychology published in 1955, with the following introduction:

> *Many changes in behavior occur in a regular, predictable sequence that is not influenced significantly by normal environmental variations. Such changes occur as the result of what is usually termed "Maturation," and the concept is an important one for the teacher. The readiness of a pupil for learning is, in part, related to his stage of maturation. Educational plans that expect a child to learn skills which, maturationally, he is not "ready" to perform are, at best, inefficient.*
>
> *This study, conducted by Dr. Josephine R. Hilgard in the Psychological Laboratories of Yale University, has two-fold value for the student. First, its substance provides convincing demonstration of the relationship between motor-skill learning and maturation in preschool children. Its second and more general value lies in the fact that it serves as a competent illustration of one of the methods used in studying the relationship between the phenomena of learning and maturation (p. 45).*

The study was made on the effects of practice on the ability of children between the ages of 24 and 36 months to button, cut with scissors, and climb a ladder. The subjects were thirty Merrill-Palmer Nursery School children who were divided into two matched groups according to chronological age, mental age, sex, and approximate initial ability in the three skills. Ten children completed the experiment. The socio-economic background of the children is not given, but an inference can be made by comparing chronological and mental ages of the children and the fact that they were enrolled in the Merrill-Palmer Nursery School. The practice group had a CA of 28.3 and an MA of 29.1, and the control group had a CA of 28.6 and an MA of 29.9. The inference is that the group consisted of average middle class children whose parents were interested in promoting their maximum development.

In her review of the research, Hilgard refers to animal studies by Spalding, Shepard and Breed, Carmichael, and Coghill, all of which demonstrate the importance of maturation in the learning process. She cites studies by Blackhurst, Hildreth, Goodenough, Barrett and Koch, Gates and Taylor, Gesell and Thompson, and Hicks. Hilgard concludes from this review: "The author believes, therefore, that improvement in skill may result from factors other than specific practice, such as the influence of structural maturation and of general practice" (Coladarci, 1955, p. 49).

The experiment consisted of having the experimental group practice buttoning, climbing, and cutting with scissors for twelve weeks; the control group received intensive training for one week, the thirteenth week. Both groups were pre-tested; the experimental group was re-tested at the end of the third week and every two weeks thereafter. The control group was only retested at the end of the twelfth and thirteenth weeks.

The climbing consisted of going up and down a two and one-half feet, three step ladder from the floor to a table. Performance was measured by timing the rate of ascent and descent. Initially, the buttoning consisted of buttoning four buttons which were already matched with the button-holes. More difficult tasks required matching of buttons and holes before buttoning. The child's performance was scored according to the number of buttons he could button and the time required to do so. The cutting with scissors consisted of asking a child to cut along a red line drawn on graph paper. The children started with a vertical line ten centimeters high and then a line fourteen centimeters long drawn at a forty-five degree angle from the base of the paper. The child's performance was measured according to the length of his cut and adherence to the line.

Apparently the children enjoyed climbing and their interest was maintained throughout the experiment, but the interest in buttoning varied. Hilgard commented that "the interest in buttons was far from spontaneous toward the end," and a variety of techniques were used to maintain interest. The cutting test held considerable interest for the children (p. 55).

The results as reported by Hilgard are: At the end of the thirteen weeks covered by the study, when the practice group had been trained for twelve weeks and the control group had been given a final week of intensive training, the outstanding result is a marked similarity in the gains made by the two groups. Though the practice group leads in the gain made in cutting and buttoning, the groups are practically the same in climbing. In the buttoning test the practice group gained 21.4 points and the control group 15.6, or 73% as much. In cutting, the practice group gained 47.5 points and the control group 40.4, or 85% as much. The difference between the two groups in climbing is slight and unreliable, 9.2 for the practice and 9.6 for the control.

The conclusions Hilgard drew from the study are:

> *"In this experiment, we cannot certainly distinguish between the gain to be attributed to maturation alone and that due to maturation plus practice in activities related to the specific skills studied. What does appear is that maturation, plus this related*

360

general practice, accounts for the great gain made between the initial test and the initial retest of the control group, and that specific training throughout the twelve-week period was a far less important contributing factor in the development of these three abilities than was this general development trend (Ibid. p.62)."

The results of this study plus the related research cited in the study is persuasive. It is easy to understand why many psychologists and educators have concluded that early training is of little value, but hindsight is a valuable tool in evaluating research. First let's examine some details of the study and then look at some broader questions.

On the buttoning test the difference would have been greater if the scores for each group at the end of the practice period had been compared because the experimental group scored about three points higher at the end of the twelfth week than they did at the end of the thirteenth week. This comparison would change the percentage the control learned compared to the experimental group from 73% to about 64 or 65%. Since motivation was a problem, the decrease for the experimental group in the thirteenth week is no surprise. The difference on cutting between the experimental and control group is small, but consistently favors the experimental group. There are no differences in climbing at the end of twelve weeks, but this may be a limitation of the test itself. How fast can one climb a three step ladder that is two and one-half feet tall? The same kind of question can be asked about the buttoning test. With the cutting test, a score of one-hundred would mean "no cutting at all" and zero would mean perfect adherence to the red line. The mean scores for the experimental group dropped from about sixty-four to below twenty which would indicate that some children must be approaching a perfect score. Obviously as they approach a perfect score, the amount of change possible with additional practice decreases.

Although it is not stated it seems to be a fair assumption from the mental and chronological ages given that no environmentally deprived children were included in the group. Also, the fact that the children were enrolled in a famous child growth and development center in the early 1930's indicates that all of the children were in home environments that approached optimal conditions for the kind of learning being tested. The good nursery schools of that period centered around spontaneous play with an emphasis upon motor development and social activities. Merrill-Palmer, a leader in the field, was reportedly no exception. If these assumptions are correct, one might expect little or no difference as a result of specific practice because the home environment generally provides this kind of learning with its built-in curriculum. In reality, the emphasis in Hilgard's conclusions should be upon "this related general practice" instead of on maturation. The other interesting notion that

361

appears throughout the study is that these three motor skills are related to intelligence.

The crux of the matter is the fact that on two of the three tasks, there were small, but significant differences which could be interpreted under these circumstances to mean that specific training did make a difference, and considering the nature of the tasks it is predictable that if the children were tested six months later there would be no significant differences because most of the children easily would be able to climb a two and one-half feet ladder, button clothes together and cut along a ten centimeter line. What would the differences be if the tasks the children were learning were cognitive in nature, did not have an upper limit that could be reached in a short span of time, and one group had no opportunity to learn the task while another group received persistent practice over a long period of time? This is the question that is germane in dealing with environmentally deprived children.

We recognize the role that maturation plays in some forms of human development, but our concern is with the environment and some of the conclusions that have been reached on the importance of the level of maturation even when the effects of the environment have been overlooked.

An excellent example is the study we have just completed at New Jersey School on the ability of children to make the sounds of the consonants and certain digraphs such as *th* and *sh.* According to the norms provided with the tests certain digraphs are usually not conquered by children until they are seven or eight. For our purpose it wouldn't make much difference if these norms were set at five and six years or three and four years. We found that among three groups of children (middle class Anglo, lower class Spanish-surnamed and lower class Anglo) there was a wide variation in the ability to make certain sounds (see Figure 9).

The assumption that middle class Anglo children as a group have a faster rate of maturation than lower class Spanish-surnamed children who, in turn, mature faster than lower class Anglos, seems to be an untenable hypothesis. A far more reasonable hypothesis is that there are differences in the environments of the three groups which account for at least part of the variability in making certain sounds correctly.

We are proceeding on the basis of this hypothesis and expect the environmentally deprived children to show significant improvements in their ability to reproduce certain sounds.

Omar K. Moore's work also raises serious questions about establishing the mental or chronological ages when certain tasks can be performed without specifying the environmental conditions. Middle class children under normal conditions usually do

362

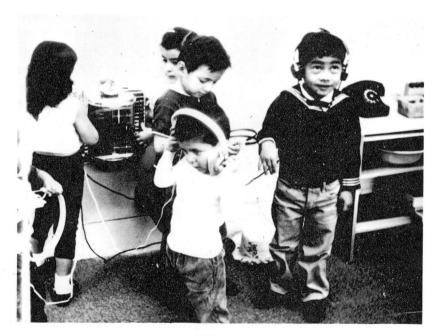

FIGURE 9

The telephone, which is attached to a tape recorder, enables us to study the linguistic patterns of children from various backgrounds (upper); a juke box, equipped with multiple headphones, serves as a random access self-selection source of varied auditory input (lower).

not read until after they are six years old, but under special circumstances three and four year old children learn to read in a matter of months and kindergarten children are capable of publishing their own newspaper (Moore, 1963, p. 14). Other researchers (Bloom, et al, 1965; Bruner, 1964; Deutsch, 1964; Fowler, 1962; Hunt, 1961 and 1964; Rosenzweig, 1966; Torrance and Strom, 1965; and others) are reporting confirming evidence that early training in cognitive development is probably worthwhile for all children and essential for environmentally deprived children.

The notion that early teaching of cognitive activities was inherently harmful probably stems from the emphasis upon teaching rather than learning and the inclination of parents and educators to ignore the significance of maturation. If it is true that twenty per cent of the middle class children in the study quoted earlier have not reached the level of maturation to allow them to make the blend sounds, then early instruction based upon rewards and punishment can be harmful and the net results will probably be that twenty per cent of the children find the experience distasteful and try to avoid it in the future. In this instance one strategy is to avoid speaking to those individuals who do the correcting. For twenty per cent of the children to pay such a price for early instruction makes the price too high and we had better postpone the teaching until more children are likely to be successful. But this is based upon the erroneous assumptions that the approach must emphasize teaching with rewards and punishments and that all children must be taught the same thing at the same time. By reversing this procdure, placing the emphasis upon learning through autotelic activities and making the learning self pacing, the fear of trying to make children learn something that is beyond their maturational level is gone; opportunities for a variety of levels is present and the teacher-researcher is free to discover empirically what a child can and will learn or what a child cannot or will not learn under certain environmental conditions (see Figure 10). This is the position we have taken at the New Nursery School.

A legitimate question that can be asked is, "Assuming that you discover that young children do learn many intellectual tasks at an early age, how do you know it is of any value?" Our response to the question is (1) we already know from other research and our own studies that young children can and do learn many cognitive skills in addition to speech and (2) the relationship between early cognitive development and school success is well established, therefore we must conclude that such learning has value. In fact, the only assumption that we make in advocating education for three and four year old children is that education has worth—it is better to read than not to read; it is better to have a skill than not to have a skill. Only when an individual possesses a skill can he choose to use it or not to use it or choose how it will be used. White's cogent case for feelings of competence (1959) as important aspects of motivation and performance bolster the validity of our assumption.

364

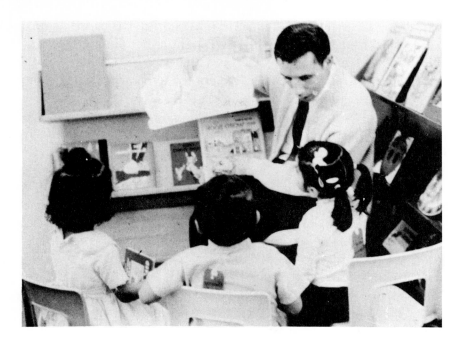

FIGURE 10

These children, who joined the group voluntarily and may leave when they wish, are learning numerous communication skills as they listen to the story and discuss it with their peers and the learning-assistant.

The only way, however, that the teacher-researcher can be certain that the child is not being pressed beyond his ability or development is to insist upon adherence to the notion of self-pacing and autotelic activities. Because of his eagerness to obtain results, a teacher often has a tendency to start teaching instead of responding and offering assistance of one sort or another to encourage children to try something the learner wants to master. At this point the teacher runs the risk of pushing the child beyond his ability or development, and as a consequence of building psychological blocks to future learning and perhaps creating more serious mental health problems. With this caution in mind we have concluded that early cognitive training is not only permissible, but extremely important for environmentally deprived children.

Before we can proceed, however, we must become more specific about what we mean by cognitive development. In order to design learning episodes we have been somewhat arbitrary in the way we have broken down cognitive activities into more operational terms. The first breakdown is into concept formation, memory and problem solving. The term "concept" is extremely broad and the definition varies with different writers. For example, some of the things Piaget refers to as concepts, Russell (1956) calls precepts. But there seems to be general agreement that such terms as dog, cat and fruit are concepts. They imply a generalization and

365

delimitation at the same time, and constitute categories and classification systems. Another kind of concept is an abstract idea or notion that does not form a category in a classification system. For example, "over, under, beside, behind, the same as," are all abstract ideas or simple concepts. We are concerned with teaching both kinds of concepts at the New Nursery School.

Memory, of course, is the ability to recall something that has been learned previously. We are concerned with helping the children learn to remember specific things, that is, exact recall, and to learn to remember something in a general way, but not necessarily exact recall. Exact recall of specific information is usually associated with rote learning or drill, while general recall is associated with meaningful learning that enables the learner to arrive at a fact without specifically remembering it. Learning multiplication tables is a good illustration of the two approaches. Specific recall can be achieved by constant drill until the learner will automatically think "seventy-two" when someone asks, "What is nine times eight?" This can be learned without any clear notion of why nine times eight equals seventy-two. To learn the multiplication tables in a meaningful way, the learner would first have to understand why nine times eight equals seventy-two. After that he might memorize the fact through drill or he might not memorize the specific fact, but rather rely upon his general knowledge of multiplication to figure out the answer. For example, when he is asked what nine times eight equals he might think, "I don't know, but eight times ten equals eighty, so nine times eight is eight less than that and therefore, must equal seventy-two."

We are concerned with both approaches. There are some specific facts we would like for the children to remember such as the names of the colors, names of letters of the alphabet, numbers up to ten, etc. With these specific facts we provide the child with the opportunity to drill and learn by rote by listening to records or playing with the Language Master. Beyond this we are concerned with helping children learn how to arrive at specific facts without memorizing them. Categories and classification systems are obviously related to this kind of mental operation.

Problem solving refers to a variety of cognitive activities. As we stated in Chapter III, problems can be classified as physical, interactional, and affective. Physical problems are those that deal with our physical world. Puzzle solving, learning to eliminate wrong responses to arrive at a correct answer, learning to discover the rules of a game, and learning how to extend a geometric pattern are different kinds of physical problems. The most common kind of interactional problems involve two or more people who interact with each other. When an interactional problem has emotional overtones, it is also an affective problem. Most of the interactional problems the children learn to solve are affective—such as finding a place in the group, getting along with the adult learning assistants, and learning to take turns. These are all interactional problems with emotional overtones. At the New Nursery School the

366

best defined learning episodes deal with physical problems. Interactional problem solving is more a general part of the environment, but specific learning episodes have not yet been worked out.

The following learning episodes are organized according to the most important function they serve.

LEARNING THE CONCEPTS "SAME" AND "NOT THE SAME"

Since a concept is an abstract idea generalized from specifics or concrete experiences, there must be enough of the "specifics" in the learning situation to enable the child to make the abstraction. For example, the child must have experiences with *things* colored red, blue, yellow, and green before he can think about the concept of color. He must have experience with things that are larger, smaller, big, little and the same size with the appropriate terms before he can think about the abstraction "size."

Most children develop these concepts at home, but children from an impoverished home usually do not. The school should provide appropriate "particularized instances" to help the child build important concepts. We know that most of our children should learn the concepts of "same" and "not the same" or "different."

The terms "alike," "unlike" or "different" and "similar" - "dissimilar" were discarded as allowing too many subtle distinctions for honest teaching. Pink and red, for example, are "similar" but are not the same color. Two squares of the same color but differing slightly in size are "alike," but are not the same size. The letters C and O are "similar" and "alike," but they are certainly not the same. After the child has the simpler ideas of "same" and "not the same" he can advance to the ideas that allow more variation.

These concepts were chosen for several reasons: (1) They are not too difficult; (2) They are important concepts; (3) Children are expected to have these concepts and be fairly skilled in using them by the time they start school; (4) Appropriate materials, which the children could see, feel, compare and play with could be developed; and (5) Most of our children did not know the meaning of the terms "same" and "different" when they entered the New Nursery School.

It was decided that the concept "same as" could best be grasped by associating it with a particular characteristic of an object, i.e., same color, same size, same length, same shape. Also, it was decided that the children should know "same" before they were exposed to learning "not the same" except in a casual way.

367

FIGURE 11

The head learning assistant holds up a colored Masonite square which the children try to match in size and color.

The suggested materials can be obtained and cut to size at any lumber yard (see Figure 11). Paint four sets of 4″ by 4″ or 3″ by 3″ Masonite squares different colors. Start with 6 or 8 colors that are easily distinguished from each other, perhaps red, yellow, blue, green, white and black. After the children have had several days to play with the squares, building, sorting, laying out patterns, and stacking, a teacher can help an interested group sort the squares into sets with each set having one of each color. She can then hold up a square and say, "Find a square that is the same color as this square." As the child finds a square that he thinks is the same color, he can compare it with the one the teacher is holding and make his decision about whether or not he has the right color. If he cannot decide, the teacher can say, "that's right, that square is the same color as this square."

As the children become adept at finding the square that is the same color as the one presented, other colors can be added to keep interest high and to make the game more difficult. Gradually add gray, light blue, light green, turquoise, pink, and orange. It is not necessary that the child learn the names of these colors. In fact, it is perferable to omit all mention of color names except as they come up incidentally. Keep in mind the purpose of the equipment, at this time, is to teach the child the concepts "same" and "not the same."

368

Four sets of Masonite squares, graduated in size by ¼" steps from 4" squares down to 2" squares can be used to help the children grasp the idea of "same size." These squares should be presented for free play first, and should include only the ½" gradations; that is, the 2", 2½", 3", 3½", and 4". At an appropriate time, a teacher can hold up one of the squares and say, "Find a square which is the same size as this square."

Again, the child can compare his selection with the one the teacher holds up, and find out for himself if he judged accurately. As the children become proficient in judging the ½" gradations, the other squares can be added to make the necessary discrimination even finer. For the convenience of sorting, each set can be marked with a numeral or letter on the back of each square.

Four sets of dowel rods, cut in graduated sizes by ½" steps from 5" to 10" in length can be used to help the children grasp the idea of "same length." Initial presentation should be of the 1" gradations only. After the children have had a chance to become familiar with the rods through free play, a teacher can say, "Find a rod which is the same length as this rod," as she holds up one. The child has his own set of rods in a tray (for the convenience of sorting, each set can be marked with a numeral or letter on the end of each rod.) He selects from his tray the rod he thinks is the same length, compares it with the teacher's and decides if it is "the same length" or "not the same length." The in-between rods can be added as the children need more challenge. Cuisenaire Rods could be used instead of rods, but the rods are superior for this purpose because they are all the same color.

There are many other opportunities for the casual use of the words "same" and "not the same."

"Bring all the blocks that are the *same length* as this block."

"All the children walk in the *same direction.*"

"That letter is the *same shape* as this one."

Different textures of cloth can be used to "find a piece of cloth that *feels the same* as this one."

Suitable manipulative toys can also be used to reinforce these concepts and to test to find out if the child is able to use the concept in a variety of situations. For example, pegs and disks can be used for a game "find the same color." Cuisenaire rods and blocks can be used for "find the same shape or length." As games are developed, be sure that "same" is tied to a particular characteristic. Avoid such

369

directions as "find a peg that is the same as this one." Does that mean color, length, shape, or what? If a child proudly shows you the design he has made on a hammer board and says, "They're all the same," you can work toward refinement of his observation and description by echoing "Yes, they are all the same shape" . . . 'same color" . . . "same length," or whatever characteristic is appropriate at that time.

After the child is secure in his knowledge of "same" related to a particular characteristic, the teacher can change the games by saying, "Find a rod which is *not the same length* as this one." As the child compares his choice with the teacher she can confirm his decision (if he is correct), and increase his vocabulary by saying, "Yes, that is *not the same*; it is different." The next step, of course, is to use the word "different" in the instruction. Say, "Find a square which is a *different color* from this square."

Playing with this type of manipulative material also sharpens the child's senses and perceptions. He must compare visually colors, sizes, lengths, and then make a decision about the comparison. The first comparison, made from some distance, is really an estimate. The second comparison, made with the two objects together, is easier because the distance is less.

Acquisition of a vocabulary of comparison also enhances the child's powers of observations. As he compares, hears, and then starts to use such phrases "larger," "smaller," (squares of different sizes), "longer," "shorter" (rods of different lengths), he is acquiring another way of looking at and talking about the objects in the world around him.

THE CONCEPT OF RELATIVE SIZE

Children are inclined to size objects as either big or little, or as many of our children did, "mama and baby." The idea that judgment of size is relative, that an object may be the tallest think in a group one time and the shortest another time is one which is easily emphasized in an environment rich with objects that can be manipulated and changed and compared to show changing relationships.

An important aspect in the formation of this concept, as well as any other, is the accuracy with which the adult uses words describing what is happening. (See Language Guides for Teachers of Young Children.)

Most of the suggestions for helping the child form the concept of relative size takes place in unstructured situations, as the opportunity arises. This places extra responsibility on the teacher for seeing these situations, and for being ready with the correct comparative terms. The importance of this can hardly be overemphasized.

370

For years elementary school teachers and parents have been confusing children by referring to the hands on the clock as being "big" and "little." "Which hand is "big," the longer narrower one or the shorter, wider, one?" They might easily have the same area. It is much less confusing to the child, and far more accurate, to say, "the longer hand" and "the shorter hand."

Of course, not all relational situations lend themselves to this comparative treatment, either because of long established usage or because of subtleties which are probably beyond the range of three and four year old culturally deprived children. Some of these we present initially as opposites such as loud and soft which can later be refined into loud, louder, loudest and soft, softer, softest.

Others are treated as opposites only, such as up and down.

Others, because of moralistic connotations, and vagueness of meaning, are not mentioned at all. Examples of these are "bad-good," "dirty-clean," "pretty-ugly."

The terms of comparison are most appropriate to use in the nursery school are listed below.

longer (referring to two objects)	
longest (referring to three or more objects)	
shorter	larger
shortest	largest
taller	smaller
tallest	smallest
heavier	bigger
heaviest	biggest
lighter	littler
lightest	littlest
narrower (less likely	wider
narrowest to be used)	widest

I. Longer-longest; shorter-shortest

   A. Unit blocks should be sized according to their one changing dimension, length. Silhouettes of the blocks on storage shelves with the length gradations displayed, will help the child see the gradations. The half-unit block is the shortest in most sets and the quadruple unit is the longest. (See equipment list)

371

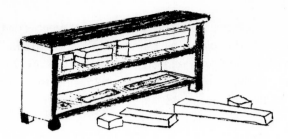

Arrange the blocks so they proceed logically from the shortest to the longest or from the longest to the shortest. Leave some space between the sizes so the differences are easily seen.

Much of the learning that takes place in unit block play is informal. It occurs as the children arrange and rearrange the blocks, put together end to end and side to side, stack and sort. The alert teacher will see many opportunities to respond to the children's play with the verbal interpretation so necessary for concept formation. This does not imply that the teacher keeps up a running commentary on the children's play, sports commentator style. That would only bore the teacher and annoy the child. It does mean being alert to give the right response at the right time.

The following examples will illustrate what we mean.

1. "Gary, you have all the longest blocks. Let Jesse have some for his road."

2. "It is time to put away the blocks. Gary, get one of the longest blocks, pretend you are a bulldozer and push the blocks back to the shelves."

3. "Jesse, find all the shortest blocks and put them on the shelf."

4. To share a moment of triumph when a child calls you over, say, "Your building is even longer that the shelf."

5. "Those boys have all the longer blocks; see what you can build with these shorter ones."

6. If the teacher has to intervene in block play long enough to get a disorganized group going again, she can get the children involved by saying, "We need some blocks. Gary, see if you can find some blocks that are shorter than this one (Holding up

372

sample)." As the child brings blocks, they can be compared to the sample and a decision made as to whether or not the blocks he brought were shorter.

7. For informal evaluation, the teacher can give the following directions:

"Go get the longest block from the shelf.
Go get the shortest block from the same shelf.
Go get a block that is longer than this one (holding up sample).
Go get a block that is shorter than this one.
Now suppose you were building a house and someone had used all the longest blocks. What could you use instead?"

B. Cuisenaire rods have only one changing dimension, length, and should be referred to as shorter, shortest, longer, longest.

During the weeks of free play, the teacher should be alert to echo inexact and groping comparisons such as "He beeg, beeg. . .He lee-al." with, "Yes, the orange rod is longer than the blue rod." (For further suggestions, see Cuisenaire rods.)

C. Dowel rods used for forming the concept "same" also illustrate the concept of relative length. As the child, attempting to find a rod the same length as the teacher's compares the two, the teacher can say, "No, they are not the same length. Your rod is longer (or shorter) than mine."

As the child advances in confidence and understanding, the teacher can ask, "Are the rods the same length? .... Is your rod longer or shorter than mine?"

When playing the game of finding a rod which is not the same length as the teacher's, the teacher and child can decide, "They are not the same length. This rod is shorter than that rod."

D. Clay and dough play gives the opportunity for many verbal responses to what the children are doing. As round balls of clay turn into snakes that grow longer and longer, leading to such remarks as "Mine beeger 'n hers," the teacher can work toward refinement of discrimination and language by suggestions such as the following: "put the rolls of clay side by side, like this, and then we can see which is the longest. Jose's roll of clay is the longest, Sherry's is next to the longest, and mine is the shortest."

373

II. Taller-Tallest; Shorter-Shortest

A. At the beginning and end of the school year, when children are measured for growth, comparisons of their height with each other, with other marks on the measuring tape, and with earlier measurements can be made. Informal comparisons of this type can be made at any time.

"Joe is taller than Mary, Joe is the tallest boy in the class."
"You are taller than you were last fall. See the mark; that is how tall you were then."
"You are shorter than Juanita is. Look at yourselves in the mirror and you can see."

B. Nesting cups, barrels, rings on the color cones, and other manipulative toys can be used to build towers of different heights. (See Manipulative Toys.) As the relative heights of these are changed by adding to or subtracting from the number of cups, the child. learns that "tallest" or "taller", "shortest" or "shorter" can be a changing thing.

C. Block structures frequently lend themselves to height comparison.

III. Wider-Widest; Narrower-Narrowest

A. Unit blocks offer opportunities for building understanding of these terms.

"Try making our building wider and shorter, then maybe it won't fall."
"The road is too narrow for the cars. Make it wider."

Gestures and demonstrations can help the child pin down the meaning of these terms. Structures made with Cuisenaire rods often illustrate this concept.

IV. Larger-Largest; Smaller-Smallest; Bigger-Biggest; Littler-Littlest

These sets of terms are often used synonymously and will be done in this case, since the subtle differences are in adult usage, not applicable to actual size gradations.

A. Use these terms with unit blocks only when the size distinctions are obvious. Usually structures take such disparate forms that overall dimensions can hardly be compared.

374

B. Nesting cups, barrels, rings on the color cones, and certain other manipulative toys that vary in all dimensions from smallest to largest demonstrate this concept.

> "Put the largest cup on the bottom. Look at the cups that are left. Find the largest one of them and try it next." (See manipulative toys)

C. Masonite squares of different sizes, such as those used for building the concept "same" (see concept formation), can be used.

> "The squares are not the same size. This square is smaller than that square."
> "Find a square which is larger (or smaller) than this square."

D. After geometric shapes have been introduced, (see concept formation - Geometric Shapes) the teacher (or child) can put on the flannel board circles, squares, triangles, or rectangles of varying sizes.

> "Point to the largest circle. . .Point to the smallest circle" . . . . .The teacher then starts removing or adding circles so that the comparative sizes change. "Now point to the largest circle." "Now point to the smaller circle." (when there are only two left)

> Do not play this game with the "Form Board", a puzzle where graduated sizes of circles, squares and triangles fit into corresponding cut-outs. In this puzzle the "largest circle" might be removed, but the outline of it, still the largest circle, remains.

E. Clay and dough balls of various sizes can be compared and labeled as smaller - smallest; larger - largest.

F. The books THE VERY LITTLE GIRL and THE VERY LITTLE BOY by Phyllis Krasilovsky, can be used to show that a child's growth changes the relative size of things. The table, fence and the doorknob, don't seem as high as the little girl begins to grow bigger.

USING MANIPULATIVE TOYS TO SHOW PATTERNS

The ability to see patterns and extend them is an aid to memory and information retrieval similar to categories or classification systems. The extension of patterns is also one form of problem solving.

375

Patterning can be done with color, shape, length, size or any other characteristic of manipulative toys. The material that is most appropriate to use for patterning includes plastic disks, Cuisenaire rods, geometric shapes, blocks, and so forth. It is essential that enough of the example be laid out that the pattern is apparent.

Patterns should be extremely simple in the beginning, such as the ones below.

Color patterns with plastic disc.

Shape patterns with triangle puzzle.

Size patterns with Masonite squares.

Color and length patterns with Cuisenaire rods.

As the child discovers the notion of extending a particular pattern, the patterns can become more complex. For example, with the Cuisenaire rods one can progress from:

to . . . .

If the child has some difficulty, the same kind of pattern with added rods can be extended; otherwise, a new pattern such as the following can be introduced.

376

Three dimensional patterns can also be used.

Plastic disks which fit together.

Masonite squares.

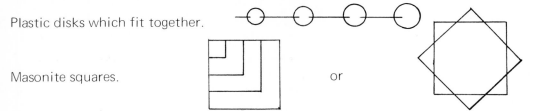

or

Select the material you plan to use and lay out the pattern. When a child wants to know what you are doing, show him, then let him take over the materials, or lay out a pattern and leave the materials there for a child to come to later.

This is a good place to assess a child's ability to perceive a pattern. Does he see no pattern at all, but just some toys? Does he duplicate the pattern rather than extend it? Does he see the pattern, start to extend it, then lose the idea as he goes along? Does he carefully extend the pattern correcting his mistakes by referring back to the original? Some children become elated by their ability to "keep going" on a pattern, such as Frank did when he alternated triangles and circles the length of the classroom and halfway back, finally stopping when he ran out of materials.

Don't give verbal help; if you have to tell the child what to do, he is probably not ready for this. The idea is to let the child find out how to do it by himself. When more than one child becomes involved, you can move from one to another, starting a pattern for each child to continue, or have all of the children make the same pattern that you have started.

After the children have the basic notion, invite them to make patterns for other children (or you) to complete.

CONCLUSION

The notion of the learner's freely exploring in a self-pacing environment, where he learns immediately about the consequences of his actions, is meaningless unless he discovers worthwhile things about himself and his physical, cultural, and social world.

In view of both the disastrous consequences of being caught up in the poverty cycle and our commitment to early educational intervention as an antidote, it is incumbent upon us to devise a responsive pre-school environment which will enable each child to begin to become as fully self actualized and competent to cope with his world as possible. We believe that the aforementioned objectives and concomitant procedures provide a cogent basis for a set of criteria, including measurable

377

behavioral outcomes, against which we can evaluate (Meier, 1967) any given child's present state of emergence from his defeating and debilitating milieu. This emancipation is our ultimate criterion of success. Thus far, the short term results have been most encouraging (Nimnicht and Meier, 1966). As our sophistication in creating and an autotelic responsive environment increases, we would anticipate an even better performance on the part of our "graduates"; thus far, they have done significantly better than their matched controls on standardized tests and in the opinion of kindergarten and first grade teachers. However, on account of the longitudinal nature of the program's objectives, it is too early yet to draw any firm conclusions about the overall efficacy of this approach to early educational intervention for preventing and reversing the undesirable effects of environmental deprivation on young children.

APPENDIX

SOME RESULTS OF RESEARCH AT THE NEW NURSERY SCHOOL

Our criteria for selection of the children are:

1. All children must be from impoverished homes, i.e., on welfare rolls, no steady wage earner in the home, low educational achievement of the parent, living in sub-standard housing, a history of anti-social behavior in the family, and a history of poor school achievement of older siblings. Not all conditions must be present in the background of every child, but a combination of three or more must be present in the background of each child.

2. Thirty children must be Spanish surnamed.
   a. Ten, three years old with no previous nursery school experience.
   b. Ten, four years old with no previous nursery school experience.
   c. Ten, four years old with one year of previous nursery experience at the New Nursery School.

3. Fifteen children must be environmentally deprived, but not Spanish surnamed.
   a. Eight, four years old.
   b. Seven, three years old.

The overall objective of the program is to facilitate the development of the kind of coping behavior which is exigent for efficient dealing with everyday problems and more particularly, with school related tasks. This attempt to augment the children's rational, problem-solving approach to life is consistent with the general goal of educational efforts toward producing individuals who can successfully participate in a rapidly changing world society. We are seeking to enable the children to become "System 4" individuals:

> *System 4 functioning, the more abstract end of the continuum, is viewed as the consequence of childhood freedom to explore both the social and physical aspects of one's environment, to establish and rely upon values derived from one's own experience and thought, and for deviating from established truth. The System 4 representative who is the recipient of diversity along with stability as a developing child, and who is of high perceived self-worth despite momentary frustrations and deviation from the normative, comes to have a highly differentiated and integrated cognitive structure and consequently to be more flexible, more creative and more relative in thought and action, more than persons of any*

379

other systems. The System 4 individual has a set of internal standards that are more truly independent of external criteria, in some cases coinciding with social definitions and in other not (Harvey, 1966, pp. 45-46).

This overall objective to increase the probability of each individual's becoming inner-directed (Reissman, 1962) is approached by zeroing in on the four more specific operational objectives dealing with self-image, language, perception, and cognition explained earlier.

In order to evaluate the effectiveness of the New Nursery School program we have used conventional tests such as the PEABODY PICTURE VOCABULARY TEST and the REVISED STANFORD-BINET TEST OF INTELLIGENCE. Both of these tests purport to measure intelligence, which is assumed to be a fairly valid measure of an individual's intellectual or cognitive functioning at the time and within the parameters of the test. We are using these tests not only as validated predictors of school success but as partial measures of the effectiveness of our nursery school program, especially in terms of language and cognitive development. Previous research (Deutsch, 1964) indicates that an intelligence test score is fairly reliable for middle-class children and for environmentally deprived (ED) children who score average or above in intelligence but not for lower class children who score below average. Therefore, we expected some changes in scores for ED children who scored below average on the initial test since we hoped not only to arrest but even to reverse the phenomenon of cumulative deficit; however, to stabilize a previously decreasing IQ would in itself represent a positive effect.

We have also experiemented with Caldwell's PRE-SCHOOL INVENTORY, Banta's CINCINNATI AUTONOMY TEST BATTERY, Nimnicht's "C" TEST, Brown's IDS SELF-REFERENTS TEST, the Meier TV TEST BATTERY, the Templin and Darley ARTICULATION TEST, A COLOR IDENTIFICATION TEST, and we gathered extensive data on the LEARNING BOOTH performances. The local school district gave the METROPOLITAN READING READINESS TEST to all kindergartners and shared the results of our graduates' performance as compared to the control group's performance. We used the Kindergarten teachers as sensitive instruments by having them rank their pupils according to their judgment of those who were most likely to succeed in first grade.

Since a comprehensive monograph is being prepared to fully describe and discuss the research which has been going on for four years now, we will attempt to only briefly report some of the highlights. Both parametric and non-parametric analyses of the data are to be made and the following observations are based on the results of some

380

of the initial parametric analyses. We are certain, from inspection of the data, that non-parametric approaches are more suitable and will yield more noteworthy information but at this writing such calculations have not been completed, let alone interpreted.

On account of the relatively small numbers of cases which are in any given category and the correspondingly few degrees of freedom, we will mention herein only those differences which are at least at the ten percent level of confidence. Since significance levels under these circumstances would be misleading, we will mention differences which are supported by at least this ten percent level of confidence. although in many cases differences are significant at the one percent level. The trends we report suggest that in ninety to ninety-nine cases out of one hundred the differences reported are probably due to real factors and in only one to ten cases out of one hundred would they be due to chance factors.

In analyzing the data we used a pre-test - post-test design or made comparisons between groups when both pre-test and post-test data were not available. Our population consists of three sub-groups of New Nursery School children (NNS's), (1) three-year-old environmentally deprived children who are attending the school for the first time (NNS-3), (2) four-year-old environmentally deprived children who are attending the school for the first time (NNS 4-1) and (3) four-year-old environmentally deprived children who are attending the school for the second year (NNS 4-2), plus an experimental group of middle-class children who attend the Responsive Environment Nursery (REN) school. The REN children are sub-divided into comparable groups (REN 3, REN 4-1, REN 4-2). All of the NNS children attended school three hours a day, five days a week for a school year. The attendance of REN children varied from two to three days a week over approximately the same period of time.

The REVISED STANFORD-BINET (RSB) and the PEABODY PICTURE VOCABULARY TEST (PPVT, form A) were both administered in September of 1966, and the PPVT (form B) was administered in May, 1967. The RSB will not be given until the Fall of 1967. At that time we will also test a matched control group of environmentally deprived children who have not had experience at the New Nursery School (some will have attended a summer Head Start program) in order to establish the base for the longitudinal study of each child in the control group.

There are some noteworthy comparisons and contrasts between the performances of the environmentally deprived children and the REN environmentally privileged children. REN has a similar program but is operated under private auspices for children from the relatively enriched environments of middle and upper-class homes.

381

Generally speaking, the REN children did far better on practically all pre and post tests. They started out performing better and they not only maintained but in many instances widened the gap during one or two years of nursery experience. This finding tends to support our thesis that properly devised early childhood experiences, such as available in an autotelic responsive environment, can enhance the performance of all children, regardless of the socio-economic status of their home background. A corollary of this would state that more and earlier enrichment is necessary for children such as our environmentally deprived group in order to effectively close the gap between their performance and that of their privileged peers. The new pilot PARENT-CHILD CENTER movement seems to be a national step in this direction.

With regard to the specific findings, let us simply take one instrument or procedure at a time and mention the significant trends. Tabular presentations showing all of the nitty-gritty will appear in subsequent publications.

The REVISED STANFORD BINET has been administered in the fall of each year to experimental and control groups. NNS children who have been in the program one year and are tested at the beginning of their second year at the NNS had a mean IQ of 99 in Fall of 1966; REN children had a mean IQ of 116 after one year's experience. These scores reveal remarkable intellectual growth, especially when reversal of the cumulative deficit, which is only stabilized in the one-year NNS children is considered. The 1967 Fall testing has not begun yet and thus additional comparisons as well as any conclusions would be premature. Last fall several first year NNS children did not even achieve a base on the RSB pre-test which makes comparisons with post-test data impossible for them; the fact that they were able to all be post-tested and had a mean IQ in the low 80's was quite encouraging since they were originally probable candidates for special education for educable mentally handicapped children.

The PEABODY PICTURE VOCABULARY TEST yielded a mean pre-test IQ of about 76 for NNS children and 116 for REN children; post-test mean IQ's for 1966-67 year were about 82 and 113, respectively. The deprived group made substantial gains and the privileged group continued to grow at a relatively rapid rate, since a mean IQ of 100 would indicate that the REN group had made one year's mental growth during the passage of one chronological year. The standard error of measurement and some regression toward the mean would account for the slightly lower REN mean IQ on the post-test.

The PRE-SCHOOL INVENTORY was administered to only NNS children and just once during the Spring of 1967. (1) There is a consistent pattern of increase in scores from NNS 3's to NNS 4-1's to NNS 4-2's. (2) The mean percentile scores for

382

the NNS 4-2's are consistently higher than for the NNS 4-1's. (3) The NNS 4-2's scored highest on Factor B - ASSOCIATE VOCABULARY and lowest on Factor A - PERSONAL - SOCIAL RESPONSIVENESS which is consistent with the program emphasis of the New Nursery School. (4) The mean percentile score for the NNS 4-2's is at the 95th percentile while the NNS 3's and NNS 4-2's are at or near the 50th percentile; this finding suggests that our group of deprived children is not significantly different from the norm (Headstart) group at entry into our program and that our program has had a positive effect on the children especially on those who have been in the school for two years. All of the factors have a fairly high and uniform correlation with the PPVT; one would expect Factor B, Associative Vocabulary, to correlate most highly with the PPVT and the data show this prediction to be accurate (r = .55). Our conclusion at this time is that the PRE-SCHOOL INVENTORY may prove to be very useful in evaluating some of the effects of a nursery school program.

The CINCINNATI AUTONOMY TEST BATTERY grew out of a study of the development of children from three to five years of age especially the developmental study of autonomy in thinking, perception, and social behavior. Autonomy is defined by Banta as "the self-regulating abilities which facilitate effective problem solving behavior. Holt's (1964) description of intelligence, "not how much we know how to do, but how we behave when we don't know what to do" succinctly describes the focus of this test.

The REN children as a group scored higher on the Curiosity Box subtest than did the NNS children, but the NNS-3 group scored higher than the NNS 4-1's and about the same as NNS 4-2's. The pattern is the same within the REN group. We can only speculate that children may lose or have stamped out some of their curiosity (or expression of it) from three to four years of age and that the program may have intervened to aid in the retention of curiosity or the feeling of freedom to explore. In general, the REN children scored higher than comparable NNS children on all subtests that we decided to analyze on basis of Banta's reliability data (these included Curiosity Box, Impulse Control, Intentional Learning, Innovative Behavior and Field Independence) and children who have been in either program for the second year generally do considerably better than those attending for the first year, regardless of age.

The pattern of the scores on the "C" Test, which requires children to simply match miniature concrete objects according to categories (e.g. a glove and a shoe), is somewhat different from what we have observed before. The REN 3 and 4-1 children as a group have higher scores than the NNS 3 and 4-1 children, with the 4-1 mean scores being higher than the 3's; however, the NNS 4-2 mean score is higher

383

than the REN 4-2. The correlations of the "C" TEST with the PRE-SCHOOL INVENTORY and the PPVT are unusually high, and we will need to do more extensive testing with the "C" TEST to determine its reliability before interpreting the data at face value. If the correlations persist, we will have a very simple, easily administered test that requires no verbal response, can be easily translated into other languages and can be used meaningfully in a test battery for three- and four-year-old deprived children. The "C" TEST correlates with Innovative Behavior (.14) and there is a negative correlation with Impulse Control (-.26). Since Impulse Control correlated positively with the PPVT (.38), the "C" TEST may be accounting for different dimensions of the PPVT and PRE-SCHOOL INVENTORY. The numerous implications of visual, auditory, and kinesthetic encoding and decoding combinations (see Kirk, 1962) will not be explored in this report but are certainly germane and warrant additional consideration.

The CHILDREN'S CATEGORIES TEST is the only part of the TV TEST BATTERY (Meier, 1967) which was administered to a sufficiently large sample of children to be analyzed by conventional statistical procedures. This non-verbal, "culture-free" test assesses biological intelligence and fundamental problem-solving processes, such as the elimination or confirmation of previous hunches within a series of progressively more complex problems. It is noteworthy that the rather consistent pattern we have noted before on other measures is not evident. In some instances, the 4-1's perform better than the 4-2's. There are some apparent differences in scores, with the REN group obtaining a higher average score than the NNS group; to what degree these differences are important is open to question until we have more data to analyze and interpret. Once again, the correlations with the PRE-SCHOOL INVENTORY are fairly high (.58 with Concept Activation-Sensory and .56 with Total) and the CHILDREN'S CATEGORIES TEST correlates with Intentional Learning (.40), Innovative Behavior (.37), and Field Independence (.37). Since this test seems to be relatively free from a reliance upon previous learning and does correlate with the complex cluster of items mentioned above, it also appears to warrant continued research and development.

We have developed a COLOR IDENTIFICATION TEST to measure a child's ability to name the basic colors. This test utilizes the Language Master, but it can be administered nearly as well without such special equipment. The colors of black, white, red, orange, yellow, brown, green, purple, and blue are painted on nine different Language Master cards, one color on each card. The name of the color is recorded on the instructor's channel, "The color of this paint is blue." The tester presents one card at a time and asks, "What color is the paint on this card?" The teacher waits up to ten seconds for a response. If the child does not respond or gives a wrong answer, we assume that he cannot name that color. In any event, the tester lets the child run the card through the machine to hear the correct answer. (If the Language Master is not used, the tester tells the child the correct answer.)

384

The results show that the first-year NNS children are significantly less able to identify colors than the REN children both on the pre-test (NNS 3 and 4-1 mean = 1.7, REN 3 and 4-1 = 5.5) and the post-test (NNS 3 and 4-1 mean = 5.9, REN 3 and 4-1 = 7.9). However, the second-year NNS children did somewhat better on both the pre-test (NNS 4-2 mean = 7.8, REN 4-2 = 7.3) and the post-test (NNS mean = 9.0, REN = 8.3). By the end of two years at the NNS, all the children could recognize and name nine colors. This ability seems quite helpful in many primary school activities (Wilson and Robeck, 1963).

The IDS SELF CONCEPT REFERENTS TEST makes use of the notion of "significant others" by using the children's mother, friends, and teacher as referents. That is, the child is asked to look at a Polaroid picture of himself while he answers a series of fourteen questions such as "Now can you tell me, is (child's name) happy or is he sad?" Then the child is asked the same question using the mother as a referent, i.e. "Does (child's name)'s mother think that (child's name) is happy or sad?" The test is repeated four times each time changing the referent. The test is more direct and easier to interpret than standard projective techniques. The different questions and referents offered the possibility of generating data on different aspects of the child's self-image.

The results of the pilot testing with NNS and matched deprived youngsters without NNS experience at the first grade level indicated some significant differences between the groups in favor of NNS graduates. However, there were not many negative responses from either of the deprived groups. Item 2 *(clean-dirty)*, 12 *(strong-weak)*, 14 *(likes the way his face looks - doesn't like the way his face looks)*, and the ***total score*** discriminated best. REN children unhesitantly made all positive responses toward themselves with each referent. Modifications have been made on the basis of the pilot study and a modified form of this procedure will be used in the future.

The first set of scores on the METROPOLITAN READING READINESS TEST indicates that the mean performance of those NNS graduates, who were in kindergarten and tested in the Spring of 1967, was thirty-five percentile points higher than their matched control group. The mean score for NNS kindergartners was at the seventieth percentile as compared with the thirty-fifth percentile for a randomly selected control group of kindergarten children in the same classes who had not attended the NNS.

When teachers were asked to rank all of their students in terms of most likely to succeed in first grade, before the readiness tests had even been given, NNS children were more frequently in the upper half than their control group counterparts. We had hoped to keep the variable of NNS attendance confidential from the kindergarten teachers, but the children revealed themselves in one way or another quite early in the school year.

385

An ARTICULATION TEST was administered to NNS and REN children in the Fall of 1966 and Spring of 1967. The results dramatically illustrate the deceptive nature of norms when used to develop school programs for children's speech acquisition. For example, the REN children were, on the average, a full two years advanced beyond the norms whereas the NNS children were an average of at least one year behind the norms; a school program designed to meet the needs of one group would miss the other group and a program aimed at the mean of the two groups would fail both. The one-year NNS children showed some growth in measured articulation skills, but the two-year NNS group truly made the continuous efforts for precise speech seem worthwhile.

The periodic tape-recorded telphone interviews (each child every fifteen days) gave us some insight into the psycholinguistic aspects of speech acquisition with several children. At this juncture the data are too limited and our analytic procedures too unsophisticated to draw any conclusions.

The LEARNING BOOTH information is quite revealing. Extensive data were gathered for NNS and REN children on four salient variables: 1. cumulative number of minutes in the booth; 2. phase level or number at end of school program; 3. cumulative number of strokes; and 4. the number of times a given child chose to go to the booth. One finding was that, even though the REN children spent significantly less time in the booths, their average phase level (which reflects magnitude of achievement) was significantly higher. They simply learned faster and more efficiently. Of course they entered with a considerably greater amount of experience and interest in symbolic, abstract activities, which was indicated on the intelligence tests.

There is a positive relationship between the number of times the children go to the booth, the time they spend in it, and achievement in booth activities. Older children and/or more intelligent based on IQ scores) children achieve more in the booth in the same amount of time.

In conclusion, then, we must reiterate that it is too early to make any firm statements based on the inadequate data and tentative inferences they allow. We can only be somewhat encouraged to continue with the longitudinal study and to carefully analyze whatever lends itself to meaningful research and evaluation. Additional data collection and analysis will give us information about interaction among variables and new meaningful avenues to explore as well as meaningless avenues to eliminate from our future explorations. The non-parametric analysis promises to yield additional important leads which will warrant further pursuit. As mentioned at the outset of this section, these results will all appear in a much more extensive research monograph at a later date.

386

References

Alper, A. E., and Horne, B. M. "Changes in I. Q. of a group of institutionalized mental defectives over a period of two decades." AMER. J. MENT. DEFIC., 64: 472-475, 1959.

Anderson, A. R. and Moore, O. K. "Autotelic folk-models." Sociological Quarterly, 1: 203-216, 1960.

Argy, W. P. "Montessori versus orthodox: A study to determine the relative improvement of the pre-school child with brain damage trained by one or two methods." REHABILITATION LITERATURE, 26: 294-304, 1965.

Ausubel, D. P. THE INFLUENCES OF EXPERIENCE ON INTELLIGENCE. Unpublished mimeographed paper read at the NEA Conference in Productive Thinking. Wash., D. C. 1963.

Ausubel, D. P. THEORY AND PROBLEMS OF CHILD DEVELOPMENT. New York: Grune and Stratton, 1957.

Bandura, A. and Walters, R. H. SOCIAL LEARNING AND PERSONALITY. New York: Holt, Rinehart and Winston, Inc., 1963.

Beller, E. K. THE IMPACT OF PRE-SCHOOL EXPERIENCE ON INTELLECTUAL DEVELOPMENT IN EDUCATIONALLY DEPRIVED CHILDREN. Unpublished paper presented at A.E.R.A. meeting, Reb., 1966.

Bendix, R. and Lipset, S. CLASS STATUS AND POWER. New York: Basic Books, 1957.

Bereiter, C. et. al. AN ACADEMICALLY-ORIENTED PRE-SCHOOL FOR CULTURALLY DEPRIVED CHILDREN. Unpublished mimeographed paper, 1964.

Bernard, H. W. HUMAN DEVELOPMENT IN WESTERN CULTURE, 2nd edition. Boston: Allyn and Bacon, 1966.

Bernstein, B. "Language and social class." BRITISH JOURNAL OF SOCIOLOGY, 11: 271-276, 1960.

Biber, B. THE EDUCATIONAL NEEDS OF YOUNG DEPRIVED CHILDREN. Bureau of Child Development and Parent Education, Department of Education, Albany, N. Y. Filmed lecture for Project Head Start.

387

Blatt, B., "Some persistently recurring assumptions concerning the mentally subnormal." TRAINING SCHOOL BULLETIN, 57: 48-59, 1960.

Bloom, B., Davis, A., and Hess, R. (Eds.) COMPENSATORY EDUCATION FOR CULTURAL DEPRIVATION. New York: Holt, Rinehart and Winston, 1965.

Bloom, B. S. STABILITY AND CHANGE IN HUMAN CHARACTERISTICS. New York: Wiley, 1964.

Bolling, R. W. "Sociatry: A new concept for the culturally deprived." JOURNAL OF HUMAN RELATIONS, 12: 471-475, 1964.

Boucher, S. W. (Ed.) Colorado state mental health planning committee: needs survey report; region 4, Weld County. Unpublished paper, 1964.

Bruner, J. S. 'The cognitive consequences of early sensory deprivation." In P. Solomon (Ed.), SENSORY DEPRIVATION. Cambridge: Harvard University Press, 195-207, 1961.

Bruner, J. S. "The growth of mind." AMERICAN PSYCHOLOGIST, Dec., 1007-1017, 1965.

Bruner, J. TOWARD A THEORY OF INSTRUCTION. Cambridge, Mass.: Harvard University Press, 1966.

Buckingham, W. ."The great employment controversy." THE ANNALS, "Automation," C. C. Killingsworth, (Ed.), Vol. 340, American Academy of Political and Social Science, Philadelphia, March, 46-52, 1962.

Burgess, E. VALUES IN EARLY CHILDHOOD EDUCATION, 2nd edition. Pasadena, Calif.: Pacific Oaks College, 1965.

Carmichael, L. MANUAL OF CHILD PSYCHOLOGY, 2nd edition. New York: Wiley, 1954.

Coleman, J. S. et. al., EQUALITY OF EDUCATIONAL OPPORTUNITY. Wash., D. C.: U. S. Department of Health, Education and Welfare, U. S. Government Printing Office, 1966.

Coll, B. D. "Deprivation in childhood: its relation to the cycle of poverty." WELFARE IN REVIEW, March, 1966.

Cutts, R. A. "Differentiation between pseudo-mental defectives with emotional

388

disorders and mental defectives with emotional disturbances." AMER. J. MENT. DEFIC., 61; 761-776, 1957.

Davis, K. HUMAN SOCIETY, N. Y.: Macmillan, 1949.

Demos, G. D. "Attitudes of Mexican-American and Anglo-American groups toward education." JOURNAL OF SOCIAL PSYCHOLOGY, 57: 249-256, 1962.

Dennis, W. "Causes of retardation among institutional children." JOURNAL OF GENETIC PSYCHOLOGY, 96: 47-59, 1960.

Deutsch, C. P. "Education for disadvantaged groups." REVIEW OF EDUCATIONAL RESEARCH, 35: 140-146, 1965.

Deutsch, C. P. EFFECTS OF ENVIRONMENTAL DEPRIVATION ON BASIC PSYCHOLOGICAL PROCESSES: SOME HYPOTHESES. Unpublished paper delivered at A.E.R.A. 1965 Convention.

Deutsch, M. "Early social environment and school adaption." TEACHERS COLLEGE RECORD, 66: 699-706, 1965.

Deutsch, M. A PROGRAM TO DEMONSTRATE THE EFFECTIVENESS OF A "THERAPEUTIC CURRICULUM" FOR THE SOCIALLY DEPRIVED CHILD. Unpublished paper, 1962.

Deutsch, M. "Facilitating development in the pre-school child: social and psychological perspectives." MERRILL-PALMER QUARTERLY, 249-263, 1964a.

Deutsch, M. "Minority group and class status as related to social and personality factors in scholastic achievement." MONOGRAPHS FOR THE SOCIETY OF APPLIED ANTHROPOLOGY, No. 2, 1960.

Deutsch, M. "Nursery Education: The influence of social programming on early development." JOURNAL OF NURSERY EDUCATION, 18, 1963a.

Deutsch, M. REVERSING DEPRIVATION EFFECTS IN THE PRE-SCHOOL CHILD. Institute for Developmental Studies, New York Medical College, Unpublished paper, 1963b.

Deutsch, M. "Social and psychological perspectives on the development of the disadvantaged learner." JOURNAL OF NEGRO EDUCATION, Summer, 232-244, 1964b.

389

Deutsch, M. SOME PSYCHOLOGICAL ASPECTS OF LEARNING IN THE DISADVANTAGED. New York Medical College: Institute for Developmental Studies, in press.

Deutsch, M. "The disadvantaged child and the learning process." In A. H. Passow (Ed.), EDUCATION IN DEPRESSED AREAS. New York: Bur. Pub., Teachers College, Columbia University, 163-179, 1963c

Deutsch, M. "The influence of early social environment on school adaptation." In Schreiber, D. (Ed.) THE SCHOOL DROPOUT. Wash., D. C.: N.E.A., 89-100, 1964c.

Deutsch, M. and Brown, B. "Social influences in Negro-white intelligence differences." JOURNAL OF SOCIAL ISSUES, 24-35, April 1964.

Dowley, E. M. "On the research side: doing research in a nursery school." JOURNAL OF NURSERY EDUCATION, 16: 22-32, 1960-61.
Eisenberg, L., Emotional determinants of mental deficiency, A.M.A. ARCHIVES OF NEUROLOGY AND PSYCHIATRY, 80: 114-124, 1958.

Ellis, N. (Ed.). HANDBOOK IN MENTAL DEFICIENCY: PSYCHOLOGICAL THEORY AND RESEARCH. New York: McGraw-Hill, 1963.

Eron, L. O., Walder, L. O., Laulicht, J. H., and Hladky, F., Jr. "The psychosocial development of aggressive behavior in children." PROCEED. RIP VAN WINKLE CLINIC, 9: 10-35, 1958.

Feldmann, S. "A pre-school enrichment program for disadvantaged children." THE NEW ERA, 45: 79-82, 1964.

Ferman, L. A., Kornbluh, J. L., and Haber, A. (Eds.) POVERTY IN AMERICA. Ann Arbor, Mich.: University of Michigan Press, 1965.

Fiske, D. W. and Maddi, S. R. FUNCTIONS OF VARIED EXPERIENCE. Homewood, III.: Dorsey Press, 1961.

Fowler, W. "Cognitive learning in infancy and early childhood." PSYCHOLOGICAL BULLETIN, 59: 116-152, 1962.

Fowler, W. "A study of process and method in three-year-old twins and triplets learning to read." GENETIC PSYCHOLOGY MONOGRAPHS, 72: 3-89, 1965.

Fowler, W. "Concept learning in early childhood." YOUNG CHILDREN, 21: 81-91, 1965.

390

Fowler, W. LONGITUDINAL STUDY OF EARLY STIMULATION IN THE EMERGENCE OF COGNITIVE PROCESSES. Paper delivered at a Conference on Pre-School Education, Social Science Research Council, University of Chicago, Feb., 1966.

Freedman, L. and Hollinshead, B. "Neurosis and social class." AMER. J. PSYCHIATRY, 113: 769-776, 1957.

Frumkin, R. M. "Occupation and major mental disorders." In A. M. Rose (Ed.), MENTAL HEALTH AND MENTAL DISORDER. New York: W. W. Norton, 1955.

Gage, N. L. (Ed.) HANDBOOK OF RESEARCH ON TEACHING. Chicago: Rand McNally, 1963.

Galbraith, J. K. THE AFFLUENT SOCIETY. Boston: Houghton-Mifflin Co., 1958.

Galbraith, J. K. THE AFFLUENT SOCIETY. New York: The New American Library, 1958.

Garfield, S. L. and Affleck, D. C. "A study of individuals committed to a state home for the retarded who were later released as not mentally defective." AMER. J. MENT. DEFIC., 64: 907-915, 1960.

Garfield, S. L., Wilcott, J. B., and Milgram, N. A. "Emotional disturbance and suspected mental deficiency." AMER. J. MENT. DEFIC., 66: 23-29, 1961.

Goodlad, J. THE CHANGING AMERICAN SCHOOL. Chicago, Ill.: Univer. of Chicago Press, 1966.

Goodman, M. E. RACE AWARENESS IN YOUNG CHILDREN. New York: Collier, 1964. Gordon, I. J. (Ed.) HUMAN DEVELOPMENT: READINGS IN RESEARCH. Chicago: Scott Foresman, 1965.

Gotkin, L. G. Cognitive development and the issue of individual differences. JOURNAL OF PROGRAMMED INSTRUCTION. 3: 1-10, 1963.

Gotkin, L. G. et. al. STANDARD TELEPHONE INTERVIEW. Unpublished memo report. New York: Institute for Developmental Studies, 1964.

Gray, S. W. and Klaus, R. A. "An experimental pre-school program for culturally deprived children." CHILD DEVELOPMENT, in press.

GUIDELINES: SPECIAL PROGRAMS FOR EDUCATIONALLY DEPRIVED CHILDREN. U. S. Dept. H. E. W., Wash., D. C.: U. S. Gov't. Printing Office, 1966.

Harlem Parents Committee, New York. THE EDUCATION OF MINORITY GROUP CHILDREN IN THE NEW YORK CITY PUBLIC SCHOOLS. Unpublished paper, 1965.

Hartup, W. W. Early pressures in child development. YOUNG CHILDREN, 271-283: 1965.

Harrington, M. THE OTHER AMERICA, New York: Macmillan Company, 1962.

Harvey, O. J. (Ed.) EXPERIENCE AND ADAPTABILITY New York: Springer Press, 1966.

Hollingshead, A. B. and Redlich, F. C. SOCIAL CLASS AND MENTAL ILLNESS: A COMMUNITY STUDY. New York: Wiley, 1958.

Holt, J. HOW CHILDREN FAIL New York: Pitman, 1964.

Hunt, E. P. and Huyck, E. E. MORTALITY OF WHITE AND NON-WHITE INFANTS IN MAJOR U. S. CITIES. U. S. Dept. H. E. W., Washington, D. C.: U. S. Gov't. Press, 1966.

Hunt, J. and Cofer, C. "Psychological deficit." In J. McV. Hunt, (Ed.), PERSONALITY AND THE BEHAVIOR DISORDERS, New York: the Ronald Press Co., 971-1032, 1944.

Hunt, J. McV. INTELLIGENCE AND EXPERIENCE. New York: Ronald Press, 1961.

Hunt, J. McV. "The psychological basis for using pre-school enrichment as an antidote for cultural deprivation." MERRILL-PALMER QUARTERLY, 10 (3): 209-243, 1964.

Ilg. F. L. and Ames, L. B. SCHOOL READINESS. New York: Harper and Row, 1964.

Institute for Developmental Studies -- ANNUAL REPORT. New York: New York Medical College, 1965.

Jensen, A. "Learning abilities in Mexican-American and Anglo-American Children." CALIFORNIA JOURNAL OF EDUCATIONAL RESEARCH, 12: 147-159, 1961.

392

Jensen, A. R. VERBAL MEDIATION AND EDUCATIONAL POTENTIAL. Address, A.P.A. Convention, 1965. Mimeographed paper.

John, V. P. A BRIEF SURVEY OF RESEARCH ON THE CHARACTERISTICS OF CHILDREN FROM LOW-INCOME BACKGROUNDS. Unpublished paper, 1964.

Kephart, N. C. "Influencing the rate of mental growth in retarded children through environmental stimulation." NAT'L. SOC. STUD. EDUC., 39th YEARB., PART II. Chicago: University of Chicago Press, 223-239, 1940.

Kirk, A. EARLY EDUCATION OF THE MENTALLY RETARDED. Urbana, Ill: University of Illinois Press, 1958.

Kirk, S. A. EDUCATING EXCEPTIONAL CHILDREN Boston: Houghton-Mifflin, 1962.

Kirk, S. A. and Kolstoe, P. "The mentally retarded." Rev. of Educ. Res. 23: 400-416, 1953.

Knobloch, H. and Pasamanick, B. THE DISTRIBUTION OF INTELLECTUAL POTENTIAL IN AN INFANT POPULATION. New York: Unpublished paper, 1956.

Kuhlen, R. G. and Thompson, G. G. PSYCHOLOGICAL STUDIES OF HUMAN DEVELOPMENT, 2nd edition, New York: Appleton-Century-Crofts, 1963.

Lampman, R. J. "Approaches to the reduction of poverty." AMERICAN ECONOMIC REVIEW, 181, May 1965.

Lawrence, P. COMPENSATORY EDUCATION. Address given to California Council on Education of Teachers, Santa Barbara, California, 1965.

Leacock, E. "Three social variables and the accurance of mental disorders." In A. H. Leighton, J. A. Clausen, and R. Wilson, (Eds.). EXPLORATIONS IN SOCIAL PSYCHIATRY. New York: Basic Books, 1957.

Lewis, O. THE CHILDREN OF SANCHEZ. New York: Random House, 1961.

Mackintosh, H. K. and Lewis, G. M. Head Start for children in slums. AMERICAN EDUCATION, 1, 1965.

Martin, K. K., Meier J. H., Reed, I., and Welch, A. GUIDELINES FOR ESTABLISHING A PROGRAM FOR THE EMOTIONALLY HANDICAPPED. Denver, Colorado: University of Denver Bureau of Educational Research, 1963.

393

Masland, R. L. "The Prevention of Mental Retardation, A Survey of Research." AMER. J. OF MENT. DEFIC., 62: 991-1112, 1958.

Masland, R. L., Sarason, S. B., and Gladwin, T. MENTAL SUBNORMALITY. New York: Basic Books, 1958.

McClelland, D. THE ACHIEVING SOCIETY. New York: Van Nostrand, 1961.

McCord, H. "Increase in measured I. Q." J. Develop. Read. 5: 214-215, Spr., 1962.

McNemar, Q. "Last: Our intelligence? Why? "Amer. Psychol., 19: 871-882, 1964.

Meier, J. H. AN EXPLORATORY FACTOR ANALYSIS OF PSYCHODIAGNOSTIC AND CASE STUDY INFORMATION FROM CHILDREN IN SPECIAL EDUCATION CLASSES FOR THE EDUCABLE MENTALLY HANDICAPPED. Unpublished Dissertation, Ann Arbor, Mich.: University Microfilms, 1965.

Miller, G. A., Galanter, E. H., and Pribram, K. H. PLANS AND THE STRUCTURE OF BEHAVIOR. New York: Holt, 1960.

Mittlebach, F. G. and Marshall, G. THE BURDEN OF POVERTY. Advance report 5 of the Mexican-American study project, U. C. L. A., 1966.

Montessori, M. DR. MONTESSORI'S OWN HANDBOOK. New York: Schocken, 1964a.

Montessori, M. EDUCATION FOR A NEW WORLD. Wheaton, Ill.: Theosophical Press, 1959.

Montessori, M. SPONTANEOUS ACTIVITY IN EDUCATION. New York: Schocken, 1965.

Montessori, M. THE MONTESSORI METHOD. New York: Schocken, 1964b.

Moore, O. K. "Autotelic responsive environments and exceptional children." In J. Hellmuth (Ed.) THE SPECIAL CHILD IN CENTURY 21. Seattle: Special Child Publications, 87-138, 1964.

Moore, O. K. "Orthographic symbols and the pre-school child -- a new approach." In E. P. Torrance (Ed.) CREATIVITY: 1960 PROCEEDINGS OF THE THIRD CONFERENCE ON GIFTED CHILDREN. University of Minnesota, Center for Continuation Study, 91-101, 1961.

394

Moore, O. K. TECHNOLOGY AND BEHAVIOR, Luncheon Address, Invitational Conference on Testing Problems, Educational Testing Service, Princeton, N. J., 1965.

Moore, O. K. and Kobler, R. EDUCATIONAL APPARATUS FOR CHILDREN. Pat. No. 3,112,569, U. S. Patent Office, granted 1963.

Moore, O. K. THE RESPONSIVE ENVIRONMENTS PROJECT AND THE DEAF. Unpublished paper, 1962.

Mowrer, O. H. LEARNING THEORY AND BEHAVIOR, New York: Wiley, 1960

Munn, N. L. THE EVOLUTION AND GROWTH OF HUMAN BEHAVIOR, 2nd edition, Boston: Houghton Mifflin, 1965.

Mussen, P. H. HANDBOOK OF RESEARCH METHODS IN CHILD DEVELOP-MENT. New York: Wiley, 1960.

Newton, M. R., Brown, R., and Crumley, J. CRISIS INTERVENTION IN PRE-SCHOOL AND EARLY SCHOOL YEARS: THE SUMTER CHILD STUDY PROJECT. Unpublished paper given at American Orthopsychiatric Association Meeting, 1965.

Nimnicht, G. P., Meier, J. H., McAfee, O., and Anderson, D. FIRST YEAR PROGRESS REPORT OF A PROJECT IN NURSERY SCHOOL EDUCATION FOR ENVIRONMENTALLY DEPRIVED SPANISH-AMERICAN CHILDREN Unpublished paper. Greeley, Colorado: The New Nursery School, 1966.

Otis, J. THE PRESIDENT'S COMMITTEE ON JUVENILE DELINQUENCY AND YOUTH CRIME AND ITS IMPLICATIONS FOR EDUCATION. Unpublished address delivered at the Tri-chapter Annual Banquet Meeting of Phi Delta Kappa, Annapolis, November, 1963.

Perlman, R. DELINQUENCY PREVENTION -- THE SIZE OF THE PROBLEM. Wash., D. C.: Children's Bureau, Health Education and Welfare, U. S. Gov't. Printing Office, 1960.

Perlman, R. et. al. EXPERIMENTAL PRE-KINDERGARTEN PROGRAM IN THE BOSTON PUBLIC SCHOOLS: PROGRAM AND RESEARCH DESIGN, unpublished preliminary draft, Action for Boston Community Development, Inc. January, 1964.

Peter, L. J. PRESCRIPTIVE TEACHING. New York: McGraw-Hill, 1965.

Piaget, J. THE GROWTH OF LOGICAL THINKING IN THE CHILD. New York: Basic Books, 1958.

Piaget, J. THE ORIGINS OF INTELLIGENCE IN CHILDREN. New York: International Univ. Press, 1962.

Piaget, J. THE PSYCHOLOGY OF INTELLIGENCE. Paterson, N. J.: Littlefield Adams and Co., 1960.

Pines, M. What the talking typewriter says. THE NEW YORK TIMES MAGAZINE, May 9, 1965.

Pinneau, S. CHANGES IN INTELLIGENCE QUOTIENT. New York: Houghton - Mifflin, 1961.

Raab, S., Deutsch, M. and Freedman, A. M. "Perceptual shifting and set in normal school children of different reading achievement levels." PERCEPTUAL AND MOTOR SKILLS, 10: 187-192, 1960.

Rambusch, N. M. LEARNING HOW TO LEARN: An American Approach to Montessori, Baltimore: Helicon Press, 1962.

Read, K. H. THE NURSERY SCHOOL: A HUMAN RELATIONSHIPS LABORATORY. Philadelphia: Saunders, 1960.

Reitan, R. MANUAL FOR ADMINISTERING AND SCORING THE REITAN-INDIANA NEUROPSYCHOLOGICAL BATTERY FOR CHILDREN (AGED 5 THROUGH 8 YEARS). Unpublished paper, no date.

Riessman, F. THE CULTURALLY DEPRIVED CHILD, New York: Harper and Row, 1962.

Robinson, H. B. THE PROBLEM OF TIMING IN PRE-SCHOOL EDUCATION. Unpublished paper, 1965.

Rosenzweig, M. R. "Environmental complexity, cerebral change, and behavior." AMERICAN PSYCHOLOGIST, 21: 321-332, 1966.

Rothstein, J. H. MENTAL RETARDATION: READINGS AND RESOURCES. New York: Holt-Rinehart and Winston, 1961.

Ryan, I. A NEW ATTACK UPON RURAL POVERTY. Unpublished proposal, Northern Michigan University, 1965.

Scott, J. P. "Critical periods in behavioral development." SCIENCE, 138: 949-955, 1962.

Scott, W. S. "Some implications for improved school learning of the pre-school approach with the culturally disadvantaged." SCHOOL PSYCHOLOGIST, 20: 10-22, 1965.

Sears, P. S. and Dowley, E. M. "Research on teaching in the nursery school." In H. L. Gage, HANDBOOK OF RESEARCH ON TEACHING. Chicago: Rand McNally, 814-864, 1963.

Sears, R. "The 1958 Summer research project on identification." JOURNAL OF NURSERY EDUCATION, 16, 1960-61.

Skeels, H. M. and Skodak, M. A. "A Follow-up study of children in adoptive homes." J. GEN. PSYCHOL. 66: 21-58, 1945.

Skodak, M. A. A STUDY OF MENTAL DEVELOPMENT. Univ. of Iowa Studies in Child Welfare, 16, No. 1, 1939.

Smilansky, S. PROGRESS REPORT ON A PROGRAM TO DEMONSTRATE WAYS OF USING A YEAR OF KINDERGARTEN TO PROMOTE COGNITIVE ABILITIES, IMPART BASIC INFORMATION AND MODIFY ATTITUDES WHICH ARE ESSENTIAL FOR SCHOLASTIC SUCCESS OF CULTURALLY DEPRIVED CHILDREN IN THEIR FIRST TWO YEARS OF SCHOOL. Unpublished paper, 1965.

Sonis, M. "Controversy and conflict in child development." JOURNAL OF NURSERY EDUCATION, 18: 160-167, 1963.

Standing, E. M. MARIA MONTESSORI: HER LIFE AND WORK. Fresno, Calif.: Academy Library Guild, 1957.

Stein, Z. and Susser, M. "The social distribution of mental retardation." AMERICAN JOURNAL OF MENTAL DEFICIENCY, 67: 811-821, 1963.

Stevens, J. J. DEVELOPMENT AND TESTING OF A MODEL FOR THE IDENTIFICATION OF POTENTIAL SCHOOL DROPOUTS. Unpublished Dissertation, Ann Arbor, Michigan: University Microfilms, 1964.

Stine, R. M. PRE-SCHOOL ENVIRONMENTAL ENRICHMENT DEMONSTRA-TION. Bureau of General and Academic Education, Department of Public Instruction, Harrisburg, Penn. Project No. S-229, Proposal No. 5-310-64, 1965.

Taba, H. CURRICULUM DEVELOPMENT: THEORY AND PRACTICE. New York: Harcourt, Brace and World, 1962.

Todd, V. E. and Heffernan, H. THE YEARS BEFORE SCHOOL: GUIDING PRE-SCHOOL CHILDREN, New York: Macmillan, 1964.

Torrance, E. P. and Strom, R. D. MENTAL HEALTH AND ACHIEVEMENT: INCREASING POTENTIAL AND REDUCING SCHOOL DROPOUTS, New York: Wiley, 1965.

Tuddenharn, R. D. Jean Piaget and the world of the child." AMERICAN PSYCHOLOGIST, 21: 207-217, 1966.

Tunley, R. "America's unhealthy children." HARPERS, May, 1966.

Wallach, M. A. and Kogan, N. MODES OF THINKING IN YOUNG CHILDREN. New York: Holt, Rinehart and Winston, 1965.

Watson, R. I. PSYCHOLOGY OF THE CHILD. 2nd edition, New York: Wiley, 1965.

Wechsler, D. "The I. Q. is an intelligent test." THE NEW YORK TIMES MAGAZINE, June 26, 1966.

White, R. "Motivation reconsidered: The concept of competence." PSYCHOLOGICAL REVIEW, 66: 297-333, 1959.

White, S. H. BIBLIOGRAPHY: PSYCHOLOGICAL STUDIES OF LEARNING IN CHILDREN. Unpublished, Harvard University, 1962.

Wilson, J. A. and Robeck, M. C. KINDERGARTEN EVALUATION OF LEARNING POTENTIAL Santa Barbara, Calif.: Sabox Publishing Co., 1963.

Yinger, J. M. A MINORITY GROUP IN AMERICAN SOCIETY. New York: McGraw-Hill, 1965.

Young, E. THE NURSERY SCHOOL PROGRAM FOR CULTURALLY DIFFERENT CHILDREN. Menlo Park, California: Pacific Coast Publishers, 1965.

398

NEW YORK CITY HEAD START: PLURALISM, INNOVATION AND INSTITUTIONAL CHANGE

Susan Ginsberg,
Project Director, New York University Head Start In-Service
Training Program, School of Continuing Education, New York City;
Formerly Recreation Consultant and Training Coordinator,
New York City Head Start Central Staff

Muriel Greenhill, Grants Officer,
Kingsborough Community College,
The City University of New York.
Formerly Educational Programs Officer,
Anti-Poverty Board, New York City
Economic Opportunity Commitee

MURIEL GREENHILL

SUSAN GINSBERG

Project Head Start in New York City was conceived and implemented as a community action and thus a change-oriented program, rather than as an extension of existing professionally run programs for pre-school children. The consequences of interpreting Head Start as an early childhood program in the actual context of community action have been manifest in the emphasis expressed in the title of this article.

Needless to say, however, the full story of how the New York City Head Start program has attempted to encourage innovation and demonstrate pluralistic approaches to institutional change is well beyond the scope of this paper. It will also be apparent that these observations have not been organized according to topics that explicitly reflect the various components in a Head Start Child Development Center. Rather, each dimension was considered at relevant points in developing the description of the programs and processes selected for analysis here.

After a retrospective description of the launching of Head Start in New York,we will attempt to provide illustrations of some of the ways that Head Start has stimulated change through the reexamination of individual as well as community and institutional roles. By presenting a few of these examples in depth, it may be possible to suggest a picture of the significant problems and potential for action leadership inherent in the development of a big city Head Start program.

SCOPE OF INITIAL HEAD START PROGRAM IN NEW YORK CITY

A brief overview indicates the scope of the program which was mounted in response to the urgent tone of its inception from Washington in the spring of 1965.

Project Head Start in New York City was one of the largest programs in the country. It involved about 25,000 children who were enrolled in 286 centers. There were over 1700 classes in public and parochial schools; 300 classes were in programs sponsored by private and community based organizations. Staff included more than 1200 teachers, 1600 assistant teachers, 7000 aides and 1500 volunteers. There were 157 program directors, 148 parent coordinators and 430 family assistants.

401

COMMUNITY ACTION THROUGH EDUCATION IN NEW YORK CITY

In 1965, objectives for community action through education in New York were identified with an emphasis on the following four themes:*

1. The importance of institutional adaptation and new cooperative arrangements, including the support and formation of new and specially designed institutional models when needed to reach the roots of poverty.

2. The need to discover and encourage productive interraction between educational institutions at every level-and the community.

3. The importance of increasing the opportunities, understanding and support for constructive one-to-one relationships between children, youths and adults.

4. The need for increased inquiry and effort directed towards more promising ways of preparing persons for more effective interaction with the poor. This was to include the whole range of professional, pre-professional and non-professional persons to be involved in community action and other anti-poverty programs. High in importance among these was the child's family which often needs help and encouragement in order to add new dimensions to a child's growth and positive experience.

PLURALISTIC SETTING FOR HEAD START PLANNING AND OPERATIONS

When Head Start was initiated many institutions were already operating early childhood programs in New York City. Day Care programs were sponsored jointly by the Department of Welfare with churches, teacher training institutions, settlement houses and other private organizations. The Board of Education had started early childhood programs in a few public schools, some in cooperation with Martin Deutsch, others under the More Effective Schools Program. Private, non-profit schools of many types under various auspices also ran pre-school programs and a number of teacher training colleges were running model laboratory schools. Few, if any, cities in the country started out with such extensive early childhood programs and such a variety of institutions and agencies which historically provided support for them.

Long before Head Start, the work of several city agencies also directly affected the operation of early childhood programs. A multiplicity of bureaus and divisions shared the authority and responsibility for defining the steps and granting the approvals necessary before the doors of a Head Start program could be opened.

In contrast to most other places, standards for young children's programs had been

---

*Muriel Greenhill, "Part II . . . New York City's Approach to the Solution of . . . Educational Problems Through Community Action Under Title II, Part A, of the Economic Opportunity Act of 1964, (46 pp. mimeo, plus component projects) with the assistance of Sue Olsen, March 1965.

402

an issue for many years in New York at both the city and state levels. Concern for the welfare of children sparked by the interest of philanthropic and citizens' groups has led not only to high standards and genuine leadership in this field, but has made the question of standards - in itself - a continuing issue in the social and political dialogue of New York City.

Furthermore, a good deal of research focused on disadvantaged children and their families, as well as a number of community-based experimental action programs, were centered in New York City. Outstanding contributors to the research were Kenneth Clark, Frank Reissman and Martin Deutsch; notable programs included those initiated by Haryou-Act Inc., Mobilization for Youth and the Bank Street College of Education.

This range of views and plurality of concerns may be seen as both an asset and a liability. The individuals and institutions mentioned are known to have influenced Head Start nationally but, in fact, they have had considerable local impact as well. At the same time, while the very high standards for teacher certification and the licensing of premises undoubtedly contributed to the quality of the overall program, they also caused much bureaucratic red tape, many delays in getting centers started and, indirectly, much adverse publicity for the New York city program as a whole.

STRATEGIES FOR INSTITUTIONAL CHANGE AND RESOURCE DEVELOPMENT

General Strategy Conceived by EOC to Launch Head Start as a City-Wide Effort
Even with this rich and complex base to work from, it was clear that the many agencies and institutions involved in early childhood programs in New York would have to be encouraged to interact in new ways and to participate in positive strategies for change so that Head Start could be a vehicle for genuine progress rather than social gimmickry or more of what already existed.

In the winter of 1964-65 and well before Head Start was announced, New York City anti-poverty staff (Economic Opportunity Committee)* together with an informal and ad hoc advisory group of interested experts laid the groundwork for future planning by joining together to consider the predictable need for greatly enhanced resources for early childhood programs to serve thousands of children, their families and the communities in which they lived within the objectives of the new federal anti-poverty program.

*The formal aegis for Head Start and other city-wide anti-poverty efforts. It is now known as the Community Development Agency and since the spring of 1967 has been a unit within the Human Resources Administration with a new superagency set up by Mayor Lindsay with responsibility as well for welfare and manpower programs.

403

In the spring of 1965 by which time Head Start was formally launched, Washington had issued only an illustrative booklet and sketchy application forms for local communities to use as a base to initiate their Head Start activities.

The EOC staff felt that the opportunity to interpret and build on these ambiguous guidelines could be utilized to identify questions and generate specific program objectives and broad policy considerations. These, in turn, would serve as the basis for substantive strategies in particular program areas and criteria against which institutional activity could be designed and evaluated.

As a further strategic step towards this goal, the informal group which had been brought together in the late winter served as the nucleus of an expanded committee formally organized as the city-wide policy advisory structure for Head Start in New York.

Included were representatives of all types of relevant agencies and institutions—settlement houses, religious organizations, municipal licensing agencies, community groups, the early childhood establishment, both academic and operational, and the public school system—which would be concerned with mounting the Head Start effort in New York City. *

The committee provided an acceptable pragmatic means to ensure the participation of a group of influential individuals in the confrontations—both with each others' ideas and with different views—about the underlying social problems which arose as the planning process took place.

At the same time, it was hoped that new ways of looking at the problems and working together to solve them would generate more creative and productive interaction among the institutions and agencies represented by the group and the other resources to which they had access.

The "transactional" value of the Committee's function was clear from the outset and may well have been regarded, at the time, as its greatest advantage. In retrospect however, the formation and functioning of this body may also be identified as one of the first major instances of the "action leadership" philosophy which character-

*In the Winter of 1965, EOC Staff formally recommended that the Head Start Committee be re-constituted to include parents and representatives from the community. During late summer and early fall 1966, three agency directors and two parents were added to the Committee.

In the late summer of 1967, in order to implement revised guidelines for the Parent Advisory Committees, OEO insisted that the Head Start Committee be disbanded and replaced by a city-wide Policy Advisory Committee with twenty-six parents, representing the twenty-six poverty areas in the city, and to also include nine public and private agency representatives and five staff members from within HRA.

404

ized the city's program and also as an illustration of the underlying belief that program and process are inseparable in program implementation and in long range planning for social action objectives.

Laying the Base for Long Range Planning and Policy Development

This interaction between process and program was also implicit in the development of new staff roles and of programs to identify and train persons to fill these positions.

In considering manpower needs for Head Start, staff and committee discussions tended to focus initially on the most tangible view of the people needed to meet Head Start objectives; classroom teachers and persons to help them, people to provide appropriate curriculums and others to offer supportive social and related services. It was obviously necessary to move ahead in ways which focused immediately on the operational needs of the Head Start sponsors preparing for the actual conduct of the program. In taking steps to meet these needs, it was also clear that a new kind of reality-oriented dialogue was needed among academicians and various professionals to strengthen and articulate the program's underlying theory and lay the base for planned development of manpower and other resources in ways which were really consistent with Head Start objectives.

In other words, it was necessary that the two dimensions of concern - social policy and other theoretical considerations, and concrete needs - be continually balanced out against each other so that attention to immediate needs for program implementation would not preclude simultaneous attention to how long term needs would be met.

This synthesis provided the frame of reference within which the new staff roles in Head Start and the university-sponsored 'multipurpose' centers (and other training programs to be described in another section) were conceived and organized.

Substantive Resources and New Institutional Models

New staff roles

A third paid position, that of assistant teacher (in addition to teacher and teacher aide), for New York City Head Start programs was designed to be filled by a college or graduate student during the summer or other periods with limited course work responsibility. While seen as a source of sub-professional assistance for the classroom teacher the position had implications for future as well as current manpower needs.

In terms of immediate needs, it increased the range of perspective as well as the numbers of people involved in the program by deliberately attracting college stu-

405

dents from many academic programs and different disciplines - social work, public administration and health services, as well as education - to work in Head Start Child Development centers. The involvement and experience gained in Head Start was seen as a way of developing or deepening a commitment on the part of these students and their peers to future careers in teaching, or to related work with disadvantaged children and their families, as well as providing a realistic contact with the new type of setting which Head Start offered.

The ability to experiment with this new staff role was also a reflection of the constructive atmosphere which prevailed during the initial stages of Head Start but could not - for budgetary and other reasons - be sustained. This was the only point in the history of the program when it was not necessary to choose between alternatives. It was then possible, for example, to argue that college students and community people each brought a new way of looking at children in the classroom and to insist that the use of indigenous personnel and steps taken to enrich the pool of future Head Start teachers were *both* important and, in fact, that each had a greater value when they were pursued simultaneously.

In the social service area, a new category of non-professional personnel was designed which had a different purpose and emphasis.

The job of family assistant at $100 per week without a minimum requirement of formal education or paid work experience was built in to the staffing pattern to insure the involvement of someone with first-hand familiarity and know-how in using neighborhood resources and to establish a new position for the poor which would have a marked impact on their own lives through a new and well paid position of responsibility. This was one clearly defined step upward from the aide level job through which low income persons were being generally introduced to employment under anti-poverty auspices.

Resistance to utilizing this position for employing poverty level persons from the community was fairly widespread at the outset and unfortunately the city guidelines were ambiguous at the beginning of the program. OEO support for restricting the position to indigenous personnel also vacillated, but the general proposition held with substantially positive results.

This job was seen as strengthening the Head Start program by augmenting the limited number of trained social workers and at the same time having the potential for influencing the agencies or institutions which would train and employ this personnel by encouraging a reevaluation and redefinition of functions traditionally associated exclusively with professional social service efforts.

406

The family assistant bridged the gap between professional social workers (to the degree that they were available) and aides, who were neighborhood people with no training and little or no job experience. By employing as family assistants, indigenous personnel with successful personal experience, for instance, in local PTA's or community groups, to work with Head Start families in the development of parent programs and the use of community resources, it was recognized that community knowledge combined with a degree of experience would make a contribution that was more sophisticated than could be expected from the aides. It would also automatically create a second step in a potential career ladder program which hopefully would come to include a number of further steps as time went on.

New Institutional model - Multipurpose center

In order to insure the development and utilization of viable new resources for early childhood community action programs, a plan was developed by EOC staff in the fall and winter of 1965 to provide one newly designed multipurpose action-research-demonstration center in each of the nine major poverty areas throughout the city.

The first three were to be sponsored by teacher training institutions and the next six under the auspices of schools of social work, public health and other relevant research and training institutions which would play a lesser but important role in the first group.

The underlying purpose was to devise an institutional structure in poverty areas that brought together higher education training and research personnel from the whole range of appropriate disciplines and professions to develop, demonstrate and foster more creative direct action programs grounded in solid theory as well as the realities of the communities to be served.

Recognizing that in big cities, at least, personal, family and neighborhood problems are so intermeshed, complicated and non-static that they tend to appear idiosyncratic, it was important that this organizational framework itself be susceptible to change and redefinition as experience accrued, community involvement increased and program priorities shifted. Just as "program and process" were viewed as inseparable in the setting up of the city-wide planning mechanism for Head Start, "program and structure" in this case could not be divided.

The first two multi-purpose centers were established by Bank Street College of Education and Queens College and vary in their emphasis and program. The Bank Street Early Childhood Center is largely concerned with theory, process and conceptualization in the context of a pre-school program for children and their families. Queens College Parents and Children Center is far more pragmatic in emphasis with close ties to social action groups in the community as the base for their parent program.

407

Footnote on the present

In the course of negotiations for the summer of 1966, OEO Washington's previously expressed negative position on the funding of three paid positions in the classroom (successfully reversed during negotiations in earlier program periods) finally prevailed and the role of assistant teacher, which was seen as the source of future manpower needs for agencies of all types, was eliminated from OEO-approved staffing patterns in Head Start funded programs in New York City.

Fortunately, Superintendent Donovan and Rebecca Winton, Director of the Early Childhood Division of the Board of Education, affirmed the value of this innovation from the outset and continued until recently to fund this position in the public school pre-kindergarten programs using Title 1 of the Elementary and Secondary Education Act. *

The position of family assistant has been retained in New York City Head Start agencies and is also being continued in many of the Board's pre-kindergarten programs. In addition, six indigenous women who were family assistants in the Board of Education program during the summer of '65 now work on a city-wide basis as members of the field staff of the central Head Start office in New York as Family Service Advisors.

As predicted, new designs have been developed for the training of family assistants. Since the fall of 1966, N.Y.U. (through their School of Continuing Education) has received OEO grants for a continual series of eight-week training programs (one of the three prototype training models nationally funded by OEO) for non-professional family assistants and teacher aides.

In developing the curriculum for this program, field oriented research was done by a member of the N.Y.U. Graduate School of Social Work faculty on the precise role of family assistant as it had evolved since the program began.** The results of this study, combined with experience with the first few groups of trainees, made it apparent that the shortage of experienced social workers in the agencies as well as the new demands of this innovative and integrative role made it necessary to develop a curriculum which not only included skills and knowledge from many different disciplines but which trained family assistants to take on a number of the responsibilities heretofore only assumed by professionally trained social workers.

---

* For private agency Head Start, substitutes for assistant teachers were provided during the Summer months by the Urban Corps - an urban work experience for college students funded by the U. S. Office of Education with support from the city of New York.

** Oscar H. Rosenfeld, "The Family Assistant in Project Head Start," Graduate School of Social Work, New York University 1966. (19 pp. mimeo)

408

It is clear then that the development of training models generated by the redefinition of traditional roles, as well as the creation of new ones for Head Start, has emerged as one of the more important contributions of the program.

It is also important to note here that many school systems are no longer limiting the use of auxiliary personnel to classroom settings. In some places they are experimenting with jobs modeled on that of the family assistant in Head Start. The role of these "community aides" in secondary schools is also seen as involving parents, providing social service resources to families and as being a bridge to the community. The implications are clear that new kinds of generic training which would make it possible for a social service aide from Head Start, for example, to move into the school system or into a hospital setting with equal ease, are called for at this time. *

New Perspectives on Organizing Resources within Institutions and Among them

Special orientation program - spring 1966
A program developed jointly in the spring of 1966 by the Bank Street College of Education, the New York City Board of Education and Head Start through the Economic Opportunity Committee, is an illustration of how strategically planned, short term and problem-oriented interaction between public agencies and educational institutions can help to support change within a large school system.

This program - even with its limited goals - was possible because of the long history of positive and productive relations between the college and the New York City school system. This crucial factor of on-going communication is also described in the study of a group of projects which placed auxiliary personnel in school systems throughout the country: "coordination was facilitated when a sponsoring institution of higher learning had previously formed extensive contacts with school systems, either through working relationships involving placement of student teachers or through other services rendered by the college or university to the system." **

As a consultative model for the in-service training of administrators, this program also demonstrated a design for the involvement of administrative and supervisory personnel working for new objectives at each planning stage and at every level of the school system. It also has implications for the implementation of new federal programs within big city school systems by focusing on administration as an organic process and clearly demonstrating that what happens at every level affects and reinforces every other level of the system.

---

* Women's Talent Corps, "College for Human Services: A Model for Innovation in Urban Higher Education" (New York: Women's Talent Corps, 1967).

** Garda W. Bowman and Gordon J. Klopf, New Careers and Roles in the American School: Report of Phase One, A Study of Auxiliary Personnel in Education (New York: Bank Street College of Education, 1967), p. 26.

409

Due to delayed funding for all of Head Start in the fall of 1965, it was not till January, 1966 that the Board of Education could hire the personnel necessary to expand their pre-kindergarten classes into Head Start programs. When the funds were finally released, large numbers of non-professionals from the community were hired as teacher aides and family assistants and other Head Start components were provided with the addition of social workers and psychologists.

Neither the principals, nor other supervisory personnel within the schools had been adequately prepared for this influx. However, the dissent and confusion which arose could be constructively interpreted in terms of problems of procedure, supervision and role definition. Therefore, at the suggestion of the Economic Opportunity Committee, Dr. Donovan, Superintendent of Schools, invited the Bank Street College to cooperate in developing an orientation sequence for superintendents, principals and other personnel who were involved in the newly expanded Head Start program in the schools.

The college worked in a consultative capacity with a planning committee of representative superintendents, principals, early childhood personnel and EOC staff. Together they developed a format for a series of meetings with Bank Street providing the recorders and organizational services as well as the keynote speakers and resource persons. School system and anti-poverty staff presented statements reflecting the views and concerns of their agencies and shared in the shaping of the enterprise as a whole.

A series of sessions was held with major supervisory staff beginning at the top of the 'administrative pyramid' with the district superintendents and adding, step by step, principals, assistant principals, social work, guidance and early childhood supervisors. The major purpose of the meeting was to examine Head Start goals with the focus of discussion on how day-to-day problems and resentments might be resolved so that the effectiveness of auxiliary personnel in the schools could be improved.

In the discussions and recommendations it was repeatedly recognized that there are countless ways in which the goals of the Head Start program can be supported or undermined within each school setting by the attitudes and practices of the entire range of administrative and supervisory personnel.

The experience in the schools during the spring of 1966 and the results of this orientation sequence point up how vital it is that not only top planning administrators, but staff at every level of the system who are responsible for incorporating new personnel or program models into their schools, be aware of the intent and design of these innovations. And, as Bowman and Klopf recommend in their study:

410

That there be orientation of both the administrators and the professionals with whom the auxiliaries will be working, including an opportunity for the expression of any doubts or resistance which may exist, and for consideration of the new and challenging leadership role of the professionals vis-a-vis the non-professionals, and also the supervisory * role of administrators vis-a-vis teacher-auxiliary teams.

New York University In-Service Training Program

The New York University in-service training program which was developed for all private agency personnel in New York City and initiated in the fall of 1966 is currently in operation. This program demonstrates how new ways of organizing resources within the academic community, and of stimulating interaction between institutions at many different levels, can be developed through an innovative undertaking sponsored by a major urban university as part of a city-wide community action effort under federal anti-poverty auspices.

Consistent with the pattern established during the summer forty-hour Head Start orientation programs, the New York University School of Continuing Education, working closely with the School of Education and the Graduate School of Social Work, agreed (under a contract with the New York City Community Development Agency) to provide training for the full range and number of professional and non-professional staff in the 47 private agency programs. These programs which are operating in 105 premises throughout the city are the sole recipients of "full-year" Head Start funds at present in New York.

Consultants assembled and employed by the university for this project are drawn from the faculties of virtually all the schools of social work and many of the schools of education in the New York area, and include directors of day care centers, private, nursery schools and some community agencies. These consultants work one and one-half days a week in the capacity of training specialists, organized into teams of one social worker and one early childhood educator. Each team is permanently assigned to a group of Head Start agencies within a specified geographic area. Sixteen such areas within the five boroughs of New York were defined by the project staff with the concurrence of the city and the Head Start agencies themselves. These areas were formed to insure a viable base and structure through which project activities could facilitate interagency communication and the sharing of resources among Head Start centers while also attempting to strengthen more effective long-term relationships within each community.

Consultant teams experiment with many different training models and combinations

*Ibid

411

of arrangements; individual consultation with directors and various other supervisory personnel; small meetings with staff in one particular category, for example teachers or family workers; interdisciplinary seminars with the total staff of one center; and workshops held with the entire staff of a group of agencies.

Workshops are led by outstanding resource specialists as well as by local community leaders. The broad range of topics that are covered include language development, art, music, parent involvement and Negro and Puerto Rican history and culture.

Central coordination makes it possible to identify and use outstanding staff from within the Head Start operating agencies as well as from the communities themselves to lead workshops in geographic areas other than their own. All training is done in the field and the Head Start agency directors and their staffs are actively involved in the planning, design and implementation of project activities which serve their own respective programs. Visits to other schools and community facilities are also an important part of the program as is the development and dissemination of new and varied teaching and training materials, many especially designed for Head Start use.

At a time when the need for greater university involvement to meet the problems of metropolitan centers is generating widespread interest and activity, this program takes on special significance.

It has evolved into a realistic new design for directing the resources of a private urban university—drawing as well, on those of its neighboring institutions—into uninterrupted and constructive undertakings with individuals and agencies in low-income communities.

By providing a vehicle for continuous cooperation between the academic community and the personnel of a field-based, action-oriented program, Head Start has served to utilize and enrich the research, theory and practices of current concern in colleges and universities. Without the immediacy of confrontation and willingness to learn from what actually exists in each Head Start center and its surrounding community, Head Start as a national program can hardly be expected to foster effectively new approaches to the development of curriculum, experimentation in teaching styles, new ways of training and involving para-professional personnel and more effective ways of integrating the work of multi-disciplinary staffs.

In short, the program may be seen as defining a model for institutional interaction and progress on many levels. Interaction outside of the university is manifested by a close working relationship between a city agency and a university center. Interaction within the university is stimulated by means of a dialogue which sidesteps the accus-

412

tomed frontiers between various disciplines, as well as among the organizational divisions of the academic community, by highlighting concerns and objectives which they share. Interaction between institutions of higher learning is encouraged by fostering a sense of common cause among their respective faculties. In the city as a whole, a corps of experienced trainers from these many different institutions is being developed. These highly experienced people are available and committed to work not just on today's Head Start program but with the whole range of new staff and new programs being designed in the schools and in the communities.

AN OPERATIONAL VIEW OF RECREATION AS A PROGRAM AREA REFLECTING THE MAJOR THEMES AND STRATEGIES DEVELOPED FOR NEW YORK CITY HEAD START

A new strategy for institutional change and creative programming through centralized financing and leadership from the top of the city Head Start organization was developed in New York during the first summer of Head Start. As a result of the Recreation program, unique to New York, two heretofore unrelated program components - children's trips and parent activities - were stimulated to function as an organic whole within a comprehensive, city-wide effort which involved both the public and private sector in supporting and working with Head Start agencies.

As a result of the Head Start Committee's concern with the lack of adequate recreational facilities in poverty areas throughout the city, New York City applied for, and was granted, a budget of $138,632 for the summer of 1965. This was to be centrally administered by the city Head Start office and was to cover the costs of trips and other activities not then specifically determined, for the 25,000 children in the program.

As the program evolved, the use of the term "recreation" was recognized as having little relation to recreation as traditionally defined; rather, it meant that a program with children's trips as its core became the catalyst for a wide variety of other activities ranging from broad parent participation to the dissemination of trip information to staff and the opening up of institutional resources within and around New York for Head Start children and their families. In addition, it came to include a program of special events (concerts and puppet shows) centrally arranged and made available to Head Start centers all over the city.

Central Planning to Encourage Institutional Involvement
Central planning for the trip program proved to be vital because transportation and recreational facilities in New York are administered by a number of government and private agencies most of whom need to be contacted at the top administrative level to enlist their cooperation.

413

The recreation staff (which was made up of one early childhood educator and one part-time consultant with a background in city planning and recreation) was able to contact personnel in a number of agencies to make specific city-wide arrangements for Head Start groups. Free subway and bus passes were arranged for off-peak hours, special hours were set aside for groups of Head Start children at zoos and museums. Contact was made centrally with the major library systems and with the Fire, Police and Park Departments in an effort to secure reduced bus parking and entrance fees, to develop special programs and to arrange for various personnel from these agencies to visit Head Start groups at their centers.

The central staff also familiarized government and private agencies with the purposes and philosophy of Head Start and enlisted their support for special visits, activities and contributions. Many offers were made by commercial firms which could not be taken advantage of because of the difficulties of deployment due to the small central staff and, generally, to the crash nature of that first summer's program.

Central Coordination and Budgeting to Stimulate Creative Programming
While the New York City Head Start central office has professional staff in each of the major disciplines involved in Head Start, its basic role is seen as coordinating and supervising the carrying out of OEO guidelines rather than formulating program content, except in isolated areas.

Because of the central fiscal control built into the recreation program, the staff was able to stimulate new curriculum ideas by helping the agencies develop interesting and appropriate trip plans when they submitted their budgets for approval. In addition, a clear understanding of the importance of first hand experience for disadvantaged youngsters was encouraged through a series of guidelines which also included research into trip possibilities within and around the city. These were circulated to the agencies so that staff would not have to do all the telephoning to check locations, times and facilities for trips which would have been very difficult in such a short, hectic summer program.

During this first summer of Head Start, no support was available to subsidize parent activities. In many ways the children's trip program was an impetus for parent involvement and served as the core around which a wide variety of parent programs were built.

The desire to involve parents in their children's curriculum and the need to recruit extra adult help for trips encouraged teachers and social service personnel to make maximum use of parents in the planning and carrying out of the youngsters' trip program. In addition, some money had been allocated in the central recreation budget for family outings and every agency was strongly encouraged by the central staff

414

to arrange for these outings. Parent meetings became forums to discuss possible sites, dates and plans for family outings. Committees were set up to provide refreshments or to organize entertainment.

The children's trips and the family outings thus provided a focus around which to organize the parents, an incentive to come together, to be part of a group, to share common concerns and experiences and then to plan for further social and educational activities together. A parent trip program which closely paralleled that of the children's was one of the important results of these meetings.

Special Events
The special event component of the recreation program scheduled entertainment at central locations, mostly in public school auditoriums, where children from private agencies, public and parochial school Head Start centers could attend. The performers included Tom Glazer, the noted folk singer, and two groups of puppeteers.

At least one of these programs was provided for each of 20,000 children during the summer of 1965 and about the same number when it was continued for the second and third summers of Head Start. It was felt to be a success for many reasons: it brought diverse groups of Head Start children and staff together; it provided a completely new experience for the children - their first live theatre, their first exposure to music in a 'concert' setting. It was an experience not only to carry over into the classroom but to become an integral part of their lives. One teacher summed up the less tangible benefits:

> These experiences gave the children something to talk about, thus enriching their language arts. They found new ways of expressing their delight and enjoyment of the things they saw and heard. They spoke more freely to the teachers and to each other. They laughed more freely and more often.

Follow-up of Recreation Program
Although a central New York City recreation budget was included in the second and third summers of Head Start, money for children's trips and parent activities was budgeted separately within each agency's application, rather than on a city-wide basis.

The logistics of fiscal disbursement which presented a problem during 1965 were thus improved, but the momentum and direction of the first summer's program have not been sustained. However, the original trip guidelines have been updated and distributed to all the centers in the city and the special events program has continued to bring Head Start groups together for concerts and puppet shows.

415

Untapped Potential for Institutional Change

The experience of the Head Start groups during the first summer and consistently since then, points up the fact that few of the popular and traditional recreation places to take children in New York have had the impetus or the opportunity to develop optimum programs for four and five year old children.

Although they serve large numbers of Head Start groups throughout the year, and are aware of the need for better programming, these institutions are not prepared to train new staff and mount special programs unless they receive a good deal of support as well as constructive pressure from groups who are concerned about developing appropriate and interesting programs for young children.

Such large and experienced institutions as the Museum of Natural History, the New York Zoological Society (which operates the Bronx Zoo and other facilities) and the Museum of Modern Art have indicated a desire to work more closely with trained early childhood personnel to develop programs especially designed to meet the needs and capture the interest of Head-Start age children. However, the Head Start central recreation staff was cut back in the summers of 1966 and 1967 and was not able to follow through on this opportunity.

A similar need to develop more programs which are suitable and worthwhile for four and five year old children is evident in the field of children's entertainment. In both these areas, Head Start can provide the impetus for meaningful institutional change - change which originates from a need to serve Head Start children more effectively and then broadens to include the whole community.

CONCLUSION

At this point it is possible to look back in time over a 3½ year period, to the fall of 1964 in New York, when the pre-school needs of poor children and their families were first considered in the early "anti-poverty" planning which later served as the base from which the city's Head Start effort could be launched.

It seems fair to conclude that under Head Start auspices here, some important changes in institutional functioning and in the development and utilization of personnel and other resources were fostered through the action leadership of the city anti-poverty effort, as the particular programs selected for discussion in the body of this article illustrate. It seems equally clear, as we have pointed out in some instances, that at least certain of the accomplishments have so far remained in effect and seem likely to continue, in their original form or with modifications; and that some important instances of "ripple effect" stimulated by these new developments can also be identified and seen as likely to continue.

416

In this final section, we shall attempt to show, in more general terms, how the impact of the city's approach may be seen to have affected the Head Start program as a whole in New York. In doing so, it will be necessary to make certain observations about how the administrative style and program emphasis at the city-wide and regional OEO levels have shifted. The many other changes that have taken place both in the general milieu of social action and in the underlying concerns of anti-poverty leadership also appear too closely linked to Head Start operations to be overlooked entirely here. However, it should be made clear that reference to these factors is included only incidentally and is not intended to suggest a complete or thorough analysis of the circumstances or events which have occurred.

As in all large cities, the Head Start program in New York has been subject to constant criticism which reflects some very real problems. Much of its potential strength has gone unrealized, many of its original accomplishments negated, and most of the more important tangential benefits - for example, the positive impact it has had on the lives of the community people employed in the program - have been overlooked in the constant concern caused by erratic funding, uncertain and divided leadership and administrative weakness, especially at the federal and municipal levels.

Under these circumstances it has been exceedingly difficult for Head Start sponsoring agencies to devote their attention primarily to Head Start programs rather than Head Start politics. It has been almost impossible to gauge the extent to which the children, the parents and the community have gained because of their involvement in Head Start activities. The indices which should have been apparent by this time have been effectively submerged in a seemingly endless succession of overlapping crises which have had little or nothing to do with the creation of productive dissent and increased autonomy at the community level which would constitute the natural and desired outgrowth of a more effective program.

Despite these many difficulties, Head Start in New York City has demonstrated in its overall design and by the nature of the strategies employed at the outset of the program, how major school systems (both publicly and religiously affiliated), settlement houses, anti-poverty organizations, child welfare agencies, church groups, colleges and universities and city and federal offices, - can work together, or at least side by side, and be effectively stimulated to interact within a structured setting that demands the best of each.

The original decision to fund both the school system and the private agency programs in New York Head Start met with great resistance. It seemed evident however, that the goals of Head Start for the city as a whole, which included institutional change, could not be accomplished by excluding the very institution in which the change would have the most impact. Only the public school system has the future responsibility for the education of Head Start children; only the public school system has the capacity to serve such a large number of Head Start children and their families.

In order to effect change in the school and the community, whether it is a large city or a small town, the authors feel that Head Start funds should be channeled in a way that makes productive interaction between privately sponsored programs and the school systems virtually unavoidable.

If funding is limited to independent agencies (thus excluding the schools) it is more difficult for the teachers or enlightened leadership within or outside the school system to find some kind of systematically viable means with which individual or group efforts may be coupled to create momentus and staying power to bring about real change.

Similarly, if funds are directed exclusively to the school system as is the case in many communities, it is too easy to absorb and "bureaucratize" innovation - which might also occur to a lesser degree, in more conservative private agencies - and there is neither enough incentive nor a strategic framework to force recognition of a common stake in making the program a success because there are shared objectives which go beyond local differences.

Currently the Board of Education in New York City uses Title 1 ESEA funds during the winter and relies on Head Start for supplementary funds for summer programs. Even this sporadic involvement has been enough to keep Head Start very much alive in the school system. For the summer program, the use of teacher aides and family assistants from the community and a degree of parent participation are enforced by OEO guidelines and Board personnel participate in the pre-service forty hour Head Start orientation given by the colleges in the area.

Inter-agency communication and planning at the top level is still operative at least in formal terms, as Board of Education representatives have maintained their seat on the city-wide Head Start advisory committee.

But is has become clear for at least a year, that opportunities for negotiation and day-to-day cooperation must be deliberately brought about to make a real impact on individuals or institutions, and that the current leadership is indifferent to this approach. The more effective plans and strategies initiated in the early years of the program were by their nature limited in time and scope and succeeded precisely because they were arrived at with sensitivity to the needs and perspectives of the institutions involved and the problems they were confronting at a particular point in time. The positive effects that they generated are bound to diminish if they are not replenished and renewed.

418

Even though important ground has been lost and many lines of communication cut off in recent months, there was no expectation at any time that Head Start alone could revitalize the school system. At its most dramatic, it gave some indication, in microcosm however, of what might be accomplished.

Of the many innovations in the New York City school system as a result of the Head Start program, perhaps the most important in the long run will be the realization that the involvement of parents in the education of their children has ramifications not only wtthin the family but within the community itself.

Larger issues and events will determine whether or not the school itself can evolve with community support into a responsive and self-renewing institution. At the base of this challenge is the terrible disparity between the needs and potential of the children, the perspectives and aspirations of their parents and the attitudes of teaching personnel and their classroom practices. Beyond that, no amount of genuine concern and sincere effort can offset the negative effects of the basic inadequacies in the preparation for teachers and school administrators which plague every school system.

In New York lately, there has been a sharp increase in the number of community groups vocally concerned about the schools and considerable debate and controversy over decentralization of the entire system as well as other reforms designed to achieve goals in some respects similar to Head Start.

But the language of debate and the very content of the more 'innovative' proposals has tended to be dominated by concern over achieving and retaining status and perquisites and they have been grounded in what are essentially political strategies and intervention techniques rather than by a sensitive and openminded commitment to attacking the realities of social problems.

The extent to which leadership at the federal level may be counted on to recast the language of debate into more productive terms is, at this writing, quite problematical. There is an encouraging trend towards productive realignment of federal-local relationships, New procedures for communications are being developed and tested to shape more comprehensive attacks on basic problems in our cities.

But much remains to be done. Federal models still must be reexamined and modified to eliminate unrealistic demands for predictability, uniformity and quantification. In their place, we need to conceive a better framework for supporting and evaluating creative programs and community action which would reflect and foster a true regard for the complex intangibles of human needs and development.

419

A young clergyman who ran a Head Start program in New York in the summer of 1965 expressed his feelings and ours, in terms that give meaning to these recommendations and to the many thousands of words that have been written elsewhere about the Head Start experience:

> *The Head Start program is more than just a way to get minority-group kids from below the 'poverty-line' ready for kindergarten and first grade. It symbolizes an all-out, across-the-boards attack on the consequence of poverty.*
>
> *If this program is not strengthened and we do not act on all the new things we have learned, poverty in vast areas will be perpetuated when it could have been worked on, young children will be only barely prepared for a kind of educational system that is not at all prepared for them, welfare workers will continue to visit only a few of the families in the overwhelming caseloads, and a multitude of citizens shall continue to wonder why those "poor folks" can't take better care of themselves, stop all that rioting, and leave the rest of us alone.*

SUBCULTURE VALUES:
THE PIVOT TO THE AMERICAN DREAM

Betty L. Broman, Ph.D.,
Assistant Professor, University of Tennessee,
Knoxville, Tennessee;
Formerly Director of Chattanooga-Hamilton
County, Tennessee, Head Start

BETTY L. BROMAN, Ph.D.

Every September thousands of four, five, and six year old children from culturally deprived homes ("deprived" when compared with middle-class white homes) enter our schools. According to THE GREAT CITIES SCHOOL IMPROVEMENT STUDIES, 1960, one of every three children in our fourteen largest cities was culturally deprived.* As defined by Frank Riessman, in THE CULTURALLY DEPRIVED CHILD, such a child is one "not benefiting from education, books, and formal language."**

Not only have they "not benefited from education, books, and formal language" but they have experienced first hand all of the base things in life--illicit sex, murder, beatings, alcohol, dope, and other degrading factors.

Another element contributing to the slow development of the deprived four, five, and six year old entrants lies in their concept of themselves. These children come to school believing that they are already failures. As do other children the culturally deprived ones absorb attitudes, values, and overt behavior problems from their family environment. Ordinarily this environment offers only crowded, inadequate living space where the children most often grow up in aggressive disturbances far removed from mature, refining physical inhibitions, either at home or in the neighborhood. Such experiences striking the children at their most susceptible ages frequently lead either to withdrawal and isolation or to surrender and imitation of their environment with all the warping it offers.

Generally two types of children emerge from the culturally deprived areas--the over-stimulated and the isolated. The challenge to pre-school personnel, therefore, is the fundamental one of providing experiences which develop healthy social attitudes and skills for both the over-stimulated and the isolated child.

*THE GREAT CITIES SCHOOL IMPROVEMENT STUDIES, Ford Foundation Project, mimeographed, 1960.

**Riessman, Frank. THE CULTURALLY DEPRIVED CHILD (New York: Harper and Row, 1962), p. 3.

Most nursery, kindergarten and readiness programs now in operation are based on middle-class white needs, and cannot fit the needs of the deprived because these children are more sophisticated and mature in the ways of violent behavior than are middle-class children. Their sub-culture moreover, forces them into situations which more protected children rarely meet. As their sub-culture is constantly changing, as are most sub-cultures, the deprived child experiences degrading insecurity in many insidious guises.

For these children some educators have suggested regular kindergarten activities, such as the ones stated by Helen Heffernan and Vivian Edmiston Todd in THE KIN-DERGARTEN TEACHER. These activities include dramatic play, problem solving, discussions, study trips, painting, modeling, music, art, planting, physical activities, and others.*

Other educators have suggested an extended first grade readiness program; as for instance, Hazel M. Lambert describes: One that "provides many experiences, experiences that help children learn about their environment, that give them the opportunity to explore, that challenge their growing powers, and that help them adjust socially."**

Both programs have merit for the culturally deprived children and for privileged children also; but the beginning point for deprived and advantaged children in concept development and early childhood experiences must differ: A child who has existed on little food, care, love, or adult adoration simply cannot begin his schooling or his communication on the same level that invites and challenges a child who has thrived under loving, protecting parents and such mentors as patient grandparents. When a program is being developed for the deprived child, all concerned must use great caution in stressing the role of the home, if the father is missing, if no one in the family works, if meals consist of beans, bread and soft drinks, if the "home" is two rooms for four or five persons; if the immediate neighborhood is a vista of dingy buildings, cluttered paved streets, and inadequate battered garbage cans; if the only animals in the district are rats, stray starved dogs, and mangy cats. These things make teaching the standard units on **Pets, The Family, The Home** and others completely irrelevant, and almost impossible for the teacher even to suggest matters of responsibility, cleanliness, and balanced meals.

Before teaching can take place, teachers must decide how and where these children

*Heffernan, Helen and Vivian Edmiston Tod. THE KINDERGARTEN TEACHER (Boston: D. C. Heath and Company, 1960), pp. 54-55.

**Lambert, Hazel M. EARLY CHILDHOOD EDUCATION (Boston: Allyn and Bacon, Inc., 1960), p. 162.

424

can fit into the sequeled types of activities and experiences that the majority of the American people feel are acceptable, worthwhile, and important for developing responsible, creative, and productive individuals.

The responsibility to help these children rests upon public schools and other agencies operating pre-school programs. Staffs must struggle with many problems to determine how to supply a flexible program in order to create the beneficial social, emotional, and physical experiences that these children fail to receive at home or in their neighborhoods. They must labor, also, to supplant the destructive with positive constructive experiences, especially those experiences most fruitful for learning.

Evidence indicates that problems which contribute to educational retardation begin early in life and become intensified and more complex through failure to correct children's deficiencies in language development. These deficiencies manifest themselves in the kind of performance first grade children begin to exhibit. Many of the deprived children come to school with a handicap so deep-seated that only frustration and failure will result from their first attempts at academic work unless teachers are so alert and informed that they will constructively meet each symptom.

To be aware of this new world, these children need many first-hand experiences. They need to touch, to taste, to smell, to hear, and to experience the joy of discovery. If a program provides many opportunities for sensory explorations, these first-hand experiences will broaden children's concepts and stimulate them to ask questions about something that is enriching and acceptable. In turn, perhaps the child will want to tell a bit about his new adventures. As a result of such experiences the child will come in time to understand more fully the books that are read to him and those which he will later be taught to read for himself.

In general, a program should be planned around the following developmental areas:

COMMUNICATION SKILL DEVELOPMENT

Teachers should make a major effort to place children in situations where language is necessary and where they will feel encouraged to talk because someone is enthusiastically interested. Teachers should engage children in group discussions concerning the activities they like; the stories they have heard; in re-telling stories and in making up their own by adding new ideas; in dramatizing stories; repeating rhymes, jingles, poetry and playing games which require oral language. Teachers should help children to listen for recognition of likenesses and differences in sounds. ("All the sounds were high sounds."); to recognize and identify sounds ("That's the sound a pig makes."); to reproduce sounds ("The horn went "honk, honk"); to detect visual likeness or difference in oral language ("Here's a big cat and here's a big cat.") or ("This dog is little and this one is big.").

425

Most important, too, is the patience of the teacher to give the child enough time to comprehend and then communicate what he has seen or heard. Language development depends upon time. The teacher should give the child time to look, to find details, to relate what he is seeing to what he has studied and to ask skillful questions which will enable the child to see major objects which be overlooked. The hope behind these suggestions is that the questioning be fun for the child and not develop into a frustrating experience for him, or put him in the position of being unsuccessful. A sensitive teacher will build success upon success for the child, depending upon her awareness of what concepts the child already knows and her skill in broadening them.

PERCEPTUAL AND CONCEPT DEVELOPMENT

Ordinarily the development of visual perception of children occurs between 3½ and 7½. As environmental factors can inhibit or enhance it, the culturally deprived are often perceptually deprived also. Visual perception skills are vital to a child's readiness for formal school work. Children may not have an eye problem but still they can have a visual problem. A child's eyes may be healthy and he may be able to read small letters at 20 feet, but a check on his visual abilities may show that he is unable to focus and control his eyes. His visual ability will determine his speed of perception, his accuracy in looking from one object to another, and whether he can keep his eyes focused on a moving object. Vision is more than just seeing. It also involves the ability to understand what is seen and to get meaning from it. Concept development is therefore, closely related to perceptual development.

Children should find and name visual objects indoors and outside. Locating and describing these objects, as precisely as possible, gives children experience in classification, and in developing a vocabulary. This progress also helps children organize and communicate their ideas. The common guessing game of children, "I see something . . ." ("I hear something that sounds like a . . .," or "This tastes like . . .,") directs their attention to the object which someone has defined, such as "two red things" in the room; or to objects with "a round shape," or objects "longer than this stick."

As young children learn to recognize shapes, they are better able to describe what they see about them. Something may be "shaped like a circle." It is important for the teacher to realize that figures, such as circles, squares, and rectangles make up a child's environment.

Play equipment, art activities, and stories will reinforce these concepts.

426

HEALTH AND PHYSICAL DEVELOPMENT

Health and physical development are interwoven with all phases of a developmental program for four, five, and six year olds. Physical development is facilitated through skill, agility and coordination development such as eye and hand coordination. Skill development helps children learn to control body movement through walking, hopping, jumping, leaping, running, galloping, skipping, sliding, bending, stretching, swinging, swaying, and twisting. At the same time that skills are being developed, agility and coordination are being developed through the proper and safe use of indoor and outdoor equipment.

Teachers should provide opportunities for frequent changes in posture during work and play. Rest and relaxation is also very important during school hours. In addition good nutritional habits and desirable social habits should be encouraged at home as well as at school. Teachers should be constantly aware of the physical limitations of four, five, and six year olds and should expect gradual development of large and small muscles coordination.

SOCIAL LIVING DEVELOPMENT

The deprived child needs many first hand experiences outside the classroom as well as inside. Short walking trips in the immediate neighborhood are best during the first months of school but sufficient time should be allowed for the children to gain enough self control to be safe on trips.

City children may walk to see neighborhood police stations (the image of a policeman to deprived children is one of fear and mistrust for this is the man that arrests fathers or other family members; he takes people to jail and you hide from him). They may also discover that nearby fire stations and grocery stores furnish many fascinations. In rural communities similar experiences may be found near the school. Occasionally a farm is practically next door to the school, thereby offering a fine opportunity not only for a special field trip but for continuous observation of the activities of the farmer throughout the year such as the care of animals, the planting of grain and the harvesting of the crops.

Through re-living these experiences children work out their concepts, identity and feelings. If full potential of a field trip is to take place, the trip should occur early in the week in order that it may have maximum carry-over in re-living the experience.

During the freeplay or the work periods within the classroom, the children will

427

clarify their new concepts. Using blocks, doll houses, dress-up clothes, records, and art materials as props they can enjoy recreating a past experience. Each trip suggests many such activities and sometimes a teacher can bring out a new or stored piece of equipment to stimulate this play. A steering wheel, for example, contributes to the follow-up play of any field trip by bus or car. Another time the teacher may develop opportunities for art experiences such as drawing a picture of something they saw, making a fireman's hat, or painting an animal. Freedom to use clay, crayons, chalk, scissors, paste and paints for interpreting the trip in their own way is very important. Opportunities for language expression about the trip are likewise of prime value to all children but are especially important to the deprived. They enjoy enumerating everything they saw, how they felt, how it smelled, etc. They happily fall into innumerable opportunities for vocabulary growth and creative language expression, if the teacher will discover the uncommon in the common and cleverly arrange the situation so as to be amazed at *their* discoveries.

Firsthand experiences with animals such as ducks, chickens, dogs, cats, fish, etc., stimulate questions and need to be a part of the child's daily activities. All motivation toward sensory learning brings about distinctions between sweet, sour, soft, hard, smooth, shiny, dull, bright, sticky, loud, harsh, etc.

After a teacher makes tentative plans for new experiences and further concept development she should listen to each child's play time conversations before deciding specifically which ideas to follow. During this time while they are engaged in dramatic play, she should also watch their activities. What roles are they playing? What do they know? What do they need to know to understand these activities more fully? Which children have had what experiences? Which children need more in-depth experiences? She must listen as they look at books and talk together over the pictures. What are they curious about? During story time the teacher may read a story and then start a discussion to find out more about the children's concepts discussed in the story.

A teacher can reinforce all experiences by films, filmstrips, pictures, stories, books, tapes, and records. Often placing a book on a library shelf will cause the children to recall their trip and playing a record may also serve to remind them of the many things they saw and heard. At the conclusion of a new field trip the teacher can reread their own stories and thank-you letters from a previous trip which had similiar experiences.

AESTHETIC DEVELOPMENT THROUGH ART, MUSIC, AND LITERATURE

Art: Children who have had limited experiences in art activities when compared to other children their age will require sufficient time for exploring with many differ-

428

ent kinds of media before they "make something." They should not be made to talk about their beginning work unless they volunteer to discuss it. Each art activity should be uninhibited and successful in itself and be completed when the child says he is through. Often teachers talk children into "filling the page." This approach at the beginning stages of self expression stifles the desire to create on his own.

After they have developed the "feel" of the media then they should begin an art activity to express their ideas. Trying the same idea with different media and manipulating various materials may provide an exploratory experience with such materials as paste, clay, crayons, paint, cloth, paper, water, brushes, sponges, soap, wood, etc.

Music: In music as in other areas of pre-school experience, culturally deprived children start at a base or point quite remote from middle class youngsters' awareness of musical activities centered around animals, the circus, the zoo, birds, farms, safety, seasons, toys, community helpers and special days (Halloween, Thanksgiving, Christmas, Valentine Day, and Easter).

Teachers need to adjust musical experiences to individual and group rates of learning, maintaining and developing skills in a rich musical environment which provides an atmosphere for pleasurable living. Children grow musically through direct, active and enjoyable participation in singing, rhythmetic activities, listening, the use of musical instruments, and in creative expressions.

A program for a pre-school group of children should develop a child's natural desire to sing, provide opportunities for individual security and group cooperation through participation in singing, dancing, or playing an instrument, and provide a basic song repertoire leading to in-depth relation of the content to the rhythms.

Literature: Interest in stories during a child's early years leads to interest in books, pictures, words, and in reading in his later life. Deprived children come from homes where "book learning" is taboo, disrespected, and ignored. This early lack of participation in one type of oral language development results in a basic deficiency that is not easily remedied at a later time. Stories often contain factual information that help children develop basic attitudes, skills, and generalizations that lead them to perform at a different level of maturity. Stories, therefore, become the beginning steps for changed behavior or for beginning concept development and social adjustment.

Through stories children should learn to discriminate between real and make-believe; to sense movements and motives of the characters; to listen attentively for clues to what might happen next; to tell stories in sequences of events with cause and effect; to dramatize stories they know; and to learn how to handle and care for books.

429

SUMMARY

A program for deprived children does not differ greatly from a program for advantaged children, but the imperatives for a teacher working with the disadvantaged are:

1. Establishing a program with the most important aspects of learning developed first. (a) oral language development, (b) basic knowledge of respect for others, (c) and activities or experiences valued by Americans as important for young children (having pets, taking trips, knowing traditional literature, etc.)

2. Not taking for granted that socially and economically deprived children are necessarily also intellectually deprived.

3. Accepting the standards of a subculture as a basis for beginning work. (This she must gradually add to, and change to the culture standards that enlightened members of the nation feel are important.)

4. To develop these new concepts and values without deriding the subculture from which the child came.

References

I. BOOKS

Back, Kurt W. SLUMS, PROJECTS, AND PEOPLE. Durham, N. C.: Duke University Press, 1962.

Bloom, Benjamin, *et al.* COMPENSATORY EDUCATION FOR CULTURAL DEPRIVATION. New York: Holt, Rinehart and Winston, Inc., 1965.

Caudill, Harry M. NIGHT COMES TO THE CUMBERLANDS. Boston: Little, Brown and Company, 1962.

Conant, James B. SLUMS AND SUBURBS. New York: McGraw-Hill, 1961.

Davis, Allison. SOCIAL-CLASS INFLUENCES UPON LEARNING. Cambridge: Harvard University Press, 1948.

Deutsch, Martin. MINORITY GROUP AND CLASS STATUS AS RELATED TO SOCIAL AND PERSONALITY FACTORS IN SCHOLASTIC ACHIEVEMENT. Monograph No. 2, Published by the Society for Applied Anthropology, 1960.

Educational Policies Commission. EDUCATION AND THE DISADVANTAGED AMERICAN. Washington, D. C.: National Education Association, 1962.

Ginsberg, Eli. THE NEGRO POTENTIAL. New York; Columbia University Press, 1956.

Greenberg, Norman C. and Gilda Greenberg. EDUCATION OF THE AMERICAN INDIAN IN TODAY'S WORLD. Dubuque, Iowa: Wm. C. Brown Book Company, 1964.

Halsey, A. H., Jean Floud, and C. Arnold Anderson. Editors. EDUCATION, ECONOMY, AND SOCIETY. New York: Free Press of Glencoe, 1961.

Harrington, Michael. THE OTHER AMERICA; POVERTY IN THE UNITED STATES. Baltimore, Maryland: Penguin Books, 1962.

Hunt, J. McV. INTELLIGENCE AND EXPERIENCE. New York: Ronald, 1961.

Kephart, Newell C. THE SLOW LEARNER IN THE CLASSROOM. Columbia, Ohio: Charles E. Merrill Books, Inc., 1960.

Myrdal, Gunnar. AN AMERICAN DILEMMA. New York: Harper and Row, 1962.

Passow, Harry A. EDUCATION IN DEPRESSED AREAS. New York: Columbia University Bureau of Publications, 1963.

Potts, Sharmon, and McCanne, Eds. PROVIDING OPPORTUNITIES FOR DISADVANTAGED CHILDREN. Denver, Colorado: Colorado State Department of Education, 85 pp. $1.00.

Riessman, Frank. THE CULTURALLY DEPRIVED CHILD. New York: Harper and Brothers, 1962.

Sears, Robert *et al.* PATTERNS OF CHILD REARING. Evanston, Illinois: Row, Peterson, 1957.

Sexton, Patricia Cayo. EDUCATION AND INCOME. New York: The Viking Press, 1961.

Silberman, Charles E. CRISIS IN BLACK AND WHITE. New York: Random House, 1964.

Sutton, Elizabeth. THE MIGRANT CHILD. Department of Health, Education and Welfare, Office of Education, 1963.

II. ARTICLES, BULLETINS AND PAMPHLETS

American Public Welfare Association, POVERTY, Selected Reading Reference, Revised edition. Chicago: The Association, 1963.

Association for Childhood Education. CHILDHOOD EDUCATION. Children in Crowded Areas, May, 1963.

Association for Supervision and Curriculum Development. EDUCATIONAL LEADERSHIP. Issue on Poverty and the School. May 1965.

Ausubel, David P. A TEACHING STRATEGY FOR CULTURALLY DEPRIVED PUPILS: COGNITIVE AND MOTIVATIONAL CONSIDERATIONS, School Review, LXXI (1963) 454-63.

Baynham, Dorsey. THE GREAT CITIES PROJECTS. NEA Journal, pp. 17-20, April, 1963.

Black, Millard H. CHARACTERISTICS OF THE CULTURALLY DISADVAN-TAGED CHILD, The Reading Teacher, XVIII,465-470, (March, 1965).

Clark, Erma. A NURSERY SCHOOL ON THE UTE INDIAN RESERVATION, Childhood Education, XXXXI 407-410, (April, 1965).

Cutts, Warren G. SPECIAL LANGUAGE PROBLEMS OF THE CULTURALLY DEPRIVED, Clearing House, XXXVII, 80-83, (1962).

Cutts, Warren G. READING UNREADINESS IN THE UNDERPRIVILEGED. NEA Journal. pp. 23-24, (April, 1963).

Daugherty, Louise G. WORKING WITH THE DISADVANTAGED PARENTS; NEA Journal, pp. 18-20, (December, 1963).

Education Supplement, EDUCATION AND POVERTY, Saturday Review, 68-89, (May 15, 1965).

Edwards, Thomas J. THE LANGUAGE-EXPERIENCE ATTACK ON CULTURAL DEPRIVATION. The Reading Teacher, pp. 546-551, (April, 1965).

Figurel, J. Allen. LIMITATIONS IN THE VOCABULARY OF DISADVANTAGED CHILDREN: A CAUSE OF POOR READING, Improvement of Reading Through Classroom Practice. Proceedings of the Annual Convention. International Reading Association, IX, 164-65, (1964).

Frost, Joe L. SCHOOL AND THE MIGRANT CHILD, Childhood Education, XXXXI, 129-32, (November, 1964).

Heffernan, Helen. NEW OPPORTUNITY FOR THE PRESCHOOL CHILD, Childhood Education, XXXXV, 227-30, (January, 1965).

Klaus, Rupert A. and Susan W. Gray. EARLY TRAINING PROJECT, INTERIM REPORT, Nashville, Tennessee: George Peabody College for Teachers, (November, 1963).

Metfessel, Newton S. TWENTY-ONE RESEARCH FINDINGS REGARDING CULTURALLY DISADVANTAGED YOUTH SUPPORTED BY INFORMATION OBTAINED FROM PRE-SCHOOL CRITICAL INCIDENT OBSERVATION RECORDS Los Angeles: Center for the Study of Educationally Disadvantaged Youth, University of Southern California, 1964.

433

N.E.A., PROGRAMS FOR THE DISADVANTAGED. EDUCATIONAL RESEARCH SERVICE CIRCULAR. Washington: National Education Association, (January, 1965).

Newton, Eunice S. THE CULTURALLY DEPRIVED CHILD IN OUR VERBAL SCHOOL, Journal of Negro Education, XXXI, 184-87, (1962).

Olson, James L. and Richard G. Larson. CULTURALLY DEPRIVED KINDER-GARTEN CHILDREN, Educational Leadership, XXII, 553-48+, (May, 1965).

Riessman, Frank. TEACHING THE CULTURALLY DEPRIVED, NEA Journal, pp. 21-22, (April, 1963).

Riessman, Frank. THE CULTURALLY DEPRIVED CHILD: A NEW VIEW, Education Digest, XXIX, 12-15, (November, 1963).

Shepard, S. A PROGRAM TO RAISE THE STANDARD OF SCHOOL ACHIEVE-MENT, U. S. Office of Education, Programs for the Educationally Disadvantaged. Washington: Government Printing Office, 1963.

Smith, Mildred B. READING FOR THE CULTURALLY DISADVANTAGED, Educational Leadership, XXII, 398-403, (March, 1965).

U. S. Office of Education. PROGRAMS FOR THE EDUCATION OF THE DISAD-VANTAGED, OE-35044, Bulletin No. 17, 1963.

U. S. Office of Education. IMPROVING ENGLISH SKILLS OF CULTURALLY DIFFERENT YOUTH. Bulletin No. 5, Doc. No. OE-30012. Washington: Government Printing Office, 1964.

Utter, Lawrence W. HELPING OUR CULTURALLY IMPOVERISHED CHILD-REN, National Education Association Journal, LII, 28-30, (N, 1963).

434

PRESCHOOL INTERVENTION THROUGH A HOME TEACHING PROGRAM

David P. Weikart, Ph.D.,
Director, Special Services,
Ypsilanti Public Schools, Michigan

Dolores Z. Lambie,
Research Associate, Special Services,
Ypsilanti Public Schools, Michigan

DAVID P. WEIKART, Ph.D.　　　　　DOLORES Z. LAMBIE

Preschool intervention programing has been widely hailed as an effective technique for preventing the academic and intellectual deficits agreed to be common among culturally disadvantaged children. Programs such as Operation Headstart have received extensive and nation wide popular support from educators, businessmen, and social service groups alike. Many school districts are involved in preschool programs for selected groups of children either as a local effort or in conjunction with state educational and welfare agencies. There is little precedent for such massive and rapid growth of a new form of general education. Without a doubt, preschool programing represents a commitment by a broad segment of the general population to the amelioration of the plight of many lower class children. Yet the informed and cautious observer is not overly enthusiastic about the possible long term outcomes from preschool intervention as presently conducted. Preschools can hardly be the sole solution for the educational problems produced by a myriad of social conditions. Current knowledge about the appropriate curriculum for these children is still too primitive, and effective designs of program style have yet to be identified.

The basis for the interest in preschool intervention programing is that early childhood seems to be the most promising time for effecting desired improvement in intellectual development patterns. Bloom (1964) pointed out in his summary of the research on child development that before four years of age is the time of greatest intellectual growth and is therefore the optimal time. Working with animals, Scott (1962) developed the concept of "critical period." He observed the effect of various kinds of deprivation, such as isolation, on lambs and puppies and concluded that timing was a crucial factor in early environmental conditions. He hypothesized that various kinds of experiences have effect when they occur at one period in time but not at another. "Organization can be strongly modified only when active processes of organization are going on." Krech (1960), Rosenzweig (1964), Bennett (1964) and others, in carefully controlled studies with laboratory rats, have successfully identified and measured physiological changes in the brain which relate directly to early experience. Pasamanick and Knoblock (1961) have documented the impact of deprivation most vividly in their study of infant development. They employed

437

samples of Negro and white infants selected for equal birth weights and absence of defects or premature birth. Using the Gesell Development Scale, they found no significant difference between the two groups at 40 weeks of age. The white babies obtained a developmental quotient of 105.4 and the Negro babies a DQ of 104.5. At three years of age, the first 300 of the original 1000 children involved in the study were retested and a highly significant difference was found. The developmental quotient of the white children rose to 110.9 while the DQ of the Negro children fell to 97.4. They conclude that, "It appears to be life experiences and the sociocultural milieu influencing biological and physiological function that in the absence of organic brain damage make human beings significantly different behaviorally from each other" (p. 86).

While this theoretical basis would seem to point to an unusual potential for success in preschool education, the research in the field is equivocal. Reviews of the research literature by Fuller (1960), Sears and Dowley (1963), and Swift (1964) indicate that for middle class children, on the whole, there are few if any differences between groups attending and not attending preschool by the time the groups reach third grade. There is a suggestion, however, from the extensive work of Skeels (1966), Skodak (1949), and others at the Iowa Child Welfare station and from Kirk (1958) that youngsters described as culturally deprived may be directly and permanently aided by preschool experience. Recent reviews by Robinson (1966) and Fowler (1966) also support cautious optimism.

The information on current preschool research projects has been summarized by Brittain (1966), Gordon and Wilkerson (1966), and Weikart (1966b). The most recent data from the Perry Preschool Project in Ypsilanti, Michigan, as representative of the current studies, indicate that preschool experiences for groups of children from disadvantaged homes (in a small urban northern community) will not greatly change the measured intellectual level but may provide the foundation necessary to produce improved academic achievement. With preschool, the child from a limited environment may be able to better utilize the general intellectual ability he has in a school setting. These findings are based upon a three year follow up of children who received a one year structured curriculum preschool experience. (Schwertfeger and Weikart, 1967; Weikart, 1967).

The difficulties in maintaining long term intellectual growth may come from several sources.

1) It may be that the general inability of present preschool programs to "cure" the deficits present in deprived children stems from the failure to start early enough to alter the child's environment. As the essential framework and basis for intellectual growth is apparently complete by age four, intervention after that age can effect

438

mild change of at least a temporary nature but not long term or dramatic shifts in performance. Several projects are currently exploring the area of early intervention. Most extensive is the program under the direction of Caldwell (1966) at Syracuse University. Work in infant stimulation begins as early as possible and extends through preschool. A day care center accepts children of working mothers and a developmental program is initiated. Early results indicate that the intervention program can successfully increase the intellectual level of the child and compensate for deprived environments to some extent. Schaefer (1967) at the National Institute of Mental Health is working with infants starting at 18 months of age. His teachers go to the homes and work individually with the infants. The mother is not directly involved. Kirk at the University of Illinois is also exploring tutorial service to infants (Colwell, 1966). After initial observation and diagnosis, planned tutoring sessions are initiated. Sequenced activities are employed to assist the child in making the transition from concrete to symbolic material. The role of the parents in the tutoring sessions is not described. White (1966) has explored the impact of early visual stimulation on institutionalized infants under 6 months of age. His results suggest that visual-motor development can be accelerated with generally beneficial results to the child's total well being. These programs, then, are efforts at early intervention before the child reaches four years of age. The Skeels' (1966) 30 year follow up report of an early Iowa study is suggestive of the extensive and positive impact that may be anticipated from these projects if the alternative for any of the children involved be a state of severe deprivation equivalent to institutional placement.

2) It may be that preschool programs have not evolved adequate curricula to meet the needs of the deprived child. Fowler (1966) suggests this point in his criticism of projects, such as the Perry Preschool, which fail to maintain initial intellectual gains. A number of workers are active in the development of new approaches and activities designed to teach reading. Blatt (1965) has employed O.K. Moore's responsive environment to introduce reading at the preschool age. Many preschool teachers have turned to the early work of Montessori, McMillian and others (Braun, 1964). Deutsch (1965) and his co-workers have evolved many specific methods which have wide application. The tape recorder listening center is an example. Smilansky (1964) has suggested many practical ideas, especially the use of social-dramatic play. Perhaps most promising are the efforts to apply broad theories of intellectual growth and development to preschool curriculum. McNeill (1966) and Cazden (1966) present summaries of key ideas in the area of language development. The use of Piaget's developmental concepts are being widely used, (Sonquist, 1967; Stendler, 1965; Sigel, 1964; Almy, 1963; and Sprigel, 1967). Bruner (1966) has suggested specific methods and outlined immediate goals. Guilford (1966) has designed a model to facilitate the teaching of cognitive processes. These efforts may hold the solutions to the development of adequate programs to accomplish the basic tasks of preschool education. Much work is necessary as yet, before a given curriculum can be depended upon to produce a desired outcome.

3) It may be that preschool follow up data are discouraging because elementary education is not willing to alter curricula so that children given a start in preschool can continue to progress with the assistance of programs designed especially for them. For example, Long (1966) has found evidence that where poor elementary teaching is current, effects of preschool wear off more quickly than where better teaching is available. Educators evaluating Head Start have reported the same trends.",...because of poor teaching or uninspired curriculum the thirst of Head Start children for further knowledge went largely unquenched and the advantages of preschooling rapidly dissipated." (Wolf, 1967) A preschool research conference sponsored by the Social Science Research Council in 1966 concluded that it was too much to ask that an experience for several hours a day for several weeks or months permanently alter all future performance without further intervention. The job of preschool was to prepare the child for the next stage of development that schools with adjusted curricula can offer. This position has been the theme of officials concerned with compensatory education today (Gordon and Wilkerson, 1966).

Altering the curriculum of the elementary school has been the major focus of much of the current work with the so called "effective school" and other similar plans many schools have introduced under Title 1 of the Elementary and Secondary Education Act. Deutsch (1965) is actively studying the effect of early elementary education curriculum alteration. Little other research is underway evaluating the effectiveness of such curriculum alteration, however.

4) It may be that preschools are simply attacking the wrong problem with the wrong person, Rather than provide enrichment and training to a disadvantaged child, it might be wise to regard his learning deficits as a symptom and look for amelioration of the problem through retraining his mother in essential areas such as language, teaching, and child control patterns. Most preschool work to date has been done in a fairly standard style focused on the child with classroom settings, teachers, aides, social workers, psychologists, referrals to local physicians and a range of curricula from traditional (Henderson, 1965) to structured, (Connor, 1964; Gray and Klaus, 1965; Weikart 1967) to task-oriented (Bereiter and Engelmann, 1966). Most headstart and general research projects, however, have employed group meetings and parent activities to involve the parents closely in the goals of preschool education. A number of projects have been directed at the mother as well as the child. The Perry Project has included weekly home visits to provide direct instruction to the child and to share with the mother information about the educative process. The Gray and Klaus project, operating preschool classes only in the summer, includes a home visitor who brings educational counseling and materials into the home on a weekly basis throughout the year. Gordon and Wilkerson (1966) record other projects for parents oriented toward teaching basic literacy and child care methods. While the importance of the mother in the educative process has been recognized,

440

her involvement has been primarily passive with the emphasis on obtaining her cooperation with the school so that the teacher may teach the child. It is this secondary role of the mother that is being increasingly questioned.

The insightful work of Hess and Shipman (1967) at the University of Chicago has documented the importance of the mother in establishing the essential basis for cognitive and language development of the child. Looking within social class groups, certain patterns of mother behavior have been identified as more effective in producing growth than other patterns. The extent of the growth seems to be determined by the mother's ability to provide learning task expectancy and learning sets, corrective feedback of information as the task is learned or performed, and positive reinforcement as the child works toward a desired goal. Hess and Shipman believe that, "The lack of cognitive meaning in the mother-child relationship is a central factor contributing to the problem of the 'culturally disadvantaged' child." They state further:

It appears, then, that in spite of a mother's good intentions, if she fails to inject sufficient cognitive meaning into her interactions with her child, she may end up structuring the situation so that he not only fails to learn, but develops a negative response to the experience. It seems possible that for many children such experiences occur frequently enough to lead to generalization resulting in negative valence for all cognitive learning situations. By this route, then a mother may induce negative attitudes, not by the child's imitating the mother or interjecting her views, but by his reacting adaptively to her well meant but harmful teaching behavior. We believe that this kind of communication failure is a primary factor in the mother-child interaction patterns of the culturally disadvantaged and that it has far-reaching and cumulative effects which retard the child's cognitive development. (1967)

It would seem, then, that preschool programs that are directed at the disadvantaged child and do not involve the mother are accepting a challenge beyond the capacity of any educational curriculum. The problem is not to provide enrichment opportunities for the child or even child welfare information to the mother, but to restructure the mother-child interaction pattern. It is to this end that preschool education must turn.

There is little doubt that the answers to effective programing for the disadvantaged child will require extensive investigation in each of the four problem areas outlined. It is most likely also true that programs will need to be developed exploiting all of the avenues open for intervention. Just as preschools can hardly be the sole solution for the educational problem produced by a myriad of social conditions, neither can elementary curricula reorganization or mother training programs serve that function

441

alone. However, there has been a distinct tendency to deal with the critical problems in the education of the disadvantaged by doing more of the same or by simply extending what is done with one age group or one social group to another group. More adventurous efforts are necessary. Sufficient basic research is available to permit extensive experimentation at this time.

THE YPSILANTI HOME TEACHING PROJECT

The Problem

The Ypsilanti Home Teaching Project was an effort to explore the feasibility of sending teachers into the homes of disadvantaged families to provide a training program for the mother and a tutoring program for the preschool child without an accompanying classroom program. While it is felt essential to initiate a home teaching project at the birth of a child in high risk disadvantaged families, for the purpose of this study, only four year olds and their mothers were included. While the Perry Preschool project has been sending teachers into the homes of the families enrolled in the program on a weekly basis for the last five years, as part of the total program, there has been no indication that parents would permit a project that did not provide out-of-the-home service in a school classroom. Then too, while the home teaching aspect of the Perry project has been highly attractive to teachers, it was unknown whether or not teachers would accept the peculiar circumstances home teaching alone would entail. It was also doubted that any "hard" dependent variables could be identified which would reflect the work of the project. Two specific objectives were selected for this limited pilot study. The first objective of the project was to develop the techniques necessary to operate a home teaching program, and the second was to evaluate the immediate acceptability and effectiveness of the program upon the child and his mother.

Related Research

While many projects have been involved with parents, few have developed a home teaching program of the type envisioned for this project. An exception was a short term project operated in New York State. No other home teaching projects are known to the authors at this time.*

A home teaching project, Project REACH, was operated by Schwartz, Phillips and Smith (1965) in a rural setting where preschool classes seemed impractical because of sparse population and resulting transportation problems. The study was designed for disadvantaged four year olds to 1) improve attitudes and skills necessary for school, 2) assess the extent of parent cooperation for such a program style, 3) im-

---

*Gray and Miller at George Peabody College in Nashville, Tennessee have developed a home teaching program which began operation in May of 1966.

442

prove parental attitudes toward school and education and 4) develop possible methods of teaching which could be adapted later for television instruction. As with all programs for the disadvantaged, the instruction focus was to overcome the deficiencies normally found in lower class disadvantaged children.

The experiment employed three groups, a home teaching experimental group, a home visitation group (termed a placebo group as untrained volunteers associated with the children on a regular basis but did not carry out an educational program), and a traditional control group. Each child in the experimental group received two 45 minute sessions with a trained teacher each week for 21 weeks. The project was styled as an enrichment program with emphasis on language development, social concepts and enhancement of self concept. The lessons were planned in advance to obtain specific learning goals. The teachers encouraged the parents to continue the lessons taught at the sessions during the week for their children.

The placebo group was visited by concerned middle class non-professionals, i.e., wives of faculty, college students, and others in similar status positions. The goal was to provide the second group with as much attention as the home teaching experimental group received; simple toys were brought for the child, but no direct educational program was initiated by the visitors. Time was spent talking with the parents.

As is usual in preschool programs, the qualitative findings based on teacher observations were that "valuable learning" had taken place (Weikart, 1967). Also, it was found that teachers in a home teaching program can gain the cooperation of disadvantaged families. The Stanford-Binet and Peabody Picture Vocabulary Test were used to measure intellectual development. While few actual data are presented, the researchers report that there were no significant differences among the three groups at the end of the 21 week experiment. Indeed, the home visitation (placebo) group was consistently better than either the experimental teaching group or the control group. The rationale given for these findings on the IQ tests was that the tests cannot adequately measure the skills and knowledge that the program taught the participating children.

Overview of the Ypsilanti Project

The basic educational procedure of the Ypsilanti Home Teaching project was a one and a half hour per week home visit to each participating family. The visits allowed a carefully individualized program to be initiated involving the mother and her four year old child. The contact was to permit the systematic development of the *foundations* necessary for intellectual functioning by the child through direct tutoring of the child by the teacher and to give occasion for the development of language, teaching, and child management skills of the mother through direct mother-teacher

443

interaction during the tutoring session. In addition, the mothers were involved in a small core group for group meetings. Every effort was made to assist the mothers in the utilization of the community to enrich the experiences of their children. The children did not attend a preschool class as such in a school.

The project operated with four state certified teachers, four part time community aides and a curriculum development supervisor. Each teacher handled a core group of nine disadvantaged families. In addition, a research staff with the extensive cooperation of the teachers collected the data necessary to evaluate the program.

The Home Teaching Session
During the sessions the direct tutoring of the child occurred and the active involvement of the mother and her training took place. To enable the mother to give full attention to the child and the teacher, teacher aides were employed when necessary to supervise the other children who might be present. When the teacher, mother, and child left the home for a field trip or group meeting the teacher aide remained in charge of the children at home.

In tutoring the child, the primary emphasis was given to activities identified as necessary foundations for cognitive growth. These activities will be discussed in detail in the next section of this report.

In consulting with the mother, the teacher planned opportunities for her to participate actively in the program. The mother was involved in the educative process and provided with the training necessary for the daily implementation of the program through observing the teacher work, functioning as a teaching assistant, and discussing educational problems that she and her child faced. The project teacher provided the necessary equipment and supplies so that the mother could immediately effect the planned program.

Group meetings were planned to broaden the effect of the individual home-visits and to reinforce the movement of mothers toward the best possible educational plans for their children. Only a few of these were held because of the short duration of this overall project.

Sample
The sample for this study was drawn from the available four year old disadvantaged children in the Ypsilanti Public School attendance district. These children were located through a survey based upon school census information, school principal recommendation and agency referral. Both Negro and white families were included. The selection criterion was a low score on the cultural deprivation scale developed

444

in the Perry Preschool project. The scale provides a gross index of cultural deprivation based upon occupation, education, and number of persons in housing unit.

Once the sample was drawn, the children were tested and the mothers were interviewed. The families were assigned to either the experimental or control group on a random basis initially. Then several members of the groups were exchanged to obtain a group match on mean cultural deprivation rating of the family and mean Stanford-Binet IQ of the children. Where possible the groups were equated for race and sex. Table 1 gives some characteristics of the two groups. While the initial Binet mean IQ's were matched, the loss of six subjects from the control due to incomplete data created some difference in mean scores. A statistical test (t-test) indicated that the difference was not significant. The members of this control group who were unavailable for complete follow up seemed to be a fair representation of this total sample. It is assumed that no bias was operating.

TABLE 1

Characteristics of the Experimental and Control Groups

Characteristic	Experimental (N=35)	Control (N=29[a])
Stanford-Binet IQ (mean)[b]	95.3	98.6
Peabody Picture Vocabulary IQ (mean)	89.0	94.1
Cultural Deprivation Rating (mean)[b]	9.5	9.8
Boy (percent)[b]	48.5%	72.4%
White (percent)[b]	74.2%	58.6%
Father in home (percent)	77.1%	82.7%
Education of mother (mean grade)	10.3	10.3
Education of father (mean grade)	9.1	10.0
Occupation of father		
unskilled-unemployed	77.1%	68.9%
semiskilled	17.1%	31.0%
skilled	2.8%	0%
Professional	0%	0%
Number of children (mean)	3.5	3.8
Welfare assistance (percent)	22.8%	20.6%
Number of rooms (mean per person)	1.06	1.04
Number of persons in home (mean)	5.6	6.2

[a]Six control children are not included in the analysis.
One family moved, one child was found to be too young and four families had incomplete data.

[b]Characteristics considered in the original matching of the two groups.

445

Data Collection

Data were collected through a number of instruments. The functional intelligence level of the child was assessed through use of the Stanford-Binet Intelligence Scale, Form LM'. The level of vocabulary development was measured by the Peabody Picture Vocabulary Test, Form A. These tests were administered by state certified psychologists. The general attitude of the mother toward education was assessed by the Weikart Educational Attitude Test (1967c). General cognitive press was measured by the Cognitive Home Environment Scale, a measure developed locally from the scales of Wolf (1964) and Dave (1963). Various environmental and demographic variables were collected through interview and observation by the teachers during initial and follow up contacts with the home. During the teaching sessions, program variables were collected on a program report form. The data were analyzed on the University of Michigan IBM 7090 computer. The next sections will present a description of the actual teaching curriculum for the child. The data on the effectiveness of the project will be presented in the form of statistical data followed by case studies of families who represent those who responded least and those who responded most to the project in terms of child IQ change and mother attitude change. The last section is a general discussion and summary of the project.

THE HOME TEACHING CURRICULUM

Introduction

The curriculum employed in the home teaching project was organized around five basic areas: 1) Manipulative activities, 2) Dramatic play, 3) Perceptual discrimination, 4) Classification, and 5) Language. While no single source can be identified as influencing the specific curriculum content, liberal use was made of the ideas from Piaget, (Inhelder, 1958), Deutsch, (1965), Smilansky, (1964), Peel, (1960); and other sources. The project also drew heavily upon the ideas the staff had developed in prior work with children. The specific curriculum was not fully developed before the project began, but was evolved as the teachers worked with the curriculum supervisor to resolve the very real problems faced in the teaching sessions.

While the project curriculum was specifically designed by the staff, the program did meet the criteria necessary in successful preschool programing for disadvantaged children. The curriculum provided step-by-step opportunities for each individual to proceed at his own rate toward predetermined cognitive goals, i.e., a structured curriculum. And the curriculum was closely supervised so that an individual teacher could maintain a perspective of the objectives to be obtained.

The design of the home teaching visits did not follow set patterns of time allotted to specific curriculum activities as commonly found in nursery schools. The unique teacher-mother-child interaction situation permitted wide latitude for individualized

446

programing. Initially the attention span of the project's four year olds seemed brief and a variety of play-oriented and problem solving activities were essential. The teachers planned activities by alternating tasks of high interest with those less well received, continually using an aura of enthusiasm, surprise, or mystery to keep the child interested and participating. It was apparent after the first round of visits to all families that the group was very heterogeneous and that a uniform curriculum could not meet the needs of each child and mother. Thus, appropriate activities for various curriculum areas were listed as a guide for the teacher. This procedure allowed for a flexible program which the teachers could adapt for each child and mother.

Individualizing the curriculum for each child placed a heavy emphasis on the teachers' ability to identify the concepts and skills that are necessary for each child's growth. Deficits in communication, classification, and perceptual discriminations were readily apparent. More difficult was the task of finding what sequence of presentations would provide a base for meaningful learning. Close observation of the children offered clues for the identification and clarification of the level of concept development. For example, after putting some beads in a container covered with a realistic picture of the beads, one child asked, "Are beads in the box?" indicating that he did not understand that beads could exist when not visible. The teacher's immediate response was, "Let's open the box and see...Are the beads in the box?" This activity was repeated to the satisfaction of the child and then games of hiding and finding objects under, in, and behind other objects were played. The follow up activity selected by the teacher was identifying familiar objects concealed in paper sacks by touching them.

Frequently the child was given a choice of activities as a reward for completing a task. When the child's performance was satisfactory he could choose one or more games to keep at home for the week. When toys, games, books or materials repeatedly were not properly cared for, the child was not given any articles to keep for one week. Only one such restriction was usually necessary and only three or four children experienced this sanction.

In addition to the variety of enrichment experiences, lessons were planned to follow sequential patterns of learning whenever possible, especially in the areas the child showed the greatest deficit. Although attempts were made to arrange the tasks by level of difficulty, many children fluctuated between levels, returning to simpler levels whenever new concepts were presented.

Educative deficits were discovered as the teacher observed the child's performance and used informal diagnostic materials, such as figure drawings, shape games, situational pictures, and other samples of the usual kinds of learning tasks master teachers frequently employ when getting to know a child. It is likely that a combination of data from sound diagnostic materials and teacher analysis of individual performance is the best procedure for assessment. The ongoing analysis primes the teacher for making immediate decisions on how to adapt the planned lesson to the child's level of development. Sometimes, however, the teachers recognized cues only as they recalled a visit while preparing the required home teaching summary or participating in the weekly group discussions on curriculum and problems encountered when working in the homes. The standard exclamation was "Oh, I missed it. I should have....." These insights were applied to planning the content of subsequent visits.

The close attention to the behavior of the individual child permitted incidental or "episodic" learning. An unusual occurrence that piqued the child's curiosity was exploited as an occasion for the introduction of new concepts. The utilization of the "novel" experience seemed to provoke more visible development of insight by the child than any of the other techniques practiced by the teachers. An illustration will be given later.

Structured Curriculum

This curriculum was formulated to improve the child's perceptual discrimination, conceptual abilities and communication skills. In establishing a hierarchy of tasks upon which to build a curriculum three spiral principles were assumed: 1) concrete, i.e., tangible, manipulations facilitate learning abstraction and the more abstraction learned the greater the ability to gain new information from manipulation; 2) household materials and everyday experiences with which the child has some degree of familiarity could be used as an introduction to new and unfamiliar concepts and these concepts provoke increased awareness of the environment; 3) teaching specific discriminations, e.g., difference between a circle and a rectangle precedes generalization, e.g., a sphere and a cylinder can be made from many circles or a block and a bar can be made from many rectangles, and these generalizations provide a basis for more difficult discriminations such as a circle is to a square as a sphere is to a cube.

The various curriculum areas will be discussed as units. Of course the actual instructional setting was an admixture, but five specific areas are discussed separately for convenience: 1) Manipulative activities, 2) Dramatic play, 3) Perceptual discrimination, 4) Classification, and 5) Language.

Manipulative Activities

All activities in which the child is the experimenter and not the passive receiver of information can be called exploration or manipulation activities. Whenever the child uses physical action, the activity can be categorized as concrete, and is both tangible

448

and motor. The components of this area of the curriculum were: 1) exploration and manipulation of objects for familiarity and labeling; 2) art activities as media for reproducing forms, shapes, and visual impressions; and 3) motor-coordination tasks to reinforce perceptual abilities. The primary uses of these activities were to support other areas of the curriculum, evaluate the child's progress in perceptual discrimination and as a change of pace following intensive work in another curriculum area such as classification.

1) Exploration and manipulation of objects. This area was treated as an integral part of concept development. As a child handled objects and played with them he discovered some of the properties that gave them identity. The teacher's role was to facilitate this identification by planning activities that drew attention to specific properties and by accompanying the child's actions and discoveries with appropriate language ("verbal bombardment"). Initially, it was efficient to use objects with which the child already had some familiarity, such as furniture used by the child, cooking or eating utensils, and the child's toys and articles of clothing. It seemed more likely that the mother would replicate the activities because the articles were readily available to her and they would serve as a reminder of what she could do with the child.

In addition to labeling the objects and identifying their parts and characteristics, manipulation of objects was frequently used to teach the meaning of common prepositions that refer to position is space (e.g., over, under, behind).

2) Art activities. Creating images or representations of objects and shapes is inherent in primary art activities such as paper collage, fingerpainting, modeling clay, drawing, pasting and cutting. These activities also provide an excellent means of involving passive mothers and relaxing overly anxious mothers. For children who had difficulty using crayons or paints the teachers started with more plastic, easily controlled media such as clay and playdough. The children were encouraged to make models of familiar objects. When accurate modeling was difficult, the teacher directed the child's attention to the various parts of the object and reinforced the teaching by playing "What's Missing?" games, in which parts of an object are removed and the child finds or guesses the missing part (i.e., wheels on a car, leg of a chair). The game also is effective when the child makes an incomplete object for mother or the teacher to guess what is missing.

Frequently art projects were started at the end of a visit and left for the mother and child to complete during the week (i.e., cutting and pasting shapes for a scrapbook, painting pictures to illustrate a trip or story). Art activities are easily accepted by mothers as "good" programing for their children.

449

3) Motor-coordination activities. A few children showed gross motor deficiencies. The teachers provided typical running and jumping games and encouraged mothers to take their children to nearby parks and to enroll them in recreation programs when feasible. Activities long associated with motor development such as ball games were also used to develop language and will be discussed in that section.

Dramatic Play

Both simple and complex pretending games were employed which required visual and auditory decoding, motor encoding and recalling sequence of stories and activities. Initially, these games were played with extraneous props using actual objects, then miniatures, and finally pictures and materials such as blocks with only a slight resemblance to the actual object. Some play was enacted without props as determined by the child's ability. The most complex game was dramatizing a story or experience with attention to the sequence of activity. The following outline gives typical examples of those employed.

1) Pretending with props.
   a. Actual objects.
      1. Coffee time with mother's cups but no water, sugar, etc.
      2. Child is given objects like those mentioned in a story and uses them in the same way the story character does. (Ex. "The Five Pennies, "Erik Blegvad.)
   b. Miniatures: Playing house with doll furniture.
   c. Other materials: Using blocks for gas station, pumps, attendant and car.

2) Pretending with pictures.
   a. Child is shown pictures of people in various positions and is asked to do what the person in the picture is doing. (Frostig, Teachers' Guide)
   b. Child adventure, picture story book is read aloud, child re-enacts story using pictures as guide.

3) Pretending without props.
   a. Isolated activities.
      1. Bouncing ball, raking leaves, opening door, walking upstairs.
      2. Pretend you are: happy, sad, angry, hurt, naughty, scared.

450

    b. Activities in sequence.
      1. Sleeping, getting up, washing, dressing, fixing breakfast.
      2. Dramatize a familiar story.

Perceptual Discrimination

From the myriad of identified components of perception the four areas chosen for use in teaching the project four year olds were: 1) body image, 2) form and color recognition, 3) size relationships, and 4) spatial arrangement.

1) Body image. This concept has been defined by McAninch (1966) as "a referential point;-a conceptual and operative image which includes an awareness of the body in relation to the physical world..." (p. 140) The reason for its inclusion in this curriculum is described in her statement:

> Since percepts are representation of the physical world, the individual must develop a structure and hierarchial order to these sensory impressions. Our bodies become a reference point from which this structure and order develops. The spatial world exists only in relationship to our own bodies since it is from this point that objects within the environment are perceived. (p. 144)

Several activities related to body image were utilized in the initial diagnostic appraisals. The child was asked to draw a picture of himself and to put together a six piece puzzle of a boy or girl (head, arms, legs and torso as separate pieces). In a singing game, the child was asked to name the parts of his own body while simultaneously touching them with a finger puppet. Pictures of people in various positions were shown for the child to "do what the person in the picture is doing." The puzzle was not an effective assessment tool because most of the children had no previous experience with puzzles. After some practice with puzzles one of the "people" puzzles was given to each child to keep at home.

The first teaching activity for body image was to make a life size outline of each child. The teachers had the children lie down on a large sheet of white or brown paper and traced around the child's body. Then the mother and teacher helped the child draw and paint features and clothing. Most mothers allowed the "image" to be put on the wall for a while and it was referred to often in subsequent lessons. Although most of the children thoroughly enjoyed this activity, two children seemed to be extremely frightened of their "image" and instructed the teacher to "take it away." After other activities they were slightly more responsive to their drawings.

451

Other activities for body image included making people of clay or playdough, jointed cardboard puppets and more "people" puzzles, Mirrors, photographs and pictures were used to identify body parts as well as family "roles" (mother, father, big sister, etc.) "Finding the Missing Part" was a popular game played with clay, take-apart dolls and pictures.

On the last visit the child was again asked to draw a picture of himself. The overall improvement was so obvious that a systematic collection of drawings will be done in future projects.

2) Form and color recognition. Recognition of forms, shapes and visual differences, such as identifying "roundness," served as a beginning for grouping objects by their physical properties.

As an introduction to shapes, the teachers concentrated on illustrating and labeling the difference between *curved* and *straight* lines. Drawing and cutting curved and straight lines in art activities, for example, were related to the new words. Three basic shapes (circle, rectangle and triangle) were presented separately. Modeling clay, playdough and emery paper served as tangible media for reproducing the shapes. A box of form blocks were also used periodically in games to strengthen identification.

After the introduction to the characteristics of the shapes (*circle*--curved, no straight sides; *rectangle*--four corners, four straight sides; *triangle*--three corners, three straight sides) the teacher's reviewed *same* and *different,* words previously presented in other lessons and began simple matching activities.

The simplest activities began with the teacher placing three objects exactly alike except for the quality to be isolated (i.e., *color:* three chairs, two red, one blue; *size: three* blue cars, two small, one large; *shape:* three yellow form blocks; two round, one square) in front of the child. The child was either given one object and asked to find another one that was the same or he was given all three and asked to find the two that were the same.

After these properties were isolated the teacher and mother played simple matching games with the child. A favorite color game was spinning a primary color wheel and then choosing an object from a box of miniatures that was the same color as the one on the wheel. The teacher's adapted the color wheel by pasting on colored shapes (circle, square, triangle, etc.) and using a box of form blocks instead of miniatures.

For those children who became proficient in matching this way the staff devised games which required the child to be aware of more than one quality at a time.

452

(Example: Domino type game made with one primary colored circle, square or triangle on each end instead of number dots. This required attention to both color and shape.)

3) Size relationship. The major goal was to make the children aware of gross differences in objects or people that were *tall-short, (long-short)* and *large-small, (big-little)* and that *tall-short* refers to height while the others usually refer to mass or bulk. This differentiation was complicated by the fact that everyday usage inadvertently employs *large* or *big* to mean the same as *tall* or *long.* No attempt was made to differentiate between *big* and *large* or *little* and *small* as the discrimination is minor and not commonly considered.

The first planned presentation of *tall-short* most often included comparisons of people, trees, and buildings, two at a time. Teachers limited the use of *long* to linear observations (strings of beads, yarn, strips of paper and rows of blocks), except when referring to time.

Comparisons between *large* and *small* were aided by using toys, kitchen materials, and pictures. In each case the objects or pictures were identical except for size. This precaution helps the child associate the size words with the proper quality. It was also necessary to exchange positions of the objects in front of the child so that the large one isn't always on the left and small one on the right or vice versa.

When the children could consistently choose the one that was *tall, long, big, large,* etc., they were given three painted tubes (from paper towels and tissue rolls) and taught *shortest* and *tallest.* A set of cans of equal height but not circumference were used for *smallest* and *largest* (or *biggest).* The cans were especially effective when the child hid the smaller one under the larger and the teacher asked him to tell what was hidden. Eventually the number of articles to be ordered by size was increased. Paper shapes, measuring cups and spoons, nesting blocks and cans were most readily available. An important consideration, however, is that in teaching single concepts, such as height, materials must be used which vary on only that dimension. Nesting blocks and cans (as one, two, and three pound coffee cans) require attention to two factors, height and circumference or perimeter. This can be confusing for a child unless they can grasp that one can is both the *tallest* and *largest* or *shortest* and *smallest.*

4) Spatial arrangement. Activities for this area followed those related to body image, form, color and size. Some children were able to use the new discriminations in complex arrangements that depended on the relationship of each object or part to another. Initially the children had learned the words that referred to spatial placement, such as *top, bottom, left, right, beside, next to, under, over,* etc., as described in the section on language.

453

Now three types of activities were utilized employing the perceptual discriminations already learned: 1) reproducing simple to complex patterns using beads and blocks, 2) constructing abstract pictures of people and objects from geometric shapes, nicknamed "Make-It-Puzzles," and 3) making "maps" of rooms in the house, furniture in a room, objects on the table, houses in a block, etc.

The sequence of *bead patterns* were inherently linear as the string was necessary to keep them from rolling, etc. However, some children enjoyed stacking them more than blocks. (Block patterns were not limited to linear arrangements but similar principles were applied to their sequence of difficulty so only the bead patterns will be discussed.) The order of difficulty followed for presenting a bead pattern was a complete sample on a separate string from which the child matched each piece, a partial sample to be repeated until all the beads were used, a demonstration of the pattern which was then removed from view, and verbal instructions given for very simple patterns without any concrete sample to follow. The following list includes an example of each type of stringing required of the child.

> a) Color only (all blue beads)
> b) Shape only (all square beads)
> c) Simple patterns of two
> > 1) color (blue bead-red bead)
> > 2) shape (square-barrel)
> > 3) color and shape (only red squares or blue squares, yellow spheres)
> d) Complex patterns of three or more colors, shapes and combinations (red square, -blue disc-yellow barrels)

Make-It-Puzzles were abstract pictures constructed from simple flat geometric shapes. The easiest was a tree made from a large circle or triangle and a narrow rectangle. The most difficult was a train with nineteen pieces. Other pictures were a snowman, wagon, boy, girl, house, rabbit, etc. The shapes were pasted on cardboard and the children given an identical set of shapes and an empty cardboard (same size as sample) to reconstruct the picture. The teacher aided learning by having the child compare the completed puzzle with the actual object and showing him how the picture was constructed.

More children were able to arrange objects (doll furniture, toy cars, dishes) to reproduce patterns found in the house, on the street, or set up by the teacher on the table, than were able to draw approximate shapes on *maps* to represent the arrangements they saw. The girls preferred mapping rooms in the house, furniture, and dish arrangements. The boys liked streets, cars, and buildings found close to home. The children made frequent referrals to the "territory" they were trying to represent, and a final comparison of the map to the actual set up.

454

Classification

In choosing an activity for a child, at least three dimensions were considered: 1) level of difficulty of the concept to be used for classifying the objects, 2) the degree of abstraction required by the materials used, and 3) the number and size of objects presented in each activity. Classification activities were used to organize objects by attributes of physical properties (such as color and shape) and by their function or use as related to the child's experience.

1) Level of difficulty. Primary level activities require discriminations based on properties that were visually apparent. The child grouped objects that were exactly the same in color, shape or form, size, position in space, and combinations of these properties (i.e., grouping red chairs, and small blue beads). When the child became accustomed to putting things together because they had one or more qualities in common the teacher introduced sorting of types or sets of objects. Each set contained several versions of an article (chairs, trucks, cars, balls) but all had visually similar characteristics.

Secondary activities are defined as those that require identification of an object's function (purpose) or use. Grouping by function is related to grouping sets of objects in the primary level, except the child cannot rely on visual clues (broom-vacuum cleaner, glass-cup). The more expansive groups have a multitude of members (toys, clothes, food). Activities that require grouping of objects because they are used together or are necessary to complete an action or activity are included at this level (soap-towel-washbowl, spoon-cereal-milk-bowl).

2) Level of abstraction. Representations of real objects used in an activity were sequenced by the teachers according to the degree of abstraction. The criteria for determining the degree of abstraction were *dimension* (from three dimensional objects to pictures), *size* (actual size to miniatures), and the *number of visual clues* relating the representation to the real object (realistic to impressionistic). These variations were used as a guide in choosing the type of materials suitable for each child's level of symbolization.

    a) actual size three dimensional facsimile
    b) realistic miniatures
    c) colored photographs and/or black and
       white realistic pictures
    d) silhouette
    e) stylized miniatures (not realistic but
       definitely representative of properties
       that identify objects)
    f) black and white line drawings

455

g) impressionistic drawings having minimal
visual clues

3) Number and size. These dimensions are important because they may mislead the teacher into believing a child has learned a concept. Actually the child may be responding to cues of number or size as he might to a teacher's facial expression. In order to insure that the child was organizing the objects according to the concept being taught, it was necessary to control for differences in size and number.

For example, a child is to select *vehicles* from a group of three objects, a truck, a car, and a bunch of grapes. The car and truck are apparently the same size. The child may select them on this basis alone, or he may reject the grapes because they have many parts. Thus size (or number) may determine the choice rather than the concept, *vehicle.*

4) Matching physical properties. Color, shape, and size, were the three visually apparent properties carefully controlled in form discrimination activities; and, as explained initially, only gross differences were compared. Sorting objects by color was the most obvious and all but two children could do this before they learned the color names.

After the child learned to identify shapes or could match and sort them (as described in Perceptual Discrimination), the teacher, mother, and child played simple classification games such as finding objects or parts of objects in the house that were round or had curved parts. Several mothers repeatedly confused their children by instructing them to find *round* circles. Thus, the teachers became aware that the explanation for a circle (round, no straight sides) was not sufficient. In the limited time remaining the teachers attempted to rectify the confusion by demonstrating that circles are equidistance from a central point and that other related shapes with roundness are not circles, such as the oval. A similar difficulty occurred with square and rectangle. It was not as easy to change the general usage of square to rectangle.

Most of the mothers delightedly relayed their child's progress in finding all the round shapes on the table, etc. One very successful activity, especially for the boys was identifying the shapes on the teacher's car. (*circle*-wheels, horn, gascap, knobs; *square* or *rectangle* parts of seat, glove box, ashtray, side window; *triangle*-vent window, divisions in steering wheel, divisions between spokes of hubcaps.)

As the children became adept at recognizing similarities they sorted cards or objects by visual criteria requested by the teacher (animals with four legs, furniture with drawers, utensils with and without moveable parts). At this point it was important to introduce the idea that everything belongs to several groups at one time, if the

456

child had not already made this observation. The one activity which helped the most was describing the separate attributes of an object (red, square, has a lid, can hold something inside, etc.)

5) Classifying by use or function. As a transition to classifying without visual clues, each mother helped her child make a scrapbook of magazine pictures, grouping the objects into classes such as: toys clothing, food, people, animals and vehicles. From these general classes the children could choose specific objects that they liked such as clocks, chairs, trucks or cars, and make small books or sets of objects called "Things That Tell Time," etc. (For those children who could not use pictures for grouping, the teachers had miniatures to be sorted into boxes by the same type classes mentioned above.)

Matching by function was usually done only with pictures. The teacher made sets of cards with objects that belong together because they serve the same function (i.e.,: broom-vacuum cleaner; cup-glass; shoe-boot, glove-mitten). For independent use the edges of the cards were cut like a puzzle so that only matching pairs would fit together in a frame. An alternative kind of belonging together was grouping objects used to complete an activity, (iron-ironing board, washbowl-soap-towel; bowl-cereal, milk-spoon.)

Language
The basic scheme for teaching language was the "verbal bombardment" approach which included:

> 1) exposing the child to a variety of language patterns by having the teachers frequently explain personal actions and external occurrences that gained the child's attention supplemented by identification of specific words using objects and motoric activity to demonstrate their meaning;
> 2) directing the child's attention to the importance of recalling events and their sequence in time and objects in their placement in space;
> 3) giving immediate "feedback" when the child gives a verbal response;
> 4) encouraging inquiry through positive responses to questions, pursuing answers to the satisfaction of the child, and making use of unique occurrences interrupting the session which attract the child.

1) Exposing the child to a variety of language patterns. At frequent intervals during each activity the teachers commented on what was happening or about to happen in

457

the teaching session. ("I am going to give you some blocks. Here are the blocks. Mother gets some blocks too") This process was followed in identifying and categorizing objects found in or near the house. In order to clarify specific word meanings it was decided that the teachers would combine verbalization with a physical activity performed by the child whenever possible. This was obviously useful with action verbs (run, walk, go, stop) and adjectives that describe tangible qualities (smooth-rough). However, the function words which received prime attention were dichotomous prepositions that refer to direction (up-down, into-out of), place (over-under, behind-in front of), and time (before-after, during-since), as well as emphasizing specific conjunctions (and, or, if-then, and because). While engaged in typical sensory, motor or manipulative activities (texture cards, ball games, drawing and painting, playing with cars and trucks) the teachers combined a familiar noun with the new word. (The ball is *under* the chair. Hold the ball *over* the chair. Roll the ball *under* the table.) Usually the child first performed the action by mimicking the teacher or his mother until he was able to respond to a request without clues. In other lessons the function words were used in conjunction with color names ("Park the *red* truck *next* to the *yellow* truck. Where is the *red* truck?"

To reinforce, as well as learn new words, the children were taken on experience trips. The most common trips were to pet shops, nursery and greenhouse, the library, grocery stores, bakery, department stores and nearby parks to acquaint mothers with convenient facilities. At every opportunity during the trip, the teacher identified and labeled the animals, plants, objects, etc. She also related the things the child observed to the concepts being taught in the home teaching sessions. For example, in a greenhouse the teacher pointed to flats of flowers and said, "These plants are *tall*. These plants are *short*." Having child touch leaves, she said, "This leaf is *smooth*. This leaf is *rough*. This plant has *red* flowers. Can you find another plant with *red* flowers?" After observing this kind of interaction, some mothers began to take their preschool child with them to get groceries or on special walks to the shopping district to try out the same teaching styles.

On each visit the teacher took a book to be read aloud to the child. Whenever possible, the book was chosen or adapted to complement the lesson. Following a trip to the supermarket teachers read "Miranda Goes to the Supermarket." To review prepositions such as up-down, in-out, under-on top of, etc. teachers read "The Up Side Down Book," "Go Dog Go" or similar books concentrating on spatial placement. These books were in addition to "fun" storybooks.

At first, the children were encouraged to look at the pictures, find things they recognized, name the objects, and tell what was happening. For those children who seemed unable to listen to stories, objects like those pictured in the book or essential to the plot were introduced to the child. With these less abstract representations,

458

the child either enacted the story as it was read or matched them to the pictures. These books and equipment were left in the home for the week.

2) Recall and sequence. Providing each child with practice in remembering simple objects and pictures and in learning to identify them from partial clues was considered a prerequisite to recalling events from stories or experience trips in sequence. The primary activities consisted of hiding an object or objects in clay, playdough, paper bag, box and under or behind furniture in the house. Depending on ability, the child was requested to choose objects identical to the ones hidden, name the object or return to niding places and indicate what would be found there. This was first played with only one or two items. Then the number was gradually increased. The teachers introduced sequence by indicating which item was hidden first, which last.

Alternate activities included "guessing games." Two or more objects (blocks, beads, cars, etc.) are placed in front of the child. After the child had handled and named them he closed his eyes and the teacher removed one. Then the child guessed which one was missing. Mother, teacher, and child took turns removing and guessing. If a child had difficulty remembering the item, it was placed in a bag so he could touch it without seeing it.

To facilitate remembering a story, several activities were helpful: 1) enacting story with props as it was told, 2) using pictures as clues to retell the story to mother and teacher, 3) finger and hand puppets to re-enact story in sequence (either with or without pictures as needed). Sequential story pictures similar to those found in reading readiness workbooks were drawn or cut from magazine advertisements and arranged in order by the child.

Experience trips also provided a valuable opportunity for recall and sequencing. The children were primed to relate their trip to father or other relatives living in the home. Mothers aided in carrying out this assignment. In most instances teachers utilized a variety of activities to help the child recall events of the trip such as examining photographs taken on the trip, drawing pictures or making murals of the key episodes to be completed by mother and child, reading stories related to trip experiences, finding pictures in magazines of objects, people, etc., seen on the trip and adding them to a scrapbook, and activities unique to the trip destination (greenhouse-planting seeds; grocery store-preparing a simple lunch).

3) Reinforcement of child's verbal responses. Two major conditions determined the inclusion of consistent reinforcement by the teacher of clear verbal responses from the child. The majority of the project mothers did not realize that it was important to reinforce their child's spontaneous attempts to tell them of exciting observations.

459

Pronunciation and usage was frequently unique to each family. In one family the mother had to interpret the child's speech for the first few visits and in another, only an older sibling could understand the preschooler and acted as interpreter for the family as well as the teacher. In addition, understanding each child's speech was hindered by the usual mispronunciations resulting from common consonant substitutions and dropped ending and representation of a variety of ethnic and culture groups in the sample such as Mexican, Negro, Southern White, and German.

As a result of these factors the patterns of reinforcement adopted by the staff included:

a) reinforcing the child's response by smiling, praising, and rewarding (i.e., giving the child a choice of materials to keep for the week) when the child gave a verbal response rather than pointing, grunting, etc.

b) repeating the child's conceptually correct one-word responses with a clear inclusion of all syllables and pronunciation most generally used in the area, followed by including the word in a sentence.
   Example: (child looking at picture)
   Teacher: "Where is the house?"
   Child: "tween"
   Teacher: "Yes, between. The house is between the trees."

c) expanding the child's phrase or sentence to include a concept taught in the lesson or in a previous lesson.
   Example: (child sorting toy vehicles)
   Child: "These trugs."
   Teacher: "these are small trucks."

The amount of vocabulary growth for project children (to be discussed in the analysis of results) indicates some success for these teaching methods in a project of this short duration. In retrospect, one of the major deficiencies of the language program was not requiring productive language from the child when the teacher was convinced the child understood the concept. (For an extensive account of language programing the reader is referred to Bereiter and Engelmann, 1966).

4) Encouraging inquiry. Formulating a question about attractive objects and phenomena was not a typical response for some of the children. From teacher observation

460

it seemed that the mothers did not share the teacher's enthusiasm and interest when the child asked a question. In spite of the teacher's obvious joy, many mothers would usually reprimand the child, saying, "You 'jest' hush and listen to the teacher!" In an attempt to salvage the teacher-child relationship under such barrages, the teachers carefully explained that questioning was a necessary part of learning and the child would be expected to ask questions in school and would do better if he could ask questions that would help him understand. Unfortunately, a few were not convinced and expressed this in statements such as, "You just aren't firm enough with him." To the minor unhappiness of these mothers, the teachers continued to praise and reward the child. Except for one family, this did not seem to unduly affect the communication between mother and teacher. In this exception, the child, being acutely aware of the gross contrast between negative and positive treatment, refused to perform a task for his mother. He then turned to the teacher, performed the task and said, "See, I do for teacher." This mother assumed a withdrawn, defeated, "there's nothing I can do" attitude in spite of the teacher's attempts to include her.

In addition to reinforcing the children for questioning, the teachers helped them pursue activities that would offer answers, assisted them by formulating questions that might be the most likely ones occurring to a child with a puzzled look, and made immediate use of the surprise element inherent in an unexpected interruption of the lesson, i.e., a loud or unusual noise, the unavoidable breakage of materials, etc. by asking with gross inflection similar to that used by many middle class mothers with toddlers, "What's that? What happened?" The latter method triggered enough unpredicted questions in subsequent visits to warrant further investigation as a major teaching technique.

Mother Participation

Each of the four teachers was responsible for working with nine preschoolers and their mothers in a weekly 90 minute scheduled visit to the home. During the visit, the teacher presented educational materials and ideas to enable her to continue the work with the child during the week.

At the beginning of the project, the mothers were informed that their presence at the teaching session was required. Of course, requiring the mother's presence did not guarantee active parental involvement; but, it did give the teachers an opportunity to demonstrate and discuss preschool training and the mother's role as her child's first and most important teacher.

The mothers' reactions were varied, but several categories were apparent. 1) The "resistive" mothers were those who abused the teaching arrangement by using the

461

teachers as baby sitters while they made telephone calls, went back to bed, cleaned house, ran errands, watched television, visited with friends, or were not home during the specified time (which the mothers had chosen themselves). During the initial phases of the project 17% of the mothers tended to use the teacher's visit in this way. By the end of the project, only 3% were in this category. 2) The "curious" mothers were those who stood in the doorway or sat nearby but would not join the teacher and pre-schooler, almost as if they were afraid to admit their interest in such "childish activities." Initially, 20% of the mothers showed this reluctance to openly commit themselves, and in the final stages of the program 14% still reacted this way, for at least part of each visit. 3) The "silent observer" mothers were those who appeared quiet and reserved throughout but sat with the teacher and child during the entire session. Approximately the same number of mothers were reserved at the beginning of the visits as at the end of the project, 20% and 21%, not necessarily the same mothers. Towards the end of the visits it became evident that almost half of these "silent observer" mothers were working with their children during the week and selectively following the teacher's suggestions. 4) The "talkative and demonstrative" mothers were those who, in a few cases, sometimes seemed intent on adopting the teacher as one of the family and involving her in the economic, social and emotional episodes of the family, but who sometimes tended to ignore the teacher's focus on the intellectual growth of the child. On the whole, these were the most cooperative mothers. Although only 23% of the mothers were talkative and open at first, at the end of the project 41% were reacting this way. 5) The "concerned" mothers were those who were usually very sensitive about their child's performance for the teacher. Although most mothers showed some concern on one or more occasions, only 20% consistently displayed behavior in each visit that indicated to the child, as well as the teacher, that the mother was somewhat apprehensive. Both categories 4 and 5, the "talkative" and "concerned" mothers, were more receptive to suggestions from the teacher, asked questions about child development and education, and generally were more cooperative than were mothers in the other categories.

The teachers attempted to involve inactive mothers who did not respond to frank discussions about their participation by asking the mother to save house hold items such as cans, jars, food cartons and scraps of material for the teacher to use, choosing or making games that required three people to play, asking the mother for an article from the kitchen to help teach new concept, handing the mother clay to be softened, scissors and paper, etc., saying something like, "Will you help us cut these out?" The teacher then used these opportunities to discuss what she was doing with the child, why the activity was important and adding comments about things that the mother could do during the week to help the child learn. Once a mother became even minimally involved during the session, the teachers started an activity at the end of the visit that could not be finished in the allotted time and left all the mater-

462

ials in the home for its completion. The teacher provided support by praising the mother's efforts and demonstrating the child's growth as a result of these activities with her child.

One of the most difficult problems was the talkative mother who continually wanted to use the teacher as a friend and confidant. For these mothers the teachers allotted short periods of time for conversation during which they tried to relate the topics brought up by a mother to her child's educational needs. In addition, it was possible to introduce some of these mothers to a neighboring project mother either in a group meeting or on an experience trip. From this introduction some mothers got their children together for trips to the park, etc. on their own.

One indication of the concern some mothers felt for their child's performance was evidenced by a tendency to press the children for answers or ridicule them for incorrect responses, immature products, and failure to learn on the first attempt. These detrimental reactions were treated openly by the teacher through discussions on establishing reasonable expectations for performance, recognizing improvement, praising the child, displaying the child's work and listing ways to help the child improve his skills. These mothers also required similar support from the teachers for their efforts.

The mothers' participation during the teachers' visits was extended throughout the week by having the mothers help their children with specific concepts and activities related to curriculum, reading stories from books left in the home, completing art projects. Each teacher left magazines in the homes for the mothers to show their children, talk about the pictures, and help the child choose pictures to add to the classification pages of his scrapbook.

In addition to the activities suggested to the mothers during the lesson, each mother received a set of booklets designed by the Perry Preschool staff specifically for mothers. The booklets were: "It's Fun to Pretend", "The First Book of Shapes: Circles Are Everywhere:, "The Second Book of Shapes: Rectangles Are Everywhere:, "The Third Book of Shapes: Circles and Rectangles", and "Counting All Around Us". These provided additional activities for the mothers to do with their child, reminders on ways to support their child's effort and simplified illustrations to demonstrate why the activities were important. About half of the mothers thoroughly enjoyed the booklets and used the information to create new activities for their children.

Case Studies
This section presents case studies of two disadvantaged families who participated in the project. These studies were selected to represent the extremes in responsiveness

463

to the intervention program. They include a description of the physical home environment, the family, the specific educational program for the child, and the teacher observed changes in the mother and child. Of special importance is the practical illustration of curriculum implementation described in an earlier section of this paper.

Case No. 20. Represents one of the most responsive families in the project.

I. Description
  A. Home Environment (Physical)

  This family lives in a rather dilapidated 2 story house converted into apts., one upper, one lower. The house is located next to commercial stores and at the side of a busy thoroughfare. The exterior of the house is brown shingle; it seems to just rise from the ground as no grass or trees surround it. After entering a hall, one immediately notices peeling walls and a rather rickety, steep staircase that leads to the upper apartment where this family lives. The door opens directly onto a living room which contains two well worn couches, a TV set, coffee table, and rocking chair. Linoleum which is worn bare, covers the floor. There are many objects and bric-a-brac cluttering the living room. The small kitchen contains rather old equipment. The kitchen sink is about the size of a bathroom sink. The kitchen is quite dark and a bare light bulb is constantly burning even on sunny days. The bathroom also contains very old equipment and is small and dark. The parents sleep in a small bedroom. The two children sleep in a room in back of the parents' bedroom.

  B. Family Members and Others

  The family unit is a mother, father, and two children. The older, child, a girl, is involved in the teaching program. The younger child is a boy of two years old. The parents were both raised in the Ypsilanti area and have lived here their entire lives. The mother was fourteen years old when she gave birth to her first child. She is a thin, small woman who always looks presentable. The father, a laborer, is employed on a road crew and since it is seasonal work he is often at home. He is short and stocky and dominates his wife with remarks such as, "You don't know anything because you are so dumb." When saying this, he usually has a smile on his face. Sometimes he takes care of the younger brother when teacher, sister, and mother are involved in teaching sessions. At times the teacher observed him lying on the bed, plucking a guitar. The younger child rarely had anything on but diapers, rubber pants, and a polo shirt even on the coldest days. Often his face was covered with

464

food and his diaper was dirty. The girl, however, was quite attractive, clean, and always neatly dressed. A cousin, of about 19 years of age, is living with the family temporarily. The teacher usually observed him glued to the TV when he was at home.

C. Teaching Conditions

The teaching sessions were always held in the kitchen. The table was usually cleared and ready for the session to begin. On two occasions, the mother had not cleared the table of breakfast dishes and apologized profusely to the teacher. The child was usually waiting for the teacher either on the top of the hall steps or in the living room. She had a broad grin on her face and was eager to talk of things she had done during the week or would ask the teacher, "What are we going to do today?," and look into the teacher's bag for the equipment. The younger brother would sometimes wander into the kitchen and grab some of the toys being used during the session or try to climb onto the table. Mother immediately shoved child out and would say, "Go to daddy," or "A., come take the baby away!" Occasionally the mother would leave session for a few minutes, to attend to the baby's needs, but she would return immediately.

II. Development of Teacher's Personal Relationship with Family
  A. Mother

The mother established an immediate warm relationship to the teacher. She would often talk to the teacher about what the child had done during the week and how well she was able to manage materials. She expressed admiration of the teaching materials and would talk about how she felt the teacher was helping her child. She felt free to talk to the teacher about her child's development and would often ask for suggestions on how to help her child grow and learn. She would offer the teacher a cup of coffee after the session ended and sit and talk. If she purchased something new for the house, she would proudly show it to the teacher. When people came into the house she would immediately introduce the teacher. During the month of May, the mother said, at one teaching session, "Next week you will have a surprise!" The next session the teacher was handed a small doll, made out of a toilet paper roll and ribbon. At Easter time, mother and child made an Easter basket for the teacher from a cottage cheese carton.

  B. Child

The child also established an immediate positive relationship with the teach-

465

er. She would greet the teacher with a large smile and run into the kitchen where we worked. She talked freely and was relaxed while we worked. She would involve the teacher in games she had made up. As she was working she kept up a steady flow of conversation. Before the teaching began, there would often be a stack of drawings on the table that the child had done. The child would talk about the drawings in great detail; how she made them the colors she had used and what they were. Mother said the child always anxiously awaited the teaching session and would ask the mother, "When is the teacher coming?"

C. Father

This father was quite antagonistic toward the teacher from the very beginning. He would often remark, "I don't trust teachers," or in a nasty tone, "Why are you doing that?" (with child). Sometimes he would come in and peer at what teacher, mother and child were doing. He would smile, shrug his shoulders, and walk out of the room. When the mother, child and teacher came back from the last testing session, father almost demanded to know IQ of child. Teacher said that she would be glad to tell him how the child had progressed as soon as the tests were scored. Father's remark then was, "However she did, you will tell me she did well to make me feel good." He then went on to say that teachers never tell the truth about children. While he was talking he was smiling.

III. Developmental Steps in Educational Growth
    A. Initial Appraisal of Child's Educational Level

The teacher's initial impression of this child was that she was very talkative. But at times her attention span was short and she would get fidgety. However, the teacher was able to bring her back to the activity and she could see it through. This child could name most of the objects in the home, especially those in the kitchen and had some conception of their use. She had trouble making specific discriminations as evidenced when the child could not sort saucers with indentations for cups from plates of the same size. She was able to name and match primary and secondary colors except blue and purple. She could match shapes when they were presented two at a time. She did not know the shape of labels and was not able to recognize them when presented with three or more at one time. No understanding of one-to-one correspondence was found, but the child could perform rote counting.

In body image activities the child could label parts of her body in detail, but

466

became frustrated with complex body puzzles when attempting to place the arms on the nearly completed puzzle. When she could not complete the task, she messed the puzzle up and said, "I can't do it", then asked if it could be put away. She was also extremely reluctant to use her body in pretending and singing games so the teacher had to employ props to encourage her. Another difficulty immediately found by the teacher was that the child had not developed the understanding that objects exist even when they are not visible.

B. Description of Stages to Current Level

Although the child was talkative, it became obvious that she frequently did not know the meaning of words she used except when labeling. She especially had difficulty with dichotomies such as *rough-smooth, wet-dry,* and *thick-thin.* The teacher presented tangible materials to demonstrate the differences in these words. The mother's help was enlisted to reinforce these new concepts by comparing objects and helping the child with activities such as rolling playdough to *thick* and *thin* consistencies.

At the onset of teaching, this child's ability to reproduce her body image was immature. As the sessions ended, her reproduction of the body was more detailed. The child also improved in her attention to the materials and concepts presented. At the beginning she had some difficulty sustaining interest in the more directed activities. Toward the end of the sessions, she was more able to concentrate on a task without squirming or talking to teacher about something that did not pertain to the task. She also became very adept at creating games to reinforce the concepts she had learned. For instance, initially the child could not identify or find hidden objects. At the end of the project she would delightedly hide an object for herself. Then she would look under all the materials on the table, saving the real hiding place for last. The teacher used this game to reinforce sequential recall by helping the child pretend to hide an object in several places and then to follow the same sequence in the search each time. The child also questioned some of the more abstract concepts presented to her such as *alive* and *dead.* While on a trip to a florist, she picked up a flower from the floor and said it did not look good. She commented that the flower was dead but that she was going to take it home, put it in water, and make it come alive again. The mother followed through and the next time the teacher saw the child she said the flower did not "get alive, it stayed dead." At the end of the project the child still had some difficulty discriminating blue from purple, but she could match complex bead and block patterns when blue and purple were not presented together.

467

She incorporated these form and color activities into her play by devising a game in which she chose a set of beads such as an orange barrel, a blue square, and a green disc, and then reproduced the set twice, giving one to mother and one to teacher. As a result of this, the teacher requested a one-to-one correspondence task and found the child could perform this easily with up to five objects as she counted.

C. Materials Employed to Develop Growth

Since reproduction of body image was weak, materials were employed with this child to strengthen the area. Play dough was used to make a body to take apart and put together again, a life size drawing was made of the child, pictures of people were shown and parts of the body were named, songs were sung in connection with body parts. Drawings of a man with missing parts were introduced for the child to identify missing parts. The child was also asked to put together body puzzles first with the completed form before her then without it. Manipulative materials such as doll furniture, cups, saucers, and blocks were introduced for language development, such as up-down, under-over, top-bottom, in-on, same-different and big-little. To try to eliminate confusion between naming colors blue and purple, objects such as crayons, plastic shapes, and sticks were introduced to the child for matching. The teacher and mother also helped her find all the objects that were blue, then find all that were purple. Two scrapbooks were made by the child and mother to classify objects (Foods; and Things in My House) Creative Playthings' Perception Placques (faces only) were given to this child to supplement activities in recognizing likenesses and differences. The child was praised by the teacher and mother when she performed tasks well, and she was encouraged by the teacher to attend to each task for longer periods of time. Tactile materials such as emery paper cut into basic shapes and finger paint paper cut into the same shapes were used to clarify difference between smooth and rough. Earth, both wet and dry, was used to clarify difference between wet and dry. An experience trip was taken to reinforce new concepts and to familarize mother with things she could do to enhance child's development.

IV. Observed Changes in Mother
   A. Understanding Educative Process

The mother quickly took clues from the teacher and implemented them by working with the child. When she worked on a scrapbook, she had child cut out a picture of a salad. She told the teacher she wanted to show the child how vegetables can be made into a salad. She kept all of her child's materials

468

in a special bag so they would not be disturbed by younger child. She also told teacher that you don't have to be rich to have fun doing things with children. She worked and encouraged child to draw and would label drawings as the teacher did. She even questioned the teacher on why she had used lower case letters when labeling and when this was explained followed teacher's example. She talked about joining the PTA next year at her child's school and said she would visit the kindergarten room at school during registration week.

B. Towards Child

Mother began to see what her child was capable of accomplishing and would often say with a smile, "I didn't know she could do that!" She began to see how to help her child learn and was very much involved in creating activities to help her child.

Case No. 34. Represents one of the least responsive families in the project.

I. Description
   A. Home Environment (Physical)

This family lives in a low-cost housing development, and the physical characteristics of this development are not at all pleasant. Paint is peeling from the exterior of the apartment, garbage is often strewn on the walls and front lawns, open garbage pails are placed at the entrance of each apartment; and lines of laundry are hung up in front of each house. Once in a while a flower will be seen, but this is rare. There is little or no grass and children play in holes of dry earth or mud, if it has rained. The windows are often cracked and when no glass is in the windows at all, they are protected by a sheet of heavy paper. The apartment this family lives in is a duplex. The living room and kitchen are downstairs; the bedrooms and bathroom upstairs. The teacher has never seen the upstairs part of the apartment. The door opens onto the kitchen which is quite dark and small, but neat and clean. The kitchen contains equipment which is old but clean and in good condition. The living room is average size and also quite dark. The teacher rarely saw a light burning in this house even on the most dismal winter days. Three children live here and rarely is a voice heard. The furniture in the living room consists of 2 couches. a TV set, a coffee table and a cabinet where various bric-a-brac is kept. The walls are painted a dull beige and seem to blend in with the area of dreariness that pervades.

   B. Family Member and Others

469

The family consists of three children and a mother. The oldest child is a girl of 6, the middle child, who was involved in the home teaching project, is a boy of four and the youngest child is a girl of about three years of age. The mother is a short, heavy set woman whose clothes seemed worn but always starched and well ironed. She rarely smiled, rarely talked and appeared to be dour and completely uninvolved with the child. When she did talk, it was usually in monosyllables and so softly it was barely audible. She usually moved slowly and often would sit on the couch and stare into space. The child with whom teacher was involved was of average height and sturdy build. His face was set tight, and his jaws were clamped together. He showed little or no animation; hardly talking, smiling or showing happiness or sadness. The older and younger children seemed more animated. They would talk in low voices and smile frequently.

C. Teaching Conditions

Mother, child and younger sister were usually in the living room watching TV or just sitting when the teacher arrived. Neither the mother or the child would get up when the teacher walked in; they just sat. When the teacher suggested that the session start the child would come very hesitantly. The mother would remain on the couch, saying nothing until teacher asked her if she would join too. She usually did, saying nothing. The teaching sessions were held at the kitchen table. The first few sessions, mother had a starched tablecloth on the table. After this teacher suggested this be removed to prevent it from getting soiled, it was never seen again. The table was always clear. Several times work that this child had done during the week was on the table. The teacher was never told about this, she just observed it there. When the teacher commented on the child's work, no response was made by either the mother or the child.

II. Development of Teacher's Personal Relationship with Family
  A. Mother

Mother was always very distant and very removed. The teacher could barely get any negative or positive response from her. She would only talk to the teacher if she was asked direct questions, and then she found answering difficult. She seemed to be immobile and completely disinterested in the teacher's presence. Several times the teacher would directly ask her how she felt about the home-teaching project and would receive a nod of the head or a response that could be barely heard. The teacher told her many times that if she had any questions about the program, to feel free to ask but nothing

470

came of this. She remained "stonelike" and did not attempt to relate to teacher in any way. Toward the end of the teaching sessions, the mother would smile just a little bit. She still did not talk very much but did not seem as rigid, a little more relaxed. At the last session she was able to say to the teacher, "You know I am a nervous person." Even when she said this to the teacher she had difficulty expressing herself and finding the proper words. This must have been quite an effort for her to reveal this to the teacher.

B. Child

The child responded to the teacher in much the same manner as the mother. He showed no visible emotions; never happy, never sad, just there. He would rarely talk to the teacher and would only respond when she insisted. As the beginning, he would remain on the couch, showing no recognition that teacher had appeared. After several sessions, the teacher noticed he ran to the door and opened it. He had a smile on his face, not a broad smile but a tight small one. When the teacher took this child to the park on a trip, the mother refused to go along. The teacher asked the child if he would like to go with her. He nodded affirmatively and went willingly to the car. On the way to the park, the teacher told him what there was in the park and that some children would be there. When the park was reached, he looked quite sad. The teacher asked what was the matter, but the child did not reply. After the teacher said that he looked sad, tears started to roll down his eyes, and he said in a low voice, "I want to go home." The teacher immediately took the child home and stressed idea of talking by saying, "If you tell me what you want, I can help you." At the end of each session the child seemed to perform the tasks required of him more easily. When the next sessions started he seemed to have regressed to his previous state of rigidity and non-performance. Whatever methods the teacher used to try to make this child respond seemed to fail. The teacher began to feel that this state of "inaction" may very well be a manipulative device to control teacher and to get what he wants. Therefore she confronted him with, "If you do what I want you to, then I will do what you want me to do." He refused to follow directions, so the teacher waited on a chair in the kitchen while he stood immobile in the living room. Teacher reinforced the idea that she would not proceed to the next activity unless he performed task required of him. When the child finally performed the task, the teacher immediately rewarded him by giving him material he liked, the toy cars. The following week, the session seemed to go much better. He could talk to the teacher with less resistance and seemed to better understand what the expectations were. After the last visit the teacher reminded the child that it was the last time she would be teaching him. He helped her to the car with her equipment. When he got to

471

the car he opened the door and sat down. He looked quite disappointed. Then he opened the car door and walked out. The teacher accompanied him back to the house and said good-bye.

III. Developmental Steps in Child's Educational Growth
A. Initial Appraisal of Child's Education Level

The teacher found it almost impossible to evaluate this child's educational strengths and weaknesses for a long period of time. He would often not perform tasks required of him and when he did participate getting him to perform just one task took almost an entire session. Therefore appraisal was done over an extended period of time. He could match colors, but not name them. He was able to match shapes but not name them. He was able to tell the difference between large and small objects and order nesting barrels by building them up from smallest to largest. He had no motoric difficulty as he could play ball, but with scissors, etc. His drawing of himself was quite small but detailed. Teacher could not get him to response to games which required naming. His drawings were quite representational. He could draw a truck, airplane, birds; and one drawing contained three figures. The teacher could not validly assess his ability to name objects since getting child to talk was so difficult.

B. Description of Stages to Current Level

At first child was so rigid and immobile that to get him to physically move from the living room to the kitchen took almost half the session. There were sessions with accomplishment and sessions that were devoted only to breaking down the barriers that prevented teaching from taking place. It varied from session to session and the teacher could not clearly assess whether or not growth was taking place. He did begin to name colors, not always naming them accurately. He was beginning to understand the properties of circle and naming objects that were round. He began to understand the meaning of words such as **near, next to, top, bottom, in,** and **out.** He could name some parts of his body toward the end of the program. Whether he could do this before, teacher really did not know, since he had initially refused to participate in activities of this sort. He was able to talk about some of his drawings in sentences. One drawing was of a tractor, and he said, "This is a tractor. It pulls up rocks." Toward the very end of the visits he could perform simple tasks for the teacher and move physically from area to area without cajoling. The teacher did not have to pull answers from him. He would respond more quickly. When sessions first began he responded to some materials by handling them over and over again. When given the color wheel, he twirled the

472

arrow round and round and could not use it in any other way. He opened and closed the brad attached to the arrow again and again. This fixed behavior seemed to stop about half way through the project.

C. Methods Employed to Develop Growth

Emphasis was placed on concrete, manipulating objects that would encourage the child to "loosen up" and talk, Since he was fond of trucks, these were used many times to stimulate dramatic play, naming of colors, and understanding function words such as *top, bottom, in, out, next to, between* and *in back of.* A garage was made by teacher and child out of a cardboard box to use with the toy vehicles. This enabled the teacher to get child to talk more freely and for child to see what specific properties a garage has, where they belong, (i.e., door, roof, walls) and what function a garage has. Other objects such as clothes pins, plastic shapes and blocks were used for matching and naming colors. Form blocks were also employed for sorting. Play dough was useful, successful media for gross discriminations of big and little. Eventually more structured activities were possible such as ordering colored tubes by height combined with manipulative activities such as reinforcing concept of "round" by rolling the tubes on the table. Paint and finger paints were used to introduce the child to aid color recognition. Since the teacher felt that child's concept of "self" was not developed, a life size drawing was made on heavy cardboard. Stories were read to encourage child to talk and name objects in the pictures. Towards the end of sessions teacher would withhold materials if he would not perform and reward him with special materials if he would. The first trip attempted was to a nearby park. Since the mother would not accompany the child, he became frightened and the trip was terminated. A second trip to a pet store with mother and child was more successful. At first in the store he stood stiffly in the middle of the room unable to talk or move. Eventually he could walk around the room, pointing rigidly at the animals. Finally he was able to pet a guinea pig and seemed to enjoy it. Mother hardly spoke a word on the entire trip even when the teacher repeatedly direct questions and comments to her.

IV. Observed Changes in Mother
  A. Understanding Educative Process

Teacher felt that there was little change in the mother's attitude toward the teaching sessions. However, when mother was asked to evaluate program her remark was "I thought the sessions were only for the child but now I know they were for me too." Teacher was quite surprised that mother could make this judgement and had not previously noticed this understanding.

473

B. Towards the Child

Teacher felt at times change was taking place and then it would be lost. For example when child first produced drawings the mother would stuff them in a closet. After talking with her about displaying the child's work, at the next sessions the drawings the child had done during the week were on the table. Once the mother said she had worked with him. For the next three or four sessions, however, there was no visible change in her interaction with her child. Then unexpectedly she said she had worked with the colored tubes the teacher had left. Her attitude toward her child was abrupt and distant and changed very little in this respect.

FINDINGS

Results

Mother Reaction. One of the basic reasons for having a preschool program in the homes was to actively involve the mother in her child's intellectual development. The actual accomplishment of this objective was evidenced by overwhelming participation of the mothers in the home visits, despite their initial reluctance. Table 2 gives the percent of possible home visits completed. It is important to note that almost 92% of the total possible visits were completed. Of those not completed, less than 3% were due to the teacher finding no one at home. This low percentage of appointments not kept by mothers indicated the general acceptance of the program and greatly encouraged the staff. The high morale of the teaching staff was evidenced by less than 1% of the cancelled visits resulting from teacher absence. The remaining 4% of the visits were cancelled because of mother or child illness, etc.

The completed home visits were of two types: (1) teaching sessions taking place in the home and (2) teaching sessions outside the home, such as experience trips and

TABLE 2

Home Teaching Attendance

Category	Number	Percent
Total possible home visits	329	100.0%
Completed home visits	301	91.6
Cancelled home visits	28	8.4
No one home	9	2.7
Teacher absent	2	.6
Child ill	10	3.0
Mother ill	3	.9
Miscellaneous	4	1.2

474

group mothers' meetings. Mothers working outside the home generally made arrangements for the teacher to come on their day off. When this was not possible, the mothers had some other member of the family present to work with the teacher and the child, usually the father or grandmother. The data in Table 3 show that only 4.3% of the visits took place without the mother being present.

TABLE 3

Mother Participation in Completed Home Visits
(N=35)

Category	Number	Percent
Total home visits completed	301	100%
With mother actively participating	288	95.7%
In the home	229	76.1%
Outside the home (Experience trips and group meetings	59	19.6%
Without mother participation	13	4.3%

TABLE 4

Reaction of Mothers to Program
(N=35)

Category	Number	Percent
Favorable Reaction	32	91.5%
Approves of one 90 minute visit per week for one semester.	14	40.0%
Desires more than one visit per week for one semester.	10	28.6
Prefers one visit per week for *more* than one semester.	8	22.9
Unfavorable Reaction	3	8.5
Too much time	2	5.7
Child should be away from home.	1	2.8

475

Table 4 documents the mothers' reaction to the general program style. These data are part of the information obtained in a final, structured interview with the mothers. Only three mothers expressed any unfavorable attitudes toward the project. Two of these were mothers with large families holding part-time jobs, and they felt the program "took too much time." However, these data are only indicative as they were collected by the teachers and therefore subject to considerable favorable response bias.

Intellectual Development Data. The primary area of critical concern in any preschool intervention project is the impact of the program upon intellectual development as measured by standardized tests. It is not enough that teachers and other participants report that they observed gains in the children. Systematic measures must also be obtained. For this project the Stanford-Binet Intelligence Scale and the Peabody Picture Vocabulary Test were selected as measures of intellectual ability. The Stanford-Binet was adopted as the best measure of intellectual ability available at this time, although it has been criticized as being unable to provide an accurate estimate of the functioning level of culturally disadvantaged children. As alternatives, non-verbal tests have been suggested as more culture fair. In a study of intelligence test data from the Perry Preschool Project, it was found that the Stanford-Binet Scale consistantly produced the highest IQ estimate when compared to results from the Illinois Test of Psycholinguistic Abilities, the Leiter International Performance Test, and the Peabody Picture Vocabulary Test (Weikart, 1967).

The Peabody Picture Vocabulary Test was selected as it seems to be very sensitive to immediate growth in language as measured by vocabulary extension. As language development is a critical area of concern in the education of the disadvantaged child, such a measure was deemed essential. In this project, where the teacher maintained limited direct contact with the child, it was assumed that the Peabody would give some estimate of the impact even though the time expended was miminal.

Table 5 presents the data for both of these instruments from the pretest and posttest assessments of the experimental and control groups. On the Stanford-Binet there are no significant differences between group means of experimental and control groups on either pretest or posttest measurements. However, there is a statistically significant difference in the growth rate of the two groups. The experimental group recorded a significantly greater mean change score than the control group. It may be concluded that the experimental intervention increased the intellectual development of the participating children when change on the Stanford-Binet is employed as a dependent variable.

On the Peabody, the experimental group also recorded greater gains than the control group. However, these gains are not statistically significant. It would seem that

476

TABLE 5

Comparison of Groups on Intelligence Scales

Scale	Experimental (N=35)	Control (N=29)	Difference	t-Test
Stanford-Binet				
Pretest, March 66	95.3	98.6	-3.3	-.839
Posttest, June 66	103.3	99.4	3.9	.902
Change score	8.2	.9	7.3	2.925**
Peabody				
Pretest, March 66	89.0	94.1	-5.1	-.762
Posttest, June 66	98.9	98.0	0.9	.141
Change score	9.9	4.0	4.9	1.242

**$p < .01$

while the home teaching sessions were sufficiently powerful to significantly affect general intellectual functioning, they were not able to significantly alter vocabulary growth patterns, given the short time involved.

While the two groups were matched initially for cultural deprivation rating and Stanford-Binet IQ, loss of six families* in the control group altered the initial Stanford-Binet mean for that group. The groups were not matched on the Peabody. To correct for these initial matching problems an analysis of covariance was run, and Table 6 presents these data. The analysis, taking into account the initial difference of the Stanford-Binet mean group scores, gives a statistically significant difference on retest mean scores. There is no significant difference on Peabody Picture Vocabulary Test. Thus, on the Stanford-Binet the experimental group obtained both a significant mean gain score and a significantly higher adjusted mean score than the control group.

Relationship with the Environment. It is generally accepted that various environmental factors and processes greatly influence the expression of intellectual ability. Tables 7 and 8 present the correlation of selected family and developmental variables with pretest and posttest assessment of the two intelligence test measures used in the program. The data in Table 7 indicate the general pattern of correlation to be found in a test-retest situation with no intermediate intervention. The general pattern described is for most variables to increase in relationship to the intellectual measures upon retesting. While only seven correlations were significantly different from

*One family moved, one family was dropped because the child was found to be too young and four families had incomplete pre or post data.

477

TABLE 6

Analysis of Co-variance of the Groups on the Intellectual Scales

Test and Group	Actual Mean	Adjusted Mean	F Ratio
Stanford-Binet Intelligence Scale			
Experimental	103.3	104.5	6.90**
Control	99.4	97.8	
Peabody Picture Vocabulary Test			
Experimental	98.9	100.9	1.18
Control	98.3	95.9	

$**p < .01$

TABLE 7

Correlation of Family History Data and Intellectual Development

Control Sample

Variable	N	Pretest S-B	Posttest S-B	Pretest PPVT	Posttest PPVT
Education of mother, years	29	.30	.16	.23	.39*
Education of father, years	28	.21	.36*	.08	.22
Cultural deprivation rating, low to high	29	.28	.43*	.18	.36*
Number of children home	29	-.39*	-.37*	-.38*	-.42
Number of younger children	17	-.48*	-.35	.01	-.11
Number of older children	23	-.47*	-.63**	-.41	-.42*
Labor severity, easy to hard	26	-.12	-.21	-.03	.01
Labor length, short to long	26	-.26	-.29	-.21	-.07
Birth weight, ounces	28	-.34	-.48**	-.31	-.43*
Age walking, months	27	.13	.40*	.27	.38*
Age talking, months	25	.08	.30	.46*	.49**
Age first tooth, months	22	.53**	.21	.27	.38
Age of toilet training, slow to fast	26	.22	.03	.02	-.15

$*\quad p < .05$
$**\ p < .01$

zero upon initial testings, 13 reach that level upon final testing. In all, 19 correlations show an increase in relationship with the two intellectual measures at retest while only seven show a decrease. Most of the correlations are in the expected direction. For example, the higher the cultural rating of the family the higher the child's measured intellectual level, and the more older children in the home the lower the measured intellectual level. However, the correlations with developmental indices such as age talking, walking and first tooth are not as expected. Also, birthweight is negatively correlated with IQ. This significant correlation is contrary to that reported by such researchers as Pasamanich and Knoblock (1961). These correlations would seem to be artifacts of the sample as these correlations do not appear in the experimental sample drawn from the same population (see Table 8).

Two important points may be made from Table 7. The first is that general environmental determiners and indicators of intellectual growth and development such as level of parent education, number of children, birth conditions, etc. hold true for this sample of a culturally deprived population. Second is that while the mean intellectual level of the group can be determined by a single initial test, a second testing for the group gives substantially better ratings for individuals in the group. Table 5 reports only a 0.9 IQ point gain for this control group upon retest after a 12 week period. This finding of stability in group means on the Stanford-Binet has been reported by Goldstein (1965) and Strodtbeck (1963). However, Table 7 indicates a far stronger relationship with the second testing than the first to important environmental determiners. It would seem that research studies involving other than group means can not depend upon an initial testing to give adequate indication of individual performance. While the difficulty of accurately assessing the intellectual abilities of culturally disadvantaged children has been widely acknowledged, it would appear that this problem can be partly solved by retesting after a relatively short period of time. When taken as a group, the mean performance level is not increased but the test experience or rehearsal allows more accurate individual scores.

Table 8 presents the same environmental variables in relation to the intellectual functioning of the experimental group. Using initial testing scores only, two correlations are significantly different from zero for this group. Upon retesting, the same two are still significantly related. The general pattern is one of decreased correlation with environmental variables after the intervention of the home teaching program. Of the 26 relationships involved, 19 decrease, two do not change, and five increase. The contrast with the control group is striking as the experimental group reverses the pattern of the control group. It would seem from these data that the home teaching program has the effect of "freeing" the culturally disadvantaged child from the environmental determiners of intellectual growth.

With the need to develop action programs to counter the effects of deprivation on

479

TABLE 8

**Correlation of
Family History Data and Intellectual Development**

Experimental Sample

Variables	N	Initial S-B	Retest S-B	Initial PPVT	Retest PPVT
Education of mother, years	35	.27	.09	.25	.22
Education of father, years	31	.33	.29	.37*	.43*
Cultural deprivation rating, low to high	35	.25	.18	.23	.21
Number of children home	35	-.23	-.19	-.37*	-.32*
Number of younger children	23	.22	.19	.32	.03
Number of older children	25	-.16	-.13	-.32	-.21
Labor severity, easy to hard	35	-.17	-.26	-.30	-.23
Labor length, short to long	35	-.18	-.24	-.21	-.09
Birth weight, ounces	35	.04	.00	-.07	.03
Age walking, month	32	-.13	-.00	.03	-.11
Age talking, month	31	-.19	-.19	-.14	-.14
Age first tooth, month	28	-.26	-.15	-.09	-.11
Age of toilet training, slow to fast	34	.21	.16	.10	.09

*$p < .05$

cognitive growth, increased attention has been given to the assessment of environmental processes which, it is hypothesized, either stimulate or support intellectual growth. Wolf (1964) and Dave (1963) developed an environmental process scale for use with middle class families. Wolf identified three key areas 1) press for achievement motivation, 2) press for language development and 3) provision for general learning. He reports a multiple correlation of .76 between the environmental process scale ratings and the child's IQ. Other researchers are working with this approach. Caldwell and Honig at the University of Syracuse have developed a scale called the Inventory of Home Stimulation. Researchers at George Peabody College have been exploring possible uses of Wolf and Dave Scale. Little information on these initial attempts is yet available other than they are showing promise.

The Home Teaching Project, working from the initial Wolf and Dave scale, evolved the Cognitive Home Environment Scale (Weikart and Radin revision) for use with lower class families. While the data are very tentative, and the scale is still undergoing extensive revision, some initial findings are presented.

480

A 25 item scale was constructed of greatly modified Wolf and Dave items. Based on a sample of 157 families from the Perry Preschool Project and The Home Teaching Project, five factors were identified.

Factor I   Availability and use of educational materials in the home
Factor II   Expectation of child's educational attainment
Factor III Educational materials specifically provided for child
Factor IV   Concern for educational activities
Factor V   Educational effort by parent

Factor II, **Expectation of Education Attainment,** proved to be significantly related to initial and final IQ's for the control group and to the final Stanford-Binet IQ scores for the experimental group. The data are confounded by the collection procedure which employed the home visit teachers in obtaining the experimental sample information during the first two or three visits. There is strong suggestion that the mothers altered their responses to conform with what they felt the teacher might desire. Thus the experimental group data are regarded as biased. The control group data present a clearer picture. As with the other environmental measures reported, the cognitive scale factor score relationship with IQ increases upon retesting. Of the ten possible correlation comparisons that the five factors present with the initial and retest Stanford-Binet and Peabody tests, eight increase upon retesting. While the Cognitive Home Environment Scale is an initial instrument, it offers promise of an effective way of determining cognitive practices in lower class homes.

Home Teaching Program variables. In order to determine what aspect of the home teaching program provided the impetus for growth in the child, the teachers maintained detailed records of the home visits. These records included information about the conditions in the home affecting the visit, who participated, the material used in the session, and teacher observations of the mother and her response to the program. Tables 9, 10, and 11 give these findings.

Table 9 presents some of the data from these records on home teaching conditions and mother participation. The very low correlations of these variables with posttest intelligence and change scores from the IQ test results are stark documentation of the lack of relationship between parent participation and IQ level and IQ change in a short term 12 week program. In fact, the tendency is for variables such as total minutes of teaching, mother participation and evidence of implementation of preschool program goals between teaching sessions to relate negatively to the Stanford-Binet and Peabody change scores. The only significant correlation is a positive one between mean number of children present during the teaching session and change on the Stanford-Binet. This finding is parallel to that reported by Radin and Weikart (1967) in some preliminary data from the Perry Preschool Project.

481

There is a suggestion in Table 9 that the children of less "cooperative" and "positive" mothers benefited from the program more than those who were from homes regarded as "cooperative." In short, children from homes where the mothers participated less, tended not to apply suggestions from the teaching sessions, experienced shorter teaching sessions, etc., had greater gains in IQ than children whose mothers were more cooperative. In order to explore this trend further, an analysis of ratings of the mother completed by the teacher after each visit is presented.

Table 10 gives the results of the teacher appraisal of the mother based on an average of nine visits to each home. The instrument employed was styled after the Osgood semantic differential model. The teacher rated the mother on a one to seven scale for each of 16 adjective pairs which are listed in the table. For each adjective pair, a total score was obtained from all teacher ratings of the mother, and then a mean score was computed based on the number of visits actually completed with the mother present.

The correlations of the rating scale items and the pretest Stanford-Binet are in the expected direction. Mothers who are seen by teacher as being *deep, going some-*

TABLE 9

Correlation of
Home Teaching Variables and Intellectual Growth

Variable	Posttest S-B	Change S-B	Posttest PPVT	Change PPVT
Total number of visits to home	.06	.11	.07	.09
Total minutes teaching spent with family	.08	-.03	.02	.06
Mean minutes per visit	.09	-.28	-.06	-.03
Total minutes of mother participation when present	-.04	-.19	-.16	-.18
Mean minutes of mother participation when present	-.02	-.12	-.23	-.29
Mean number of children present per visit	-.09	.38*	-.22	.24
Percent of total time other children participated	-.14	-.03	-.05	.19
Mean number of visits observed implementation between visits	.00	-.10	-.16	-.17

$*p < .05$

482

TABLE 10

**Correlation of Adjective Scale Rating
of Mother and Intellectual Growth**

Variables	Initial S-B	Retest S-B	Change S-B	Initial PPVT	Retest PPVT	Change PPVT
bad-good	.32	.10	-.38*	.00	.12	.15
erratic-steady	.25	.07	-.34*	.02	.04	.03
shallow-deep	.45**	.22	-.37*	.18	.18	-.03
hard-soft	.20	.01	-.34*	.00	.11	.14
dead-alive	.26	.16	-.16	.07	.12	.04
aimless-going	.34*	.26	-.11	.20	.09	-.17
tight-loose	.02	.00	-.10	.01	.21	.27
uncooperative-cooperative	.21	.05	-.31	-.01	.06	.09
insensitive-sensitive	.36*	.13	-.38*	.13	.12	-.04
stale-fresh	.35*	.16	-.33*	.09	.13	.03
cool-warm	.19	.09	-.17	.03	.05	.02
closed-open	.26	.18	-.12	.13	.12	-.04
dry-wet	-.13	-.15	-.03	-.18	-.22	-.02
cloudy-sunny	.30	.10	-.37*	.01	.15	.17
apart-together	.37*	.23	-.22	.13	.22	.08
passive-active	.18	.14	-.03	.12	-.04	-.21

[a]Scale was from 1 to 7, e.g., bad, erratic = 1 and good, steady = 7. Eleven dimensions have been reversed to facilitate reading of table. Table 15 gives the original format.

* $p < .05$
** $p < .01$

where, sensitive, fresh, and together have children with higher IQ's. Those items which do not reach statistical significance are uniformly in the expected direction. The impact of the program is shown in the rating scale correlations and the posttest Stanford-Binet scores. There are no correlations significantly different from zero and, while the same "good mother" relationship exists, every correlation has been reduced. The correlation pattern of the rating scale with the Stanford-Binet change scores is an unexpected finding. These correlations seem to indicate that children of mothers who are least open to home teaching intervention as indicated by "poor mother" ratings by teachers are, in fact, the youngsters who benefit most from the program. High IQ gain is significantly associated with children whose mothers are rated by teachers as being bad, erratic, shallow, hard, insensitive, stale, and cloudy. On all adjective pairs, high IQ change is associated with qualities in mothers that teachers regard as "poor." This finding is consistent with data in table 9.

483

The Peabody Picture Vocabulary Test data are presented in the right side of the table. As will be recalled from Table 5, the Peabody change did not discriminate between the control and experimental groups. This finding is not unexpected in that the teachers maintained a contact for only an hour and a half each week, hardly enough time to teach language to the extent necessary to improve the performance on the Peabody. The pattern of correlations is only suggestive. In all but five ratings the correlations increase upon the retest and the change score correlations are in the opposite direction from that found on the Stanford-Binet change score correlations on all but six items. It maybe that children of "good" mothers were better prepared to absorb the language stimulation. Or, it is suggested that "good mothers" profited from the home teaching experience and were able to carry it over into language development. In short, mothers rated as "good" had brighter children to begin with and they utilized the contact with the teaching program to improve their own skills which are in turn reflected in language development on the part of their children. Those mothers rated "bad" by the teachers were unable to exploit their opportunity as much as the "good" mothers but their children profited from the opportunity for general cognitive stimulation as is shown by the consistent change pattern on the Stanford-Binet Scale.

The teachers were asked to rate the nature of the mothers' participation in the preschool home teaching sessions. These ratings were done after each visit and the teacher attempted to identify salient features of the mothers' behavior. Table 11 presents these data. It may be assumed that these behaviors represent traditional or habitual modes of behavior by the mother. As the program was too short to obtain change scores, the ratings are used as total scores adjusted for number of ratings. Again, all the relationships are in the expected direction with the mothers more attentive to their children having brighter children. While the over all results are slight, the correlations both before and after intervention between IQ and the extent of mother attention and positive reinforcement given to the child are the largest. The findings from work with the mother-child interaction tests such as Hess and Shipman (1966) and Wiegerink and Weikart (1967) suggest that these areas are essential for adequate cognitive growth. In these tests, the successful mother employs positive reinforcement as a preferred teaching tool. On the ratings in Table 11, no change scores are significantly correlated with the nature of mother's participation.

High and Low IQ Change Children. In order to explore the possibility that certain intervention procedures or environmental determiners are critical of IQ change, a sample of high and low gainers on the Stanford-Binet was drawn from the experimental group. The 12 highest gainers (mean gain 18.2) were compared with the 13 lowest gainers (mean gain 0.2). These data were analyzed to compare the significance of difference in mean scores on important variables. Tables 12 through 15

484

TABLE 11

Correlation of
Nature of Mother's Participation and Intellectual Development

Variable[a]	Pretest S-B	Posttest S-B	Change S-B	Pretest PPVT	Posttest PPVT	Change PPVT
Controlled preschool child	.08	.12	.09	.19	-.01	-.28
Gave attention to preschool child's activity	.25	.25	.06	.18	.07	-.17
Gave positive reinforcement	.27	.26	.04	.33*	.14	-.30
Stimulated preschool child to respond	.11	.07	-.03	.04	-.06	.13
Paralleled preschool child's activity on peer level	.05	-.02	-.13	.08	-.05	-.18
Modeled teacher's role	.14	.12	.01	.09	.00	-.13

a the scale was from 1 = often to 4 = never, signs are reversed.

* $p < .05$

give these results. Table 12 presents the information as it relates to intellectual test data. As would be expected, the two sub-groups differ significantly on mean change scores. Important, however, is the verification of the relationship suggested by the correlations of Stanford-Binet IQ with adjective ratings of mothers by the teachers given in Table 10. The finding was that "poor" mothers had children with greater Stanford-Binet, IQ change although their initial IQ's are lower than children of "good" mothers. The high change sub-group mean Stanford-Binet IQ is initially (but not significantly) below that of the low change sub-group. At the final testing the high change sub-group is as much above the low change sub-group as they were below initially. Change scores obtained on the Peabody do not follow the pattern established by change scores on the Stanford-Binet. The low gainers on the Stanford-Binet have slightly greater change scores on the Peabody than do the high gainers. The independence of Peabody change scores from Stanford-Binet change scores was seen in tables 9 and 10. The small sample as well as its *post hoc* nature limit the value of the table.

Table 13 presents the comparison of the two sub-groups on several environmental variables selected for study. While there are no significant differences between the two subgroups, the tendency again is for the high gainers to be "worse off" environmentally. For example, their mothers and fathers had less education; they had lighter birthweights; and they walked, talked, and obtained their first tooth later than

485

TABLE 12

Gain Differences in Intellectual Development by Change Groups

Test	High Gainers Mean (N-12)	Low Gainers Mean (N-13)	t-Test
Stanford-Binet Intelligence Scale			
Pretest, March 66	93.9	101.5	-1.107
Posttest, June 66	111.9	101.7	1.480
Change score	18.0	.2	8.631**
Peabody Picture Vocabulary Test			
Pretest, March 66	93.2	89.6	.312
Posttest, June 66	104.3	103.4	.099
Change score	11.2	13.8	- .337

**$p < .01$

TABLE 13

Differences in Environmental Variables by Change Groups

Environmental Variable	High Gainers (N-12)	Low Gainers (N-13)	t-Test
Pre-test CA, in months	57.7	56.7	.728
Cultural deprivation rating	9.2	9.1	.219
Education of mother, years	10.2	10.7	- .685
Education of father, years	8.6	9.2	- .569
Number of children home	3.6	3.4	- .313
Number of younger children	1.2	1.7	-1.416
Number of older children	2.1	1.8	.508
Number of persons in home	5.7	5.7	- .029
Labor severity, easy to hard	1.8	1.8	- .046
Labor length, short to long	1.7	1.8	- .060
Birthweight, ounces	119.8	129.1	- .033
Age of walking, months	12.2	11.2	1.139
Age of talking, months	14.1	13.2	.478
Age of first tooth, months	8.1	6.8	1.216
Age of toilet trained, years	1.9	2.0	- .561

486

did low gainers. They also tended to come from larger families and tended to be the younger children of the family rather than the older. High gainers, in other words, tend to come from situations more suggestive of poor development potential than do the low gainers. These data are congruent with the lower mean Stanford-Binet scores for the high gainers reported in Table 12.

Table 14 presents information from teacher ratings of the home teaching conditions and other program variables. None of the mean program variable scores is significant-

TABLE 14

Gain Group Differences on Program Variables

Program Variables	High Gainers	Low Gainers	t-Test
Number of home visits	9.1	8.8	.365
Total number of visit minutes	780.0	794.2	- .241
Mean number of minutes per visit	85.4	89.4	-1.606
Total minutes mother participated	599.1	703.5	-1.097
Mean number of minutes mother participated	74.6	80.8	- .747
Percent of time other children participated	11.1	11.1	.001
Number of times teacher observed implementation	3.8	4.2	- .445
Mother control child[a]	2.3	2.3	- .133
Mother pays attention to child[a]	1.4	1.5	- .196
Mother gives positive reinforcement to child[a]	2.5	2.4	.430
Mother stimulated child[a]	2.2	2.1	.329
Mother enters activity on peer level[a]	2.3	2.2	.535
Mother models teacher role[a]	2.3	2.2	.261
Mother ready for visit[b]	1.6	1.6	- .008
Mother prepared place to work[b]	1.5	1.2	1.193
Mother did other activities[b]	2.8	3.1	- .831
Mother asked questions about session[b]	2.2	1.8	1.050
Mother raised personal problems[b]	2.8	2.6	.471

a Scale is 1 = often to 4 = never. Teachers rated the mother after each visit and the mean of these rating is presented.

b Scale is 1 = often to 4 = never. The teachers made a single summary rating upon the completion of the home teaching project.

ly different for the two groups. As is suggested throughout the evidence presented, the high gainers had mothers who were less involved in the program than mothers of low gainers. For example, while the total number of minutes the teacher provided the family was almost identical for the two subgroups, the total number of minutes the mother participated in the teaching session was less for the high gainers than for the low gainers. She also seemed to pay less attention to the child and to afford him less positive reinforcement. In an overall rating by the teacher of the home visit the mother of the high gainers less often prepared a place to work, she more frequently chose to do other activities in the house rather than working with the teacher and the child, and she less often asked questions about the teaching sessions. She also less often raised personal problems with the teacher, suggesting the reserve between the teacher and the mother. The tendency of high gainers to have "poor" mothers in terms of the program and its goals is a constant one across all variables.

Table 15 gives the data relating to the teacher's systematic rating of the mother on the basis of each visit. As was suggested by the correlation table on IQ change and

TABLE 15

Gain Group Differences on Adjective Ratings

Adjectives[a]	High Gainers	Low Gainers	t-Test
Good-bad	3.2	2.3	1.910
Steady-erratic	3.0	2.8	.578
Shallow-deep	4.1	4.9	-1.500
Hard-soft	4.2	5.4	-2.399*
Alive-dead	3.4	3.0	.898
Going-aimless	3.1	3.0	.134
Loose-tight	3.8	3.3	.898
Cooperative-uncooperative	2.7	2.1	1.491
Sensitive-insensitive	3.6	2.8	2.147*
Stale-fresh	4.3	5.0	-1.403
Warm-cool	2.9	2.3	1.311
Open-closed	2.9	2.3	1.181
Wet-dry	4.0	3.8	.576
Sunny-cloudy	3.4	2.8	1.411
Together-apart	3.3	2.9	1.135
Passive-active	4.6	4.8	- .380

[a] Scale was from 1 to 7, e.g., good, steady = 1 and bad, erratic = 7.

*$p < .05$

488

the adjective ratings, the "poor" mother has the child with the greatest change. For example, while only two statistically significant differences between the two groups were found by the teachers, teachers rated mothers of high gain children uniformly as bad, hard, uncooperative, insensitive, etc., more often than mothers of low gainers. All of the adjective comparisons uniformly support these observations although the differences do not reach statistical significance on most individual items.

Sex Differences. The data were analyzed for sex differences on most variables. In general, there were no significant differences in environmental variables except girls tended to have significantly more younger siblings than boys ($p < .05$). Table 16 presents the data on intellectual development. On initial Stanford-Binet Scale scores, the girls scored significantly higher than the boys, primarily due to scores of the girls in the control group. This suggests that boys are more vulnerable to the impact of deprivation than girls. Upon retesting, the final group mean scores are not significantly different, primarily because of the rapid growth of the boys in the experimental group. On the Peabody Picture Vocabulary Test the boys score higher than the girls initially, however, the difference is not significant. Upon retesting, the girls in both experimental and control groups gained at a more rapid rate than their male counterparts so that the final Peabody scores are almost identical.

Race Differences. As with sex differences, few significant differences are found on environmental variables. Negro mothers report their labor during child birth was of greater severity ($p < .05$). Also, the cultural deprivation rating was lower for Negroes than for Caucasian families participating in the study ($p < .05$). Both are indices of low intellectual development.

The major race differences are in measured intellectual development and in reported child behavior; as with environmental variables, few significant differences were found. Table 17 presents the data on intellectual development. At the time of initial testing, the Negro group obtained lower Stanford-Binet and Peabody IQ scores than did the Caucasian group. Both Negro and Caucasian experimental subgroups gained as a result of the preschool intervention and the difference in the amount of the gains is not statistically significant. On the Stanford-Binet, the initial mean scores show relatively little difference between the total Negro and Caucasian groups though the Negro group points lower. Upon retesting, which is hypothesized to give a better estimate of actual functioning level, the control group reflects a statistically significant difference between the two races (Caucasian 104.2 and Negro 95.9). It is important to note that the experimental Negro subgroup profits from the program sufficiently to maintain the close relationship with the experimental Caucasian subgroup (Caucasian group 104.4 and Negro 100.1). All subgroups do somewhat poorer on the Peabody initially than on the Stanford-Binet. The Negro subgroups, however, are as much as 13 points lower than their obtained Stanford-Binet IQ scores. While

489

TABLE 16

Mean Sex Differences in Intellectual Development

Test and Group	Boys[a]	Girls[b]	t-Test
Stanford-Binet			
Initial testing			
Experimental	91.5	98.8	-1.276
Control	95.8	105.7	-1.800
Total	93.9	101.0	-1.802*
Final Testing			
Experimental	102.3	104.4	- .301
Control	96.8	106.4	-1.634
Change			
Experimental	10.8	5.7	1.678
Control	.9	.6	.070
Peabody Picture Test			
Initial Testing			
Experimental	91.9	86.2	.611
Control	94.3	93.6	.061
Total	93.2	88.5	.699
Final Testing			
Experimental	100.6	97.3	.405
Control	96.9	100.9	- .317
Change			
Experimental	8.7	11.2	- .359
Control	2.6	8.1	- .696

[a]Experimental boys = 17; Control boys = 21; Total = 38.
[b]Experimental girls = 18; Control girls = 8; Total = 26.

*$p < .05$

both Caucasian and Negro subgroups profit from the experimental program, it is the Negro subgroup which records the greatest gains, 13.1 points, on the Peabody. It would seem from inspection of the change scores that the mean intelligence level of the Negro sample as a whole is underestimated on initial Peabody Picture Vocabulary Test and overestimated on initial Stanford-Binet Intelligence Scale scores. Limited sample size precludes further analysis of such subgroups as Negro males, etc.

490

TABLE 17

Mean Race Difference in Intellectual Development

Test and Group	Caucasian[a]	Negro[b]	t-Test
Stanford-Binet			
Initial Testing			
Experimental	95.5	94.7	.124
Control	101.5	94.4	1.396
Total	97.9	94.5	.806
Final Testing			
Experimental	104.4	100.1	.585
Control	104.1	92.8	2.200*
Change			
Experimental	8.9	6.1	.751
Control	2.6	- 1.6	1.122
Peabody Picture Test			
Initial Testing			
Experimental	91.6	81.4	.945
Control	101.3	83.8	1.886*
Total	95.4	82.8	1.807*
Final Testing			
Experimental	100.5	94.5	.634
Control	103.6	90.1	1.217
Change			
Experimental	8.9	13.1	- .549
Control	2.4	6.2	- .544

[a]Experimental Caucasians = 26; Control Caucasians = 17; Total = 43
[b]Experimental Negroes = 9; Control Negroes = 12; Total = 21.

*$p < .05$

Table 18 presents information on the mothers' rating of her child on a variety of areas relating to how she perceives his behavior. The data were collected during the initial project interview. The striking observation based upon the table is the systematic and consistent tendency for the Negro mother to regard her child less favor-

491

TABLE 18

Race Difference in Reported Child Behavior

Behavior[a]	Caucasian N=43	Negro N=21	t=Test
Difficulties in relationships with siblings and peers.			
Fights	2.5	2.3	1.152
Argues	2.4	2.0	1.593
Complains of playmates	3.4	2.8	2.420*
Fears playmates	3.9	3.4	2.717
Shunned by playmates	3.5	3.2	.909
Difficulties in relationships with parents			
Disobedient	2.6	2.4	.780
Irresponsible	3.0	2.3	2.879*
Wants adult help	2.4	2.3	.323
Does things by self	1.4	1.4	.230
Play Activities			
Plays alone	2.8	2.7	.535
Plays with others	2.3	2.3·	- .158
Uses imagination in play	1.9	2.1	-1.098
Active play	1.7	1.7	- .232
Inactive play	3.2	3.2	- .345

[a] Scale: 1=often to 4=never.

*$p < .05$

ably than the Caucasian mother. For example, the Negro mother significantly more often than the Caucasian mother states that her child complains about playmates, fears playmates and is irresponsible. There is a tendency for the Negro child more often to fight, argue, be shunned by playmates, be disobedient, want help from adults, play alone, and to fail to use imagination in play activities. Considering the general tendency of the social desirability set that Negro lower class mothers frequently assume, it is amazing that these mothers chose to portray their youngsters in so inadequate a light.

Mother Attitudes toward Education. The Weikart Educational Attitudes Test (1966a) was employed to assess the attitude of the mothers toward education. The semi-

492

structured projective test presents a series of projective style educational situation pictures with incomplete sentences to be completed by the mother. An analysis of covariance was done to account for initial differences in control and experimental mothers. Of the eight areas assessed by the test one attitude area changed significantly as a result of the intervention program. The difference was found on Factor VI, **Parent Image Attributed to Teacher.** The mother in the home teaching experimental group attributed favorable attitudes towards mother to teachers significantly more often than did mothers of control children (F Ratio= 10.23, $p. < .01$). There was no difference in this area at the start of this program between control and experimental group parents.

CONCLUSIONS

This preschool project was designed to explore the feasibility of home teaching as a method of preschool intervention in the cognitive development of disadvantaged children. Three questions were studied to determine feasibility. 1) Would the mothers accept a training program for themselves and a tutoring program for their children without school classroom attendance? 2) Would teachers accept the problems and conditions associated with working in the homes? 3) Could the program significantly alter the cognitive growth of participating children?

Reaction of Mothers. Based on the available data, there is little doubt that the mothers who participated in the project accepted home teaching with enthusiasm. Of course, there were wide differences in the individual feelings expressed by mothers. But in terms of permitting teaching to take place and of participating directly in the teaching session, mothers in this project were overwhelmingly cooperative. These mothers had a strong desire for their children to do well and, although a mother may have been totally ignorant of the correct steps to produce educational growth in her child, she was willing to learn.

Reaction of Teachers. Public school teachers who participated in the project demonstrated unusually high morale and consistently expressed interest in continuing work in the homes. While all teachers found wide variation in the mothers and children they were serving as far as extent of cooperation, acceptance, etc. were concerned, strong teacher cooperation in implementing home teaching projects in small northern communities may be expected.

Cognitive Growth. It is clear from the data presented in the paper that two things happened to youngsters participating in the project. First, there was significant increase in general intellectual ability (when compared to a control group) within the 15 hours of tutoring the project provided. This rapid increase in functional IQ is a frequent finding in structured preschool classroom program (Weikart, 1967). Se-

493

cond, there was a reduction in the relationship between environmental variables generally accepted as predictors of intellectual functioning, such as education of mother, number of children in family, etc., and measured IQ. During the same period, the relationship between these variables and IQ greatly increased for the control group. It may be concluded that the home teaching program had significant positive impact upon the general intellectual growth of the child independent of environmental conditions.

The data were also analyzed for race and sex differences, with few significant differences recorded. The small sample size in several subgroups limited meaningful analysis of this particular sample.

Two additional findings are of importance from the project. First is evidence related to the conditions that support cognitive development in a disadvantaged population. Second in data regarding the identification of disadvantaged children who will respond to short term cognitive training programs.

Conditions Supporting Cognitive Development. A review of Tables 7 and 8 which present general correlations of environmental variables with the Stanford-Binet demonstrates the well known relationship between parent education, number of children in family, birth order, etc. and level of cognitive development. Surprisingly, it is the teacher ratings of the mother along a general "good-bad" dimension that defines cognitive development more significantly. Mothers who are seen over a 12 week period as being "deep, going somewhere, sensitive, fresh, and together:" have children who are brighter than mothers who are rated as having less of these qualities. The data are consistent for all ratings. These ratings by teachers are related directly to the mothers' general warmth and willingness to maintain verbal communication (not defined as verbal ability). This finding that "good" mothers have brighter children is congruent with the data from tests of mother teaching style reported by Hess and Shipman (1966) and Wiegerink and Weikart (1967). More effective mothers are those who give positive verbal reinforcement for the child's learning behavior. The finding also gives meaning as to why number of children and birth order so dramatically affect cognitive development. The more children the mother has to care for, given the extensive and realistic pressures of lower class problems of daily existence, the less she can spread what general warmth and communication she has among the children. Thus each younger child gets proportionately less during a key period of cognitive development. It must be noted that the correlations, while consistent, are not large and are only appropriate for use in a general way.

Children Responding to Program. Perhaps equally critical is the finding of which children change as a result of the program's intervention. The ones who change are clearly those children whose mothers are rated by teachers as "hard, in-sensitive,

494

etc." and give evidence of being somewhat resistant to the program. Schaefer (1967) noted, "The lower the initial social-economic status of children or the greater the initial deprivation, the greater the increase in mental test scores in response to a specified level of intellectual stimulation." The contribution that this project makes to this position is that it is not social-economic status that determines cognitive deprivation but lack of warmth and verbal communication by the mother. When this ingredient is supplied by an outside tutor through a structured preschool program, the child demonstrates improved performance on tests of cognitive ability.

An important question is why did the children of mothers who had "good" ratings not show as much improvement as children of mothers rated "bad." Are these data supportive of a position that IQ has an upper limit? Basically it would seem that the program was too short to offer the children of warm and verbal communicative mothers much stimulation. Even though the program was individually designed for each child, the discrepancy between what the teacher offered and what the child had already been offered in the home was not great enough to induce rapid IQ growth. For those children from more disadvantaged families, as defined in this study, the discrepancy was great enough to induce rapid growth. Replication of this project should aid in clarifying this question.

The home teaching project presented in this paper represents an attempt to explore a style of preschool intervention that is considerably different from the traditional nursery school programs. The introduction of the mother as a major partner in the education of the young child for school is a unique aspect of the project. Working in the homes of disadvantaged children by certified teachers offers new potential for education to realize its responsibilities. The focus upon the mother-child relationship, gives a basis for the development of training programs. The feasibility of this style of intervention has now been demonstrated. It is important to concentrate upon its further development as a useful tool in the remediation of the education problems faced by this disadvantaged child.

The research reported herein was supported by Section 4 funds of the 1966 State Aid Act of the State Board of Education, State of Michigan and the Ypsilanti Board of Education. An extensive replication of the project is planned for the spring of 1967 funded by the State of Michigan Board of Education and the Ypsilanti Board of Education. Special appreciation is extended to Mr. Benjamin Hamilton of the State Department of Education for his extensive support and assistance. For their professional pioneering, the teachers who worked in the study, Mrs. Judy Borenzweig, Mrs. Patricia Moss, Mrs. Linda Rogers, and Mrs. Gail Wilkins deserve recognition for their excellent service.

References

Almy, M. New views on intellectual development: a renaissance for early education. Unpublished manuscript. May, 1963.

Bennett, E. L., Diamond, M. C., Krech, D., & Rosenzweig, M. R. Chemical and anatomical plasticity of the brain. SCIENCE, 146: 610-610, 1964.

Bereiter, C., & Englemann, S. LANGUAGE LEARNING ACTIVITIES FOR THE DISADVANTAGED CHILD. New York: Anti-Defamation League of B'nai B'rith, 1966.

Blatt, B., & Garfunkel, F. A FIELD DEMONSTRATION OF THE EFFECTS OF NONAUTOMATED RESPONSIVE ENVIRONMENTS ON THE INTELLECTUAL AND SOCIAL COMPETENCE OF EDUCABLE MENTALLY RETARDED CHILDREN. Boston: Boston University, 1965.

Bloom, B. S. STABILITY AND CHANGE IN HUMAN CHARACTERISTICS. New York: John Wiley and Sons, 1964.

Braun, S. J. Nursery education for disadvantaged children: an historical review. Community Research and Services Branch, National Institute of Mental Health. Unpublished manuscript. 1964.

Brittain, C. V. Some early findings of research on preschool programs for culturally deprived children. CHILDREN, 13, 4: 130-134, 1966.

Bruner, J. S. TOWARD A THEORY OF INSTRUCTION. Cambridge, Mass.: Harvard University Press, 1966.

Caldwell, B. M., *et al.* A day-care program for disadvantaged infants and young children--observations after one year. Paper read at the Annual Meeting of the American Pediatric Society, 1966.

Cazden, B. Some implications of research on language development for preschool education. Paper read at the Social Science Research Council Conference on Preschool Education. University of Chicago, 1966.

Colwell, R. (Ed.) Tutorial services with infants. ALUMNI BULLETIN, University of Illinois, College of Education, June, 1966.

Connor, F. P., & Talbot, M. E. AN EXPERIMENTAL CURRICULUM FOR

496

YOUNG MENTALLY RETARDED CHILDREN. New York: Bureau of Publications, Teachers College, Columbia University, 1964.

Dave, R. H. The identification and measurement of environmental process variables that are related to educational achievement. Unpublished doctoral dissertation, University of Chicago, 1963.

Deutsch, M. INSTITUTE FOR DEVELOPMENTAL STUDIES: ANNUAL REPORT 1965. New York: New York Medical College, 1965.

Fouracer, M. S., Connor, F. P. & Goldberg, I. I. THE EFFECTS OF A PRESCHOOL PROGRAM UPON YOUNG EDUCABLE MENTALLY RETARDED CHILDREN. VOL. II, THE EXPERIMENTAL PRESCHOOL CURRICULUM. New York: Department of Special Education, Teachers College, Columbia University, 1962.

Fowler, W. Longitudinal study of early stimulation in the emergence of cognitive processes. Paper read at Social Science Research Council Conference on Preschool Education, University of Chicago, 1966.

Fuller, E. VALUES IN EARLY CHILDHOOD EDUCATION. Washington, D. C.: National Education Association, 1960.

Goldstein, L. S. Evaluation of an enrichment program for socially disadvantaged children. New York: Institute for Developmental Studies, New York Medical College, 1965. (Duplicated.)

Gordon, E. W., & Wilkerson, D. A. COMPENSATORY EDUCATION FOR THE DISADVANTAGED, PROGRAMS AND PRACTICES: PRESCHOOL THROUGH COLLEGE. Princeton: College Entrance Examination Board, 1966.

Gotkin, L. G. LANGUAGE LOTTO, New York: Appleton-Century-Crofts, 1966.

Gray, S., & Klaus, R. A. An experimental preschool program for culturally deprived children. CHILD DEVELPM., 36: 877-898, 1965.

Guilford, J. P. Intelligence: 1965 model. AMER. PSYCHOLOGIST, 21: 20-26, 1966.

Henderson, A. S. 1964-1965 ANNUAL PROGRESS REPORT TO THE FORD FOUNDATION ON THE PRESCHOOL AND PRIMARY EDUCATION PROJECT. Harrisburg, Pa.: Council for Human Services, 1965.

497

Hess, Robert D. & Shipman, Virginia C. "Cognitive elements in maternal behavior", chapter in FIRST MINNESOTA SYMPOSIUM ON CHILD PSYCHOLOGY' Minneapolis: University of Minnesota Press, in press, to appear in 1967.

Hess, Robert D. & Shipman, Virginia C. Maternal attitudes toward the school and the role of pupil: some social class comparisons. Chapter in H. Passow (Ed.) FIFTH WORK CONFERENCE ON CURRICULUM AND TEACHING IN DEPRESSED AREAS, in press, 1967, New York: Columbia University Teachers College.

Hess, Robert D. & Shipman, Virginia C. Maternal influences upon early learning: the cognitive environments of urban preschool children, chapter in Hess, R. D. & Bear, Roberta (Eds), EARLY EDUCATION: REPORT OF THEORY, RESEARCH AND ACTION. Chicago: Aldine Press, in press, to appear in 1967.

Inhelder, B., & Piaget, J. THE GROWTH OF LOGICAL THINKING FROM CHILDHOOD TO ADOLESCENCE. New York: Basic Books, 1958.

Kirk, S. A. EARLY EDUCATION OF THE MENTALLY RETARDED. Urbana: University of Illinois Press, 1958.

Krech, D., Rosenzweig, M. R., & Bennett, E. L. Effects of environmental complexity and training on brain chemistry. J. COMP. PHYSIOL. PSYCHOL., 53: 509-519, 1960.

Long, E. R., Jr. THE EFFECT OF PROGRAMMED INSTRUCTION IN SPECIAL SKILLS DURING THE PRESCHOOL PERIOD ON LATER ABILITY PATTERNS AND ACADEMIC ACHIEVEMENT. Chapel Hill, N. C.: University of N. C., 1966.

McAnich, M. Body image as related to perceptual-cognitive-motor disabilities. In J. Hellmuth (Ed.) LEARNING DISORDERS, Vol. 2. Seattle, Washington: Special Child Publications, 1966.

McNeill, D. Developmental psycholinguistics. In F. Smith & G. Miller (Eds.), THE GENESIS OF LANGUAGE, Cambridge, Mass.: MIT Press, 1966.

Pasamanick, B. & Knoblock, H. Epidemiologic studies on the complications of pregnancy and the birth process. In C. Caplan (Ed.), PREVENTION OF MENTAL DISORDERS IN CHILDREN. New York: Basic Books, 1961, pp. 74-94.

Peel, E. A. THE PUPIL'S THINKING. London: Oldbourne Book Co., 1960.

PIAGET, J. THE ORIGINS OF INTELLIGENCE IN CHILDREN. (2nd ed.) New York: International Universities,Press, 1952.

498

Radin, N. & Weikart, D. P. A home teaching program for disadvantaged preschool children. In D. P. Weikart (Ed.) PRESCHOOL INTERVENTION: PRELIMINARY REPORT OF THE PERRY PRESCHOOL PROJECT. Ann Arbor, Michigan: Campus Publishers, 1967.

Robinson, H. B. The problem of timing in preschool education. Paper read at Social Science Research Council Conference on Preschool Education. University of Chicago, 1966.

Rosenzweig, R., Bennett, E. L. & Krech, D. Cerebral effects of environmental complexity and training among adult rats. J. COMP. PHYSIOL. PSYCHOL., 57: 438-439, 1964.

Schaefer, E. Infant education and intellectual development. A paper read at the Convention of Council for Exceptional Children, St. Louis, 1967.

Schwartz, A. N., Phillips, L. W. & Smith, M. B. REACH. (Raising educational aspirations of the culturally handicapped). Unpublished report on Cooperative Research Project 5-8072-12-1, State University of New York College at Plattsburgh, 1965.

Schwertfeger, J. & Weikart, D. P. The nature of preschool benefits. MICH. EDUC. J., 44: 18-20, 1967.

Scott, J. P. Critical periods in behavioral development. SCIENCE, 138: 3544, 1962.

Sears, P. S. & Dowley, E. M. Research on teaching in the nursery school. In N. L. Gage (Ed.), HANDBOOK OF RESEARCH ON TEACHING. Chicago: Rand McNally, 811-864, 1963.

Sigel, I. S. The attainment of concepts. In M. L. Hoffman & L. W. Hoffman (Eds.), CHILD DEVELPM. RES. New York: Russell Sage Foundation, 1964.

Skeels, H. M. Adult status of children with contrasting early life experiences: a follow-up study. MONOGRAPHS OF THE SOCIETY FOR RESEARCH IN CHILD DEVELOPMENT, 32: 2, 1966.

Skodak, M. & Skeels, H. M. A final follow-up study of one hundred adopted children. J. GENET. PSYCHOL., 75: 85-125, 1949.

Smilansky, S. Progress report on a program to demonstrate ways of using a year of kindergarten to promote cognitive abilities. Henrietta Szold Institute, Israel. Unpublished manuscript. 1964.

Sonquist, H. D., & Kamil, K. Applying Piagetian concepts in the classroom for the disadvantaged. In D. P. Weikart (Ed.), PRESCHOOL INTERVENTION: PRELIMINARY REPORT OF THE PERRY PRESCHOOL PROJECT. Ann Arbor, Michigan: Campus Publishers, 1967.

Sprigle, H. A. Curriculum development and innovations in learning materials for early childhood education. Paper read at Southern Conference on Early Childhood Education, University of Georgia, 1967.

Stendler, C. B. A Piaget-derived model for compensatory preschool education. Unpublished manuscript. University of Illinois, 1965.

Strodtbeck, F. L. Progress report: The reading readiness nursery. The Social Psychology Laboratory, University of Chicago, 1963 (Duplicated.)

Swift, J. W. Effects of early group experience: the nursery school and day nursery. In M. L. Hoffman & L. W. Hoffman (Eds.), REVIEW OF CHILD DEVELOPMENT RESEARCH. New York: Russell Sage Foundation, 1964, 249-288.

Weikart, D. P. A semi-structural projective test for measuring educational attitudes. Unpublished doctoral dissertation, University of Michigan, 1966_a.

Weikart, D. P. Results of preschool intervention programs. Paper read at University of Kansas symposium on the Education of Culturally Disadvantaged children. Ypsilanti Public School, Ypsilanti, Michigan, 1966_b.

Weikart, D. P. (Ed.) PRESCHOOL INTERVENTION: PRELIMINARY REPORT OF THE PERRY PRESCHOOL PROJECT. Ann Arbor, Michigan: Campus Publishers, 1967.

White, B. Infant Stimulation. Paper read at Social Science Research Council Conference on Preschool Education, University of Chicago, 1966.

Wiegerink, R. & Weikart, D. P. Measurement of mother teaching styles. Proceeding, 75th ANNUAL CONVENTION, AMER. PSYCHOL. ASSOC. p. 33-334, 1967.

Wolf, M. In PLAIN TALK, 5-Creative Playthings. Princeton, New Jersey, 1967.

Wolf, R. M. The identification and measurement of environmental process variables, related to intelligence. Unpublished doctoral dissertation. University of Chicago, 1964.

500

A RETROSPECTIVE LOOK AT THE EXPERIENCES OF A COMMUNITY CHILD GUIDANCE CENTER WITH PROJECT HEAD START

Robert Shaw, M.D.,
Director, Children's Mental Health Services, Lincoln Hospital;
Assistant Professor, Dept. of Psychiatry,
Albert Einstein College of Medicine,
Yeshiva University, New York, New York

Carol J. Eagle, Ph.D.,
Chief Psychologist, Children's Mental Health Services, Lincoln Hospital;
Assistant Professor, Dept. of Psychiatry,
Albert Einstein College of Medicine,
Yeshiva University, New York, New York

Franklin H. Goldberg, Ph.D.,
Psychologist,
New York University Reading Institute,
New York, New York

In the summer of 1965, the Coney Island Mental Health Service for Children and Youth of the Jewish Board of Guardians became involved with a variety of services on behalf of the new Head Start program sponsored by the Board of Education of New York in Coney Island. As a community-oriented child guidance clinic we were interested in exploring and evaluating the ways in which a clinic can develop a meaningful role in providing new and hopefully innovative services to the children of a disadvantaged urban slum. The work we carried out has been reported in its general aspects in AN ACCOUNT OF THE EXPERIENCES OF A COMMUNITY CHILD GUIDANCE CENTER WITH OPERATION HEAD START, SUMMER 1965, (Shaw and Eagle, 1966); in one special aspect of our function in A CLINIC AS CATALYST IN HEAD START, (Shaw and Eagle, 1967); and the evaluation data we gathered at that time has been reported in HEAD START CHILDREN AND THEIR MOTHERS, (Goldberg and Eagle, 1966).

The possibility of early intervention, of offering truly preventive services, and of being able to extend services to a larger segment of our population, cannot help but attract the interest and thought of those planning the activities of children's community mental health programs. It seems axiomatic to us that given the current concern with community mental health, individual programs will make increasing efforts to reach out to their surrounding community. Among these attempts will be found modifications of direct treatment services, the establishment of consultative programs to child care institutions and the initiation of community mental health projects on the social action model or on the public health model.

The question of compensatory programming for pre-school children had been of interest and under discussion from the inception of our clinic in the fall of 1964. We had many doubts about the ultimate usefulness of programs that focused on cognitive development through sensory stimulation of kindergarten children (i.e., Deutsch, 1962, Forgays, 1965) and would have preferred a program focused on the total emotional growth of the child and the facilitation of his mother's efforts to promote his maturation and development. When faced, however, with the possibility

503

of a large scale Head Start program in our catchment area, we decided to explore the role a community child mental health service could play in such a program.

At that time the clinic was less than one year old and we were strongly concerned with the way we would represent ourselves to the community. We had on arrival requested community support for and acceptance of a mental health consultation program to all the schools in our district which would include in it an attempt to deal with most children within their school setting and to refer for treatment only those children considered by the consultant to be the cases most likely to benefit. By active participation in Head Start we hoped to combat the possibility that our preference for consultation to direct treatment services would lead to our being perceived as just talkers rather than doers, or just evaluators rather than clinicians.

The district served by our clinic consisted of the western half of Coney Island and included two health areas with a population of some 65,000 people. *A neighborhood in transition, formerly quite solidly middle class, it had over the past ten to fifteen years become the repository for a large welfare population of mixed racial and ethnic origins. By any measure of social disruption such as number of Aid to Dependent Children recipients, infant mortality, incidence of tuberculosis, or juvenile delinquency, this area clearly qualified as a socially-disadvantaged neighborhood.

The advent of the Head Start program offered an opportunity for us to conceive of ways in which the clinic could serve usefully the community at large. The air of optimism and enthusiasm that accompanied the innovation of Head Start offered the possibility of initiating dialogue between professional and community people, as well as between white and non-white populations. Furthermore, we saw as a possibility that the clinic through consultation could enhance the overall effectiveness of staff.

Once Head Start funding had become a reality we became active in the following ways:

> 1. Community organization and recruitment. Our experience within the community suggested to us that there was a large pool of children who desperately needed the kind of help that might be possible through a well-conceived pre-school experience. It seemed likely that without intervention one of two possibilities would eventuate: 1) either the school system would grossly

---

* 1960 census tracts. It is estimated the community has grown by approximately 20,000 within the last six years (Quiroz, 1965).

504

underestimate the number of possible children and therefore not plan for them, or, 2) even if they did, the community might not cooperate to the extent of actually delivering the children to school for whatever program was finally planned.

A working committee was established including the neighborhood leaders (both formal and informal) as well as representative professionals from agencies operating healt'.. services in the area. We hoped that this group could provide the liaison work necessary to make contact with families unavailable to typical community-based programs and might also become the nidus around which future programs might be developed. This group recruited volunteers and provided the necessary facilities for mounting a door-to-door and apartment-to-apartment campaign. By the use of a street parade they reached into every home in the most disadvantaged area and recruited over 200 children within several days. Out of the ranks of this working group and through liaison with the Director of the Early Childhood Education Division of the Board of Education, neighborhood people who had demonstrated their abilities were assigned to the new jobs that became available for community people in the Head Start program.

2. The development of liaison relationships within the community. The success of the program clearly depended upon the degree to which adequate liaison could be developed between the school and the community. Our staff, therefore, worked at all hierarchial levels to encourage understanding and mutual acceptance by all participants. Liaison with parents of prospective Head Starters provided the means to maintain their motivation thereby ensuring good attendance as well as aiding the parents in perceiving the program as helpful and non-threatening. Liaison with school personnel supported their perception of the volunteers as useful and helpful collaborators in the common goal of educating children.

3. Consultation services. In conjunction with liaison activities we wanted to be of benefit to the school personnel in their efforts at programming adequately for the children. Also in our role as mental health consultants, we would be in a position to provide the special help needed in the understanding of a particular child's or family's problems.

505

The clinic provided a common meeting ground for the staffs of the two schools. Consultation to the combined staffs was related mainly to community issues and attempts to involve the entire family in aspects of the program.

Consultation to the classroom teachers included our participation in the evaluation of 30 children in two classes; visits to their homes by a clinician;[*] and discussions of classroom management. Our educational consultant[**] participated in the two classrooms in the programmed visits of each child's mother and used these visits as educational experiences for the mothers.

4. Evaluation and research. The program provided the opportunity to study the so called "disadvantaged" child and his "hard core" family. Data was collected on the 30 children in the two classes to which we offered consultation. Visits were made to the homes of twenty-four of the thirty children.[***] Because of our liaison activities and consultative services our data collection was viewed as evidence of a positive concern on our part for these children by both the school personnel and their parents.

Our interest in assessing community mental health variables and investigating the relation between school functioning and possible family pathology led us to formulate the following questions in our study:

1. What proportion of our experimental population would be regarded as "emotionally disturbed"? What are the salient psychological characteristics of children so described?

2. What is the relationship, if any, between ratings of "emotional disturbance" in children and their mothers?

3. Is the number of behavior symptoms recorded for the child, as reported by both teachers and mothers, a reliable index of degree of emotional disturbance?

4. Does degree of emotional disturbance affect school functioning and attitudes?

[*] Mrs. Kathleen Walke
[**] Mrs. Dorothy Boguslawski
[***] Five families subsequently applied to our clinic for diagnostic and treatment services, interestingly enough not for the Head Start child. These visits seem to reflect the positive link that had been made to our clinic when one considers this as a group who traditionally underutilizes psychiatric service.

506

5. Are certain characteristics and attitudes of the mothers related to their child's (and their own) emotional disturbance and/or his school functioning?

6. How do mothers of Head Start "drop-outs" (children who were registered for the program but did not attend) differ, if at all, from mothers whose children participated in the Head Start program with respect to the accessibility to educational intervention and degree of emotional disturbance?

Two classes were chosen for intensive study; one for each of the schools we served as consultants. One was a morning class, the other was an afternoon class. One class consisted of 16 children (10 boys and 6 girls), the other had 14 children (6 boys, 8 girls) all between the ages of 4½ to 6. Demographic data indicated that most children belonged to families from lower socio-economic levels (19 families were on welfare) while a few could be considered lower-middle class families. With respect to ethnic background, 14 families were Puerto Rican, 9 families were "white" (4 Jewish, 4 Italian, 1 Protestant) and 7 families were Negro. None of the "white" families were receiving welfare funds. All children had at least 2 siblings; many had three or more brothers and sisters. In 1/3 of the homes, the father was absent. Interestingly, the women in these homes tended to be the more "disturbed" mothers. In 3 families both parents were high school graduates; only 2 other mothers in the entire sample completed high school. These characteristics identified our sample as a disadvantaged one.

There were three major sources of data. First there was the socio-economic identifying data, obtained from the Head Start Information Forms (1 and 3) which had to be filled out for each Head Start child and were made available to us. These forms contained medical-dental history as well as family data such as educational, work and income information for both parents, number of people living in the household, etc. Secondly, each teacher made the following ratings during the last week of the program for each child in her class in consultation with the psychologist:

A. Child Description Checklist (a Head Start instrument involving a general description of the child according to one or more of nine categories such as disruptive, provocative, isolated, fearful, unhappy, etc.)

B. Behavior Inventory (a 50 item rating scale devised by Zigler for the Head Start program which we divided, on an intuitive ad hoc basis, into six subscales (we are awaiting the results of a factor analysis of this Inventory performed by Head Start). These 6 sub-scales are:

507

1. *task involvement* which includes such items as being methodical and careful in tasks undertaken, sticking with a job until it is finished, working earnestly at classwork or play, being easily distracted, giving up easily, etc.

2. *intellectual motivation* consisting of such items as welcomes change and new situations, asks many questions for information, is imaginative, prefers the habitual and familiar, etc.

3. *affect control* as indicated by such items as: carefree, even tempered, becomes aggressive or enraged when frustrated, emotionally over-responds to usual classroom problems, etc.

4. *self reliance* involving ratings on items such as: tries to figure out things for himself, appears to trust his own abilities, needs a minimum of assistance from others, excessively seeks the attention of others, lets other children boss him around, etc.

5. *extroversion* which includes such items as: talks eagerly to adults about his own experiences, often keeps aloof from others, is reluctant to talk to adults, etc.

6. *cooperativeness* as exemplified by such items as considerate, does what is asked, is jealous, has little respect for the rights of others. It should be noted that some items were stated in a positive form while others were phrased negatively which was taken into consideration in scoring protocols.

C. Symptom Checklist, devised by Glidewell (1956), which yields an index of the number of different behavioral difficulties (i.e. symptoms) reported for the child. The symptoms were rated when disturbances were reported in such behaviors as sleeping, eating, getting along with other children, having unusual fears, etc.; and

D. a rating of "Emotional Disturbance" along a six-point scale (adapted from Glidewell, 1956).

Evaluation of mothers of twenty-four Head Start children were made by Mrs. Walke, who went into the home for an interview and then rated the mother for degree of "Emotional Disturbance" and the child on the Symptom Checklist. She also rated the mother on twelve scales mostly derived from the Fels series along such dimensions as sociability of family, defensiveness, mother-child rapport,

508

academic-intellectual stimulation of the child, enforcement of discipline, withholding of help, emotional control, affectionateness and vocational outlook. The social worker tried to make similar evaluations of six mothers who did not send their child to the Head Start program.

The following results were obtained which reflect upon the major questions raised.

1. Nine of the thirty children (30%) were rated by teachers as "emotionally disturbed". There were six boys and three girls so rated though none of these children were considered "seriously disturbed" (the sixth point on the scale).

Teachers seemed to hesitate placing a child into a moderately or seriously disturbed category despite what appeared to us to be highly disruptive classroom behavior. They felt positively about the youngsters and may have felt also that such ratings might be regarded as reflecting adversely upon their adequacy as teachers. The "disturbed" children fell into two descriptive categories: either disruptive, provocative and hyperactive (4 boys) or isolated, silent and unhappy (the remainder).

The social worker, probably being more sensitive to pathology, regarded thirteen of twenty-three mothers (57%) as showing some degree of emotional disturbance, including two mothers who were regarded as "seriously disturbed".

2. A significant ($P < .01$) r of .53 was found between the social worker's rating of emotional disturbance of the mother and the teacher's rating of emotional disturbance of the child. This is an important finding because it indicates a consistency in the reflection of a child's disturbance from home to school even when the symptom pictures are different (see below).

3. The very significant relationship ($r = .86$) between the teacher's ratings of emotional disturbance and the number of symptoms in the child is in part due to the same person making both ratings. However, the r between the social worker's rating of symptoms and the child's emotional disturbance (as rated by the teacher) was also significant ($r = .53$, $P < .01$). Present findings were consistent with Glidewell's results suggesting that two symptoms or less indicated no disturbance, three to four symptoms were characteristic of those with some degree of disturbance and six or more symptoms

were only found in children of at least moderate disturbance. The most frequent symptoms reported by the mothers were disturbances in sleeping, eating (disturbances the teacher would not see in the half-day program) and temper tantrums; the teachers most frequently reported difficulties in getting along with other children, overactivity and underactivity (seen in daydreaming, withdrawn behavior).

4. All six sub-scales of the Behavior Inventory correlated significantly with teacher ratings of emotional disturbance. Thus there was a negative relationship between each of the following and emotional disturbance: task involvement (-.67), intellectual motivation (-.46), affect control (-.81) self-reliance (-.45), extroversion (-.63), and cooperativeness (-.77). In other words, those pre-schoolers rated emotionally disturbed are the seemingly disinterested, difficult to manage or withdrawn children who according to middle-class teacher and psychologist standards already seem well on their way to being considered "problem" children, i.e., non-achievers, delinquents, drop-outs, etc.

5. Efforts to relate aspects of mother functioning and attitudes to child behavior were not too successful. However, there was some evidence suggesting that the aggressive, acting-out child usually had a disciplinary lax, emotional mother where considerable mother-child friction was present. The isolated, withdrawn child tended to have a mother who showed little warmth or intellectual stimulation, who was strict with little disciplinary friction, who withheld help and showed little emotion and who expressed little concern or hope for the future. Several mother scales correlated significantly with ratings of mother emotional disturbance (i.e. disciplinary friction, withholding of help, defensiveness and emotional expression). Thus, a mother who was rated as disturbed tended not to be able to respond emotionally to others, not to be able to give help to her child and to become involved in fights and struggles over issues of discipline.

6. It was difficult to find and interview mothers of "drop-out" Head Start children (a finding itself suggestive). Of the six mothers with whom a meaningful interview could be held *all* six were considered moderately or severely disturbed and their children (where ratings could be reliably made) had four or more symptoms.

510

The results indicate that teachers can identify suspected emotionally disturbed pre-school children through a number of techniques (direct ratings, behavior description, symptom checklist) and that these children seem to have mothers who are considered emotionally disturbed. The 30% of the Head Start children judged to be in need of treatment corresponds closely with the number reported by Johannet in his clinical evaluation of the emotional health of Boston Head Start children.

The indication that the emotionally disturbed child tends to do poorly, is the least motivated, causes the most difficulties in class and is described as either aggressive or withdrawn is not surprising except for the implication that such observations can be reliably and validly made, using relatively crude instruments by regular classroom teachers in children so young and in so short a period of time (i.e., after about seven weeks). The suggested relationships between mother and child behaviors require more intensive investigation with more reliable instruments.

To determine the consistency of these judgements over time, we had teachers rate the children in May-June, 1966 and again in May-June, 1967, on the Glidewell Emotional Disturbance Scale (ED) and the Symptom Checklist (SC)[*]. The progression of the children to new teachers each year made it impossible for any teacher to rate the same child twice.

As the children grew older we of course became interested in their adaptation and success in their school work. Therefore, beginning in 1966 we had the teacher also rate the child as to his potential "academic ability" (as these were largely kindergarten children) on a four-point scale: 1) superior; 2) above average; 3) average; 4) below average. We found a positive significant relationship between the teacher's judgement of the child's emotional disturbance (ED) and the teacher's judgement of his academic ability (AA): i.e., 1966 $r = .53^{**}$, 1967 $r = .56^{***}$. Over time the ED becomes more strongly related to the AA -

$$1965 \text{ ED to } 1966 \text{ AA, } r = .23$$
$$1965 \text{ ED to } 1967 \text{ AA, } r = .36$$
$$1966 \text{ ED to } 1967 \text{ AA, } r = .46^2$$

and we would hypothesize that our next year follow-up would bring us even stronger relationships between the earlier detected emotional disturbance and present academic trouble. While in the original ratings it is possible that the "halo" effect reported by many investigators was operating, the long term trend makes this seem less likely.

[*] The reliability coefficient for the teacher's ratings between their ED and SC ratings is always high lending confidence in the reliability of their judgements on these two scales. In 1965, $r = .86$, 1966, $r = .76$, 1967, $r = .84$.

[**] $P < .01$

[***] $P < .05$

511

TABLE I

Relationship between Emotional Disturbance Scale
and
Symptom Check List over Three-Year Period

	1966a ED	1967 ED	1966 SC	1967 SC
1965 ED	.47*	-.01		
1965 SC			.47*	.45*
1966 ED		.64**		
1966 SC				.52**

a In 1966, N = 21. The nine missing children had moved leaving no forwarding address.
In 1967, by chance we found one of our original 30 children in school bringing our 1967 N up to 22.

*P <.05
**P <.01

Our results indicate a positive relationship between emotional disturbance ratings and the symptom checklists from 1965 to 1966, and 1966 to 1967 and even from 1965 to 1967 for the symptom checklist.

Another interesting finding is obtained when one looks at the consistency of year to year ratings. We define consistency as deviation of no more than one rating point difference in the three ratings and demand at least two out of the three ratings be the same. With this definition, 46% of the group so qualify. Children who are consistently rated by the teachers over the three years strikingly fall within the moderate disturbance to healthy end of the continuum. Inconsistency is evaluated by the ratings varying more than one point, with no two ratings identical, which describes 41% of the sample. The striking finding in viewing the data in this way is that 70% of the inconsistent children show an improvement in the evaluation of the severity of their emotional disturbance. All of these children were rated a "four" or a "five" in 1965 and today, in 1967, have moved to the "three" to "one" range of the scale.* No sex difference is found on this; although generally for the whole group as was found in 1965 the boys were more often rated as more disturbed.

* Another earlier finding was checked on, i.e., the significant correlation (.53, P <.01) between a psychiatric social worker's rating of emotional disturbance of the mother (on the basis of a home interview) and the teacher's rating of emotional disturbance of the child. Correlating the 1965 rating on the mother to the child's ED in 1966 and 1967 yielded insignificant relationships.

Since in general, the group's rating moved toward healthier rating, there was little possibility of a significant correlation between the child's later rating and mother's ratings (in 1965) being attained. In 1965, 10 of the mothers received a rating of four and over, and six of the children did so; but by 1967, only two of the children received such a serious rating.

512

Thus the group as a whole has moved towards ratings of less severe emotional disturbance (with the exception of two boys). Four possible explanations of this finding occur to us. The original ratings were made by the teacher in consultation with a psychologist and may therefore have led to a greater appreciation of more subtle pathology in the child. Without consultation with a mental health professional, teachers may be reluctant to emply the more serious ratings on the scales as indicating a non-acceptance by them of the child or a failure in their role as a teacher. The second possiblity is that of course the children, as a group, have indeed become better adjusted, or emotionally healthier. If this finding were to be substantiated, particularly longitudinally, then one would wonder if the early Head Start experience had not in some way aided the children in better adaptation to kindergarten and subsequently first grade.

A third possibility is that a number of children originally rated as disturbed because of conduct and habit disorder are now perceived solely as educational failures because of the symptom picture having shifted into cognitive spheres. A fourth possibility is that the teacher's stereotype of a slum child includes a range of symptomatology that she no longer considers especially "disturbed".

It is worthwhile, now, three years later to retrospectively review the experience and the findings reported above.

It must be clear to the reader that at the time of clinic commitment to the support of the Head Start program that this activity was predicated on several assumptions. Among them were:

1. A program of a brief compensatory pre-school attendance might make a significant impact on the child's initial adaptation to school and this in turn might contribute substantially to the degree of success that that child would experience in his subsequent school career.

2. That without some intervention the Head Start program would be so poorly attended by the children most in need of such a program, that the net contribution to subsequent educational success would not materially affect the overall level of educational attainment in our area.

3. Early childhood compensatory education compared to programs for older children seemed sufficiently conflict free for both community and professionals that there would be the highest likelihood of promoting an adequate degree of readiness for a conflict-avoiding, collaborative model of community social action (Peck, *et al,* 1966.)

513

4. That the beginnings of a social action program of a collaborative nature would help to develop local neighborhood leadership that would be capable of extending the range and depth of future social action projects.

5. That consultative services to the Head Start program, working within the educational system, might offer the possibility of a degree of institutional change that would make it more likely that the program would attain its objectives.

6. That the clinic would benefit in several ways from active participation. This benefit would accrue from the experience gained, the data collected, the possibility of a contribution to the mental health of severely disadvantaged children, and the establishment of close working relationships with both members of the community at large and the various people in the educational system involved in the new program.

It is clear that the ultimate validity of the first assumption has not been crucially tested and must await really systematic investigation and longitudinally controlled studies.

Although there is an ever-burgeoning literature on the effects of pre-school enrichment, few studies have focused on the emotional health of the child. By and large there is contradictory evidence as to their merit. Experimental versus control group gains have not been found by Alpern (1966), Phillips (1965), and not found in certain measures, by Deutsch (Institute for Developmental Studies, 1965) and DiLorenzo (1967). Yet significant gains have been demonstrated by Deutsch in certain measures (*ibid.*) and DiLorenzo (1967), Weikart (1964), Gray and Klaus (1965), Holmes (1965) and Wolf (1966). Although there is evidence that these gains can be obtained, Wolf (1966) and Holmes (1965) have demonstrated their "wash out" later in the regular school setting. It would seem that the contradictory evidence from these well designed studies points to an obvious conclusion. The most important gains or positive effects seem to be taking place in studies where the programs are specially designed to introduce special teaching techniques (cf. Deutsch; Weikart, etc.), where the home is involved actively in the educational process (Gray & Klaus) and/or special program combinations involving home and school.

Our findings aimed as they were at the emotional "health" of the child have provided us with a baseline for following these children through their public school academic careers and observing the relationship between their emotional disturbance and adaptation in school.

514

We feel quite confident about the accuracy of our second assumption and the importance of the role that the clinic played in the enlisting of community participation in the successful recruitment of large numbers of children. In contrast to the oversubscription of the Coney Island program leading to the establishment of two extra classes at the last moment, in many areas in New York City the registration fell well below the number of openings for Head Starters, and the attendance fell far below the number actually registered. We had attempted to demonstrate the importance of community participation in the recruitment by using a neighborhood school in a similar ghetto slum area as a control school with regard to registration. Within a few days the principal of that school only seven blocks away called the clinic in anger. He considered that the recruitment drive had "pirated" most of the available children from his district and that this was unfair to his program. Only ten children had been recruited for his school by the fourth day of registration.

The volunteer group who had responded to their great success with enormous pride were delighted to repeat the recruitment for the second school. A new campaign was mounted. In addition to the door-to-door work of the volunteer group, the principal of the second school sent a class of children with their teacher to help in the recruitment drive. These efforts filled that school's eight classes within two more days.

Even though we are convinced of the value of this contribution we can still examine the question as to whether our role in recruitment was of help to the larger issues involved. Would it have been better to wait and use a failure of the program as the issue for a conflict oriented social action program? This will be more fully discussed below.

The third assumption seemed to be quite accurate in the sense that collaboration around early childhood education was rather easy to institute and the community people who were involved, were accepted into the schools with much less difficulty than we might have expected.

Other factors that must be kept in mind that facilitated this acceptance of community people into the school program included the high enthusiasm associated with this innovative program, the fact that the program was limited to the summer, and this, in turn, relaxed the usual restrictions associated with New York City school programming.

The fourth assumption turned out not to be totally true. The spirit of the recruitment drive steadily diminished. Our key volunteers were coopted by the salaried positions offered by Head Start and became professional school workers.

515

While this was an important gain and one with which we were initially quite pleased, in retrospect we would question the benefit for the community at large of this outcome. The clinic's committment to direct and consultative services was so great and the importance of continuous community organization efforts was so poorly understood that we did not sustain our initial success. The result of this was the gradual dissipation of our original community group as a potential leadership unit. The gains made by the individuals in the volunteer group seemed stable and clearly demonstrated the worthwhileness of this approach from the expected "ripple effect" of the development of leadership. Also, it was our impression that the experience in and of itself contributed to the mental health of the participants primarily through enhancing their self-esteem. Some of these people subsequently took active roles in the development of the Community Development Corporation when that possibility arose and were instrumental in the funding of O.E.O. sponsored projects at a later date. The experience suggests to us that to develop a stable community based group one of two types of situations is necessary. A group is more likely to remain stable in a conflict-free community organizational drive if they have a degree of power to make decisions that have a visible effect on external circumstances. The recruitment phase satisfied these conditions and if they had the power to disburse funds or select ongoing programs as in the Community Progress Centers or Community Development Corporation, that might have continued. The other possibility is that of the conflict model as most vividly demonstrated by Alinsky. Had we avoided any participation at all and, then, entered the situation only after a total recruitment failure, on a conflict-based model, we might have maintained a viable group. This ultimately might have made possible genuine institutional change in the schools that would have contributed more effectively to educational benefit for a wider group of children. The possibility of individual success through salaried employment neutralized the original group adhesiveness.

With regard to the fifth assumption one cannot ever demonstrate conclusively that it is impossible to achieve institutional change from within the system but our own experience as well as extensive review of the literature leads us to feel that there is little likelihood of true institutional change that can be achieved through consultation to the programs run by the New York City Board of Education. While temporary amelioration is often possible, to some degree, it usually depends on a person or two with whom the consultant has developed a special relationship and the change vanishes when personnel changes. . .There are some degree of carryover the following year in that there was some attempt at recruitment but the efforts were so inadequate that classes had to be closed and the scope of the program was less.

The general benefits to the clinic (our sixth assumption) were great. The good will engendered among community residents led to self referrals for clinical services and

516

subsequently, with the advent of the community corporation the clinic was invited to sponsor special programs for parents and youth. Our consultation programs were supported. The District Superintendent helped develop the degree of cooperation on the part of the staff of one elementary school that led to the participation in Project Catch-up, a therapeutic remedial program for slum children bussed into a middle-class school (Shaw *et al.*, 1967). The opportunity to observe these Head Start children and their families helped us to develop a full day program of compensatory schooling for a group of severely disadvantaged three-year olds and their families. The good will that the consultation program in general achieved for the clinic led to the Board of Education allowing us to temporarily house our own later independent Head Start program in an ongoing neighborhood school. And, finally, continuation, as a group, for our own Head Start children was provided by the public school they entered the following Fall.

The approach to the educational disability of ghetto children such as described here or for that matter in almost all programs is a partial one and does not really address itself to the changes that will have to be brought about in the larger social context in which these children will have to find their paths. Authors such as Levin (1967) and Hechinger (1965) have raised the question of "Headstart to where?" These issues are beyond the scope of the small, primarily clinically-oriented children's mental health service.

One must always keep in mind that given a community mental health conceptual model such as Leighton (1959) and Caplan's (1964) nutritional analogue in which chronic deprivation of vital physical, psychosocial and socio-cultural supplies is associated with a distinctly higher risk of mental illness, any approach to this massive socio-cultural problem through compensatory educational approaches alone is doomed to failure.

With a new range of competing modes of mental health intervention those responsible for the allocation of trained professional time will have to set priorities and decide the relative proportion of staff time that will be assigned to direct treatment, to consultation, to community action or direct community service. One obvious question raised by this experience is: should mental health professionals use their training to produce a good "hard sell?" Perhaps this account will be of some help to those faced with this decision.

We would say, finally, to the interested clinic or clinician that while the problems of these children have not as yet been solved, the efforts on their behalf have produced much that is useful in comparison to the effort that was expended. The clinician need feel no shame at efforts aimed at less than cure. Palliation and first aid are not demanded by society at large but have a respected place in the history of the healing

517

arts. We feel that these endeavors should be considered as trials or as action research, to be reported as freely and as rapidly as possible, so that efforts toward clarifying concepts of both theory and practice can be expedited.

This work was carried out when the authors were at the Coney Island Mental Health Service for Children and Youth of the Madeleine Borg Child Guidance, Institute, a Division of the Jewish Board of Guardians, New York.

References

STUDIES OF PRE-SCHOOL EDUCATION
FOR THE DISADVANTAGED CHILD [*]

Adams, Arlin M. and Charles H. Boehm, PROPOSAL TO THE FORD FOUNDATION FOR A PRE-SCHOOL AND PRIMARY EDUCATION PROJECT. Submitted for the Council on Human Services of the Commonwealth of Penna. Harrisburg: Department of Public Instruction, May, 1963.

Alinsky, S. Citizen participation and community organization in planning an urban renewal. Chicago: Industrial Areas Foundation, 1962.

Allen, Winifred Y. & Doris Campbell. The Creative Nursery Center: A Unified service to children and parents. NY:FASS, 1948.

Almy, Millie, "New Views on Intellectual Development in Early Childhood Education." In INTELLECTUAL DEVELOPMENT: ANOTHER LOOK. Washington: Association for Supervision and Curriculum Development. 1964.

Alpern, Gerald D. "The Failure of a Nursery School Enrichment Program for Culturally Disadvantaged Children." Paper presented at 1966 Annual Meeting, American Orthopsychiatric Assn.

[*] Prepared by Mrs. Marilyn Seide, Research Assistant, Children's Mental Health Services, Lincoln Hospital.

Alpern, G. D. A program that failed: 3 Dimensional Consequences. Paper presented at 1967 Annual Meeting A A P C C Washington, D. C.

Anastasi, Anne and Rita D'Angelo. "A Comparison of Negro and White Pre-School Children in Language Development and Goodenough Draw-a-Man I.I., "JOURNAL OF GENETIC PSYCHOLOGY, 81:147-65, 1952.

Anderson, H. H. "Domination and Social Integration in the Behavior of Kindergarten Children and Teachers,"GENETIC PSYCHOLOGY MONOGRAPHS, 21:285-385, No. 3, 1939.

Ausubel, D. P. How reversible are the cognitive and motivational effects of cultural deprivation? Implications for teaching the culturally deprived child. Paper read at a conference on the teaching of the culturally deprived child, Buffalo, N. Y., March 28-30, 1963.

Baltimore City Public Schools Early Admission Project, PROMISING PRACTICES FROM THE PROJECTS FOR THE CULTURALLY DEPRIVED. Chicago: Research Council of the Great Cities School Improvement Program, April, 1964.

Beilin, H. and L. Gotkin. "Psychological Issues in the Development of Mathematics Curricula for Socially Disadvantaged Children, "Paper presented to the Invitational Conference on Mathematics Education, Chicago, April, 1964.

Bereiter, C., J. Osborn, S. Engelmann, and P. A. Reidford. An academically-oriented preschool for culturally deprived children. Univer. of III.: Institute for Research on Exceptional Children, 1965 (Manuscript).

Bereiter, C. E., & Engelmann, S. Observation on the use of direct instruction with young disadvantaged children. Journal of School Psychology, IV, number 3, Spring 1966.

Bereiter, C. E., & Engelmann, S. TEACHING DISADVANTAGED CHILDREN IN THE PRE-SCHOOL. Englewood Cliffs, N. J.: Prentice Hall Inc. 1966.

Bernstein, B. "Language and Social Class," BRITISH JOURNAL OF SOCIOLOGY, 11:271-276, 1960.

Bernstein, Basil. "Social Class and Linguistic Development: A Theory of Social Learning." In A. H. Halsey, Jean Floud and C. Arnold Anderson (eds.), Education, Economy and Society. New York: The Free Press of Glencoe, 1961, pp. 288-314.

519

Bing, E. "Effect of Child-Rearing Practices on Development of Differential Cognitive Abilities," CHILD DEVELOPMENT, 34:631-648, 1963.

Bloom, Benjamin S., Allison Davis and Robert Hess, COMPENSATORY EDUCATION FOR CULTURAL DEPRIVATION. New York: Holt, Rinehart and Winston, 1965.

Brittain, C. V. Preschool Programs for Culturally Deprived Children. CHILDREN, 13 (4), 1966.

Brodbeck, A. J. and O. C. Irwin. "The Speech Behavior of Infants Without Families," CHILD DEVELOPMENT, 17:145-156, 1946.

Bronfenbrenner, U. "Socialization and Social Class Through Time and Space." In E. E. Maccoby, T. M. Newcomb and E. L. Hartley (eds.), READINGS IN SOCIAL PSYCHOLOGY. New York: Holt, Rinehart and Winston, 1958, pp. 400-425.

Brown, F. "An Experimental and Critical Study of the Intelligence of Negro and White Kindergarten Children." JOURNAL OF GENETIC PSYCHOLOGY, 65:161-175, 1944.

Bruner, J. S. "The Cognitive Consequences of Early Sensory Deprivation." In P. Solomon (ed.), SENSORY DEPRIVATION. Cambridge: Harvard University Press, pp. 195-207, 1961.

Bruner, J. S. "The Course of Cognitive Growth," American Psychologist, 19:1-15, 1964.

Bruner, Jerome S. TOWARD A THEORY OF INSTRUCTION. Belknap Press of Howard University Press, 1966.

Caldwell, Bette M. & Julius R. Richmond. Programmed Day Care for the Very Young Child - a Preliminary Report. JOURNAL OF MARRIAGE AND THE FAMILY, 26:482-88, 1964.

Caplan, G. PRINCIPLES OF PREVENTIVE PSYCHIATRY, New York: Basic Books, 1964.

Care of Children in Day Care Centers. Geneva: WHO, 1964.

Cherry, Estelle. Children's Comprehension of Teacher and Peer Speech. Institute for Developmental Studies, June, 1964.

520

Chilman, Catherine S. "Child-Rearing and Family Relationship Patterns of the Very Poor," Welfare in Review, 3:9-19, January, 1965.

Clark, K. B. and M. K. Clark. "The Development of Consciousness of Self and the Emergence of Racial Identification in Negro Pre-School children, "Journal of Social Psychology, 11:159, 1940.

Clark, K. B. and M. K. Clark. "Skin Color as a Factor in Racial Identification of Negro Pre-School Children," Journal of Social Psychology, 11:159, 1940.

Dennis, W. "Causes of Retardation Among Institutional Children in Iran," JOURNAL OF GENETIC PSYCHOLOGY, 96:47-59, 1960.

Deutsch, Cynthia P. Brief partial review of activities related to urban education. New York: Institute for Developmental Studies, November 1964.

Deutsch, Cynthia P. Education for some Special Groups. REVIEW OF EDUCATIONAL RESEARCH, 35 (2):140-146, 1965.

Deutsch, Cynthia P., & Deutsch, M. Brief reflection on the theory of early childhood enrichment programs. Paper read at Social Science Res. Council Conference on Early Childhood Education, Chicago, Illinois, February 1966.

Deutsch, M. Minority group and class status as related to social and personality factors in scholastic achievement. Monogr. No. 2, Ithaca, New York, The Soc. for Applied Anthropology, 1960.

Deutsch, Martin. The Disadvantaged Child and the Learning Process. W. H. Parson (Ed): EDUCATION IN DEPRESSED AREAS. N. Y. Teachers College Bureau of Publications, 1963.

Deutsch, Martin. Nursery Education: The Influence of Social Programming on Early Development. JOURNAL OF NURSERY EDUCATION, 18 (3), 1963.

Deutsch, Martin. "Facilitating Development in the Pre-School Child: Social and Psychological Perspectives," MERRILL-PALMER QUARTERLY, 10:249-263, July, 1964.

Deutsch, M. The role of social class on language development and cognition. AMER. J. ORTHOPSYCHIAT., 35:78-88, 1965.

Deutsch, Martin. What We've Learned about Disadvantaged Children. NATION'S SCHOOLS, April, 1965.

Deutsch, M. Some aspects of early childhood programs. In: FIRST STEPS TOWARD THE GREAT SOCIETY - PERSPECTIVES. Washington, D. C., 1965.

Deutsch, Martin. Some Psychological Aspects of Learning in the Disadvantaged, TEACHERS COLLEGE RECORD, 67 (4):260-65, 1966.

Deutsch, M. Some psychosocial aspects of teaching the disadvantaged. Teachers College Record, 67 (4):1966.

Deutsch, Martin. Some Elements in Compensatory Education. (Revision of Talk given in Sausalito, Calif.)

Deutsch, M., & Ellis R. Curriculum guidelines for use with the disadvantaged pre-school child. (In preparation - Inst. for Developmental Studies).

Deutsch, M., Ellis R. Nimnicht, G., & Covert, A. Memorandum on Facilities for Early Childhood Education. Prepared for Educational facilities Lab., New York.

Deutsch, Martin and Alfred Freedman. A Program to Demonstrate the effectiveness of a "Therapeutic Curriculum" for the Socially Deprived Pre-School Child. New York: Institute for Developmental Studies. January, 1962.

DiLorenzo, Louis T. A study of year-long prekindergarten programs for educationally disadvantaged children. Paper presented at 44th Annual Meeting, American Orthopsychiatric Assn., March, 1967.

Ellis, R. Applications of research: The enrichment program for disadvantaged children. Associated Public School System 18th Annual Conference Report, 1966, New York: Teachers College.

Ellis, R. Educational programming for pre-school children. CHILD STUDY Bull. of Inst. for Child Study, University of Toronto, Canada, 28, 2 (109), Summer 1966.

Ellis, R. Pre-kindergarten education for the disadvantaged child. In: Hellmuth, J. (ed.) THE DISADVANTAGED CHILD, Vol. I, Seattle: Special Child Publications, 1967.

Ellis, R., Deutsch, M., Nimnicht, G. & Covert, A. Memorandum on: Facilities for Early Childhood Education, Sociology, 1960, 33.

Feldman, Shirley. A Preschool Enrichment Program for Disadvantaged Children. THE NEW ERA, 45 (3):79-82, 1964.

522

Filippi, R. School-centered intervention with children of low-income families. Paper presented at 44th Annual Meeting, American Orthopsychiatric Association, Washington, D. C., March, 1967.

Fleiss, Bernice H. Pre-school enrichment. CAMPUS SCHOOL EXCHANGE, Spring 1964.

Forgays, D. Individual differences in the effects of early experience on later behavior. Address given at Fourth Annual Invitational Conference on Urban Education, Yeshiva University, Ferkauf Graduate School of Education, New York, April, 1965.

Gardner, Dorothy E. M. and Joan E. Cass. The Role of the Teachers in the Infant and Nursery School. Pergamon Press, 1965.

Garwood, Dorothy S. and Bernice Augenbraun. The Head Start Child: Relationship between psychosocial maturity and familial factors. Paper presented at 44th Annual Meeting, American Orthopsychiatric Assn., Washington, D. C., March, 1967.

Glidewell, J., Mensha, I. and Gilden, Margaret - Behavior Symptoms in Children and Degree of Sickness. Paper presented at the American Psychiatric Association, Chicago, Illinois, 1956.

Goldberg, F. H. and C. J. Eagle. Head Start Children and Their Mothers: Relationships among Mental Health, School Functioning and Maternal Attitudes. Paper presented at Eastern Psychological Assn. Meeting, April 16, 1966.

Goldberg, Miriam L. Adapting Teacher Style to Pupil Differences: Teachers for Disadvantaged Children, MERRILL-PALMER QUARTERLY, 10:161-178, 1964.

Goldfarb, W. Emotional and intellectual consequences of psychologic deprivation in infancy: a reevaluation. In P. H. Hoch and J. Zubin (Eds) PSYCHOPATHOLOGY OF CHILDHOOD. N. Y.: Grune and Stratton, 1955. pp. 105-119.

Goldfarb, W. Psychological privation in infancy and subsequent adjustment. AMER. J. Orthopsychiat., 1945, 15, 247-255.

Goldsmith, Cornelia. Developments in Pre-School Education and implications for philosophy and practice in Day Care. JOURNAL OF JEWISH SERVICE, 42 (2):192-97, 1964.

Goldstein, L. S. Evaluation of an enrichment program for socially disadvantaged children. Institute for Developmental Studies June 1965.

Goldstein, L. S., & Deutsch, M. An enrichment program for socially disadvantaged children: some preliminary findings. (In preparation, Institute for Developmental Studies).

Gordon, Edmund W. Characteristics of Socially Disadvantaged Children. REVIEW OF EDUCATIONAL RESEARCH, 35 (5):377-388, 1965.

Graff, Patrick J. Culturally Deprived Children: Opinions of Teachers on the Views of Riessman. EXCEPTIONAL CHILDREN, 31:61-65, 1964.

Graham, Jory. Handbook for Project Head Start N. Y.: ANTI-DEFAMATION LEAGUE OF B'NAI BRITH, 1965.

Gray, Susan W. and R. A. Klauss. An experimental preschool for culturally deprived children. CHILD DEVELPM., 36:887-898, 1965.

Grotberg, Edith H. Learning Disabilities, and Remediation in disadvantaged children. REVIEW OF EDUCATIONAL RESEARCH, 35 (5):413-425, 1965.

Hechinger, F. M. Headstart to where? SATURDAY REVIEW, 75:58-60, December 18, 1965.

Hechinger, Fred M. (Ed) PRE-SCHOOL EDUCATION TODAY. Doubleday, 1966.

Hellmuth, J. (ed.) THE DISADVANTAGED CHILD, Vol. I. Seattle, Wash.: Special Child Publications, 1967.

Hess, R. and V. Shipman. "The Cognitive Environment of Preschool Children." Paper presented to the Research Conference on the Education of the Culturally Deprived, University of Chicago, June, 1964.

Hilgard, J. "Learning and Maturation in Pre-School Children," JOURNAL OF GENETIC PSYCHOLOGY, 41:36-56, 1932.

Holmes, D. and M. B. Holmes. Evaluation of Two Associated YM-YWCA Head Start Programs (Final Report) Dec. 30, 1965, New York.

Hunnicutt, C. W. (ed.) URBAN EDUCATION AND CULTURAL DEPRIVATION. Syracuse: Syracuse University Press, 1964.

524

Hunt, J. McV. The psychological basis for using preschool enrichment as an antidote for cultural deprivation. MERRILL-PALMER QUART., 10:209-248, 1964.

Institute for Developmental Studies: Selected papers from the Arden House Conference on pre-school enrichment of socially disadvantaged children. Merrill-Palmer Quarterly, 10:3, 1964.

Institute for Developmental Studies. ANNUAL REPORT, 1965, N. Y.: N. Y. Medical College, 1965.

Jensen, A. R. "Learning in the Pre-School Years," JOURNAL OF NURSERY EDUCATION, 18 (2): 133-138, 1963.

Johannet, P., and Nancy Rodman. "The therapeutic nursery school as an adjunct in the treatment of children with anti-social development." Paper presented at 44th Annual Meeting, American Orthopsychiatric Assoc., Washington, D. C., March, 1967.

John, Vera P. "A brief survey of research on the characteristics of children from low-income backgrounds." Report prepared for U. S. Commissioner on Education, August, 1964.

John, Vera P. The intellectual development of slum children: Some preliminary findings. AMERICAN JOURNAL OF ORTHOPSYCHIATRY, 33 (5), 1963.

John, Vera P. and Leo S. Goldstein. "The Social Context of Language Acquisition," MERRILL-PALMER QUARTERLY, 10:266-275, July, 1964.

Johnson, Nancy. "Psychological Report Covering Seven Pre-School Centers." New Haven, Conn.: New Haven Public Schools, June 3, 1964.

Karp, John N. and Irving Siegel. Psychoeducational appraisal of disadvantaged children. REVIEW OF EDUCATIONAL RESEARCH, 35 (5):401-412, 1965.

Kendler, H. and T. Kendler. "Inferential Behavior in Pre-School Children," JOURNAL OF EXPERIMENTAL PSYCHOLOGY, 51:311-314, 1956.

Kitrell, Flemmie P. "A Nursery School Program within Day Care Hours for Culturally Deprived Children and Parents." Howard Univ., Washington, D. C., Dec. 1966.

Koch, M. B. and D. R. Meyer. "A Relationship of Mental Age to Learning-Set

Formation in the Pre-School Child," JOURNAL OF COMPARATIVE PHYSIOLOGICAL PSYCHOLOGY, 52:387-9, 1959.

Kohn, M., Dorothy W. Gross, Blanche Saia, Helen Silverman and Roslyn Solomon. Individualized teaching with therapeutic aims of disturbed pre-school children. Paper presented at 44th Annual Meeting, American Orthopsychiatric Association, Washington, D. C., March, 1967.

Knobloch, Hilda and B. Pasamanick. "Environmental Factors Affecting Human Development Before and After Birth," PEDIATRICS, 26:210-218, 1960.

Kraft, Iwer: Are we overselling the Pre-School Idea? SATURDAY REVIEW, December 18, 1965.

Larson, R. and J. L. Olson. "Method of Identifying Culturally Deprived Kindergarten Children," EXCEPTIONAL CHILDREN, 30:130-134, November, 1963.

Leighton, A. MY NAME IS LEGION. New York: Basic Books, 1959.

Leighton, A. Poverty and social change, SCI. AM., 212:21-27, 1965.

Levenstein, P., and R. Sunley. An effect of stimulating verbal interaction between mothers and children around play materials. Paper presented at 44th Annual Meeting, American Orthopsychiatric Assoc., Washington, D. C., March, 1967.

Levin, T. Preschool Education and the Communities of the Poor. In J. Hellmuth (Ed.), DISADVANTAGED CHILD, Vol. I, Seattle, Washington: Special Child Publications, 1967.

McCarthy, Dorothea. LANGUAGE DEVELOPMENT OF THE PRE-SCHOOL CHILD. Minneapolis: Institute of Child Welfare Monographs, No. 4, 1930.

Mackie, J. B., Anabel Maxwell and F. T. Rafferty. Psychological development of culturally disadvantaged Negro kindergarten children. A study of the selective influence of family and school variables. Paper presented at 44th Annual Meeting American Orthopsychiatric Association, Washington, D. C., March, 1967.

Montague, D. O. "Arithmetic Concepts of Kindergarten Children in Contrasting Socio-Economic Areas," ELEMENTARY SCHOOL JOURNAL, 64:393-397, 1964.

Montessori, Maria. SPONTANEOUS ACTIVITY IN EDUCATION: The Advanced Montessori Method. Cambridge, Mass.: Bentley, 1964.

THE NEW NURSERY SCHOOL. Greeley: Colorado State College.

Newton, E. S. Planning for the language development of disadvantaged children and youth. Journal of Negro Education, 33, (3), 1964.

Nimnicht, G., and J. Meier. "A First Year Partial Progress Report of a Project in an Autotelic Responsive Environment Nursery School for Environmentally Deprived Spanish-American Children." JOURNAL OF RESEARCH SERVICES (Bureau of Research Services, Colorado State College, Greeley), Vol. 5, No. 2 (6/66) pp. 3-34.

Norcross, K. J., & Spiker, C. C. The effects of stimulus pretraining on discrimination performance in pre-school children. CHILD DEVELOPMENT, 28, 1957.

Ozer, M. N. & N. A. Milgram. The effect of a summer Head Start program: A neurological evaluation. Paper presented at 44th Annual Meeting, American Orthopsychiatric Association, Washington, D. C., March, 1967.

Passow, A. H. (ed.) EDUCATION IN DEPRESSED AREAS. New York: Teachers College Bureau of Publications, 1963.

Peck, H. B., Roman, M. and Kaplan, S. R. Community action programs and the comprehensive mental health center. Presented at the American Psychiatric Association Regional Research Conference, Boston, Massachusetts, 1966.

"Pennsylvania Preschool and Primary Education Project," Progress report, Harrisburg, Pa., 1967.

"Pre-Kindergarten: Plenty Amid Poverty," EDUCATION U.S.A., October 29, 1964.

Phillips, L. W., et al. "Reach (Raising Educational Aspirations of the Culturally Handicapped)" Unpublished report on Cooperative Research Project 5-8072-2-12-1, State Univ. of N. Y. College, Plattsburg, 1965.

Quiroz, A. Selected social & demographic characteristics of the area immediately surrounding Coney Island Hospital. Community Mental Health Documents, 5.

Radin, Norma and Constance Kamil. The child-rearing attitudes of disadvantaged Negro mothers and some educational implications. JOURNAL OF NEGRO EDUCATION, 34:138-146, 1965.

Ralph, Jane B. Language development in socially disadvantaged children, REVIEW OF EDUCATIONAL RESEARCH, 35 (5):389-400, 1965.

Ralph, Jane B., Alexander Thomas and Stella Chess. Social behavior in nursery school children as a function of age and length of school attendance. Paper presented at 44th Annual Meeting, American Orthopsychiatric Association, Washington, D. C., March, 1967.

Riessman, F. THE CULTURALLY DEPRIVED CHILD. New York: Harper and Row, 1962.

Ruderman, Florence A. Conceptualizing needs for day care: Some conclusions drawn from the Child Welfare League day care project. CHILD WELFARE LEAGUE, 44:207-213, 1965.

Sands, Rosalind M. A Preventative Clinical and Educational Program for Children from 2 to 3 and their mothers. Paper presented at American Orthopsychiatric Assn., March, 1965.

Schacter, S. O., & Wolitsky, D. L. A therapeutic nursery group in a settlement house. Paper presented at Mid-Winter meeting of Academy of Psychoanalysis, New York City, December 6, 1964.

Shaw, R., Bernstein, S., Boguslawski, D. B. and Eagle, C. J. A new community mental health approach to learning problems in the elementary grades. Presented at the American Orthopsychiatric Association Meetings, 1967.

Shaw, R. and C. Eagle: An Account of the experience of a community Child Guidance Center with Operation Head Start, Summer, 1965. Paper presented at the American Orthopsychiatric Association, 1966.

Shaw, R. and Eagle, Carol J. A Clinic as catalyst in a Head Start Program, Jx. Amer. Acad. Child Psych., VI, 3, 1967.

Silver, Archie A., Esbeth Pfeifer and Rosa Hagin. Therapeutic Nursery As an Aid in the Diagnosis of Language Development.

Skeels, Harold M. "An Interim Brief on the NIMH-Iowa Follow-up Studies Relative to Mental Retardation, Dependency and Maternal Deprivation," National Institute of Mental Health, Bethesda, Md., March 31, 1964.

Skeels, H. M. Some Iowa studies of the mental growth of children in relation to differentials of the environment: a summary. Yearb. Nat. Soc. Stud. Educ., 39, Part II, 281-308, 1940.

Smilansky, S. "Progress Report on a Program to Demonstrate Ways of Using a Year of Kindergarten to Promote Cognitive Abilities, Impart Basic Information and Modify Attitudes which are Essential for Scholastic Success of Culturally Deprived Children in their First Two Years of School." Paper presented to the Research Conference on the Education of the Culturally Deprived, University of Chicago, June, 1964. (Israeli Project, unpublished manuscript.)

Starkweather, E. K. Potential Creative and the Preschool child. Oklahoma State Univ.

Swift, Joan W. Effects of early group experience: the nursery school and day nursery. In M. L. Hoffman and Lois W. Hoffman (Eds.), REVIEW OF CHILD DEVELOPMENT RESEARCH, Vol. I. N. Y.: Russell Sage Foundation, 249-288, 1964.

Taba, Hilda. Cultural Deprivaton as a factor in school learning. MERRILL-PALMER QUARTERLY, 10:147-159, 1964.

Thomas, Alexander, Stella Chess, Herbert G. Birch, Margaret E. Hertzig, and Sam Korn. BEHAVIORAL INDIVIDUALITY IN EARLY CHILDHOOD. New York: New York University Press, 1964.

Thomas, D. "Oral Language, Sentence Structure, and Vocabulary of Kindergarten Children Living in Low Socio-Economic Urban Areas." Ph.D. Dissertation, Wayne University, 1963.

Tomlinson, H. "Differences Between Pre-School Children and Their Older Siblings on the Stanford Binet Scales," JOURNAL OF NEGRO EDUCATION, 13:474-479, 1944.

Trager, H. S. and M. R. Yarrow. THEY LEARN WHAT THEY LIVE. New York: Harper, 1952.

Vosk, J. S. Study of Negro Children with learning difficulties at the outset of their school careers. AMERICAN JOURNAL OF ORTHOPSYCHIATRY., 36 (1), 1966.

529

Wann, K. D., Mirian Dorn, and Elizabeth Liddle. FOSTERING INTELLECTUAL DEVELOPMENT IN YOUNG CHILDREN. New York: Teachers College Bureau of Publications, 1962.

Weikart, D. P. et al Perry Preschool Project Progress Report. Michigan: Ypsilanti Public Schools, 1964.

Wellman, Beth L., and B. R. Candless. "Factors Associated with Binet I.Q. Changes of Pre-School Children." Psychological Monographs, 60, 2 (whole No. 278), 1946.

Wilkerson, D. F. Prevailing and needed emphasis in research on the education of disadvantaged children and youth. JOURNAL OF NEGRO EDUCATION, 33 (3), 1964.

Wilkerson, Doxey A. Programs and practices in compensatory education for disadvantaged children. REVIEW OF EDUCATIONAL RESEARCH. 35 (5):426-440, 1965.

Wolff, Max and Annie Stein. Six Months Later: A comparison of children who had Head Start, Summer 1965, with their classmates in kindergarten. A case study of the kindergartens in four public elementary schools, N. Y.C., 1966.

Wortis, Joseph. Prevention of mental retardation. AMERICAN JOURNAL OF ORTHOPSYCHIATRY, 35 (5):886-895, 1965.

Wortis, H. and A. M. Freedman. "The Influence of Environment Upon the Development of Premature Children." Paper read at American Orthopsychiatric Association, Chicago, March, 1964.

Wright, J. G. and J. Kagan (eds.). "Basic Cognitive Processes in Children," SOCIAL RESEARCH AND CHILD DEVELOPMENT MONOGRAPHS, 28, No. 2, 1963.

530

HEAD START - MEASURABLE AND IMMEASURABLE

Eveline Omwake, Ph.D.,
Chairman, Dept. of Child Development,
Connecticut College,
New London, Connecticut

EVELINE OMWAKE, Ph.D.

The program from which the illustrations are drawn and the curriculum described is the year round Head Start Project in New Haven, Connecticut. This was opened on a small scale in 1962 as the New Haven Pre-kindergarten Program of the New Haven Board of Education supported by funds from the Ford Foundation. The program now serves about 650 children and is OEO funded through Community Progress Incorporated - a community action program. The Director of Head Start is Mrs. Adelaide Phillips and the Curriculum Coordinator is Mrs. Lois Rho. The writer has been a consultant to the project since its inception. Dr. John Santini is Superintendent of Schools.

While waiting for "evidence" as to the full effectiveness of this type of experience for 3 and 4 year old children, the city authorities' efforts to expand and implement rather than to change the curriculum might be accepted as "testimony" to its suitability. With few exceptions the Elementary School principals and the Kindergarten teachers welcome the children who have been to Head Start because they feel that the children have an advantage over those who have not. It is conceded by all who have observed the development of the program that very successful parent-involvement aspect is an essential factor in the total picture. Mrs. Grace Dowdy has been the Coordinator of the parent program since the beginning.

While the Head Start watchers are patiently waiting out the years ahead for the returns of follow-up studies of the children now enrolled in the program, it might be of benefit to all concerned to give attention to a few of the under-developed aspects to the children's experiences. These refer to the unplanned incidental learning events of every child's day - events often unobserved because the adults' research eye and interest are focussed elsewhere, and immeasurable because no two are alike, also because a part of their importance to the child is the history and context of experiences they reflect. Because of the popular focus on planning very specific learning experiences for very young children whose learning functions are in a condition of emergence, the opportunity for incidental learning of a positive sort is fast disappearing for children in all sectors of society. The short-lived but frequent sponta-

533

neous learning situations which mean so much to those to whom they happen are being either inadvertently crowded out because the day is so full of scheduled set tasks or deliberately extinguished. The latter may occur because the adults in charge of planning consider the time to be wasted for learning or because they think that out-of-school time provides them enough opportunity. Unhappily the latter is not true.

There are many types of unplanned, unscheduled events which go down on each child's own unique unwritten record of successes and failures. One time as I arrived on a visit to a Head Start Child Development Center a boy pedaled by on his trike calling, "Did you come to watch us Head Start kids?" I said that I had and asked, "What's going on today?" "Ask the teacher," he replied as he circled backwards to eye my advance to the door. This episode has stayed in my mind along with dozens of others in which "Head Start kids" have demonstrated a use of knowledge and learning skills in spontaneous self-initiated encounters with the environment. In this particular 60-second incident I could glimpse age appropriate motor skill, language, perception, and the ability to differentiate, organize his thoughts, and select a response appropriate to the occasion. In addition, he seemed to have an enviable degree of self-esteem, or at least esteem for "Head Start kids."

Sometimes the unscheduled event occurs as an exchange of free and friendly foolishness between several children, such as might take place in any situation where children feel that the adults in charge are interested in all forms of behavior and learning whether or not they happen to approve of what goes on. An example of "friendly foolishness" could be the snack table behavior classic of youngsters supporting each other in autonomy development as they blow bubbles with milkstraws or bite the milk carton spout wearing it like a mask to make their agemates laugh and to tease their teachers. Obviously the adult neither needs to condone nor encourage such actions, but whether she tolerates it to its natural finish or stops it at the point where the children show that even for their amusement the returns are beginning to diminish, she owes the event due respect for the part it plays in mental health and learning at the three- or four-year-old level. It should be noted for the skeptical reader that it would be highly inappropriate for the teacher to appear to encourage such goings on by participating or joining in the fun. If this were to happen the children would indeed be confused in their learning about what adults expect of children and how adults themselves should behave. She plays her part by letting the children have their fun before signaling the time to stop.

But however the adults view children's nonsense, to the child himself inclusion in an epidemic of infectious mischief represents an experience of acceptance by agemates which in many cases leads more directly to self-esteem than the adult approval which might be gained for refraining from joining in the other children's own fun.

534

This kind of "togetherness" of children in behavior admired and initiated only within their own world also provides an opportunity for learning by imitation and for elaborating someone else's idea with variations of one's own creation. The shared laughter which ensues, however boisterous, provides an important moment of tension release, followed by the need to control the exuberance when the teacher decides it's time to call for order.

Such behavior is not specific to any particular environment so long as two or more children are together. It can be observed in the middle class Nursery School, Head Start Child Development Center, Day Care Centers from New York to California, the Childhavens of Denmark, and the Kibbutzim of Israel. In households where the children eat with the grownups it takes place at the family dinner table - at least once. In a scene from a film* sequence a "milk bubbling" exchange is beautifully pictured in a shot intended to demonstrate conversation at mealtime and how a teacher introduces the concepts of equal parts as orange sections are considered visually and verbally by herself and those nearest her at the table. In this scene a few children appear to be involved with her activity and conversation and perhaps are truly learning about halves and quarters. At the opposite end of the table a couple of youngsters are watching a boy engrossed in blowing into his milk carton. The viewer can only speculate as to whether the one type of interaction - adult to children - provided a more meaningful experience than the other which was child to child, and to wonder which activity inspired the children in between to want to join in for the fun and challenge of mastery.

From such typical three- and four-year-old initiated events does the feeling of belonging to one's own crowd emerge. Many an understanding teacher has inwardly rejoiced as she has outwardly put her foot down on these and other infectious fun experiences because she notes at least mentally that "even Mario (or some other withdrawn little outcast from the in-group) joined in." Perhaps she even let the noise and unruliness continue past its prime in the interest of that child's self-esteem and good humor so essential to his eagerness to make the best use of the other more formalized learning exercises on her schedule.

The point is not to debate whether children need to behave thusly in order to have a good growing-up experience, although this writer tends to put a good deal of faith in the educational as well as ego-healing powers of many forms of natural childish behavior such as have been described above. The important point is the need for adults who are studying and planning for children to take note of the timelessness and universality of "silliness" as the children are inclined to call it. While in adult terms it may be "mischief," the form it takes does not necessarily lead to

*A CHANCE FROM THE BEGINNING, a film made at the Institute for Developmental studies, New York University, Washington Square, New York City

535

harm or danger so long as an adult is in the vicinity to help the children to stop when they have reached the point where the relaxation of controls deteriorates into disorganization.

Because the nature of the learning involved is less easily identified in such situations than it is when observed under conditions of completing structured tasks, the ordinary incident tends to be ignored for its usefulness to adult research as well as to the children's pleasure in early learning. It is true that a spontaneous short-lived learning event is indeed hard to study for its contribution to the child's cognitive growth. In the interests of research one favors the structured task. This is defensible on the grounds that controlled conditions are necessary in order to conduct the study in such a way as to produce statistically significant data. However, it is important to avoid conveying, by virtue of their exclusion, that the innumerable self-initiated acts in which a child calls on his cognitive and other powers to carry out his intent are of less significance in his overall learning experience than the set task under the scrutiny of the researcher.

Perhaps even more significant is the fact that the possible importance of such incidents in the child's growth experiences tends also to be ignored at the level of planning and evaluating programs. It is true that a kind of token appreciation is casually offered to the idea that children need some time to use in their own way, but the spirit of acceptance of a play life for children is quite unlike the whole-hearted adult respect reserved for the more formal structured activities so readily recognized and recommended as "educational."

Another memory of an early pre-kindergarten program visit involves a boy who looked up from his position at the table where he was erecting a structure from plastic fit-together toys to ask of me, "Do you want to look at a book?" This scene took place in April in a year-round program and the child recognized me from earlier visits. We have no way of knowing if he conscientiously remembered the earlier occasions when I was accustomed to "looking at books" with children in the group. In the fall season consultation visits always meant working along with the teachers because at that time the sense of organization which can only develop as a group lives and learns together had not yet set in. All hands present, regular staff, volunteers and visiting consultants were needed to engage the children in activities which would lead to independent play and learning. On the day in question this boy pushed his toys over to his neighbor, whose impatience to get them was mounting to the grabbing point, and hurried to the book corner, anticipating my positive response to his invitation. There he arranged for me to sit on a child's chair and took his position opposite me, proceeding to read a book in true teacher style with the cover backed against his chest so I could see the print and pictures as he looked down over the top. He mimicked the teacher in pointing and asking questions to hold my attention

536

and check my knowledge. At the sight of the story-telling, two other children joined us and flanked the "teacher."

This simple charade invites analysis of what the boy had actually been learning and what it meant to him. Because of my familiarity with the enthusiasm which had gone into the development of that particular program, I was enjoying some inner amusement as well as satisfaction at this youngster's appealing demonstration of interest in books which his teachers had been so freshly eager to inspire. They were determined to help children love learning and books in the hope that in the near future of the first grade they might love to learn to truly read them. However, although this episode clearly suggests that the goal of the program for helping the boy enjoy and use books was being realized, as will be indicated later all the supportive experiences he had had were not sufficient to produce an adequate beginning reader when he was faced with the academic approach of his traditional first grade.

Many observers to Project Head Start, along with many of the teachers in the program, have been examining situations such as these for what they reveal about the nature of learning and the conditions which influence it. The more formal research of those whose business it is to design, conduct, and report it, is providing us with a great deal of new knowledge about children which is specific to certain types of situations and particular conditions. New ideas and a sharper inspection of old ones have helped considerably in the recent upgrading of the ordinary nursery school and in the enrichment of teacher preparation programs. The emphasis on "programming" and "structuring" has challenged many nursery school teachers to examine their practices to see if they could be improved. As a result, puzzles, lotto, and other matching, sorting, naming, counting, and discrimination games which have long been popular in the schools seem now to be introduced and supervised in ways which suggest greater awareness of the service of such items to cognitive learning.

Also, there appears to be an increased respect for the idea that such activities should be more logically structured and require more supervision than has been customary in programs too loosely organized to convey to the children or their teachers that learning and mastery were indeed taking place. Teachers are hopefully becoming more cognizant of the need to consider the logic and structure of their own spoken language in the interests of helping children to learn to speak effectively.

The very teachers who may have been paying too little attention to the contribution of structure in the environment to the children's learning and mastery are probably the ones who are well convinced of the contribution of the informal unscheduled learning events such as are being illustrated herein. However, they, as well as the casual observer to these incidents, are not usually in a position to structure their studies and formalize their findings. This is because they are engaged in teaching,

537

not research. Taking time out to record would reduce their effectiveness on the job. The result is that the group teachers' professional explorations into theory usually take place in informal discussions and staff meetings rarely becoming a part of the published record so as to be available to others engaged in the same type of work.

The problem of balance here could be easily worked out. If the very informal teachers of young children have discovered that they can offer the child a richer opportunity by considering how and when to introduce appropriate structuring, those formal teachers who lean heavily on structured tasks as a way of providing learning opportunities and controlling behavior need to study the subject of incidental learning more closely. If the researchers feel safer with the controlled study which permits measuring and counting, it might be fruitful for them to consider designs for studying whatever happens, (the unplanned, educational events) rather than only what they go in to observe and examine with hypotheses, problem, and method firmly in mind. The present condition seems to be that although the place of incidental learnings or the unplanned educational event is not denied, neither is it offered up for accounting when the child's progress, or, as in the case of Head Start, the program is assessed.

In another Center a group of three girls "dressed to the teeth" in flowered hats, veils, long skirts and high-heeled shoes, accompanied by two boys in men's hats and ties, were parading along one side of the play room "going shopping." The subject of this pantomime was easily recognized as they stopped at intervals pretending to look, handle, and stuff some imaginary product in their bags. The teacher's only observable contribution was to remind them to stop at the check-out counter, and to quickly suggest to a boy whom she had been teaching at a nearby table that he might be the cashier and to help him to arrange a box and stool near the end of their line of march.

Elsewhere in the same room a crowd of children was busy climbing on and off a "train" of chairs and boxes. The steering wheel at the front indicated that a vehicle of some sort was being engineered by a driver. The knowledge that during the previous week this group, with their teachers and all the mothers, had taken a twenty-minute round trip train ride suggested that the trip had provided, among other things, a dramatic play theme useful in their continuing learning. In this instance the play had been initiated, organized, and conducted entirely by the children. It drew to its natural finish after about ten minutes of repeated getting on and off the train-like arrangement of boxes and chairs. An interesting note was that the engineer, whose role was assumed by different children with each trip, always turned to see that his passengers were seated before signalling "Time to go" - (not the traditional "All Aboard" of the trainman) the familiar more meaningful phrase of the teacher preparing for any departure time.

538

The group in question had only recently learned how to carry on this kind of age-appropriate dramatic play. When the children had entered the program six months previously, the sight of dress-up clothes, housekeeping corner with a good assortment of furniture, dishes, etc., block shelf surrounded by the usual accessory block toys, and an indoor climber had failed to inspire the children with ideas for their use. Even the occasional doll bathing and rolling of small cars on the floor or table had needed strong encouragement, and, in some cases, demonstration by the teachers for the idea to catch on that the materials were there for the children to use.

Without the natural home setting for development of this important mode of learning, play must be "taught" and teachers must develop the essential understanding of its nature, as well as techniques in supporting the children's independence in it. In the program described above, the teachers had achieved their goal of establishing the importance of play activity for its learning and its pleasure, as well as for its tension release and anxiety relief aspects. They had done this through regularly responding to play with the same quality of positive interest that they showed in the cognitive skill tasks and educational games. They had kept the conversation going around familiar themes - going away, going to work, coming home, going to bed, watching TV, carrying out the trash and garbage, going to the clinic, etc., making use of any flicker of interest or response to include a child in the conversation. Books, stories, pictures, and trips within the neighborhood were used not only to increase the children's knowledge of their environment, but also to give them something to play as well as talk and ask about. Until the children learned how to be playmates of each other, the teachers had served as playmates, contributing ideas, language, imagination, and enjoyment around central themes which it was clear that all the children shared in fact, if not in quality - household, family, and neighborhood life.

Another equally important issue closely related to that of emphasis in research, program planning and evaluation, is that of the changing view of the goals of Head Start. It is now becoming evident that even from its inception it has been hoped by many authorities that children attending Head Start would be able to compete scholastically when they joined their more richly nurtured agemates in the elementary school. In 1964 this writer attended a discussion of the possibilities of a program such as has come into being. At that meeting various of the authorities present held to a realistic goal that children might be helped to enter school with more pleasure, confidence, and courage if they had a preliminary experience in which teachers would help them to feel more positively towards themselves and school. It was the sense of that meeting that school success in academic terms could not be expected as a result of such a program. In short, children themselves might indeed benefit but the elementary school would still face the problem of large numbers of poor learners. Now, three years later, it seems that new experiences, greater self-confi-

539

dence, and a positive feeling about school is not considered sufficient reason for so expensive and elaborate a program; children must have made up for their deficiencies in academic skills and knowledge, as well as in their confidence and courage, in order to be ready for the primary school. This seems to be the result of adults being carried away by fantasies of their own magical powers, because there is no sign from child study to tell us that the school environment, however benign, supportive, or stimulating, can offset the learning deficiencies developing as a result of a depressing home life.

The disadvantaged child lends himself well to description when it comes to his deficits in learning and experience. It has been conveyed in a variety of current writings that self and other concepts are remarkably underdeveloped and unclear and that life experiences have not engendered the eagerness, hopefulness and trust as essential for strong and solid early learning patterns as motor, verbal, and other specific skills. In addition, the mixture of independence and dependence is often improperly balanced. Obviously, his needs are many. It is probably safe to say that we have learned more about his problems than we have about the best ways of helping him. There is, however, general agreement that whatever is offered to the children in the Head Start programs, it is not sufficient to carry over into the kindergarten and first grade without continued supplemental help for them.

This condition confirms the predictions of the original planners that the most that might be achieved would be a better school adjustment which might or might not enable the children to get more out of the kindergarten or first grade than they might have without the head start. It also suggests that it is important to continue to review and revise the goals, inasmuch as these have considerable bearing on both the research and the program planning.

Whereas at the start we were concerned about children's feelings toward school, reporting now focuses on how the school feels about the Head Start child and the program proper. There was a brief period in the first year when it was fairly well accepted that it was too early to expect convincing data about the difference between Head Start and non-Head Start children. The reports then were informal and subjective comments from teachers and observers who didn't pretend to measure the effects of the summer program on the children's attitudes. However, the question has changed from "Did you notice any differences?" to "How are they doing academically?" One hears, "What exactly did they learn in Head Start?" "How much did Head Start help?" rather than, "Did the children change?" These wordings suggest the subtle difference between evaluating the effort for what it means to the children and reviewing it to discover whether or not the school's job is being made easier as a result of the program.

540

In the earlier era of generous and benign thinking about the terrible neediness and hopelessness of the extremely disadvantaged children, child development center staffs were encouraged to draw in volunteer and auxiliary services so as to be able to give help and attention in all areas of need - rightfully including the family's home conditions. It was intended to support the self-esteem, initiative, independence and good health of the children and their families under a program which was basically educational in nature. Now one hears complaints that the Head Start children enter the next level of school *expecting* a continuance of personal and individual attention. For this they are described as "spoiled." This is an important aspect to the total experience deserving of careful examination. It may well be that the abundance of unaccustomed help to some children who, not having encountered the joys of either dependence or independence which healthy four- and five-year olds strive for, sat back to passively permit having good done to them.

Here it is appropriate to question the nature of the attention-giving practices rather than to conclude that the children are used to so much help that they are "spoiled." Children of all sorts become dependent on others to do their work for them ("spoiled") if adults regularly do for them what they could do for themselves, given a little help at the strategic moment. It is quite likely that many of the adults "helping" as volunteers, aides, assistants, or even teachers, were inclined to do things *for* the children instead of showing them how. One frequently observes an adult inserting puzzle pieces for a child as if the goal were to complete the puzzle instead of to pick up some experience in looking for clues to solve a problem and to sharpen one's observational powers. Many adults, eager to avoid spillage, pour liquids for children instead of steadying the smaller hand to pour it. Others tend to lift a child down from high spots to which he has climbed, instead of supporting his effort to climb down himself. To help a growing child to help himself is a highly specialized teaching skill acquired through experience, training, and knowledge of growth and development. It also involves a special variety of judgment which usually is best learned through first-hand experience with young children individually and in groups.

To do a puzzle while a child watches, or to play with the doll, fire engine, dump truck, or game until the child wants to do it, too, is one thing, but to continue to do it for him once he starts offers no help to his learning.

The fact that performance in the academic skills is fast becoming the accepted measure of Head Start success suggests that the goals have narrowed since January, 1965, when so many people wholeheartedly began to participate in a program designed to support the administration's wish "to open the eyes of children to the wonders of the world." Despite the fact that the researchers and planners have zoomed in on the "cognitive skills" there is still no evidence to say that school success can be counted on as a result of any kind of preschool experience. This condi-

541

tion has been belabored repeatedly in regard to research in the regular nursery school, which program differs less in goals, procedures, etc., from a good Head Start Center than many persons believe. The contribution of the nursery school to later school success is, of course, attested to by the increasing demand for such schools and the large number of their graduates who have been progressing successfully through the various levels of school. It has not been possible, for a variety of reasons, and probably never will be, to pinpoint the advantages in such a way that it can be said, "nursery school children do better in school than non-nursery school children." The same condition may have to apply to Head Start as well.

Learning is so complex, performance so vulnerable to influence from a number of external forces, and school practice is so subject to conditions beyond the control of the teacher, that for the present we might serve the children in sounder ways if we withheld our concern for primary school success until the children reach that level after due process of appropriate educational experiences suited to their immediate learning needs.

Even though the literature in child development, child psychology, and early childhood education teaches, regardless of the point of view being propounded, that the early years are a period of the emergence of learning skills and that the learning environment should support their development in this critical period, implementation of the "learning to learn" idea tends nevertheless to promote the development of a few specialized learning skills instead of total learning. In total learning the skills must become integrated in the service of overall functioning. To consider the subject of a child's overall functioning requires extensive as well as intensive study of his daily life. We have apparently not yet reached the point of examining our goals for Head Start to discover if we can accept improved adjustment in social, physical and self-esteem terms without grade-adequate reading or number skills.

For a child to be more confident, to have greater self-esteem, to smile more often, laugh and engage in foolish interaction with his peers might represent an important gain due in large part to a Head Start experience which served his family also when this same child could not dependably perform specific cognitive tasks. The boy described in the story-reading charade is a case in point. Despite the fact that with obvious self-esteem he demonstrated fine motor control with the manipulative toys, recognized the visitor, showed good bodily control as he got up from his chair and hurried to the books with agile, graceful movements, had memory and perception appropriate to setting up a story-reading situation, and displayed the ability to interact socially in a way suited to the conditions, he did not, as it turned out, know which book he was showing me. When I looked at other books with him later I discovered that he was quite unable to accurately name familiar items, colors, or book titles and he brought me two crackers when I asked for three.

542

This boy's teachers had been working steadily in more and less formal ways on his concepts; he had had many individual and group looking and listening experiences; and he had been having regular help in counting sticks, stones, cubes, crackers and children from the beginning of the year. Months later his kindergarten teacher found him lively, responsive, independent in self-care, and well-behaved. However, because he could not name colors and seemed to require much individual help in completing tasks correctly, his teacher raised the question as to why he had not been "taught" to do such things in Head Start. It might be speculated that by the time he reached first grade this boy could be cited by critics of Head Start as an example of the failure of the program to produce children who performed better than non-Head Start children. Only those who would have known this boy all along would recognize the positive effects of the group experience. These were manifest in a brightened facial expression, pleasure in movement, friendliness toward others, in social behavior and in faith in the school as an agency that could accept him as he was and offer him continuing appropriate help with his learning problems. Psychological studies which had been a part of his Head Start background confirmed the teacher's hunches that he was dull and slow but not mentally retarded and would continue to need individualized help if he were to learn. Depending on one's goals, this boy could be viewed either as a Head Start success or a Head Start failure.

When the project first came into being a reason for it was that the schools were reporting that children entering at the first level were without even the basic knowledge that the five- or six-year old should bring with him. A year later the Head Start programs were being opened to three-year olds. They, too, showed signs of depressed learning functions in not knowing how to use the ordinary, simple toys with which their more advantaged agemates are so familiar. The ordinary youngster's learning functions are challenged by toys and play activities which serve the purpose of helping to give expression to ideas, deal with anxieties, make friends and convey to adults their skills, knowledge, concerns and confusions. This resulted in many experimental programs.

The program in which the children described herein were enrolled offered what might be described as a good nursery school curriculum, featuring a combination of adult structured and child structured activities containing rich and regular experiences in art, music, science, and physical fitness. They spent much time buying and cooking food to eat and talk about. In its thirty separate centers one observes many differences from group to group. These are due to the fact that each teacher develops her program using to best advantage the physical space, play materials, the assets of the neighborhood, and her own particular skills, as well as those of her aide, assistant, or whatever supportive personnel implement the staff. The particular combination of children within her group and the different experiences that the various ones of them might have had also contribute to her guide as to how to balance her program and adjust the schedule.

543

The primary goal in such a program is to encourage the child's interest in his immediate environment and to help him gain mastery over himself and those aspects of the environment with which he must learn to deal. Mastery over himself refers to the usual listing of the emerging learning functions - motor, language, perceptual and conceptual development, memory, problem-solving, logical thinking, behavioral controls, pleasure, and the ability to organize and integrate knowledge. The teachers view themselves as investors of the learning process through their efforts to make it possible, meaningful, and gratifying. Inter-personal relationships, child to child and child to adult are considered important. It is expected that effective approaches to other people must, for Head Start children, be taught and fostered. Teacher help is offered with the aim of helping the child not only to "learn to learn" but also to begin to comprehend the learning skills idea - to know that looking, listening, remembering, figuring out, telling and asking of his everyday life are the very ways of learning that the teachers value for him.

In summary, the writer points out that the present trend in Head Start planning and evaluation is moving away from the original idea that children were to receive overall enrichment and wonder-provoking experiences so that they might enjoy going to school. The current emphasis is to place a big burden on the Head Start teachers to focus their teaching efforts on activities structured to foster the development of certain of the cognitive skills. Implicit in such an approach is a failure to respect and recognize the seriousness and importance to the children themselves of the generally personal rather than purely intellectual aspects of their lives. These other aspects include incidental events which may in the long run matter more to the children than those on the teacher's schedule. Such events are examined and illustrated. A type of program which places emphasis on both the structured task and the child structured play, and aims to improve the children's skills in both areas is presented. It is suggested that the learnings from these incidental, brief encounters and continuing dramatic play are probably not measurable due to their spontaneous and changing nature. However, regardless of whether or not their value to the child's total development can be proven, they are of immeasurable value in a positive sense in the children's own estimate of their experiences. In program planning, teacher preparation, research and evaluation we need to attach greater importance to the children's present overall experiences in the Centers. Attention to cognitive development must continue to be a major concern but in itself will not lead to an accurate picture of early learning.

544

AN ANALYSIS OF CURRENT ISSUES IN THE EVALUATION OF EDUCATIONAL PROGRAMS

Herbert Zimiles, Ph.D.,
Chairman, Research Division,
Bank Street College of Education,
New York, New York

HERBERT ZIMILES, Ph.D.

During this era of educational innovation, it is becoming increasingly unpopular to make assumptions about the validity of an educational program, or even an idea, without amassing objective, systematically collected data bearing directly upon its value. Each new program is met with the demand for its evaluation, and is challenged to demonstrate that in fact it brings about the changes claimed for it. Soon, it may be predicted, libraries, museums, summer camps, and other familiar institutionalized efforts to effect a psychological influence, will undergo the same systematic evaluation as more formal educational programs. Ultimately, perhaps, no program of action will escape this form of review. If the behavioral sciences were sufficiently developed in theory and method to support so rigorous an empirical attitude, there would be no reason to question what is fact becoming a tradition (if not an industry) of program evaluation. Unfortunately, however, most of the results of evaluation studies are open to a wide range of interpretation; the ambiguity of the findings usually seriously impairs their utility. The concept of evaluation itself, therefore, deserves more careful examination.

The Dominance of Outcome Evaluation

If one looks at the problem of evaluating educational programs for young children as an example, it is possible to identify at least three levels at which evaluation can be conducted: by examining the stated objectives of the program, or its mode of operation, or its actual accomplishments. Each of these approaches requires different skills. A theoretically-oriented educator whose breadth of vision is combined with a sense of practicality and knowledge of child development, who can formulate developmentally desirable goals and foresee viable modes of operation, could be asked to examine the objectives of the program. In order to judge the mode of operation of the program, the evaluator would have to be an expert in educational operations and know the relationship between particular forms of operation and a set of specified goals. Finally, evaluation of the outcome of a program would require the skills of a psychometrician because such an approach calls for sophistication in sampling, statistical analysis, and measurement of relevant behaviors.

547

Among these various levels of evaluation, it is the third alternative which is almost invariably preferred. There may be agreement that the goals of a program are admirable, yet it may fail because it is not being executed properly. Further, the goals may be judged to be exemplary, and the operation of the project equally outstanding, but it may fail to produce the outcomes that were expected for it. Thus, the evaluation of outcomes gives the appearance of being most definitive, and it is not surprising, therefore, that ambitious evaluation studies of substance usually take this form. It is generally agreed that systematic, empirical assessment of actual accomplishment is preferably to subjective judgment of potential success.

As a result, the evaluation of educational programs has almost always entailed a comparison of pre-post scores of participating children with an appropriate control group. It is reasoned that if it cannot be demonstrated that the consumers of an educational product can perform distinctively on a specified, observable criterion task, the value of the product is thrown into doubt. For this simple paradigm to be workable, however, one must specify at what point the task should be given to the consumer, and more important, criteria must be established for designating the nature of this critical evaluation task.

Deficiencies of Outcome Evaluation
The psychometrician-evaluator must first define outcome in order to establish the criterion task which will serve as an index of change. For practical reasons, including the pressure upon him to deliver results quickly, he is most likely to decide to study the immediate outcome of a program by comparing the child's performance on the criterion task at the end of the year with what it was at the beginning. Such evaluation will reveal nothing about the long-term effects of participation in a program -- about the durability of immediately visible effects, which, it may be argued, constitutes the true payoff of a program. Nor can we learn about "incubation" effects which first begin to manifest themselves at later points in time (as a result of their interaction with subsequent experiences at later developmental stages). The problems associated with long-term evaluation are obvious; long-term outcomes can be studied with precision only where there is control over the influence of the intervening period so as to provide assurance that differences in outcome many years later can reasonably be attributed to previous participation in the program in question. Where such control is not possible, as it seldom is, then at least frequent periodic assessment during the intervening period is necessary to estimate the influence of interpolated experiences. Such a program is so expensive and time-consuming that it is seldom undertaken. Nevertheless, without provision for long-term study, outcome evaluation lacks the definitiveness it appears to have at first glance.

A second, and perhaps more important issue, is that the validity of measurement of outcomes is seldom known; when it is known, it is often disappointingly low. The

548

psychometrician engaged in outcome-assessment research is likely to invest his greatest effort in those areas over which he has the most control and the greatest expertise. He will take pains to achieve proper sampling, and can be expected to provide for suitable comparison groups. His choice of measuring instruments is likely to be dictated by their convenience for mass administration and efficient data processing. As to the psychometric credentials of the instrument itself, the availability of norms and the level of reliability will probably be given a higher priority than the nebulous issue of validity. By temperament and training, the psychometrician-evaluator is ill-equipped to deal with questions regarding the relevance of the instrument; therefore, such questions are likely to get less attention than the host of other factors to which he must also attend. That psychological processes in children at age four and five, for example, have not been sufficiently delineated, and therefore methods for measuring these processes remain crude, is a fact he may learn from consultants, since he himself is probably not a specialist in child development. Such unsettling information simply reinforces his decision to invest his energies in other aspects of the assessment problem, while resolving to do the best he can with regard to the difficult question of validity. As a result, the methods of measurement used to evaluate outcomes may often be only dimly related to the hypothetical processes affected by the program itself.

Furthermore, outcome evaluation is also bedeviled by the fact that only a portion of the possible outcomes can be studied. The possible outcomes produced by Head Start, for example, are multitudinous and complex. They range from changes in a child's factual knowledge, language comprehension and expression, curiosity, mastery of materials, attitude toward school and relatedness to his peer group, to dramatic changes in his physical health, and to the sundry effects his attendance in Head Start may have upon his mother and the rest of the family -- from fostering a meaningful relationship between the mother and the school and extending her orbit of relationships in the community, to simply providing relief from caring for her child while he is in school, or freeing her to attend to other family members and other household duties. The list of all possible outcomes is obviously very long. The evaluator, of necessity, must invest in but a handful of dimensions for study -- those he believes will show the greatest impact. But his wager may be wrong, and whatever his choice, he will be sampling but a fragment of the effects produced by the program.

Furthermore, because classes vary in their procedures and goals, a given evaluation procedure, while peculiarly apt for some classes, may be inappropriate for others. In addition, the relative importance of the various influences of a program can be expected to vary from child to child and family to family. This will result from the differential receptivity of individual children and their families to their particular program. This interaction effect means that whatever the dimension under assess-

549

ment, it is likely that for some children the gains will be large, for others modest, and for still others nil. By averaging the gain in a single dimension of influence over all the children in the evaluation study, a misleading leveling of the effect is accomplished. It may be argued that only a case study of individual children and their families will begin to reveal the total effect of a program like Head Start and the particular pattern of influence experienced in each case.

For outcome evaluation to be effective, it should have a quality it almost always lacks -- comprehensiveness. Partial evaluation of outcome can lead to an unwarranted denigration of a program; yet, only a program with the most explicitly and narrowly defined goals is likely to receive comprehensive evaluation. Furthermore, it is not merely the actual accomplishment of a program that matters, but whether it has the potential within its fabric for achieving its stated goals. This latter consideration is one which the evaluator-psychometrician with an empirical bent may be unprepared to cope with.

The question of program potential leads to the issue of the timing of an outcome evaluation. In the case of Head Start, it may be argued that the program is still too new for its potential usefulness to be judged; and that it should be evaluated only when its operations have been stabilized, and properly trained professional staff and fully-equipped plants made available. Adequately trained personnel are not at present available in sufficient numbers to staff Head Start classrooms; in some regions they are not available at all. The very concept of Head Start, by design, called for experimentation with professional roles, new ways of teaching children whose backgrounds and skills were strange to most preschool teachers, much more intensive involvement with parents and the community, and new methods of plant utilization and recruiting children. All these considerations indicate that the program is bound, initially, to go through a formative, transitional period, thus seriously calling into question the timing of the evaluation to which this complicated program is being subjected so early in its evolution.*

Thus, the timing, the completeness, and most important of all, the validity and relevance of outcome-evaluation methods may be questioned. This is not to say that outcome evaluation is not an inherently sound procedure, but rather that it is more complicated than it first appears to be, and that present limitations in knowledge and technology seriously curtail its usefulness. Although the problems of timing and even of comprehensiveness can be met with great effort and expense, the fundamen-

* It should be noted that the current national evaluation of the Head Start program differs from the earlier, independently undertaken, local studies, which were intent on demonstrating whether or not Head Start was a "success". The national evaluation, more realistically, is examining the relationship between variations in program on the one hand, and corresponding variation in pupil performance and impact on parents on the other.

550

tal problem of validity of measurement remains as a powerfully restrictive factor. This means that only modest claims can be made for outcome-evaluation studies. They may offer suggestive leads about the benefits and shortcomings of a program, but the life of a program should not depend upon their findings. The evaluator-psychometrician does not now possess an infallible, definitive yardstick against which a program can be compared. Just as psychologists have adopted the concept of construct validity in recognition of the fact that the theoretical network invoked to test the validity of a particular method of measurement may be as faulty as the method of measurement itself, so too, negative evaluation findings may be attributable more to the procedures employed to assess a preschool program than to the preschool program itself. Unfortunately, the psychometrician-evaluator frequently becomes so habituated to the shortcomings of his methods that he may hardly notice them as he proceeds to gather his data. As a result, he becomes party to an unwitting conspiracy of silence regarding the deficiencies of existing evaluation procedures.

Outcome Evaluation Viewed as Research

The most disturbing consequence of the image of adequacy and, sometimes, even of invulnerability fostered by outcome evaluation, aside from the misleading information it generates under the guise of scientific fact, is that it fails to exploit a valuable opportunity for the research-minded psychologist to refine and extend existing methodology. The outcome evaluation provides an opportunity to study an influence process with a specified beginning and end, and challenges him to identify the psychological processes activated therein. He is then asked to find or devise valid methods of measuring these behavioral variables. Further, the influence process itself constitutes a criterion against which he can validate his methods of measuring the variables affected. For example, intensive study of an experimental class may lead the researcher to conclude that the child's "symbolic functioning" is most directly affected by the program. He would then proceed to find or devise a measure of "symbolic functioning" appropriate to the age level under study, and administer it on a pre-post basis in a number of classes in the experimental program. The pre-post change data would then contribute to the validation of his measure and the confirmation of his hypothesis. Thus, an evaluation study offers the researcher intensive exposure to sets of similar transactions involving many different children in different classrooms over a relatively long period of time. This maximizes the likelihood of abstracting the most significant dimensions of behavior affected by classroom events and at the same time provides both a design and a ready field setting for validating the theoretical inferences drawn from the previous period of intensive observation. In contrast with the relatively modest efforts of the researcher who attempts to measure the tenuous psychological changes he manages to induce in the laboratory, the evaluation worker has access to a program of psychological

551

change of much greater intensity and duration, without the distortions produced by the artifacts of the laboratory setting.

However, the psychometrician-evaluator almost never describes his evaluation procedure as a study of the construct validity of his methods, nor does he view the evaluation task as an instrument for learning. The theoretical excursion into the delineation of the psychological processes involved in his study is cut short if not entirely bypassed; the re-evaluation of validity seldom occurs. Along similar lines, he views himself as unrelated to the program he is evaluating; in fact, the objectivity of his position as an outside judge is thought to be enhanced by eliminating his exposure to the program under evaluation. This can lead to an evaluation procedure which relies exclusively on test findings, and can result in the remarkable occurrence of an evaluator not setting foot inside even one of the classrooms whose programs he is evaluating. The pre and post test data become like the blood or urine samples taken in a physiology experiment in their mechanistic quality and their physical remoteness from the level at which the experimental intervention itself is introduced. Unfortunately, the psychologist does not possess the physiologist's knowledge of the nature of the functional relationship between his test data and the process under study. What is perhaps needed most in current evaluation work is intensive study of the influence process itself so as to identify the principal variables affected and the nature of their interplay.

In addition, it should be noted that an evaluation method remote from the actual operation of a program, nevertheless, may influence the program it assesses even before its results are made known. Program directors and teachers may often look upon the evaluation procedure as embodying a scientific summary statement of the learning activities which are supposed to take place. As a result, it is not uncommon to find elements of the evaluation testing procedure incorporated into the daily teaching program of a given classroom, not only because the teacher is interested in having her children give a favorable impression upon being evaluated, but because she perceives the tests used by the examiner as specifying the scope and character of learning which scientific analysis indicates should take place. Thus, an evaluation can affect the program not only by the substantive data it provides regarding the psychological functioning of young children in school, but by the guidelines it may implicitly set for programming among teachers who interpret the evaluation procedure as constituting a summary of standards and expectations.

Absolute vs. Operational Evaluation

In the light of the limitations in outcome evaluation discussed above, current attempts to evaluate innovative educational programs should be more varied and "operational" in their approach, focusing more heavily on the influence process of

552

the program in conjunction with more modest, exploratory assessments of outcome. By way of contrast with such an approach, outcome evaluation may be conceived as an "absolute" form of evaluation because it makes no assumptions about the validity of the principles underlying the program. It places the burden on a program to demonstrate its effectiveness by producing change in designated criterion variables. An "operational" evaluation, on the other hand, begins with an assessment of the goals of a program and its design for operation. Proceeding from there, it assumes that whatever merits a given program may have, it will benefit from systematic monitoring and study by an evaluation agency whose work is closely coordinated with the execution of the program. In so doing, the operational evaluation actively supports program implementation while contributing to the eventual development of sound methods for absolute evaluation.

An operational evaluation would begin with a theoretical analysis of the program by addressing itself to such questions as:

1. Are the stated goals of the program coordinated with generally accepted goals for educating young children? If not, is it clear how they are different?
2. Does the proposed form of the program maximize the probability of achieving its stated goals? Is the proposed mode of implementation suitable to the objectives sought?
3. Is the statement of goals and proposed operations sufficiently differentiated according to age, developmental level and cultural background of the participating children, to guide local practitioners in developing their program?

Following an examination of the total program in the abstract, the operational evaluator subdivides the program into its component parts, and proceeds to evaluate the degree to which each is being implemented according to the original plan. He identifies obstacles to proper implementation and recommends how these can be eliminated. Always with an eye upon the goals of the program (and with a readiness to recommend that the statement of goals be revised), the evaluator studies the mode of teaching, the program for the parents, if any, the utilization of auxiliary personnel, etc., in terms of whether these conform to the originally-stated plan of operation, helping to identify the patterns of variation which exist. With all the improvisation often required, especially if the program is large and/or a crash program, an operational evaluation has an additional advantage in that it will include in its study the compromises which have become necessary -- in modification of program, in plant, in selection and utilization of personnel -- on the basis of which adjustments in policy can be recommended.

Less on the order of "trouble shooting," but still operational in character, is evaluation work stimulated by specific researchable questions raised by the practitioner. For example, there may be interest in evaluating two different ways of teaching perceptual discrimination ability, or in studying the ways in which peer group behavior changes as a function of preschool experience. The program's administrator may be interested in the difference between church and secular agencies' programs, or may need help in recruiting, selecting and placing teaching personnel. How can new recruits be assessed so that their placement will maximally exploit their talents? What are the areas of teacher functioning in which intensively-trained recruits are competent and which are the areas in which the new teachers function least effectively?

Perhaps the most important facet of operational evaluation is that it requires the evaluation worker to become saturated with the life of the program he is studying. Unlike the absolute evaluation worker who studies children in isolation to examine the effects of a program, the operational evaluator is process-oriented; his main work requires him to study classroom life intensively. Virtually all his assignments will require him to record some aspect of classroom interaction -- how the teacher uses a particular method, how the children respond to a given phase of the program, etc. The phenomena he will be asked to study are in the classrooms themselves, because his job is to service the operation of the program. In this manner he will gain the opportunity to advance current knowledge regarding how children's behavior is influenced by school experience, and ultimately to formulate a series of hypotheses regarding the effects of the program with sufficient elaboration and supporting methodology to mount a meaningful absolute evaluation.

Thus, operational evaluation is seen as a first stage in the development of a sound evaluation study, one which cannot be bypassed if effective absolute evaluation is to follow. This means abandoning for the moment, at least, traditional modes of absolute evaluation, with their psychometric dominance, in favor of a long period of intensive operational evaluation geared toward delineating the influence process of the program. It implies, too, that evaluation work must be conducted by people who are theoretically sophisticated as well as technically competent to study the day-to-day operation of a program in terms of its principal psychological transactions.

The helpful editorial comments of Jacqueline Rosen and Doris Wallace are gratefully acknowledged.

THE LONG VIEW

Sargent Shriver,
Director, Office of Economic Opportunity,
Washington, D. C.

One of the great dangers lying in ambush for any new program is the short view method of planning. The quick result, the new statistic, the startling discovery, the overnight success: these cliches are the motor on which the short view runs.

The trouble is, it's a weak motor. After the first result or the first success, it peters out.

Applied to a program such as Head Start, the short view may get things going, but it can't *keep* things going.

That's why a lot of short view people are satisfied just to have a Head Start that has gotten things going. They don't have a long enough view to see that Head Start has to keep them going, or else it's just another bureaucrat's plaything -- one more program in a list that is already too long.

Because Head Start was planned and launched in an incredibly short time, the skeptics said it would fall flat on its face. They said it would reach only a small number of children. Its benefits wouldn't last.

In three short years, Head Start has proved the skeptics wrong.

-- more than 2 million pre-school children have already been enrolled.

-- their families have been drawn into the total life of the community.

-- more than a million youngsters have entered regular school with aroused minds and livened hearts.

-- 325,000 neighborhood people have volunteered to work in the program.

None of this was happening before Head Start.

Fortunately, everyone concerned with the program, from the architects at headquarters to the workers in the field, have dedicated themselves to the long view: finding ways to make the program grow in effectiveness, and to sustain and increase its influence.

When a child leaves Head Start -- whether year round or summer program -- his records must not be stamped "Graduated" and filed in a drawer. The work has only begun.

In the first place, we must continue to encourage and support *family* neighborhood strength. Poverty-held families tend to isolate themselves -- from each other and from the outside world. That is the nature of poverty. Head Start planners and workers must continually seek ways in which families can help each other. Together they can identify problems and seek solutions -- alone they can only be victimized by those problems. Head Start families can start neighborhood baby-sitting pools, form consumer coops, or combine efforts to combat housing problems. That's only a few things that can be done. The knowledge gained by parents in Head Start that in coordinated action there is effective and productive strength must never be lost. The means to good health should always be available to the child and his family. It is not sufficient to give a five-year old medical and dental examinations and treatment if, at ten or twelve years old, these are neglected or out of reach.

When the child enters Head Start, both he and his family must be "hooked in" to a source of health and welfare services lasting far beyond the term of the program. The facilities offered by agencies such as the OEO Child and Parent Centers, clinics, the OEO Neighborhood Health Centers, medical assistance under welfare, crippled children's programs, and of course, the physicians themselves, must be constantly mobilized on behalf of these families. There must be alert watchdogs along the route to ensure that families receive proper and adequate direction to these sources.

Head Start parents, properly involved in the program, have become motivated to take an active part in their children's early development. They have learned that they have a vital role to play, and they want to go on playing it. This motivation must be given continued and strong support. Parents must remain as participants in the planning and operation of their children's education and development; they must be given opportunities to work in the classroom as employees, volunteers or observers; they must be confident they can have free and frank exchanges of ideas with those in charge; educational opportunities offered them by Head Start must be continued and progressively expanded.

Doubtless the voices of the skeptics will be raised, crying that herein lies an unrealistic, whimsical never-never-land. Many of these will be the same voices which, before

558

the first summer Head Start in 1965, said the program would never reach even 10,000 children. It reached 561,000.

Little if any new legislation will be required for the sustained carrying forward of the innovations born in Head Start. The mechanism for adult education is already in existence. It could easily be made complementary to this sustained effort. Local communities will need to develop personnel, and to upgrade the skills of non-professionals. (Head Start's exciting new program of Career Development is discussed elsewhere in this volume.)

A nationwide effort would be required to bring about the effective involvement of volunteers and the mobilization of every available local resource.

Already, more and more school systems are engaging non-professional aides, usually parents, to work with the teacher in the classroom. More and more, parents are being invited to serve on advisory councils, helping to blue-print their children's education, in close liaison with the professionals.

There is an encouraging change in thinking about early childhood development, which is also having an impact upon the regular school system. Slowly, some of our flat-footed ideas are being thrown out, and replaced by ideas that are current, imaginative and flexible. For much of this change, Head Start deserves credit.

NEW CAREERS IN HEAD START

William J. Benoit,
Director, Career Development and Technical Assistance,
Project Head Start, Office of Economic Opportunity,
Washington, D. C.

THE NEED FOR TRAINING AND CAREER OPPORTUNITIES

A well-trained staff may have more impact than any other single factor in accomplishing Head Start's overall objective of providing low-income young children with the best possible Head Start; at the same time we must recognize the growing problem of finding personnel experienced in child development and related fields to staff individual programs.

Since Head Start was initiated in the summer of 1965, it has served some 2 million children in summer and full year programs. Head Start proposes to create career opportunities where they do not exist at this time in this pool of 100,000 paid positions concentrating on those employed in full year programs. Building career opportunities from presently existing jobs is a complicated administrative procedure, and Head Start is committed to making a strong beginning in the direction of career opportunity during the coming year.

Jobs with relevant training accompanying them can become careers if certain system changes are included. For instance, before training begins, arrangements must be made to open the job system for those who perform well both in their job and in training which accompanies it so that they can transfer laterally into different kinds of jobs, diagonally into different jobs at a more responsible level, and, when appropriate, vertically in the same area of work. The training given must be immediately relevant to the performance of the job in question, and it must also receive academic credit which is marketable in our credential-oriented society. We are talking about a job rather than a career, if a position does not allow movement into similar work outside OEO with no sacrifice in responsibility or income.

When a career progression program is set up to provide opportunity for individuals in poverty, it must certainly offer income at the entry level which is above the poverty scale, and it should include frequent advances in income, perhaps three a year, which reward performance and achievement rapidly. It is particularly important that

563

a program supported by the Office of Economic Opportunity provide training which leads to marketable degrees and certificates, in that the Office of Economic Opportunity is dedicated to moving people permanently out of poverty. Thus Head Start in its Career Development Program is working closely with school systems and human service agencies at all levels to provide career opportunities for persons who wish to move outside OEO in terms of job responsibility.

Head Start, then, is seeking to provide maximum opportunity for professionals and non-professionals to develop according to their individual interests and capacities. Skills and understandings gained from effective training benefit the employee, the program, and the local community by helping to meet the real needs of young children and their families; training can also help to lift the employee to greater responsibility and income. Within the Head Start system, Community Action Programs and delegate agencies that operate Full Year Head Start Programs are being asked to create agency-wide position development plans which establish clearly defined paths for career progression opportunities and which include the training necessary for advancement or transfer. Rapid salary advancement as a reward for competent performance is an essential part of each career development plan.

Head Start presently has three existing training programs other than special institutes and training sessions for particular local or regional purposes. **In-service Training** which is offered through the staff of a given program and as a part of the working day routine; **Summer Orientation Training** which is typically forty hours long and conducted on university campuses for a week preceding the operation of the summer programs; and **Eight Week Training** which is a residential university experience for selected staff members from the Full Year Head Start Programs. In addition, Head Start has recently initiated a new program as part of its career development emphasis called Supplementary Training. This supplements the three existing types of training previously mentioned, and is one part of a major attempt to provide career opportunities for Head Start staff members from presently existing jobs.

SUPPLEMENTARY TRAINING

Supplementary Training is conducted by colleges and universities in Head Start facilities. The program is developed jointly by Head Start and Community Action Agencies, and the Colleges and Universities. Training received in a Supplementary Training Program must be given academic credit which can be used toward both an Associate and a Bachelor's Degree. This provides the opportunity for staff members who elect to leave Head Start to move into other fields with their marketable two-year and four-year degrees. It means that a mother with four children who serves as a teacher aide in Head Start can begin to think of her job as a career in that there is a real possibility of permanent employment for her, when she acquires a two-year

564

degree, be the employment within Head Start, in the new program Project Follow Through, in a local public school system, or in some other human service agency in the community. She can also consider the position to be a career because she receives frequent salary increases for her performance which move her closer to a professional income level, and she has the option of transferring into another field from teaching such as neighborhood organization or social work. In effect, she is moving toward the flexibility that a middle-class college graduate has in terms of career opportunity. Because the system has been set up in advance for her, she will find that all of her credits in an Associate of Arts degree will be transferable into a four-year program, and she hopefully will not face the unpleasant situation where perfectly good academic credit cannot be transferred because of the requirements of an inflexible system.

Community Action Programs and delegate agencies, such as school systems which operate Head Start programs, must establish a career development plan in the year to come which includes "jobs with training built in," salary increases for good performance, and lateral, diagonal, and vertical transfer opportunities. The agency must also have a long term training plan responsive to the needs of a varied staff, and this plan must be supported by a counseling program with effective evaluation being an integral part of the system. Each agency operating a Full Year Head Start Program will, in the coming year, establish a Career Development Committee composed of both professional and non-professional staff members representing the various types and levels of employees in the program, and the non-professional staff members will fill at least fifty percent of the Committee positions.

The Career Development Committee will work with other public and private agencies on an ad hoc basis to help coordinate training opportunities. The Career Development Committee serves in a staff advisory capacity to the Program Director, and has the responsibility for developing criteria for selection of staff members to be involved in training; it will also work with staff specialists to establish criteria for overall agency personnel procedures, including selection of staff, promotion policies, compensation scales, and evaluation of staff performance.

COLLEGE AND UNIVERSITY INVOLVEMENT
IN
SUPPLEMENTARY TRAINING

From the early stages of planning for Supplementary Training there seemed to be little doubt that staff members in Head Start would be delighted with the possibilities offered in a program which could give them academic credit for training courses conducted for the most part in Head Start facilities. The response of institutions of higher education, on the other hand, seemed questionable because we asked for so much. The objectives of the program included training, not only professional persons used to university regulations, but a large number of non-professionals, one-third of whom had not completed high school. The non-professionals are for the most part women, ten to twenty years older than typical college students. Frequently they have large families for whom they provide sole support. There is little research available to describe the ability of non-professionals, but those who have worked most closely with them feel those working as aides in Head Start are the "cream" of an able population that has never been utilized in our society. They learn quickly and, not surprisingly, are most effective in working with low-income young children.

Many schools of education have been pleased with internship programs which prepare middle-income college graduates to become elementary and secondary teachers. This is a modern day version of the apprenticeship concept wherein a person learns to teach by teaching under supervision, not by observing a master teacher teach. Many universities have given graduate credit for this type of experience and this, in effect, is what we ask institutions to do for non-professionals from Head Start; the credit is given at the lower division or Associate of Arts level, however. The whole program is built from this basic premise: professional skills in human services can best be acquired through a combination of on-the-job training with good supervision, supported by formal course work for breadth and depth of understanding offered in the framework of a small seminar.

Much of the seminar work should cross over disciplinary lines, making use of a team of instructors interacting with students and with each other. In the short range view, this is very expensive; in the long range it is economical, because it really works much better than one instructor lecturing at thirty students about issues which they often do not see as relevant to their concerns.

The majority of people to be trained under the Head Start Supplementary Training program will be non-professionals with family responsibilities which require them to maintain full-time employment while participating in an academic course of study. This will require that colleges and universities conduct a major portion of their course work after working hours and on Saturdays. In addition, it will be desirable to conduct classes on an extension basis within the community, such as a centrally located Head Start facility.

Colleges, universities and Head Start staff will need to work closely together in identifying those situations where course work and job experience can be combined into a comprehensive course of study. Programs will need to stimulate the interest and efforts of universities in creating new child development curricula specifically

566

designed for persons working with disadvantaged children and to tailor their courses to meet the special needs of Head Start professionals and non-professionals.

If individuals participating in an academic course of study are to gain long-term benefits from the training, universities will need to award academic credit. This credit should tie into an accredited two-year and subsequently a four-year degree. Acceptance of a new population taking revised or new courses requires special adjustment in other areas such as financial aid policies, testing and counseling services-- in fact, practically every service of the university needs to make a special response to the non-professional.

At this point it is customary for the university to begin thinking of its essential mission. If so many adjustments are necessary to accommodate a program such as Supplementary Training, can the university justify expenditure of its limited faculty and supportive resources for this task? After considering the needs of the local community or area served by the university, the answer has frequently been yes, with certain conditions tied to this positive response.

The Office of Economic Opportunity must carry most of the financial burden in the early years of the program so that the university can sense whether its faculty has continuing interest in this type of program. At the same time it must find increasing financial support for the program within its constituency, Also, OEO must be willing to adjust its contractual arrangement to the regular flow of university committee and fiscal procedures.

The future of Supplementary Training is hopeful if OEO continues to operate Head Start. Educational Projects, Inc. conducted a feasibility study in the spring of 1967, which included a survey of 215 institutions of higher education across the country, assessing their interest in participation in Supplementary Training; 88% of these institutions responded favorably. The program was announced informally in early July, 1967, and 19 proposals were submitted by the application deadline in mid-August. Twelve programs were initiated in September, 1967, many of them cooperative arrangement where junior colleges serve those who are completing their final two year of undergraduate work. Professional persons working in Head Start programs are also eligible for Supplementary Training; they will pay one-half the costs of training, whereas the non-professionals will receive it at no cost. Professionals may take upper division courses in Child Development and related fields or graduate work in the same disciplines as appropriate. OEO hopes to have 70 programs operative by July of 1968 in this new venture to serve the needs of children and families in poverty.

567

Articles for reference for NEW CAREERS in HEAD START

CAREER ORIENTED TRAINING vs JOB ORIENTED TRAINING, (Riessman, Frank).
> School of Education
> New York University
> Washington Square
> New York, New York 10003

CURRICULUM DESIGN FOR TRAINING THE TRAINERS OF NON-PROFESSIONALS
> New Careers Training Laboratory
> 184 Fifth Avenue
> New York City, New York 10010

INDIGENOUS NON-PROFESSIONAL (THE), (Reiff and Riessman)
> Community Mental Health Journal
> Box 23
> Lexington, Massachusetts 02173

ISSUES IN TRAINING THE NEW NON-PROFESSIONAL, (Riessman, Frank)
> School of Education
> New York University
> Washington Square
> New York City, New York 10003

JOB ORIENTED GROUP TRAINING FOR HIGH SCHOOL DROP-OUTS: THE ISSUES, RELATIONSHIPS AND OUTCOME, (Bloomberg, Claire M.)
> Center for Youth and Community Studies
> 2400 6th Stree, N. W.
> Washington, D. C.

MODEL FOR TRAINING NON-PROFESSIONALS DELINQUENCY STUDY AND YOUTH DEVELOPMENT PROJECT, (Naylor, Naomi LeB.)
> Southern Illinois University
> Edwardsville, Illinois

PROFILE OF THE NEW CAREERS TRAINING PROJECT (Sponsored by Institute for Youth Studies, Howard University), Bank Street College of Education
> 216 West Fourteenth Street
> New York City, New York 10011

568

Books

CULTURALLY DEPRIVED CHILD (THE), (Riessman, Frank)
Harper and Row Publishers, Inc.
49 East 33rd Street
New York City, New York 10016

NEW CAREERS FOR NON-PROFESSIONAL IN EDUCATION
University of California Extension
University of California at Riverside
Riverside, California 92502

NEW CAREERS FOR THE POOR, (Pearl and Riessman)
The Free Press
866 Third Avenue
New York City, New York 10022

TEACHER EDUCATION IN A SOCIAL CONTEXT, (Klopf and Bowman)
Mental Health Materials Center, Inc.
104 East 25th Street
New York City, New York 10010

Pamphlets

NON-PROFESSIONAL IN THE EDUCATIONAL SYSTEM (THE)
Office of Economic Opportunity
Publications Office
1200 19th Street, N. W.
Washington, D. C. 20506

TAP - THE TEACHER AIDE PROGRAM
Washington School of Psychiatry
1610 New Hampshire Avenue, N. W.
Washington, D. C.

ISSUES IN TRAINING (Edited by Weschler and Schein)
National Training Laboratories (NEA)
1201 16th Street, N. W.
Washington, D. C. 20006

FOLLOW THROUGH:
FULFILLING THE PROMISE OF HEAD START

Robert L. Egbert, Ph.D.,
Director "Follow Through" Program,
U. S. Office of Education,
Washington, D. C.

ROBERT L. EGBERT, Ph.D.

The success of Head Start's enriched preschool activities has been established. Few will deny that children with Head Start experience enter school better prepared to meet the challenge of the classroom.

Through Head Start they have learned how to identify colors, distinguish shapes, enlarge their vocabularies. They have moved beyond their own neighborhoods, many to see for the first time a department store, a zoo, a museum. They have had health checkups their parents could not afford. Nutrition, psychological, social work and speech therapy services have all helped remove impediments to learning. Head Start has helped to put disadvantaged youngsters -- children who are deprived education- ally as well as economically -- on a more equal basis with the other children with whom they will compete in school.

Yet unless the Head Start child continues to receive special attention, he tends to lose all that he has gained. One summer or one year of Head Start is not enough to overcome the cumulative effects of deprivation in the early years. For the children of poverty the benefits of Head Start must be continued in elementary school. Fol- low Through is essential.

Dr. Max Wolff pointed this up rather clearly in his New York City follow-up study of Head Starters in kindergarten. He states, "The desire to learn dies because it is unfed." In comparing Head Start children who entered kindergarten in September 1965 with classmates who had no preschool experience, Dr. Wolff found "Head Start children do better than their classmates when both have good teachers." But in sharp contrast, these youngsters "do worse and are more damaged by poor kinder- garten teaching than their classmates. More damage is done to the child who looks forward eagerly to an educational program he has learned to enjoy than to the child who has had no previous knowledge of what to expect, if the later school experience is poor."

To bring equal opportunities to those Head Start graduates who have tasted a school

573

world rich with understanding adults and meaningful and interesting activities, President Johnson called for a Follow Through program in his February Message on Children and Youth to the Congress:

> *The achievements of Head Start must not be allowed to fade. For we have learned another truth which should have been self-evident--- that poverty's handicap cannot be easily erased or ignored when the door of first grade opens to the Head Start child.*

> *Head Start occupies only a part of a child's day and ends all too soon. He often returns home to conditions which breed despair. If these forces are not to engulf the child and wipe out the benefits of Head Start, more is required. Follow Through is essential . . . the benefits of Head Start must be carried through the early grades.*

Follow Through has been designed to carry the benefits of Head Start into the regular school system by offering graduates of Head Start and other similar preschool programs continued special attention not only in the field of instruction but also in a wide range of other areas -- medical, dental, nutritional, psychological and social.

Administration of the program has been delegated by the Office of Economic Opportunity to the U. S. Office of Education. Policies and program guides governing the operation of Follow Through are developed jointly by the two agencies.

Forty pilot Follow Through programs were initiated in selected school districts across the Nation in the 1967-68 school year. The pilot projects -- located in city ghettos, in rural America, in the outer city -- will serve as the nucleus of a program scheduled for expansion in the future, hopefully to all disadvantaged children who have been in pre-school programs.

In its first year, Follow Through will expend approximately $3.1 million and involve approximately 4,000 children. The number of children has been deliberately kept small so that schools can provide a comprehensive program of quality services. Each school district participating in the program serves as a pilot for its region and for similar communities throughout the country. The pilot centers are open for visits by other school administrators and teachers, parents, community leaders, anyone interested in the program. Follow Through has a built-in evaluation-information program that provides for wide distribution of program results so that other school districts may benefit from the pilot experience.

Although during the first year only kindergarten or first grade children will participate in Follow Through, it is anticipated that services will be extended in future years to children through the third grade.

574

As other programs for the disadvantaged, Follow Through recognizes that children of poverty live under definite hazards -- physical, social and psychological -- which seriously hamper their growth and development. They enter school without many of the preschool skills that more privileged children bring with them from their homes.

The aim of most educational programs for youngsters from poor families has been to compensate for environmental deficiencies, raise levels of aspiration, and improve self-concepts so that disadvantaged children will be able to compete with their more privileged peers. The Follow Through pilot programs have these same basic aims but a number of other crucial objectives as well:

Individualized instruction that builds on listening and speaking skills in an atmosphere that generates curiosity, success and positive self-concept

An uninterrupted experience that builds on the Head Start experience

Social, racial and economic integration

Meaningful parent participation

Maximum use of school, neighborhood, and other resources

Continuous training for professional and non-professional staff

Evaluation designs that assess the growth of individual children and overall program effectiveness.

Follow Through focuses on the total needs of each child and thus requires a comprehensive, yet individualized, approach to learning. It means looking beyond the immediate classroom to the many environmental factors which affect the learning of a particular child. Thus, Follow Through calls for an interdisciplinary approach which provides services in the areas of health, nutrition, social services, guidance and psychology to support an individualized program of instruction. Significant involvement of parents and community agencies is vital to the program.

One of the major program goals is to help disadvantaged children develop and use language more effectively -- especially important for youngsters who must learn English as a second language. In Puerto Rico, for example, where children also speak a sub-standard Spanish, a linguistic analyst and researchers help Follow Through children develop better language skills. From this research, Puerto Rico school officials hope to create their own specialized materials for teaching language. Corpus Christi, Texas, is comparing the effectiveness of the bilingual approach and the English as a second language approach in its program for Mexican-American children.

Follow Through emphasizes developing and reinforcing self-esteem in children and introducing them to a wide, new range of experiences. A variety of enrichment activities are available to children at any given moment. Activities have been designed to allow for success, self-discovery, and awareness of individual potential so that children can be helped to view themselves realistically.

Since Follow Through monies can be used only for non-curricular, health, welfare, and special remedial services, other resources (primarily Title I of the Elementary and Secondary Education Act, as well as State and local monies) are being used in conjunction with program funds. Follow Through funds can be used to hire resource specialists, aides, and non-teaching professionals. Title I or local funds can finance additional teachers to guarantee individualized instruction. Local health and welfare agencies are being tapped to provide ancillary services to children.

With a teacher, professional specialists, and such auxiliary personnel as aides, volunteers, and parents, youngsters are provided the individualized instruction and specialized attention so vitally needed. In Prince George's County, Maryland, for instance, ten to twelve highly skilled professionals plus a large complement of aides and volunteers enable school officials to provide 1 teacher for every 14 students and an overall ratio of 1 staff member for every 8 children.

Some of the pilots are experimenting with changes in the organization and atmosphere of the classroom. In Duluth, Minnesota, one classroom in each of the three target schools has been transformed into a Kindergarten-Primary Laboratory, a comfortable "living room" for children and their parents, with an "open school" philosophy. Children attend regular kindergarten class half a day and are in the laboratory for the remainder. Each lab has six centers: listening, viewing, library, play therapy, science, mathematics, and humanities. Team teaching and a staff-student ratio of one to three are features of the individualized instructional program.

Districts must concentrate as much as possible on disadvantaged children who have participated in full-year preschool programs. Yet rather than isolate project classes from the regular school program, Follow Through children are grouped to reflect the fullest possible social, racial, and economic integration. The findings of the Equal Educational Opportunity Survey (the Coleman report) reveal the importance of providing for disadvantaged children peer models from a variety of socioeconomic groups. At least one-half of the children in a Follow Through project must be Head Start graduates; the other children can come from any social, racial, or economic group as long as a proper mix is achieved. All children receive the instructional benefits of the program; but only poor children receive health and welfare services which for middle-class children are provided by the home.

Several districts, such as Rochester, New York, and Racine, Wisconsin, are reaching

576

the above goal by sending inner city children to modern, well-equipped schools in the outer city. Youngsters participate in a morning session that is racially and economically integrated. Each afternoon they attend a special education center for lunch, a rest period, and educational activities that reinforce their morning experiences.

Universities and colleges are intimately involved in many Follow Through projects. University personnel often help in program planning and evaluation or conduct inservice training. In New Haven, Connecticut, a team of psychiatrists and social workers from the Yale Child Study Center observe Follow Through children in the classroom and provide specialist services on a regular basis. A special center on the grounds of a former college encompasses five Follow Through classes, two pre-school, one first grade, and one second grade. The entire school is geared to a search for educational alternatives. An intimate relationship is established between researchers, clinicians, and teachers.

Staff development on a continuing basis has been integrally woven into each Follow Through project. The Morgantown, West Virginia, project video-tapes and plays back immediately a series of classroom sessions so that teachers and consultants can analyze how children form their values through classroom activities. This technique should help staff find new and better ways to modify the attitudes and performances of individual students. In Tupelo, Mississippi, a noted educational author instructs staff in the techniques of teaching thinking skills to children. A system of "mail-order" micro-teaching developed in cooperation with the University of South Mississippi permits teachers to tape one-concept lessons which are mailed to the university for evaluation and returned with suggestions as to how teachers can improve techniques and methods.

Parental action can unquestionably reinforce classroom learning. In the early years, it is especially critical that parents understand the important role they play in the development of their children. For this reason, Follow Through places heavy emphasis on parent participation. Parents should be able to observe, participate in, discuss, learn about, and challenge existing school procedures. Their questions, concerns, and suggestions should be treated seriously.

Parents need to be brought closer to the learning process so that they can stimulate their children to learn at home -- so that a unity characterizes the learning that takes place in and out of the classroom. Teachers should show parents what they are doing and explain what they are trying to accomplish. Given insight into the educational process and involved in the learning experiences of their children, parents will become skilled in fostering the intellectual, emotional, and social development of their children.

577

The pilots secure parent participation by encouraging long visits in the classroom, arranging home visits by the staff team, enlisting parents to serve as classroom aides and volunteers, forming parent committees to discuss substantive issues affecting the education of their children, starting adult activities which parents plan themselves, scheduling teacher-parent conferences that focus on positive features of a child's performance as well as areas of deficiency, and providing adult and parent education and job placement services when necessary.

In San Diego, California, a Human Resource Coordinator performs home counseling and supervises the social work component; and adult education coordinator conducts basic skills classes for parents. A special program in Boulder, Colorado, emphasizing the cultural tradition of the Southwest, instructs parents and staff in the methods of home reinforcement of language.

Each Follow Through project has formulated an advisory committee composed of representatives of community action agencies, persons from the neighborhood and other appropriate community leaders to assist in the planning, implementation, and operation of the program. At least half of the advisory committee members are parents.

The community action agency has a key role in Follow Through. Although grants are made to local education agencies, school officials must develop and implement Follow Through programs in conjunction with community action agency officials. The CAA, from its administration of the Head Start program, has extensive experience in programs for young children. Furthermore, the CAA has had experience with parent involvement and mobilization of community resources that the school typically has not. It also has access to the poor. To maintain continuity with Head Start programs, it is essential that school officials responsible for Follow Through programs examine preschool records, discuss effective techniques and approaches, and draw on the experience that preschool staff have had with individual children. The home, the school, the community -- three areas of vital concern to the young disadvantaged child -- all, then, are focal points in Follow Through.

Already, it seems, Follow Through programs are advocating two concepts which have wide application for all school populations: continuity and the team approach.

Too often when a child moves from preschool to kindergarten and then on to the primary grades, he is confronted with a different atmosphere and organizational scheme at each level. He moves from an unstructured to a structured learning situation. Goals and activities vary. Often there is no logical progression from one stage to another. Follow Through is designed to remove the barriers which clearly divide nursery school from kindergarten and both of these from elementary school. If edu-

578

cation from pre-kindergarten through grade three is viewed as a unity, development is a more natural, uninterrupted progress. Transition from one stage to another is smooth, and continuity is thereby insured.

The child and his family frequently have contact with various school or school-related staff -- the teacher, nurse, social worker, and perhaps physician, community worker, elementary guidance counselor, and psychologist. Too often the efforts of these staff members are not coordinated in an effective manner. Each may act somewhat autonomously, having little interaction with other staff members, neglecting to exchange pertinent information and coordinate various services. To integrate the efforts of all personnel working with the child, Follow Through recommends the formulation of an inter-disciplinary team. The team can consult frequently on the progress of individual children and the effectiveness of the overall program. Communication, interaction, and feedback guarantee that the needs of the whole child are not treated in a fragmented manner.

Technical assistance is being provided each of the pilot programs by OE and OEO staff, special consultants and State educational agency personnel. The State will play an increasingly important role as the Follow Through program expands. The Office of Education will rely on the assistance of SEA staff in the evaluation of project proposals and in the extension of aid to individual school districts in program development, operation, and evaluation.

Many districts have initiated preschool follow-up activities under Title I, and some States are already actively promoting follow through programs of their own. The California legislature has enacted a bill encouraging school districts to solidify the preschool experience in the primary grades. No funds were originally appropriated for this program. Yet many invaluable practices require no expenditures whatsoever: transmission of preschool records, communication between and exchange of information by preschool and primary staff, dialogue between school and parents, volunteer services. Other activities cost relatively little and, in fact, are economically efficient: joint inservice training for preschool and primary staff, sharing of specialists such as psychologists, medical personnel and speech therapists who may not be used on a full-time basis for one program.

In school year 1968-69, Follow Through will probably continue on a pilot basis. More demonstration programs will be financed to broaden geographical representation and add further momentum to the pilot phase. The second year, the program will encourage further school district-university cooperation in developing innovative programs. The pilot effort will enable school districts to experiment with creative approaches to primary education. Their endeavors will undoubtedly have an effect not only on education for the disadvantaged but on all of early childhood education as well.

The necessity for early childhood education programs cannot be disputed. Bloom, in his STABILITY AND CHANGE IN HUMAN CHARACTERISTICS, reports that, in terms of intelligence measured at age 17, 80 percent is developed by approximately age 8. Because a child's future is largely determined by the age of 8, it is essential that the school and community exert themselves strenuously to counteract the effects of an early life of deprivation. In terms of financial investment alone, preventive measures are less costly than remedial efforts. Moreover, early childhood intervention will enable disadvantaged children to become, not social liabilities, but rather self-sustaining individuals able to produce and contribute and control their own destinies.

Follow Through, by financing small group instruction, language development classes, cultural enrichment opportunities, parent activities, staff development, and an array of ancillary services, will permit school systems to reinforce the gains that children make in Head Start and focus on reversing the cumulative effects of economic and educational deprivation.

BIBLIOGRAPHIES

HEADSTART

A complete Bibliography from
ERIC Information Retrieval Center
on the Disadvantaged*

Clark, Erma. "A nursery school on the Ute Indian Reservation." In: THE DISADVANTAGED CHILD: ISSUES AND INNOVATIONS, edited by Joe L. Frost and Glenn R. Hawkes. N. Y., Houghton Mifflin, p. 189-192, 1966. FROM CHILDHOOD EDUCATION, April, 1965, pp. 408-410."

Connecticut State Department of Education. Office of Program Development, PRESCHOOL EDUCATION IN DANBURY, Danbury, 24p., 10 ref., 1966. (A Demonstration City Project Report.) Bulletin No. 97.

Dept. of Public Instruction, Harrisburg, Penn., PRESCHOOL AND PRIMARY EDUCATION PROJECT, 1965-1966 annual progress report to the Ford Foundation. 46p., 1967.

Deutsch, Martin. Early social environment: its influence on school adaptation. In: THE SCHOOL DROPOUT, edited by Daniel Schreiber. Washington, D. C., National Education Association, Project School Dropouts, p. 89-100, 1964.

Deutsch, Martin. "Nursery education: the influence of social programming on early development." JOURNAL OF NURSERY EDUCATION, 18, 7 p., 5 ref. April 1963. (reprint)

Deutsch, Martin and Freedman, Alfred. A program to demonstrate the effectiveness of a "therapeutic curriculum" for the socially deprived pre-school child. 31p. 1962.

Deutsch, Martin. "What we've learned about disadvantaged children." NATION'S SCHOOLS, 75:50-51, April, 1965.

Duhl, Leonard J. "K-4/ a new school." TRANS--ACTION, 1, 4 p., March 1964. (reprint)

Elinger, Bernice D. "Literature for Head Start classes." ELEMENTARY ENGLISH, 43: 453-459, 120 ref. May 1966. (photo copy)

Englewood, New Jersey. Public Schools, PUBLIC SCHOOL BEGINS AT FOUR. Englewood, 2 p., 1965.

*Ferkauf Graduate School, Yeshiva University, 55 Fifth Avenue, New York, N. Y. 10003

ERIC Information Retrieval Center on the Disadvantaged, New York, N. Y., PRESCHOOL EDUCATION--a SELECTED BIBLIOGRAPHY. New York, N. Y., 9 p., 1967.

"Even after kindergarten: what if they're still not ready?" GRADE TEACHER 83, 134, September 1965. (xerox copy)

Feldmann, Shirley. "A preschool enrichment program for disadvantaged children." NEW ERA, 45:79-82, 8 p., 1964. (reprint)

"For the child who has nothing." From: THE NEW REPUBLIC. December 26, 1964, pp. 7-9. In: THE DISADVANTAGED CHILD: ISSUES AND INNOVATIONS, edited by Joe L. Frost and Glenn R. Hawkes. N. Y., Houghton Mifflin, p. 38-41, 1966.

Foster, Florence P. "The impact of early intervention." YOUNG CHILDREN, 21 (6), 354-360, 10 ref. September 1966.

Foster, Florence P. "The song within: music and the disadvantaged child." YOUNG CHILDREN, 20: 373-376, 2 ref. September 1965.

Getzels, J. W. "Preschool education." IN WHITE HOUSE CONFERENCE ON EDUCATION, A MILESTONE FOR EDUCATIONAL PROGRESS' Washington, D. C., Committee on Labor and Public Welfare, p. 116-125, 26 ref. 1965.

Goldstein, Leo S. EVALUATION OF AN ENRICHMENT PROGRAM FOR SOCIALLY DISADVANTAGED CHILDREN. 31 p., 1965.

Goldstein, Kenneth M. and Chorost, Sherwood B. A PRELIMINARY EVALUATION OF NURSERY SCHOOL EXPERIENCE ON THE LATER SCHOOL ADJUSTMENT OF CULTURALLY DISADVANTAGED CHILDREN. NYC Staten Island Mental Health Society, Wakoff Research Center, 35 p., 15 ref. 1966.

Gore, Lillian L. and Koury, Rose. EDUCATING CHILDREN IN NURSERY SCHOOLS AND KINDERGARTENS. Washington, D. C., Office of Education, 80p., 50 ref. 1964.

Graham, Jory. HANDBOOK FOR PROJECT HEAD START. NYC, Anti-Defamation League of B'nai B'rith, 22p., no date. (Prepared under the direction of the Urban Child Center, University of Chicago.)

Hunt, J. McVicker. "The psychological basis for using pre-school enrichment as an antidote for cultural deprivation." MERRILL-PALMER QUARTERLY, 10: 209-248, 133 ref., July 1964.

Illinois Univ., Urbana. Institute for Research on Exceptional Children. AN ACADEMICALLY ORIENTED PRESCHOOOL FOR CULTURALLY DEPRIVED CHILDREN, A PROGRESS REPORT; Prepared by Carol Bereiter. 8 p. 1965.

Indiana Univ. Foundation, Bloomington. "The development and evaluation of a diagnostically based curriculum for psycho-socially deprived preschool children; proposal and interim reports by Walter L. Hodges, Boyd R. McCandless, and Howard H. Spicker. 53 p. ref. 1964-1966.

John, Vera P. POSITION PAPER ON PRE-SCHOOL PROGRAMS: A BRIEF SURVEY OF RESEARCH ON THE CHARACTERISTICS OF CHILDREN FROM LOW-INCOME BACKGROUNDS. 12p., 34 ref., 1964.

Jones, Edgar L. EARLY SCHOOL ADMISSIONS PROJECT. NYC, Ford Foundation, 18 p. 1965. (A Ford Foundation Reprint from Southern Education Report, Vol. 1, No. 1, July-August 1965.)

Karracker, Cyrus. "Denmark's "save the children." YOUNG CHILDREN, 21 (6), 365-370, 5 ref. September 1966.

Klein, Donald C. and Lindemann, Elizabeth. APPROACHES TO PRE-SCHOOL SCREENING. Journal of School Health, 34: 365-373, 2 ref. October 1964. (reprint)

Larson, Richard G. and Olson, James L. A PILOT PROJECT FOR CULTURALLY DEPRIVED KINDERGARTEN CHILDREN: final report. Racine, Wisconsin Unified School District No. 1, 118p., 40 ref. 1965.

Levin, Harry. PRESCHOOL PROGRAMS FOR DISADVANTAGED CHILDREN. 27p., 8 ref. 1964. (Presented to the U. S. Commissioner of Education.)

Little Neighborhood Schools, Philadelphia. A PROPOSAL WITH THE IMMEDIATE GOAL OF OPENING AND OPERATING 100 NURSERY SCHOOLS FOR 2000 CHILDREN. 9 p. 1964.

WATER, SAND AND MUD AS PLAY MATERIALS. New York, N. Y., National Association for the Education of Young Children, 19p. ref. c 1959.

584

Gray, Susan W., et. al., THE EARLY TRAINING PROJECT: A HANDBOOK OF AIMS AND ACTIVITIES. Nashville, George Peabody College for Teachers and Murfreesboro, Tennessee City Schools, 96 p., 27 ref., 1965.

Gray, Susan W. and Klaus, Rupert A. "An experimental preschool program for culturally deprived children." CHILD DEVELOPMENT, 36 (4): 887-898, 12 ref., December 1965. (xerox copy)

Harding, John. "Effects of compensatory preschool programs." In: PROJECT LITERACY REPORTS NO. 4: report of the fourth research planning conference. Ithaca. N. Y., Cornell University, Project Literacy, p. 43-48, 1964.

Hartman, Allan S. PRESCHOOL DIAGNOSTIC LANGUAGE PROGRAM--a curriculum guide for use by teachers in compensatory preschool education programs. Harrisburg, Pennsylvania, 70 p., 4 ref., 1966.

Harvard Information Center on Individual Differences in Education, Cambridge, Massachusetts, BIBLIOGRAPHY ON INFANTS AND PRE-SCHOOL. Cambridge, Mass., 6 p., 64 ref., 1965.

Hechinger, Fred M., ed. PRE-SCHOOL EDUCATION TODAY: NEW APPROACHES TO TEACHING THREE-, FOUR-, AND FIVE-YEAR OLDS. Garden City, N. Y., Doubleday, 156 p., 64 ref., 1966.

Heffernan, Helen. "A challenge to the profession of early childhood education." In: THE DISADVANTAGED CHILD: ISSUES AND INNOVATIONS, edited by Joe L. Frost and Glenn R. Hawkes. N. Y., Houghton Mifflin, p. 168-174, 8 ref., 1966. (From the Journal of Nursery Education, September, 1964, pp. 237-241.)

Hess, Robert D. and Shipman, Virginia. "Early blocks to children's learning." In: THE DISADVANTAGED LEARNER: knowing, understanding, educating, edited by Staten W. Webster. San Francisco, Chandler, p. 276-285, 1 ref., 1966. (From Children, 12 (5), September-October, 1965.)

Hess, Robert D. SCHOOL REPORT: PERRY PRESCHOOL PROJECT; Ypsilanti, Michigan. 8 p., 1964. (Report to Conference on Compensatory Education, University of Chicago, June 1964.)

Hillsborough County, Fla. Public Schools. PROJECT HEAD START HANDBOOK. 31p., 52 ref., 1965.

585

National Association for Nursery Education, WHAT IS MUSIC FOR YOUNG CHILDREN? by Betty Jensen Jones. New York, N. Y., National Association for the Education of Young Children, 52p. ref. c1958.

Newark Pre-School Council, New Jersey. A PROGRAM FOR THE CHILDREN OF NEWARK, NEW JERSEY. By the Newark Pre-School Council and the Child Service Association, 43 p. no date.

Board of Education. SCHOOL RETENTION AND PRE-EMPLOYMENT PROGRAMS AND PROJECTS. NYC, 22 p., 38 ref. 1963.

Office of Navajo Economic Opportunity, Window Rock, Ariz. PRE-SCHOOL AND KINDERGARTEN PROJECT. 7 p., no date.

Ohio University, TO CONDUCT A MULTIPLE ATTACK ON POVERTY WITH UNIVERSITY STUDENTS AND TEENAGE TEACHER AIDES FROM POOR FAMILIES WORKING WITH PRE-SCHOOL CHILDREN IN APPALACHIA. 2p. no date.

Olson, James L. and Larson, Richard G. "An experimental curriculum for culturally deprived kindergarten children." In: THE DISADVANTAGED CHILD: ISSUES AND INNOVATIONS, edited by Joe L. Frost and Glenn R. Hawkes. N. Y.,Houghton Mifflin, p. 175-182, 8 ref. 1966. (From Educational Leadership, pp. 553-558, 618, May 1965.)

Pennsylvania. Departments of Health, Public Instruction, and Public Welfare. PRESCHOOL AND PRIMARY EDUCATION PROJECT, A LONG RANGE ATTACK TO REDUCE THE EDUCATIONAL DISADVANTAGE OF PRESCHOOL CHILDREN FROM POVERTY BACKGROUNDS. Harrisburg, 55p. 1965.

PROGRESS REPORT OF THE EXPERIMENTAL NURSERY SCHOOL PROGRAM. Philadelphia, School District and Philadelphia Council for Community Advancement, 110 p., 6 ref. 1965?

Pierce-Jones, John. OUTCOMES OF INDIVIDUAL AND PROGRAMMATIC VARIATIONS AMONG PROJECT HEAD START CENTERS, 1965. 84 p. 1965.(Presented to the Office of Economic Opportunity's Conference of Independent Investigators for Project Head Start.)

PRE-SCHOOL EDUCATIONAL PROGRAMS. (In IRCD Bulletin, 1(2)/1-9, March 1965.)

586

Rasmussen, Margaret. NURSERY SCHOOL PORTFOLIO. Washington, D. C., Association for Childhood Education International 1961.

Robinson, Halbert B. THE PROBLEM OF TIMING IN PRESCHOOL EDUCATION. 35 p., 81 ref. 1966. (Paper prepared for Social Science Research Council Conference on Preschool Education, University of Chicago, February 7, 8, 9, 1966.)

Robison, Helen F. and Mukerji, Rose. "Language, concepts--and the disadvantaged." EDUCATIONAL LEADERSHIP, 23:6p., November 1965. (reprint)

Robison, Helen F. and Spodek, Bernard. New directions in the kindergarten, New York, Columbia Univ., Teachers College Press, 214p. ref. 1965. (Early Childhood Education Series)

Sacadat, Evelyn and Liddle, Gordon P. "Reaching the culturally handicapped." EDUCATION, 87 (6)/323-327, February 1967.

Sacramento, California. City Unified School District. PARENTS' HANDBOOK FOR PARENT PARTICIPATION PRESCHOOL CLASSES. Sacramento, 88p., 78 ref. 1965.

Schwartz, Sydney. PRE-SCHOOL CHILD DEVELOPMENT CENTERS IN DISADVANTAGED AREAS OF NEW YORK CITY—SUMMER 1966. NYC, Center for Urban Education, 91p. 1966.

Seattle Day Nursery Association. VOLUNTEER JOBS AT SEATTLE DAY NURSERIES. Seattle, 11p. 1964.

"Skid Row child bypassed." SCIENCE NEWS, 89: 167, March 12, 1966. (xerox copy)

Spodek, Bernard. "Early childhood education at the crossroads." In: SEMINAR SELECTIONS ON THE DISADVANTAGED CHILD, edited by Elizabeth H. Brady. NYC, Selected Academic Readings, 11p., 1966. (Speech at ASCD Conference, March 1966.)

Spring Valley, New York. Ramapo School District II. A PRE-SCHOOL PROGRAM FOR CHILDREN IN A SUBURBAN VILLAGE COMMUNITY. 3 p., 1964.

Stern, Carolyn. THE PRESCHOOL LANGUAGE PROJECT: A REPORT OF THE FIRST YEAR'S WORK.Los Angeles, University of California, 21p., 1966.

Stine, Ray M. PRE-SCHOOL ENVIRONMENTAL ENRICHMENT DEMONSTRATION. 30p., 1964. Cooperative Research Project S-229.

Stott, Leland H. and Ball, Rachell S. INFANT AND PRESCHOOL MENTAL TESTS: REVIEW AND EVALUATION. Monographs of the Society for Research in Child Development, 30 (3), 151p., 209 ref., September 1965. Published by Child Development Publications of the Society for Research in Child Development, Inc., Purdue University, Lafayette, Indiana. (Serial No. 101)

Strodbeck, Fred L. THE READING READINESS NURSERY: SHORT-TERM SOCIAL INTERVENTION TECHNIQUE, PROGRESS REPORT. 72p., 4ref., 1964.

Tannenbaum, Abraham J. AN EARLY INTERVENTION PROGRAM THAT FAILED. Columbia Univ., N. Y., Teachers College, 14p., 1966.

"Teaching kids before they start school." CHANGING TIMES, 4p., August 1965.

TEACHING THE DISADVANTAGED CHILD, film series. McGraw-Hill Test-Films, N. Y., 4p., 1966.

Texas Education Agency, Austin. PRESCHOOL INSTRUCTIONAL PROGRAM FOR NON-ENGLISH SPEAKING CHILDREN. Austin, 132p., 96ref., 1966.

Urban Child Study Center, Chicago. CONDENSED INVENTORY OF PRESCHOOL PROJECTS FROM AN INVENTORY OF COMPENSATORY EDUCATION PROJECTS. 25p., Chicago, 1965.

U. S. Office of Economic Opportunity. Community Action Program. PROJECT HEAD START. Washington, D. C., 48 p., 1965.

U. S. Office of Economic Opportunity. HEAD START CHILD DEVELOPMENT PROGRAMS. Washington, D. C., 64p., 1965?

U. S. Office of Economic Opportunity. POINTS FOR PARENTS: 50 SUGGESTIONS FOR PARENT PARTICIPATION IN HEAD START CHILD DEVELOPMENT PROGRAMS. Washington, D. C., 32p., 1966?

Walker, Richard N. BODY BUILD AND BEHAVIOR IN YOUNG CHILDREN, I. BODY BUILD AND NURSERY SCHOOL TEACHERS' RATINGS. Monographs of the Society for Research in Child Development, 27: No. 3, 94p., 66ref., 1962.

Wann, Kenneth D. TEACHING THE VERY YOUNG. New Jersey Education

588

Association (NJEA) Review, 4p., May 1965.

Weber, Evelyn, ed. PRIMARY EDUCATION: CHANGING DIMENSIONS. Washington, D. C., Association for Childhood Education International, 77p., 23ref., 1965.

Weikart, David P. PERRY PRESCHOOL PROJECT 1962-1963: A PROGRESS REPORT. Ypsilanti, Michigan, Public Schools, 52p., 35ref., 1963.

Weikart, David P. PERRY PRESCHOOL PROJECT PROGRESS REPORT. Ypsilanti, Michigan, Public Schools, 101p., 35ref., 1964.

Wolff, Max. APPENDIX: ORIGINAL INSTRUMENTS USED AND BIBLIOGRAPHY. 22p., 19ref. 1966.

Wolff, Max and Stein, Annie. FACTORS INFLUENCING THE RECRUITMENT OF CHILDREN INTO THE HEAD START PROGRAM, SUMMER 1965: A CASE STUDY OF SIX CENTERS IN NEW YORK CITY. 30p., 1966.

Wolff, Max and Stein, Annie. LONG-RANGE EFFECT OF PRE-SCHOOLING ON READING ACHIEVEMENT. 16p., 1966.

Wolff, Max and Stein, Annie. SIX MONTHS LATER: A COMPARISON OF CHILDREN WHO HAD HEAD START, SUMMER, 1965, WITH THEIR CLASSMATES IN KINDERGARTEN: A CASE STUDY OF THE KINDERGARTENS IN FOUR PUBLIC ELEMENTARY SCHOOLS, NEW YORK CITY. 83p., 1966.

Wolman, Thelma G. "Pilot project for pre-kindergarten pupils." THE ELEMENTARY SCHOOL JOURNAL, 66 (8), 403-412, May 1966. (xerox copy)

Wolman, Thelma G. "A PRESCHOOL PROGRAM FOR DISADVANTAGED CHILDREN--THE NEW ROCHELLE STORY." YOUNG CHILDREN, 21(2), 98-111, 45ref. November 1965. (xerox copy)

Young, Ethel. THE NURSERY SCHOOL PROGRAM FOR CULTURALLY DIFFERENT CHILDREN. Menlo Park, Cal., Pacific Coast Publishers, 44p., 80 ref., 1965.

Preschool Education
A Selected Bibliography*

Brunner, Catherine. More than an ounce of prevention. Childhood Education, 42: 35-43, September 1965.

Chicago. Urban Child Study Center. Condensed inventory of preschool projects from an inventory of compensatory education projects. 25p, 1965.

Crow, Lester D.; Walter I. Murray; and Hugh H. Smythe. Educating the culturally disadvantaged child: principles and programs. New York: David McKay, 315 p., 30 ref., 1966.

David, Allison. The future education of children from low socio-economic groups. In: New dimensions for educational progress: the report of a symposium sponsored jointly by Phi Delta Kappa International, Xi Campus Chapter of Phi Delta Kappa, the School of Education, University of Pittsburgh. Bloomington, Inc.: Phi Delta Kappa, p. 27-43., 1962.

Bereiter, Carl E. Academic instruction and preschool children. In: Language programs for the disadvantaged: the report of the NCTE Task Force on teaching English to the disadvantaged. Champaign: National Council of Teachers of English, p. 195-203, 1965.

Bereiter, Carl E.; and Siegfried Engelman. Teaching disadvantaged children in the preschool. Englewood Cliffs: Prentice-Hall, 312 p., 1966.

Bloom, Benjamin S.; Allison Davis; and Robert D. Hess. Compensatory education for cultural deprivation: based on working papers contributed by participants in the Research Conference on Education and Cultural Deprivation. Chicago: Holt, Rinehart and Winston, p. 12-20, 1965.

Deutsch, Martin. Facilitating development in the pre-school child: social and psychological perspectives. Merrill-Palmer Quarterly, 10: 249-263, 11 ref., July 1964.

Deutsch, Martin. What we've learned about disadvantaged children. Nation's Schools, 75: 50-51, April 1965.

Englewood (N. J.) Public Schools. Committee on Education of

*Ferkauf Graduate School, Yeshiva University, 55 Fifth Avenue, New York, N. Y. 10003

590

Four-Five-and-Six-Year-Olds. Guidelines for the education of four-five-and-six-year-olds. 106 p., 80 ref., 1964.

Fleiss, Bernice H. The continuity of education, from pre-kindergarten to primary. Young Children, 22: 78-82, November 1966.

Foster, Florence P. Premature independence in preschools for the disadvantaged. Young Children, 21: 142-150, January 1966.

Frost, Joe L.; and Glenn R. Hawkes, eds. The disadvantaged child: issues and innovations. Boston: Houghton Mifflin, p. 135-199, 1966.

Getzels, J. W. Preschool education. In: White House Conference on Education, a milestone for educational progress. Washington, D. C.: U. S. Government Printing Office, p. 116-125, 26 ref., 1965.

Gordon, Edmund W.; and Doxey A. Wilkerson. Compensatory education for the disadvantaged: programs and practices, preschool through college. New York: College Entrance Examination Board, p. 47-53, 1966.

Gore, Lillian L.; and Rose Koury. Educating children in nursery schools and kindergartens. Washington, D. C.: U. S. Office of Education, 78 p., 50 ref., 1964.

Granite, Harvey R. Language beacons for the disadvantaged. Elementary School Journal, 66: 420-425, May 1966.

Gray, Susan W.; and Rupert A. Klaus. Deprivation, development and diffusion. unpublished. 25 p., 1966 ("Presidential address, Division of School Psychologists, American Psychological Association, September 4, 1966.") (Authors' affiliation: George Peabody College for Teachers.)

Hechinger, Fred M., ed. Pre-school education today: new approaches to teaching three-, four-, and five-year olds. Garden City, N. Y.: Doubleday, 156 p., 64 ref., 1966.

Hunt, J. McVicker. The psychological basis for using pre-school enrichment as an antidote for cultural deprivation. Merrill-Palmer Quarterly, 10: 209-248, 130 ref., July 1964.

John, Vera P. Position paper on pre-school programs. unpublished. 12 p., 34 ref. 1964, ("A brief survey of research on the characteristics of children from low-income backgrounds—prepared for Commissioner Keppel," December 1964.) (Author's affiliation: Ferkauf Graduate School, Yeshiva University.)

McIntyre, John P. Education for the culturally different. The National Elementary Principal, 45: 65-68, February 1966.

Mackintosh, Helen K.; Lillian Gore; and Gertrude M. Lewis. Educating disadvantaged children under six. Washington, D. C.: U. S. Bureau of Educational Research and Development, 31 p., 42 ref., 1965. (Disadvantaged children Series No. 1)
Mukerji, Rose. Roots in early childhood for continuous learning. Childhood Education, 42: 28-34, 3 ref., September 1965.

New York City. Board of Education. Pre-kindergarten curriculum guide. 159 p., 150 ref., 1965 (?) (Curriculum Bulletin, 1965-1966, no. 11.)

Olson, James L.; and Richard G. Larson. An experimental curriculum for culturally deprived kindergarten children. In: The disadvantaged child: issues and innovations, edited by Joe L. Frost, and Glenn R. Hawkes. Boston: Houghton Mifflin, p. 175-182, 8 ref., 1966.

Porter, Para; and A. D. Castle. Practical ideas and activities for pre-school enrichment programs. Wolfe City, Tex.: Henington, 48 p., 1966.

Robinson, Halbert B. The problem of timing in preschool education. unpublished. 35 p., 79 ref. 1966, ("Paper prepared for Social Science Research Council Conference on Preschool Education, University of Chicago, February 7-9, 1966.") (Author's affiliation: University of North Carolina.)

Silver, Archie A.; Elsbeth Pfeiffer; and Rose A. Hagin. The therapeutic nursery as an aid in the diagnosis of delayed language development. unpublished. 19 p., 1966, ("Paper read at the annual meeting, American Orthopsychiatric Association, April 1966.") (Authors' affiliation: Department of Neurology and Psychiatry, New York University.)

Smilansky, Mosche. Intellectual advancement of culturally disadvantaged children. New York: John Wiley and Sons, 1967.

Smilansky, Sarah. Socio-dramatic play for culturally disadvantaged pre-school children. New York: John Wiley and Sons, 1967.

Spodek, Benjamin. Poverty, education and the young child. Educational Leadership, 22: 593-604, 15 ref., May 1965.

Stern, Carolyn. Language competencies of young children. Young Children, 22: 44-50, 11 ref., October 1966.

Teaching kids before they start school. Changing Times, 19: 32-34, August 1965.

Wylie, Joanne, ed. A creative guide for preschool teachers: goals, activities, and suggested material for an organized program. Racine: Western Publishing, 173 p., 130 ref., 1965.

The young child—today's pawn? Education Leadership, 23: 98-142, November 1965. (Special section on preschool education.)

Research

Beller, E. Kuno; and Allan Nash. Research with educationally disadvantaged pre-school children. unpublished. 13 p., 1965. ("This paper was presented on February 12, 1965 at the Annual Meeting of the American Educational Research Association in Chicago, Illinois.") (Authors' affiliation: Temple University.)

Blatt, Burton; and Frank Garfunkel. A field demonstration of the effects of nonautomated responsive environments on the intellectual and social competence of educable mentally retarded children. Boston: Boston University, 233 p., 1965. (Cooperative Research Project no. D-014.)

Caudle, Fairfid M. Prereading skills through the "talking typewriter." The Instructor, 75: 39-40, October 1965.

Cazden, Courtney B. Some implications of research on language development for preschool education. unpublished. 28 p., 25 ref., 1966. ("A paper prepared for the Social Science Research Council Conference on Preschool Education, Chicago, Febraury 7-9, 1966.") (Author's affiliation: Harvard University.)

Deutsch, Martin. Progress report—April 29, 1965—June 30, 1966—and continuation proposal—July 1, 1966—June 30, 1967—for Regional Research and Resource Center in Early Childhood. unpublished. 195 p., 1966. (Project no. NY-CAP-65-9457.) (Author's affiliation: Institute for Developmental Studies, Department of Psychiatry, New York Medical College.)

Fearn, Leif. A dual-directional approach to initial reading instruction: a pilot study. unpublished. 8 p., 1966. ("Conducted in the Lukachukai Pre-school under the auspices of the Office of Navajo Economic Opportunity.") (Author's affiliation: Navajo Demonstration School, Lukachukai, Ariz.)

Goldstein, Kenneth M.; and Sherwood B. Chorost. A preliminary evaluation of nursery school experience on the later school adjustment of culturally disadvantaged

593

children. New York: Wakoff Research Center, 31 p., 15 ref., 1966. (Cooperative Research Project no. S-323.)

Goldstein, Leo S. Evaluation of an enrichment program for socially disadvantaged children. unpublished. 25 p., 1965, (Author's affiliation: Institute for Developmental Studies, Department of Psychiatry, New York Medical College.)

John, Vera P. A study of language change and homogeneous classrooms. unpublished. 22 p., 18 ref., 1966. (Project proposal submitted June 2, 1966 to the Office of Economic Opportunity.) (Author's affiliation: Ferkauf Graduate School, Yeshiva University.)

Kamii, Constance K.; and Norma L. Radin. A framework for a preschool curriculum based on some Piagetian concepts. unpublished. 23 p., 21 ref., 1966. (Authors' affiliation: Perry Preschool Project, Ypsilanti Public Schools, Ypsilant, Mich.)

Kamii, Constance K.; Norma L. Radin; and David P. Weikart. A two-year pre-school program for culturally disadvantaged children: findings of the first three years. unpublished. 7 p., 1966.

Osser, Harry. The syntactic structures of 5-year-old culturally deprived children. unpublished. 5 p., 1966, ("presented at the Symposium on The Concept of Structure in Language and Thinking, Eastern Psychological Association Annual Meeting, New York City, April 15, 1966.") (Author's affiliation: School of Medicine, Johns Hopkins University.)

Robinson, Helen F.; and Rose Mukerji. Concept and language development in a kindergarten of disadvantaged children. Washington, D. C.: U. S. Office of Education, 218 p., 31 ref., 1966. (Cooperative Research Project no. S-320.)

Schwartz, Sydney. Pre-school development centers in disadvantaged areas of New York City—Summer 1966. New York: Educational Practices Division, Center for Urban Education, 60 p., 1966.

Smilansky, Mosche; and Sarah Smilansky. Bases for intellectual advancement of culturally disadvantaged children. unpublished. 57p., 1965. ("A revision of a paper presented at the 7th annual research roundup of children and youth at the University of California, Los Angeles, July 1965.") (Authors' affiliation: Szold Institute, Jerusalem, Israel.)

Smilansky, Sarah. An experiment to promote cognitive abilities, impart basic information and modify attitudes of pre-school culturally disadvantaged children,

594

through the development and improvement of their socio-dramatic free play. unpublished. 36 p., 1965. (Paper presented at the annual meeting of the American Orthopsychiatric Association, New York, March 1965.)

Sonquist, Hanne D.; and Constance K. Kamii. The application of some Piagetian concepts to teaching in a preschool for disadvantaged children. unpublished. 17 p., 9 ref., 1966. (Authors' affiliation: Perry Preschool Project, Ypsilanti Public Schools, Ypsilanti, Mich., March 1966.)

Stearns, Keith; Walter Hodges; and Howard Spicker. Interim report: a diagnostically-based language curriculum for psycho-socially deprived preschool children. unpublished. 13 p., 7 ref., 1966. ("Presented at a symposium on 'Early First-Language Instruction for the Culturally-Different Child' on Saturday, February 19, 1966 at the 50th annual Meeting of the American Educational Research Association, Pick-Congress Hotel, Chicago, Illinois.") (Authors' affiliation: Indiana University.)

Stine, Ray M. Pre-school environmental enrichment demonstration. Harrisburg, Penn.: Bureau of General and Academic Education, Department of Public Instruction, 32 p., 12 ref., 1964. (Cooperative Research Project S-229 OE-5-10-153.)

Stodolsky, Susan B. Material behavior and language and concept formation in Negro pre-school children: an inquiry into process. unpublished. 90 p., 51 ref., 1965. (Doctoral dissertation, University of Chicago, 1965.)

Programs

Alpern, Gerald D. The failure of a nursery school enrichment program for culturally disadvantaged children. American Journal of Orthopsychiatry, 36: 244-245, March 1966.

Baltimore (City) Public Schools. An early school admissions project: progress report, 1962-1963. 96 p., 4 ref., 1963.

Baltimore (City Public Schools. An early schools admissions project: progress report, 1963-1964. 1964.

Bereiter, Carl E.; and others. An academically oriented pre-school for culturally deprived children. In: Pre-school education today: new approaches to teaching three-, four-, and five-year-olds, edited by Fred M. Hechinger. Garden City, N. Y: Doubleday, p. 105-135, 5 ref., 1966.

595

Bereiter, Carl E.; and Siegfried Engelman. Language learning activities for the disadvantaged child. New York: Anti-Defamation League of B'nai B'rith, 34 p., 1965 (?).

Boston Public Schools. Action for Boston Community Development. The Demonstration Pre-Kindergarten Program. 16 p., 1966.

Brunner, Catherine. Project Help: program for early school admissions. Education Digest, 29: 22-25, March 1964.

Champaign, Ill. National Council of Teachers of English. Language programs for the disadvantaged: the report of the NCTE Task Force on teaching English to the disadvantaged. p. 39-73, 3 ref., 1965.

Clark, Erma. A nursery school on the Ute Indian Reservation. In: The disadvantaged child: issues and innovations, edited by Joe L. Frost and Glenn R. Hawkes. Boston: Houghton Mifflin, p. 189-192, 1966.

Deutsch, Martin. Nursery education: the influence of social programming on early development. The Journal of Nursery Education, 18: 191-197, 5 ref., April 1963.

Deutsch, Martin; and Alfred Freedman. A program to demonstrate the effectiveness of a "therapeutic curriculum" for the socially deprived pre-school child. New York: Institute for Developmental Studies, Department of Psychiatry, New York Medical College, 32 p., 1962.

Feldmann, Shirley C. A preschool enrichment program for disadvantaged children. The New Era, 45 (no. 3): 79-82, 1964.

Foster, Florence P. The impact of early intervention. Young Children, 21: 354-360, September 1966.

Fresno City (Cal.) Unified School District. The Compensatory Education Program pre-school department guide for 1964-65. 66 p., 1965.

Gray, Susan W.; and others. The Early Training Project: a handbook of aims and activities. Nashville: George Peabody College for Teachers; and Murfreesboro, Tenn.: Murfreesboro City Schools, 96 p., 27 ref., 1965.

Gray, Susan W.; and Rupert A. Klaus. An experimental preschool program for culturally deprived children. Child Development, 36: 887-898, 12 ref., December 1965.

Harding, Alice C. Project Get Set: Philadelphia prekindergarten program aimed at giving underprivileged children a better change for a fair start in life. NEA Journal 55: 16-18, October 1966.

Hardy County Public Schools, Moorefield, W. Va. Preschool program in Hardy County, West Virginia under the Office of Economic Opportunity Community Action Program: guide book for teachers. 40 p., 6 ref., 1965.

Hess, Robert D. School report: Perry Preschool Project, Ypsilanti, Michigan. unpublished. 8p. 1964. (Report to Conference on Compensatory Education, University of Chicago, June 1964.) (Author's affiliation: University of Chicago.)

Jones, Edgar L. Early School Admission Project. New York: Office of Reports, Ford Foundation, 18 p., 1965.

Knight, Robert. The Harlem Action Group pre-school and day care program. New York: Harlem Action Group, 36 p., no date.

Levens, Dorothy. A special preschool program at Vassar. Young Children, 22: 16-19, October 1966.

Lipchik, Margaret. A Saturday school for mothers and preschoolers. In: Pre-school education today: new approaches to teaching three-, four-, and five-year-olds, edited by Fred M. Hechinger. Garden City, N. Y.: Doubleday, p. 137-143., 1966.

Martin, John H. Freeport Public Schools Experiment on Early Reading Using the Edison Responsive Environment Instrument. New York: Responsive Environments Corporation, 8 p., 1964 (?).

Newark, N. J. Pre-School Council; and Child Service Association. A program for the children of Newark, New Jersey. 40 p., 1965 (?).

Oakland (Cal.) Public Schools. Interagency Project. Preschool program. 11p., 28 ref., 1965.

Philadelphia. Public Schools. 1964-1965 progress report of the Experimental Nursery School Program. 78 p., 6 ref., 1965 (?).

Platoff, Joan. Preschool prototype: an integrated semicooperative nursery school. Young Children, 21: 205-211, March 1966.

Ponder, Eddie G.; and Laura Schneider. Early childhood enrichment program for

597

disadvantaged children. In: Preparing teachers of disadvantaged young children, edited by Bernard Spodek. Milwaukee: University of Wisconsin, p. 6-19. 1965. ("Summary of Proceedings of a Conference of Directors of N.D.E.A. Institute for Teachers of Disadvantaged Youth, July 16-17, 1965, Kenwood Conference Center, University of Wisconsin, Milwaukee.")

Preschool programs for the deprived child in New Haven, Connecticut, Dade County, Florida, and Baltimore, Maryland. In: The disadvantaged child: issues and innovations, edited by Joe L. Frost and Glenn R. Hawkes. Boston: Houghton Mifflin, p. 192-199., 1966.

Radin, Norma; and David Weikart. A home teaching program for disadvantaged preschool children. unpublished. 14 p., 6 ref., 1966. (Authors' affiliation: Ypsilanti Public Schools, Ypsilanti, Mich.)

Ramapo School District II, Spring Valley, N. Y. A preschool program for children in a suburban-village community. 3 p., 1964 (?).

Rassmussen, Margaret, ed. Nursery School Portfolio, Washington, D. C. : Association for Childhood Education International, Unpaged., 1961.

Sacramento (Cal.) City Unified School District. Parents' handbook for parent participation preschool classes. 93 p., 78 ref., 1965.

Special report: preprimary programs. Nation's Schools, 77: 48-68, June 1966.

Strodtbeck, Fred L. The reading readiness nursery: short-term social intervention technique, progress report. Chicago: Social Psychology Laboratory, University of Chicago, 72 p., 3 ref., 1964.

Tannenbaum, Abraham J. An early intervention program that failed. unpublished. 14 p., 1966. (Author's affiliation: Teachers College, Columbia University.)

Texas Education Agency, Austin. Preschool instructional program for non-English speaking children. Revised edition. 137p., 16 ref., 1964.

Viscovich, Andrew J. A pre-school project. Childhood education, 42: 44-45, September 1965.

Weikart, David P. Perry Preschool Project: progress report, 1962-1963. Ypsilanti, Mich.: Ypsilanti Public Schools, 52 p., 35 ref., 1963.

598

Weikart, David P. Perry Preschool Project: progress report, 1963-1964. Ypsilanti, Mich.: Ypsilanti Public Schools, 108 p., 35 ref., 1964.

Wolman, Thelma G. Pilot project for pre-kindergarten pupils. The Elementary School Journal, 66: 403-412, May 1966.

Wolman, Thelma G. A preschool program for disadvantaged children—the New Rochelle story. Young Children, 21: 98-111, 45 ref., November 1965.

Young, Ethel. The nursery school program for culturally different children: a notebook. Menlo Park, Cal.: Pacific Coast Publishers, 44 p., 80 ref., 1965.

Project Head Start

Brainin, Sema. A study of changes in school-related behaviors of pre-school children: observed in connection with Operation Head Start as conducted by Bronx River Neighborhood Center, Summer 1965. New York: Bronx River Neighborhood Center, 13 p., 1965 (?).

Brazziel, William F. Head start on a new kind of life: an assessment of gains in two summer programs. Integrated Education, 4:42-46, August-September 1966.

Butler, Annie L. Will Head Start be a false start? Childhood Education, 42:163-166, 3 ref., November 1965.

Carleton, Charles S. Head Start or false start? American Education, 2:20-22, September 1966.

Eisenberg, Leon; and C. Keith Conners. The effect of Head Start on developmental process. unpublished. 11 p., 1966. ("Presented at the 1966 Joseph P. Kennedy Jr. Foundation Scientific Symposium on Mental Retardation, April 11, 1966, Sheraton-Boston Hotel, Boston, Massachusetts.") (Authors' affiliation: School of Medicine, Johns Hopkins University.)

Feinberg, Harriet. Some problems in preschool education for disadvantaged children: with special emphasis on "Project Head Start." unpublished., 1965, (Author's affiliation: Graduate School of Education, Harvard University.)

Head Start: a special section. Grade Teacher, 83: 63-81, December 1965.

Head Start or false start? American Child, 48: 5-24, Spring 1966. (Special issue on Head Start.)

Hess, Robert D.; and others. Techniques for assessing cognitive and social abilities of children and parents in Project Head Start. unpublished. 115 p., 1966. ("Report on Research Contract OEO-519 with the U. S. Office of Economic Opportunity, July 1966.") (Authors' affiliation: University of Chicago.)

Hudson, Catherine R. The Child Development Center: a program to provide children a "Head Start" in life and implications for primary education. The Teachers College Journal, 37: 8, 41-47, October 1965.

Operation Head Start. The Reading Teacher, 19: 323-363, February 1966. (Special issue on Head Start.)

Reiff, Donald G.; and Pere Julia. The language-situation in Project Head Start centers, 1965: a survey conducted for the Office of Research and Evaluation, Project Head Start. 1966, unpublished. Unpaged. (Contract OEO-932.) (Authors' affiliation: University of Rochester.)

Slaven, James J. Montessori Head Start. Audiovisual Instruction, 11: 546-549, September 1966.

Waller, David A.; and C. Keith Connors. A follow-up study of intelligence changes in children who participated in Project Head Start. unpublished. 19 p., 7 ref., 1966. ("This study was supported by funds from the Office of Economic Opportunity: Head Start Contract no. 510") (Authors' affiliation: School of Medicine, Johns Hopkins University.)

Bibliography on Preschool and Early Childhood Education
from
National Laboratory on Early Childhood Education
ERIC Clearinghouse
University of Illinois, Urbana, Ill.
Brian W. Carrs, Director

Association for Childhood Education International. TOWARD BETTER KINDERGARTENS. Washington, D. C.: A C E I, 64 p., 1967. (PSOOO 110)

Blatt, Burton and Garfunkel, Frank. A FIELD DEMONSTRATION OF THE EFFECTS OF NONAUTOMATED RESPONSIVE ENVIRONMENTS ON THE INTELLECTUAL AND SOCIAL COMPETENCE OF EDUCABLE MENTALLY RETARDED CHILDREN. Boston, Massachusetts: Boston University (Cooperative Research Program of the United States Office of Education, Project No. D-014), 237 p., 1965. (ED010 289)

Caldwell, Bettye M. "What is the Optimal Learning Environment for the Young Child?" AMERICAN JOURNAL OF ORTHOPSYCHIATRY, 37 (1): 8-21, 1967. (PS000 018) Caldwell, Bettye M. and Richmond, Julius B. "Programmed Day Care for the Very Young Child--A Preliminary Report." JOURNAL OF MARRIAGE AND THE FAMILY, 26 (4): 481-488, 1964. (PS000 024)

Cazden, Courtney B. "Subcultural Differences in Child Language: An Interdisciplinary Review." MERRILL-PALMER QUARTERLY, 12 (3): 185-214, 1966. (PS000 301)

Clark, Ann D. and Richards, Charlotte J. "Auditory Discrimination Among Economically Disadvantaged and Nondisadvantaged Preschool Children." EXCEPTIONAL CHILDREN, 33: 259-262, 1966. (PS000 067)

Concannon, Sister Josephina. AN EXPERIMENTAL STUDY OF THE INFLUENCE OF INDIVIDUAL vs GROUP INSTRUCTION ON SPATIAL ABILITIES IN PRESCHOOL CHILDREN (Final Report). Chestnut Hill, Massachusetts: School of Education, Boston College (United States Office of Education, Contract No. 5-10-288), 161 p, 1966. (PS000 096)

Deutsch, Cynthia P. "Auditory Discrimination and Learning: Social Factors." MERRILL-PALMER QUARTERLY, 10 (3): 277-296, 1964. (ED001 116)

Deutsch, Martin. "Facilitating Development in the Pre-School Child:Social and Psychological Perspectives." MERRILL-PALMER QUARTERLY, 10 (3): 249-263, 1964. (ED002 356)

601

Fleiss, Bernice H. "The Continuity of Education, From Prekindergarten to Primary." YOUNG CHILDREN, 22 (2): 78-82, 1966. (PS000 308)

Glaser, Robert. PSYCHOLOGICAL BASES FOR INSTRUCTIONAL DESIGN (Research Report). Pittsburgh, Pennsylvania: University of Pittsburgh, Learning Research and Development Center (United States Office of Education, Contract No. 3-16-043), 7 p, 1966. (PS000 173)

Glaser, Robert. THE PROGRAM FOR INDIVIDUALLY PRESCRIBED INSTRUCTION. Pittsburgh, Pennsylvania: University of Pittsburgh, Learning Research and Development Center (United States Office of Education, Contract No. 3-16-043), 8 p., 1966. (PS000 150)

Hartman, Allan S. "Preprimary Programs: How to Improve Preschool Programs." NATIONS SCHOOLS, 77 (6): 57-58, 1966. (PS000 309)

Harvey, O. J. et al. "Teachers' Belief Systems and Preschool Atmospheres." JOURNAL OF EDUCATIONAL PSYCHOLOGY, 57 (6): 373-381, 1966. (PS000 276)

Hechinger, Fred M. (Editor). Pre-School Education Today. Garden City, New York: Doubleday and Company, Inc., 150 p, 1966. (PS000 311)

Hess, Robert D. and Shipman, Virginia. "Early Blocks to Children's Learning." CHILDREN, 12 (5): 189-194, 1965. (PS000 312)

Hunt, Joseph McV. The Psychological Basis for Using Preschool Enrichment as An Antidote for Cultural Deprivation. In O. J. Harvey (Editor). EXPERIENCE, STRUCTURE, AND ADAPTABILITY. New York: Springer Publishing Company, Pp. 235-276, 1966. (PS000 313)

John, Vera P. and Goldstein, L. S. The Social Context of Language Acquisition. MERRILL-PALMER QUARTERLY, 10 (3): 265-275, 1964. (PS000 314)

Johnsen, Kathryn P. and Leslie, Gerald R. Methodological Notes on Research in Childrearing and Social Class. MERRILL-PALMER QUARTERLY, 11 (4): 345-358, 1965. (PS000 315)

Karnes, Merle et al. ACTIVITIES FOR DEVELOPING PSYCHOLINGUISTIC SKILLS WITH PRESCHOOL CULTURALLY DISADVANTAGED CHILDREN. Urbana, Illinois: University of Illinois, Institute for Research on Exceptional Children, 108 p, 1966. (PS000 302)

Kellogg, Ralph E. A STUDY OF THE EFFECT OF A FIRST-GRADE LISTENING INSTRUCTIONAL PROGRAM UPON ACHIEVEMENT IN LISTENING AND READING. San Diego, California: San Diego County Department of Education (United States Office of Education, Cooperative Research Project No. 6-8468), 158 p., 1966. (PS000 097)

Levens, Dorothy. A Special Preschool Program at Vassar. YOUNG CHILDREN, 22: 16-19, 1966. (PS000 316)

Levin, Tom. The Child Development Group of Mississippi: A Hot Sector of the Quiet Front in the War on Poverty. AMERICAN JOURNAL OF ORTHOPSYCHIATRY, 37 (1): 139-145, 1967. (PS000 317)

Moore, Omar K. The Responsive Environments Project and the Deaf. AMERICAN ANNALS OF THE DEAF, 110 (5): 604-614, 1965. (PS000 167)

Moore, Omar K. and Anderson, Alan R. THE RESPONSIVE ENVIRONMENTS PROJECT. Pittsburgh, Pennsylvania: University of Pittsburgh, Learning Research and Development Center, 35 p, 1966. (PS000 175)

Painter, Genevieve. The Effect of a Rhythmic and Sensory Motor Activity Program on Perceptual Motor Spatial Abilities on Kindergarten Children. EXCEPTIONAL CHILDREN, 33 (2): 113-116, 1966 (PS000 310)

Radin, Norma and Weikart, David. A HOME TEACHING PROGRAM FOR DISADVANTAGED PRESCHOOL CHILDREN. Ypsilanti, Michigan: Ypsilanti Public Schools (Cooperative Research Program of the United States Office of Education, Project No. 2494), 13 p, 1966. (PS000 318)

Ralph, Jane B. Language Development in Socially Disadvantaged Children. REVIEW OF EDUCATIONAL RESEARCH, 35 (5), 389-400, 1965. (PS000 104)

Rice, Joseph P. and Plowman, Paul D. A Demonstration Center with Differential Programming for Gifted Pupils in California in Grades one Through Nine: Enrichment, Acceleration, Counseling and Special Classes. CALIFORNIA SCHOOLS, 34 (5): 139-154, 1963. (PS000 062)

Weikart, David P. PRELIMINARY RESULTS FROM A LONGITUDINAL STUDY OF DISADVANTAGED PRESCHOOL CHILDREN. Paper presented at the convention of the Council for Exceptional Children, St. Louis, Missouri, 20 p, 1967. (PS000 303)

Weikart, David P. (Editor). PRESCHOOL INTERVENTION: A PRELIMINARY REPORT OF THE PERRY PRESCHOOL PROJECT. Ann Arbor, Michigan: Campus Publishers, 171 p, 1967. (PS000 304)

Weikart, David P. RESULTS OF PRESCHOOL INTERVENTION PROGRAMS. Paper presented at the University of Kansas Symposium on the Education of Culturally Disadvantaged Children, University of Kansas, Lawrence, Kansas, May, 60 p, 1966. (PS000 305)

Weikart, David P. et al. PERRY PRESCHOOL PROJECT: A PROGRESS REPORT, 1962-1963. Ypsilanti, Michigan: Ypsilanti Public Schools (Project sponsored by Ypsilanti Board of Education; Washtenaw County Board of Education; and Michigan Department of Public Instruction), 52 p, 1963. (PS000 306)

Weikart, David P. et al. Perry preschool project: PROGRESS REPORT, 1963-1964. Ypsilanti, Michigan: Ypsilanti Public Schools, June, 105 p, 1964. (PS000 307)

Wolff, Max. STUDIES I, II, and III:ORIGINAL INSTRUMENTS USED AND BIBLIOGRAPHY (Appendix). New York, New York: Yeshiva University (The Office of Economic Opportunity, Project No. 141-61 Ia), 23 p, no date. (PS000 284)

Wolff, Max and Stein, Annie. A COMPARISON OF CHILDREN WHO HAD HEAD START, SUMMER, 1965, WITH THEIR CLASSMATES IN KINDERGARTEN: A CASE STUDY OF THE KINDERGARTENS IN FOUR PUBLIC ELEMENTARY SCHOOLS, New York City (Study I). New York, New York: Yeshiva University (The Office of Economic Opportunity, Project No. 141-61), 94 p, 1966. (PS000 281)

Wolff, Max and Stein, Annie. FACTORS INFLUENCING THE RECRUITMENT OF CHILDREN INTO THE HEAD START PROGRAM, Summer, 1965: A CASE STUDY OF SIX CENTERS IN NEW YORK CITY (Study II). New York, New York: Yeshiva University (The Office of Economic Opportunity, Project No. 141-61), 31 p, no date. (PS000 282)

ED------numbers are available on microfilm from EDRS, National Cash Register Company. The clearinghouse holds all this material in hard copy form. It is available to anyone on request for a nominal charge to cover mailing and photoreproduction.

SUBJECT INDEX

607

608

609

610

611

EPILOGUE

Dr. Edgar A. Doll passed away the day after he wrote the following for this volume. Here he speaks of what might now be called his "last will and testament" to the field of education, namely his new Preschool Attainment Record.

Jerome Hellmuth, Editor
October 23, 1968

Some things are almost self-evident after reading this volume. They may be briefly enumerated as follows:

1. need for orientation
2. need for explicit purposes
3. need for specific direction of education
4. need for empathic relationship to child, etc.

For these purposes there are relatively few specific instruments. To offset this lack we have developed the Preschool Attainment Record[1] as a device which contains all the above endeavors. This is actually a specific rearrangement of the VSMS[2]. This new Scale affords a developmental record of child growth in preschool years. The substantial material is available in many publications on child development.

We might think of the Preschool Attainment Record (PAR) as a time schedule as well as an inventory in early childhood development. It affords a "before" and "after" measurement device which tells us specifically where a child stands at the time educational therapy or developmental instruction is first offered to him. We might also in successive measurements at particular time intervals by readministration of the same schedule, record the amount and rate of progress. This Scale also affords an implicit curriculum for developmental instruction.

This scale has been recently developed in association with Dr. Geraldine L. Doll and has had nearly two years of exploratory application. However, an adequate statistical organization of the material has not been accomplished but is being undertaken in various Centers. We might consider this endeavor as "hot off the griddle" but somewhat less than fully baked.

---

1. Doll, Edgar A., Preschool Attainment Record, American Guidance Service, Inc., 1966, Circle Pines, Minnesota.

2. Doll, Edgar A., Measurement of Social Competence, A Manual for the Vineland Social Maturity Scale, Educational Test Bureau, 1953.